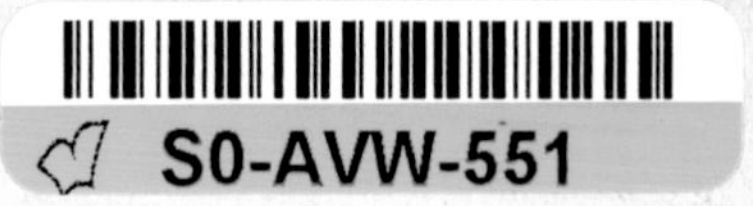

Substance Abuse

Eight good reasons why you need this new edition of *Substance Abuse*. . .

1. New sections on evidence-based treatment (Chapter 8), evidence-based prevention (Chapter 15), moderation management (Chapter 10), national drug control strategy (Chapter 15), and alcohol marketing (Chapter 15) introduce you to the most current approaches to addiction treatment.
2. A new section on Internet addiction (Chapter 14) offers guidance on the fastest growing area of addiction.
3. New sections on counseling persons with disabilities and the elderly and assessment of alcohol problems in women provide support for working with often underserved populations.
4. Updated data on assessment instruments offers information on the newest tools available to you.
5. Survey data on prevalence of tobacco, alcohol, and other drug use among youth and diverse populations; treatment admissions; emergency room admissions; and prevalence of addiction has been updated to reflect the most current statistics.
6. New bulleted chapter summaries, discussion topics for each chapter, and Internet resources for each chapter encourage both quick review and extended research.
7. The importance of ethics and confidentiality are highlighted by a revised chapter order.
8. And cross references (assignments) at the ends of many chapters open up the robust resources of Pearson's MyHelpingLab for you!

Substance Abuse

Information for School Counselors, Social Workers, Therapists, and Counselors

FOURTH EDITION

Gary L. Fisher
University of Nevada, Reno

Thomas C. Harrison
University of Nevada, Reno

Boston • New York • San Francisco
Mexico City • Montreal • Toronto • London • Madrid • Munich • Paris
Hong Kong • Singapore • Tokyo • Cape Town • Sydney

Series Editor: Virginia L. Blanford
Series Editorial Assistant: Matthew Buchholz
Marketing Manager: Danae April
Editorial Production Service: Omegatype Typography, Inc.
Composition Buyer: Linda Cox
Manufacturing Buyer: Linda Morris
Electronic Composition: Omegatype Typography, Inc.
Cover Administrator: Linda Knowles

For related titles and support materials, visit our online catalog at www.pearsonhighered.com.

Library of Congress Cataloging-in-Publication Data

Fisher, Gary L.
Substance abuse : information for school counselors, social workers, therapists, and counselors / Gary L. Fisher, Thomas C. Harrison. — 4th ed.
p. cm.
Includes bibliographical references and index.
ISBN-13: 978-0-205-59176-3 (pbk.)
ISBN-10: 0-205-59176-0 (pbk.)
1. Social work with drug addicts—United States. 2. Social work with alcoholics—United States. 3. Drug addicts—Counseling of—United States. 4. Alcoholics—Counseling of—United States. 5. Drug addiction—United States—Prevention. 6. Alcoholism—United States—Prevention. I. Harrison, Thomas C. II. Title.

HV5825.F566 2009
362.29—dc22

2007039936

Printed in the United States of America

10 9 8 12 11

Allyn and Bacon is an imprint of

www.pearsonhighered.com

ISBN-10: 0-205-59176-0
ISBN-13: 978-0-205-59176-3

To our beautiful and loving wives,
Carole and Terianne,
and our children,
Colin, Aaron, and Brooke,
and Iain, Ryan, Becky, and Jordan

About the Authors

Gary L. Fisher is professor of Health and Human Sciences at the University of Nevada, Reno. He was the founder and first director of the Center for the Application of Substance Abuse Technologies where he developed undergraduate, graduate, and continuing education activities for addiction counselors, prevention specialists, and allied professionals. Dr. Fisher's career has spanned 33 years and includes work as a private practice clinician and a public school psychologist. In addition to this textbook, he is the author of *Rethinking Our War on Drugs: Candid Talk about Controversial Issues,* published in 2006, and the coauthor of four books for learning disabled children and their parents.

Thomas Harrison is professor and chairman of the Department of Counseling and Educational Psychology at the University of Nevada, Reno. He developed the drug testing program for the University of Florida Athletic Department and has been a consultant for the State of Nevada Bureau of Alcohol and Drug Abuse. Dr. Harrison's career has spanned 30 years in the field, including private counseling and consulting practice. He is the author of *Consultation for Contemporary Helping Professionals,* published in 2004, and of several articles in professional journals.

Contents

11 *Children and Families* 199

12 *Adult Children and Codependency* 228

13 *HIV/AIDS* 255

14 *Gambling and Other Addictions* 276

15 *Prevention* 311

Preface

We teach in a counseling department that offers training in school counseling, marriage and family therapy, college student development, mental health counseling, and school psychology. Our department requires that all students take a course titled "Models of Prevention, Treatment, and Recovery in Addictions." The goal of the course is to familiarize students with the alcohol and other drug (AOD) field, including basic pharmacology, conceptualizations of AOD, assessment, models of prevention, family issues, and the like.

In teaching this course, we reviewed many textbooks. Many were focused primarily on the pharmacology of alcohol and other drugs. Others were directed toward the person who wanted to work in AOD treatment. Some espoused a narrow orientation to understanding addiction. We never found a book designed for the mental health professional in generalist settings that included all the information we believe to be necessary, and that presented a balanced view of addictions. So we wrote one.

That this book is now in its fourth edition is gratifying, but more importantly: It confirms the need for a generalist text in this area. In Chapter 1, we provide our rationale, explaining why we think mental health professionals (school counselors, social workers, marriage and family therapists, mental health counselors, rehabilitation counselors) need this information. We also offer an overview of the topics covered in this book. Both of us have done most of our clinical work in generalist settings (schools, private practice, community mental health centers, universities), and we have used our experiences to select these topics. Our clients have ranged from those with no alcohol or drug problems to those who have been in numerous treatment programs—and everything in between. We hope that this results in a balanced presentation of some controversial areas.

While writing and revising this book, we have tried to keep in mind the common complaints that students have about textbooks: We have illustrated the application of concepts with many examples from our own clinical experiences; we have tried to personalize the writing and avoid the more stilted language of traditional academia. Let us know if this has worked to make the book more interesting and accessible.

What's New in This Edition

With each revision, we update the content throughout. This fourth edition includes a new section on Internet addiction (Chapter 14), which offers guidance on the fastest-growing area of addiction, as well as significant new material on evidence-based treatment (Chapter 8), evidence-based prevention (Chapter 15), moderation management (Chapter 10), National Drug Control Strategy (Chapter 15), and alcohol marketing (Chapter 15). In addition, new sections on counseling persons with disabilities and the elderly, and assessment of alcohol problems in women, provide support for working with often underserved populations.

Content on assessment instruments offers information about the newest tools available to practitioners. Survey data on prevalence of tobacco, alcohol, and other drug use among youth and diverse populations; treatment admissions; emergency room admissions; and prevalence of addiction have been updated to reflect the most current statistics.

We have also reordered the chapters to highlight the increasing importance of ethics and confidentiality. Finally, new bulleted chapter summaries, discussion topics for each chapter, and Internet resources for each chapter encourage both quick review and extended research.

MyHelpingLab

myhelpinglab Pearson's MyHelpingLab is available packaged with this text at no additional cost. MyHelpingLab is an online destination designed to help students in social work, counseling and psychotherapy, marriage/family therapy, and human services make the transition from their academic coursework to their professional practice. It includes video footage of actual therapist–client sessions, a rich archive of case studies including case worker–client interactions, and information about licensing.

New end-of-chapter activities link some of the topics in this book to appropriate content in MyHelpingLab. To access MyHelpingLab, visit www.myhelpinglab.com.

Acknowledgments

As with any effort such as this, many people have contributed to the final product. We want to thank Gary Pregal, Katie Swanson, Susan Malby-Meade, Frank Tirado, Priscilla Wu, and the late Cheri Dunning for their efforts on the first edition of this text. Julie Hogan, director of the Western Center for the Application of Prevention Technologies, and Nancy Roget, director of the Center for the Application of Substance Abuse Technologies at the University of Nevada, Reno, provided valuable insights in the development of the second edition. In preparing the third edition, we relied on the work of the Addiction Technology Transfer Centers (funded by the Center for Substance Abuse Treatment) and the Centers for the Application of Prevention Technologies (funded by the Center for Substance Abuse Prevention). These outstanding networks helped us identify relevant issues and concepts. We are also grateful to John Chappel, emeritus professor of psychiatry and behavioral sciences at the University of Nevada, Reno. We also thank reviewers of the earlier editions, including Peggy D. Campbell, Florence Darlington Technical College; Robert O. Choate, Stephen F. Austin State University; and Christopher Wagner, Virginia Commonwealth University.

In preparing the fourth edition, we thank Sabina Mutisya, doctoral student at the University of Nevada, Reno, for her invaluable assistance with research, and the reviewers who provided helpful suggestions for revision: Debra Morrison-Orton, California State University, Bakersfield; Nadine Panter, University of Nebraska, Kearny; and George M. Andrews, Baltimore City College.

Gary L. Fisher
Thomas C. Harrison

Substance Abuse

1

The Role of the Mental Health Professional in Prevention and Treatment

It has become almost trite to recite the problems related to the use of alcohol and other drugs (AOD)[1] in our society. Various statistics are reported in newspaper articles, surveys, and research studies that become mind-numbing with the array of graphs, percentages, and dollar amounts in the billions. It is not our purpose to contribute to the data avalanche in an effort to convince you that the abuse of AOD causes a variety of serious problems in our country. If you are reading this book, you are probably in a training program to prepare for a career in one of the helping professions and, one hopes, you have some awareness of the severity of this problem. On the other hand, our experience in training mental health professionals has taught us that there is a need for a framework to understand the extent to which AOD issues affect not only the lives of those individuals you will be working with, but your own lives as well and the society in which we live. Therefore, allow us to provide this framework with a few facts.

[1]As is the case with many areas in the helping professions, terminology can be confusing. In this book, we will use the term *alcohol and other drugs* (AOD) to clearly indicate that alcohol is a drug and to avoid having the reader omit alcohol from any discussion about drugs. If tobacco is relevant to a discussion, we will generally refer to "alcohol, tobacco, and other drugs." The term *illegal drugs* will be used to refer to substances such as marijuana, heroin, cocaine, methamphetamine, and ecstasy which are illegal under most or all circumstances. *Illicit drugs* are illegal drugs as well as legal drugs used inappropriately, such as prescription pain medications.

The use of terms such as *alcoholism, drug addiction, chemical dependency,* and *substance abuse* can also be problematic. In Chapter 2, we will give some definitions of terms used in the field, and, in Chapter 5, we provide the criteria to diagnose certain AOD conditions. However, since these terms are used in this chapter, you should think of *alcoholism* as an addiction to the drug alcohol. *Drug addiction* refers to the addiction to drugs other than alcohol. *Chemical dependency* includes addiction to AOD. *Substance abuse* means that there have been individual or societal problems as a result of AOD use. After reading Chapters 2 and 6, you should have a more useful understanding of these terms.

According to survey data, more than 23 million Americans age 12 and over need treatment for an alcohol or illicit drug problem. In 2005, 7.5 million needed treatment for illicit drugs and 19.4 for alcohol problems (Substance Abuse and Mental Health Services Administration, 2006). (The two numbers total more than 23 million because people who need treatment for both alcohol and illicit drugs are counted in both groups.) The Substance Abuse and Mental Health Services Administration conducts a yearly survey on the use of all drugs, legal and illegal in the United States (Substance Abuse and Mental Health Services Administration, 2006a). In 2005, 8.1% of all individuals age 12 and above reported using an illicit drug in the past month. In the 12 to 17 age group, 16.5% had used alcohol in the past month and 9.9% had engaged in binge drinking. In the same age group, 10.8% smoked cigarettes. According to *Scientific American* (1996), more than 100,000 annual deaths in the United States are attributable to alcohol. In 1992, 24% of these deaths were a result of accidents, primarily drunk driving. Eleven percent of the deaths resulted from homicide and 8% from suicide. Cirrhosis of the liver caused nearly 27,000 deaths in 1999 (Yoon, Yi, Grant, Stinson, & Dufour, 2002). The death rate from drug abuse has doubled over the past two decades (Centers for Disease Control and Prevention, 2000). The Centers for Disease Control and Prevention (2002) reported 440,000 annual deaths in this country as a result of tobacco use.

The relationship between AOD, crime, and violence has also been clearly established. The Center on Addiction and Substance Abuse published an extensive study of this relationship. It was determined that 80% of adult inmates were under the influence at the time they committed their crimes, engaged in illegal activity to buy drugs, had a history of drug or alcohol abuse, or some combination of these factors. AOD were a factor in nearly 40% of violent crimes, and alcohol was more closely associated with violent crime than any other drug (Center on Addiction and Substance Abuse, 1998). Kelleher, Chaffin, Hollenberg, and Fischer (1994) studied the relationship between AOD abuse and child abuse. They found that adults who physically abused or neglected their children were significantly more likely to have a substance abuse or dependence disorder. Similarly, in a study of domestic violence, Brookhoff, O'Brin, Cook, Thompson, and Williams (1997) found that 92% of assailants used alcohol or other drugs on the day of their arrest, and 72% had prior arrests for substance abuse-related offenses. More than half of adult male arrestees test positive for illicit drug use (National Institute of Justice, 2001).

The monetary costs of AOD abuse also provide tangible evidence of the significance of these problems. In a study for the National Institute on Drug Abuse and the National Institute on Alcohol Abuse and Alcoholism (Harwood, 2000), the 1998 costs of alcohol abuse were estimated at $185 billion and other drug abuse costs at $143 billion. Nearly 50% of the costs of alcohol abuse were due to illness, over 20% were attributable to premature death, and the remaining costs were due to healthcare, crime, and other factors. For other drug abuse, nearly 60% of the costs were related to crime, with illness, premature death, and healthcare accounting for nearly all of the remaining costs.

The nation's total cost for smoking-related medical costs and lost job productivity due to premature death was estimated to be nearly $160 billion (Centers for Disease Control and Prevention, 2000). Ironically, for every dollar that states spend on substance abuse and addiction, 96 cents is spent on shoveling up the wreckage caused by AOD use and 4 cents is spent on prevention and treatment (Center on Addiction and Substance Abuse, 2001).

We risk contributing to the data avalanche to illustrate that the abuse of AOD is like a tree with many branches. The trunk is AOD abuse but the branches are the multitude of other problems caused by or related to AOD. To avoid totally clogging your mind with statistics and/or completely depressing you before you read the rest of this book, we neglected to describe other branches of the tree such as the decreased work productivity, excessive school truancy and work absenteeism, and detrimental effects on partners, children, and fetuses resulting from AOD abuse. However, these and other branches exist and are the concern of all helping professionals.

The Need for Generalist Training

A few years ago, one of your authors was asked by a local school district to conduct an independent psychological evaluation of a 14-year-old student who was a freshman in high school. The young man's parents were dissatisfied with the school district's evaluation of their son and had asked for another opinion. The youngster was failing most of his classes and was skipping school frequently. The parents were quite sure that their son had a learning disability that would explain his difficulties. The district's school psychologist had tested the student and not found a learning disability. The school counselor had suggested that there may be an emotional problem and recommended family counseling. In addition, a weekly progress check was initiated at school so the parents could be kept informed of assignments and homework that their son needed to complete. They had also hired a tutor. However, none of these interventions seemed to be helping, so the independent evaluation was requested.

In reviewing the test information, no indications of a learning disability were found. An AOD assessment (which will be discussed in Chapter 6) was conducted and there was evidence that the young man was using AOD on a daily basis. The parents said that they allowed their son and his friends to drink in their home because they believed that this would prevent them from using "drugs" and from drinking and driving. The parents were defensive about their own AOD use and rejected suggestions that the cause of their son's problems could be related to his AOD use. A couple of months later, there was a request for the young man's records from an AOD treatment program. He was referred to the program following an arrest for stealing alcohol from a convenience store.

One of us was supervising a master's student who was in a marriage and family therapy internship. The intern had been seeing a family of four (mom, dad, and two children, aged 3 and 9) who were referred to our university counseling clinic by Children's Protective Services. A child abuse report had been filed at the 9-year-old's elementary school because of bruises on the youngster's face. The father explained that he had slapped his son because of his frustration with the boy's behavior and "back-talking." The parents complained of frequent conflicts related to parenting techniques and family finances. The intern had developed an intervention plan that included referring the parents to a parent education program and working with the family on "communication skills" including "I-messages" and conflict resolution procedures. The intern was frustrated because the parents had failed to follow through on the parent education classes and had not made much progress in improving their communication patterns. It was suggested that the intern assess the AOD use of the parents and she did so at the next session. The mother and father had a heated argument about the father's drinking behavior. They did not show up for their next appointment and, when the intern called, the mother said that they were discontinuing counseling because the father said it was a waste of time.

We regularly consult with a social worker in private practice. One of her clients is a woman in her early 30s who sought counseling for "depression." The woman had been married twice, and described a series of failed relationships. Her first husband was an alcoholic and the second was a polydrug abuser. For two years she had been living with a man who was in recovery from cocaine addiction. However, she found out that he had been having numerous affairs during their relationship. The woman, who has a master's degree, could not understand why she continued to become involved with these kind of men. She felt that there must be something wrong with her because the men in her life needed alcohol, other drugs, or other women. Her father was an alcoholic and verbally abusive, and she had also been sexually molested by her paternal grandfather.

In the three situations described, the "helping professionals" (school psychologist, school counselor, marriage and family therapy intern, social worker) were not involved in providing substance abuse treatment, but they needed information and skills in the AOD field to perform their job functions in a competent manner. Your two authors have worked in schools as teacher and school psychologist, in a mental health clinic, in a university athletic department, and in private practice. We currently train school counselors and marriage and family therapists, as well as substance abuse counselors. We have found that the frequency of AOD-related problems is so pervasive in the helping field that the lack of training in this area would result in inadequate preparation for mental health professionals. When you read the statistics on the relationship between domestic violence, child abuse, other crime, and AOD, it should be clear that this also applies to criminal justice personnel.

It would be unreasonable to expect all helping professionals to have the same set of skills as substance abuse counselors. We don't expect substance abuse counselors to be able to plan educational interventions or to do family therapy. Similarly, school and mental health counselors, social workers, and marriage and family therapists do not need to be able to monitor detoxification or to develop treatment plans. However, all mental health professionals will encounter individuals who need assessment and treatment for AOD problems and clients who are having problems as a result of relationships with individuals with AOD problems. Included in the related problems that mental health professionals (school counselors, mental health counselors, rehabilitation counselors, psychologists, social workers, and marriage and family therapists) will encounter are children who have been fetally affected by parental AOD use, the psychological impact on children and adults who live or have lived with caretakers who abuse AOD, and the intrapersonal and interpersonal problems of individuals who are in relationships with people who abuse AOD. Many of you have read about fetal alcohol syndrome, adult children of alcoholics, and codependency, which are included in these "related" problems. All of these issues will be discussed in this text.

We hope that you are convinced that mental health professionals need training in the AOD field, not only to identify those clients who need further assessment and treatment but for the multitude of related problems that all mental health professionals will encounter on a regular basis. As with many areas in the mental health field, there are differing views on the causes and treatment of alcoholism and drug addiction based on the variety of disciplines concerned with these problems and the philosophical orientation of different individuals.

Philosophical Orientation

Jerome is a 47-year-old African American man who had been arrested for a DUI (driving under the influence). It was his third DUI and he had previously been in an alcohol treatment program. There had been previous arrests for writing bad checks and spousal abuse. He was unemployed and dropped out of school in the tenth grade. An assessment revealed a long history of AOD use beginning at age 12. Jerome's mother was an alcoholic and he was raised by his grandmother. He does not know his biological father.

Jerome's problem may be viewed in different ways by different professionals, depending on their training and experiences. A sociologist may focus on the environmental and cultural factors that modeled and encouraged AOD use. Some psychologists might attend to the fact that Jerome experienced rejection by his biological parents that led to feelings of inadequacy. The use of AOD might be seen as a coping mechanism. A physician might be impressed by the family history of alcoholism and hypothesize that Jerome had a genetic predisposition for chemical dependency. A social worker may think that Jerome's unemployment and lack of education resulted in discouragement and consequent AOD use. A criminal justice worker may see his behavior as willful misconduct and believe that punishment is necessary.

These differing views of the causes and treatment of Jerome's problem are not unusual in the mental health field. However, what is unique in the AOD field is that many drug and alcohol counselors, others involved in the treatment of chemically dependent people, and many people who are recovering from AOD problems believe that Jerome has a disease that has affected him mentally, physically, socially, emotionally, and *spiritually.* This spiritual component separates AOD problems from other mental health problems and has had implications for the understanding and treatment of AOD problems. One implication is that methods to attend to the spiritual aspect of treatment (e.g., Alcoholics Anonymous) are a common component of treatment. Another implication is that there are many individuals involved in the treatment of AOD problems who do not have formal training as counselors but who are "in recovery" and hold a fervent belief in a particular orientation to treatment. This belief may be based not on scientific evidence but on their own experience and the experience of other recovering individuals. This phenomenon is similar to an individual's religious beliefs that cannot (and should not) be disputed by research since the beliefs are valid for that individual. Clearly, the potential for disagreement and controversy exists when scientific and spiritual viewpoints are applied to the same problem, which has certainly been the case in this field.

In Chapter 3, we will discuss the different models of addiction and will thoroughly discuss the "disease concept" of chemical dependency. Our point here is that we believe that the AOD field requires an openness on the part of the mental health professional to a wide variety of possible causes of AOD problems and to a multitude of methods by which people recover from these problems. We have worked with people who discontinued their use of AOD without any treatment, individuals who stopped after walking into a church and "finding Jesus," clients and students who swear by AA, and people who have needed a formal treatment program.

If you work in a treatment program, you tend to see people who have experienced many life problems related to AOD use. It is easy to develop a viewpoint about chemical dependency based on these clients' experiences. It is important to remember that treatment providers do not see those people who modify or discontinue their AOD use through methods other than formal treatment.

This book is written from the perspective of the mental health professional working in a generalist setting rather than from the perspective of a substance abuse counselor in a treatment setting. Therefore, we will provide the type of information we believe all mental health professionals need in the AOD field to work effectively in schools, community agencies, and private practice, rather than providing all the information needed to work as a substance abuse counselor in a treatment setting. We want to provide a balance in the types of viewpoints that exist in this field so that you can understand these perspectives. We will describe the popular literature in certain areas (e.g., adult children of alcoholics) and contrast this with research in the area so that you can understand that clinical impressions and research do not always match. Finally, we want to communicate our belief that it is not advisable to adopt universal concepts of cause and treatment in this field. In other areas of mental health treatment, we encourage practitioners to assess a client and to develop treatment strategies based on the individual and group characteristics of the client. The same rules should apply in the AOD field.

Attitudes and Beliefs

Close your eyes for a minute and visualize an alcoholic. What did your alcoholic look like? For most people, the alcoholic is a white male, middle aged, who looks pretty seedy. In other words, the stereotypical skid row bum. Did you visualize somebody who looks like Betty Ford, the former First Lady? Did you visualize one of your professors? Did you visualize a professional athlete?

Attitudes and beliefs about alcoholics and drug addicts have an effect on the mental health professional's work. Imagine that you are a mental health counselor and a well-dressed middle-aged woman comes to see you complaining of symptoms of depression. If you hold false beliefs about alcoholics, such as that they must be dirty and drunk all the time, you might fail to diagnose the Betty Fords of the world. The first author tells his students in his substance abuse class about his own alcoholism and drug addiction to dispute stereotypes about the educational level and employment of alcoholics and drug addicts.

To help students understand their own attitudes about alcoholics and drug addicts, we have our students attend an Alcoholics Anonymous (AA) or Narcotics Anonymous (NA) meeting as a class assignment. We encourage you to do this as well (if you do go to a meeting, make sure you attend an "open" meeting [see Chapter 10]). In addition to acquiring a cognitive understanding of this type of support for alcoholics and addicts, students report interesting affective reactions that provide information about their attitudes. For example, many students report that they want to tell others at the meeting that they are there for a class assignment and that they are not alcoholics. Our response is that unless you believe that alcoholism or drug addiction is simply a condition that some people develop and has nothing to do with morals or a weak will, you would not care if you were mistakenly identified as alcoholic or drug addicted. If you do care, you must believe that alcoholics and drug addicts have some type of character flaw. This realization helps many potential mental health professionals modify their attitudes and beliefs about alcoholism and drug addiction.

A second type of affective reaction that students report is surprise with the heterogeneity of the group. At most meetings, they see well-dressed businessmen and women, young people, blue-collar workers, unkempt people, articulate individuals, and people obviously impaired from their years of using AOD. Seeing such a variety of people tends to destroy any stereotypes the students may have.

Although we believe that potential mental health professionals may hold any belief system they want, the belief that alcoholism or drug addiction is due to a moral weakness or a character flaw may have a detrimental effect on providing or finding appropriate help for those with AOD problems. For example, imagine that you are a marriage and family therapist and that you are seeing a couple in which one partner is drinking excessively. You believe that changing heavy drinking to moderate drinking is largely a matter of willpower and desire, and you communicate this to the drinking partner. If this individual is addicted to alcohol, your belief system will be incompatible with this client's reality. Your client may experience shame, because he or she is not strong enough, or anger at your lack of understanding. Resistance and termination are frequent outcomes, and the client fails to get the proper help. Therefore, if you do believe that excessive AOD use is largely due to moral weakness or character flaws, you would be well advised to refer these cases to others.

Denial, Minimization, Projection, and Rationalization

Imagine (or maybe you don't have to imagine) that you are in love with someone you believe to be the most wonderful person in the world. You cannot imagine living without this person and firmly believe that you need this person to survive. Your mother sits you down one day and tells you that you must no longer associate with this person. She tells you that this person is destroying your life, that you have changed since becoming involved with this person, and that all your family and friends believe that you need to break off the relationship before something terrible happens to you. How would you react? You might tell your mother that she is crazy and that all her complaints about this person are untrue (denial). Perhaps you acknowledge that your person does have some little quirks, but they really don't bother you (minimization). You tell your mother that she and the rest of your family and friends are really jealous because they do not have someone as wonderful as you (projection) and that you may have changed but these changes are for the better and long overdue (rationalization).

We use this analogy so you can develop an empathic understanding of what many AOD-addicted individuals experience. Obviously, the "love object" in this case is the individual's drug of choice. The addicted individual may be seen as having an intimate and monogamous relationship with alcohol or other drugs and believe that he or she needs the drug to function and survive. In the same way that people deny that a relationship has become destructive, the addicted individual may deny that alcohol or other drugs have become destructive in spite of objective evidence to the contrary. The defense mechanisms of denial, minimization, projection, and rationalization are used so that the person does not have to face a reality that may be terrifying: a life without alcohol or other drugs.

While we know that it may be easy for you to intellectually understand these concepts as applied to alcoholic and other drug-addicted people, we have found it useful for our students to have a more direct experience with their own use of defense mechanisms. At the first class session of our substance abuse class, we ask the students to choose a substance or activity and abstain from this substance or activity for the semester, and that the first thing that popped into their heads and was rejected because it would be too hard to give up is the thing they should choose. Students usually choose substances such as alcohol, coffee, chocolate, or sugar, or activities such as gambling (we live in Nevada where gambling is legal) or watching television. Some choose tobacco and an occasional courageous student will choose an illegal drug. The students record their use of the defense mechanisms through journal entries and write a paper about the experience at the end of the semester.

If you are wondering whether some students "blow off" the assignment and just make up the material in their journals and papers, the answer is "of course." When the assignment is given, this issue is discussed. The students are told that they can do anything they want to; the instructor will never know the difference. However, there is some reason for potential mental health professionals to take a close look at themselves if they are unwilling to abstain from a substance or activity for 15 weeks, particularly when mental health professionals will be encouraging clients to abstain from alcohol or other drugs for a lifetime.

We encourage you, our reader, to examine your own use of denial, minimization, projection, and rationalization, particularly in regard to your own use of AOD. Mental health professionals are not immune to AOD problems and are just as likely to use these defense mechanisms as anyone else is. As you read the rest of this book, take some time to examine your own substance-using behavior. If there is a problem, this would be the ideal time to get some help. This would certainly be preferable to becoming one of the many impaired professionals who may cause harm to their clients and themselves.

Helping Attitudes and Behaviors

Although we have encountered many mental health professionals with AOD problems, we have found that a more pervasive problem may be the potential mental health professionals who gravitate to the helping professions because of unresolved issues in their lives. Although there may be a sincere desire to help others, these potential mental health professionals may actually be unhelpful to clients. For example, in our counselor education program, we find that many of our students are adult children of alcoholics. Now, that is no problem in and of itself. In fact, as we will discuss in Chapter 12, many adult children of alcoholics have the same or fewer problems than other adults. However, being raised by one or more alcoholic caretakers may lead to certain characteristic ways of behaving that could have implications for a mental health professional's effectiveness. For example, a graduate student in marriage and family therapy whom we will call Debbie (we are changing all of the names of students and clients we are using in this book to protect anonymity) decided to pursue a career in the helping professions because everyone told her that she was easy to talk to and was a good listener. Debbie said that she was one of those people to whom total strangers immediately told their life stories.

Debbie was raised by her biological parents, both of whom were alcoholics. Within her family, she had developed a method of behaving that would minimize the probability of conflict developing. She did most of the cooking and cleaning at home, took care of her younger siblings, and worked very hard at school. Debbie reported being in a constant state of anxiety due to her worry that she had "missed" something that would send one of her parents into a rage.

In hindsight, it is easy to see that Debbie developed a false belief that she could control her parents' moods and behavior by making sure that everything was perfect at home and by her achievements at school. It is not unusual for children raised by alcoholic caretakers to develop a role designed to divert attention away from the real problem in the family. (Again, this will be discussed in detail in Chapter 12.) However, the development of this childhood role had implications for Debbie's work as a marriage and family therapist. We noticed that she was quite hesitant to confront clients and that she seemed very uncomfortable with conflict. Debbie had more than the usual anxiety for a student when counseling and brooded excessively when her clients did not immediately feel better. Clearly, the characteristic ways Debbie had learned to behave as a child were having a detrimental effect on her development as a marriage and family therapist in spite of the fact that people found her easy to talk to.

Another of our graduate students in counseling, Patricia, was taking our substance abuse counseling course. She failed her midterm examination. Patricia came to see the instructor and explained that the content of the course generated a great deal of emotion for her since her parents were alcoholics, and she had been married to a drug addict. Because of these emotions, she said that she had difficulty concentrating on the lectures and the reading material and in following through on class assignments (students were required to attend an Alcoholics Anonymous and an Alanon [for family members of alcoholics] meeting). The instructor communicated his understanding that the course could have that impact on people with history and experiences in the substance abuse area and suggested that Patricia drop the course (he offered a passing withdrawal) and pursue counseling for herself. Patricia chose to avoid working on these issues, she stayed in the course, and failed.

Since most of you who are reading this text are graduate students, this may strike you as rather harsh. However, consider the alternative. Let's say that the instructor had offered his understanding and allowed Patricia to remain in the course without dealing with these issues and passed her. Would Patricia be able to work effectively with individuals and families in which there were alcohol or other drug problems, with adult clients who were raised by chemically dependent caretakers, or with clients living with alcohol- or other drug-abusing partners? In an attempt to avoid these problems, she might do a poor job of assessment, or she might ignore the signs and symptoms of alcohol or other drug problems. Or she might ignore or fail to inquire about substance abuse in the family of origin or in the current family of her clients. In short, we believe that her unwillingness to face these problems would result in her being a less effective counselor.

What about Debbie? Her excessive anxiety and concern with her performance prevented her from objectively looking at her clients and her own counseling behaviors. Debbie's fear of conflict resulted in an unwillingness to confront her clients, which limited her effectiveness. Fortunately, Debbie was receptive to feedback and suggestions. She did some work on her own issues, and she has become a fine marriage and family therapist.

This discussion is not meant to discourage those of you who are adult children of alcoholics, are in recovery from an alcohol or other drug problem, or have lived or are living with a chemically dependent person from pursuing your careers. It is our experience that most people who want to become helping professionals have a need or desire to help people that is based on family of origin issues that may adversely affect their work. This is certainly the case with both of us. It is not a problem if you enter a training program in one of the helping professions because of your own need to be needed. It is a problem if you avoid examining your own issues and fail to take steps to resolve these issues in order to avoid ineffective (or in some cases, harmful) work with clients.

In this particular field, we find helping professionals who cannot work effectively with clients because of their own AOD use or their experiences with AOD use in their families of origin and/or with partners. In the rest of this book, we will attempt to provide you with information that will enable you to deal effectively with the direct and indirect problems resulting from AOD use that social workers, school counselors, mental health counselors, marriage and family therapists, and other helping professionals will encounter. However, all of this information will be useless if your own use patterns or issues are unresolved and if they impact your work. Since denial is so pervasive, we encourage you to seek objective feedback regarding the necessity to work on your own use of alcohol or other drugs or on other issues and, if necessary, to choose a course of action with professional assistance. But please, for your own benefit and for the benefit of your future clients, don't choose to avoid.

Overview of the Book

In our choice of chapter topics and the orientation of each chapter, we have tried to maintain a primary goal of providing useful information in the AOD field to general mental health professionals. Therefore, Chapter 2 (Classification of Drugs), Chapter 3 (Models of Addiction), Chapter 8 (Treatment of AOD Problems), and Chapter 10 (Twelve-Step and Other Types of Support Groups) are overviews of these topics. We have attempted to provide enough detail about treatment and Twelve-Step groups to reduce any myths about these activities and to allow mental health professionals to make informed referrals. Issues that usually provoke some controversy among generalists (e.g., the disease concept, relative dangers of different drugs, etc.) are also discussed.

In several chapters, we have attempted to integrate the role of the mental health professional in working with clients with AOD problems with the specialist in the field. In Chapter 6 (Assessment and Diagnosis), Chapter 7 (Client Engagement and Brief Interventions), and Chapter 9 (Relapse Prevention and Recovery), our goal is that you will understand the types of AOD services that mental health professionals in generalist settings provide.

Chapter 11 (Children and Families), Chapter 12 (Adult Children and Codependency), and Chapter 14 (Gambling and Other Addictions) involve issues related to AOD problems. In many instances, mental health professionals may work with clients having these problems. In each of these chapters, we have attempted to provide sufficient depth of coverage so that you will have a conceptual framework to understand the relationship of these topics to AOD and to understand the implications for treatment.

Chapter 4 is an in-depth discussion of multicultural issues in the AOD field. As with all mental and other health-related topics, it is essential to understand both individual and group characteristics of clients. The cultural context of AOD use is of crucial importance in both prevention and treatment. We have chosen to highlight its importance by devoting a chapter to the topic rather than integrating multiculturalism into each chapter. Therefore, we encourage you to maintain an awareness of diversity issues as you read the remaining chapters.

Chapter 5 concerns confidentiality and ethics. In teaching a substance abuse counseling class to mental health generalists, we have found nearly universal ignorance of the fact that almost all mental health professionals are bound by federal confidentiality regulations. Students often perceive this topic as "dry." However, we have seen the consequences of lack of awareness of confidentiality regulations. So, please have the stamina to wade through this chapter.

The relationship between HIV/AIDS and substance abuse is discussed in Chapter 13. Our inclusion of a chapter on this topic reflects the increasing need for awareness among all mental and other health professionals regarding transmission and prevention of this and other communicable diseases.

Having only one chapter on prevention (Chapter 15) does not imply that the subject is unimportant. Indeed, if prevention efforts were more successful, there would be less need for the rest of this book. Clearly, school counselors and school social workers must be well informed about effective prevention approaches. However, successful prevention involves all aspects of a community, and all helping professionals must be involved. We are particularly interested in increasing your awareness of our perverted public policy regarding the marketing of legal drugs (alcohol and tobacco) and its effect on prevention efforts.

At the ends of chapters, major points are bulleted in a Summary section. We have added Internet resources for those of you who want more information on subjects in the chapters. Finally, there are some discussion questions designed to provoke your thinking about issues.

We need to mention two aspects of writing style so you understand what we are trying to do in this book. First, there are many examples from clinical cases included. We both maintain clinical practices and believe that such cases can illuminate concepts and increase interest. Second, the tone of our writing may be less scholarly than you are accustomed to. We have taught many university courses and have used a lot of textbooks. We also were students for a *long* time. From these experiences, we found that many textbooks were marvelous, nonpharmaceutical methods to induce sleep. Although accurate and scholarly, the stilted style was often a barrier to acquiring information. It has been our intention to make this book accurate and informative but with a lower probability of causing drowsiness. Let us know if it worked.

2

Classification of Drugs

As we noted in Chapter 1, this textbook is designed for the mental health professional (e.g., school counselor, mental health counselor, rehabilitation counselor, social worker, marriage and family therapist) who will encounter AOD problems with clientele but who, generally, will not provide treatment for these problems. Therefore, the goal of this chapter is to provide an overview of the drugs (including alcohol and tobacco) that are most often abused and drugs that are used in the treatment of some mental disorders. However, a thorough understanding of the pharmacology of drugs and related issues (e.g., medical management of overdose, use of psychotropic medications in the treatment of mental disorders) would require far more attention than one chapter can offer. Also, information in this area changes rapidly as a result of research. For example, there is no medication that has been found to be effective in significantly reducing cocaine craving. However, there is considerable research in this area. By the time you read this book, there may be pharmacological management of cocaine withdrawal that does not currently exist. We are including an additional reading list at the end of this chapter if you want to acquire more comprehensive information on the topics discussed. In addition, we encourage you to develop contacts with AOD treatment providers who are likely to remain current with regard to research in this area. This will reduce the probability that you will pass along misinformation or outdated information to your clients.

Different methods exist that are used to classify drugs (Jacobs & Fehr, 1987). We will use the method that classifies drugs by their pharmacological similarity. Drugs exist that do not fit nicely into one classification, and these will be noted. For each drug classification, we will mention the common drugs contained in the classification and some common street names, the routes of administration, major effects, signs of intoxication, signs of overdose, tolerance, withdrawal, and acute and chronic effects. First however, we will present information on the federal schedule of drugs, some simple definitions of terms that will be helpful in understanding the rest of the chapter, and a brief discussion of the concept of "dangerousness."

Comprehensive Drug Abuse Prevention and Control Act

In 1970, the Comprehensive Drug Abuse Prevention and Control Act (often referred to as the Controlled Substances Act) was passed by the U.S. Congress. As part of this law, drugs are placed in one of five "schedules," with regulatory requirements associated with each schedule. Schedule I drugs have a high potential for abuse, no currently accepted medical use in treatment in the United States, and a lack of a safe level of use under medical supervision. Drugs on Schedule I include heroin, methaqualone (Quaalude), LSD, and marijuana. Schedule II drugs also have a high abuse potential and can lead to psychological or physical dependence. However, these drugs have an accepted medical use in treatment. These drugs include morphine, PCP, cocaine, and methamphetamine. As you can probably surmise, the criteria for the other schedules involve less abuse potential, increased medical uses, and less likelihood of psychological and physical dependence.

As you will see from our discussion of the classification of drugs, the way some drugs are classified is clearly illogical. For example, benzodiazepines such as Valium and Xanax are Schedule IV drugs, with part of the criteria for inclusion being that the drugs have a lower abuse potential than drugs on Schedules I, II, and III. In reality, these drugs have at least the same if not greater abuse potential than marijuana, a Schedule I drug. However, the inclusion of a drug on a certain schedule is related to public policy, which will be discussed in Chapter 15. For example, the reclassification downward of a drug such as marijuana would be politically unpopular, and the reclassification of benzodiazepines upward would be resisted by the manufacturers of these drugs.

The Concept of Dangerousness

Related to the preceding discussion of schedules of drugs is the concept of the inherent dangers of certain drugs. Tobacco, alcohol, and other drugs are not safe to use. There are acute and chronic dangers, and these dangers vary by drug. For example, there is little acute danger from the ingestion of a glass of wine by an adult. The acute danger of shooting cocaine is far greater. Chronic use of any drug (including alcohol) has an increased risk, but the danger of smoking one pack of cigarettes a day for 40 years is greater than the dangers from drinking one can of beer a day for 40 years. Danger is also related to the method used to administer a drug. Smoking a drug or injecting it produces the most rapid and intense reaction, while ingesting a drug generally produces effects with longer duration, although less intensity. Snorting drugs is in between but has more similarities to smoking and injecting than ingesting. Although any method of administration may be dangerous both acutely and chronically, smoking or injecting drugs tends to result in the most acute problems since these routes of administration rapidly introduce the drug to the bloodstream and, subsequently, to the brain. Also, smoking drugs causes damage to the respiratory system, and the intravenous use of drugs may cause serious problems including abscesses, blood clots, allergic reactions to the substances used to "cut" the drug, and communicable diseases such as hepatitis and HIV.

It is certainly important that you understand the acute and chronic effects of different drugs and the addictive potential of tobacco, alcohol, and other drugs. However, it is essential that you understand that any of the psychoactive drugs we discuss in this chapter can be used in an addictive manner. You will learn that hallucinogens are not physically addicting in the sense that body tissues require these drugs for normal functioning. However, this does not imply that people are immune from serious problems resulting from the use of hallucinogens. Alcohol is clearly an extremely dangerous drug in spite of the fact that many people use the drug without problems. Marijuana is not as acutely or chronically dangerous as cocaine, but that does not mean it can be used safely. We have worked with clients who have serious life problems from marijuana use. This is not a sermon to "Just Say No." It is a caution to avoid concluding that you can direct clients away from some drugs to other drugs, and a caution to avoid using your own experience with AOD as a basis for determining which drugs are safe and which are dangerous.

Definitions

Terminology in the AOD field can be confusing. One author may have a very specific meaning for a particular term while another may use the same term in a more general sense. An analogy might be the use of the term *neurotic* in the mental health field. While one professional may use this term when referring to some very specific disorders, another may use it to describe a wide variety of mental health problems. However, there is no universal agreement about how some of these terms should be used. Therefore, the following definitions should assist you in understanding this chapter and the rest of the book, but you may find differences in definitions as you read professional and popular literature in the AOD field.

Addiction: Compulsion to use alcohol or other drugs regardless of negative or adverse consequences. Addiction is characterized by psychological dependence (*see below*) and, often (depending on the drug or drugs) physical dependence (*see below*). As we will discuss in Chapter 14, the term *addiction* is sometimes applied to behaviors other than AOD (e.g., eating, gambling).

Alcoholism: Addiction to a specific drug: alcohol.

Chemical dependency: A term used to describe addiction to alcohol and/or other drugs and to differentiate this type of addiction from nonchemical addictions (e.g., gambling).

Dependence: A recurrent or ongoing need to use alcohol or other drugs. Psychological dependence is the need to use alcohol or other drugs to think, feel, or function normally. Physical dependence exists when tissues of the body require the presence of alcohol or other drugs to function normally. All psychoactive drugs can produce psychological dependence and many can produce physical dependence. Dependence will also be defined in Chapter 6, based on the criteria in the *Diagnostic and Statistical Manual of Mental Disorders, Fourth Edition, Text Revision* (*DSM-IV-TR*) (American Psychiatric Association, 2000), to diagnose AOD dependency disorders.

Intoxication: State of being under the influence of alcohol or other drugs so that thinking, feeling, and/or behavior are affected.

Psychoactive drugs: Natural or synthetic chemicals that affect thinking, feeling, and behavior.

Psychotropic drugs: Chemicals used to treat mental disorders.

Substance abuse: The continued use of alcohol and/or other drugs in spite of adverse consequences in one or more areas of an individual's life (e.g., family, job, legal, financial). Abuse will also be defined in Chapter 6 according to the criteria in the DSM-IV-TR.

Tolerance: Requirement for increasing doses or quantities of alcohol or other drugs in order to create the same effect as was obtained from the original dose. Tolerance results from the physical or psychological adaptations of the individual. *Cross-tolerance* refers to accompanying tolerance to other drugs from the same pharmacological group. For example, tolerance to alcohol results in tolerance to minor tranquilizers such as Xanax, even when the individual has never used Xanax. *Reverse-tolerance* refers to a condition in which smaller quantities of a drug produce the same effects as did previous larger doses.

Withdrawal: Physical and psychological effects that occur when a drug-dependent individual discontinues alcohol or other drug use.

Central Nervous System Depressants

Central nervous system (CNS) depressants (also referred to as *sedative-hypnotics*) depress the overall functioning of the central nervous system to induce sedation, drowsiness, and coma. The drugs in this classification include the most commonly used and abused psychoactive drug, alcohol; prescription drugs used for anxiety, sleep disturbance, and seizure control; and over-the-counter medications for sleep disturbance, colds and allergies, and coughs. In general, CNS depressants are extremely dangerous. In 1996, there were over 110,000 deaths caused by alcohol in the United States, the third leading cause of death (National Institute on Alcohol Abuse and Alcoholism, 2001). Alcohol in combination with other drugs accounted for about one-third of drug abuse-related emergency room episodes in 2005 (Substance Abuse and Mental Health Services Administration, 2007).

Drugs in This Classification

Alcohol is the most well-known CNS depressant because of its widespread use and legality. The alcohol content of common beverages is beer, 3% to 6%; wine, 11% to 20%; liqueurs, 25% to 35%; and liquor (whiskey, gin, vodka, etc.) 40% to 50%. The "proof" on alcohol beverages is computed by doubling the alcohol content. Therefore, a bourbon that is described as "90 proof" is 45% alcohol. It is important to remember that the amount of alcohol in one 12-ounce beer is the same as the amount of alcohol in 6 ounces of wine or in 1.5 ounces of liquor (all standard drinks). The alcohol in beer is simply contained in a larger amount of liquid.

Barbiturates are prescription drugs used to aid sleep for insomniacs and for the control of seizures. These drugs include Seconal (reds, red devils), Nembutal (yellows, yellow jackets), Tuinal (rainbows), Amytal (blues, blue heaven), and Phenobarbital. There are also non-barbiturate sedative-hypnotics with similar effects but with different pharmacological properties. These include Doriden (goofballs), Quaalude (ludes), Miltown, and Equinil. Being a Schedule I drug, Quaalude cannot be legally prescribed in the United States.

The development of benzodiazepines or minor tranquilizers reduced the number of prescriptions for barbiturates written by physicians. These drugs were initially seen as safe and having little abuse potential. Although the minor tranquilizers cannot be easily used in suicide as can barbiturates, the potential for abuse is significant. The benzodiazepines are among the most widely prescribed drugs and include Valium, Librium, Dalmane, Halcion, Xanax, and Ativan.

Finally, certain over-the-counter medications contain depressant drugs. Sleep aids such as Nytol and Sominex, cold and allergy products, and cough medicines may contain scopolamine, antihistamines, or alcohol to produce the desired effects.

Routes of Administration

Obviously, alcohol is administered by drinking. Some over-the-counter medications are also in liquid form. The barbiturates, nonbarbiturate sedative-hypnotics, and minor tranquilizers come in pill form. As with many psychoactive drugs, liquid forms of the drugs are produced and administered by injection.

Major Effects

The effects of CNS depressants are related to the dose, method of administration, and tolerance of the individual, factors that should be kept in mind as the effects are discussed. At low doses, these drugs produce a feeling of relaxation and calmness. They induce muscle relaxation, disinhibition, and a reduction in anxiety. Judgment and motor coordination are impaired, and there is a decrease in reflexes, pulse rate, and blood pressure. At high doses, the person demonstrates slurred speech, staggering, and, eventually, sleep. Phenobarbital and Valium have anticonvulsant properties and are used to control seizures. The benzodiazepines are also used to clinically control the effects from alcohol withdrawal.

Overdose

Alcohol overdose is common. We refer to this syndrome as being "drunk." The symptoms include staggering, slurred speech, extreme disinhibition, and blackouts (an inability to recall events that occurred when the individual was intoxicated). Generally, the stomach goes into spasm and the person will vomit, helping to eliminate alcohol from the body. However, the rapid ingestion of alcohol, particularly in a nontolerant individual, may result in coma and death. This happens most frequently with young people who participate in drinking contests.

As these drugs depress the central nervous system, overdose is extremely dangerous and can be fatal. Since the fatal dosage is only 10 to 15 times the therapeutic dosage, barbiturates are often used in suicides, which is one reason they are not frequently prescribed. It is far more difficult to overdose on the minor tranquilizers. However, CNS depressants have a synergistic or potentiation effect, meaning that the effect of a drug is enhanced as a result of the presence of another drug. For example, if a person has been drinking and then takes a minor tranquilizer such as Xanax, the effect of the Xanax may be dramatically enhanced. This combination has been the cause of many accidental deaths and emergency room visits.

Tolerance

There is a rapid development of tolerance to all CNS depressant drugs. Cross-tolerance also develops. This is one reason why overdose is such a problem. For example, Bob, a very heavy drinker, is quite anxious and is having difficulty sleeping. He goes to his physician with these symptoms. The physician does not ask about his alcohol use and gives him a prescription of Xanax. Bob follows the directions and takes one pill. However, because he is tolerant to alcohol, he is also cross-tolerant to Xanax and the pill has no effect. He can't sleep so he takes three more pills and has a glass of brandy. The synergistic effect of these drugs results in a coma.

The tolerance that develops to the CNS depressants is also one reason that the use of the minor tranquilizers has become problematic. People are given prescriptions to alleviate symptoms such as anxiety and sleep disturbance that are the result of other problems such as marital discord. The minor tranquilizers temporarily relieve the symptoms but the real problem is never addressed. The person continues to use the drug to alleviate the symptoms, but tolerance develops and increasing dosages must be used to achieve the desired effect. This is a classic paradigm for the development of addiction and/or overdose.

Withdrawal

The withdrawal syndrome from CNS depressants can be medically dangerous. These symptoms may include anxiety, irritability, loss of appetite, tremors, insomnia, and seizures. In the severe form of alcohol withdrawal called delirium tremens (DTs), additional symptoms are fever, rapid heartbeat, and hallucinations. People can and do die from the withdrawal from these drugs. Therefore, the detoxification process for CNS depressants should include close supervision and the availability of medical personnel. Chronic, high-dosage users of these drugs should be discouraged from detoxifying without support and supervision. For detoxification in a medical setting, minor tranquilizers can be used, in decreasing dosages, to reduce the severity of the withdrawal symptoms.

The dangerousness of withdrawal from CNS depressants is one reason why supervised detoxification is needed. In addition, supervision and support are usually required because the withdrawal symptoms are unpleasant and rapidly alleviated by using CNS depressants. For example, a 47-year-old man decides that he has been drinking too much and wants to quit. He doesn't tell anyone and is going to "tough it out." Although he doesn't have any medically dangerous symptoms, he is anxious, irritable, and has trouble sleeping. His family, friends, and coworkers remark about how unpleasant he is, and he is quite uncomfortable. He has a few drinks and finds that the symptoms are gone. Very rapidly, he is drinking heavily again.

Acute and Chronic Effects

In terms of damage to the human body and to society, alcohol is the most dangerous psychoactive drug (tobacco causes far more health damage). Alcohol has a damaging effect on every organ system. Chronic effects include permanent loss of memory, gastritis, esophagitis, ulcers, pancreatitis, cirrhosis of the liver, high blood pressure, weakened heart muscles, and damage to a fetus including fetal alcohol syndrome and fetal alcohol effect (see Chapter 12). Other chronic effects include family, social, occupational, and financial problems. Acutely, alcohol is the cause of many traffic and other accidents and is involved in many acts of violence and crime. The yearly monetary cost to the United States attributable to alcohol is estimated to be $185 billion (Harwood, 2000).

Certainly, the other CNS depressants can cause the same acute problems that are the result of injury and accident and chronic effects on the individual and family due to addiction.

Central Nervous System Stimulants

CNS stimulants affect the body in the opposite manner as do the CNS depressants. These drugs increase respiration, heart rate, motor activity, and alertness. This classification includes highly dangerous, illegal substances such as crack cocaine, medically useful stimulants such as Ritalin, drugs with relatively minor psychoactive effects such as caffeine, and the most deadly drug used, nicotine. Cocaine was mentioned in 55% of the drug abuse-related emergency room episodes (Substance Abuse and Mental Health Services Administration, 2007).

Drugs in This Classification

Cocaine (coke, blow, toot, snow) and the freebase or smokeable forms of cocaine (crack, rock, base) are the most infamous of the CNS stimulants. Cocaine is found in the leaves of the coca shrub that grows in South America. The leaves are processed and produce coca paste. The paste is, in turn, processed to form the white hydrochloride salt powder most of you know as cocaine. Of course, before it is sold on the street, it is adulterated or "cut" with substances such as powdered sugar, talc, arsenic, lidocaine, strychnine, or methamphetamine. Crack is produced by mixing the cocaine powder with baking soda and water and heating the solution. The paste that forms is hardened and cut into hard pieces or rocks. The mixing and heating process removes most of the impurities from the cocaine. The vaporization point is lowered so the cocaine can be smoked, reaching the brain in one heartbeat less than if it is injected. Therefore, crack is a more pure form of cocaine than is cocaine hydrochloride salt powder.

Amphetamines are also CNS stimulants, and one form in particular, methamphetamine, is a major drug of addiction. The amphetamines include Benzedrine (crosstops, black beauties), Methedrine or methamphetamine (crank, meth, crystal), and Dexedrine (dexies). There are also nonamphetamine stimulants with similar properties such as Ritalin and Cylert (used in the treatment of attention deficit-hyperactivity disorder) and Preludin (used in the treatment of obesity). These drugs are synthetics (not naturally occurring), and the amphetamines were widely prescribed in the 1950s and 1960s for weight control.

Some forms of CNS stimulants are available without a prescription and are contained in many substances we use on a regular basis. Caffeine is found in coffee, teas, colas, and chocolate as well as in some over-the-counter products designed to help people stay awake (e.g., No Doz, Alert, Vivarin). Phenylpropanolamine is a stimulant found in diet-control products sold over-the-counter (e.g., Dexatrim). These products are abused by individuals who chronically diet (e.g., anorexics). Pseudoephedrine is a substance in many nasal decongestants. Since it is used in the manufacture of methamphetamine, federal and state laws have been passed to restrict the quantities of these over-the-counter medications that can be purchased.

Although it has mild euphoric properties, nicotine is the highly addictive stimulant drug found in tobacco products. According to the Centers for Disease Control and Prevention (2000), an estimated 440,000 Americans die each year from smoking-related illnesses. This is four times as many deaths as result from alcohol. By a wide margin, nicotine is the most deadly drug we will discuss. Ironically, it is not only legal, it is marketed. We will mention this contradiction in public policy in Chapter 15.

Routes of Administration

With CNS stimulants, every method of administration is possible and utilized. Caffeine is consumed in beverage form, but it is also eaten (e.g., chocolate) or taken in pill form (e.g., No Doz). Nicotine is obviously smoked but can be chewed (chewing tobacco, nicotine gum) or administered through a skin patch. Cocaine and amphetamines can be snorted, smoked, injected, and ingested.

Major Effects

The uses of CNS stimulants have an interesting history. Many of you know that Sigmund Freud wrote "Uber Coca," which described the use of cocaine to treat a number of medical problems. Originally, Coca-Cola contained cocaine. In the 1980s, cocaine was depicted in the popular press as a relatively harmless drug. Amphetamines were used in World War II to combat fatigue and were issued by the U.S. armed forces during the Korean War. These drugs have a long history of use by long-distance truck drivers, students cramming for exams, and women trying to lose weight.

As with most of the psychoactive drugs, some of the CNS stimulants (cocaine and methamphetamine) have a recreational use. The purpose is to "get high," or to experience a sense of euphoria. Methamphetamine and cocaine users report a feeling of self-confidence and self-assurance. There is a "rush" that is experienced, particularly when cocaine is smoked and when cocaine and methamphetamine are injected. The high from methamphetamine is generally less intense but longer acting than cocaine.

CNS stimulants result in psychomotor stimulation, alertness, and elevation of mood. There is an increase in heart rate and blood pressure. Performance may be enhanced with increased activity level, one reason why athletes use CNS stimulants. These drugs also suppress appetite and combat fatigue. That's why people who want to lose weight and people who want to stay awake for long periods of time (e.g., truck drivers) will use amphetamines.

Overdose

CNS stimulants stimulate the reward center of the brain. The most powerful of these drugs result in the body's not experiencing hunger, thirst, or fatigue. There is no built-in satiation point, so humans can continue using cocaine and methamphetamine until there is no more or they die. Therefore, the compulsion to use, the desire to maintain the high, and the unpleasantness of withdrawal make overdose fairly common. There may be tremors, sweating and flushing, rapid heartbeat (tachycardia), anxiety, insomnia, paranoia, convulsions, heart attack, or stroke. Death from overdose has been widely publicized because it has occurred with some famous movie stars and athletes. However, far more people experience chronic problems from CNS stimulant addictions than from overdose reactions.

Tolerance

There is a rapid tolerance to the pleasurable effects of cocaine and methamphetamine and the stimulating effects of tobacco and caffeine. If you drink five or six cups a day of combinations of coffee, tea, and colas, you probably know this with regard to caffeine. You will find that if you stop using caffeine for a couple of weeks and then start again, the initial doses of caffeine produce a minor "buzz," alertness, and/or restlessness.

The rapid tolerance to the euphoric effects of cocaine and methamphetamine leads to major problems with these drugs. The pleasurable effects are so rewarding, particularly when the drugs are smoked or injected, that the user is prone to compulsively use in an effort to recapture the euphoric effects. When injected or smoked, the effects are enhanced but of relatively short duration. Continual use to achieve the high leads to rapid tolerance. The user is then unable to feel the pleasure but must continue to use the drug to reduce the pain of withdrawal.

A sensitization or reverse tolerance can occur, particularly with cocaine. In this instance, a chronic user with a high tolerance has an adverse reaction (i.e., seizure) to a low dose.

Withdrawal

Unlike the withdrawal from CNS depressants, the withdrawal from these drugs is not medically dangerous. However, it is extremely unpleasant. If you have an addiction to caffeine and want to get a small taste of the withdrawal from CNS stimulants, discontinue your use of caffeine. The symptoms you can expect include a chronic headache, irritability, restlessness, and anxiety. You may have trouble sleeping and concentrating.

The withdrawal from cocaine and methamphetamine is called "crashing." The severe symptoms usually last two to three days and include intense drug craving, irritability, depression, anxiety, and lethargy. However, the depression, drug craving, and an inability to experience pleasure may last for several months as the body chemistry returns to normal. Suicidal ideation and attempts are frequent during this time, as are relapses. Recovering cocaine and methamphetamine addicts can become very discouraged with the slow rate of the lifting of depression, and, therefore, support is very important during this time.

If you have been or are addicted to nicotine, you probably have experienced the unpleasant withdrawal symptoms during attempts to quit (we are assuming that nearly everyone addicted to nicotine has tried to quit or has succeeded). Enhance the severity of your experience dramatically, and you may be able to achieve an empathic understanding of the withdrawal syndrome for cocaine and methamphetamine addicts.

Acute and Chronic Effects

As previously stated, the acute effects of CNS stimulants can be dramatic and fatal. These include heart attacks, strokes, seizures, and respiratory depression. However, the results of chronic use cause the most problems. The addictive properties of these drugs are extremely high. Individuals with addictions to cocaine and methamphetamine spend a tremendous amount of money to obtain drugs, and they encounter serious life problems related to their addiction. Also, there is an increased risk of strokes and cardiovascular problems, depression, and suicide in chronic users. Symptoms of paranoid schizophrenia can occur. If cocaine or methamphetamine is snorted, perforation of the nasal septum can occur. Injection of CNS stimulants has the same risks as injecting other drugs (e.g., hepatitis, HIV). Since these drugs suppress appetite, chronic users are frequently malnourished.

If you are smugly saying to yourself that the only CNS stimulant you use is caffeine, see the caffeine-induced disorders that are described in the *DSM-IV-TR* (see Chapter 6). Also, caffeine may precipitate panic attacks in individuals predisposed to panic disorders, and the drug may be detrimental to some heart patients (Julien, 2005). A woman who is considering having a baby should reduce caffeine intake, and pregnant and breastfeeding women are advised to abstain (Julien, 2005).

Clearly, the chronic effects of nicotine addiction are damaging to health. The number of health-related problems, deaths, and days of work missed due to the chronic use of tobacco products is astounding.

Opioids

The opioids[1] are naturally occurring (opium poppy extracts) and synthetic drugs that are commonly used for their analgesic (pain relief) and cough-suppressing properties. This includes injectable morphine for severe pain and prescription drugs, such as Loratab, Darvocet, and Percocet, for less serious ailments. Codeine is often an ingredient in prescription cough medicines.

Opium was used by early Egyptian, Greek, and Arabic cultures for the treatment of diarrhea since there is a constipating effect to this drug. Greek and Roman writers such as Homer and Virgil wrote of the sleep-inducing properties of opium, and recreational use of the drug in these cultures did occur (Julien, 2005). Morphine was isolated from opium in the early 1800s and was widely available without prescription until the early 1900s when the nonmedical use of opioids was banned.

One particular opioid that has been mentioned frequently in the news in the past few years is OxyContin (oxycodone). This time-released drug was designed for chronic pain control. By crushing the tablets and snorting or injecting them, users experience an effect similar to heroin. Tolerance and physical dependence occur rapidly. Since OxyContin is available by prescription, it can be obtained legally through physicians. However, abuse of this drug has led to prescription fraud and robbery of pharmacies.

[1]We will use the term *opioid* to refer to any natural or synthetic drug that has an analgesic (pain relieving) effect similar to that of morphine. The terms *opiate, narcotic,* and *analgesic* are also used to describe this classification of drugs.

Drugs in This Classification

The opioids include opium, codeine, morphine, heroin (smack, horse), Vicodin, Loratab, Dilaudid, OxyContin, Percodan, methadone, Darvon, Demerol, Talwin, and buprenorphine.

Routes of Administration

We are familiar with many of these drugs in the pill or liquid form when used for pain relief or cough suppression. When used illicitly, the opioids are often used intravenously, but this is also a route of administration when these drugs are used medically for pain relief. Heroin, which is used only illicitly in the United States, can be snorted or smoked in addition to the common intravenous method. As the danger of disease from dirty needles has been widely publicized, alternative routes of administration for heroin have become more popular. Opium has been smoked for centuries.

Major Effects

Opioids have medically useful effects including pain and cough suppression and constipation. Obviously, there is also a euphoric effect that accounts for the recreational use of these drugs. They can produce nausea and vomiting and itching. A sedating effect occurs, and the pupils of the eyes become constricted.

Methadone or Dolophine is a synthetic opioid that does not have the dramatic euphoric effects of heroin, has a longer duration of action (12 to 24 hours compared with 3 to 6 hours for heroin), and blocks the symptoms of withdrawal when heroin is discontinued. This is the reason for the use of methadone in the treatment of opioid addiction (see Chapter 8). The action of levo-alpha acetyl methedol (LAAM) has an even longer duration. Buprenorphine is now being prescribed in an office setting to treat opioid dependence.

Overdose

Death from overdose of injectable opioids (usually heroin) can occur from the direct action of the drug on the brain, resulting in respiratory depression. Death can also occur from an allergic reaction to the drug or to substances used to cut it, possibly resulting in cardiac arrest. Heroin accounted for 20% of drug abuse-related emergency room episodes in 2005 (Substance Abuse and Mental Health Services Administration, 2007). Overdose of other drugs in this classification may include symptoms such as slow breathing rate, decreased blood pressure, pulse rate, temperature, and reflexes. The person may become extremely drowsy and lose consciousness. There may be flushing and itching skin, abdominal pain, and nausea and vomiting.

Tolerance

Frequency of administration and dosage of opioids is related to the development of tolerance. Tolerance develops rapidly when the drugs are repeatedly administered but does not develop when there are prolonged periods of abstinence. The tolerance that does develop is to the euphoric, sedative, analgesic, and respiratory effects of the drugs. This tolerance results in the individual's using doses that would kill a nontolerant person. The tolerant individual becomes accustomed to using high doses, which accounts for death due to overdose in long-time opioid users who have been detoxified and then go back to using.

Cross-tolerance to natural and synthetic opioids does occur. However, there is no cross-tolerance to CNS depressants. This fact is important, because the combination of moderate to high doses of opioids and alcohol or other CNS depressants can (and often does) result in respiratory depression and death.

Withdrawal

When these drugs are used on a continuous basis, there is a rapid development of physical dependence. Withdrawal symptoms are unpleasant and uncomfortable but are rarely dangerous. The symptoms are analogous to a severe case of the flu, with running eyes and nose, restlessness, goose bumps, sweating, muscle cramps or aching, nausea, vomiting, and diarrhea. There is significant drug craving. These symptoms rapidly dissipate when opioids are taken, which accounts for relapse when a person abruptly quits on his or her own ("cold turkey"). When the drugs are not available to the dependent individual, the unpleasant withdrawal symptoms also result in participation in criminal activities in order to purchase the drugs.

Acute and Chronic Effects

As we have already stated, there is an acute danger of death from overdose from injecting opioids, particularly heroin. Also, the euphoric effects of opioids rapidly decrease as tolerance increases, and, as this tolerance occurs, the opioid use is primarily to ward off the withdrawal symptoms.

Compared with the chronic use of CNS depressants, chronic use of the drugs themselves is less dangerous to the body. However, the route of administration and the lifestyle associated with chronic opioid use clearly has serious consequences. Obviously, there is the risk of communicable disease from the intravenous use of opioids and sharing needles. The lifestyle of heroin addicts often includes criminal activity to secure enough money to purchase heroin. Women may participate in prostitution, which adds the associated risks of diseases and violence. Nutrition is frequently neglected. However, those individuals who have been involved in methadone maintenance programs for long periods of time do not experience negative health consequences from the use of methadone (which is taken orally).

Hallucinogens

Many of the hallucinogens are naturally occurring and have been used for thousands of years. Some have been (and are currently) used as sacraments in religious rites and have been ascribed with mystical and magical properties. Today, many types of hallucinogens are synthetically produced in laboratories. Some of the hallucinogens became very popular in the 1960s and 1970s, with a drop in use in the 1980s. While there was a resurgence of use from 1992 to 2001 among youth, recent surveys have shown the lowest use of hallucinogens since the surveys were started in 1975 (Johnston, O'Malley, & Bachman, 2006).

Drugs in This Classification

As Julien (2005) points out, this classification comprises a group of heterogeneous compounds. Although there may be some commonality in terms of effect, the chemical structures are quite different. The hallucinogens we will discuss include LSD (acid, fry), psilocybin (magic mushrooms, shrooms), morning glory seeds (heavenly blue), mescaline (mesc, big chief, peyote), STP (serenity, tranquility, peace), and PCP (angel dust, hog). PCP is used as a veterinary anesthetic, primarily for primates.

Routes of Administration

Hallucinogens are usually swallowed. For example, LSD may be put on a sticker, stamp, or sugar cube. Psilocybin is eaten. However, hallucinogens can also be snorted, smoked, or injected. PCP is often sprinkled on a marijuana joint and smoked.

Major Effects

These drugs produce an altered state of consciousness, including altered perceptions of visual, auditory, olfactory, and/or tactile senses and an increased awareness of inner thoughts and impulses. Sensory experiences may cross into one another (e.g., hearing color). Common sights and sounds may be perceived as exceptionally intricate and astounding. In the case of PCP, there may be increased suggestibility, delusions, and depersonalization and dissociation. Physiologically, hallucinogens produce a rise in pulse and blood pressure.

Overdose

With the exception of PCP, the concept of "overdose" is not applicable to the hallucinogens. For example, Julien (2005) reports that the lethal dose of LSD is 280 times the normal dose. "Bad trips" or panic reactions do occur and may include paranoid ideation, depression, undesirable hallucinations, and/or confusion (Julien, 2005). These are usually managed by providing a calm and supportive environment. An overdose of PCP may result in acute intoxication, acute psychosis, or coma. In the acute intoxication or psychosis, the person may be agitated, confused, and excited, and may exhibit a blank stare and violent behavior. Analgesia (insensibility to pain) occurs that may result in self-inflicted injuries and injuries to others when attempts are made to restrain the individual.

Tolerance

Tolerance to the hallucinogenic properties of these drugs occurs, as well as crosstolerance between LSD and other hallucinogens. No cross-tolerance to cannabis has been demonstrated. Tolerance to PCP has not been demonstrated in humans (American Psychiatric Association, 2000).

Withdrawal

There is no physical dependence that occurs from the use of hallucinogens, although psychological dependence, including drug craving, does occur.

Acute and Chronic Effects

A fairly common and well-publicized adverse effect of hallucinogens is the experience of flashbacks. Flashbacks are the recurrence of the effects of hallucinogens long after the drug has been taken. Reports of flashbacks more than five years after taking a hallucinogen have been reported although abatement after several months is more common.

With regard to LSD, there are acute physical effects including a rise in heart rate and blood pressure, higher body temperature, dizziness, and dilated pupils. Mental effects include sensory distortions, dreaminess, depersonalization, altered mood, and impaired concentration. "Bad trips" involve acute anxiety, paranoia, fear of loss of control, and delusions. Individuals with preexisting mental disorders may experience more severe symptoms. With regard to chronic effects, we have already mentioned the rare but frightening experience of flashbacks. According to Julien (2005), most heavy users of LSD discontinue use at some point because they get tired of it or have no further need for it.

On the other hand, PCP does result in significant adverse effects. We have already discussed some of these effects. Chronic use may result in psychiatric problems including depression, anxiety, and paranoid psychosis. Accidents, injuries, and violence occur frequently.

Cannabinols

Marijuana is the most widely used illegal drug. Nearly 17% of adults in the 18 to 25 year range reported using marijuana in the previous month (Substance Abuse and Mental Health Services Administration, 2006). The earliest references to the drug date back to 2700 B.C. In the 1700s, the hemp plant (*Cannabis sativa*) was grown in the colonies for its fiber, which was used in rope. Beginning in 1926, states began to outlaw the use of marijuana since it was claimed to cause criminal behavior and violence. Marijuana use became popular with mainstream young people in the 1960s. Some states have basically decriminalized possession of small amounts of marijuana although, according to the federal government, it remains a Schedule I drug. However, emergency room episodes in which marijuana was mentioned comprised 30% of the total drug abuse-related emergency room visits (Substance Abuse and Mental Health Services Administration, 2007).

Drugs in This Classification

The various cannabinols include marijuana (grass, pot, weed, joint, reefer, dube), hashish, charas, bhang, ganja, and sinsemilla. The active ingredient is delta-9-tetrahydrocannabinol (THC). Hashish and charas have a THC content of 7% to 14%; ganja and sinsemilla, 4% to 7%; and bhang and marijuana, 2% to 5%. For simplicity, we will refer to the various forms of cannabinols as "marijuana."

Routes of Administration

Marijuana is usually smoked in cigarette form or pipes. It can also be ingested, normally by baking it in brownies or cookies.

Major Effects

Marijuana users experience euphoria; enhancement of taste, touch, and smell; relaxation; increased appetite; altered time sense; and impaired immediate recall. An enhanced perception of the humor of situations or events may occur. The physiological effects of marijuana include increase in pulse rate and blood pressure, dilation of blood vessels in the cornea (which produces bloodshot eyes), and dry mouth. Motor skills and reaction time are slowed. According to the National Institute of Health (1997), marijuana may be medically useful in reducing nausea and vomiting from chemotherapy, stimulating appetite in AIDS and other wasting-syndrome patients, treating spasticity and nocturnal spasms complicating multiple sclerosis and spinal cord injury, controlling seizures, and managing neuropathic pain. However, further clinical studies are necessary to reach conclusions on the value of marijuana in medical treatment.

Overdose

Overdose is unusual because the normal effects of marijuana are not enhanced by large doses. Intensification of emotional responses and mild hallucinations can occur, and the user may feel "out of control." As with hallucinogens, many reports of overdose are panic reactions to the normal effects of the drug. In individuals with preexisting mental disorders (e.g., schizophrenia), high doses of marijuana may exacerbate symptoms such as delusions, hallucinations, disorientation, and depersonalization (Julien, 2005).

Tolerance

Tolerance is a controversial area with regard to marijuana. According to Palfai and Jankiewicz (1997), mild tolerance may develop. However, Inaba and Cohen (2000) stated that, "Tolerance to marijuana occurs in a rapid and dramatic fashion" (p. 241). The difference of opinion as to whether tolerance develops slowly or quickly may be due to type of subject studied and various definitions of "dosage." For example, tolerance rapidly occurs in animals but only with frequent use of high doses in humans (Hanson, Venturelli, & Fleckenstein, 2006). At the least, chronic users probably become accustomed to the effects of the drug and are experienced in administering the proper dosage to produce the desired effects. Cross-tolerance to CNS depressants, including alcohol, has been demonstrated (Palfai & Jankiewicz, 1997).

Withdrawal

A withdrawal syndrome can be observed in chronic, high-dosage users who abruptly discontinue their use. The symptoms include irritability, restlessness, decreased appetite, insomnia, tremor, chills, and increased body temperature. The symptoms usually last three to five days.

Acute and Chronic Effects

As you are all aware, marijuana has been and continues to be controversial. Ballot measures in several states have involved marijuana laws. This controversy is related to the facts and myths regarding marijuana's acute and chronic effects. However, the professional community has as many views of the "facts" regarding marijuana as does the general public. While our interpretation of the research may be different than others, we are confident in saying that this issue is not "black and white." Marijuana should clearly not be a Schedule I drug. However, no psychoactive drug is safe. Marijuana can and does result in significant life problems for many people.

Marijuana is certainly not acutely or chronically dangerous when death is the measure of dangerousness. However, the effect on motor skills and reaction time certainly impairs the user's ability to drive a car, boat, plane, or other vehicle.

Chronic use of marijuana does seem to have an adverse effect on lung function, although there is no direct evidence that it causes lung cancer. Although an increase in heart rate occurs, there does not seem to be an adverse effect on the heart. As is the case with CNS depressants, marijuana suppresses the immune system. Chronic marijuana use decreases the male hormone testosterone (as does alcohol) and adversely affects sperm formation. However, no effect on male fertility or sexual potency has been noted. Female hormones are also reduced, and impairment in ovulation has been reported.

Although marijuana has been reported to cause amotivational syndrome, which is characterized by apathy, loss of goal directiveness, and dulled emotions, no causal relationship has been established (Schwartz, 1987).

In addition, the National Institute on Drug Abuse (1998) provides evidence that marijuana produces adverse effects on the brain, lungs, reproductive system, attention, memory, and learning. However, other investigators reviewing marijuana research have arrived at different conclusions (Zimmer & Morgan, 1997). For an objective review of the literature on all aspects of marijuana, we recommend *Cannabis Use and Dependence: Public Health and Public Policy* by Hall and Pacula (2003).

Inhalants and Volatile Hydrocarbons

Inhalants and volatile hydrocarbons consist largely of chemicals that can be legally purchased and that are normally used for nonrecreational purposes. In addition, this classification includes some drugs that are used legally for medical purposes. As psychoactive drugs, most of these substances are used mainly by young people, particularly in low socioeconomic areas. Since most of these chemicals are accessible in homes and are readily available for purchase, they are easily used as psychoactive drugs by young people who are beginning drug experimentation and by individuals who are unable to purchase other mind-altering substances due to finances or availability.

Drugs in This Classification

The industrial solvents and aerosol sprays that are used for psychoactive purposes include gasoline, kerosene, chloroform, airplane glue, lacquer thinner, acetone, nail polish remover, model cement, lighter fluid, carbon tetrachloride, fluoride-based sprays, and metallic paints. Volatile nitrites are amyl nitrite (poppers), butyl and isobutyl (locker room, rush, bolt, quick silver, zoom). Amyl nitrite has typically been used in the gay community. In addition, nitrous oxide (laughing gas), a substance used by dentists, is also included in this classification.

Route of Administration

As the name of this classification implies, these drugs are inhaled, a method of administration referred to as "huffing" or sniffing. The industrial solvents and aerosol sprays are often poured or sprayed on a rag and put in a plastic bag. The individual then places his or her head in the plastic bag and inhales rapidly and deeply.

Major Effects

The solvents and sprays reduce inhibition and produce euphoria, dizziness, slurred speech, an unsteady gait, and drowsiness. Nystagmus (constant involuntary movements of the eyes) may be noted. The nitrites alter consciousness and enhance sexual pleasure. The user may experience giddiness, headaches, and dizziness. Nitrous oxide produces giddiness, a buzzing or ringing in the ears, and a sense that the user is about to pass out.

Overdose

Overdose of these substances may produce hallucinations, muscle spasms, headaches, dizziness, loss of balance, irregular heartbeat, and coma from lack of oxygen.

Tolerance

Tolerance does develop to nitrous oxide but does not seem to develop to the other inhalants.

Withdrawal

There does not appear to be a withdrawal syndrome associated with these substances.

Acute and Chronic Effects

The most critical acute effect of inhalants is a result of the method of administration, which can result in loss of consciousness, coma, or death from lack of oxygen. Respiratory arrest, cardiac arrhythmia, or asphyxiation may occur. Many of these substances are highly toxic, and chronic use may cause damage to the liver, kidneys, brain, and lungs.

Anabolic Steroids

Anabolic steroids are synthetic drugs that are illicitly used to improve athletic performance and increase muscle mass. These drugs resemble the male sex hormone, testosterone.

Although some anabolic steroids are approved for use in the United States for medical purposes, the abuse of these drugs led Congress to pass the Anabolic Steroids Act of 1990. This law regulated the distribution and sale of anabolic steroids and added these drugs to Schedule III of the Controlled Substances Act. In 2005, 1.5% of high school seniors reported steroid use in the previous year (Johnston et al., 2006).

Drugs in This Classification

Anabolic steroids approved in the United States include Depo-Testosterone, Durabolin, Danocrine, and Halotestin. Some veterinary anabolic steroids are illicitly sold for human use and include Finiject 30, Equipoise, and Winstrol. Delatestryl, Testex, and Maxibolan are sold legally only outside of the United States.

Routes of Administration

Anabolic steroids are taken orally or injected. "Stacking" refers to combining oral and injectable steroids.

Major Effects

Anabolic steroids are used medically for testosterone replacement and treatment of muscle loss, blood anemia, and endometriosis. However, the abuse of these drugs by athletes and by those who wish to improve their physical appearance is prompted by the effects of anabolic steroids on muscle strength, body mass, and personality. These drugs increase muscle strength, reduce body mass, and increase aggressiveness, competitiveness, and combativeness.

Overdose

When used illicitly to improve athletic performance or physical appearance, the dosage is well beyond the therapeutic dose. For example, Brower, Blow, Young, and Hill (1991) found that weight lifters used from 2 to 26 times the recommended dose of anabolic steroids. Although there is no immediate danger of death or serious medical problems from high dosage levels of anabolic steroids, there are serious complications from long-term use. These effects will be described later in this section.

Tolerance

No evidence of tolerance to anabolic steroids exists.

Withdrawal

Physical and psychological dependence on anabolic steroids does occur, and there is a withdrawal syndrome. The symptoms of withdrawal include depression, fatigue, restlessness, insomnia, loss of appetite, and decreased interest in sex.

Acute and Chronic Effects

For males, atrophy of testicles, impaired production of sperm, infertility, early baldness, acne, and enlargement of the breasts occurs. In females, there are masculinizing effects including increased facial and body hair, lowered voice, and irregularity or cessation of menses. There is an increased risk of coronary artery disease due to reduced "good" cholesterol (HDL) and increased "bad" cholesterol (LDL). An association has also been established between oral anabolic steroids and jaundice and liver tumors (Julien, 2005). Mood swings, with periods of unreasonable and uncontrolled anger and violence, have been noted.

Club Drugs

Rather than sharing pharmacological similarities, the drugs that will be discussed in this section are grouped together because of the environment in which they are commonly used. The use of these drugs is primarily by youth and young adults associated with dance clubs, bars, and all-night dance parties ("raves").

It would not make sense to discuss the common characteristics of overdose, tolerance, withdrawal, and acute and chronic effects since the drugs are not related pharmacologically. However, we felt that it was important to reference these drugs as a separate class because of the wide media coverage of club drugs. We will refer to the most appropriate pharmacological classification for each drug, and you can refer to the characteristics in the designated section.

Rohypnol (roofies) is a benzodiazepine (CNS depressant) that is illegal in the United States, but widely prescribed in Europe as a sleeping pill. When used in combination with alcohol, Rohypnol produces disinhibition and amnesia. Rohypnol has become known as the "date rape" drug because of reported instances in which women have been unknowingly given the drug while drinking. When women are sexually assaulted, they cannot easily remember the events surrounding the incident.

MDMA (ecstasy) has the properties of the CNS stimulants and hallucinogens. It is taken in tablet form primarily, but can also be found in powder and liquid forms. It is relatively inexpensive ($10 to $20 per pill) and long lasting. Ecstasy is primarily used by youth and college-age adults. The euphoric effects include rushes of exhilaration and the sensation of understanding and accepting others. Some people experience nausea, and depression may be experienced following use. Deaths have been reported from ecstasy use primarily as a result of severe dehydration from dancing for long periods of time without drinking water. Ecstasy can be used compulsively and become psychologically addictive.

Ketamine (K or special K) is generally considered to be a hallucinogen. It is used as a veterinary anesthetic and is usually cooked into a white powder from its liquid form and snorted. The euphoric effect of ketamine involves dissociative anesthetics or separating perception from sensation. Users report feeling "floaty" or outside their body. Higher doses expand this experience. They may have some numbness in extremities. Ketamine is very dangerous in combination with depressants, since higher doses depress respiration and breathing. Frequent use may lead to mental disorders due to the hallucinogenic properties of the drug. Psychological dependence also occurs in frequent users.

GHB (gamma hydroxybutyrate) is actually a synthetic steroid originally sold over the counter in health food stores as a body-building aid. GHB is usually sold as an odorless liquid that has a slight salty taste. The effects are similar to CNS depressants, with low doses resulting in euphoria, relaxation, and happiness. However, higher doses can cause dizziness, drowsiness, vomiting, muscle spasms, and loss of consciousness. Overdoses can result in coma or death, as can mixing GHB with other CNS depressants such as alcohol. Physical dependence can occur.

Other drugs, such as LSD, PCP, mescaline, and marijuana are sometimes classified as club drugs. However, since these drugs have a wider use, we have discussed them in other drug classifications.

Drugs Used in the Treatment of Mental Disorders

Mental health professionals will work with clients who are taking a variety of legally prescribed drugs to treat many mental disorders. These drugs generally have little or no euphoric effects and, therefore, are not used for recreational purposes. However, it is certainly important for helping professionals to have some familiarity with the uses and effects of these drugs.

Drugs Used in the Treatment of Psychotic Disorders

Antipsychotic or neuroleptic drugs are used in the treatment of schizophrenia and other psychotic disorders. These major tranquilizers produce psychomotor slowing, emotional quieting, and an indifference to external stimuli. Although these drugs are called "tranquilizers," the effects are not euphoric or pleasant. Therefore, they are not drugs of abuse. The phenothiazines (Thorazine, Stelazine, Prolixin, Mellaril) and nonphenothiazines (Navane, Haldol) control agitation and hallucinations. Disturbed thinking and behavior is reduced. These effects have allowed many schizophrenic individuals to live in noninstitutional settings and to function more effectively. However, if the drugs are discontinued, the psychotic symptoms reappear. The drugs do not produce tolerance or physical or psychological dependence. Acute side effects include a dry mouth and Parkinson-like symptoms such as disordered motor movements, slow motor movements, and underactivity. Chronic effects include repetitive, involuntary movements of the mouth and tongue, trunk, and extremities. Massive overdoses are usually not lethal.

A new generation of antipsychotics is now on the market. These drugs include Risperdal, Zyprexa, Clozaril, Seroquel, and Zeldox. They have fewer side effects than the earlier drugs.

Drugs Used in the Treatment of Affective Disorders

Antidepressant drugs elevate mood, increase physical activity, improve appetite, reduce insomnia, and reduce suicidal ideation in most depressed clients. They are used for the treatment of acute and chronic depression. There are three types of antidepressant drugs. The MAO (monoamine oxidase) inhibitors (Nardil, Parnate) are used infrequently today because these drugs can raise blood pressure if foods with tyramine (cheeses, herring,

Chianti wine) are consumed. The tricyclics (Tofranil, Elavil, Sinequan) were widely used as antidepressants until the development of the "second generation" antidepressants (Prozac, Luvox, Paxil, Zoloft). These drugs, although no more effective than the tricyclics, have a more rapid onset of effect and fewer adverse side effects. The tricyclics may take two to three weeks to produce the desired effects, while the newer drugs take about one week. This time difference can be critical with depressed clients. The tricyclics can produce cardiac problems and potentiate the effects of alcohol. Lethal overdoses are also possible. The media has widely publicized claims that Prozac has caused homicidal or suicidal behavior, but no cause-and-effect relationship has been scientifically established. However, these drugs have warnings for adolescents as there has been an established relationship between the use of antidepressants and the risk of suicidality in youth (Hammad, Laughren, & Racoosin, 2006). Second-generation antidepressants have also been used in the treatment of obsessive-compulsive disorder and panic disorders.

Lithium is used in the treatment of bipolar disorder. It is an antimanic, rather than an antidepressant, drug. Clients who take lithium must be closely monitored, since high concentrations can cause muscle rigidity, coma, and death.

The treatment of panic attacks has included antianxiety agents (benzodiazepines) that were discussed in the Central Nervous System Depressants section of this chapter (Librium, Valium, Xanax, Ativan). However, these drugs are dependence producing and are abused. Nonbenzodiazepines that are used to treat panic disorders but are noneuphoric include Atarax, Buspar, and many antidepressants.

Drugs Used in the Treatment of Attention Deficit Disorder

There has been a great deal of attention directed toward children and adults who have attention deficit disorder. This condition may exist with or without hyperactivity and is characterized by distractibility, inability to concentrate, short attention span, and impulsivity. It has been found that Ritalin, Cylert, and amphetamines reduce many of these symptoms. Ritalin and amphetamines have a rapid onset of effect and a short duration. Cylert is longer acting but also takes longer to work. These drugs are CNS stimulants and can be abused. The use of stimulants to control the symptoms of attention deficit disorder has always seemed paradoxical. However, it may be that this disorder is due to unfocused electrical activity in the brain, and the stimulant drugs may improve the ability of the individual to concentrate and focus. Rather than calming the person down, the affected client is simply better able to focus his or her energy, concentrate, and reduce attention to extraneous stimuli. This may also reduce the anxiety that often accompanies attention deficit disorder.

Since these drugs are CNS stimulants, there are the associated side effects of appetite suppression, sleep disruption, and growth disturbance when these drugs are continuously used by preadolescents. A small number of individuals experience lethargy and emotional blunting. If these symptoms occur, the physician should immediately be contacted to adjust the dose or to prescribe a different drug.

It should also be mentioned that these drugs should not be prescribed to control unruly behavior in children. Attention deficit disorder should be diagnosed only after a careful multidisciplinary assessment. The best protocol to evaluate the efficacy of medication is a double-blind procedure in which neither the school nor parent is aware when a placebo or active drug has been taken. Behavior should be observed at school and at home, and the case manager can then determine whether medication will be helpful.

There has been speculation that children with attention deficit hyperactive disorder (ADHD) who are treated with stimulant drugs would be more likely to develop problems with alcohol or other drugs later in life. However, in a meta-analysis of studies, Wilens, Faraone, Biederman, and Gunawardene (2003) found that ADHD children treated with stimulant drugs are *less* likely to develop substance abuse problems later in life than ADHD children who do not take medication. Since 2002, nonstimulant drugs (e.g. Strattera) have been approved by the FDA for treating ADHD in children and adults.

Summary

- The federal Controlled Substances Act classifies drugs into five schedules based on the addictive potential and medical uses of the drug.
- The classifications of drugs include central nervous system depressants (alcohol, minor tranquilizers), central nervous system stimulants (cocaine, methamphetamine), opioids (heroin, pain pills), hallucinogens (LSD, magic mushrooms), cannabinols (marijuana), inhalants and volatile hydrocarbons, anabolic steroids, and club drugs (ecstasy).
- Drugs are used to treat various mental disorders such as psychotic disorders, affective disorders (depression, anxiety), and attention deficit-hyperactivity disorder.

Additional Reading

Abadinsky, H. (2007). *Drug abuse: An introduction* (6th ed.). Chicago: Nelson-Hall Publishers.

Hanson, G., Venturelli, P. J., & Fleckenstein, A. E. (2006). *Drugs and society* (9th ed.). Boston: Jones and Bartlett.

Inaba, D. S., & Cohen, W. E. (2000). *Uppers, downers, all arounders* (4th ed.). Ashland, OR: Cinemed Inc.

Inciardi, J. A., & McElrath, K. (2007). *The American drug scene: An anthology* (5th ed.). Los Angeles: Roxbury Publishing.

Julien, R. M. (2005). *A primer of drug action: A concise, nontechnical guide to the actions, uses, and side effects of psychoactive drugs* (10th ed.). New York: W. H. Freeman and Company.

Schuckit, M. A. (1998). *Educating yourself about alcohol and drugs: A people's primer.* New York: Plenum Press.

Internet Resources

Comprehensive Drug Abuse Prevention and Control Act
www.usdoj.gov/dea/pubs/csa.html

Facts about specific drugs
www.nida.nih.gov/drugpages.html

Drug Use Surveys

National Household Survey on Drug Use and Health
http://oas.samhsa.gov/nsduh.htm

Monitoring the Future
www.monitoringthefuture.org/index.html

Further Discussion

1. Do you agree with the classification of marijuana as a Schedule I drug? Why or why not?
2. Compare the monthly rate of use of alcohol for minors compared to the rate of use of illicit drugs for 8th, 10th, and 12th graders (from the Monitoring the Future website). What conclusions do you reach and what are the implications?
3. Which classification of drugs is the most dangerous in your opinion? What are the public policy implications of your view?

3

Models of Addiction

You may have heard of Charles Manson, the leader of a cult of people who committed some horrible murders in 1969 in California. He ordered his cult members to kill some famous and wealthy people with the hope of creating a race war. Manson is currently serving a life sentence in prison and has been the subject of popular books and periodic media interviews, particularly whenever he has a parole hearing. Manson has been variously described as being possessed by evil spirits, as being the victim of an abusive and violent childhood, as being a sociopath, and as having a chemical imbalance that created a psychosis including delusions of grandeur and persecution. When one reads about Manson, all of these explanations of his behavior seem to make some sense. Certainly, whatever explanation makes the most sense probably depends on a person's values and beliefs, formal and informal training, and experience. However, it is important to critically examine the explanations of the behavior of someone such as Charles Manson, since different explanations have different implications for the proper method to deal with him. For example, if you believe that he is possessed by evil spirits, there may be a spiritual method to treat him (i.e., exorcism). If you accept the explanation that he is a sociopath, then the appropriate method may be firm punishment for his actions. If his behavior is due to his violent and abusive childhood, he may be deserving of our sympathy and in need of therapeutic interventions. Finally, if Manson's behavior is due to a chemical imbalance, then he is not responsible for his behavior and may need medication to manage his condition.

You can see that values and beliefs play a role in whichever explanation you accept. If you believe in evil spirits, this explanation may appeal to you. Formal and informal training will have an effect, since you may have taken some courses in sociology or social psychology and been taught that abusive childhood experiences are related to violent behavior in adulthood. Maybe you work in law enforcement and have directly seen the victims of brutality, and, from these experiences, you have come to believe that the perpetrators must be lacking in conscience to commit such crimes.

However, it may be that all of these explanations for the abnormal behavior of a Charles Manson have some validity. He may have a spiritual deficit, lack a conscience in the manner in which most of us understand this concept, be influenced by his childhood experiences, and have some form of physiological abnormality. The "amount" of explanation of his behavior may not be equally divided among these factors (they may not have equal weights in explaining Manson's behavior), and it may be necessary to consider a number of different variables in determining the most appropriate course of action. For example, the brutality of the murders, Manson's lack of remorse, and his potential for future violence may lead to a decision to incarcerate a person such as Manson, no matter what the "true" explanations are for his behavior.

The AOD field has also been characterized by a variety of explanations for the same behavior. This is certainly not unusual in the mental health or medical field. However, the fervor and inflexibility with which some proponents of certain models of addiction adhere to their models has produced controversy in this field. Furthermore, the use of AOD interests and elicits extensive involvement from the legal system, business, government, the religious community, as well as from the medical and mental health fields. The differing goals and orientations of these disciplines has resulted in sharp differences regarding the explanation of problematic use of AOD. Consequently, the manner in which those people with AOD problems are dealt has also been a controversial issue. We will discuss some of the various "models" or explanations of addiction, giving particular attention to the popular "disease concept." Also, we will discuss some cases that illustrate that one explanation alone for addictive behavior may be insufficient.

The Moral Model

The moral model explains addiction as a consequence of personal choice. Individuals are viewed as making decisions to use AOD in a problematic manner and as being capable of making other choices. This model has been adopted by certain religious groups as well as by the legal system. Drunkenness is viewed as sinful behavior by some religious groups (Miller & Hester, 1995), and the use of alcohol is prohibited by certain religions (e.g., the Mormon Church). From this perspective, religious or spiritual intervention would be necessary to change behavior. Several years ago, we conducted an AOD workshop for clergy, and the moral model was strongly advocated by many of the members who were present. Many saw acceptance of a particular religious persuasion as the necessary step to overcome AOD problems.

A 1988 Supreme Court decision found that crimes committed by an alcoholic were willful misconduct and not the result of a disease (Miller & Hester, 1995). Certainly, the manner in which states deal with drunk driving violations may relate to the moral model. In states where violators are not assessed for chemical dependency and where there is no diversion to treatment, the moral model guides policy. If excessive alcohol use is the result of personal choice, then violators should be punished.

The moral model is a common way that the general public has of conceptualizing alcoholics and addicts. For example, when you see a homeless person who is obviously affected by alcohol or other drugs, do you experience disgust, laugh at him or her, or express a moral judgment? Furthermore, as William White (2001), a well-known recovery advocate, notes, the language in the field is related to the moral model:

> Terms such as *alcohol abuse, drug abuse, substance abuse* all spring from religious and moral conceptions of the roots of severe alcohol and other drug problems.... to suggest that

> the addict mistreats the object of his or her deepest affection is a ridiculous notion.... Addicts, more than anyone, treat these potions with the greatest of devotion and respect. (p. 4, italics in original)

As White and other recovery advocates have noted, the moral model of addiction has contributed to creating a stigma about addiction and addicts. This stigma may cause barriers to getting help. For example, if you are having problems with alcohol or other drugs and if those around you believe that alcoholics and addicts are weak-willed and/or immoral, then you are more likely to try to solve the problem yourself or hide it than you would be to seek outside help.

Sociocultural and Psychological Models of Addiction

While the moral model explains addiction as a matter of personal choice caused by spiritual or character deficiencies, other explanations of addiction focus on factors that are external to the individual, such as cultural, religious, family, and peer variables or psychological factors. For example, Stanton Peele (1989), in his book criticizing the disease concept of alcoholism, points to the low rate of alcoholism among Chinese and Jewish populations. He provides a cultural explanation for this, since the Chinese and Jews do not disapprove of the use of alcohol but do disapprove of excessive drinking, particularly if it leads to inappropriate behavior. In these groups, young people use alcohol in social or ceremonial situations along with adults, but they also observe the prohibitions against excessive use and perceive the judgments made of those who violate the cultural sanctions regarding alcohol use (Peele, 1989). Cultural acceptance of heavy drinking has also been postulated to account for the high rate of alcoholism among certain groups such as Irish-Americans (Peele, 1984).

While the prohibition against the use of alcohol and other drugs by certain religious groups would seem to limit the number of AOD addicts among members of the group, this is not always the case. Those who believe that the problematic use of alcohol and other drugs is the result of environmental factors point to the moderate use of alcohol among certain religious groups (e.g., Jews) and their corresponding low rate of alcoholism, and they attribute this to the fact that members are taught to use alcohol responsibly. Those who are raised in a religion that prohibits the use of alcohol never observe moderate use and, therefore, if use is initiated, the individual is more likely to use in an excessive manner. Thus, in this conceptualization, the religious prohibition against the use of alcohol may actually contribute to excessive use for those who violate the prohibition or leave the religion.

Regardless of the model of addiction one adheres to, the use patterns and attitudes about alcohol and other drugs of family members and peers is highly related to addiction. Lawson, Peterson, and Lawson (1983) found that 30% of children with alcoholic parents developed alcoholism, compared with 5% of children with moderately using parents and 10% of children with abstaining parents. (These results have been used to support both genetic and environmental explanations of addiction.) Parental use of alcohol and other drugs has been identified as one of the most important factors in early use by adolescents (Barnes, Farell, & Cairns, 1986), and parental permissiveness toward use is highly correlated with adolescent AOD abuse (Johnson, Shontz, & Locke, 1984; McDermott, 1984). Furthermore, proponents of a sociocultural model of addiction believe that certain family environmental patterns predispose children for alcoholism. For example, A. W. Lawson (1992) found that disengaged, rigid families who are conflict-oriented and repress the expression of feelings and rigid, moralistic families were more likely to produce alcoholic offspring. In the effort to identify risk factors for adolescent substance abuse, Hawkins and his colleagues found that family history of alcoholism, family history of criminality or antisocial behavior, family management problems, parental drug use and positive attitudes toward use, and friends who use drugs were all predictive of adolescent AOD problems (Hawkins, Lishner, & Catalano, 1985; Hawkins, Lishner, Catalano, & Howard, 1985). Having friends who use drugs was among the strongest predictors.

While sociocultural or external factors have been used to explain addiction, psychological explanations of addiction also exist. It is beyond the goals of this text to discuss each of these theories, but we will spend some time on the most widely held psychological explanations of addiction. Perhaps the most accepted view, particularly by those outside the addiction field, is that the problematic use of alcohol and other drugs is secondary to some other psychological problem or condition. The primary psychological problem causes emotional pain, and alcohol and other drugs serve to temporarily relieve this pain. For example, a woman was sexually molested as a child by a relative. She does not tell anyone, or her story is not believed, and she does not receive any assistance. The woman experiences anger, guilt, embarrassment, and anxiety as a result of the experience and gravitates toward alcohol and other drugs to relieve these uncomfortable feelings. Another example would be the person who suffers from endogenous depression and self-medicates with stimulants to relieve the constant symptoms of depression.

John Bradshaw, the popular author and lecturer, has described compulsive behavior, including alcohol and drug addiction, as a reflection of an individual's effort to escape shame from the family of origin (Bradshaw, 1988). In support of this view, Coleman (1982) found that 33% to 62% of female alcoholics had suffered neglect or sexual abuse in their families of origin.

Related to the view that AOD problems are secondary to other psychological problems is the question about whether an alcoholic or addictive personality exists. Clearly, there are alcoholics and drug addicts who seem to be free of any identified psychological problems prior to their problematic use patterns. Proponents of psychological explanations of addiction believe that there may be an "addictive personality" that could be identified and that would explain why individuals with AOD addictions often have problems with nondrug addictive behavior (e.g., gambling, food, work, sex) following successful recovery from their drug of choice. However, this effort to identify the "addictive personality" has largely been unsuccessful. As Miller (1995) noted, "alcoholics appear to be as variable in personality as are non-alcoholics" (p. 90).

An additional psychological theory that has been used to explain addictive behavior is social learning theory. As a leading proponent of this theory, Alan Marlatt, has stated, "From a social-learning perspective, addictive behaviors represent a category of 'bad habits' including such behaviors as problem drinking, smoking, substance abuse, overeating, compulsive gambling, and so forth." (Marlatt, 1985, p. 9). In this conceptualization, drug use is initiated by environmental stressors or modeling by others and is reinforced by the immediate effects of the drug on the feelings generated by the stressor(s) or by acknowledgment or recognition from role models with perceived status. One example would be the case of the sexually molested woman we discussed earlier. From a social learning viewpoint, this woman used alcohol and other drugs to avoid the unpleasant emotions generated by her molestation (environmental stressor). Since there is an immediate (although temporary) relief from these negative feelings, alcohol or other drug use is reinforced. Another typical example would be the individual who uses alcohol to "unwind" after a stressful day at work. Since tolerance to alcohol develops, over time this person must use an increasing amount of alcohol to experience the reinforcing effects of alcohol on tension. A "bad habit" is developed.

The first author has a vivid recollection of his initial experience with alcohol and how modeling contributed to this experience and subsequent alcohol use. In his house, there was a wide variety of alcohol, and he saw it used daily with few observed negative consequences. One night when he was 12, the author was alone at home and began experimenting with a variety of alcoholic beverages. He became quite ill. Although his parents were upset, there was also a lot of talking about their first experiences with becoming sick from alcohol and some laughter about the situation. He also got a lot of attention from his friends when he told them about the incident. Therefore, in spite of some negative consequences (nausea and parental anger) there was sufficient positive reinforcement to increase the probability of repeated use.

In a social learning model, the sociocultural factors we discussed play a role in determining what type of drug is used, when it is used, and how it is used. For example, social use of alcohol may be acceptable, but drinking alone may be perceived as deviant. Snorting or smoking drugs may be within the behavior parameters of a social group, but intravenous use of drugs may result in ostracism. Furthermore, the psychological state of the person is also important. For example, if a child sees the parents using alcohol excessively in social situations, the child may be more likely to see drug use as acceptable in a social situation as a means of creating social comfort and fun. In contrast, imagine that the father in a family isolates himself and drinks in response to negative emotions. The child may see drug use as the appropriate reaction to negative emotions. The psychological state of the individual would be important, since social discomfort might elicit the desire for alcohol or other drugs in the first example, while negative emotions would elicit this desire in the second example.

Eventually, as the individual uses more and more, a physiological state of dependence occurs, and, consequently, withdrawal symptoms are experienced if the drug is removed. The use of the drug to relieve withdrawal symptoms is highly reinforcing, since an immediate and effective reduction or elimination of symptoms occurs (Tarter & Schneider, 1976). The social learning model of addiction has been widely used in the development of relapse prevention strategies, a topic that will be discussed in detail in Chapter 9.

Disease Concept of Addiction

This popular and controversial model of addiction is credited to E. M. Jellinek, who presented a comprehensive disease model of alcoholism (Jellinek, 1960). This model has become an implicit component of the Alcoholics Anonymous and Narcotics Anonymous programs, as well as a guiding model for many treatment programs (Kurtz, 1990). The World Health Organization acknowledged alcoholism as a medical problem in 1951, and the American Medical Association declared that alcoholism was a treatable illness in 1956. Following Jellinek's work, the American Psychiatric Association began to use the term *disease* to describe alcoholism in 1965, and the American Medical Association followed in 1966 (Royce, 1989). As with many concepts and theoretical models in the addiction field, the disease concept was originally applied to alcoholism and has been generalized to addiction to other drugs.

The disease of addiction is viewed as a primary disease. That is, it exists in and of itself and is not secondary to some other condition. This is in contrast to the psychological models discussed earlier in which addictive behavior is seen as secondary to some psychological condition. In Jellinek's (1952) own words:

> The aggressions, feelings of guilt, remorse, resentments, withdrawal, etc., which develop in the phases of alcohol addiction, are largely consequences of the excessive drinking…these reactions to excessive drinking—which have quite a neurotic appearance—give the impression of an "alcoholic personality," although they are secondary behaviors superimposed over a large variety of personality types…. (p. 682)

Jellinek (1952) also described the progressive stages of the disease of alcoholism and the symptoms that characterize each stage. The early stage, or prodromal phase, is characterized by an increasing tolerance to alcohol, blackouts, sneaking and gulping drinks, and guilt feelings about drinking and related behaviors. The next stage, the middle or crucial phase, is defined by a loss of control over drinking, personality changes, a loss of friends and jobs, and a preoccupation with protecting the supply of alcohol. The issue of "loss of control" has come to be a central defining characteristic of alcoholism and one of the more controversial aspects of the disease concept. We will examine this issue when discussing criticisms of the disease concept. The late stage, or chronic phase, is characterized by morning drinking, violations of ethical standards, tremors, and hallucinations.

It is important to conceptualize these stages as progressive. In other words, the stages proceed in sequence and, in the disease model of addiction, are not reversible. Therefore, an individual does not go from the middle stage back to the early stage of alcoholism. The rate at which this progression occurs depends upon factors such as age, drug of choice, gender, and physiological predisposition (Royce, 1989). For example, adolescents progress more rapidly than adults, females faster than males, and users of stimulants more quickly than alcohol users (Royce, 1989). Proponents of the disease concept also do not believe that the progression of addiction disease is affected by a period of sobriety, no matter how long the period of sobriety lasts. As David Ohlms (1983), a physician, has stated:

> let's say that Jack or Jane stops drinking. Maybe because of some formal treatment: maybe he or she just goes on the wagon, and there is a prolonged period of sobriety for, say, 10 or 15 or even 25 years…. then for some reason,…Jack or Jane decides that they can drink again, and tries to return to the normal, social, controlled type of drinking that any non-alcoholic can get away with. But poor alcoholic Jack or Jane can't. Within a short period of time, usually within 30 days, the symptoms that the alcoholic will show are the same symptoms showed when drinking was stopped 25 years before. And usually worse. It's as if the alcoholic hadn't had that 25 years of sobriety, as if they meant nothing. An alcoholic cannot stay sober for awhile and then start over and have early symptoms of alcoholism. (p. 5)

Consistent with this concept (that the individual with addictive disease does not reverse the progression of the disease even with a prolonged period of sobriety) is the notion that addictive disease is chronic and incurable. That is, if an individual has this disease, it never goes away, and there is no drug or other treatment method that will allow the alcoholic or addict to use again without the danger of a return to problematic use. One implication of this notion is that the only justifiable goal for the alcoholic or addict is abstinence, which is the stance of Alcoholics Anonymous (Bratter, 1985; Ward, 1990). Furthermore, the idea that addiction is chronic and incurable is the underlying rationale for alcoholics and addicts who are maintaining sobriety for referring to themselves as "recovering" as opposed to "recovered" or "cured" (Royce, 1989).

In addition to the idea that abstinence must be the goal for those with addictive disease, there are other implications to the disease concept. First, if addictive disease is progressive, chronic, and incurable, then it is logical to assume that a person with this condition who does not enter "recovery" will eventually die. Death occurs as a result of accidents or the physical effects of alcohol and other drugs over time. However, most of these individuals are not identified as dying from addictive disease. For example, in 1994 a member of the Houston Oilers professional football team was involved in a traffic accident in which his best friend was thrown from the car and killed. The football player was so distraught at the sight of his dead friend that he took a shotgun from his car and killed himself. Both men were well over the legal limit for blood alcohol level. The football player's friend had a blood alcohol level over three times the legal limit. Although we cannot diagnose these men as alcoholics, whether they were or not, their deaths would not be classified as the result of alcohol use. These deaths were a result of a traffic accident and a suicide. However, if the men were indeed alcoholics, a proponent of the disease concept would attribute these deaths to alcoholism. Similarly, consider the individual who, after many years of heavy drinking, develops a liver disease. Eventually, he dies of liver failure. Is the cause of death liver failure or alcoholism? Again, in the disease concept of addiction, these deaths are the result of untreated addiction.

A further implication of the disease concept of addiction is that, if a person has this disease and, for example, the drug of choice of the person is alcohol, the person will continue to exhibit all the symptoms of the disease if he or she discontinues the use of alcohol and begins to use some other drug. This is true no matter what the drug of choice is. As Royce (1989) stated, "We mentioned the recovered alcoholics who relapse when given a painkiller by the dentist and have seen long-recovered alcoholics whose doctor prescribed tranquilizers after a mild heart attack relapse into alcoholic drinking within three weeks and death in six months" (p. 132). This phenomenon is not restricted to alcohol. "Based on extensive clinical experience, use of any psychoactive drug will usually lead back to use of the primary drug or addiction to the secondary drug (drug switching). I believe the only safe path to follow is complete abstinence from all psychoactive drugs" (McCarthy, 1988, p. 29).

Evidence to Support the Disease Concept

The evidence to support the disease concept is based on the similarity of alcoholism and drug addiction to other chronic diseases and on research on the brain chemistry and brain changes in addicts. McLellan, Lewis, O'Brien, and Kleber (2000) reviewed the literature on chronic illnesses, such as diabetes, asthma, and hypertension, and compared the characteristics of these diseases to addiction. They found that the genetic heritability, established by examining rates of diseases in identical versus fraternal twins, was very similar for alcoholism and drug addiction compared to the other chronic illnesses. In addition, response to treatment is similar. Left untreated, the condition of most alcoholics and drug addicts becomes worse. Remission is unusual. This also occurs with diabetes, asthma, and hypertension. McLellan et al. (2000) also showed that the percentages of clients who comply with treatment and the relapse rates of addiction and other chronic illnesses are the same. Addiction, diabetes, asthma, and hypertension are all conditions in which there is no "cure." However, all these problems can be managed through proper treatment, and this treatment must be followed for life.

McLellan et al. (2000) also discuss the issue of the "voluntary" nature of alcohol and other drug use. Again, they compare the choice to use alcohol and other drugs to other chronic illnesses. For example, diet, physical activity, and stress level are all factors affecting hypertension. These factors are all within voluntary control. However, what is not in voluntary control is the person's physiological response to these factors, and the physiological response is strongly influenced by genetic factors. Therefore, addiction is similar to other chronic diseases in that the management of the condition requires voluntary treatment compliance. However, the development of the disease is not due to choice, but to factors beyond voluntary control.

In addition, the National Institute on Drug Abuse (NIDA) has funded a great deal of research on the neuroscience of addiction. For example, Alan Leshner (2000), former director of NIDA, stated:

> Researchers have already identified some of the changes involved in two of the key phenomena associated with addiction: drug tolerance and drug craving.... we now know that drugs significantly increase the availability of dopamine, a neurotransmitter that activates the brain's pleasure circuits. When cells are exposed to repeated surges of dopamine due to chronic drug abuse, they may eventually become less responsive to dopamine signals.... As for drug craving...researchers have shown that it is related to widespread alterations in brain activity, especially to changes in the nucleus accumbens area of the forebrain. (p. 1)

Critics of the Disease Concept

As we said earlier, the disease concept is controversial and not without critics. For example, "because the majority of the treatment programs are based on the disease concept of alcoholism, their lobbying, public relations, and advertising efforts inevitably propagate the disease theme" (Fingarette, 1988, p. 23). Probably, the two most famous critics are Stanton Peele and Herbert Fingarette, both of whom have written books (Fingarette, 1988; Peele, 1989) as well as articles disputing the disease concept of addiction. Some of their arguments will be summarized here.

Since the disease concept is widely attributed to Jellinek, much criticism has been directed at his research, which was the basis for his conclusions about the disease concept. Jellinek's data were gathered from questionnaires distributed to AA members through its newsletter, *The Grapevine.* Of 158 questionnaires returned, 60 were discarded because members had pooled and averaged their responses. Also, no questionnaires from women were used. Jellinek himself acknowledged that his data were limited. Therefore, one might wonder why Jellinek's concept of the disease of alcoholism received such widespread acceptance. One reason is that the disease concept is consistent with the philosophy of AA, which is by far the largest organized group dedicated to help for alcoholics. Second, as Peele (1988) noted:

> The disease model has been so profitable and politically successful that it has spread to include problems of eating, child abuse, gambling, shopping, premenstrual tension, compulsive love affairs, and almost every other form of self-destructive behavior.... From this perspective, nearly every American can be said to have a disease of addiction. (p. 67)

Furthermore, Fingarette (1988) accuses the alcohol industry itself of contributing to the public perception of alcoholism as a disease:

> By acknowledging that a small minority of the drinking population is susceptible to the disease of alcoholism, the industry can implicitly assure consumers that the vast majority of people who drink are *not* at risk. This compromise is far preferable to both the old temperance commitment to prohibition, which criminalized the entire liquor industry, and to newer approaches that look beyond the small group diagnosable as alcoholics to focus on the much larger group of heavy drinkers who develop serious physical, emotional, and social problems. (p. 27, italics in original)

The progressive nature of addiction has also been criticized. George Vaillant (1983), a proponent of the disease concept, has suggested that there is no inevitable progression of Jellinek's stages of alcoholism:

> The first stage is heavy "social" drinking.... This stage can continue asymptomatically for a lifetime; or because of a change of circumstances or peer group it can reverse to a more moderate pattern of drinking; or it can "progress" into a pattern of alcohol abuse.... At some point in their lives, perhaps 10–15 percent of American men reach this second stage. Perhaps half of such alcohol abusers either return to asymptomatic (controlled) drinking or achieve stable abstinence. In a small number of such cases...such alcohol abuse can persist intermittently for decades with minor morbidity and even become milder with time. (p. 309)

Similarly, Royce (1989), in describing the patterns and symptoms of alcoholism, stated, "Even when progression occurs, it does not follow a uniform pattern. The steps may be reversed in order, or some steps may be omitted. Symptoms progress, too; something that was minor in an early stage may appear later in a different form or to a greater degree.... Rate of progression varies also" (p. 89). As with Vaillant, Royce takes a favorable position toward the concept of addiction as a disease.

As we have seen, some of those with sympathetic views toward the disease model of addiction have recognized that the concept of a rigid and inevitable progression of stages is not consistent with reality in working with individuals with AOD problems. However, the issue of "loss of control" has been a more contentious one. As Fingarette (1988) stated, loss of control may be "the central premise of the classic disease concept of alcoholism" (p. 31). Certainly, the first step of the Twelve Steps of Alcoholics Anonymous implies this loss of control: "We admitted that we were powerless over alcohol—that our lives had become unmanageable" (Alcoholics Anonymous, 1981, p. 5).

Several arguments have been advanced to dispute the notion of loss of control. Fingarette (1988) pointed out that if alcoholics lack control only after first consuming alcohol, then they should have no difficulty abstaining. Obviously, however, alcoholics do have difficulty abstaining. If loss of control exists before the first drink (which would explain the difficulty in abstaining), it implies a difficulty in exercising self-control or willpower, which is a much different model of addiction. Furthermore, experimental studies have demonstrated that alcoholics do exert control over their drinking and that variables such as the amount of effort to get alcohol, the environment in which drinking occurs, the belief about what is being consumed, rewards, and the like influence how much is consumed by an alcoholic (Fingarette, 1988; Peele, 1989). As one example, Marlatt, Demming, and Reid (1973) divided alcoholics into four groups. One group believed that they were taste-testing three brands of a vodka-tonic beverage when they were actually drinking tonic water only. A second group believed that they were taste-testing tonic water only, when they were actually drinking vodka and tonic. The third group was correctly told they were drinking a vodka and tonic beverage, and the fourth group was correctly told they were drinking tonic water only. The results showed that it was the alcoholic's belief about what they were drinking that determined the amount they drank and not the actual alcohol content of the beverage they consumed. The alcoholics who expected tonic and got alcohol drank an almost identical amount to those alcoholics who expected and got tonic. Both of these groups drank considerably less than the groups who expected alcohol, and the alcoholics who received and expected alcohol drank nearly the same amount as those alcoholics who expected alcohol but got tonic.

Defenders of the disease concept point out that "experimenters took too literally the idea that one drink always means getting drunk," and "Many research projects set out to disprove the 'one drink' hypothesis in laboratory or hospital settings so artificial and with criteria so wooden that nobody with real experience in alcoholism could take the results seriously" (Royce, 1989, p. 135). Loss of control has been modified to mean that the alcoholic or addict cannot predict the situations in which he or she will exercise control and the situations in which he or she will lose control. Therefore, this loss of predictability is thought to define the alcoholic or addict (Keller, 1972). Fingarette's (1988) response is that "This new approach to loss of control so emasculates the concept that it becomes useless in explaining or predicting drinking behavior" (p. 44).

Advantages of the Disease Concept

Perhaps the greatest advantage to the articulation that addiction is a disease has been to remove the moral stigma attached to chemical dependency and to replace it with an emphasis on treatment of an illness. We do not punish a person for having a disease; we provide assistance. In a more functional sense, defining addiction as a disease has also resulted in treatment coverage by insurance companies. Using medical terminology to describe addiction has also led to greater interest in scientific research. Few medical scientists would be interested in investigating the physiological correlates of a lack of willpower or to a moral deficiency. For the individual who has problems with alcohol or other drugs (and for the family as well), the concept of a disease removes much of the stigma and associated embarrassment, blame, and guilt. You would not feel guilty if you were diagnosed with diabetes and, therefore, a person with addictive disease need not feel guilty for having this disease. As we have said, people who believe that addiction is due to a lack of willpower or to a moral deficiency may avoid treatment, since the admission of the need for help is an admission that some character flaw exists. Therefore, an acceptance of the disease concept may make it easier for some people to enter treatment. Another advantage of the disease concept is that it is clearly understandable to people and provides an explanatory construct for the differences in their alcohol and other drug-taking behavior compared with others. To reuse the well-worn analogy with diabetes, it is quite clear to the people with diabetes that they cannot use certain foods in the same manner as those who do not have diabetes. If they do, there will be certain predictable consequences. Knowledge about the disease allows the alcoholic or addict to understand that he or she is physiologically different from others. In the same way that it may be unwise for the diabetic to eat a hot fudge sundae (in spite of the fact that friends may do so without consequences), the alcoholic learns that it would be unwise to drink (in spite of the fact that friends may do so without consequences). Finally, the disease concept has a logical treatment objective that follows from its precepts: abstinence. If you have a physiological condition that results in severe consequences when alcohol or other drugs are used, you can avoid these consequences by abstaining from alcohol or other drugs. If you attempt to use moderately, you will eventually lose control, progress through predictable stages, and suffer the consequences. Since most individuals who seek treatment for alcohol or other drug problems have experienced some negative consequences already, this argument can be compelling.

Disadvantages of the Disease Concept

As the critics of the disease concept have pointed out, the orthodox precepts of the disease concept may not be accurate. There is not an inevitable and completely predictable progression of symptoms and stages, nor a consistent loss of control. Therefore, individuals with alcohol or other drug problems who may need some form of intervention or treatment may avoid help since they do not fit the "disease model." For example, we were told by a substance abuse program counselor about an inquiry from a man whose girlfriend thought he had a drinking problem. Although he drank on a daily basis, his use of alcohol had not progressed in the last few years. When asked if he was having any financial, occupational, legal, or family problems, he said that he was not. Now certainly, denial may be at work here, but the point is that the intake counselor did not encourage the man to seek help since he did not fit the classic "disease" characteristics, while the program in which the counselor works is based on this model.

An adherence to the disease model may also result in a purely medical model of treatment:

> While this may have the advantage of motivating physicians to treat the alcoholic in a nonjudgmental way...the average American physician is still both reluctant to treat alcoholics and often ignorant about alcoholism.... Medical models tend to put the physician in full charge, focus almost exclusively on physical damage, and perpetuate a medical "revolving door" which is more humane than the drunk tank but equally ineffective for long-range treatment. It implies that nonmedical persons are unable to treat the illness.... (Royce, 1989, p. 123)

The notion that the disease concept removes responsibility from the alcoholic or addict for his or her behavior is frequently cited as a disadvantage of this model (Royce, 1989). Since the alcoholic or addict is "powerless" over the disease, inappropriate or even criminal behavior may be attributed to the "disease." Relapse may also be blamed on the disease, "If alcoholics come to view their drinking as the result of a disease or physiological addiction, they may be more likely to assume the passive role of victim whenever they engage in drinking behavior if they see it as symptom of their disease..." (Marlatt & Gordon, 1985, p. 7). In other words, if an alcoholic believes the disease concept and the AA slogan "one drink away from a drunk," then a slip (return to use) may result in the alcoholic's giving up responsibility for maintaining sobriety and returning to a previous level of use, since the slip is symptomatic of the loss of control. Proponents of the disease concept counter this argument by saying that the addict is not responsible for the disease but is completely responsible for recovery. In addition, court rulings have rarely allowed a defense of addiction for criminal behavior (Miller & Hester, 1995).

Biopsychosocial Model of Addiction

We want to describe six people we have known or worked with. Each has a history of heavy alcohol or other drug use. Bill, a bartender, was diagnosed as alcoholic at the age of 50. He was drinking over a fifth of whiskey a day. On his own volition, he went to a treatment program that used aversive conditioning techniques (see Chapter 8). At the time he entered treatment, his liver functioning was at about 20% of normal. In other words, if he had continued to drink much longer, he would have died. After completing the program, Bill returned to his job as a bartender. He never attended an AA meeting or returned to the treatment program for follow-up. Bill once said, "I'll drink myself to death rather than go back to that (treatment center) place." In 19 years, he never had a slip or relapse. Bill finally died of lung cancer, because he could not quit smoking.

Marty was a 15-year-old special education student with a diagnosis of learning disability. He was having continual problems with the law due to his use of alcohol. When Marty would consume a small amount of alcohol, he would suffer blackouts and become violent. He went through several in-patient treatment programs but quickly relapsed each time. When he was 20, Marty broke into a house while intoxicated and was discovered by the owner. He stabbed the man to death and is now in prison for life.

Loretta, a 30-year-old woman, was on probation for possession and distribution of methamphetamine. She lived with a man who used drugs and who was physically abusive to her and to her daughter. Another daughter had been removed from her custody. She lost her license to work in her profession due to her felony conviction. After her "boyfriend" was sent to prison, she found a job and a new place to live and was on the road to regaining custody of her other daughter. However, a random urinalysis by her probation officer came up dirty, and she was placed in an in-patient treatment program as an alternative to prison. Loretta lost her job, home, and custody of her children. Before this relapse, she had been sober for six months and was attending NA meetings.

Marvin, a 63-year-old man, had been a heavy drinker for 40 years. He was retired and relatively healthy. He developed a respiratory illness that required prolonged use of a medication that affected liver functioning. Marvin was told that he could not drink alcohol while taking the medication and that he was to take the medication for one year. It was suggested that his withdrawal from alcohol be medically supervised due to his prolonged and heavy use. Marvin rejected this suggestion, discontinued his alcohol use, and has been clean and sober with no slips for 10 years. He has never attended an AA meeting or any other form of treatment.

Hector, a 30-year-old man, began using alcohol and other drugs at the age of 13. He was in street gangs, involved in crimes, and incarcerated as a juvenile. Hector was placed in a drug treatment program at the age of 16 and attended NA meetings after treatment. He remained sober for about six months, at which time he again began to use cocaine, marijuana, and alcohol. At age 23, he married, had a child, and discontinued his heavy use. He continues to use alcohol and marijuana on an irregular basis. Hector is a successful officer in a small company, although he cannot read or write at a functional level.

Rebecca is currently 43 years old and has been sober for seven years. She reported that her husband expressed concern about her level of alcohol use prior to their marriage and that she "just decided to stop." Rebecca did not go through any treatment program, nor has she attended any AA meetings. She says that she has problems doing anything on a moderate basis, and, as a result, she has to monitor her eating behavior and work habits. Rebecca says, "I can't eat just a couple of M & Ms. If I start, I'll keep eating until they are all gone." She likes to drink nonalcoholic beer and wine, saying "It makes me feel like a grown-up."

Although we have changed the names of these people, these cases are all real. We are not implying that they are typical or atypical, and we did not include those individuals who completed traditional treatment programs or use AA as a primary method of maintaining sobriety, although we know plenty of people who do so. These cases are meant to illustrate the concept that is well articulated by Pattison and Kaufman (1982):

> Most scientific authorities in the field of alcoholism now concur that the construct of alcoholism is most accurately construed as a multivariate syndrome. That is, there are multiple patterns of dysfunctional alcohol use that occur in multiple types of personalities, with multiple combinations of adverse consequences, with multiple prognoses, that may require different types of treatment interventions. (p. 13)

Bill, Marty, and Loretta had patterns of use that could well fit within the disease model of addiction. In particular, Marty had a very unusual response to alcohol that certainly would make one suspicious of physiological differences. Bill's progression was very similar to that described by Jellinek (1952), but he responded to a treatment that was quite unlike the traditional models based on the disease concept. Loretta also continued to use in spite of having every reason to stop, which certainly seems like a loss of control.

In contrast, Marvin's drinking remained at a heavy but nonproblematic stage of use for many years with no apparent progression. In opposition to what might be expected, he had no physical or psychological problems discontinuing his use when faced with a strong motivation to stop. Hector, who seemed to have serious problems with alcohol and other drugs, reverted to moderate use when he matured and acquired responsibilities for others. His behavior could be explained from a social learning perspective. Rebecca seemed to demonstrate an "addictive personality." She constantly had to be aware of her characteristic of going overboard. Her use of nonalcoholic beer and wine is contrary to what is recommended by most treatment programs, but it works for her.

It's quite natural for treatment providers to develop a concept of addiction based on the clients they come in contact with. Helping professionals who work in substance abuse treatment programs see individuals who have had some pretty serious life problems as a result of their alcohol and other drug use. They are not likely to see individuals who have successfully discontinued their use on their own or through a nontraditional method, or to work with clients who interrupt their use patterns before they experience serious life problems. Finally, alcohol and other drug treatment providers do not usually see clients who are heavy users but who do not have life problems as a result of their use. Therefore, it is logical that those professionals who work in the substance abuse treatment field may develop a concept of addiction that is based on a biased sample. This is not to say that the disease concept does not fit many alcoholics and addicts or that traditional treatment approaches and Twelve-Step recovery programs are not useful. Certainly, as we illustrated with Bill, Marty, and Loretta, many alcoholics and addicts fit the characteristics of the disease concept, and many, many people have been helped by traditional treatment programs based on the disease concept and utilizing AA and NA. We are arguing that other explanations for problematic alcohol and other drug use and a variety of treatment options should be considered. Interestingly, Jellinek (1960), who is credited with developing the disease concept, identified five different types of problem drinking patterns, only two of which were thought to demonstrate the characteristics of the disease. This seems to be ignored by many disease concept proponents.

People begin AOD use on an experimental basis for lots of different reasons. They continue using because there is reinforcement for doing so through a reduction of pain, experience of euphoria, social recognition and/or acceptance, success, and so forth. Some people progress to abuse and addiction. Why?

It is certainly possible that progression in some people is due to a genetic predisposition and that this genetic predisposition may be understood through physiological differences. It is also plausible that personality characteristics may explain some progression, or that physical or emotional pain may explain some problematic use, or environmental circumstances may provide answers. Any combination of these factors may also be possible. With a certain client, we may find that the reduction of chronic back pain leads to a reduction in alcohol use. Another client (as with Hector) may have a change in environmental factors that leads to a change in use. Through therapy, another client may come to a greater self-awareness with regard to personality characteristics, and modification of use may occur. With other clients, reduction of pain, change of environment, and self-knowledge does not affect their use at all.

In an effort to reflect the multivariate nature of addiction, many authors now refer to the "biopsychosocial" model of addiction (e.g., Galizio & Maisto, 1985; Kumpfer, Trunnell, & Whiteside, 1990; Wallace, 1994). In the biopsychosocial model of addiction, the interactions of biological, psychological, cognitive, social, developmental, and environmental variables are considered to "explain" addiction. According to Kumpfer et al. (1990), the biopsychosocial model is a reasonable conceptualization because it incorporates the other models into a single model. Therefore, important factors in the treatment of a particular client are not ignored when all variables are considered. For example, the parents of Loretta (our methamphetamine user) were alcoholics. She was sexually and physically abused as a child. Her parents introduced her to alcohol at the age of 9. She consistently became involved with men who abused alcohol and other drugs. As you can imagine, all of these factors would be crucial in understanding Loretta's addiction and in designing a treatment program for her.

We suggest that mental health professionals, whether or not they work with substance abuse problems, thoroughly assess clients (see Chapter 6), develop multiple hypotheses to explain the client's AOD problem based on the assessment, avoid forcing the client to fit a rigid or preconceived notion of addiction, and utilize a variety of treatment methods and interventions (see Chapter 8) evolving from the assessment, hypotheses, and most important, the needs of the client.

Summary

- The moral model is not widely accepted and discourages people from seeking treatment.
- Sociocultural and psychological models explain addiction as a result of environmental or personality factors.
- The disease model is widely accepted because of its medical orientation and because abstinence is logically related to the model.
- The disease model has helped to reduce the stigma of addiction and has enlisted the support of the medical community in treatment.
- A disadvantage of the disease model is that some addicts blame their behavior on the "disease."
- The biopsychosocial model incorporates all the relevant variables in the etiology and treatment of addiction.

Internet Resources

Disease concept of addiction
www.bhrm.org/papers/Counselor1.pdf

Addiction as a brain disease
www.drugabuse.gov/scienceofaddiction

Criticism of the disease concept
www.peele.net/index.html

Further Discussion

1. Think about some celebrity you have heard about who has an AOD problem. Given what you know about this person, use different models of addiction to explain their condition.
2. Which model of addiction appeals to you the most? Why?

Models of Addiction

Case Study Activity

Read Substance Abuse, Case 2: An Emergency Room Patient Who Is a Chronic Alcoholic.

- Use one of the models of addiction to conceptualize this 42-year-old alcoholic/addict.

To access the case for this activity, log on to MyHelpingLab at www.myhelpinglab.com. Select the **Counseling & Psychotherapy** tab to locate the **Counseling Case Archive.**

4

Culturally and Ethnically Diverse Groups

As mentioned in Chapter 3, it is quite natural for treatment providers to develop a concept of addiction based on the clients with whom they come in contact. An important ingredient in this tentative formulation is the treatment provider's possession of a sound theoretical basis of the general nature of addictions. The same holds true when working with individuals and groups of different cultural and ethnic backgrounds. One needs to be well grounded in the understanding of the cultural values of that individual or group so that the formation of tentative hypotheses about alcohol and other drug use, abuse, and addiction are more likely to be accurate. This is especially true now because, by the time you read this, more than one-third of all Americans will be persons of color, and Delva, Wallace, O'Malley, Bachman, Johnston, and Schulenberg (2005) assert that the Hispanic population alone will make up 25% of the total U.S. population. This significant increase is not relegated only to people of color. As the U.S. population grows, so will the number of persons with disabilities. Reilly, Bocketti, Maser, and Wennet (2006) maintain that there are 40 million Americans with disabilities, and the number will likely increase, since having a disability is possible for anyone regardless of ethnicity or cultural background.

Without sensitivity to cultural differences and cultural competency, providers will likely be ineffective from the outset, because attempts to assess alcohol and other drug involvement will be met with both cultural and therapeutic resistance. This double whammy will undoubtedly preclude an accurate assessment of any type, let alone that of drug involvement.

Room (2005) maintains that ethnic and cultural identity in a diverse society is partly assigned and partly constructed. Ethnic and cultural assignment are particularly amenable for "visible minorities" who are identifiable by skin color, language differences, age, physical disability, or some other such external sign(s). However, ethnic and cultural assignment is also made for the more "invisible minorities" as well, such as those with learning disorders/differences and those differing in sexual orientation. Although little is known about adolescents with disabilities and their AOD use, the few studies published consistently show significantly higher substance use rates for youth with disabilities (e.g., Hollar

& Moore, 2004; McMillen, McMillen, & Simeonsson, 2002; Simeonsson, McMillen, McMillen, & Lollar, 2002).

When assigned (and thus, stereotyped), individuals and groups will often act out or perform the identity. This can serve to delineate and maintain sharper differences and separation between groups of people. Some of the acting out includes AOD use and abuse. For example, Lurie (1971) believes that the heavy drinking by Native Americans can be likened to the world's oldest ongoing protest demonstration, which serves to demark and maintain the Indian–Euro-American boundary. Stivers (2000) found that drinking in Ireland in the 1800s eventually lead to the British stereotyping of the Irish as heavy drinkers, and when the Irish came to America in the mid-nineteenth century, they acted that stereotype out in the United States so that drinking made the Irish "more Irish."

According to Malcolm, Hesselbrock, and Segal (2006), although Native Americans and Alaska Natives comprise less than 1% of the population in 2002, alcohol dependence among them is two times higher than that found in the general population. Moreover, Alaska Natives have an alcohol morbidity rate seven times higher than the general population. Together, these two groups account for roughly 2.4% of all admissions to publicly funded AOD and mental health treatment facilities (National Institute of Health, 2004).

Based on the need for cultural awareness, sensitivity, and competency, this chapter will present information on Native Americans and Alaska Natives, Asian and Pacific Islanders, African Americans, and Latino and Hispanic populations. We will also examine persons with disabilities and the elderly. Concerns for helping professionals when working with members of these populations will conclude the chapter.

Native Americans and Alaska Natives

Native Americans (which include American Indians, Alaska Natives, and Aleuts) have been separated by the United States government into three categories: (1) federally recognized tribes and bands, (2) nonfederally recognized tribes and bands, and (3) urban Native Americans. According to Napoli, Marsiglia, and Kullis (2003), Native Americans number about two million and approximately 300,000 to 400,000 are of school age, which represents about 1% of the nation's student population. There are over 558 tribes and 253 different languages. As of 2000, the Native American, Alaskan Native, and Aleut populations residing in the United States tended to live in one of ten major cultural areas: Northeast, Southeast, Plains, Arctic, Subarctic, Northwest Coast, Plateau, Great Basin, California, and the Southwest (U.S. Bureau of the Census, 2000). These cultural areas are further subdivided into urban or reservation lifestyles. In general, about one-half of Native Americans live in cities, and the other half reside on reservations or in other remote, widely separated areas (Lex, 1987).

If you were to spend a moment reflecting upon the differences between the Euro-Americans living in the northeastern United States and the South, or between the Southwest and the Midwest, or between California and the rest of the United States, you would begin to see that there are now and always have been vast differences in the ways that people speak, eat, dress, and approach life in general. The Native American populations are no different. Alaska Natives, for example, can be seen as differing along geographic lines that reflect a difference in cultures (Attneave, 1982). Alaskan Eskimos inhabit the coastal areas to the north while the Aleuts occupy settlements along the Aleutian Islands. Fairbanks is the cultural hub for the Athabascan-speaking tribes who reside in the surrounding mountains and valleys. Yet, very different are the coastal tribes who reside on the islands close to Juneau and Ketchikan and along the coast of the Alaskan panhandle. In attempting, then, to summarize and underscore the geographic distribution and variety of Native American cultures, it can be said that, in all probability, most Native Americans living outside of the Southwest would look at the silver and turquoise jewelry of the Southwest Pueblo Indians as being as much an exotic art form as would the non–Native American—regardless of whether they lived in urban centers, on reservations, or in rural settings (Attneave, 1982).

Background

According to Attneave (1982), there is no Native American or Alaskan Native person today who categorically lives out a traditional lifestyle. All are involved in the non–Native American United States culture to some degree. For example, more than half of the Native American and Alaskan Native populations do not use the reservation as their principal residence. Since urban centers offer different opportunities for work, education, and other endeavors, thousands of Native Americans can be found residing in these urban areas for varying lengths of time.

In the late 1700s, trappers, traders, and frontiersmen introduced alcohol as a social beverage to Native Americans on a widespread scale. Prior to that, little or no use of alcohol existed among Native Americans north of Mexico, with the exception of use for certain ceremonial purposes. For woodland and plains tribes especially, methods of obtaining altered states of consciousness as a means to communicate with the Great Spirit and the spirits of nature were achieved mainly through dancing, fasting, drumming, sleep deprivation, and isolation (Westermeyer and Baker, 1986).

As the concept of Manifest Destiny became the accepted orientation fueling the exploration of the lands to the West, so did alcohol become the most important item exchanged for furs (Chittenden, 1935). With little history to guide alcohol consumption, Native Americans as a group were uncertain about how to view it. Many tribes came to believe that alcohol had magical powers associated with curing disease. Other tribes simply viewed drunken people as unaccountable for their behaviors. It has been stated that perhaps Indians first learned to drink in a binge pattern at the trade fairs where drinking parties often lasted several days, accompanied by games, acts of bravado, and fighting (Westermeyer & Baker, 1986). Still others saw drinking as more social and economic. Although they were cautioned by leaders to abstain, alcohol was accepted by many Native Americans as a gesture of friendship from the white-skinned traders. Thus, alcohol took on an economic value. Accepting alcohol, even drinking with the whites, was believed to cement good trade relations.

Many Native American leaders became so disturbed by the spate of drinking among their people that they appealed to government officials for help. Federal intervention finally came in 1832 with the Indian Prohibition Act. This act prohibited the selling or providing of liquor to American Indians. However, it was deemed largely unsuccessful: Alcohol was deeply infused into the trading economy and social practices of many tribes by the 1830s, creating a demand for the drug. As a result, many Native Americans as well as whites turned to smuggling alcohol, and they made good profits. Moreover, by the 1830s, Native Americans had learned to ferment alcohol from their plethora of carbohydrate sources. Although the Indian Prohibition Act was ineffective, the United States government did not revoke the law until 1953. In its absence, many Native American leaders remained vigilant about the potentially destructive nature of alcohol, so that currently 69% of all United States reservations are under a self-imposed system of prohibition (Young, 1991).

The Native American relationship with alcohol has also been mitigated by the historical events of forced relocation of tribes, the break-up of Native American families, and the constant harassment from settlers and soldiers. In an attempt to assess the influence of these historical events upon Native American drinking behaviors, as many as 42 theories have been promulgated—the most notable of which is the sociocultural explanation (Young, 1991). This theory maintains that, as a culture, Native Americans are continuing to mourn the loss of their heritage and culture and are reacting to the stresses of acculturation and the demands to integrate into the mainstream of Euro-American society. In this theory, alcohol is seen as salubrious, anesthetizing the pain associated with the multiple losses incurred by Native Americans. Aside from whatever biophysiological proclivities that exist among Native Americans (and the jury is still out on this issue), the current state of anomie or normlessness is seen as acting to maintain the abuse of alcohol.

It becomes important, then, to examine the values that are purported to be at the heart of this grieving process. Sadly, it will become apparent that Native American values were functional prior to the introduction of alcohol but may have now become seriously problematic in the development of current Indian drinking patterns. The grieving process for the Native Americans and Alaskan Natives thus includes not only mourning the loss of a culture, but mourning the deleterious effects of alcohol on their peoples.

Values

In spite of the enormous diversity among Native American populations, there are some basic values that are thematic for Native Americans and Native Alaskans. These values focus upon orientation to time, the relationship between humans and the natural world, social relationships, and the concept of "noninterference." Many of these values are held by both Native American and Euro-American cultures, but they usually vary in philosophy or in the emphasis placed on them.

Time. Attneave (1982) and Ivey, D'Andrea, Bradford-Ivey, and Simek-Morgan (2007) explain that Euro-American culture is concerned with present time in terms of minute-by-minute awareness: What time is it? How much time do I have left? How long will it take me to drive to Long Island? Native Americans and Native Alaskan peoples also view time in the present. However, for them, present time is cyclical or universal rather than linear. Native Americans view present time as it relates to personal rhythms (not unlike the popular notion of biorhythms) and seasonal rhythms that encompass days, months, and even years. Native American life is thus organized in broad context around these various rhythms and not organized by traditional calendars and watches—both of which are seen as external.

Attneave (1982) and Ivey et al. (2007) point out that the Native American concept of past time has little or nothing to recommend its revival to the Native American population. The immediate past is measured in one or two generations, and this timeline is filled with a grim and depressing past. The future, no longer anchored to the seasonal variations, remains unknown and unpredictable. In spite of it all, though, it is important to note that today Native Americans will likely have preserved some of their original concept of time and, because of the clash of cultures, some distortions of it as well.

Humans, the Natural World, and Social Relationships. Since the Industrial Revolution, the prevailing view of nature in Euro-American culture is that it is wild and capricious. Therefore, nature is seen as needing to be controlled, and increasing or improving technology is viewed as increasing control over nature. For Native Americans and Native Alaskans, nature cannot be controlled. They advocate the need to understand the natural forces of nature and the need to harmonize with them rather than attempting to control or dominate these forces. Thus, Native American populations aim to surrender control. Surrendering with regard to alcohol meant that if one was going to drink, so be it. But surrendering to the forces of nature is not the same as being passive. Moreover, becoming drunk might be met with temporary ostracism.

Native Americans believe that the group takes precedence over the individual, which may go a long way in explaining the rapid spread of alcohol among earlier Native American peoples. In the past, there was little ability to preserve perishables from season to season. Sharing of food, clothing, and transportation was the norm as well as the necessity. For example, imagine you and a group of friends were camping in the desert during the summer and you had a gallon of milk as your only source of nourishment. You would likely share it immediately with everyone until it was all gone or risk the probability of its spoiling and becoming useless before nightfall. This concept of sharing of goods has existed in the Native American culture for many centuries, so it can be easily seen how, in Native American culture, alcohol would have been passed around until it was gone. For this reason, some consider this idea the underlying explanation for "binge drinking" (Attneave, 1982).

Noninterference. Another source of grieving, and a source of explanation for early Native American alcohol use patterns, revolves around a concept called "noninterference." Although the Native American peoples respected the idea of the group, there was an underlying principle explaining the proper place of the individual. Just as there was respect for the natural forces of nature, there was also respect for the natural unfolding of the potential in each person. "Noninterference" is an academic term used to describe this approach to human behavior (Attneave, 1982). This philosophy allows Native American parents to nurture their children while allowing them to learn from their mistakes. In this process, there is much more emphasis placed upon having the child learn by doing, so the children can learn from their own mistakes. Noninterference is also practiced with the elderly. For example, no matter how senile or ill the elders in the tribe may be, they still retain the right to determine their own courses of action. This notion of allowing one to learn from mistakes may have had a significant impact upon the development of alcohol abuse and alcoholism among Native Americans throughout generations.

Risk Factors for Alcohol and Other Drug Abuse

Sociocultural Factors. Native American youth start using alcohol, tobacco, and other drugs at an earlier age than does the general population (Napoli et al., 2003). In a review of literature, Marlatt and VandenBos (1997) suggest that modeling variables, peer pressure, and experimental substance use as an expression of stage-related rebelliousness are correlates of substance abuse in the Native American youth population. In addition, other related variables include the use of substances for tension coping, as well as general feelings of alienation.

Andre (1979) found that 75% of all Native American deaths are related to alcohol in some way. Aside from the sociocultural theories pointing to mourning as a significant risk factor, Westermeyer advances another risk factor. In citing studies that examine drinking patterns among various subgroups of Native Americans, Westermeyer (1991) found differences between Native Americans living in the West and those residing in other geographic locations. Motor vehicle crashes and injuries, usually associated with intoxication, are elevated among Western mountain tribes. Given that the Western states are significantly larger than other states and the fact that most reservations prohibit the sale of alcohol, those Native Americans living in the West and desiring alcohol have greater distances to travel in order to purchase it. Therefore, Westermeyer (1991) believes that the sheer number of miles involved in procuring alcohol may contribute significantly to the higher incidence of alcohol-related accidents.

Ross (2004) states that female Native American adolescents are more likely to have significant depression and/or anxiety disorders, and Walters and Simoni (2002) assert that these co-occurring disorders are associated with increased AOD use and abuse in Native communities. In addition, these women are disproportionately affected by violence, and the resulting posttraumatic stress is also associated with elevated AOD use. Paltrow (2004) maintains that another factor that influences the maintenance of AOD problems is the criminal justice system. This includes racial profiling as well as judges who believe in the myth that using drugs is a choice for Natives rather than seeing female AOD use associated with oppression and socioeconomic injustices. Both Paltrow (2004) and Owen (2004) claim that drug laws along with subsequent incarceration destroy the lives of women. This makes it almost impossible for female Native Americans to recover from such punishing policies. Current laws and morality related to homosexuality also influence AOD use and recovery from it for Native Americans. For example, Gilley and Co-Cké (2005) see that Native American gay males often feel alienated from their tribal, ceremonial, and social communities because of homophobia. As with the gay population in general, the gay bar scene makes healthy living difficult for Native American gay males.

Physiological Risk Factors. High rates of abstinence also occur among Native American populations, but this is often overlooked because a gross examination of drinking prevalence appears to support the idea that these populations have a higher alcohol consumption rate than other ethnic groups or subgroups in the United States (Hill, 1989). Upholding this stereotypical view is the popular folklore theory called "firewater." This theory maintains that Native Americans have an inherent weakness for alcohol. According to Westermeyer (1991), early studies have failed to show consistent and significant differences in alcohol metabolism among Native Americans. A recent study conducted by Ehlers and Wilhelmsen (2007) examined the genetic variants that increase the rise for consumption of AOD among southwest California (SWC) Indian families. Results provide some evidence for a linkage between body mass index and substance abuse suggesting that "consumption phenotypes" may share some genetic determinants. However, more studies are needed to definitively establish this relationship.

Patterns of drinking behavior were studied by Weisner, Weibel-Orlando, and Long (1984), who caution those in the helping profession against making drinking level synonymous with drinking style. For Native Americans, drinking styles are influenced by socioeconomic status, degree of Native American identity, and extent of tribal affiliation. Through their research, these same authors identified "teetotalers," "serious drinkers," and "white man's drinking" patterns in urban-dwelling Native Americans and offered some interesting profiles of those falling into each category. Teetotalers are seen as comprising two different groups: those who never drink and those former drinkers now abstaining. Older Native American women primarily make up the former group, while older men tend to make up the latter group. The "white man's drinking" patterns were noted in both women and men who were profiled as having "more white collar jobs, higher and more stable incomes, and more formal education" (Weisner et al., 1984, p. 245). Younger, more-often unmarried individuals, and those individuals from lower socioeconomic backgrounds were seen as the "serious drinkers." These individuals were thought to participate less in traditional Native American activities.

Psychological Risk Factors. Psychological risk factors may have important implications for treatment and prevention. Jones-Saumty, Hochhaus, Dru, and Zeiner (1983) conducted a seminal study investigating the extent to which the apparent higher incidence of depression in their sample of Native Americans was the cause of or the result of compulsive drinking. In their study, they compared the psychological adjustment and drinking behaviors in one group with one or more first-degree (directly related) alcoholic relatives and a group without a history of familial alcoholism. Results indicated no differences between these groups. A second study by these same authors compared the group of Native Americans with a family history of alcoholism and a group of Euro-Americans with similar family history. Results indicated a significant difference between these two groups in level of depressive symptoms (Jones-Saumty et al., 1983). The authors conclude that there are differences in psychological adjustment and drinking behavior between these two groups. Although neither group obtained clinical levels of depression, the "consistency of symptoms across two different instruments seems to indicate a prevalence of depressive tendencies within American Indians with a history of family alcoholism" (Jones-Saumty et al., 1983, p. 788). Rather than concluding these differences as categorical, these same authors suggest that "possibly, we have begun to identify some potential areas of risk for American Indian social drinkers in developing an alcohol problem" (p. 789).

Along those lines of previous research, Marlatt and VandenBos (1997) have developed 16 substance abuse risk categories for Native American youth. These categories include: (1) smoking tobacco, (2) use of smokeless tobacco, (3) family smoking, (4) peer smoking, (5) family smokeless tobacco use, (6) peer smokeless tobacco use, (7) experimentation, (8) intentions to use, (9) peer use of alcohol, (10) inhalants, marijuana, and crack/cocaine, (11) quality of family relationships, (12) school adjustment, (13) orientation, (14) non–substance-related deviant behaviors, (15) perceived deviance in school environment, and (16) cultural identification and religiosity. According to Marlatt and Vandenbos, the category with the highest positive correlation to overall risk is reported lifetime smokeless tobacco use. The next highest correlation is reported lifetime tobacco use. The next risk factor is lifetime alcohol use. Remember that these are correlations and, therefore, cannot be interpreted as causative. Knowing that, mental health professionals can still focus on these categories when examining issues surrounding the risk factors for substance abuse among Native American youth. Perhaps, in addition to this research, one should be mindful of what Gordon (1994) stated. In a review of the literature, Gordon summarized that there is no one cause of heavy drinking or recognizable, common response to alcohol ingestion. There are various alcohol-related behaviors. It appears as though the outcomes vary according to tribal background, acculturation level, and individual inclination (Coyhis, 2000; Gordon, 1994).

Asian Americans and Pacific Islanders

From your reading of the section on Native Americans, it is hoped that you would anticipate the Asian population to be diverse. Asians include Asian Indians (India), Pakistanis, Thais, Filipinos, Vietnamese, Laotians, Cambodians, and the Hmong peoples (Highland Laotian). The peoples of East Asia include Chinese, Japanese, and Koreans. Pacific Islanders include Hawaiians, Samoans, and those from Guam.

Typical Western observers tend to view all East Asians as being very similar—if not the same. Nothing could be further from the truth. Asian/Pacific Islanders comprise more than 60 discrete racial/ethnic groups and subgroups, and these groups are heterogeneous with vast variation within. Language is the most apparent difference. Yet, the histories of China, Japan, and Korea reveal vastly differing social and economic development. Moreover, once living in the United States, all Asian groups demonstrate significant within-group differences that will become more pronounced in future years.

Virtually all of the world's great religions are represented in this culturally and ethnically diverse group of Asian and Pacific Islander Americans, including Animism, Hinduism, Buddhism, Judaism, Christianity, and Islam. The culturally and ethnically diverse populations presented in this chapter all have conflict as part of their history, and Asian Americans are no different. However, the Asian population is distinctive in that they also have a history of fighting among themselves. This single variable may distinguish Southeast Asians in another significant way: Although Asian Americans (including Southeast

Asians) tend to group themselves ethnically, Southeast Asian Americans, especially those living in urban centers, have demonstrated a lack of pulling together due to their history of internal fighting (Burns & D'Avanzo, 1993). The transitions involving acculturation and accommodation will only exacerbate this cultural tension and can increase the risk factor for alcohol and other drug abuse.

Background

Although Islamic laws eschew alcohol, and most Muslim, Hindu, and Buddhist groups avoid alcohol, many Asian and Pacific cultures do use alcohol in rituals (Shon & Ja, 1982). An example of this is found in the "tribal binge" drinking of Pacific Islanders and in ceremonial and traditional events in Japan. Drinking in Japan is reported to start as early as age 11, and alcohol use is organized and institutionalized (Tani, Haga, & Kato, 1975). Working men of all ages have their favorite drinking establishments. The more exclusive establishments have a host of taxis and private automobiles to transport their regular customers home. In less prestigious places, friends and companions transport those who drink too much. Oashi and Nishimura (1978) have categorized four types of Japanese drinking: (1) drinking at dinner done mainly by the man to relax after work; (2) drinking to celebrate annual events; (3) drinking with one's friends after work; and (4) drinking at a roundtable after meetings and conventions—usually to lessen communication barriers. Oashi and Nishimura show that the lessening of communication barriers by drinking is important in Japan and that it is acceptable for a subordinate to be very frank with one's boss when either one or both are drunk.

The Chinese not only allow the use of alcohol at social functions, it is virtually pushed on one as a display of hospitality. However, drunkenness is discouraged. Traditionally, Hong Kong has few drinking-centered establishments, generally restricts the use of alcohol to males, and values drinking alcohol at meals. In Chinese culture, alcohol is often viewed in a somewhat similar fashion to that of the abolitionist in the temperance movement in America's nineteenth century (see section on African Americans). That is, alcohol is associated with lack of restraint, but it is not generally feared that drunkenness will lead to violence. Chafetz (1964) has noted that Taiwanese have well-defined ways of behaving, have strong social sanctions against excessive drinking, and encourage drinking only at meals or at special events. He also found that the Taiwanese have little official concern about alcohol treatment programs due to the overall lack of psychiatric resources and the low level of alcoholism in the dominant Chinese population.

Koreans generally view alcohol as part of their culture, in which drinking is for celebrations, mourning, to feel good, and to find friends (Kitano, 1982). Korea is roughly 80% Christian, and this Christian influence may be reflected in Korean males being sanctioned to drink whenever they wish, while females are often restricted to drinking at celebrations and dances.

Polynesians do not employ guilt as a means to regulate drinking and drunkenness. However, Tongans and Samoans, many of whom are Christian, do seem to use guilt to control the amount of drinking. Drinking to excess is seen as potentially threatening in the Samoan culture. In an early study, Lemert (1964) reported that a large number of Samoan wives had left their marriages because of the heavy drinking of their physically abusing husbands.

Values

When attempting to describe the values held by Asians or Pacific Islanders, the vast within-group differences prohibit any attempt at brevity. What follows are some general descriptions that would more likely apply to recent Asian immigrants and are less likely to describe earlier generations of Asian Americans. Such discrepancies are mostly due to the effects of acculturation.

Family Roles. Most Asian societies are structured with well-defined role expectations. This includes a patriarchal family structure consisting of elders or extended family members and a structure in which children are seen as subordinates. According to Fukuyama and Inoue-Cox (1992), Ivey et al. (2007), and others there is a strong sense of "filial piety" and respect for authority, which reinforces obedience and protection of the family name. The father's decisions are beyond reproach and are categorically accepted. The mother nurtures both her husband and her children. Whereas at one time it was socially desirable for the father to be the disciplinarian, the contemporary Asian father is not home as much, so the discipline is essentially left to the mother.

The male is expected to provide for the economic welfare of his family and in so doing is the one on whose shoulders falls the responsibility for the family's successes or failures. Because the physical appearance of Asians differs significantly from Euro-Americans concomitant with the presence of racial and cultural discrimination toward Asian Americans (Shon & Ja, 1982), Asian men can face extraordinary pressures when attempting to provide financially for their families. Research suggests that it usually takes about ten or more years for them to find economic security (Burns & D'Avanzo, 1993). This length of time and the pressures to succeed increase their risk for AOD abuse. Risk for substance abuse also seems to increase with the level of educational attainment for these men—especially for Chinese, Korean, and Japanese men. Chi, Lubben, and Kitano (1989) found consumption rates of alcohol increased with educational attainment.

Shame, especially the idea of "saving face," controls behaviors in the Asian family and is learned early in life. The concept of shame and loss of face involves not only the exposing of one's actions for all to see, but also family, community, or social withdrawal of confidence and support (Ivey et al., 2007; Shon & Ja, 1982). Inextricably woven into the value of shame is obligation. Obligation in the Asian/Pacific Islander community contains spoken and unspoken elements of reciprocity, and the greatest obligation is toward one's parents. According to Fukuyama and Inoue-Cox (1992), this is an obligation that cannot ever truly be repaid. Regardless of what the parents may do to the child, the child is still obligated to give respect and obedience to them. The more that Asian children are exposed to Euro-American schools, the more this sense of obligation can come into question and become a source of confusion. The transition will produce a period of anomie for the Asian offspring, and it is during this period of normlessness that they may be at an increased risk for AOD abuse.

Communication. Roles also play an interesting and important part in communication for the Asian/Pacific Islander population. Communication between individuals is governed by such characteristics as age, gender, education, occupation, social status, family background, marital status, and parenthood (Shon & Ja, 1982). These variables influence behavior in terms of who will bow the lowest, who will initiate and change topics in a conversation, which person will speak more loudly, who will break eye contact first, and who will be most accommodating or tolerant. Most of the newly immigrated Asian/Pacific Islanders are likely to want to avoid confrontation, keeping conversations on a harmonious level, and often maintaining self-control over their facial expressions while avoiding direct eye contact. This information is important when assessing for AOD problems, because it can work in reverse. If responses from Asian clients appear to upset the professional conducting the assessment, answers may not be given accurately so as to avoid confrontation.

Religion. Beliefs about health and responses to offerings of healthcare are influenced by religious beliefs in the Asian/Pacific Islander population. For example, Buddhism holds that life is suffering, and suffering emanates from desire. Pain or other suffering is seen as punishment for transgressions in this or previous lives. Alcohol and other drug problems may fall into this context. The notion of pain and suffering may so strongly influence one's beliefs that the likelihood of seeking help for AOD problems may be severely diminished (Shon & Ja, 1982). Animism is the idea that evil spirits, demons, or gods have control over one's life. Because of this, the "shaman" may be the primary caregiver or helper in situations involving alcohol or other drug abuse. However, Western helpers may be invited to aid in the process. Confucianism is prevalent among older Vietnamese and is a moral and ethical code that includes the worshipping of ancestors. Because Confucianism stresses a hierarchical order in both family and social systems, it will be the family elder who would have the final say in decisions involving treatment for AOD abuse. As a helping professional, you need to be very careful to demonstrate respect for this individual.

Taoism, which stresses harmony, is also quite prevalent among the Asian population. Burns and D'Avanzo (1993) point out that medically invasive procedures are seen as disrupting harmony. Harmony also plays a significant role in one's intention to seek help. A passive posture toward treatment may be assumed by an individual of Asian or Pacific Islander descent because anything else would disrupt harmony and perfection.

Risk Factors for Alcohol and Other Drug Abuse

According to SAMHSA's National Survey of Substance Abuse Treatment Services (U.S. Department of Health and Human Services, 2003), which examined data from 2001, the Asian population continues to have the lowest rates of illicit drug use (2.8%). This is due largely to a general pattern of emphasizing family unity, pursuing higher education for better job opportunities, and the value of self-sacrifice in order to give the next generation better opportunities.

While detailed epidemiological data and qualitative data about the Native Hawaiian community is lacking, Austin (2004) maintains that alcohol, tobacco, and other drug use and associated violent behavior has become alarming to the community since the late

1990s. Although substance use and violent behavior interact in a complex fashion, Austin found that individuals who identified strongly with being Hawaiian reported being happier and had fewer instances of witnessing, perpetrating, or being a victim of violence. Ethnic pride is seen as an important protective factor against AOD problems.

The traditional values and ethnic pride mentioned will be mediated by the adjustment patterns of Asian/Pacific Islanders once they enter the United States. The sheer number of immigrants concomitant with the age distribution of this group suggests that these families are in a constant state of transition once they arrive. The process of acculturation will impact all family members and will differentially affect their risk for AOD abuse. For example, a newly arrived Asian American homemaker will be confronted with Euro-American values of female independence, assertiveness, achievement, and work. As a result, elder Asian Americans, expecting to be cared for by family members, can experience great shock and loneliness when faced with nursing home care. Such conflicts between newly acquired values and traditional values can place these individuals at risk for AOD abuse. The effects of such reactions to stress may be seen among Cambodian women; Burns and D'Avanzo (1993) found 15% of a sample of Cambodian women residing on the East Coast reporting a family member having drug problems. Over half of that same sample said that they had used a drug for nonmedicinal purposes, such as for relieving the emotional pain of their plight.

Often, in attempting to meet security needs, all Asian family members will seek employment immediately upon arrival in the United States. That changes, however, once the family has settled in. Females will be less likely to remain working outside of the home (Gordon, 1994). According to Shon and Ja (1982), the family will often survive in dilapidated housing in order to save enough money to purchase a small business. While the family hierarchy may provide a stabilizing force to deal with the pressures of financial adjustment, youths who are exposed to the parental pressures for high achievement and financial success may fall victim to feelings of isolation and self-blame. To help brace against fear of long-term insecurity, many Asian Americans also work hard to send their children to schools in hopes that they will become high-paid professionals. This value is reflected in the sheer numbers of Asian American youth attending prestigious universities in the United States. However, attempts to further the education of their children can be met with resistance, in that the younger are likely to be attending English-speaking schools while their older siblings and parents may still prefer or use their native language. This would suggest that there might be a bicultural splitting within this population in terms of language. Language differences within families can lead to increased levels of stress, thereby increasing individual family members' risk factors for AOD abuse.

Moreover, language difficulties in school may preclude the Asian/Pacific Islanders' abilities to fulfill their parents' wishes to excel. This would be especially true for first-generation immigrants who came to the United States involuntarily or because of economic hardships faced in their homelands. The sum total of language difficulties and perceived inabilities to meet parental wishes can lead to alienation inside the family (Ivey et al., 2007; Shon & Ja, 1982). For example, the father's insistence upon obedience may be called into question and, when the father's beliefs are called into question, it may significantly contribute to a breakdown of traditional family structure. The result can be anomie, leaving the youth at risk for drug abuse. Kim (1991) states that, in families where the parents do not speak English, youths often lose filial respect because parents who have a difficult time providing for the family also find it difficult to establish the traditional authoritarian family role structure. As a result, youths are left feeling depressed and alienated, which can lead to alcohol and drug abuse as a means to cope.

Finally, in terms of risks, Ebberhart, Luczak, Avanecy, and Wall (2003) studied family history of two Asian American subgroups, Chinese and Koreans. The study aimed to explore the relationship of a positive history of alcoholism among Chinese and Koreans and the later development of alcohol dependence. Results supported the notion of the variability among subgroups in that Korean Americans reported higher rates of first-degree history of alcohol dependence.

African Americans

The role of alcohol in the contemporary African American community varies from that of many other groups. African Americans have culturally acceptable means for achieving spontaneity, sociability, and relaxation. Alcohol, then, is not seen a requisite for a feeling of celebration. In addition, specific drinking patterns of African Americans are found to be somewhat different from those of Euro-Americans. Early ethnographic studies suggest that taverns appear to be social centers for a majority of African Americans who drink (Sterne & Pittman, 1972). As would be true with any group regardless of ethnicity, African Americans who frequent taverns and bars are a group unto themselves and, as you would expect, are regarded as candidates for the underclass in African American culture rather than seen as responsible participants in community life. The exception would be a man who was a weekend tavern drinker and was otherwise a capable wage earner and family man. Women who frequent taverns and bars, however, would likely be socially compromised in the wider African American community.

In general, alcohol is often perceived to be a "party food" and is associated with being palliative, while the potential harmful effects are often overlooked or not understood. Alcohol consumption at parties or other social gatherings has a minor role in terms of setting the mood of gaiety and spontaneity. Therefore, abstaining from alcohol does not mean the person is being staid or a "party pooper."

Many African Americans drink almost exclusively on the weekends, traditionally a time of relaxation, visitation, and celebration. Brand names and the quantity of alcohol drunk reflect status in many African American communities. Several studies also report that African Americans tend to be polar in their use: They either abstain or drink heavily (Bourne, 1973; Harper, 1976, 1978). These authors also report that African Americans begin to drink at an earlier age, to purchase larger containers of alcohol than their Euro-American counterparts, to concentrate their drinking on the weekends, and to share alcohol with relatives and groups of friends. According to Harper (1978), this latter pattern appears to be more likely associated with lack of disposable income than to the atavistic, group-oriented value held by Africans and Native Americans.

The history of the relationship between African Americans and alcohol is engaging. Since the institutionalization of slavery in the early 1600s, a broad social and intellectual climate, known as Enlightenment thinking, has prevailed in American thought and has had a significant impact upon views of alcohol and its relationship to African Americans. So, to understand the history of African Americans and alcohol is to trace the institutionalization of slavery up through the prohibition period in the twentieth century.

Background

Early stereotyping of Africans (who became "African Americans" after the Emancipation Proclamation) and the institutionalization of slavery in the United States led to subsequent fears of slave insurrection and fueled numerous social measures aimed at controlling this population. Aside from legislation rigidly restricting their ability to trade, Africans were also prohibited from using alcoholic beverages. A West Jersey (New Jersey) law of 1685, for example, stated: "Any person convicted of selling or giving of rum, or any manner of strong liquor, either to a negro or Indian, except the stimulant be given in relief of real physical distress is liable to a penalty of five pounds" (Herd, 1991, p. 355). Similar laws were in effect in most of the colonial governments including Maryland, North Carolina, Georgia, Delaware, Pennsylvania, and New England (Larkin, 1965). Rather than being fueled by the fear that drunkenness would lessen their work ethic, the assumptive premise of these laws was based on the fear that intoxicated slaves would foment rebellion. While the relationship with alcohol and insurrection was presumptive, the manner in which the early African slaves were treated certainly did little to quell the fear of insurrection.

The American Revolution witnessed the abolition of slavery in most of the northern states, but not in the newly formed states of the South. And for southern slaveholders, the discrepancy between the "free north" and the "slave south" exacerbated fears of insurrection. Many new laws were instituted that further restricted the use of alcohol by slaves. However, in spite of laws, the popular views held by slave owners varied on the use of alcohol as a means of controlling Africans. As stated earlier, some believed that prohibiting slaves' use of alcohol would help guard against rebellion. This view was based on the southern planters' widely held view that alcohol was an important cause of every insurrectionary movement in the United States (Freehling, 1968). Another popular view stood in direct opposition. This view was equally concerned with controlling Africans, but held that the sober, thinking slave was the one who was dangerous and needed the constant vigilance of the owner (Douglass, 1855). Herd (1991) summarized these two views:

> One [view of alcohol] inspired images of force and rebellion, whereas the other suggested images of passivity and victimization. From the former perspective liquor was believed to be a powerful agent of disinhibition capable of unleashing violent and irrational behavior in otherwise civilized people. Hence, alcohol was regarded as a cause of crime and violence, a substance that made people commit barbaric and cruel acts. In the latter view alcohol was believed to be a powerfully addicting substance that forced men to drink and left them weak, slothful, and in a thoroughly degraded condition. (p. 357)

What were the views of alcohol held by the Africans themselves? They varied, of course. But interestingly enough, Africans were essentially split on the issue as well. Many regarded drinking as a natural reaction to being held against their will. For example, Stampp (1956) maintains that the consumption of alcohol by slaves was internally motivated as the "only satisfactory escape from the indignities, the frustrations, the emptiness, [and] the oppressive boredom of slavery" (p. 368). According to this view, there was a demand for alcohol by slaves, and Stampp offers a quote from a former slave to corroborate this assertion: To be sober during the holidays "was disgraceful; and he was esteemed a lazy and improvident man, who could not afford to drink whiskey during Christmas" (p. 370). However, during the same period, black and white abolitionists alike maintained that holidays were perhaps the paragon of travesty. To these abolitionists, when slaveowners offered libations to slaves during times of celebration, their intent was anything but to celebrate. They believed that holidays instilled more docile and passive resistance among slaves (Herd, 1991).

The views of alcohol as the enslaver and the disinhibitor, coupled with the Enlightenment philosophy of the time, inspired a spontaneous practice of temperance in the middle nineteenth century. Temperance ideology was focused on Enlightenment thinking and the role of self-control, since it was this ability to control one's irresistible desires that would free humans to be rational and productive. The temperance movement did not stop there, however. Temperance was seen in a broader scope as a vehicle for freeing the will as well as having significant social implications for freeing slaves. Freedom and self-control meant freedom for all and freedom from all. This included freedom from slavery as well as freedom from alcohol. It is not surprising, then, to see that the northern abolitionists embraced a view of alcohol as the enslaver, and therefore, the enemy. Those southern slave owners who believed in temperance adopted the view that alcohol was the disinhibitor and could unleash dangerous impulses in slaves. In describing the abolitionist view, Fredrickson (1971) writes

> What made slavery such a detestable condition was not simply that it created a bad environment; it was a severely limiting condition that was incompatible with the fundamental abolitionist belief that every man was morally responsible for his actions. (p. 37)

For many Africans, intemperance was seen as analogous to promoting slavery. The popularity of abstinence was reflected in the spate of temperance societies and in the periodicals promulgated by Africans at the time. The pledge of the American Temperance Union adopted at a New England temperance convention in 1836 demonstrates the rigid adherence to the value of abstinence:

> Being mercifully redeemed from human slavery, we do pledge ourselves never to be brought into the slavery of the bottle, therefore we will not drink the drunkard's drink: whiskey, gin, beer, nor rum, nor anything that makes drunk come. (n.d., p. 4)

Curiously, the temperance movement among Africans was less a movement toward curtailing high alcohol consumption among their own than it was part of a larger movement of social reform that marked the era. In fact, estimates of the quantity of consumption by Africans during this period are conflicting. So, it cannot be said that alcohol was the primary motivator for African interest in temperance (Sterne, 1967). Herd (1991) believes the lure of temperance was more a reflection of African abolitionist views on slavery and the lure of Enlightenment thinking that valued the social betterment of all.

At the beginning of the twentieth century, stereotyping and the perceived problems with the African American population had become central to the issue of alcohol reform for southern prohibitionists. Influenced by the Victorian Age and the preoccupation with sexual mores, women and children were now seen as needing protection from the disinhibited African Americans who were being portrayed as sexual perpetrators in the sensationalistic periodicals of the time (Sterne, 1967). The hackneyed views of African Americans spilled over into the disenfranchisement campaigns aimed at controlling both the poor white and African American vote (Herd, 1991). "Whiskey-sodden, irresponsible" African American voters "needed" to be controlled, so many politicians urged restrictive voting rights. The temperance movement, which had advocated freedom, was thus thwarted by restrictions on voting rights, and there was a decline in the movement's popularity among many African American reformists who now saw alcohol regulation as antithetical to the true tenets of the temperance movement (Du Bois, 1928). However, Herd (1991) claims that it was at the popular level where the most profound changes in views of alcohol among African Americans of the time took place. A new fascination with a sensual lifestyle overshadowed the now anachronistic temperance movement.

Accompanying this fascination were significant demographic and socioeconomic changes in the African American population. Escaping intense oppression in the South, thousands migrated to the northern "wet" cities, only to find many northern industrialists, especially those resisting the union movement, offering only low-paying jobs—primarily recruiting African Americans as strikebreakers. Many took these jobs, while many others found bootlegging much more profitable than farm and other unskilled labor. Speakeasies and cabarets, emphasizing excitement and sensual pleasure, became the arenas for this new lifestyle. As a result, the views of alcohol among African Americans shifted one hundred eighty degrees: Whereas many African Americans had embraced the temperance movement of one hundred years earlier as a means to demonstrate defiance, intemperance in early twentieth century America was the means to demonstrate defiance against an oppressive and restrictive legal system.

Values

While there is no such thing as "The African American Family," studies on the African American family structure can be used to guide a general understanding of this diverse population.

Family Roles. As you would expect, the roles of males and females in the African American family vary. Historically, the displacement of African Americans from agriculture into service and industrial employment, with little adjustment in the amount of racism, left this group as the "last hired, first fired." Unemployment was always high outside of southern agriculture, and out of necessity African American women worked outside the home. As a result, egalitarianism among the genders is more common than not and may be more pronounced in the African American culture than in the Euro-American culture of America. The egalitarian nature of the family structure stands in direct opposition to the stereotypic view that African American households are matriarchal households. Hines and Boyd-Franklin (1982) state that this misperception usually arises because African American women often assume responsibilities in their families that are less frequently taken on by women in Euro-American cultures. The emphasis upon egalitarianism in the African American family also allows for an exchange of family roles so that various members can assume responsibility for the children. Fathers and grandfathers, for example, may provide the primary care of the child while the female works.

In spite of the role-flexibility afforded by egalitarianism, stereotypical views of African American males as being irresponsible remains. For example, there is an often misunderstood concept called *peripheralness* cited in the literature that reinforces the hackneyed view of African American families being matriarchal. Simply, peripheralness suggests an absence of participation or interest on the part of African American fathers in their families. A more accurate view of the role of fathers reflects the pressures of providing for the family in a society where job ceilings exist and oppression abounds (Hines & Boyd-Franklin, 1982). These same authors also indicate that the African American father may have to spend an inordinate amount of time and energy trying to provide for the family's basic survival needs, a preoccupation that drains the psychic energy that would otherwise be infused into the family. Faced with both pressures to provide and barriers thwarting their efforts, underemployed and unemployed African American fathers may be at risk for turning to alcohol and other drugs as a means of relieving the pain.

Kinship and Extended Family Bonds. The flexibility of roles in African American culture is also influenced by an atavistic value emphasizing strong kinship bonds. While slavery certainly reinforced this value, its origins can be traced to Africa where Africanian thinking had produced the syllogism, "We are, therefore I am" (Hines & Boyd-Franklin, 1982). Prevalent among many African American families and tied to the value of kinship is a phenomenon known as "child-keeping." Child-keeping occurs when a child is informally "adopted" or reared by other family members who have more resources than the biological parents. Rather than seeing child-keeping as the disruption of the family system, Hines and Boyd-Franklin believe that this occurrence actually elevates the importance of the child. Yet African American children may be subjected to ridicule and ostracism by a mainstream Euro-American culture that fails to recognize and/or appreciate this value—believing instead that the child who is raised by grandparents reflects a broken home. As a result of these misperceptions and other factors, African American children may experience stress at school and can turn to alcohol and other drugs. This is reflected in a study of African American adults between the ages of 18 and 23 living in Harlem. Brunswick (1979) found that the initial use of marijuana, heroin, psychedelics, and alcohol occurred most commonly on the way to school. Brunswick also found that alcohol was the drug used earliest in a sample of African American young adults living in Harlem. Moreover, Brunswick found that 20% of the males in the sample had begun using alcohol by age 10, and by age 14 half of the males and 40% of the female drinkers had used alcohol.

Religion. The crucial role of the church in the emancipation of slaves in America is reflected in current views of the importance of a strong religious orientation among many African Americans. In times of slavery, cryptic messages about times and places for escape often came from the pulpit during the church service (Hines & Boyd-Franklin, 1982). Interestingly, these same authors point out that songs sung today in many African American churches, such as "Steal Away" and "Wade in the Water," often carry the remains of those messages. The power of those messages, hidden in church protocol, and their relationship to emancipation issues should leave no one surprised that some of the most notable contemporary leaders in the African American culture are or were preachers: the Reverend Martin Luther King, Jr., the Reverend Jesse Jackson, Malcolm X, and others. Although these individuals are of international stature, the local church is an important vehicle allowing for the emergence of leaders in local African American communities. Free from the oppression that exists in mainstream Euro-American culture, the church allows outlets for creative talents that otherwise might be thwarted. The racism and oppression experienced by low-paying jobs during the week may be offset somewhat by becoming a deacon or trustee on Sunday. Hines and Boyd-Franklin remind us that numerous church activities, such as dinners, trips, singing in the choir, and participation in Sunday School, provide an intricate social life for many African Americans and promote their mental health and a sense of connectedness. Although church affiliation would be expected to temper African American drinking patterns, African Americans are at a high risk for alcohol-related causes of mortality and morbidity.

Risk Factors for Alcohol and Other Drug Abuse

The results of research on the relationship between African Americans and alcohol and other drugs is mixed. Yet some interesting trends indicating use are notable. For example, Gordon (1994) found that substance abuse in the African American population is linked to three processes: (1) economic deprivation, (2) racism, and (3) stress. Caetano, Clark, and Tam (1998) and Kingree and Sullivan (2002) see risk factors for African Americans as resulting from an interrelationship of individual attributes and characteristics, environmental characteristics, historical experiences, and cultural factors. In addition, such issues as poverty, unemployment, and racism and discrimination contribute to the heightened risk.

Availability and Geographical Factors

One factor increasing risk is availability. For instance, Los Angeles had approximately three liquor stores per block in addition to those neighborhood stores offering beer and wine in 1978. Gordon (1994) found that, in 1993, there were 10 times more liquor stores in the African American communities than in predominantly Euro-American communities. Parker and Harmon found the availability of alcohol to be a contributing factor in consumption rates among African Americans. It would appear that residing in inner cities, where there is a plethora of taverns and liquor stores, is a factor that might increase the risk for AOD abuse. However, in an early study, Robins and Guze (1971) refuted the notion that impoverished urban areas were associated with increased alcohol abuse among African Americans. The absence of alcohol-related problems was associated with having come from a stable family background, good performance in school, an absence of juvenile arrests, and a lack of early drug experimentation.

Although impoverished geographical locations may not have been a significant variable in determining alcohol use patterns among African Americans in the 1970s, it may be more of a factor now. Brown and Alterman (1992) reviewed the literature regarding substance abuse in culturally and ethnically diverse populations and found that the risk for substance abuse appears to have increased among individuals residing in impoverished areas. These same authors go on to state that

> to the extent that many African Americans are and continue to be impoverished and deprived of many of the resources and benefits of our society, we should expect to find greater rates of substance abuse and more severe consequences of drug use. (p. 861)

This finding is corroborated by Boyd, Mackey, Phillips, and Travakoli (2006), who found that African American women who live in rural areas experience a disproportionate number of negative health and social consequences as a result of their AOD use when compared to the AOD use of white women.

Developmental Issues. King (1982) asked a rather intriguing question regarding African American drinking patterns: "Why is the consumption of alcohol (3+ drinks per day) most prevalent in the age decades 40 to 49 and 50 to 59 among African Americans?" He conducted a search of the literature published between 1977 and 1980 and found that most American men (regardless of ethnicity) go through a transition in the middle years. He postulated that the increase of heavy drinking in African American men during the middle years may be due to frustrated attempts at attaining satisfactory love and work aspirations. In an earlier study, Levinson (1978) had theorized that these years from 30 to 40 may be especially difficult for an African American male who is attempting to match aspirations with achievement. Failing to achieve one's goals can be expressed in depression and dependency, and this is exactly what Steer, Shaw, Beck, and Fine (1977) found in their study of African American alcoholics. These authors believe that, having failed to achieve their dreams, many African American men may turn to alcohol in their early 30s to offset feelings of inadequacy and depression. Adding support to this view is Williams (1986), who points out that unemployment can have a deleterious effect on drinking behavior in that it is correlated with increased risk of alcohol problems.

Latino and Hispanic Populations

The term *Latino American* is used to describe those persons living in the United States who share a common Hispanic cultural background. The term *Hispanic* refers to Spaniards and Portuguese, while *Latino* includes those known as Chicanos, Cubanos, Puerto Ricans, Latin Americans, and Mexican Americans. Three major groups comprise the Latino population: Mexican Americans, Puerto Ricans, and Cuban Americans. The following section will present information on these groups as well as some information on Central and South Americans. In general, differences between these three groups of people are influenced largely by educational level, socioeconomic status, immigration status, age/generation, rural versus urban residence, country of origin, and degree of acculturation (Torres, 1993).

Background

The immigration patterns among Cuban Americans, Puerto Rican Americans, Central and South Americans, and Mexican Americans are varied. Joining the 50,000 Cubans already living in the states were large numbers of Cubans who emigrated during the political unrest of the 1950s. The majority of those leaving were the highly educated, professional and business upper-class people (Burns & D'Avanzo, 1993). About 3,000 wealthy Cubans left when Fidel Castro came into power in 1959, and these were joined by another wave of middle-class immigrants who came to the United States in 1960. Finally, in 1980, came a wave of working-class Cubans, some 125,000 strong and made up mainly of African American Cubans (Burns & D'Avanzo, 1993). Puerto Rican Americans have immigrated to the United States mainly for economic reasons in low but steady rates. Central and South Americans represent the most recent Latino/Hispanic immigrants to the United States. Most of these individuals came because of political upheaval in their respective countries. Exact figures of immigrants are unavailable, mostly due to their being illegal aliens, but it is known that a majority come from Guatemala, El Salvador, and Nicaragua (Burns & D'Avanzo, 1993). These same authors note that there is a high incidence of post-traumatic stress disorder (PTSD) in this group and attribute that to the violence experienced by these individuals in their homelands as well as to the trauma, such as beatings and rape, experienced while traveling to the United States through Mexico. With the exception of those living in the southwestern United States, the majority of Mexican families living in the United States are immigrants.

The presence of Latinos/Hispanics in the southwest region of the United States dates back to the early 1500s. The outcome of the Mexican War (1846–1848), caused by conflict over Texas, witnessed the annexation of Arizona, California, Colorado, New Mexico, Texas, and portions of Utah and Nevada. Along with this annexation came over 75,000 Mexican people who were granted U.S. citizenship (Burns & D'Avanzo, 1993). The Mexican Revolution of 1910 was the cause of another influx of Latino/Hispanic immigrants to the United States. In addition, Burns & D'Avanzo point out that, between World War II and the 1960s, the Braceros Programs allowed for seasonal laborers to enter the country to work in the fields of California, Arizona, Washington, Texas, and the Midwest.

Values

As with the other culturally and ethnically diverse populations discussed in this chapter, values indigenous to the Latino/Hispanic culture come into frequent conflict with the Euro-American value system, which can cause distress for the Latino/Hispanic individual and family. Feelings of guilt, self-doubt, and even betrayal can create disharmony within and among Latino/Hispanic families. Similar disruptions can occur when individual family members take advantage of economic or educational opportunities not taken by other family members. Moreover, Gilbert (1978) has alluded to problems that can occur within a family when one member who is well adjusted to the sociological and cultural pressures of biculturalism marries one who is less well adjusted.

Familism and Cariño. Traditional Latino/Hispanic families value the family above almost everything else. However, Mexican American families do not necessarily place as much emphasis on this value. The traditional Latino/Hispanic family is private, which is especially true with problems such as AOD abuse (Burns & D'Avanzo, 1993). The family protects the individual and demands loyalty while stressing the importance of family proximity, cohesiveness, and respect (*respeto*) for parental authority. *Orgullo* (pride), *verguenza* (shame), *confianza* (confidence), *dignidad* (dignity), and *pobre pero honesto* (poor but honest) are typical values in traditional Latino/Hispanic families (Falicov, 1982). However, as Latinos/Hispanics become more acculturated into mainstream Euro-American society, these values become a source of conflict. Joining gangs, where these values operate strongly, becomes one way Latino/Hispanic youths cope with the conflict of values.

Similar to, yet different from, many African American families, Latino/Hispanic families usually live in a nuclear arrangement but do have extended families living nearby. The large size of the family, usually consisting of parents and four or five children, influences the family structure in many ways. Depending on the degree of acculturation, Latino/Hispanic families value affiliation and cooperation while placing much less value upon confrontation and competition (Falicov, 1982). Moreover, many childrearing concerns such as caretaking, discipline, financial responsibility, companionship, emotional support, and problem-solving are shared. In traditional Latino/Hispanic families, for example, the role of godparents is very pronounced.

The emphasis on intergenerational and lateral interdependence, however, does not diminish the value of *cariño,* or deep caring for the family, nor does it eliminate the need for strong adherence to a high degree of hierarchical organization in which rules are clearly organized around age and gender. Even though traditionally older male children are given the greatest authority and power, there is an unconditional acceptance of family members and an emphasis upon equality. Parents often provide much nurturance and protection for children and do not push them into achievement when it involves unhealthy competition between family members (Falicov, 1982).

Children also occupy a central role in the marriage. Because *el amor de madre* (motherly love) is seen as a much greater love than romantic love, it is the existence of the children that essentially ties the marriage together. This value is reflected in a relatively lower divorce rate for this population than for their Euro-American counterparts (Burns & D'Avanzo, 1993). Even though children enjoy a central role in the family, their status is lower than that of their parents. It is *respeto* (respect) that maintains the child's status while allowing parents to reinforce a dependence and dutiful posture among their children (Falicov, 1982).

Machismo and Marianismo. Almost everyone is familiar with the hackneyed version of Latino/Hispanic *machismo* or *muy hombre.* According to Falicov, this value dictates the need for males to be strong, brave, protective of their women (mothers, sisters, wives), aggressive, sexually experienced, courageous, and authoritarian. The implication is for women to be humble, submissive, virtuous, and devoted to their home and children. This value for females is known as *hembrismo* or *marianismo* and underscores the importance of the self-sacrificing mother. *Marianismo* also serves to counterbalance the male value of *machismo* (Stevens, 1973).

In actuality, many Latino/Hispanic men are dependent and submissive, and it is the women who are dominant and controlling (Falicov, 1982). In public, the "self-denial" of the mother is reinforced by the father's insistence that the children obey and help her. Often, however, he is much less involved with the children other than to discipline them, and, on more than one occasion, the mother may find herself in covert disagreement with him. When this occurs, she may act as a mediator between the children and the father, thus adding more to her central position in the family (Stevens, 1973).

The conflict of values arising between the male need to demonstrate *machismo* and the female value of *marianismo* can create stress for Latino/Hispanic males. Alcohol, the most commonly abused drug among contemporary Latino/Hispanics, did at one time help to build a social structure into their societies. It now appears that drinking alcohol is an accepted way of dealing with stresses of acculturation, and the value of *machismo* tends to strengthen the notion that alcohol is an accepted way of displaying this male value (Stevens, 1973). *Machismo* likely influences younger males to drink more than do their female counterparts, especially in the Mexican American youth population (Bettes, Dusenbury, Kerner, James-Ortiz, & Botvin, 1990).

Risk Factors for Alcohol and Other Drug Abuse

Sociological Risk Factors. As with other culturally and ethnically diverse populations, the resulting tensions involved in acculturation raise the level of risk for alcohol and other drug abuse among the Latino/Hispanic population. Patterns of risk vary across male and female populations and between adults and youth and appear to be influenced by both cultural acceptance of alcohol as well as by role-modeling of drinking behaviors.

Research into Latino/Hispanic youth reveals that this population may be at great risk because of language barriers, lowered self-esteem, dropping out of the educational system, early exposure to substance use and abuse by family members, and because of the daily stresses encountered in living (Bettes et al., 1990; de la Rosa, Holleran, Rugh, & MacMaster, 2005; Gilbert & Cervantes, 1986). Moreover, those Mexican American farm laborers who pick crops change residences constantly as they follow crops. The continuous changing of location disrupts a sense of continuity and can adversely affect farm workers' children, placing them at an increased risk for alcohol and other drug use and abuse.

Other sociological risk factors for substance abuse by Latino/Hispanic youth reflect the problems confronted in the schools. Varying degrees of language proficiency are excessive and can pose serious problems both in seeking and maintaining employment or when children attend English-speaking schools. Limited language proficiency can lead to decreases in self-esteem, thus elevating the risk for abusing substances. For example, in a comparative study of adolescents, it was found that Latino/Hispanic adolescents are at high risk for alcohol abuse, a fact mainly attributed to reports of lowered self-esteem (Bettes et al., 1990).

Role-modeling also influences adolescent drinking patterns. For example, Gilbert and Cervantes (1986) report that parental and sibling use of alcohol was seen as the best predictor of alcohol use by young Mexican American males. De la Rosa, Rugh, and Rice (2006) found that Latino adolescents increase drug use with gang affiliation and, after leaving the gang, use more drugs. These authors found that risk factors for Latino youth were associated family attitude toward deviance, friends' use, school truancy, and living in neighborhoods with high crime rates. According to a U.S. Department of Health and Human Services report (2003), Mexican American men and women were somewhat more likely to have drinking problems and to drink more heavily than their Cuban, Puerto Rican, or Central and South American counterparts. For the female population, this heavy use could be a result of the breakdown of traditional Hispanic culture and the concomitant loss of social supports and ensuing lack of socialization into the Euro-American culture.

In the Puerto Rican community, heavy drinking takes place most often in public and in full view of children. As long as family and social obligations are fulfilled, heavy drinking is widely tolerated (Hispanic Health Council, 1987). In general, the Puerto Rican population views alcohol as a socially approved reward for hard work or achievement and sees alcohol as a means to escape undesirable circumstances. Alcohol use allows for a "manly" activity to be shared while acting as a social facilitator and refreshment and is seen as a way to feel and act as Puerto Rican (Burns & D'Avanzo, 1993). The level of risk for AOD abuse is compounded when there exists a clash of values between the dominant Euro-American and Puerto Rican culture.

The influences of acculturation also play an important role in drinking behaviors of Latino/Hispanic youth, but research is conflicting with regards to the effects of acculturation upon the drinking patterns of Latino/Hispanic adult males (Markides, Ray, Stroup-Benham, & Trevino, 1990). For example, Latino/Hispanic high school seniors and first-year college students reported that abusing alcohol was the result of pressures faced in dealing with taking responsibility for their decisions. However, Corbett, Mora, and Ames (1991) found that Latino/Hispanic men who had the greatest consumption of alcohol also reported the greatest amount of acculturation and demonstrated the highest level of education and income. This, together with the fact that these men tended to drink with other men, raises the likely possibility that *machismo* continues to be a significant variable across Latino/Hispanic male development and appears to place this group at an increased risk for substance abuse.

Psychological Risk Factors. Bettes et al. (1990) reported that Mexican American youth were found to have the lowest ratings of internal locus of control when compared with other youth. The perception of being in control may depend on the degree of acculturation, so that a higher level of internal locus of control would likely reflect increased feelings of social adequacy and environmental mastery. Language deficiencies can severely limit one's sense of personal autonomy and perceived control, which can be reinforced if the Latino/Hispanic individual does not see much hope for economic, social, or educational improvement. The shame associated with economic and educational deprivation can exacerbate lowered feelings of self-worth and put Latino/Hispanic individuals at psychological risk for substance abuse. Moreover, the risk for substance abuse can be heightened when one experiences a conflict of values between one's family members or close friends. For example, in a study of Cuban American women who reported tranquilizer use, Kirby (1989) found that reasons for use included stress resulting from having to balance work with traditional Cuban values (for example, maintaining the household and assuming total responsibility for child care). These women also reported "extreme conflict" over these stressful roles and used drugs to "soothe nerves."

Persons with Disabilities and the Elderly

It is uncomfortable and frightening to know that the only minority group that accepts all members is the group of persons with disabilities. That is, anyone—anytime and anywhere—can suddenly become a member of this minority group. While some disabilities appear at or before birth, others can and are experienced during one's life. Disabilities can range from a specific learning disability to HIV/AIDS and everything in between.

Bombardier, Blake, Ehde, Gibbons, Moore, and Kraft (2004) report that persons with disabilities who abuse AOD have poorer psychological adjustment than the general population. This is alarming in that Taggart, McLaughlin, Quinn, and McFarlane (2007) as well as Emerson and Turnball (2005) found those with disabilities are misusing alcohol and illicit drugs at greater rates. This group is also reported to overuse prescribed medications (McGillicuddy, 2006). As with other chronic diseases where medications are required (e.g., multiple sclerosis, HIV/AIDS), alcohol and drug use can lead to dangerous central nervous system problems.

Taggart et al. found reasons that people with disabilities misused AOD centered on "self-medicating against life's negative experiences" (p. 362). Psychological trauma and social distance from the community were cited as specific reasons. Misuse is influenced by perceived (and real) trauma which, in turn, leads to physiological, psychological, financial, and relational problems. This creates more trauma, and a vicious cycle ensues which raises the risk of AOD abuse.

These same issues affect the elderly in every population. However, you can imagine the geometric impact on AOD abuse of social, political, and economic injustices on the elderly of racioethnic minorities. Aside from the social dimension, there are medical dimensions. For instance, the elderly use a larger proportion of medication than any other group. Gurnack and Johnson (2002) assert that the elderly comprise 12% of the U.S. population, yet they account for one-fourth of all drugs prescribed. It stands to reason that this population would be at greater risk for AOD abuse.

However, Gurnack and Johnson point out that while there is some information on the elderly in the Euro-American population, little is known about the elderly in racioethnic populations. In conducting an analysis of data provided by the National Household Survey on Drug Abuse (NHSDA) discussed earlier, these researchers did find a curvilinear relationship between AOD use and age. In general, AOD use increased while the person was young and decreased as the person grew older. There are differences between type of drug used and minority-group membership. For example, the prevalence and admission to treatment rates for alcohol were greater among the older Native American and Alaskan Native population than for the elderly in other groups. Older African Americans males and females had greater prevalence and treatment admission rates for illicit drugs than other elderly groups. Although we will discuss HIV/AIDS in great detail in Chapter 13, Gurnack and Johnson present some interesting findings related to this topic and elder use of AOD. Preliminary studies reveal that late-onset crack use appears to be most prominent among elderly African American males who are socially isolated. This pattern is seen as increasing the risk for exposure to HIV/AIDS because crack cocaine is often introduced to this population by younger females who exhibit high risk factors for HIV/AIDS.

Much more research is needed in this area, and Gurnack and Johnson call for more systematic investigations of the elderly minority populations. However, there are structural barriers to gathering such data. These researchers believe that policy makers continue to see AOD use and abuse as a phenomenon affecting younger populations. As a result, most of the research conducted by large-scale surveys like the NHSDA focuses on high school youth and pregeriatric adults. As a result, the epidemiological approaches only tell part of the story. Attention needs to be paid to the cultural factors which clearly shape the AOD use and misuse patterns of minority elderly populations.

Helping Culturally and Ethnically Diverse Populations

Issues for the Helping Professionals

Mental health professionals are taught to empathize with their client or clients. Moreover, helping professionals are taught to avoid power struggles and coercive relationships with their clients. Power struggles can come in many forms, and stereotyping is a subtle form of power that can be used to coerce clients of varying cultural and ethnic backgrounds. By labeling a group as having certain characteristics and certain drinking or other drug use patterns, one can create a cognitive paradigm in which to gather and filter information.

You, as a mental health professional, should take care to undertake an examination of your own worldview regarding culturally and ethnically diverse groups. Ivey et al. (2007) state that your worldview is the way that you and your clients make sense of things or make meaning of the world. These same authors go on to say that individuals make idiosyncratic meanings, but these individualized meanings also have universal human qualities. It is critical that you develop an awareness of how race/ethnicity, culture, and gender impact your view of the world. In describing "cultural intentionality," Ivey et al. suggest that mental health professionals (1) need to develop an ability and a willingness to generate additional thoughts, words, and behaviors in an effort to communicate with self and others within a given culture; (2) need to develop an ability to develop alternative thoughts, words, and behaviors in an effort to communicate with a variety of diverse groups across cultures; and (3) need to develop enhanced abilities to formulate plans, act on a variety of possibilities that may exist in a given culture, and reflect on these actions.

A critical issue for counselors relates to the understanding of a racioethnic client's story. On one level, counselors are trained to listen carefully. At the same time, when the racioethnic minority client with AOD problems brings such issues as power, powerlessness, oppression, and addiction into the counseling dialogue, Euro-American counselors will likely feel threatened on other levels. There are meaningful ways of dealing with this issue. Cartwright and D'Andrea (2005) and Pedersen (2002) support the idea that multiculturalism is not a complication as much as it is a complexity. Pedersen favors the term "culture-centered" counseling over the concept of multicultural counseling in order to emphasize the centrality of culture in the counseling process. Pedersen sees culture-centered counseling as helping with the accuracy of assessment

providing common ground for conflict management

increasing identity

increasing health through biodiversity

protection from culture encapsulation

helping the future global village survive

increasing social justice

right thinking that is both linear and nonlinear

helping people to learn about culture shock, spirituality, political pluralism, and good psychology (Cartwright and D'Andrea, 2005, p. 218)

Harper (2006), Tucker (2006), and other researchers extend the work on treating diverse populations and emphasize the necessity for counselors to be *culturally competent* (as opposed to culturally sensitive). In discussing ethical multiculturalism, Harper sees ethical treatment of a diverse clientele as including moral reasoning, cultural competence, beneficence/nonmaleficence, and respect for persons and communities. This includes the need for counselors to have cultural knowledge, awareness, sensitivity, skills, and an understanding of ethical principles. Given the stigma associated with alcoholism and being a minority, one can clearly see how important it is to embrace the level of professionalism inherent in cultural competence and culture-centered approaches.

Assessment and Treatment Issues

Remember, this book is written for the generalist in the helping field, rather than for a specialist in the field of addictive behaviors. You will likely assess your client for the extent of involvement with alcohol and other drugs, then refer him or her to a specialist if needed. In order to make an assessment, mental health professionals must understand how the client's culture views alcohol and other drug use. What may be defined as problematic drug use in a predominantly Euro-American culture may be viewed as normal in a nonwhite culture. For example, an Asian American's frank confrontation with his or her boss when both are drunk is considered appropriate. Therefore, sharing with clients that you suspect a problem with their use of alcohol or another drug without an understanding of acceptable use in their culture may be incorrect. It may also be inappropriate. Your lack of knowledge may discourage the client from seeking further assistance from you or others in the helping services. If a problem did exist, you may have missed an opportunity to help. If there were a serious problem, it may become more serious.

When working with Native Americans, remember that "Direct confrontation is limited to making sure the individual is aware of the consequences of behavior. Then, it is left to the innate forces within the individual to operate" (Attneave, 1982, p. 70). In terms of treatment, Weisner et al. (1984) point out that involvement in an alcoholism treatment program (either as a patient or as a counselor), membership in a church or Alcoholics Anonymous (AA), and the increased adherence to traditional Native American values appear to be the most significant factors in maintaining abstinence for the "teetotalers" group. Native

Americans, as a whole, are active in their recovery from alcoholism and have been working on their addictions since the early 1960s (Coyhis & White, 2002). Many support groups exist on reservations, and traditional rituals such as the sweat lodge, the talking circle, prayer, and intervention by tribal leaders are now commonplace. The federally funded Indian Health Services and other local and state agencies, such as the Billy Rogers Wellness and Recovery Program at the University of Oklahoma, are active organizations helping Native Americans to recover from alcoholism.

A hopeful treatment approach for Native American alcohol problems is illustrated by the Shuswap tribal community in British Columbia, Canada. In 1971, Chief Andy Chelsea made a commitment to stop drinking and confront the rampant problem of drinking and alcoholism in his community. According to Coyhis and White (2002), Chief Andy Chelsea proclaimed that "the community is the treatment center" and revitalized tribal traditions, confronted bootleggers, promoted AA meetings, and established educational and developmental job programs for those in recovery. Between 1971 and 1981, the sustained efforts reduced the incidence and prevalence of alcoholism in his community from nearly 100% to less than 5%. The success of his efforts prompts Coyhis and White to proclaim that "the most efficacious and enduring solutions to Native American drinking problems are the ones that emerge from the very heart of tribal cultures" (p. 163). Nevertheless, a note of caution needs to be advanced in "that no one treatment program will serve all people, all communities, or all Native American peoples" (Milbrodt, 2002, p. 41).

Bachman et al. (1991) have shown that, in many instances, the Asian/Pacific Islander populations' use of most drugs is about half that of the white population. Alcohol is the exception. Rates for consumption more closely approximate that of Euro-Americans, and Burns and D'Avanzo (1993) suggest that if trends continue, it will not be long before drugs become a significant problem. Unfortunately, there is a stigma attached to seeking professional treatment in the Asian/Pacific Islander population, and Sue (1987) points out that these folks are less likely than other groups to seek treatment for alcoholism. If, when assessing Asian/Pacific Islanders, you determine that an individual might benefit from treatment, remember that your suggestions for treatment need to be addressed through the father or elder, who will be making the decision for himself or for other family members. Whatever intervention is agreed upon, there needs to be an element of cultural sensitivity and bilingualism. There are DUI classes for Asian/Pacific Islanders, and AA groups exist for Japanese-speaking individuals.

Assessing African Americans for alcohol and other drug abuse varies from that of other culturally and ethnically diverse populations. For example, in assessing a middle-aged African American male who reports drinking heavily at the local tavern with friends on Saturday, mental health professionals might be well advised to suggest that a friend drive him home rather than referring him for assessment and potential treatment.

According to Sanders (2002), the 1980s and 1990s reflected attempts to adopt traditional recovery support networks. Networks such as Alcoholics Anonymous and Narcotics Anonymous were seen as more culturally relevant and attractive to African Americans, and treatment centers that were being developed were aimed at being more culturally sensitive. Currently, taking from Chief Andy Chelsea's proclamation that the Native American community is the treatment center, there is a strong emphasis on indigenous addiction treatment for African Americans as well. The Glide Memorial Methodist Church in San Francisco is an example of such a community-oriented treatment approach. Initiated in 1989, approximately 80% of today's community-based congregation is working on recovery. In this treatment approach, the overt expression of rage and anger is encouraged, because the expression of it is seen as an important component of recovery. Another example is the One Church–One Addict project, founded in 1993 by Father George Clements. Over 900 churches are involved with the project as of 2002. The goal of this project is to recruit faith-based communities such as churches, temples, and synagogues to provide postrelease aftercare for addicts leaving prisons. Another indigenous approach is the Free-N-One recovery program. Sanders (2002) describes this as a Christian-centered recovery program that provides various support groups for addicts and their families. Spread throughout the country, there are over 50 such programs in the state of Illinois alone (Sanders, 2002, p. 170). A fourth type of indigenous program is the Nation of Islam program. This program has been in existence since the 1950s and is aimed at helping African American male substance abusers in the criminal justice system. A fifth community-based approach is called the African American Survivors Organization. The purpose of this organization is to provide African American men a safe place to talk about issues. Often, these issues are the very ones that would not be talked about in recovery meetings where there is a racial mix of members. The format of the African American Survivors Organization is somewhat similar to the traditional Twelve-Step meetings discussed in Chapter 10. However, the opening of these African American meetings is focused on teaching group members some of the principles of African culture. The Seven Principles of Nguza Saba are read and discussed in the meetings. These principles are unity, self-determination, collective works and responsibility, cooperative economics, purpose, creativity, and faith. According to Sanders, the group meetings offer both support and challenges to group members.

It is important for mental health counselors to remember that regardless of which specific type of treatment program or project exists and is available for any given geographic location, virtually every church in the African American community is involved in helping addicts.

Traditional values may influence efforts to assess alcohol and other drug use in the Latino/Hispanic population. The traditional concept of *machismo* implies that Latina/Hispanic women are not to drink. Yet they do, and younger Latina/Hispanic women are experimenting with alcohol in greater numbers. Many older women may be reluctant to report substance abuse because of the shame associated not only with their loss of control but also with their violation of tradition. So, when assessing for substance abuse in Latino/Hispanic individuals it is important, if not crucial, to determine the extent of the client's acculturation.

Because of the strong value placed on children, an assessment of AOD abuse in the Latino/Hispanic population should include referral to a facility where there is child care or where frequent visits by children are allowed. Without such a consideration, the Latina/Hispanic woman's fear of losing her children may pose significant barriers to treatment. Initial assessment of drug use by Latina/Hispanic women might focus on the impact of use on the family system, and especially the impact on the children.

Ironically, approaching men through the *machismo* value may prove effective in assessing use. While *machismo* allows for heavy drinking, being a strong family provider is also valued and often stands in direct opposition to excessive drinking behavior. By focusing on the man's need to be a strong provider and a good role model for his sons especially, the helping professional may be able to help the Latino/Hispanic father determine whether a problem exists. Finally, the Latino/Hispanic population generally is a religious one and includes traditional and nontraditional religious practices with many Cuban Americans and Puerto Ricans following nontraditional practices. Assessment and referrals should include attention paid to services offered by churches and facilities that allow for a variety of religious practices.

In determining possible courses of action for treatment for Latinos, it is important to keep several things in mind (Delgado, 2002). Ideally, the treatment center should be close to the client's family, residence, and/or social network. Moreover, since the fear of discrimination, stigma, and other forms of oppression is very real in the lives of Latinos (and other racioethnic minorities), it is critical that this client population be allowed to "be themselves" in treatment. Hence, mental health counselors need to be aware of the extent to which the treatment facility or program promotes the use of the client's language and cultural traditions. It is also important that the facility or program employ Latinos at all levels of staff. With outpatient facilities specifically, the days and hours of operation are important considerations. When referring to a local center, be aware that clients may be working swing-shifts or nights and will need services that are congruent with their work schedules and family-care situations. Subgroups within these larger diverse populations experience risk factors for developing AOD problems, and this includes adolescents, the elderly, and persons with disabilities. For example, adolescents with disabilities face isolation, discrimination, lack of personal adjustment and success, health issues, easier access to prescription drugs, and perceived entitlement to substance use based their disability. Studies consistently show significantly higher substance use rates for youth with disabilities, while evidence from surveys on adults with disabilities reflects lower rates of AOD abuse than the general population. However, use and misuse of alcohol and illicit drugs is on the increase in persons with disabilities, and this mostly due to "self-medication against life's experiences." Elderly populations are at risk due to amount of medications prescribed, discrimination, and increasing age-related disabilities.

Summary

- Today's minority populations will increase in numbers and make up approximately one-third of the general U.S. population in the next two decades.
- In order to be more accurate and more descriptive, researchers of prevalence rates should focus on racioethnic subgroups and should examine profiles of each drug because of the varied use and effects of drugs on racioethnic and other minorities.
- Heavy drinking by Native Americans as being likened to the world's oldest ongoing protest demonstration, which serves to demark and maintain the Indian–Euro-American boundary; some populations of Native Americans have more problems than others.
- Beginning in early adolescence, Latinos and Native American youth lead the nation in alcohol and illicit drug use.

- Female Native American adolescents and women are more likely to have significant depression and/or anxiety disorders, which are associated with increased AOD use.
- Native Americans and Alaskan Natives have higher alcohol prevalence and treatment rates than other groups.
- Asian/Pacific Islanders comprise more than 60 discrete racial/ethnic groups and subgroups. These groups are heterogeneous and at the same time, have vast variation within each group.
- Chinese Americans and Korean Americans can encourage drinking at social functions as a display of hospitality; however, public drunkenness is discouraged in these and the Samoan culture.
- Research has reflected a bicultural split of language among Asian Americans based on youth acquiring English, and this may increase risks for AOD use and abuse.
- Ethnic pride is seen as an important protective factor against AOD problems in other Pacific Islander groups.
- Mexican American men and women are somewhat more likely to have drinking problems and to drink more heavily than their Cuban, Puerto Rican, Central and South American counterparts.
- The history of African Americans and alcohol is to trace the institution of slavery in the United States.
- Studies show that African Americans often either abstain from alcohol or drink quite heavily; feelings of failure related to the American Dream increases AOD use among African American males—particularly for those males in their early 30s.
- Research has found that for African Americans, AOD use and abuse is related to availability, living in rural areas (for women especially), and other sociocultural issues including chronic unemployment, prison, and discrimination.
- Adolescents, the elderly, and persons with disabilities in almost every group experience increased risk factors for AOD abuse, and this is mostly due to "self-medication against life's experiences."
- Evidence from surveys on adults with disabilities reflects lower rates of AOD abuse than the general population.
- Diverse populations traditionally mistrust the treatment system.
- Treatment for diverse groups should include family involvement because they are viewed as more culturally relevant for many minority groups.
- Asian Americans have the lowest rates for treatment admissions.
- Older African Americans are treated for illicit drug use at greater rates than for other elderly populations.
- The research suggests that there should be strong emphasis on indigenous addiction treatment for Native Americans/Alaskan Natives and African Americans.
- "Multicultural counseling" should be replaced with "culture-centered counseling," and counselors need to be competent in their understanding and appreciation of differences when engaged in treating these groups.
- Culture-centered approaches include counselor competencies in knowledge, attitudes, and skills and emphasize (among others) social justice, spirituality, political pluralism, and common ground for conflict resolution.

Internet Resources

Native Americans and AOD
www.aii.outreach.ou.edu/links.htm

African Americans Quitting AOD
www.mayatech.com/cti/jmate/pdf/Stevens_181_1.pdf

Hispanics and AOD
www.ncadi.samhsa.gov/govpubs/MS459

Asian Americans and AOD
www.tfj.sagepub.com/cgi/reprint/8/3/267.pdf

Culture-centered approaches
www.apa.org/videos/4310471.html

Further Discussion

1. What image comes to your mind when you think of minorities and substance abuse?
2. What role does discrimination play in perpetuating the assessment of AOD problems among diverse populations?
3. How does the issue of social justice influence the treatment of diverse groups with AOD abuse problems?
4. Given the view that Native Americans are engaged in the longest ongoing protest by drinking, what are your thoughts regarding the issue of responsibility?
5. Cultural sensitivity was the first step in multicultural counseling. What is the relationship of this to cultural competence?

5

Confidentiality and Ethical Issues

A high school counselor has been working with a student with multiple problems. After being caught with marijuana, the student had been referred to an AOD treatment center for an assessment. The treatment program determined that the student was not in need of formal treatment but did recommend that the school counselor work with the student on some social skills and minor family issues. During a discussion, the student tells the counselor that he is selling pot at school. What should the counselor do?

A licensed clinical social worker works in a nonprofit mental health agency. The agency does not provide AOD treatment but does provide aftercare services for recovering clients. This social worker has been working with a recovering intravenous drug user on life skills, such as hygiene, appearance, work behaviors, and leisure time activities. The client tells the social worker that he is HIV positive and has been having unprotected sex with a number of partners. What should the social worker do?

A marriage and family therapist is in private practice. She has been seeing a woman for depression. The woman works in a management position for a large company. The company has a self-funded insurance plan that pays for the woman's treatment. The personnel manager of the company contacts the therapist, reports that evidence has surfaced that the woman is using cocaine, and tells the therapist that the company is considering termination. She asks the therapist for guidance. What should the therapist do?

A very large corporation has an Employee Assistance Program counselor on staff. Any employee can see the counselor for three sessions, after which the counselor must develop a plan that, depending on the employee's problem, usually involves a referral to a private therapist or treatment program. This counselor has been contacted by the CEO of the corporation and told to see one of the vice presidents who the CEO believes is alcoholic. After talking to the vice president, the counselor believes that a referral to an alcohol treatment program is appropriate. However, the vice president refuses to follow the recommendation and tells the counselor that she will sue the counselor if he reveals any information to the CEO. The vice president claims that the discussions they have had are confidential. What should the counselor do?

In these four hypothetical situations, we have illustrated some confidentiality issues in the AOD area for mental health professionals. In the remainder of the chapter, we will discuss confidentiality laws that can assist mental health professionals in deciding on the appropriate course of action in such situations, provide guidance for helping professionals in documenting their work with clients, and bring up some of the ethical issues for helping professionals related to the AOD field.

Confidentiality: 42 Code of Federal Regulations, Part 2 (42 CFR)

Confidentiality for mental health professionals is always problematic, since many federal and state laws are often complex and confusing, as are the ethical guidelines developed by professional organizations. As a future mental health professional, you may become familiar with confidentiality guidelines in your training program and then, once in the field, be faced with specific situations that do not fit the general guidelines and legal parameters presented in courses and workshops.

In the AOD area, federal regulations exist to govern confidentiality. We will discuss these regulations in some detail, because even if mental health professionals are not providing AOD treatment services in their work setting, the regulations usually still apply. However, these regulations can be complex, and an infinite number of situations related to confidentiality can develop. We suggest the following in situations in which you might be unsure of the appropriate action to take:

1. Consult your supervisor and/or legal counsel.
2. Contact your state attorney general's office regarding state laws on privileged communication and mandatory reporting.
3. Contact the Legal Action Center,[1] an organization that specializes in legal and policy issues in the AOD area.

Does 42 CFR Apply to You?

Issued in 1975 and amended in 1987, 42 CFR contains the regulations issued by the Department of Health and Human Services related to the confidentiality of AOD abuse patient records (terminology used in the regulations). These regulations supersede any local or state laws that are less restrictive than the regulations. Federal regulations in this area were seen as necessary, because individuals with AOD problems might be hesitant to seek treatment if their confidentiality could not be guaranteed. This was particularly true when treatment for illegal drug abuse was separate from alcohol treatment and, therefore, simply contacting a drug treatment program became an admission of illegal activity.

[1]The Legal Action Center provides direct legal services to individuals, and publications, training, technical assistance and education to agencies. The Legal Action Center can be reached at 225 Varick Street, New York, NY 10014. (1-800-223-4044)

Before you conclude that these regulations are irrelevant because you will not be providing AOD treatment, please read further. 42 CFR defines a *program* as any person or organization that, in whole or in part, provides alcohol/drug abuse diagnosis, treatment, or referral for treatment and receives federal assistance. Federal assistance is defined as receiving federal funds in *any* form, even if the funds do not directly pay for AOD services. This includes tax-exempt status by the IRS, authorization to conduct business by the federal government (e.g., Medicaid provider), or conducting services for the federal government or for branches of state government that receive federal funds. This means that, if you work in a school district that has a free lunch program and also has a program that refers students to treatment, 42 CFR applies. If you work for a mental health agency that accepts Medicaid or CHAMPUS (Civilian Health and Medical Program for Uniformed Services) and diagnoses substance use disorders, 42 CFR applies. If you are an EAP counselor who works for or has a contract with a company that does business with state or federal government, 42 CFR applies. In fact, the only scenario we can imagine in which 42 CFR would not apply to readers of this text would be a counselor or therapist in private practice who does not accept Medicaid or CHAMPUS or any other state or federal insurance reimbursement and does not refer, diagnose, or treat clients with AOD problems. This scenario is unlikely.

The General Rule

The general rule in 42 CFR regarding disclosure of records or other information on AOD clients (42 CFR uses the term *patients*) is *don't.* Except under the conditions we will describe later, you are prohibited from disclosing *any* identifying information regarding clients who receive any service from a program as defined in the regulations. Clients who never enter treatment but inquire about services or are assessed to determine whether they need services are also included, as is information that would identify someone as a client. Finally, this includes information that a person (other than the patient) may already have or may be able to obtain elsewhere, even if the person is authorized by state law to get the information, has a subpoena, or is a law enforcement official.

Let's make this general rule more concrete. You work in a community mental health center that accepts Medicaid and provides a variety of mental health services, including group counseling for AOD abusers. You do an intake on a self-referred client (Frank) and recommend he join the group. Frank says, "No thanks" and leaves. A week later, you receive a visit from a detective from another state. He is looking for Frank and has reason to believe that you have seen him. He has a subpoena for any records on Frank. You must say, "Federal confidentiality regulations require that I neither confirm nor deny my contact with clients." You must not provide any records to the detective. If you fail to maintain Frank's confidentiality, you are subject to a fine of up to $500 for the first offense and up to $5,000 for subsequent offenses. Ironically, if you had not met Frank, you could legally tell the detective that Frank had never come to the mental health center, since this would mean that Frank had never been a client (had not applied for, requested, or received services) and, therefore, you are not bound by 42 CFR.

As with any good rule, there are exceptions (which we will discuss) to the general rule against disclosure. However, we want to caution you that it is best to seek advice if you are unsure about disclosure, because these exceptions can be complex and difficult to interpret in practical situations.

Written Consent

The first exception to the confidentiality rule is that disclosure can be made if the client gives written consent for the disclosure. 42 CFR specifies that the written consent must include the name of the program making the disclosure; the name of the individual or organization receiving the disclosure; the name of the client; the purpose or need for the disclosure; how much and what kind of information will be disclosed; a statement that the client may revoke the disclosure at any time; the date, event, or condition upon which the disclosure expires; the signature of the client and/or authorized person; and the date the consent is signed. A separate consent form must be signed for each individual or organization receiving information on the client. The consent form must also include a written prohibition against the redisclosure of the information to any other party.

In the case of a minor client, a parent or guardian signature is necessary only if state law requires parental consent for treatment. If parental consent is required, the parent or legal guardian and the minor client must both sign the consent. If a minor contacts a treatment program in a state in which parental consent for treatment is required, the program cannot disclose the contact to the parent(s) unless the program director believes the minor lacks the capacity to make a rational choice or represents a substantial threat to his or her life or well-being. Clearly, these decisions can be subjective.

The regulations regarding written consent for disclosure allow treatment providers to release information to third-party payers (e.g., managed care organizations) and employers. However, the release of this information also provides an opportunity for the misuse of such information. Third-party payers and employers are prohibited from redisclosing this information. Equally important is the stipulation regarding how much and what kind of information will be disclosed. Treatment providers must be careful to limit disclosure to information necessary to accomplish the disclosure's purpose. In the case of a third-party payer, this might be limited to the diagnosis, estimated duration of treatment, and services needed. Employers may need only a general statement regarding participation in treatment and progress.

Clients who enroll in treatment programs that use addictive drugs (e.g., methadone) as part of the treatment program are required to consent to disclosure to a central registry. The purpose of this disclosure is to prevent a client from enrolling in multiple programs that use such drugs. Thus, programs may confer about the client if multiple enrollment is detected. The consent remains in force as long as the client is in a treatment program that utilizes addictive drugs.

The only situation in which an irrevocable consent is allowed is in the case of criminal justice referrals. If treatment is a condition of any disposition of criminal proceedings (e.g., dismissal of charges, parole or probation, sentence), the disclosure can be made irrevocable until the client's legal status changes. For example, if a probationary status has been completed, the client may then revoke consent.

It should be noted that written consent does not mandate the program to disclose. There may be situations in which the program believes that disclosure is not in the best interests of the client. This may present an ethical dilemma for the program, which we will discuss later in this chapter. We advise you to seek legal counsel in any situation in which you believe that disclosure in accordance with a valid written consent would be contrary to the client's welfare.

Other Exceptions to the General Rule

In addition to clients' written consent for disclosure, another exception to the prohibition would be communication among staff within an organization, if such communication is necessary to provide services. For example, staffings occur in which clients are discussed among staff members who have either direct or indirect contact with the client. Also, in a multiservice agency (e.g., a hospital), information on clients can be provided to central accounting departments for billing purposes.

This exception can be delicate in public schools. Can or should disclosure of information on a student be made to the student's teachers? The regulations state that the recipient must need the information in connection with duties that are related to providing alcohol or drug-abuse diagnosis, treatment, or referral. Let's say that a student assistance program refers a student to a treatment program and the student is admitted for inpatient treatment. The student is in a special education program, and the teacher is asked to provide some assignments for the student during the time he or she is not in school. Does the teacher need to know where the student is to fulfill this responsibility? Probably not. After treatment, the student returns to school and the teacher is asked to report weekly on the student's behavior and academic performance. Again, the teacher probably does not need to know the reasons for this request. However, the teacher may be better able to help if he or she knows the purpose of monitoring the student. In such cases, the best practice is to request a written consent to disclose to teachers or other school personnel. Having such knowledge will also prevent teachers from innocently asking students where they have been. The problem in schools, as well as other large organizations, is that information is often disclosed to individuals who should not receive it. Therefore, confidentiality education for staff is often needed.

Program staff may discuss clients with people outside of the program as long as the communication does not identify the person as an AOD abuser and does not verify the client's receiving AOD treatment services. For example, case histories may be discussed as long as the client cannot be identified from the history. A treatment program may tell a newspaper reporter that 37% of its clients are cocaine users. A hospital that provides a variety of services and has an AOD treatment program can say that John Smith is a patient in the hospital, as long as John is not identified as receiving AOD treatment.

A medical emergency is another exception to the prohibition on disclosure. A medical emergency is defined as a situation that poses an immediate threat to the health of an individual and requires immediate medical intervention. The disclosure must be made only to medical personnel and only to the extent necessary to meet the medical emergency. The name and affiliation of the recipient of the information must be documented, along with the name of the individual making the disclosure, the date and time of the disclosure, and the nature of the emergency. Such an emergency might arise in social detoxification programs, when clients are withdrawing from central nervous system depressants without medication or medical supervision. If a client begins to seizure and requires medical attention, emergency medical personnel clearly need to know where the client is and why the seizures are occurring. Other situations considered medical emergencies include drug overdoses and suicide threats or attempts.

Earlier in the chapter, we gave the example of a detective with a subpoena for records on a client of a mental health center. As we discussed, the program must not provide records, since a subpoena alone is not sufficient for disclosure according to 42 CFR. However, a subpoena *and* a court order *are* sufficient. Usually, the court notifies the program and client regarding the application for a court order and provides an opportunity for a response from the program and/or client, but this is not the case when a subpoena is issued. Since these issues involve legal proceedings, we suggest you seek legal counsel if you are served with a subpoena or a court order is issued for client information.

Another exception involves disclosure to an organization with a contract to provide services to programs. These contracts are called Qualified Service Organization Agreements (QSOA). For example, in contracting for drug testing or accounting services, a program must disclose identifying information. This disclosure is allowed as long as the QSOA documents comply with the confidentiality regulations.

Another exception to disclosure includes the commission of a crime by a client on the premises of the program or against program personnel. In such an instance, the crime can be reported to the appropriate law enforcement agency and identifying information on the client can be provided.

Identifying information regarding clients can also be disclosed for research, audit, or evaluation purposes. Although the research exception does allow programs to disclose confidential client information to individuals with a proper research protocol, the researcher is prohibited from redisclosing the information. Similarly, regulatory agencies, third-party payers, and peer review organizations may have access to client information for audit and/or evaluation of the program, but the information can be used only for these purposes.

Finally, an exception to disclosure occurs in cases of actual or suspected child abuse or neglect. Confidentiality does not apply to initial reports of child abuse or neglect, as when a client is suspected of, or admits to, child abuse or neglect or when a minor client is the victim. After the initial report, any follow-up reports or contacts do require consent. For example, an adolescent female in an inpatient program reports that she has been sexually molested by her stepfather. The program must make an initial report to the appropriate county or state office of children's protective services. However, any follow-up visits by law enforcement officials or child welfare workers require the client's written consent.

One caution regarding the report of child abuse or neglect: A client with children will not be charged with abuse or neglect simply because he or she has abused alcohol or other drugs. A danger to the child must exist before authorities will take action. Child abuse and neglect frequently occur but are not inevitable or always readily apparent when parents abuse AOD.

Other Confidentiality Issues

Mental health professionals often ask about reporting past crimes of clients or clients' threats to commit future crimes. 42 CFR is clear regarding the exception to disclosure when a crime is committed on program premises or against program personnel. If a proper court order is issued, disclosure can also be made without client consent. Crimes may be reported as well if the report can be worded in such a way that the client is not identified as a client in an AOD program (remember the broad definition of program). However, state laws regarding privileged communication vary by state and by profession. Psychologists may have one set of guidelines, social workers another, and licensed professional counselors another. It is essential that you become familiar with the state laws regarding privileged communication in your profession. However, remember that, unless the state laws regarding disclosure of clients in AOD programs are more restrictive, they are superseded by the federal regulations.

Does a mental health professional have the duty to warn a potential victim if an AOD client threatens to harm the person? In *Tarasoff* v. *Regents of the University of California* [17 Cal. 3d 425 (1976)], a case often used as a precedent, the court found a counselor negligent for failing to warn a person whom the client had threatened and did harm. However, this case applies only in California (Brooks, 1992). Because a conflict may occur between the duty to warn and 42 CFR, Brooks suggests that mental health professionals warn potential victims in such a way that the client is not identified as an AOD program client.

Finally, the question of disclosure of communicable diseases, particularly HIV, has become a sticky confidentiality issue. All states mandate healthcare providers to report cases of communicable diseases to local public health authorities (Lopez, 1994). Lopez suggests several strategies that would allow compliance with such mandates as well as with 42 CFR. Clearly, the simplest strategy is to secure the client's written consent for the mandated report and for follow-up by public health authorities. If the client provides consent, public health officials would have no problem locating the client for examination (that is extremely important in the case of diseases such as tuberculosis [TB] and hepatitis), interviewing to identify partners and contacts, counseling, and monitoring compliance.

If the client does not provide written consent, program personnel could make an anonymous report. However, the client's location could not be provided if this information identified the client as an AOD client, as would be the case in inpatient settings. Also, most states require the person making the report to identify him- or herself, which could also violate 42 CFR. An alternative suggestion (Lopez, 1994) is for the program to enter a QSOA with the local public health authority, who would screen clients for communicable diseases and could then legitimately follow up with clients.

According to Lopez (1994), the "medical emergency" exception to 42 CFR would not apply in cases of sexually transmitted diseases and HIV/AIDS. In both instances, no immediate threat to life is apparent, and, in the case of HIV/AIDS, emergency medical intervention would not impact the condition. However, TB is transmitted by casual contact, is difficult to confirm, and is potentially deadly. Therefore, suspected or confirmed TB may constitute a medical emergency and, therefore, be an exception to disclosure. Although Lopez does not mention hepatitis, the same situation would probably apply.

Program personnel may feel a duty to warn sexual partners of, and those who have shared needles with, an HIV/AIDS client. Again, the best practice is to attempt to convince the client to provide written consent to disclose, but, failing this, anonymous reporting can be considered. The wording in 42 CFR would probably not justify using the medical emergency exception to disclosure.

Health Insurance Portability and Accountability Act (HIPAA)

HIPAA was passed by Congress in 1996 and requires standardization of electronic patient health, administrative, and financial data; unique health identifiers for individuals, health plans, and healthcare providers; and security standards to protect the confidentiality and integrity of individually identifiable health information. HIPAA affects healthcare providers, health plans, employers, public health authorities, life insurers, clearinghouses, billing agencies, information system vendors, service organizations, and universities. All these organizations were required to comply with the privacy provisions of HIPAA by April 14, 2003.

For most of us, the privacy and confidentiality standards in HIPAA are the most relevant part of the law. Generally, there are no major conflicts between HIPAA and 42 CFR. However, HIPAA involves general healthcare, while 42 CFR is specific to AOD. Therefore, in the areas in which the two laws overlap, providers should follow the *most restrictive* law. HIPAA's privacy and confidentiality standards involve the rights of patients to control the release of their medical information, the use of their medical information, and security of patient records. If you work for any of the applicable agencies or organizations, you should be provided with training on HIPAA. Mental health professionals should ask the agency officials responsible for HIPAA compliance about the integration of 42 CFR with HIPAA.

Drug Testing

Drug testing in the workplace and school raises serious privacy issues. The Substance Abuse and Mental Health Services administration has developed guidelines for drug-free workplaces that include drug testing, and the Office of National Drug Control Policy has a publication called *What You Need to Know About Drug Testing in Schools* (see Internet Resources at the end of the chapter). However, we should note that the current federal stance on drug testing is weighted toward "do it," while organizations such as the American Civil Liberties Union oppose many of the ways drug testing is implemented. There have been many court rulings on the topic, but it is beyond the scope of this chapter to review all the complex issues involved. The following general information is based on the court decisions up to this time.

Preemployment Testing. Employers can conduct preemployment drug tests and make offers of employment contingent on a negative drug test. A prospective employee cannot be singled out for preemployment drug testing. In other words, preemployment drug testing must be part of the hiring policy of the organization and applied uniformly.

Random Testing. Employees occupying positions of safety or security sensitivity can be randomly tested without cause. For example, the Nuclear Regulatory Commission, Department of Transportation, and Department of Defense conduct random testing of individuals in designated positions. The issue of who should be considered in a designated position has been the subject of legal actions.

Reasonable Suspicion Testing. Clearly, this is a very subjective area and has also been the subject of legal actions. However, employers with drug testing policies can require a drug test of an employee if there is evidence such as direct observation of use or possession, physical symptoms of being under the influence, erratic or abnormal behavior, or an arrest for a drug-related offense. Evidence is the critical part of this type of testing and has precipitated many of the legal challenges.

Postaccident Testing. Employers who intend to do drug testing following job-related accidents must have a clearly stated policy to that effect. In such cases, employees can be required to submit to a drug test directly after an accident. In many cases, insurance carriers require a drug test as part of the claim process.

Treatment Follow-up Testing. This is another ambiguous privacy area. An employer may have a policy of random testing of employees who return to work following drug treatment. However, in the absence of any symptoms of drug use, it is easy to see how this type of testing may be construed as an intrusion of privacy. Furthermore, it is certainly stigmatizing for the individual. Generally, this type of testing has only been upheld for individuals in positions of public safety or high security.

Drug Testing in Schools. In June 2002, the U.S. Supreme Court upheld the use of random drug testing for secondary students participating in competitive extracurricular activities. Schools can conduct random testing for cause (evidence of drug use or possession). It should be noted that a study by Yamaguchi, Johnston, & O'Malley (2003) found that drug testing had no impact on the rate of drug use in schools that conduct such testing compared to schools that do not do drug testing.

Documentation

All mental health professionals must be particularly attentive to the issue of written documentation. As Marino (1995) reported:

> By keeping good records, counselors can ensure that their clients and their own best interests are served.... Without proper records there is no way another counselor can intervene when the assigned counselor is not available, no way to defend themselves in a lawsuit and no way to verify a payable service. (p. 8)

In the AOD treatment field, accrediting bodies and state agencies often have regulations that specify the form and content of treatment plans and progress notes and the frequency with which written documentation must be made. For the mental health professional working in an agency or institutional setting, there may also be a structure to guide written documentation. However, many school counselors and private therapists must depend on their own experiences and judgment. For those mental health professionals who are uncertain about the form and content of their progress notes on clients, the guidelines developed by

Roget and Johnson (1995) for AOD counselors may be helpful. These authors recommend that progress notes should be written with the idea that they could potentially be used in a legal proceeding. Therefore, the entries should be brief and largely factual. Opinion and conclusions should be clearly labeled as such. Terms not commonly recognized in the professional vernacular (e.g., toxic codependency, wounded inner child) should be avoided. Any reports of child abuse and neglect should be clearly documented, including the name and title of the person who received the report. The person making case notes should be especially careful to document any incidents in which the health, safety, or security of the client is an issue. For example, any threat or attempt at suicide should be documented, along with the actions taken by the mental health professional.

Ethics

Professional organizations, such as the American Psychological Association, American Counseling Association, National Association of Social Workers, and the American Association of Marriage and Family Therapists, have ethical standards for their members. Many AOD counselors belong to the National Association of Alcoholism and Drug Abuse Counselors, which also has published ethical standards. You are obligated to become familiar with both the ethical standards of your profession and the state laws relating to ethical practice for licensed or certified professionals in your field. While most ethical issues are common to all mental health professionals and you will probably receive information about these ethical standards in your training program, we want to mention several areas that present particular problems in the AOD field.

Scope of Practice

Most mental health professionals recognize that their training and expertise is insufficient for an actively psychotic client and would refer such a client to an appropriate treatment setting, which would include medical personnel. However, in the AOD area, there is often a perception that any licensed or certified mental health professional is competent to treat such clients. For example, in our state, licensed psychologists can diagnose and treat AOD problems, but the state has no training requirement in this area for licensure. In most cases, it is up to the professional to determine his or her own areas of competence, and an ethical professional will refer clients who fall outside these areas of expertise to the appropriate person and/or agency. We hope that the information in this book will help you make the determination regarding whom to refer. As you will see in Chapter 6, you should have specific training in the diagnosis of Substance Use Disorders before making a diagnosis in this area. Furthermore, it is our belief that a client with a Substance Dependence Disorder diagnosis (see Chapter 6) should be referred to an AOD treatment program rather than being seen by a mental health generalist. We strongly recommend consultation with a specialist in the field regarding appropriate treatment settings and planning if a client is diagnosed with a Substance Abuse Disorder.

Scope of practice is also an issue for AOD counselors who do not have other counselor training. Although training in the field is changing, many AOD counselors have minimal formal training, and their training may be specific to AOD treatment. Therefore, the counselor may be unprepared to treat clients with co-occurring disorders (see Chapter 8) or may be unable to differentiate substance use disorders from other disorders. The ethical practice would be to consult with licensed mental health professionals and refer when there is any question regarding the client's diagnosis.

Client Welfare

The mental health professional has a primary responsibility to the welfare of the client. Therefore, if a counselor, social worker, or marriage and family therapist is seeing a client who is not benefiting from treatment, the mental health professional is obligated to terminate treatment and refer the client. This may mean that a client with an escalating pattern of AOD use may need a referral to a treatment program in spite of the rapport you have established, the client's great insurance benefits, or your own conceptualization of AOD problems. For example, if most of the programs in your area operate on the basis of the disease concept (see Chapter 3) and your point of view differs, you are not relieved of your responsibility to refer clients who need treatment. Conversely, you should not refer all clients to the same type of treatment program because you have a professional or personal relationship with a specific treatment program.

Earlier in this chapter, we discussed the fact that written consent for disclosure does not mandate that a program disclose information. Instances may occur in which the client would be harmed by disclosure. Of course, clients can revoke consent at any time (in all instances except criminal justice situations), but they may be reluctant to do so. For example, imagine you are a licensed professional counselor working at a mental health center where you are providing relapse prevention services for a recovering polydrug abuser. The client has provided a written consent to disclose treatment compliance and relapses to the client's company. One day, the client admits to a slip that you believe is an isolated event. In your opinion, the client has actually learned a great deal from the slip. On one hand, the client does not want to revoke consent because it is a condition for continued employment, while, on the other hand, you believe that reporting the slip would cause harm to the client, since termination would result. Ethically, you should not disclose the slip even though you have written consent to do so. But, we should add that it would be unethical to lie to the employer. Your best course of action would be to refuse to provide information about slips.

If a client insists that you disclose information that you believe would result in harm to the client, you should seek legal advice. However, instances may occur in which legal advice and ethical practice are in conflict. Remember, your primary responsibility is the welfare of your client.

Managed Care

Many mental health professionals are either employed by managed care companies (e.g., health maintenance organizations) or are under contract with them. Certain ethical issues have arisen as a result of managed care. While these issues involve scope of practice and client welfare, we want to specifically mention them in this section because they seem to be increasing in frequency as the managed care movement spreads.

Imagine that you are a licensed mental health professional who also has the appropriate certification for addiction counseling. You work for an agency that has contracts with a number of managed care companies. You conduct an assessment on a client and believe that the client has a cocaine and alcohol problem. However, the client's behavioral healthcare coverage does not include AOD treatment. The only way the client can get any service is if you make another mental disorder diagnosis. Another client is clearly alcohol dependent. You think an inpatient program would be the most appropriate. However, this client is in a managed care program that covers only outpatient treatment. A third client is referred to you after receiving a DUI. After a careful assessment, you determine that this was an isolated mistake and the client only needs some education. However, your agency runs an outpatient AOD program and the census has been low. Your client has coverage for outpatient treatment and your agency director is pressuring you to recommend the program to your client. A fourth client clearly needs outpatient treatment. This client's managed care company has a preferred provider arrangement with a local treatment agency. You know that this agency employs "counselors" who are not properly certified to provide AOD treatment services.

In a perfect world, mental health professionals would not be faced with these ethical dilemmas. Your diagnostic decisions and treatment recommendations would be based solely on client welfare, professional judgment, and appropriate practices. However, other issues (i.e., money) have intruded. While you are in a training program, it is very easy for others to tell you how to behave ethically. When you are employed and your boss is pressuring you, when you have clients who need help, or when your livelihood is dependent on paying clients, you may find yourself tempted to cross ethical boundaries. We won't patronize you by lecturing about the need to maintain the ethical standards of any mental health profession. However, we do believe that the frequency of these dilemmas would be reduced if all citizens had access to appropriate AOD treatment services. This might stimulate you to be proactive with policy makers in advocating for this.

Application of Confidentiality Regulations

Now that you are familiar with the confidentiality regulations, let's see how they apply to the situations presented at the beginning of the chapter. In the first case, a high school counselor is working with a student who was referred through the school's student assistance program, and the student disclosed that he had been selling marijuana on campus. The counselor is covered under 42 CFR because the school district receives federal support and the student assistance program does refer students to treatment. However, this situation would be an exception to confidentiality since it concerns a crime that is committed on the premises. In some states, the discussion between the counselor and the student may be protected as privileged communication, in which case the counselor would not have the option of reporting the crime. In such a state, the state law is actually more restrictive than 42 CFR and therefore takes precedence. If the state has no privileged communication law, the counselor is not obligated to report the crime but could legally report it under the provisions of 42 CFR. In this case, the counselor must decide the course of action that is in the best interests of the client.

In the second case, a social worker is providing aftercare services in a mental health agency. The client is a recovering IV drug user who reports being HIV positive and admits to having unprotected sex with a variety of partners. Again, the social worker must comply with 42 CFR. The social worker is providing treatment services and the agency is nonprofit and, therefore, federally supported. If the client is aware of being HIV positive, he or she has probably already been reported to public health officials. However, the social worker can probably make a report without violating 42 CFR. Since the agency provides a variety of services and the social worker does not provide AOD services exclusively, the report can be made without identifying the client as an alcohol or other drug treatment client. Of course, the social worker should attempt to get written consent for disclosure from the client. However, if the client lives in a halfway house for recovering addicts, the social worker cannot give the client's address to the public health authority because to do so would identify the client as an alcohol or other drug client.

Since the social worker is able to make a report to the public health authority without violating 42 CFR, the issue of warning sexual partners of the client's condition would best be left to public health officials. If the social worker has the names of sexual partners but the client would not give written consent for disclosure, the social worker can make anonymous reports to the partners. However, the social worker would probably not have names. Of course, we would hope that the social worker would counsel the client regarding his or her sexual behavior.

In the third situation, whether a marriage and family therapist in private practice falls under 42 CFR is questionable. Marriage and family therapists are generally not eligible for Medicaid or CHAMPUS payments, but the therapist may be a preferred provider for a state-funded insurance plan, and in such an instance would have to comply with 42 CFR. When the personnel manager contacts the therapist to inquire about the employee who is seeing her, the first issue to address is consent. If the client has not given written consent for the therapist to disclose information to the personnel manager, she should neither confirm nor deny that the woman is in therapy. If written consent has been provided, the therapist has several options for handling the suspicion of cocaine use. Since depression has been the focus of treatment, we would hope that AOD use has been assessed and ruled out as a problem. However, the therapist may feel that this issue exceeds her scope of practice, and so she refers the client for a more thorough assessment. Drug testing may also be needed. Clearly, if a therapeutic relationship has been developed, the therapist should discuss the issue of cocaine use with the client.

The EAP counselor for the large corporation will have to comply with 42 CFR if the company does any business with state or federal government. In the situation described, the counselor would have a problem if he or she did not obtain a written consent for disclosure from the vice president *before* providing services. Once the counselor interviews the vice president, the vice president becomes a client and the information discussed is confidential. The CEO has no right to be informed, regardless of who is paying the bill or the fact that the counselor is an employee of the company. However, if the company does not meet the criteria in 42 CFR for federal support, then the counselor has an ethical dilemma. The EAP counselor first needs to clearly establish the parameters of reporting before providing any services and, ethically, must then ensure that anyone who sees the counselor understands these parameters.

When an employer insists that an employee see the EAP counselor as a condition of avoiding an adverse action, such as suspension or termination, the employee must give written consent to disclose before any services are provided. However, the disclosure is limited to a report of the EAP counselor's recommendation(s) and a report about whether the employee followed the recommendation(s). Clearly, a less restrictive disclosure would inhibit most employees from being open with the counselor. However, EAP counselors should warn clients that, if employees sue employers or file Workers' Compensation claims, all records of contacts with EAP counselors and other mental health professionals may be disclosed during legal proceedings (Schultz, 1994).

Summary

- 42 CFR ensures that people who seek AOD treatment are in no more legal jeopardy than those who do not seek treatment.
- Almost all mental health professionals will have to comply with 42 CFR.
- The best advice to handle complexity in the law is to keep all identifying information confidential, including confirmation or denial regarding whether someone is a client.
- Any exceptions to confidentiality should be discussed with legal counsel.
- Mental health professionals should conform to ethical standards of professional associations and licensing boards.
- Mental health professionals should be very familiar with ethical standards regarding scope of practice and child welfare issues.

Internet Resources

42 CFR Part 2
www.lac.org/pubs/gratis.html

Drug testing
www.drugtestingnews.com

HIPAA
www.hhs.gov/ocr/hipaa

Ethics
http://naadac.org/documents/index.php?CategoryID=23

Legal Action Center
www.lac.org

Workplace drug testing
http://dwp.samhsa.gov/DrugTesting/DTesting.aspx

School drug testing
www.whitehousedrugpolicy.gov/pdf/drug_testing.pdf

Further Discussion

1. Discuss any laws or administrative regulations in your state regarding confidentiality for AOD counselors, social workers, school counselors, licensed professional counselors, and/or psychologists.
2. What do you see as the advantages and disadvantages of random drug testing in schools and the workplace?
3. If a housecleaner was seeing you for counseling, what would be the ethical concerns with trading your services for your client's housecleaning service?

Confidentiality and Ethical Issues

Case Study Activity

Read Substance Abuse, Case 1: Janis: A Mother Whose Teenage Son's Behavior Suggests a Struggle with Substance Abuse and Major Depression.

- Assess the counselor's adherence to confidentiality and ethical guidelines with Sam, particularly with regard to informed consent and client welfare.

To access the case for this activity, log on to MyHelpingLab at www.myhelpinglab.com. Select the **Counseling & Psychotherapy** tab to locate the **Counseling Case Archive.**

6

Assessment and Diagnosis

A few years ago, we were supervising a marriage and family therapy intern in our clinic at the university. The intern had just seen her first client and was eager to show the videotape of her session during supervision. The client was a middle-aged woman whose presenting problem was management of her 7-year-old son. The intern was excited about working with the woman because the intern had experience with a structured program for parenting skills and, therefore, thought that she knew exactly what to do to help. The intern asked a few questions about the discipline techniques the client used and gathered a little information on the family constellation. She then described the type of parenting strategies that they could work on in counseling. In watching the tape of the session, we noticed how anxious the client appeared to be, and it seemed that she was not really absorbing the information the counselor was presenting. We asked the intern whether she were sure that she had identified the correct problem. The intern seemed surprised because the client had clearly stated that she needed help with the discipline of her child and had given many examples that illustrated her difficulties with parenting. As the third session began, the client immediately began to cry and told the intern that she thought she was alcoholic.

If you know anything about the counseling process, you probably can identify several problems with this description of counseling. You might attribute the intern's actions to inexperience and a desire to demonstrate success. However, imagine yourself working as a school counselor or in a community mental health agency. You have an extremely heavy caseload and see people for a variety of problems, so you feel pressured to make a rapid determination of the problem and to quickly come up with interventions. When a client comes in with a clear statement of the issue and you are familiar with a course of action, it may not occur to you that there is an unstated problem. You are thinking, "Great. I know how to handle this in only a few sessions. Then I can go on to the next person."

Many clients attribute their problems to something other than alcohol or other drugs or, if concerned about their use, the client may be hesitant to discuss these concerns until he or she feels comfortable with the mental health professional. For example, a client comes to a mental health center complaining of depression. A recent relationship has ended, and the therapist works with the client on grief and loss. The therapist never finds out that the client is a frequent cocaine user. Or, a high school student makes an appointment with the school counselor supposedly to discuss his schedule, when in reality he wants to talk about his increasing use of marijuana but wants to "check out" the counselor first.

In any counseling or helping situation, the best methods to identify the "real" problem are to establish a trusting relationship with clients and to conduct a thorough assessment. In your counseling skills classes, you learn about the facilitative conditions that are necessary to build a trusting relationship (i.e., warmth, respect, positive regard, empathic understanding). Hopefully, you have also learned about the assessment process. In this chapter, we will focus on the assessment that any helping professional can (and should) perform, with an emphasis on the signs and symptoms that would indicate the possible existence of an alcohol or other drug problem. In keeping with the goals of this text, the purpose of this discussion of assessment is to ensure that school counselors, social workers, mental health counselors, marriage and family therapists, rehabilitation counselors, and other helping professionals will *always* consider the possibility of AOD problems in the normal assessment process. We believe that the prevalence of AOD problems in our society necessitates their consideration as a causal or contributing factor with nearly every client. We are not presenting an assessment protocol specific to AOD problems, because this type of assessment would be conducted by those involved in the treatment of AOD problems. However, we will describe some of the instruments that are used in the assessment process so you will be aware of the advantages and disadvantages of these tools.

We also want to discuss the diagnosis of AOD problems. Helping professionals need to be aware of the criteria that are used to determine whether someone is or is not chemically dependent. However, awareness does not imply competence in reaching diagnostic decisions. Assessment is the process of gathering information, and diagnosis is the conclusion that is reached on the basis of the assessment. Therefore, we strongly recommend that you refrain from diagnosis unless you have had thorough training specific to assessment and diagnosis of substance use disorders.

Definitions of Use, Misuse, Abuse, and Dependence or Addiction

For most helping professionals who do not have extensive training in the AOD field, it is somewhat difficult to determine whether a client's substance use is or is not problematic. They may rely on personal experience and information (or misinformation) they pick up. For example, a high school counselor gets a call from a parent of one of the students. The young man is 17 years old, came home from a party on Saturday night smelling of alcohol, and admitted to drinking at the party. His parents belong to a religious group that prohibits the use of alcohol, so neither one has any experience with alcohol or other drug use. They want to know whether their son has a problem. The high school counselor did her share of experimentation in adolescence but is a moderate user as an adult. She assures the parents that nearly all adolescents experiment and they have nothing to worry about. Is she right?

A simple conceptualization of the distinction between different levels of use can be helpful to the mental health professional in determining the type of intervention that is appropriate for a client. However, these definitions are not appropriate for diagnosis. They simply are a guide for the mental health professional in recommending the course of action for a client.

Nearly everyone uses alcohol or other drugs (including caffeine and tobacco) at some point in his or her life. We define *use* as the ingestion of alcohol or other drugs without the experience of any negative consequences. If our high school student had drunk a beer at the party and his parents had not found out, we could say that he had used alcohol. Any drug can be *used* according to this definition. However, the type of drug taken and the characteristics of the individual contribute to the probability of experiencing negative consequences. For example, it is illegal for minors to drink alcohol. Therefore, the probability that our high school student will experience negative consequences from drinking alcohol may be far greater than that probability is for an adult. The chances that an adult will experience negative consequences from shooting heroin are greater than experiencing negative consequences from drinking alcohol.

When a person experiences negative consequences from the use of AOD, it is defined as *misuse.* Again, a large percentage of the population misuses alcohol or other drugs at some point. Our high school student misused alcohol because his parents found out he had been drinking at a party and because it is illegal for him to drink. Many people overuse alcohol at some point, become ill, and experience the symptoms of a hangover. This is misuse. However, misuse does not imply that the negative consequences are minor. Let's say that an adult woman uses alcohol on an infrequent basis. It is her 30th birthday, and her friends throw a surprise party. She drinks more than usual and, on the way home, is arrested for a DUI. She really doesn't have any problems with alcohol, but, in this instance, the consequence is not minor.

You may be wondering about the heavy user of alcohol or other drugs who does not *appear* to experience negative consequences. First, remember that these definitions are meant to provide the helping professional with a simple conceptualization as a guide. Second, the probability of experiencing negative consequences is directly related to the frequency and level of use. If a person uses alcohol or other drugs on an occasional basis, the probability of negative consequences is far less than if one uses on a daily basis. However, since we are talking about probability, it is possible that a person could be a daily, heavy user and not experience negative consequences that are obvious to others. We say "obvious" because a person may be damaging his or her health without anyone being aware of this for a long period of time.

We define *abuse* as the continued use of alcohol or other drugs in spite of negative consequences. Our high school student is grounded for two weeks by his parents. Right after his grounding is completed, he goes to a party and drinks again. He continues to drink in spite of the consequences he experienced. Now, he might become more sneaky and escape detection. However, as we discussed previously, the probability of detection increases the more he uses and, if he does have a problem with alcohol, it is likely that his use will be discovered. As another example, let's go back to the woman who was arrested for a DUI after her birthday party. For people who do not have an alcohol or other drug problem, getting a DUI would be so disturbing that they would avoid alcohol altogether or drink only at home. If, a month after the DUI, the woman was at another party or a bar drinking when she would be driving, this is considered abuse.

Addiction or dependence is the *compulsive* use of alcohol or other drugs regardless of the consequences. We worked with a man who had received three DUIs in one year. He was on probation and would be sentenced to one year in prison if he were caught using alcohol.

But, he continued to drink. The man was clearly addicted to alcohol, because the negative consequences did not impact his use.

The relationship between the level of intervention and these definitions can be illustrated with our high school student. If the assessment (which will be described in this chapter) indicates that the student "misused" alcohol, he may need to suffer a significant consequence to impress upon him the fact that drinking by minors is illegal and unacceptable. He may also need education about the effects and consequences of alcohol use. Furthermore, the student may also need counseling or social skills training if his use is related to peer pressure or to a desire to fit in. If the assessment indicates that he has been abusing alcohol, a referral to a treatment program or helping professional who specializes in alcohol and other drug problems may be the appropriate intervention. Obviously, if he has been using alcohol in a compulsive manner, referral to a treatment program is appropriate.

Although the definitions of use, misuse, abuse, and dependence or addiction provide a rough conceptual framework for the helping professional, it would be erroneous to perceive these categories as discrete. Substance use can more logically be viewed as a continuum. However, as we discussed in Chapter 3, it would be inappropriate to assume that there is an inevitable progression along the continuum. The mental health professional must conduct a thorough assessment to determine a client's placement on the continuum and then decide on the appropriate intervention given the level of use, life problems, and relevant client characteristics.

Psychosocial History

We assume that you have taken (or will take) a course in assessment as part of your training program and have learned (or will learn) that a psychosocial history is a critical part of the assessment process, regardless of the client's presenting problem. We want to focus on the information that you would gather on the psychosocial history that may relate to alcohol and other drug use problems. However, a couple of remarks related to assessment in general and the psychosocial history in particular are necessary first.

Assessment is a process that should be ongoing during counseling, and a helping professional should be continually gathering information that will assist the client. The psychosocial history is a structured method of gathering information in areas that may relate to the client's difficulties. This method ensures that a helping professional rules out possible causal factors. However, a psychosocial history is not an interrogation. A helping professional must use the same facilitative skills in a structured interview as would be used in any counseling situation. Certainly, the nature of a psychosocial history necessitates that the interviewer ask questions. However, if the helping professional asks a series of questions without sensitivity to the client, the relationship may be damaged, and the interviewer may elicit resistance from the client that would hinder the assessment process. The helping professional should tell a client that the purpose of a psychosocial history is to learn as much about him or her as possible so that the best service can be provided. Often, the analogy of a physician gathering a complete health history before seeing a patient makes sense to clients. Also, it is best to begin a psychosocial history with areas that are the *least likely* to be threatening to a client.

Every assessment should consider individual characteristics and group differences of clients and, in Chapter 4, we discussed AOD issues specific to various ethnically diverse groups. Although it would be erroneous to make *a priori* assumptions about clients from ethnically diverse groups, the interviewer must be aware of group differences and must account for these differences during the assessment. The notion of cultural relativism discussed in Chapter 4 may be helpful in this regard.

Finally, we know that there are situations in which a complete psychosocial history is impractical. For example, a school counselor is rarely in a position to gather such a history due to time constraints, lack of access to the information, or to the restraints of confidentiality. Parents may not be willing to see the school counselor, or a student may ask that the counselor refrain from contacting parents or teachers. In such cases, the helping professional should gather as much information as possible but should exercise caution in reaching conclusions with incomplete information. While real-world barriers are not excuses for poor practice, these barriers do exist and must be acknowledged. However, helping professionals should make every effort to gather a complete psychosocial history to avoid missing the real problem.

With these parameters in mind, we will discuss the areas to be assessed in a psychosocial history and the signs and symptoms of alcohol and other drug use issues related to these areas. As we stated earlier, the prevalence of AOD problems necessitates consideration of these problems as a causal or contributing factor in most client difficulties. However, it would also be an error to believe that all client problems are caused by or related to AOD. If you want to do a competent job of assessment, you should be open to a variety of possible explanations.

AOD Use History

We suggest beginning the psychosocial history with an area that is least likely to elicit client resistance, and an AOD use history would generally not fit this criterion. Therefore, you probably should not begin the interview with this history. However, it certainly is the most direct manner to assess AOD problems. Clearly, assessment of substance use problems through direct questions about client use requires honesty and accuracy from the client, but this is true with regard to all areas of the psychosocial history. Certainly, some clients minimize their use, particularly if they perceive a problem. However, it is surprising how often clients report heavy use and do not perceive it as a problem, or minimize their actual use when it is still excessive compared to others.

Clients should be asked "How much (alcohol, marijuana, cocaine, etc.) do you use?" rather than "Do you use (alcohol, marijuana, cocaine, etc.)?" While the latter question elicits a "yes" or "no," the former question is more open ended. For example, when one client was asked how much alcohol he used, he said, "Not much. About as much as most guys." Follow-up revealed that this was two to three cases of beer a week.

The interviewer should ask about use in each of the psychoactive drug classifications mentioned in Chapter 2. Don't assume—based on gender, ethnicity, appearance, or other characteristics—that a client is involved only with certain drugs. Also, don't forget to ask about tobacco use. Clients should be questioned regarding quantity of use, frequency, setting (alone, at home, with friends), the methods used to procure their supply (e.g., from friends, purchased, stolen, or in exchange for sex), and the route of administration (e.g., ingestion, snorting, smoking, intravenously). With adolescents, it is helpful to ask what drugs their friends use, particularly if they deny their own use, since having friends who use is predictive of adolescent drug problems (Hawkins, Lishner, Catalano, & Howard, 1985).

The alcohol and drug use history of a client is helpful to determine progression (or lack thereof) on the continuum of use and because age of first use (prior to age 15) is also predictive of later problems (Robins & Przybeck, 1985). With regard to progression, clients who report little or no use should be asked whether there were times when their use was heavy. If so, what occurred to change this pattern—treatment, maturity, life changes, or some other event? If their use is currently heavy, how long has it been at this level? Has there been a gradual or sudden increase in use?

The information in this and other chapters of this book should be helpful to you in determining whether the client's reported use is problematic. However, one simple rule may be helpful. Ask yourself this question, "Does a normal drinker (user) drink (use) as this client does?" To answer this question, you must have some knowledge of "normal" and consider the client's *age, gender, ethnicity,* and other characteristics. For example, you are interviewing a 47-year-old man who suffered a back injury in his construction job and is applying for vocational rehabilitation. He reports drinking a six-pack of beer each night and two cases on the weekend. He has a stable marriage, has never been arrested, and had stable employment until his injury. Does he have a problem? Or, a 20-year-old college junior was found in possession of a quarter-ounce of marijuana in his dorm room. He and his friends smoke on the weekend. He does not drink alcohol, and he began his marijuana use last year. You are a college counselor, and you must determine the type of intervention or discipline required. Does he have a problem? Maybe you are a probation officer. One of your clients is a 27-year-old African American man who lives in an urban area. He was involved in a fight in a bar and was arrested. He drinks alcohol on Friday and Saturday nights and usually drinks to the point of intoxication. His drinking started at age 18 and he does not use other drugs, except tobacco. Does he have a problem?

Does a normal drinker (user) do what these individuals do? Our 47-year-old beer drinker is a heavy drinker with no reported problems. Based on what you have learned about alcohol in Chapter 2, you should know that this level of alcohol use on a daily basis is not normal. If the man has no other problems at this time (which would be surprising, but possible), he will probably have physical problems from his alcohol use in the future. The situation with the college student and probation client are less clear. They have both experienced problems related to their use of alcohol and other drugs. However, we also must consider the social and cultural context of their use. The probation client may have an alcohol problem or he may have a problem with his social group, expectations for male behavior in his culture, or the like. The college student may be using marijuana in a manner that is quite consistent with his social group and does not result in any difficulties, with the exception of the illegality of the drug. The rest of their psychosocial histories may help clarify the extent of their problems.

Family History

A psychosocial interview will always have some focus on the client's current family constellation and family of origin. With regard to AOD problems, it is well known that a history of alcoholism or other drug addiction in the family of origin is a risk factor for substance abuse (e.g., Hawkins et al., 1985). However, it is best to ask the client if there were any problems in the family with regard to alcohol or other drugs rather than asking if the parents were (are) alcoholic or drug addicted. The client may be unable to make such a diagnosis, and may be hesitant to apply these labels due to the stigma associated with them.

A variety of problems in families may be related to AOD problems (as well as other problems). These include physical and sexual abuse. Since studies have found that as many as 75% of women in alcohol treatment programs have been sexually molested (Rohsenow, Corbett, & Devine, 1988), this is particularly important to assess with women clients. Other types of family problems including financial difficulties, communication problems, and excessive conflict may be caused by or related to alcohol and other drug use, so these issues also should be assessed.

Often clients will report a divorce in the family of origin or current family or the death of a parent or caretaker. The psychosocial interviewer should investigate such events further. For example, a client may say that her parents divorced when she was young because her father was "irresponsible." The interviewer should attempt to determine whether alcohol or other drugs contributed to this "irresponsibility." A parent's death in an automobile accident may have been caused by substance abuse, as well.

The importance of assessing alcohol and other drug use in the family of origin and current family is not restricted to the client's own use. As we will discuss in Chapters 11 and 12, children who live in substance-abusing homes and adult children who were raised by alcoholic or other drug-addicted caretakers may have a variety of problems as a result. There is also the whole issue of codependency, which will also be discussed in Chapter 12. Although codependency is a controversial issue in the field, it is certainly the case that some individuals are attracted to people with AOD problems and tend to repeatedly choose such people as partners. Therefore, a positive family history of alcohol or other drug abuse may help explain the current problems of some clients, even if the clients have no alcohol or other drug use problems of their own.

Social History

When the first author was in a master's program in school psychology, he was seeing a couple for marriage counseling in the university clinic. One of the wife's complaints was that the husband never wanted to go out or have any friends over. This was quite a change from when they first got together. After fumbling around for several sessions and trying some behavioral contracts to increase their social activity (which didn't work), the husband admitted that he was happier sitting at home with his beer and watching TV. The author, who had no training in the AOD field at the time, did not know what to do. His supervisors (who also had no training in the AOD field) suggested some ways to make the marriage more exciting so that the husband would be more interested in his wife than in TV and beer. Is it surprising that the couple finally became frustrated with counseling and terminated?

Individuals who have progressed in their alcohol or other drug abuse may go through a gradual change in social activities and relationships. There may be a shift to friends who use in the same manner as the client, while nonusing friends are dropped. Parents of adolescents will frequently notice this, although the reason for the change in social groups may not be identified by the parents. Eventually, more and more isolation may occur if the social group does not "keep up."

Clients (or significant others) may report that previously enjoyed activities have been discontinued, which may be attributed to depression in adults and rebellion in adolescents. We worked with an adult who had been an avid snorkler but had greatly reduced his involvement as his alcohol and tobacco use progressed. An adolescent client had been involved in the school band but had dropped out and was spending his spare time playing his guitar in his room as a result of heavy marijuana use.

It is also important to assess the client's relationship history for involvement with partners who have alcohol or other drug problems. This may provide some evidence for codependency (see Chapter 12). One of our clients was a woman in her mid-30s who was referred by a state agency for depression following a disabling injury that prevented her from working. She was involved in a 10-year relationship with a polydrug abuser and had previously lived with an addict who had been murdered. Her father was alcoholic. In discussing relationships with this client, we found that she had absolutely no idea that it was possible to have a relationship with a man who did not abuse alcohol or other drugs. In treating this client, the social history was important since a good deal of her depression was related to the fact that she could no longer support herself, and she thought that she would be forever dependent on alcoholic and drug-addicted men.

Legal History

There is nothing very complicated about a client's report of DUIs or arrests for public intoxication or possession or distribution of drugs. However, as we discussed in Chapter 1, there is a relationship between all types of criminal behavior and AOD use. Therefore, a client's report of a history of shoplifting, assault, robbery, burglary, and other crimes may indicate alcohol or other drug problems. With adolescents, status offenses such as running away, truancy, curfew violations, and incorrigibility may be symptoms of substance abuse problems. Although this area seems very straightforward in a psychosocial assessment, we find it is the most frequently neglected. This may be due to the interviewer's own hesitancy to ask such questions.

Educational History

This is a particularly important area to assess with adolescents. Hawkins et al. (1985) found that academic failure and lack of commitment to school were risk factors for adolescent substance abuse. In addition, Karacostas and Fisher (1993) found that a higher proportion of students identified as learning disabled were classified as chemically dependent compared with non–learning disabled students. Finally, Archambault (1992) includes the following signs of adolescent substance abuse: truancy, absenteeism, incomplete assignments, sudden drop in grades, verbal abuse toward teachers or classmates, and vandalism.

With adolescents, it is particularly important to determine whether there has been a change in behavior or academic performance over time. In particular, a change that occurs from the elementary grades to middle or high school may suggest alcohol or other drug involvement. Because school counselors may be gathering information in this area from cumulative files, teachers, and parents, they should be particularly attentive to this issue of change. In addition to the signs noted by Archambault (1992), there may be an increase in suspensions or expulsions, fights, or stealing. Teachers may indicate problems with the student's falling asleep in class, belligerence, or increasing withdrawal.

A retrospective report from adults of these kinds of school problems may indicate past or current AOD problems. In addition to inquiring about behavioral and academic issues, the mental health professional should ask whether the client has a history of dropping out of educational programs, including postsecondary institutions.

Educational history can be particularly helpful with a young adult (18 to 25) who is being seen for presenting problems unrelated to AOD abuse. For example, we assessed a 24-year-old man who had been hit by a car while riding his bike. Some brain damage had resulted, and the man had requested vocational rehabilitation services. The assessment was to determine his cognitive and academic capabilities. During the psychosocial history, the man reported increasing academic problems in high school although he had graduated. Subsequently, he started and dropped out of college three times. He admitted to being under the influence of LSD when the accident occurred (no one had ever asked him if he was using). He had also begun heavy AOD use in his junior year in high school and continued to be a heavy user of alcohol and hallucinogens.

Occupational History

With many adults, work history may indicate more current problems with AOD than an educational history that occurred long ago. However, the same types of issues (poor performance, behavioral and attitudinal problems) that we discussed regarding school may occur in the work setting. For example, frequent job changes, terminations, and reports of unsatisfactory performance may be noted. For a person who maintained a job for an extended period of time, there may be a report of a gradual progression of deteriorating performance. There may also be frequent absenteeism, moodiness and irritability, uncharacteristic displays of anger, and deteriorating relationships with supervisors and colleagues. A good indication that an employee may have a substance abuse problem is frequent absence from work on Mondays (perhaps the employee has been involved in heavy use on the weekend and is too hung over or too tired to come to work).

Underemployment may be reported by a client whose alcohol or other drug use has progressed to a problematic level. Clients may gradually seek jobs that require less responsibility, skills, or time as their substance use impairs their ability to perform at work, and their AOD use becomes the primary preoccupation.

Military history should also be addressed. Alcohol, marijuana, and heroin were frequently abused in Vietnam, and many veterans from this era returned to the United States with AOD problems. Furthermore, stressful military experiences and the subsequent development of emotional problems may put a veteran at risk for difficulties with AOD.

Medical History

Not only do alcohol and other drugs cause some specific ailments, but people who abuse substances get sick more often. For example, alcohol abuse results in lowered immunity to infection. Also, substance abusers may not be as attentive to nutrition and exercise as those who abstain or use in a nonabusive manner. Furthermore, there is a relationship between substance abuse and injuries caused by accidents that result from impaired judgment, perception, coordination, reaction time, and by violence. Therefore, a medical history that includes frequent illnesses and/or accidents may indicate substance abuse problems.

In Chapter 2, we discussed some of the medical problems associated with the abuse of different drugs. For example, if a client reports a medical history that includes gastritis, peptic ulcers, or a fatty liver, the mental health professional should certainly suspect alcohol abuse. You should also keep in mind that the long-term use of legal drugs (alcohol and tobacco) may result in medical problems in clients who show no other symptoms of substance abuse.

Psychological and Behavioral Problems

When people see a mental health professional, either of their own volition or through some form of coercion, they may not recognize a causal relationship between their presenting problem and substance abuse. For example, a woman came to see us at the insistence of her husband. She had symptoms of depression, and the husband had threatened to leave her if she did not get help. The woman's physician had prescribed an antidepressant, but this had not helped. During the psychosocial assessment, we learned that the woman used alcohol and Valium on a daily basis.

The common problems cited by people seeking assistance from mental health professionals may be due to or exacerbated by alcohol or other drug use. Depression, anxiety, panic attacks, mood swings, irritability, outbursts of anger, problems in sleeping and eating, sexual dysfunction, and the like may be related to substance abuse. However, we are not implying that all psychological and behavioral problems are due to substance abuse. Certainly, a client could present with any of the problems we have listed and have no substance abuse problem at all. Nor are we saying that, if there is alcohol or other drug abuse, it is always the cause of the client's problems. A client may be highly anxious for some reason and begin to use alcohol or other drugs to relieve the symptoms of anxiety. Even if the client stopped using, he or she would still be anxious if the cause of the anxiety still existed. However, the client's use can become a *contributing factor* to the anxiety and must, therefore, be a focus of treatment.

If your reaction to reading this section is, "You seem to be saying that every problem I might see as a mental health professional could be related to AOD use," you get an *A*. That's why we are stressing the assessment of AOD use and are providing information on the signs of substance abuse that you may find on taking a psychosocial history. Ruling out substance abuse as a contributing or causal factor can save you and your clients time, frustration, and (often) money. Furthermore, given the frequency of these problems, we believe it is simply an element of good practice.

Signs of Adolescent Substance Abuse

Although many of the areas of the psychosocial history may be useful with adults and adolescents in determining the probability of an alcohol or other drug problem, there are additional signs of adolescent substance abuse. Since adolescents may not have experienced the variety or the severity of life problems as adults have, the typical psychosocial history may not assess some of these signs. However, a careful assessment of adolescents who are experiencing school or home problems is important in order to intervene in the adolescent's use pattern before more serious problems occur.

Fisher and Harrison (1992) described a protocol for the assessment of AOD abuse with adolescents who are referred in a school setting. Those of you preparing for careers as school counselors or school social workers might find these procedures useful. As part of this protocol, the authors recommend that assessment procedures involve a careful examination of changes in the adolescent's behavior in a variety of areas. As we discussed in the educational history section of the psychosocial history, these changes may involve a deterioration in academic performance, increased absenteeism and truancy, fighting, verbal abuse, defiance, or withdrawal. In addition, it is important to look at the adolescent's social relationships. There may be less and less involvement with friends who do not use and more involvement with peers who are users. The adolescent may identify with a particular school group that typically uses (i.e., "I'm a stoner"). There may be a decreasing involvement and interest in previously enjoyed activities such as athletics or social groups. Furthermore, adolescents may gravitate toward music and dress that depict AOD use in a positive manner or are associated with substance-using adolescents. Adolescents may need money to support their use and turn to stealing, selling possessions, or dealing drugs. In the latter instance, parents and teachers may become aware that the adolescent has a large amount of cash at various times that cannot be adequately explained. Finally, it should go without saying that if an adolescent is in possession or under the influence, a problem exists. It is the severity of the problem that must be assessed.

It is often difficult to differentiate adolescent behavior that may indicate alcohol or other drug problems from normal adolescent behavior. If you tell a group of parents that defiance and changes in friends can be signs of adolescent substance abuse, they may all send their children for drug testing. It is important for a mental health professional who works with adolescents to have a thorough understanding of adolescent development to differentiate "normal" adolescent behavior from unusual behavior and to examine all areas of a psychosocial history as well as the additional signs of adolescent substance abuse. It would be an error to isolate one or two signs and attach undue importance to them. For example, if a lot of kids at school are wearing T-shirts with the insignias of beer companies and a child buys one, this does not mean that he or she is using or abusing alcohol. (However, we do encourage everyone to express their disapproval of this type of drug advertising.) As with the assessment of any individual, you should consider all the information you gather before making a judgment.

Self-Report Inventories

There are many screening and assessment[1] devices and protocols that have been developed to help a clinician determine if a client has a substance abuse problem. Many of these devices and protocols have been designed for use in substance abuse treatment programs to

[1]You should be aware that screening and assessment are different. Screening is usually a brief procedure used to identify individuals with possible problems or who are at risk for developing a problem. Assessment is a more thorough process that should involve multiple procedures and is designed to result in diagnostic, placement, and treatment decisions. The self-report inventories we are discussing are used for screening but also may be part of a thorough assessment.

determine whether a client is appropriate for treatment and the type of treatment setting and services that would be the most appropriate. It is beyond the objectives of this text to discuss these various devices and protocols, but the interested reader will find reviews of the most frequently used screening and assessment devices and procedures in the Center for Substance Abuse Treatment (1993), Cooney, Zweben, and Fleming (1995), Jacobson (1989), and Miller, Westerberg, and Waldron (1995). Generally, we will discuss self-report inventories that are used in both substance abuse treatment and generalist settings. Since these instruments may be used for diagnostic purposes, they should be used only by professionals who have formal training in assessment and diagnosis and who have specific training in the diagnosis of substance use disorders.

Also, we want to caution you about self-report inventories in general. Certainly, as a part of a comprehensive assessment, self-report inventories can be useful. However, they are not meant to be used in isolation from other assessment data. Second, there is always a validity issue with any test, and self-report inventories are no exception. Since a self-report inventory is a test in which the client "self-reports," you cannot be sure that the client has responded in a truthful manner. Some tests have scales to detect intentional or unintentional distortions, but these are never foolproof. Also, the assumption is often made that the inventory is measuring what it is supposed to be measuring, and this may not always be the case.

Michigan Alcohol Screening Test (MAST)

The MAST (Selzer, 1971) is a 25-item inventory of drinking habits that is simple to administer and score. It takes about 10 minutes when self-administered but can also be read to a client. Each item is scored 0 for a nondrinking response or, depending on the item, 1, 2, or 5 for a drinking response. The total possible score is 53. A score of 0 to 4 is considered to be nonalcoholic, 5 to 6 suggests an alcohol problem, 7 to 9 is alcoholism, 10 to 20 is moderate alcoholism, and above 20 is severe alcoholism. Examples of questions on the MAST are: "Does your wife, husband, a parent or other near relative ever worry or complain about your drinking?" (No = 0, Yes = 1), "Are you able to stop drinking when you want to?" (Yes = 0, No = 2), and "Have you ever attended a meeting of Alcoholics Anonymous?" (No = 0, Yes = 5).

Based on this sample of questions, you can see that the MAST would be easy to fake. The content of the questions is obvious and this results in many false negatives (client scores in the nonalcoholic category when there is in fact an alcohol problem). Jacobson (1989) reported that studies using a cutoff score of 5 resulted in a 21% to 34% false-positive rate (indication of an alcohol problem when no problem actually exists). He suggested using a cutoff score of 12, which results in a 5% to 8% false-positive rate and a 7% to 12% false-negative rate. Obviously, the test is designed to measure only alcohol problems. It can be given to other family members (who are asked to respond about their perceptions of the client), and the results can be compared with the client's responses.

A similar instrument to measure other drug use was developed by Skinner (1982). The Drug Abuse Screening Test was derived from the MAST and contains 20 items. It is designed for use with adult clients. Also, Westermeyer, Yargic, and Thuras (2004) adapted the MAST for alcohol and other drugs (MAST-AD).

CAGE

This extremely short and simple screening instrument for alcohol problems was first reported by Ewing and Rouse (1970). The CAGE consists of four questions, each question associated with a letter in the name of the test: Have you ever felt the need to *C*ut down on your drinking? Have you ever felt *A*nnoyed by someone criticizing your drinking? Have you ever felt bad or *G*uilty about your drinking? Have you ever had a drink first thing in the morning to steady your nerves and get rid of a hangover (*E*ye-opener)? Responding "yes" to two or more questions indicates an alcohol problem.

As might be expected from such a brief test with such obvious content, the results of studies evaluating the effectiveness of the CAGE in identifying alcoholics are quite mixed (Cooney et al., 1995). Therefore, the CAGE should be viewed as a very rough screening and should be followed by further questioning when a respondent gives an affirmative answer to any item (Cooney et al., 1995; Jacobson, 1989).

Alcohol Use Disorders Identification Test (AUDIT)

This 10-item questionnaire was designed for use in primary healthcare settings (Babor, de la Fuente, Saunders, & Grant, 1992). The AUDIT can be used as a self-report survey or as part of a structured interview and then incorporated into a general health interview, lifestyle questionnaire, or medical history. The content of the questions are obvious and involve the consumption of alcohol, symptoms of alcohol dependence, and problems caused by alcohol. The respondent indicates the frequency at which the event or activity in the question occurs. For example, "How often during the last year have you failed to do what was normally expected from you because of drinking?" (never, less than monthly, monthly, weekly, daily, or almost daily). Each frequency has a point value (i.e., 0 for never and 4 for daily or almost daily). A score of 8 in men and 7 in women is considered indicative of a strong likelihood of hazardous or harmful alcohol consumption, and scores of 13 or more suggest alcohol-related harm. As the authors acknowledge, the questions may not be answered accurately because some clients may be hesitant to admit the extent of their alcohol use or the problems it is causing.

Allen, Litten, Fertig, and Babor (1997) reviewed the research on the AUDIT. They found that the AUDIT scores were moderately related to other self-report alcohol screening tests. Several studies showed that the AUDIT was correlated with biochemical measures of drinking. The reliability of the test was adequate.

Problem-Oriented Screening Instrument for Teenagers (POSIT)

The POSIT is a 139-item screening instrument developed by a panel of experts for the National Institute on Alcohol Abuse and Alcoholism to identify potential problems in a variety of areas, including substance abuse, mental and physical health, family and peer relations, and vocational functioning. The items are responded to "yes" or "no," and the test can be administered by school personnel, juvenile and family court workers, medical and mental healthcare providers, or staff in treatment programs. It is designed for 12- to 19-year-old clients and is available in English and Spanish. The reading level is advertised as being at the fifth grade level. The POSIT can be scored using templates or through computerized scoring and interpretation services. Two empirically based cutoff scores indicate low, medium, or high risk in each of 10 problem areas. Because the POSIT was developed by a federal agency, it is available at no cost (see Internet Resources at the end of the chapter).

Substance Abuse Subtle Screening Inventory-3 (SASSI-3) (Miller, 1997)

Cooper and Robinson (1987) have criticized self-report inventories because of "a continual lack of agreement on the most appropriate cutting score" and "the unacceptably high rate of misclassifications that researchers have found" (p. 180). In addition, as has been previously noted, the content of the MAST is so obvious that it would fail to detect alcoholics who deny a problem (Fisher, Mason, & Fisher, 1976). As Cooper and Robinson (1987) noted

> What is needed...is a short, inexpensive assessment tool that can accurately differentiate chemical abusers from social drinkers and general psychiatric clients. In addition, the test would need to be unaffected by denial or attempts at impression management on the part of the client. The Substance Abuse Subtle Screening Inventory...was developed by Miller to achieve these ends. (p. 181)

The first edition of the SASSI was developed in 1983 by Glen Miller. The instrument is now in its third edition (Miller, 1997). The SASSI-3 combines scales that measure obvious signs and symptoms of substance abuse with questions consisting of subtle attributes and items seemingly unrelated to substance use. A series of "decision rules" are used to categorize the adult client as high or low probability for a substance dependence disorder and the adolescent client as "chemically dependent" or "not chemically dependent" (the terminology used in the SASSI).

According to Creager (1989), the SASSI is being used in general mental health centers, university student health and mental health centers, employee assistance programs, addiction treatment programs, court-ordered substance abuse programs, and psychiatric and various medical programs. The SASSI takes 10 to 15 minutes to administer (self-report responses by the client orally or written or by computer) and takes only a few minutes to score. There is an adult version (ages 18 and above) in English and Spanish and an adolescent form, with separate scoring norms by gender for each version. The reading level of the test is supposedly 3rd to 5th grade, although Kerr (1994) indicates that it is probably higher. For clients with reading difficulty, the test may be administered using an audiotape. In addition to the test manual and users guide, training workshops are conducted frequently by the SASSI Institute.

The SASSI-3 seems to be at the forefront of efforts to make the determination of substance abuse problems more sophisticated and psychometrically sound. For both adult and adolescent versions of the test, there are Face Valid Alcohol (FVA) and Face Valid Other Drugs (FVOD) scales. The questions on these scales contain content obviously related to the use of AOD. For example, some items involve negative consequences of use (i.e., trouble on the job, in school, or at home due to alcohol or other drugs), loss of control (i.e., drinking more than is intended), or using to change thoughts or feelings. The items are scored on a 4-point Likert scale (0 = never and 3 = repeatedly).

The remainder of the SASSI-3 consists of true–false items regarding belief, value, and attitude statements. Many of these items are unrelated to AOD issues. The statements were empirically selected to differentiate those with a high probability of having a substance dependence disorder (see Diagnosis in this chapter) from those with a low probability of such a disorder. Through the scoring system, all of the SASSI-3 items are categorized in eight subscales to assist in interpretation and treatment planning.

The scoring of the SASSI is simple. For the FVA and FVOD scales, the points for each item are added. For the other scales, a template is used to determine the number of items that the client responds to in the scored direction. A profile form (males on one side and females on the other, and different profiles for adolescents and adults) is used to plot the client's scores, with raw scores converted to T scores (a T score is a standard score with a mean of 50 and a standard deviation of 10). The conversion is computed for you on the profile form. On the same form is a series of "decision rules." The clinician checks a "yes" or "no" to each rule. If any rule is checked "yes," the adult client has a high probability of having a substance dependence disorder. For adolescents, a "yes" to any rule suggests the client is "chemically dependent."

A review of the SASSI by Kerr (1994) indicates that the test does a fairly good job in identifying chemically dependent individuals. The internal consistency of the scales is low, which may be due to the method used in constructing the scales, but the test-retest reliability is acceptable. In discussing the clinical usefulness of the SASSI, Kerr (1994) states,

> The SASSI is almost as good as its promotion claims it to be. It seems to have been responsibly developed, and it is clearly created with the practitioner in mind. Its ease of administration and scoring, its clear decision rules and suggestions for interpretation, and informative and carefully written manual all make it very attractive to mental health providers who have difficult and important decisions to make about treatment. (p. 251)

Unfortunately, the claims regarding the SASSI appear to be too good to be true. In a review of 36 studies on the SASSI, Feldstein and Miller (2007) found that there was no evidence that the subtle scales on the SASSI were able to overcome denial or dishonesty of clients in order to detect substance use disorders. In fact, the SASSI was no better than screening instruments such as the MAST, CAGE, and AUDIT (which are all free) in identifying people with substance use disorders. Moreover, the SASSI did have a higher rate of false positives (identifying someone with a substance use disorder when no such problem existed), particularly among ethnic minorities, than the other screening instruments.

Like any self-report inventory, the SASSI should *not* be used in isolation from other assessment techniques. Because of its ease of administration and scoring, we have found instances in which the SASSI is the *only* assessment technique used. Second, the use of the terms *substance dependence disorders* and *chemically dependent* may tempt mental health providers to diagnose on the basis of the SASSI. As we have previously stated, diagnosis should be made only by mental health providers with formal training and experience in the AOD field and should be based on a comprehensive assessment. The fact that there is an adolescent form of the SASSI has made the test attractive to public school personnel. Although this is not a bad thing in and of itself, diagnosis of substance abuse problems is generally beyond the scope of practice of most mental health practitioners in public schools (e.g., school counselors, school social workers, and school psychologists).

For those individuals who are not qualified to diagnose but who wish to use the SASSI as part of an assessment, we suggest that the information from the SASSI be communicated to a client as follows: "Your scores are similar to those people who have alcohol or other drug problems." Whatever other data you have gathered that are consistent with this finding should also be provided.

Addiction Severity Index (ASI)

At the beginning of this section, we said that we wanted to focus on instruments that could be used in generalist and substance abuse treatment settings. The ASI is an exception. This instrument should only be used by trained professionals in substance abuse treatment settings. We are mentioning it because it has arguably become the most widely used assessment system in substance abuse treatment programs. Even if you will not be working in substance abuse treatment, you should at least have a basic understanding of the ASI.

The ASI was developed by Tom McLellan and his colleagues (McLellan, Luborsky, O'Brien, & Woody, 1980) and is now in its 5th edition. It is a semistructured interview designed to assess seven potential problems areas for clients referred for substance abuse treatment: medical status, employment and support, drug use, alcohol use, legal status, family and social status, and psychiatric status. It is designed for adults (although an adolescent version has been developed) and takes about an hour to administer. There are seven subscales and about 200 items. It can be scored by hand or through computerized scoring and interpretation. The ASI provides two scores: subjective severity ratings of the client's need for treatment (interviewer generated) and composite scores of problem severity during the prior 30 days (computer generated). The ASI has been normed on a variety of treatment groups and subject groups and has been extensively used as a basis to establish the most appropriate type of treatment setting and the intensity of treatment services needed (see Chapter 8). The ASI is available at no cost (see Internet Resources at the end of the chapter).

Referral

Earlier in this chapter, we gave an example of a high school senior (let's call him Tyrone) whose parents were concerned about an incident of alcohol use at a party. The parents contact you (the school counselor) and ask whether their son has a problem with alcohol. You interview the parents and Tyrone, contact his teachers to find out about his academic performance and behavior, review the cumulative file, and administer a self-report inventory. Based on the assessment, you have some reasons for concern. Although the parents do not use alcohol or other drugs because of their religious beliefs, the paternal grandfather and an uncle are alcoholic. Tyrone's grades have dropped, which the parents attributed to "senioritis." They have also been uncomfortable about some kids that Tyrone has been hanging around with. You really didn't know Tyrone before you interviewed him, at which time he was friendly but rather evasive. You have some doubts about Tyrone's truthfulness on the self-report inventory. What should you do?

You may still be unsure about Tyrone's placement on the continuum of use, and you do not have the time to work with him individually. So, you want to refer Tyrone and his parents to someone or someplace outside the school. Certainly, asking colleagues for referral sources is great. However, we want to discuss a few guidelines in making referrals.

If you are unsure about the results of your assessment and want another opinion, you may refer clients to any AOD treatment program that conducts assessments. Often, these assessments are free of charge. However, you should be aware that assessments are a marketing tool of for-profit treatment programs. There may be a tendency for programs to find problems and refer to themselves. Therefore, you have a professional obligation to make sure that you are referring to a program that conducts objective assessments.

You may decide that Tyrone is in the "precontemplation stage" (see Chapter 7) and referral to an individual or agency is appropriate. Be sure that your referral source has the training and experience to work with AOD-related problems, as it is erroneous to assume that all credentialed mental health professionals have this capability. In some states, licensure as a psychologist, marriage and family therapist, or other mental health professional does not require trainiionals have this capability. In some states, licenng in the AOD field. Therefore, simply having a license in one of the helping professions does not guarantee expertise in this field.

Each state has an agency to coordinate AOD treatment and prevention services. This agency will have a listing of all treatment programs and the services they offer. Generally, the state will have some sort of accrediting process for programs. Most, but not all, states also have a certification or licensing process for AOD treatment providers. There should also be a record of complaints and/or sanctions imposed on credentialed counselors or programs. There is no guarantee that licensed or certified professionals or accredited programs will always be competent or that others would not do a good job. However, you are always safest in referring to an accredited program or certified or licensed individual to ensure that some minimum standards have been met and that there is some method of monitoring competence and ethical practice.

In many work and school settings, programs exist to provide screening, assessment and referral services for employees and students. Although these programs provide services for a number of life problems, AOD issues are almost always included. In most instances, employees or students can initiate a contact with the program or work supervisors, teachers, or school administrators may refer someone whom they are concerned about. At work, the programs are usually called the *employee assistance program;* and in schools the terms *student assistance program, student intervention team,* or *student identification and referral program* are used. In the workplace, the company or organization may have its own employee assistance program personnel or it may contract with a group that specializes in providing program services. While the type of services may vary, employee assistance programs normally provide brief (one to three) sessions with a professional in order to determine a course of action for the employee's problem. In the case of alcohol or other drug problem, the employee would be referred to a treatment program. Schools vary widely in the services provided because of differing school district policies and state laws. In many cases, a team consisting of school personnel (e.g., counselors, teachers, and administrators) is trained to recognize the symptoms of many common (but serious) problems of adolescents. When a student is referred, the team may gather information from the student's teachers and one or more of the team members may meet with the student and/or the parents. After gathering information, the team meets and decides on a course of action. If an alcohol or other drug problem were suspected, the parents would normally be referred to an outside professional or a treatment program for an assessment.

Diagnosis

After all our cautions to avoid diagnosis, it might seem contradictory to include a section on this topic. The cautions involve two issues. First, diagnosing a condition not only implies that you understand the criteria for making that particular diagnosis but that you also can differentiate that condition from others. For example, if you diagnose a person as alcohol dependent, were you able to rule out dysthymia, posttraumatic stress disorder, and generalized anxiety disorder? Do any of these conditions exist concurrently? Second, there can be a scope of practice and associated liability issues involved in making a diagnosis. If your training and license or certification do not allow you to diagnose, you are exceeding your scope of practice if you do.

However, many mental health practitioners work in settings that require a diagnosis and either are qualified or are supervised by qualified professionals. Even if you do not diagnose as part of your job, knowing the criteria to diagnose substance abuse or substance dependence is important in your conceptual framework of what constitutes an alcohol or other drug problem. We will provide such a conceptual framework and then discuss the specific criteria for diagnosing "Substance Dependence" and "Substance Abuse" as defined in the *Diagnostic and Statistical Manual of Mental Disorders, Fourth Edition, Text Revised* (*DSM-IV-TR*).

The easiest conceptual framework to diagnose an alcohol or other drug problem is "trouble." Someone who has medical, social, psychological, family, occupational, educational, legal, or financial trouble as a result of alcohol or other drug use usually has a problem. However, the easiest framework is not necessarily the most accurate. In the section on "AOD Use History" on the psychosocial interview, we gave an example of a 47-year-old man who drinks large quantities of beer. No *trouble* was reported but he has a problem. We worked with a couple in which the husband drank three or four beers a week. The wife thought he was alcoholic because she was raised in a home in which no alcohol was used and she had no framework to understand moderate use. This man had family trouble related to his alcohol use, but he was not an abuser or dependent. You can see that there can be exceptions, but, usually, *trouble* equals a problem. It can also be the case that the mental health professional must assist clients in identifying trouble. We recently listened to a woman tell of her family and relationship history. Her grandfather, father, husband, brothers, and so on drank to excess on the weekends, were verbally and physically abusive when intoxicated, and spent a great deal of money on alcohol. She did not know that this behavior was abnormal because it was what she grew up with and observed in her community. Her awareness was stimulated by observations made by a nurse in an emergency room after her husband broke her nose while drunk.

The Diagnostic and Statistical Manual of Mental Disorders (DSM-IV-TR)

The *Diagnostic and Statistical Manual of Mental Disorders* published its fourth edition with text revisions in 2000. For those of you unfamiliar with the *DSM-IV-TR,* the manual contains a list of diagnostic criteria for mental disorders that are the focus of treatment for psychiatrists, psychologists, social workers, mental health counselors, marriage and family therapists, and the like. For each disorder, the manual specifies features of the condition, the diagnostic criteria, associated features and disorders, specific culture, age, and gender features, prevalence, course, familial pattern, and differential diagnosis. Mental health professionals who work in agency or private settings use the *DSM-IV-TR* for diagnosis. All insurance companies that we are aware of require a *DSM-IV-TR* diagnosis for payment. Many publicly funded agencies also require a *DSM-IV-TR* diagnosis of clients. Therefore, regardless of your feelings about labeling clients, the use of the *DSM-IV-TR* is a reality in the mental health field.

For our purposes, the most important part of the *DSM-IV-TR* (2000) involves the chapter on "Substance-Related Disorders." Included in this chapter are the "Substance Use Disorders" ("Substance Dependence" and "Substance Abuse") and "Substance Induced Disorders" ("Substance Intoxication," "Substance Withdrawal," and a variety of other disorders). We will focus most of this discussion on the Substance-Related Disorders since mental health professionals would generally be involved with diagnoses in this classification.

In the *DSM-IV-TR*, substance dependence is defined as "a cluster of cognitive, behavioral, and physiological symptoms indicating that the individual continues use of the substance despite significant substance-related problems" (p. 192). You may recall that, earlier in the chapter, we gave a working definition of addiction/dependence that specified use of alcohol or other drugs regardless of the consequences. Although more technical language is used, the *DSM-IV-TR* definition is similar. The diagnostic criteria for substance dependence are as follows:

> A maladaptive pattern of substance use, leading to clinically significant impairment or distress, as manifested by three (or more) of the following, occurring at any time in the same 12-month period:
>
> (1) tolerance, as defined by either of the following:
>   (a) a need for markedly increased amounts of the substance to achieve intoxication or desired effect
>   (b) markedly diminished effect with continued use of the same amount of the substance
>
> (2) withdrawal, as manifested by either of the following:
>   (a) the characteristic withdrawal syndrome for the substance (refer to Criteria A and B of the criteria sets for Withdrawal from the specific substances)
>   (b) the same (or a closely related) substance is taken to relieve or avoid withdrawal symptoms
>
> (3) the substance is often taken in larger amounts or over a longer period than was intended

(4) there is a persistent desire or unsuccessful efforts to cut down or control substance use
(5) a great deal of time is spent in activities necessary to obtain the substance (e.g., visiting multiple doctors or driving long distances), use the substance (e.g., chain-smoking), or recover from its effects
(6) important social, occupational, or recreational activities are given up or reduced because of substance use
(7) the substance use is continued despite knowledge of having a persistent or recurrent physical or psychological problem that is likely to have been caused or exacerbated by the substance (e.g., current cocaine use despite recognition of cocaine-induced depression, or continued drinking despite recognition that an ulcer was made worse by alcohol consumption).

Specify if:

With Physiological Dependence: evidence of tolerance or withdrawal (i.e., either Item 1 or 2 is present)

Without Physiological Dependence: no evidence of tolerance or withdrawal (i.e., neither Item 1 or 2 is present)

Course specifiers

Early Full Remission

Early Partial Remission

Sustained Full Remission

Sustained Partial Remission

On Agonist Therapy

In a Controlled Environment

Notice that the first two criteria, tolerance and withdrawal, are not necessary for a diagnosis of dependence. Remember from Chapter 2 that tolerance is the need for increasing amounts of the substance to achieve the desired effect. This may be difficult to determine in some individuals, and individuals vary considerably in initial sensitivity to AOD. Also, with some drugs (e.g., PCP) tolerance has not been demonstrated. Similarly, withdrawal signs and symptoms are not observed with hallucinogen use. Therefore, tolerance and withdrawal are not necessary or sufficient for a diagnosis of dependence. Criteria 3 through 7 are self-explanatory and involve the compulsivity and *trouble* we have previously discussed in substance dependence.

The diagnosis of substance dependence can be specified as being with or without physiological dependence so that it is clear whether tolerance and withdrawal are present. Also, a description of the status of recovery can be given after none of the criteria for dependence (or abuse) have been observed for at least one month. If the client has been in recovery for 1 to 12 months and none of the criteria for dependence or abuse are met, "Early Full Remission" is specified. If one or more criteria are met but the client cannot be diagnosed as "Substance Dependence" (i.e., does not meet three or more of the criteria), "Early Partial Remission" is specified. "Sustained Full Remission" and "Sustained Partial Remission" are the specifiers when the period of recovery is 12 months or longer. The "partial remission" specifiers are generally used to indicate recovering clients who have had one or more "slips" or returns to use but have not had full-blown relapses (see Chapter 9).

"On Agonist Therapy" and "In a Controlled Environment" are specified so that clients who have a low probability of use due to external circumstances can be identified. For example, if a recovering alcoholic is taking Antabuse (see Chapter 8), the diagnosis would specify "On Agonist Therapy." A recovering opioid addict who is incarcerated for two years has a low probability of use because he or she is in prison. Thus, "In a Controlled Environment" would be specified.

The *DSM-IV-TR* defines Substance Abuse as "a maladaptive pattern of substance use manifested by recurrent and significant adverse consequences related to the repeated use of substances" (p. 198). Again, this is consistent with the earlier definition of abuse in this chapter as continued use of alcohol and other drugs in spite of negative consequences. The criteria are as follows:

A. A maladaptive pattern of substance use leading to clinically significant impairment or distress, as manifested by one (or more) of the following, occurring within a 12-month period:
   (1) recurrent substance use resulting in a failure to fulfill major role obligations at work, school, or home (e.g., repeated absences or poor work performance related to substance use; substance-related absences, suspensions, or expulsions from school; neglect of children or household)
   (2) recurrent substance use in situations in which it is physically hazardous (e.g., driving an automobile or operating a machine when impaired by substance use)
   (3) recurrent substance-related legal problems (e.g., arrests for substance-related disorderly conduct)
   (4) continued substance use despite having persistent or recurrent social or interpersonal problems caused or exacerbated by the effects of the substance (e.g., arguments with spouse about consequences of intoxication, physical fights)
B. The symptoms have never met the criteria for Substance Dependence for this class of substance.

You may notice that tolerance and withdrawal are not mentioned in the criteria for abuse and that a pattern of compulsive use is also restricted to "dependence." The criteria for "abuse" emphasize harmful consequences from repeated substance use. Clearly, if an individual meets the criteria for Substance Dependence, the person could also be diagnosed with Substance Abuse. However, "A diagnosis of Substance Abuse is preempted by the diagnosis of Substance Dependence" (p. 198).

Following the general criteria for Substance Dependence and Substance Abuse, there are descriptions for dependence and abuse for a variety of substances including alcohol, amphetamines, cannabis, cocaine, hallucinogens, inhalants, opioids, phencyclidine (PCP), sedative, hypnotic, or anxiolytics, and other or unknown substances (e.g., anabolic steroids, nitrite inhalants [poppers], nitrous oxide [laughing gas]). A short discussion is included on the unique characteristics of the particular drug in relationship to the criteria for dependence or abuse. In addition, there is dependence for nicotine (but not abuse) and polysubstance dependency, defined as dependence on three or more groups of drugs. Caffeine is included for Caffeine-Induced Disorders (e.g., Caffeine Intoxication, Caffeine-Induced Anxiety Disorder, Caffeine-Induced Sleep Disorder), but there are no classifications for dependence and abuse.

The *DSM-IV-TR* contains a variety of Substance-Induced Disorders. As the name implies, these are mental disorders caused by the use of AOD. They may be associated with abuse or dependence. For example, Substance Intoxication "is the development of a reversible substance-specific syndrome due to the recent ingestion of [or exposure to] a substance ...[with] clinically significant maladaptive behavioral or psychological changes associated with intoxication [e.g., belligerence, mood lability, cognitive impairment, impaired judgment, impaired social or occupational functioning]" (p. 199). Substance Withdrawal "is the development of a substance-specific maladaptive behavioral change, with physiological and cognitive concomitants, that is due to the cessation of, or reduction in, heavy and prolonged substance use" (p. 201). Substance-Induced Disorders other than intoxication and withdrawal are included elsewhere in the *DSM-IV-TR* and are referenced under the appropriate substance. These include Substance-Induced Delirium, Substance-Induced Persisting Dementia, Substance-Induced Persisting Amnestic Disorder, Substance-Induced Psychotic Disorder, Substance-Induced Mood Disorder, Substance-Induced Anxiety Disorder, Substance-Induced Sexual Dysfunction, and Substance-Induced Sleep Disorder. For example, there are nine Alcohol-Induced Disorders listed in the *DSM-IV-TR*.

Summary

- Identification of the signs and symptoms of AOD problems is important for all mental health professionals to avoid misdiagnosing client problems.
- Mental health professionals must be able to differentiate AOD use, misuse, abuse, and dependence.
- Psychosocial histories, with or without self-report inventories, are the best method to identify AOD problems.
- When referring clients for treatment, mental health professionals must be sure providers have the proper license or certification to provide AOD treatment services.
- The criteria in the *DSM-IV-TR* should be utilized in making substance use disorder diagnoses but the proper training, experience, and supervision is needed before mental health professionals make these diagnoses.

Internet Resources

Screening and assessment instruments
http://lib.adai.washington.edu/instruments

Alcohol Use Disorders Identification Test (AUDIT)
http://whqlibdoc.who.int/hq/2001/WHO_MSD_MSB_01.6a.pdf

Problem-Oriented Screening Instrument for Teenagers (POSIT)
www.corr.state.mn.us/org/supportserv/umbrellarule/pdf/DHS-4141A-ENG_1.pdf

Psychosocial history example
www.ssw.umich.edu/icwtp/substanceAbuse/Sub_Abuse_Assess_Form.pdf

Addiction Severity Index (ASI)
www.tresearch.org/resources/instruments/ASI_5th_Ed.pdf

DSM-IV-TR (Note: URL provides excerpts only. Full access requires a fee)
www.psychiatryonline.com/resourceTOC.aspx?resourceID=1

Further Discussion

1. Why should screening instruments not be used to make diagnostic decisions in isolation from other assessment procedures?
2. Since the *DSM-IV-TR* has specific criteria for diagnosing substance use disorders, what is the problem with having any AOD counselor or mental health professional making diagnoses?
3. Discuss the advantages and disadvantages of computerized psychosocial histories as a way of saving time and money.

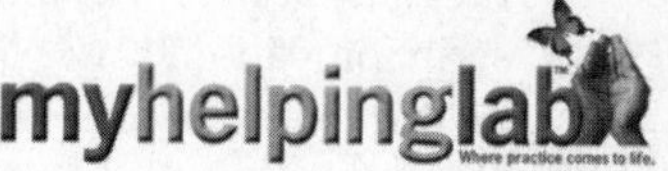

Assessment and Diagnosis

Case Study Activities

Read Substance Abuse, Case 1: Janis: A Mother Whose Teenage Son's Behavior Suggests a Struggle with Substance Abuse and Major Depression.

- Is there sufficient information for you to determine whether Sam has a substance use disorder? If so, provide the specific data to justify your decision. If not, what other questions would you ask during the psychosocial assessment to help you determine whether Sam has a substance use disorder?

Read Addictions Counseling, Case 1: A Life of Substance Abuse: The Story of Josh.

- What self-report inventory or inventories would be the most useful in the assessment of Josh? Justify your choice or choices.
- Josh clearly has a substance use disorder. Does he meet the criteria for substance dependence or substance abuse? Justify your answer.
- How would the counselor go about finding an appropriate referral for Josh?

To access the cases for this activity, log on to MyHelpingLab at www.myhelpinglab.com. Select the **Counseling & Psychotherapy** tab to locate the **Counseling Case Archive.**

7

Client Engagement and Brief Interventions

Sara is a high school counselor. One day, two students come to see her to discuss their concerns about their friend Marlow. The students describe a progression of marijuana and prescription pain pill use. Marlow is frequently under the influence at school and is selling methamphetamine to support his drug use. Sara contacts Marlow's teachers who describe absenteeism, failure to complete assignments, and sleeping in class. She calls Marlow's home and talks to his mother. The mother is a single parent who says that Marlow's father is an alcoholic who rarely has contact with the family. She tells Sara that she is also concerned about Marlow's drug use but feels completely helpless to do anything about it. In the past, she has tried to get Marlow to go to a treatment program for an assessment but he refuses. What should Sara do?

Miguel is a marriage and family counselor who works for a community mental health center. He sees a family who was referred by a child protection case worker after an incident of physical abuse of the 10-year-old son was reported by the school. After one session, the father does not return to counseling. The mother describes an increasing pattern of alcohol use and verbal and physical abuse by the father. He has had a DUI in the last month and she is concerned that he will be fired from his job. When the mother tries to talk to the father about his alcohol use, he becomes angry and leaves the house. What can Miguel do about this situation?

Angelica is a social worker who works in an employee-assistance program with a large corporation. One of the vice presidents comes to her to discuss his concerns about the deteriorating job performance of one of the managers. The manager's behavior has become unpredictable. He seems to function well one day and the next day is irritable and even explosive. The manager was rude to an important client and yelled at one of the secretaries in front of other employees. One of the manager's friends has told the vice president that the manager is a frequent cocaine user. Angelica meets with the manager who tells her that he has been under a great deal of stress in his job and that the rumors of his drug use were started by jealous colleagues. How should Angelica handle the situation?

It would be convenient if mental health professionals could learn to identify potential AOD problems in their clients, present the client with this information, refer the client to treatment, and move on to something else. Unfortunately, in most cases, this does not reflect reality. To help you understand the reasons for this reality, you must have an empathic understanding of the importance of AOD to the alcoholic or addict. Therefore, we will restate a metaphor from Chapter 1. Think about the most important person in your life. Imagine that one day, a friend comes up to you and says, "(the person you care most about) is no good for you. You need to get rid of him/her right now and never see him/her again." We don't think that your response would be, "You're right. I've been thinking the very same thing. I'll go home right now and tell him/her that it's over." It is much more likely that you would defend this person and your relationship, tell your friend to mind his own business, and leave.

Many alcoholics or addicts have developed a relationship with their drugs of choice that they believe to be critical to their functioning and of primary importance to their lives. Just as you may have difficulty imagining yourself being happy without this most important person, alcoholics or addicts may not be able to imagine functioning without their drugs of choice. Of course, problems do develop in relationships, and there may come a time when the problems outweigh the perceived importance of the relationship. Similarly, alcohol or other drug users may start to have problems as a result of their use and might not experience the euphoria that was once a part of the relationship with their drug(s). In the three situations that are described at the beginning of the chapter, you might question the relationship metaphor. After all, the people described in these situations are having significant problems in their lives as a result of their AOD use. Surely, you think, they can see the harm that AOD are having on them and those around them. If this occurs to you, we would ask whether you have ever been in love with someone and, when the relationship ended, you looked back and wondered what you ever saw in the person. If anyone criticized your lover or your relationship while you were in love, you probably responded that no one could possibly understand the depth of your feelings and the intensity of the relationship. Although in hindsight, you may now believe that the relationship was unhealthy, at the time any objective data to support this perception were ignored. Think about the alcoholic or addict as being "in love" with the drugs of choice.

The reality is that people often do not acknowledge the harm that a relationship is having in their lives, or, if the harm is acknowledged, the person may be reluctant to abandon the relationship. The old saying "Love is blind and lovers cannot see" applies to human relationships as well as the relationship people can have with AOD. Many authorities in the field attribute this "blindness" to the psychological defense mechanism of denial, which we will discuss later in this chapter. An alternative explanation is that people are fearful of abandoning a relationship that, while harmful, is familiar. For example, there is considerable interest in the fact that women who leave abusive relationships frequently return to them (Griffin, 1993). One explanation is that the women have no other concept of relationships, and, although the abuse is unpleasant, they are at least familiar with the "rules" and are afraid of the alternatives. The alcoholic or addict may be aware of the undesirable consequences of addiction but be immobilized by the fear of living without alcohol or drugs.

Whatever the explanation, the mental health professional still faces a problem: a client with alcohol or other drug problems and an unwillingness to change. What can be done? In the rest of this chapter, we will describe a model of motivating an alcohol or other drug-affected person to get help called "Motivational Interviewing" (Miller & Rollnick, 1991). Finally, we will discuss some strategies to assist clients who have not reached the stage of substance use dependence (see Chapter 6). These strategies are called *brief interventions.*

Client Engagement

Client engagement is a term used to describe the process of motivating a person to actively engage in treatment or less intensive methods of reducing the harm caused by AOD. By less intensive methods, we mean a continuum from the brief interventions that will be described later in this chapter to participation in an educational program at a school for a student caught smoking. As you will see in this chapter, some methods of client engagement are confrontational and/or coercive, while others use counseling strategies designed to elicit active participation from clients on their own volition.

In the AOD field, the term *intervention* was historically used to describe the process of moving clients from problem identification to treatment. However, intervention implies that something is being done to the client. For example, for many years the main process to motivate addicts and alcoholics to enter treatment was an "intervention" process described by Johnson (1973). The process involved a planned confrontation of the alcoholic or addict by significant people in his or her life (e.g., spouse, children, friends, employer). This emotionally charged event was designed to break through the denial system of the alcoholic or addict. Client engagement emphasizes the freedom for clients to make a choice to either genuinely participate in treatment or to resist it. For example, the court system can force a person to enter treatment (intervention), but cannot force the person to honestly involve himself or herself in the treatment process. Therefore, we prefer the term client engagement.

Motivational Interviewing

An alternative to the Johnson method of client engagement has been developed by William Miller and Stephen Rollnick and described in their book *Motivational Interviewing: Preparing People to Change Addictive Behavior* (Miller & Rollnick, 1991). Motivational interviewing is a process for assessing a client's readiness to change, and it uses procedures based on this readiness to enhance the probability of change. In motivational interviewing, it is acknowledged that a client may not be ready to benefit from a direct attack on his or her use of AOD.

Use of Confrontation and Defense Mechanisms

Miller and Rollnick (1991) dispute the commonly held belief that confrontation is necessary for the alcoholic or addict to be motivated to seek treatment:

> Confrontation of (the) harsh variety has been believed to be uniquely effective—perhaps the only effective strategy for dealing with alcoholics and addicts. Yet confrontational strategies of this kind have not been supported by clinical outcome studies. Therapist behaviors associated with this approach have been shown to predict treatment failure.... There is...no persuasive evidence that aggressive tactics are even helpful, let alone superior or preferable strategies in the treatment of addictive behaviors or other problems. (pp. 6–7)

Interestingly, Miller and Rollnick (1991) state that the use of aggressive confrontational procedures in the field are a product of practice rather than research. Furthermore, they cite statements by Bill W. (one of the founders of Alcoholics Anonymous) that are inconsistent with confrontational approaches.

However, the use of confrontation to motivate alcoholics/addicts to enter treatment came about because of the "impenetrable defense systems" (Johnson, 1973, p. 1) of the alcoholic/addict. Miller and Rollnick dispute the commonly held belief that alcoholics/addicts are "in denial." In discussing the defense mechanism of denial, they state, "there is not and never has been a scientific basis for the assertion that alcoholics...manifest a common personality pattern characterized by excessive ego defense mechanisms" (p. 10). Again, the view that alcoholics/addicts have "impenetrable defense systems" is more likely the result of perception on the part of treatment providers than as a result of research. Miller and Rollnick assert that to deny the label of "alcoholic" or "addict" and to resist the associated directives (i.e., enter treatment, abstain) are normal reactions to perceived undesirable characteristics and threats to freedom of choice. These normal reactions are labeled as abnormal by treatment providers and symptomatic of the alcoholic's "denial." Furthermore, a confrontational style of interviewing or counseling tends to evoke resistance in clients. When the client resists the confrontation of the counselor, it further confirms the counselor's perception that the client is "in denial." Therefore, it is actually the behavior of the counselor that elicits resistance and denial in the client. According to Miller and Rollnick:

> the purpose of confrontation is *to see and accept reality,* so that one can change accordingly.... [And] confrontation is a goal in many different forms of treatment for a wide variety of problems.... The question...is this: What are the most effective ways for helping people to examine and accept reality, particularly uncomfortable reality. (p. 13, italics in original)

Stages of Change

Miller and Rollnick (1991) describe the stages of change developed by Prochaska and DiClemente (1982) as a conceptual framework for motivational interviewing. The stages of change are (1) Precontemplation; (2) Contemplation; (3) Determination; (4) Action; (5) Maintenance; and (6) Relapse.

At the precontemplation stage, the individual may not be aware that a problem exists and would generally be surprised to learn that others perceive a problem. A client may need information and feedback at this stage to raise awareness. However, Miller and Rollnick believe that coercion or aggressive confrontation would be counterproductive at this stage. With regard to alcohol or other drug problems, we can imagine a 26-year-old man, named Stan, who has always lived, worked, and played with people who drink and use drugs on a regular basis. He has had one DUI and drinks heavily every day. He begins to date a woman who does not use heavily or frequently, and she talks to him about his use. Stan is genuinely surprised that his girlfriend perceives a problem.

At the contemplation stage, the individual is ambivalent about the problem. He or she has become aware that others perceive a problem and vacillates between considering change and rejecting it. For example, let's say that Stan's girlfriend convinces him to talk to a marriage and family therapist she knows to "get a professional opinion." Stan is interested in pleasing his girlfriend, so he agrees. In the course of the conversation, Stan says things such as, "My old man is an alcoholic and I sure don't want to end up like him, but he drank Old Crow and I stick to beer," and "I guess I could slow down but everyone would laugh at me." According to Miller and Rollnick, the techniques of motivational interviewing can be helpful at this stage to tip the balance toward change. However, if the therapist moves to the action stage before the client is ready, resistance may develop.

At the determination stage, the helping professional is presented with a window of opportunity to facilitate client movement toward action. If the opportunity is missed, the client moves back to contemplation. At this stage, the techniques of motivational interviewing may help the client find "a change strategy that is acceptable, accessible, appropriate, and effective" (Miller & Rollnick, 1991, p. 17). If Stan seems to be at the determination stage and talks about "slowing down," the counselor might suggest a short-term "experiment" in which he drinks no more than two drinks per day for two weeks and then comes back and discusses the experience.

The action stage is when people intentionally act, with or without assistance, to bring about change. After trying the experiment for two days, Stan goes to a bar with his friends after work. He gets drunk, gets into a fight, and suffers a broken nose and a dislocated finger. He doesn't have any sick leave at work so he loses pay, and his girlfriend tells him that she doesn't want to see him anymore. Stan is too embarrassed to go back to the therapist and admit his failure so he "goes on the wagon" on his own.

In the maintenance stage, the person tries to maintain the change that resulted from his or her actions without relapsing. However, people may need specific skills to maintain a behavior change. Stan does well for three weeks. He doesn't go out at all, and his girlfriend agrees to start seeing him again. They spend their evenings at home watching TV. One Friday, his girlfriend is going to spend the evening with her friends and Stan feels that he is ready to go out with the guys. They go to their favorite bar and Stan orders a Coke. His friends start teasing him. At the maintenance stage, Stan needs some skills to deal with this social pressure.

Since Stan does not have these skills, he relapses.[2] (In Chapter 9, we will discuss the strategies of maintaining a behavior change related to AOD use and relapse-prevention techniques.) With regard to motivational interviewing, an important issue in the maintenance and relapse stages is for the mental health professional to create an environment in the counseling relationship so that the client feels safe in discussing difficulties in maintaining the behavior change and to report relapses that often occur during the change process. Since Stan's therapist was not aggressively confrontational and did not impose a label

[2]The differences between slips and relapses will be discussed in Chapter 9.

on him, Stan felt comfortable returning after his relapse. He will again go through the stages of change but, hopefully, Stan will begin at the determination stage and avoid the relapse stage. However, the mental health professional who uses motivational interviewing strategies would recognize that clients often cycle through the stages of change several times.

A client in the determination or action stage may be amenable to a confrontational intervention. However, if the confrontation is too aggressive in the determination stage, it may alienate the client, and the client may return to the contemplation stage. We would like to motivate a client to change who is at the contemplation stage, where he or she may not have yet experienced serious consequences of AOD use, and we do not want to alienate clients at the determination stage through aggressive confrontation. Motivational interviewing is designed to accomplish these goals.

Working through Ambivalence

As Miller and Rollnick (1991) point out, clients at the contemplation stage of change are normally ambivalent about change:

> Problem drinkers, addicts, bulimics, and pathological gamblers often recognize the risks, costs, and harm involved in their behavior. Yet they are also quite attached and attracted to the addictive behavior, for a variety of reasons. To complicate the conflict further, they typically are not exactly sure what they should *do* about their situation! They want to drink (or smoke, or purge, or gamble), but they don't want to. They want to change, and they don't want to. (p. 37, italics in original)

Although this ambivalence is normal, a goal of motivational interviewing is to resolve this ambivalence (hopefully, by choosing change). Certainly, the facilitative conditions for counseling (e.g., empathy, respect, warmth, concreteness, immediacy, congruence, genuineness, and authenticity) are necessary conditions for change in any counseling situation. In addition, Miller and Rollnick suggest some traps to avoid and counseling techniques to use to resolve client ambivalence.

Perhaps the most common trap that would interfere with client resolution of ambivalence is what Miller and Rollnick call the *confrontational trap.* As the name implies, this trap would relate to our previous discussion of the practitioner's perception of the need to confront the denial of AOD-abusing clients. When confrontation is used at the contemplation stage, the helping professional can expect resistance. Rather than appearing ambivalent, the client is seen as resistant and in denial. According to Miller and Rollnick, such denial is predictable. If the client is ambivalent and the practitioner argues for the "there is a problem" side of the ambivalence, the client will argue for the "there isn't a problem" side of the ambivalence.

Additional traps mentioned by Miller and Rollnick are the question-answer trap, in which the client answers a series of closed questions by the mental health professional. Hopefully, you have been taught to avoid this type of interviewing in a basic counseling skills course. There is also the expert trap, in which there is an attempt to fix the problem by exerting expertise. Clients may elicit this from a helping professional in order to remain passive and thus minimize their responsibility for change. The labeling trap involves the attempt to attach a diagnostic label (e.g., alcoholic) to a client. As Miller and Rollnick point out, there is no research evidence that the acceptance of such a label predicts favorable treatment outcome, and, clearly, many people resist such labels. Finally, there are the premature focus trap and the blaming trap. In the former, the mental health professional focuses the client on the AOD issue before the client is ready, and, in the latter, the client perceives that blame is being assessed for his or her behavior.

The strategies that Miller and Rollnick suggest for resolving the client's ambivalence use many of the basic counseling interventions of Carl Rogers's Person-Centered Therapy. For example, the use of open-ended questions, reflective listening, affirming and supportive statements, and summarization are all recommended. However, the elicitation of self-motivational statements is the "guiding strategy to help clients resolve their ambivalence. ... *In motivational interviewing, it is the client who presents the arguments for change.* It is the counselor's task to facilitate the client's expression of these self-motivational statements" (Miller & Rollnick, 1991, p. 80, italics in original).

Self-Motivational Statements

Miller and Rollnick categorize self-motivational statements as cognitive (problem recognition), affective (statements of concern), and behavioral (intentions to act). Evocative questions can be used to elicit self-motivational statements in any of the categories. For example, "In what ways has your marijuana use been a problem for you?" (problem recognition), "What worries you about your cocaine use?" (statement of concern), and "What would be the advantages of changing your drinking habits?" (intention to act) are examples of evocative questions designed to elicit self-motivational statements.

Miller and Rollnick suggest that clients be asked for both the positive and negative aspects of their AOD use as a method to elicit self-motivational statements. Expressions of concern are often elicited when the client lists the negative aspects of use. The client can then be asked to elaborate on these concerns. Related to this technique is asking clients to describe the aspect of their use that concerns them the most, comparing the times that they experienced problems to the present, and imagining what life would be like if they changed their use pattern. The clients can also be asked to examine their goals in life and then to describe how their current use pattern facilitates or hinders their ability to achieve their goals. Finally, Miller and Rollnick suggest that the experienced helping professional may use the technique of paradox to elicit self-motivational statements. As one example of the use of paradox, the counselor and client may engage in a role play in which the counselor takes the side of arguing for the continuation of the present pattern of alcohol and other drug use and the client argues for a behavior change. Paradox techniques should be used judiciously and, again, by experienced mental health professionals.

Working with Resistance

As Miller and Rollnick (1991) note, "Ambivalence does not usually disappear, but only diminishes" (p. 87). The avoidance of traps and the use of techniques to elicit self-motivational statements should be helpful in reducing ambivalence. However, a mental health professional can expect clients to remain ambivalent in spite of these efforts and can also expect that this ambivalence will be demonstrated through client resistance.

A difference between motivational interviewing and some other counseling approaches is a "working assumption of motivational interviewing: that *client resistance is a therapist problem*" (p. 100, italics in original). While many mental health professionals view resistance as a personality characteristic of clients or a symptom of client pathology, Miller and Rollnick argue that the behavior of the helper will usually have an impact on the level of client resistance. In addition, the reduction of client resistance is seen as a favorable outcome of motivational interviewing. The logical extension of this point of view is that helping professionals must change their behavior to reduce client resistance. "[C]ounselors can change their style in ways that will decrease (or increase) client resistance. It is desirable to evoke low levels of client resistance, because this pattern is associated with long-term change..." (p. 100).

Miller and Rollnick describe four categories of resistance: arguing (challenging, discounting, hostility), interrupting (talking over, cutting off), denying (blaming, disagreeing, excusing, claiming impunity, minimizing, pessimism, reluctance, unwillingness to change), and ignoring (inattention, nonanswer, no response, sidetracking). Although it is not important for the helping professional to categorize the type of resistance, it is important to recognize resistance in order to handle it appropriately.

To illustrate the use of the techniques to minimize resistance that are recommended by Miller and Rollnick, let's look at a client statement and the helping professional's possible responses. The client name was Frank, a 37-year-old, and his drugs of choice were cocaine and alcohol. After Frank's second DUI, he was ordered by the court to attend NA and individual counseling. Based on an assessment, Frank was easily diagnosed as Psychoactive Substance Dependent (see Chapter 6). He recognized that the problems he had were the result of alcohol and cocaine use and was afraid of going to prison, but he resisted the label "alcoholic/addict" and complained about the NA meetings. During the third session with his counselor, Frank said:

> I hate going to those _______ NA meetings. Man, you should see those people, bikers with tattoos, old needle pushers, bums. And all that God _______. I'm an atheist, man. I'm not like those people. I know I can't drink or do coke any more. If I do, they'll put me away. But I'm no junkie or wino.

Frank's statements are certainly reflective of the denying category of resistance. The first strategy recommended by Miller and Rollnick is simple reflection, a skill that you have probably practiced many times in a basic counseling skills course. A simple reflecting response to Frank would be, "You really feel out of place at NA meetings." This avoids the confrontation trap and provides a sense of empathic understanding to the client that may be helpful in moving the client away from resistance and toward further exploration of the problem.

Amplified and double-sided reflections can also be used to focus on the other side of the client's ambivalence as well. An amplified reflection exaggerates the client's perception of the situation, which may result in the client's talking about the other side when he or she hears how extreme their position sounds. In Frank's case, an amplified reflection might be, "You feel like NA is completely wrong for you. You can't see any similarity between NA members and yourself, and the philosophy is totally wrong for you." The double-sided reflection presents both parts of the client's ambivalence. Such a response to Frank would be, "You don't feel comfortable at NA meetings, but you know you need to stay away from coke and booze."

With some issues that cause resistance, Miller and Rollnick (1991) suggest shifting the focus so that the client does not continue to use the issue as a barrier to movement. In Frank's case, the "God" issue in NA was consistently raised. A "shifting focus" response would be, "You know Frank, I really hear how the 'God' stuff in NA turns you off. You also mentioned that the topic of the meeting last night was gratitude. What did you think about that?" In using "shifting," it is important that the helping professional clearly reflect an understanding of the client's thoughts and feelings prior to shifting. Again, the helping professional would use this technique when the issue presented is seen as a barrier to the client's moving ahead.

Another approach to working with an issue that causes resistance is to agree with the client but with a twist. In other words, the helping professional concurs with the content of the client's concern but takes the discussion in a slightly different direction. For example, with regard to the God issue, Frank's counselor might say, "You are right. There is a heavy emphasis on spirituality in NA and 'God' is mentioned a lot. In fact, I know some people who go to AA and NA regularly but don't believe in 'God'." The twist in this counselor statement is to motivate Frank to ask about this apparent contradiction, possibly leading to clarification of his resistance to attending NA.

Miller and Rollnick (1991) also suggest that the helping professional emphasize the personal choice and control of the client as a method of reducing resistance. Although Frank may dislike NA because of a genuine philosophical difference, the fear of being labeled, or discomfort, his resistance may also be related to the fact that he was ordered by the court to attend. In this case, you might think that Frank actually does not have personal choice or control. Although, theoretically, he could choose not to attend, the consequence of such a choice would be imprisonment; therefore, it would be not be constructive to point out that he has personal choice. However, the counselor could say, "Well, you are court-ordered to go to NA and maybe that is upsetting to you. But, no one can make you believe what you hear at the meetings, and no one can make you listen. That's up to you."

A helping professional can also reduce resistance by focusing on the content of the client's statements but interpreting them in a different manner. This is called *reframing.* Reframing may result in the client's acknowledging a different point of view, especially if the counselor has developed the client's trust by clearly hearing the client's perspective. In Frank's case, a reframing response might be, "When you say 'junkie' and 'wino,' I know what you mean. But, think about (name some famous athletes or movie stars who are in recovery). They go to AA or NA, and I think you'd agree that they aren't 'junkies' or 'winos.' I wonder if you just focus on the people at the meeting who fit your stereotype and ignore the others. What do you think?"

Miller and Rollnick (1991) also discuss the use of therapeutic paradox to reduce resistance. They recommend the use of such techniques when "all change efforts are met with opposition" (p. 109). The gist of therapeutic paradox is "that the client should continue on as before, without changing, or should even increase the behavior in question" (p. 109). As with the discussion of ambivalence, paradoxical techniques should be used only by an experienced professional because the techniques can be risky.

Transition from Resistance to Change

When ambivalence is largely resolved and resistance has decreased, the client is ready to take action for change. According to Miller and Rollnick, the helping professional will be aware of this transition when the client stops resisting (arguing, interrupting, denying, and objecting), reduces the number of questions asked about the problem, seems more calm and settled, makes more self-motivational statements, asks more questions about change, talks about life after change, and experiments with changes. For the helping professional who is not an AOD counselor, this transition may present some dilemmas. Should the client be referred to an AOD counselor, to a treatment program, or to recovery groups? Or should the generalist continue working with the client? As with other people problems, helping professionals need to have a clear understanding of which types of AOD issues they can handle and which would require referral. We discussed some guidelines for referral in Chapter 6. Based on this information, should a generalist continue to work with Stan? He is young and uses alcohol only. However, he also has had a DUI and drinks heavily every day. Or, does Frank need a formal treatment program? As with many issues in the helping professions, answers are not always clear-cut. You may devise a plan, based on a thorough assessment, that seems reasonable. For example, you work on an action plan with Stan to moderate his alcohol use. You find that he is not successful in using alcohol moderately. This feedback suggests that you need a new plan. Hopefully, you will be acquiring enough information to make good judgments about when to refer and what kind of referrals to make.

Miller and Rollnick discuss the steps in the action phase such as setting goals, considering the options to achieve the goals, and deciding on a plan. We would hope that you will use this framework in your work regardless of whether you see yourself developing action plans for individuals with AOD problems. Also, we certainly recommend that you read Miller and Rollnick's *Motivational Interviewing* for more information if this approach to client engagement appeals to you.

Brief Interventions

Individuals with moderate or risky levels of AOD use may not be diagnosed with a substance use disorder but still be in need of assistance. This group is responsible for a disproportionate percentage of motor vehicle accidents and other injuries, deaths from AOD, poor workplace performance, medical illnesses, marital problems, and family dysfunction (Wilk, Jensen, & Havighurst, 1997). The techniques to engage these clients to change their AOD behaviors are called *brief interventions:*

> Brief interventions for excessive drinking should not be referred to as an homogenous entity, but as a family of interventions varying in length, structure, targets of intervention,

> personnel responsible for their delivery, media of communication, and several other ways, including their underpinning theory and intervention philosophy. (Heather, 1995)

Since brief interventions frequently are conducted in general healthcare settings, schools, or social service agencies, mental health professionals should be familiar with them. The procedures can range from a five-minute explanation of the harm of AOD by a healthcare provider, to a mental health counselor encouraging a client to see if he or she can stop drinking on his or her own, to more structured programs.

The Center for Substance Abuse Treatment (CSAT) has published a manual titled *Brief Interventions and Brief Therapies for Substance Abuse* (Center for Substance Abuse Treatment, 1999a) (see Internet Resources at the end of the chapter). We will summarize the chapter on brief interventions.

The goal for a client is to reduce the risk of harm from AOD. The stages-of-change model and techniques of motivational interviewing are the basis of the brief intervention techniques described in this manual. The type of intervention is generally related to the level of AOD use. Light or moderate users may need education about guidelines for low-risk use and the problems that may occur from increased use. If the light or moderate alcohol user occasionally has five or more drinks (defined as "binge drinking"), he or she can be encouraged to stay within the guidelines of no more than four drinks at any one time and no more than fourteen drinks per week. Pregnant women or women contemplating pregnancy can be advised to abstain from AOD. At-risk drinkers are those who frequently exceed recommended guidelines but do not meet criteria for a substance abuse disorder. At-risk drug users are determined by the frequency and level of use and the drug(s) used. For this group, brief interventions are designed to encourage moderation or abstinence. Education about the consequences of continued high-risk use may also be offered.

There are also brief interventions for the client with a substance abuse disorder or substance dependence disorder. However, these clients would normally be seen in a treatment setting, and this will be discussed in Chapter 8.

The CSAT manual (1999a) describes five basic steps in the brief intervention process. The first introduces the issue in the context of the client's health. This includes building rapport with them, defining the purpose of the discussion, obtaining the client's permission to proceed, and helping the client to understand the reason for the brief intervention.

The next step is screening, evaluating, and assessing. You already have an understanding of this step from Chapter 6. This is obviously important to determine whether the person is a light or moderate user or at-risk.

Providing feedback follows screening, evaluating, and assessing. Using information from the preceding step, an interactive discussion of the findings is conducted. A specific piece of information should be given, followed by a request for client response. In this step, it is important for the helping professional to assess the client stage of change in order to determine what to do in the next step.

After giving feedback and assessing the client's stage of change, the possibility of changing behavior and setting goals is discussed. You can see how important the stage of change is. For example, you would meet high resistance if you suggest abstinence to an at-risk drinker in the precontemplation stage. The helping professional can suggest a course of action and then negotiate with the client. For example, we worked with a young woman who was an at-risk drinker in the contemplation stage of change. We suggested she limit her drinking to no more than two drinks and no more than two days a week. She resisted this, and we finally agreed to three drinks one day a week and two drinks no more than two days a week.

The final step is summarizing and reaching closure. This is important so that both the helping professional and the client have a clear understanding of the changes that were agreed on. Scheduled follow-up is an important part of this step. Depending on the type of brief intervention and the client's level of use, this follow-up may involve another face-to-face meeting or a telephone call.

The CSAT manual also contains a brief intervention workbook. The workbook is based on the summarized steps and contains useful tools like substance use contracts.

Research evidence supports the use of brief interventions with nondependent drinkers. Wilk et al. (1997) reviewed studies that randomly assigned heavy drinkers to brief interventions or no interventions. Heavy drinkers who received brief interventions in primary healthcare settings were twice as likely to moderate their drinking as those who did not receive brief interventions. Fleming et al. (2002) found that a brief intervention conducted by primary care physicians with heavy drinkers reduced their drinking behavior, and there was an associated reduction in health problems and alcohol-related motor vehicle accidents. The positive effects of the brief intervention continued for up to four years.

Summary

- Motivational interviewing is a series of techniques that are based on the "stages of change" and are designed to engage clients in treatment.
- Brief interventions are generally used with nondependent clients to reduce the harm that may result from AOD use.
- Most brief interventions are targeted to the stage of change of the client and use motivational interviewing techniques.

Internet Resources

Motivational interviewing
www.motivationalinterview.org

Brief interventions
www.ncbi.nlm.nih.gov/books/bv.fcgi?rid=hstat5.chapter.59192

Further Discussion

1. In the helping professions, it is often said that, for someone to benefit from treatment, they must have the desire to change. In light of this, should clients at the precontemplation stage of change be forced by schools, the legal system, or employers to seek treatment for AOD problems?
2. Discuss the concept of providing screening for AOD problems and brief interventions in all primary healthcare settings and emergency rooms.

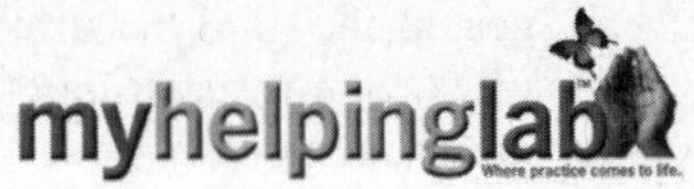

Client Engagements and Brief Interventions

Video Lab

The following modules contain videos related to the topics in this chapter:

- Module 7, Stages of Change
- Module 8, Motivational Interviewing

Case Study Activity

Read Addictions Counseling, Case 2: A Cry for Help: A Counselor and an Alcoholic Friend.

- What stage of change do you think Ellen is in? Why?
- At one point, Ellen says, "I just am, I just am . . . I drink every day, I throw up every day, I'm just, it's just too much! I'm going to die drunk, and I don't want to! My kids! What about my kids?" Her friend Jean asks, "So now what honey?" Is Jean's response an effective way to facilitate Ellen's motivation to change? Why or why not? Suggest a response that would be consistent with the concepts of motivational interviewing.

To access the case for this activity, log on to MyHelpingLab at www.myhelpinglab.com. Select the **Counseling & Psychotherapy** tab to locate the **Counseling Video Lab** > **MyHelpingLab Videos by Course** > **Addictions/Substance Abuse Counseling** modules or the **Counseling Case Archive.**

8

Treatment of AOD Problems

In a textbook for helping professionals who are not planning to work in substance abuse treatment, a thorough discussion of treatment may not seem necessary. However, we have found that helping professionals have an almost mystical conception of substance abuse treatment. Once the social worker, school counselor, mental health counselor, rehabilitation counselor, or marriage and family therapist has referred a client for treatment, there seems to be an expectation that the client will return cured. In fact, alcoholics used to say they were going for "the cure" as a euphemism for treatment. This view may be encouraged by the fact that clients often "disappear" (in the case of inpatient treatment) or discontinue other forms of counseling or therapy at the insistence of the substance abuse treatment program. The helping professional may never see the client again, which reinforces the idea that alcoholics and addicts have been cured as a result of treatment.

The questions we are asked most often in teaching helping professionals about the AOD field are "What happens in treatment?"; "What are the specific interventions?"; and "Does treatment work?" Answers to these questions are important for the helping professional, since clients referred for treatment expect that they are being directed toward an appropriate and helpful program. However, treatment programs differ in their orientation, in the specific strategies used, in the settings in which treatment occurs, and in treatment for special populations. We want to acquaint you with these aspects of treatment in order to dispel any mystical views you hold and, most important, so that you can describe evidence-based treatment strategies. Also, we will discuss the research on the effectiveness of treatment and suggest a model for matching client needs and treatment strategies. Finally, we think that it is important for you to understand some of the controversial issues in the treatment of AOD problems.

How Many Are in Treatment? How Many Need Treatment?

According to the Substance Abuse and Mental Health Services Administration (2006b), in 2005, there were nearly 1.85 million admissions to treatment programs that report data to state government agencies. Nearly 22% were in treatment for alcohol problems and another 18% for alcohol with a secondary drug involved. Almost 17.5% of the admissions involved opioids (e.g., heroin) as the primary drug problem, nearly 14% cocaine, almost 16% marijuana and over 9% stimulants such as methamphetamine. In 2005, 89% of clients were in outpatient treatment, 10% in nonhospital residential treatment, and 1% in hospital inpatient programs (Substance Abuse and Mental Health Services Administration, 2006c). Treatment settings will be discussed later in the chapter. Of the treatment facilities in this country, 61% are private, nonprofit, 27% are private for-profit, and 11% are state or local government. Thirty-eight percent of the facilities offered treatment programs for co-occurring disorders, 32% served adolescents, 14% had programs for pregnant or post-partum women, 33% served other adult women groups, 7% had senior citizen programs, 28% had programs for criminal justice populations, and 6% served gay and lesbian groups. Treatment services in sign language for the hearing impaired were available in 29% of all facilities and 47% used languages other than English (Substance Abuse and Mental Health Services Administration, 2006c).

The Substance Abuse and Mental Health Services Administration (2006a) reported that, in 2005, over 23 million Americans needed treatment for an alcohol or other drug problem (this includes people with both alcohol and drug problems). Of that number, 2.3 million or about 10% actually received treatment (the 1.85 million treatment admissions cited in the previous paragraph only includes those admissions reported to state government agencies, whereas treatment agencies or organizations that are not licensed by state government have no reporting requirements, leading to the higher figure). Of the remaining 90% of people who needed treatment, only 1.2 million felt they needed treatment. From that group, about one-quarter tried to get treatment but were unable to do so (reasons are not reported) and about three-quarters made no effort to get help.

What Happens in Treatment?

Approaches to Treatment

As you might expect after reading Chapter 3 on models of addiction, there are different approaches to treatment based on the model of addiction adhered to by the program developer(s). However, there is a growing trend toward more eclectic approaches to treatment (Miller & Hester, 1995) that combine aspects of different treatment models. While this may be good practice, it may also be driven by financial concerns, particularly in for-profit treatment programs. For example, some insurance companies pay for substance abuse treatment only if there is another mental disorder as well. This consideration has resulted in treatment programs' developing "co-occurring disorders" programs and using components from all of the treatment approaches we will discuss. Co-occurring disorders will be discussed further under Treatment and Special Populations.

Perhaps the most well-known and widely emulated approach to treatment is the Minnesota Model developed by the Hazeldon Foundation in the 1940s and 1950s. As described by Cook (1988), the Minnesota Model

> is an abstinence orientated, comprehensive, multi-professional approach to the treatment of the addictions, based upon the principles of Alcoholics Anonymous. It espouses a disease

> concept of drug and alcohol dependency with the promise of recovery, but not cure, for those who adhere to it. The programme is intensive, offering group therapy, lectures, and counselling. (p. 625)

The philosophy of the Minnesota Model can be described by four components (Cook, 1988). The first is the belief that clients can change attitudes, beliefs, and behaviors. Famous people who have completed the program, such as Betty Ford, Elizabeth Taylor, and Anthony Hopkins, are used as models to illustrate this belief. Second, the Minnesota Model adheres to the disease concept of addiction. The term *chemical dependency* is preferred to *addiction* or *alcoholism* and is seen as a physical, psychological, social, and spiritual illness. The major characteristics of the disease concept are taught. That is, chemical dependency is seen as a primary disease that is chronic, progressive, and potentially fatal. The focus of treatment is the disease and not secondary characteristics.

The third philosophical component is illustrated by the long-term treatment goals of the Minnesota Model: abstinence from all mood-altering chemicals and improvement of lifestyle. Clients are not considered cured since the disease is incurable. However, through abstinence and personal growth, a chemically dependent individual can be in the process of recovery, "an ongoing, lifelong, process of increasing insight and commitment to change" (Cook, 1988, p. 627). Finally, the Minnesota Model uses the principles of Alcoholics Anonymous (AA) and Narcotics Anonymous (NA) in treatment. While we will devote a large portion of Chapter 10 to AA and NA, at this point it is sufficient to mention that the utilization of AA and NA principles implies a heavy spiritual component to treatment in the Minnesota Model.

Cook (1988) also describes the elements and structure of the Minnesota Model program. A continuum of care including assessment and diagnosis, detoxification, inpatient, therapeutic communities, halfway houses, outpatient, and aftercare has been developed using the Minnesota Model. Group therapy is used and is concerned with present and future behavior as opposed to past causal factors. Groups are often confrontational. The family also receives therapy. Didactic experiences including lectures and videotapes are used to educate clients about the disease of chemical dependency and the consequences of the disease. While the staff is composed of professionals from a number of disciplines (physicians, social workers, psychologists, nurses, and clergy), recovering addicts and alcoholics are also used as counselors. Clients have reading and writing assignments, such as reading the AA Twelve Steps and Twelve Traditions (see Chapter 10) and writing their life histories. Attendance at AA/NA meetings is required, and clients are expected to work through the first three to five steps of AA while in treatment. There may also be work assignments and recreational activities, depending on the treatment setting. Aftercare includes attendance at AA or NA.

In contrast to the disease model of treatment exemplified by the Minnesota Model, behavioral models of treatment use techniques of classical and operant conditioning in the treatment of AOD problems. Perhaps the best-known behavioral technique applied to alcohol problems is aversive conditioning which is "designed to reduce or eliminate an individual's desire for alcohol…[by] pairing unpleasant stimuli or images with alcohol consumption" (Rimmele, Howard, & Hilfrink, 1995, p. 134). The unpleasant stimuli most widely used are nausea, apnea (paralysis of breathing), electric shock, and various images. Nausea is the oldest and most commonly used of these stimuli, with fairly wide use in the former Soviet Union and in certain hospitals in the United States. The process is to give the client a drug that, when combined with alcohol, produces severe nausea. In a supervised setting, the client is then allowed to drink. In the classical conditioning paradigm, the feeling of severe nausea should quickly become associated with drinking alcohol. Electric shock can also be administered when the client drinks, or a drug can be administered that produces apnea when alcohol is consumed. Since these procedures are painful, stressful, and potentially dangerous, careful screening of clients and medical supervision is necessary. As might be expected, there is also a high dropout rate from programs using these techniques. In Chapter 3, we described Bill, who completed an aversive conditioning program and remained sober for 19 years until his death. Although the treatment was successful, he found the whole experience extremely unpleasant, which was exactly the effect intended. While electric shock can be used in the treatment of addiction to drugs other than alcohol, most references to aversive conditioning are related to the treatment of alcoholism. It may be that drugs that produce nausea or apnea have not been developed for narcotics or stimulants.

Covert sensitization (Rimmele et al., 1995) has major advantages over other forms of aversive conditioning techniques. (This process involves pairing the consumption of the drug of choice with aversive images, such as nausea or negative consequences of alcohol or other drug use.) The advantages are quite obvious. Since the client does not actually experience nausea, electric shock, or apnea, there are no medical dangers. Clients would also be less likely to discontinue treatment, although desensitization may elicit "extraordinarily intense responses in your client" (Rimmele et al., 1995, p. 136). The question of effectiveness of covert desensitization compared with other aversive conditioning procedures and other methods of treatment will be discussed later in this chapter.

Additional behavioral techniques have been used in treatment. Pomerleau, Pertschuk, Adkins, and Brady (1975) used contingency contracting in which clients made monetary deposits that were forfeited if the client did not complete the treatment program. Behavioral Self-Control Training "consists of behavioral techniques which include goal setting, self-monitoring, managing consumption, rewarding goal attainment, functionally analyzing drinking situations, and learning alternative coping skills" (Hester, 1995, p. 148). These techniques have been used to achieve abstinence or controlled use. (Controlled use, a controversial treatment goal, will be discussed later in the chapter.)

Another form of a behavioral approach to treatment is the Community Reinforcement Approach (CRA). Although there are a variety of "twists" to this approach, the basic idea is to provide tangible rewards for achieving successful treatment goals. For example, CRA was applied in a 24-week outpatient program for cocaine addicts (Higgins et al., 1995). For each "clean" urine sample, clients were given vouchers for retail goods that increased in value with consecutive cocaine-free samples.

A comprehensive treatment approach for stimulant (e.g., methamphetamine) abuse was developed by researchers at UCLA (Rawson et al., 1995). The Matrix Model includes elements of group and family therapies, education, support groups, and relapse prevention. There is an emphasis on the relationship between the counselor and the client, with the counselor utilizing the relationship to reinforce positive behavior change. The approach is not confrontational and seeks to promote self-esteem, dignity, and self-worth. Detailed manuals have been developed to guide this approach.

Further, the National Institute on Alcohol Abuse and Alcoholism (NIAAA) has developed treatment manuals for three very different approaches to alcohol treatment. The manuals were used in a large-scale study to investigate the effects of matching clients to treatment approaches (see Treatment Effectiveness). The first approach is called Twelve-Step Facilitation Therapy and is based on the principles of Alcoholics Anonymous. The treatment protocol familiarizes clients with the AA philosophy and encourages participation in AA. This approach is similar to the Minnesota Model.

The second manual is called "Cognitive-Behavioral Therapy" and is based on a social-learning theory model. Skills to avoid relapse are taught. Many of the specific techniques in this approach will be covered in Chapter 9, when we describe the Cognitive-Social Learning Model to relapse prevention.

Finally, the third approach is "Motivational Enhancement Therapy" and is designed to help clients identify and utilize personal resources to effect change. This approach is based on motivational psychology and is related to Motivational Interviewing (see Chapter 7).

Pharmacological procedures are also used in treatment. However, it is rare to find these procedures as the only intervention. Rather, they are usually used in conjunction with other treatment methods. The philosophy of treatment and the treatment setting may also determine whether drugs are used to treat AOD problems. One would expect that treatment programs adhering to the disease concept would be adverse to using drugs in treatment. However, Cook (1988) stated that detoxification at Minnesota Model programs may use medication. Treatment programs in nonhospital settings without medical staff obviously should not use drugs in treatment.

Detoxification, the period of time in which a client is withdrawing from AOD, is frequently a time when medication is used. In the past, this process occurred in an inpatient, hospital setting. However, outpatient detoxification is now a common practice due to the high costs of hospitalization. In the detoxification process for alcohol and other CNS depressants, minor tranquilizers such as Valium or Xanax are often used to reduce the danger of seizures and the other uncomfortable and dangerous withdrawal symptoms. Careful medical supervision with a gradually decreasing dosage is necessary, since these minor tranquilizers are in the same drug classification as alcohol (see Chapter 2).

Medications are used in opioid detoxification (e.g., O'Connor & Kosten, 1998), and a variety of drugs have been tested in an effort to reduce the severity of cocaine withdrawal. However, no common detoxification protocol has emerged (Warner, Kosten, & O'Connor, 1997). Methadone is widely known for its use in treating opioid addiction. Methadone is a synthetic narcotic with a longer duration of effect than heroin, and ingestion blocks the euphoric effects of opioids. Once a client is stabilized on a particular dose, he or she takes it to reduce or eliminate any withdrawal symptoms from heroin abstinence. The client usually must visit a methadone clinic to receive the dose. However, the federal government is experimenting with distributing methadone through primary care physicians and pharmacies. This would eliminate the difficulty some clients encounter when a methadone clinic is located at some distance. Once a client is stabilized on methadone, he or she can function normally.

Recently, a new medication has been approved for use in treating opioid addiction. Buprenorphine is an opioid that has proved to be as effective as methadone. The advantages of buprenorphine are that it is taken in tablet form, daily doses do not appear to be necessary, and it has relatively mild withdrawal symptoms. In the pill form administered to opioid addicts, naloxone is added to buprenorphine. The naloxone decreases the likelihood of abuse, because it blocks the "high" that could be achieved by injecting buprenorphine alone. In addition, buprenorphine can be administered by general physicians in outpatient clinics, rather than in specialty clinics, as is the case with methadone. The approval of buprenorphine by the Federal Drug Administration has greatly increased the access to opioid agonist treatment for heroin addicts.

Antabuse (disulfiram) has been used in conjunction with other forms of alcohol treatment. When Antabuse is taken and alcohol is ingested during the following 24- to 48-hour period, the client experiences facial flushing, heart palpitations and rapid heart rate, difficulty in breathing, nausea, and vomiting. Since Antabuse takes 30 minutes to work after ingestion, it has been of limited value in aversive conditioning. The client must take Antabuse on a daily basis, and this raises an issue of the need for such medication. If an individual were motivated to take Antabuse daily, it would seem that he or she would probably be motivated to remain abstinent without Antabuse. However, some alcoholics, when tempted to use alcohol, are comforted by the fact that Antabuse will result in an unpleasant reaction if they drink. This awareness often reduces or eliminates the urge to use. Clients who use Antabuse must be warned against using over-the-counter products that contain alcohol, since the Antabuse will cause a reaction from the use of these products.

In the last several years, there has been considerable publicity on the use of naltrexone in alcoholism treatment. Naltrexone is an opioid antagonist (i.e., a drug that blocks the effects of other drugs). However, it has also been found to reduce the craving for alcohol. Therefore, it is recommended as one strategy in a comprehensive treatment program, but not as the *only* strategy. A panel of experts developed a protocol on the use of naltrexone in alcoholism treatment (Center for Substance Abuse Treatment, 1998) and reported:

> Naltrexone therapy improves treatment outcomes when added to other components of alcoholism treatment. For patients who are motivated to take the medication, naltrexone is an important and valuable tool. In many patients, a short regimen of naltrexone will provide a critical period of sobriety, during which the patient learns to stay sober without it. (p. xv)

While some recent studies have shown mixed results on naltrexone, Fuller and Gordis (2001) suggest that individuals with stable support and living situations who have been drinking for 20 years or less appear to be the most likely to benefit from naltrexone.

Treatment Strategies and Techniques

In describing the major approaches to treatment, we have already mentioned some of the techniques used in the treatment of alcoholics and addicts. For example, the disease or Minnesota Model uses group therapy, education, Twelve-Step meetings, and other strategies as well. In this section, we want to describe the most common procedures that are used in treatment. However, understand that not all of these strategies may be used in all treatment programs, or more or less emphasis may be placed on particular interventions depending on the treatment approach and setting. It is a good idea for helping professionals to contact treatment programs in their areas to determine the exact components of the particular program *before* making referrals.

Morgenstern and McCrady (1992) reviewed the literature in the substance abuse treatment field and identified 35 processes used in treatment. They categorized these processes as general psychotherapy, behaviorally oriented, disease model, or pharmacology. Examples of processes used from a disease model included facilitating the client's spiritual experience in recovery, helping the client accept the disease concept, and facilitating the client's commitment to attend AA meetings, to get a sponsor, and to work the Twelve Steps. Behavioral processes include helping the client understand that problem drinking is a learned behavior, helping the client understand the role of high-risk situations in triggering drinking, and teaching the family new ways of coping with the client's drinking-related behavior. Pharmacological processes were related to administering medications (e.g., methadone).

Clearly, the identification of these processes is not much help in understanding what happens in treatment. How do you "help" or "facilitate?" The only concrete processes are those related to providing medication. Treatment planning and the treatment plan are the methods by which treatment staff determine what the problems are and what to do about them. Any substance abuse treatment program that is accredited by a state or other accrediting body will have individual treatment plans for all clients. That does not mean that all treatment plans in all treatment programs are comprehensive or useful—just that potential for usefulness exists. Treatment planning involves the assessment and diagnosis of the client (discussed in Chapter 6), the actual written treatment plan, and an aftercare plan. While the form and content of the treatment plan may vary from program to program and state to state depending on accreditation requirements, every treatment plan should include a statement of the problem(s), long-term goals, short-term objectives that are measurable, strategies to achieve goals and objectives, and review and target dates.

To illustrate a problem statement, long-term goal, and short-term objective, we asked to look at some treatment plans at one of our local treatment programs (with names deleted, of course). As has been our experience in the past, the only differences we saw in treatment plans were the drugs of choice mentioned in the problem statement and length of client use. Goals, objectives, and strategies were almost identical. This example is certainly representative, although we will discuss the problem of applying the same strategies to every client later in this chapter.

Example of Treatment Plan

Problem Statement: (Client's Name) has used alcohol and cocaine on a daily basis for the last 16 months.

Long-Term Goal: (Client's Name) will remain abstinent from all mind-altering drugs.

Short-Term Objective: (Client's Name) will remain abstinent from all mind-altering drugs for one month.

Strategies:
1. Attend one AA or NA meeting per day.
2. Attend all program lectures.
3. Participate in two individual counseling sessions per week.

4. Participate in three group counseling sessions per week.
5. Participate in one family counseling session per week.

Let's examine these strategies more closely, along with some that are not addressed on this portion of the treatment plan.

Individual, Group, and Family Counseling

Since you are preparing for a career as a mental health professional, you have had or will have courses in individual, group, and family counseling. Although it is beyond our scope to thoroughly discuss the processes and theoretical approaches to counseling, we believe that an individual who enters a counseling relationship with any client should be trained and credentialed to perform counseling functions. At the very minimum, mental health professionals should possess the facilitative qualities of counseling, such as empathy, respect, warmth, concreteness, immediacy, congruence, and genuineness. While the need for training, credentialing, and facilitative qualities has (hopefully) been drilled into your head, making this message seem redundant, these issues are of utmost concern in the substance abuse counseling field. In many states, substance abuse counselors need only a high school diploma or GED and little formal training.

Royce (1989) described the counseling models he sees as most useful in counseling alcoholics:

> Whether group or individual, it seems that the most appropriate psychotherapeutic modes for alcoholics are those that focus on the present and future rather than on the past. Examples are the reality therapy of William Glasser, the existential here-and-now logotherapy of Viktor Frankl, the rational-emotive therapy (RET) of Albert Ellis, and other such nonanalytic therapies.... Psychodrama and role-playing can be very useful under a skilled therapist, because of their appeal to both imagination and emotion. Transactional analysis (TA)...can be useful provided one does not get too involved in analyzing the games people play or think of alcoholic addiction as merely learned behavior that can be easily unlearned. (p. 256)

In addition to Royce's suggestions, we would also include the previously discussed use of behavioral techniques of therapy, such as covert desensitization and Behavioral Self-Control Training (Hester, 1995).

Traditionally, group counseling is often the primary approach of both inpatient and outpatient treatment programs. However, in many treatment programs, group counseling may actually be a confrontation of individuals in the group who are not "working the program" or it may be dissemination of educational information. This is considerably different from the group counseling described by Corey (1990) that is probably part of your training program. It would be more useful for group work to help to develop concrete usable skills and to rehearse these behaviors in the group. In addition, such group counseling can be used to analyze drinking and drug-taking behaviors and to develop methods of coping, problem solving, and assertiveness, rather than being focused on gaining client compliance to admit to having a disease.

There has been an increasing use of family counseling in treatment programs. As with group counseling, what is sometimes called family counseling is actually education about the disease concept and the family's role in the disease process. However, family counseling is an essential component of treatment as O'Farrell (1995) explains:

> Many alcoholics have extensive marital and family problems...and positive family adjustment is associated with better alcoholism treatment outcomes at follow-up.... Marital and family problems may stimulate excessive drinking, and family interactions often help to maintain alcohol problems once they have developed.... Finally, even when recovery from the alcohol problem has begun, marital and family conflicts may often precipitate renewed drinking by abstinent alcoholics. (p. 195)

Conceptually, Kaufman and Kaufman (1992) suggested the following paradigm in working with families of substance abusers:

> Treating the family of a substance abuser is a complicated process. Treatment takes place simultaneously on many levels. In meeting the needs of the family as an entity, the spouse subsystem, the sibling subsystem, and the individual needs of each person in the family must be considered. These three areas must interlock and work in harmony. Teaching and demonstrating effective parenting is an important aspect of treatment. Encouraging families to form positive social networks aids in the total treatment. Part of family therapy is the problem-solving process that occurs. Hopefully, these techniques become internalized so that the family maintains them throughout its lifetime. (p. x)

A treatment approach for adolescents that primarily focuses on the family has been developed by Howard Liddle (Diamond & Liddle, 1996). Multidimensional Family Therapy is conducted in the treatment setting, in the home, and in community settings. Parents work on their parenting style, learn to distinguish influence from control, and develop a positive and developmentally appropriate influence on their child.

Support Groups

We will thoroughly discuss Twelve-Step and other forms of support groups in Chapter 10. However, Twelve-Step groups are such a central part of most treatment programs that there must be some mention here of this type of treatment strategy. For example, Adelman and Weiss (1989) stated that Alcoholics Anonymous (AA) is an essential component of an effective inpatient program, while Zimberg (1978a) said that outpatient treatment for addiction should include AA. In fact, many programs throughout the country utilize an Alcoholics Anonymous (AA) or Narcotics Anonymous (NA) Twelve-Step approach for both in- and outpatient treatment. Again, we will save a discussion of the components and effectiveness of Twelve-Step groups for the following chapter. However, the use of Twelve-Step meetings as a treatment strategy and the utilization of the Twelve-Step philosophy in treatment programs is consistent with the disease model of addiction and, as we have already discussed, with the orientation of the Minnesota Model of treatment.

While AA and NA are recommended for the alcoholic/addict, family members are encouraged to attend either Al-Anon or Alateen meetings. This is to introduce family members to the potential support available through Al-Anon or Alateen while the client is still in treatment. For those of you unfamiliar with these groups, Al-Anon is a support group for family members of alcoholics/addicts using the Twelve-Step model, and Alateen is a similar support group specifically for teenagers who have an alcoholic/addicted parent. Clients and family members may also be referred to ACOA (Twelve-Step support for adult children of alcoholics) or CODA (Twelve-Step support for codependents).

There are alternative support groups to those that use the Twelve-Step model. However, the acceptance of these alternatives in disease-model treatment programs may be resisted.

Lifestyle Changes

Irrespective of the orientation of the treatment program, treatment strategies designed to bring about changes in the lifestyle of the client are essential. For example, if clients return to the same friends and activities that were a part of their lives prior to treatment, relapse is highly probable. The range of lifestyle changes that must be addressed illustrates the complexity of comprehensive treatment and the need for long-term interventions for alcoholic/addicted individuals. We will discuss some of these strategies for lifestyle change in more detail in Chapter 9, Relapse Prevention, since mental health professionals may be involved in the implementation of many of these strategies. The lifestyle areas that should receive attention for a particular client should be determined during the assessment of the client and should then be included in the treatment plan.

The issue of friends, lovers, family members, and acquaintances is a focus of treatment. If a client has close associations with individuals who use AOD, some difficult and painful decisions must be made. These topics may be discussed in individual, group, and family counseling. In addition, clients may need assistance with social skills in order to enhance their ability to make new friends. Many alcoholic/addicted individuals have relied on the use of AOD to feel comfortable in social situations and/or as a common bond to those with whom they spend time. The difficulty of this particular area can often be clearly illustrated with an adolescent who is told during treatment to avoid contact with friends who use. The adolescent returns to school after treatment and perceives his or her options as returning to a previous social group or having no friends at all. If relapse is to be avoided, the adolescent who is treated for an alcohol or other drug problem clearly needs continued support and assistance to help develop a new social group.

Since many individuals with AOD problems have used these substances to avoid negative emotions or to manage stress and pain, alternative methods of dealing with common life problems must also be taught in treatment. Strategies may involve stress management techniques, relaxation procedures, and assertiveness training. The intent of such training is to provide the client with skills to use in situations or in response to situations in which alcohol or other drug use was the only perceived option available. For example, a business executive is treated for alcoholism. He returns to work after treatment and, as happens to everyone, has "one of those days." In the past, he has used alcohol to cope with the stress and tension of work. If the client is not taught alternative methods for managing stress and tension along with techniques to relax that do not involve drugs, relapse is a predictable response.

Other lifestyle areas that may be a focus of intervention include vocational and educational planning, financial planning, living environment, and nutrition. To illustrate how these factors can influence recovery, we will use the case of a client named Celest who was seen for individual counseling. Celest's drug of choice was methamphetamine and she was on probation for possession and court-ordered to treatment. After completing an inpatient, 28-day program, she was seen for counseling on a weekly basis. Celest regularly attended NA meetings and seemed sincerely interested in living a drug-free life. She lived in a small house with 14 people, including her daughter and an abusive, drug-using boyfriend. The house was owned by the boyfriend's parents. When Celest told the boyfriend that she wished to leave the relationship and the house, he threatened to kill both her and her daughter. He had a history of violence. Celest had lost her license to work in her trained profession (slot machine mechanic) due to her felony conviction. She was unemployed, had no child care, and was diabetic. When she did not manage her diet and insulin, she would experience severe mood swings.

You can easily see all the areas that required attention, any of which could result in a return to use if ignored. These practical issues in treatment go beyond the model used and are critical determinants in whether a client is able to maintain a drug-free lifestyle. So you won't be kept in eternal suspense, this particular situation had a fairly happy ending (as far as we know today). Celest's boyfriend was sent to prison for a variety of offenses, and she was able to move in with her brother. A vocational rehabilitation counselor helped her find employment, and a latch-key program through her daughter's school provided child care. Again, the point of this case is to illustrate how vocational guidance, financial planning, living arrangements, and nutritional counseling may all be necessary components of treatment.

Education

Many treatment programs, particularly those using a disease-concept model, use lectures and films to provide clients with information on the disease concept, on family issues in AOD use, and on the social, medical, and psychological consequences of AOD use. Miller and Hester (1995) discuss the rationale for the use of education in the treatment of alcoholism:

> U.S. alcohol treatment often includes a series of lectures and films.... Implicit in such strategies is the assumption that alcohol problems evolve from deficient knowledge—from a lack of accurate information. When armed with correct and up-to-date knowledge, individuals presumably will be less likely to use alcohol (and other drugs) in a hazardous fashion and to suffer the consequences. (p. 4)

Although the teaching of educational information is a commonly used strategy in treatment, there is no evidence that providing information to alcoholics/addicts changes their behavior. However, as we discussed in Chapter 7, education can be helpful for light or moderate users and at-risk users. Furthermore, as part of a comprehensive treatment program, it certainly makes sense to provide information to clients and family members. But education and information dissemination should not be expected to produce miraculous changes and, therefore, these activities should not be conducted at the expense of more useful treatment strategies. As an aside, it has always been fascinating to us that didactic methods are used to present information to clients in treatment with little or no regard for the learning capacity or learning style of the client. For example, since our own research

(Karacostas & Fisher, 1993) has found a higher-than-expected proportion of learning-disabled adolescents with probable AOD problems, it would be logical to assess clients to determine the most effective method for imparting information. However, we have found that this is rarely a part of the assessment in treatment programs.

Aftercare

For those individuals who enter AOD treatment, recovery can be conceptualized as a three-stage process. The first stage is formal treatment, the second stage is aftercare, and the third stage is ongoing recovery. *Aftercare* refers to the interventions and strategies that will be implemented after formal treatment is completed. However, it more accurately should be called "continuing care," since aftercare programs are usually continuations of many of the strategies from formal treatment. Our focus is on the issues that require attention following discharge from formal treatment.

The case of Celest described above is a good example of how issues that cannot possibly be solved in a month-long treatment program can be carried on in aftercare. Frequently, individual and family therapy will be components of an aftercare program as well as vocational, educational, and financial guidance. Attendance at Twelve-Step meetings will usually be mentioned in aftercare plans. Aftercare meetings may be a part of the treatment program, or the client may be referred to a mental health professional for management of the aftercare program. Since the aftercare program is an essential element in relapse prevention, we will discuss this in detail in Chapter 9.

Treatment Settings

The strategies and interventions described can be implemented in a variety of treatment settings. In this section, we will briefly describe these settings and then discuss some of the issues that may determine the type of setting in which a client receives treatment.

Therapeutic Communities

The therapeutic community is a residential environment usually associated with treatment for drugs other than alcohol. As Polich, Ellickson, Reuter, and Kahan (1984) explained, "The goal of therapeutic communities is to resocialize the drug abuser by creating a structured isolated mutual-help environment in which the individual can develop and learn to function as a mature participant" (p. 96). The duration of treatment is typically longer than other types of treatment, usually one year or more. Synanon, one of the earliest and most famous therapeutic communities, expected permanent involvement by clients.

The characteristics of therapeutic communities include a highly structured daily routine, a system of rewards and punishment for behavior, and frequent group confrontation, self-reflection, and confession of past wrongdoing. Because of the isolation and long-term nature of most therapeutic communities, the drop-out rates tend to be high. This type of treatment setting is often a treatment of last resort. In other words, most therapeutic community residents have failed in one or more other types of treatment setting.

Interestingly, therapeutic communities are increasingly popular as a treatment setting in jails and prisons. Obviously, the length of this type of approach is no barrier in these institutions. The needs of institutional clients are often well suited to this type of program since the primary goal of a therapeutic community is "global life-style change, including abstinence from (alcohol and other drugs), elimination of antisocial behavior, enhanced education, constructive employment, and development of prosocial attitudes and values" (Center for Substance Abuse Treatment, 1995a, p. 51).

Inpatient and Residential Treatment

Although this treatment environment is usually associated with hospitals, this is not always the case. Residential treatment may occur in nonhospital settings. The duration of treatment is shorter than in therapeutic communities, and the social isolation is reduced. Most inpatient and residential programs gradually reintroduce the client to a normal environment through community outings and home passes. These programs generally offer supervised detoxification that may involve medication in a hospital setting or social detoxification (i.e., no medication) in a nonhospital setting. The typical 28-day treatment duration has no research base. It has come about as a result of financial constraints, particularly the reluctance of insurance companies to pay for treatment. Inpatient and residential treatment settings have the advantages of 24-hour supervision, the reduced likelihood of clients using while in treatment, highly structured days, and a total immersion in treatment, with removal from the everyday stressors and pressures that may interfere with treatment. The disadvantages of this setting are the expense (a 28-day program in a hospital setting may be well over $10,000) and the artificiality of the environment. In a supervised, structured, and protective setting, a client may have little difficulty maintaining abstinence. In a well-supervised program, there may be no choice. However, the client may have little or no opportunity to practice new behaviors and may develop a false belief in self-efficacy (competence to deal with the environment). The real world may quickly dispel the client's perception of self-efficacy, and relapse results.

Partial Hospitalization and Day Treatment

As you can probably tell from the heading of this section, these types of treatment settings can also occur in hospitals or freestanding treatment centers. The client normally spends all or some of the evenings (and overnight) at home. These programs are less expensive than inpatient or residential programs and allow clients to remain involved with some normal aspects of life while they are in treatment. Since the client's life is less artificial than it would be if he or she were in 24-hour care, there is greater opportunity to apply the knowledge and skills acquired during treatment. There is also the opportunity to figure out some of the possible barriers in the client's daily life to a changed lifestyle during the time the client has frequent contact with the treatment program. This allows the client to work on solutions to these barriers before the formal treatment program ends. However, there are risks associated with partial hospitalization and day treatment. The most obvious risk involves the opportunities for the client to use AOD. Unless the client admits to using or there is drug testing, a return to use may not be discovered. Also, if the client's friends and family are using or are not supportive of the client's efforts, living in the "normal" environment for even brief periods may be counterproductive.

Intensive Outpatient and Outpatient

These types of treatment programs are usually associated with free-standing treatment programs or clinics, such as mental health centers. Intensive outpatient programs usually are held for three or four evenings in the week for 2 to 4 hours each evening. Outpatient treatment is usually less frequent (one or two evenings a week) and shorter (1 to 2 hours per session). As you might imagine, outpatient clients usually would not be classified as substance dependent (see Chapter 6) or might be involved in this type of setting as the end point of a gradual reduction in treatment intensity.

The major advantage (aside from cost) of intensive outpatient and outpatient programs is that clients can continue to work or go to school. It is often the case that a person's only expressed barrier to treatment is the perceived or actual necessity to work or go to school. Whether this barrier is real or used as an excuse, it does not exist in intensive outpatient programs.

Choice of Treatment Setting

Klar (1987) discussed the concept of "least restrictive environment" with regard to the appropriate treatment setting. Those of you with a background in special education are familiar with this concept as it relates to placement of students, and the rationale is similar for AOD treatment. Clients should be placed in the treatment setting that offers the least amount of restriction, with the highest probability of success, while all the factors identified in the assessment are considered. What are some of these factors? Nace (1987) identified criteria for determining whether outpatient alcoholism treatment was appropriate. These criteria included client motivation, ability to discontinue use, social support, employment, medical condition, psychiatric status, and treatment history. Clients who are poorly motivated to discontinue use (i.e., court mandated) or who admit to a failure to abstain if AOD are available may fail in outpatient treatment. Also, we have already discussed the importance of social support. Employment may be a double-edged sword. While continued employment may strongly motivate a client to succeed in outpatient treatment, the work environment is often a source of stress for people, or coworkers might encourage the client to use (i.e., going out for drinks after work). An individual who is unemployed (and, ironically, is probably the least able to afford more expensive inpatient treatment), may be a poor candidate for an outpatient program since the client is not occupied for a large segment of time by a job. Obviously, individuals with medical and/or psychiatric conditions may need more restrictive treatment environments. A person with liver damage may need medical supervision and an environment that ensures abstinence. Similarly, a client who is receiving pharmaceutical treatment for a psychiatric condition may (but not always) require inpatient treatment. Finally, if someone has already failed in outpatient treatment, more intensive treatment may be needed.

Unfortunately, all of these factors might not be used in determining the treatment setting for a client. In other words, money, insurance, and the availability of publicly funded treatment programs, rather than client factors, may determine where a person is placed for treatment.

As a result of "nonclient" factors being used to determine treatment setting, many states are adopting "uniform patient placement criteria" to determine the appropriate treatment setting. The most widely used patient placement criteria are those developed by the American Society of Addiction Medicine (ASAM). These criteria involve client characteristics and are used to determine the appropriate intensity of the treatment setting (outpatient, intensive outpatient/partial hospitalization, medically monitored intensive inpatient, and medically managed intensive inpatient). We certainly encourage you to ask treatment programs if they use uniform patient placement criteria (the usual question is "Do you use ASAM-2?") and to encourage clients to ask their insurance or managed care company what criteria are used to determine treatment setting.

Principles of Effective Treatment

The National Institute on Drug Abuse (NIDA) published a booklet in 1999 called "Principles of Drug Addiction Treatment: A Research-Based Guide." This short booklet is available on line (see Internet Resources at the end of the chapter) and contains evidence-based principles, methods, and programs in treatment. Thirteen principles are listed in this booklet, and it is extremely useful for all mental health professionals to be familiar with them.

1. **No single treatment is appropriate for all individuals.** Matching treatment settings, interventions, and services to each individual's particular problems and needs is critical to his or her ultimate success in returning to productive functioning in the family, workplace, and society.
2. **Treatment needs to be readily available.** Because individuals who are addicted to drugs may be uncertain about entering treatment, taking advantage of opportunities when they are ready for treatment is crucial. Potential treatment applicants can be lost if treatment is not immediately available or is not readily accessible.
3. **Effective treatment attends to multiple needs of the individual, not just his or her drug use.** To be effective, treatment must address the individual's drug use and any associated medical, psychological, social, vocational, and legal problems.
4. **An individual's treatment and services plan must be assessed continually and modified as necessary to ensure that the plan meets the person's changing needs.** A patient may require varying combinations of services and treatment components during the course of treatment and recovery. In addition to counseling or psychotherapy, a patient at times may require medication, other medical services, family therapy, parenting instruction, vocational rehabilitation, and social or legal services. It is critical that the treatment approach be appropriate to the individual's age, gender, ethnicity, and culture.
5. **Remaining in treatment for an adequate period of time is critical for treatment effectiveness.** The appropriate duration for an individual depends on his or her problems and needs. Research indicates that for most patients the threshold of significant improvement is reached at about three months in treatment. After this threshold is

reached, additional treatment can produce further progress toward recovery. Because people often leave treatment prematurely, programs should include strategies to engage and keep patients in treatment.

6. **Counseling (individual and/or group) and other behavioral therapies are critical components of effective treatment for addiction.** In therapy, patients address issues of motivation, build skills to resist drug use, replace drug-using activities with constructive and rewarding nondrug-using activities, and improve problem-solving abilities. Behavioral therapy also facilitates interpersonal relationships and the individual's ability to function in the family and community.
7. **Medications are an important element of treatment for many patients, especially when combined with counseling and other behavioral therapies.** Methadone and buprenorphine are very effective in helping individuals addicted to heroin or other opiods stabilize their lives and reduce their illicit drug use. Naltrexone is also an effective medication for some opiod addicts and some patients with co-occurring alcohol dependence. For persons addicted to nicotine, a nicotine replacement product can be an effective component of treatment. For patients with mental disorders, both behavioral treatments and medications can be critically important.
8. **Addicted or drug-abusing individuals with coexisting mental disorders should have both disorders treated in an integrated way.** Because addictive disorders and mental disorders often occur in the same individual, patients presenting for either condition should be assessed and treated for the co-occurrence of the other type of disorder.
9. **Medical detoxification is only the first stage of addiction treatment and by itself does little to change long-term drug use.** Medical detoxification safely manages the acute physical symptoms of withdrawal associated with stopping drug use. While detoxification alone is rarely sufficient to help addicts achieve long-term abstinence, for some individuals it is a strongly indicated precursor to effective drug addiction treatment.
10. **Treatment does not need to be voluntary to be effective.** Strong motivation can facilitate the treatment process. Sanctions or enticements in the family, employment setting, or criminal justice system can increase significantly both treatment entry and retention rates and the success of drug treatment interventions.
11. **Possible drug use during treatment must be monitored continuously.** Lapses to drug use can occur during treatment. The objective monitoring of a patient's drug and alcohol use during treatment, such as through urinalysis or other tests, can help the patient withstand urges to use drugs. Such monitoring also can provide early evidence of drug use so that the individual's treatment plan can be adjusted. Feedback to patients who test positive for illicit drug use is an important element of monitoring.
12. **Treatment programs should provide assessment for HIV/AIDS, hepatitis B and C, tuberculosis and other infectious diseases, and counseling to help patients modify or change behaviors that place themselves or others at risk of infection.** Counseling can help patients avoid high-risk behavior. Counseling also can help people who are already infected manage their illness.
13. **Recovery from drug addiction can be a long-term process and frequently requires multiple episodes of treatment.** As with other chronic illnesses, relapses to drug use can occur during or after successful treatment episodes. Addicted individuals may re-

quire prolonged treatment and multiple episodes of treatment to achieve long-term abstinence and fully restored functioning. Participation in self-help support programs during and following treatment often is helpful in maintaining abstinence.

Evidence-Based Treatment

Federal and state government agencies involved in AOD treatment are increasingly advocating for, and in some cases, limiting funding to treatment strategies that research has shown to be effective and that have demonstrated consistent results in multiple studies. "Evidence-based" treatment is the term generally used to describe these methods or strategies but "empirically-based," "science-based," or "research-based" are also used.

It should be noted that there is no uniform consensus on the process to award this designation to some treatment method. Federal research agencies such as the National Institute on Drug Abuse (NIDA) and the National Institute on Alcohol Abuse and Alcoholism (NIAAA) have done much of the work on funding promising practices and compiling lists of those that demonstrate effectiveness after rigorous and multiple evaluations. However, practices may be effective in clinical settings that have simply not been subjected to scientific study. Furthermore, evidence-based treatment may be implemented poorly by clinicians, applied in settings or with populations the treatment has not been validated with, or employed incompletely, thus negating the effectiveness of the process. So, don't assume that simply because a treatment is described as "evidence-based" that success is inevitable nor should you conclude that an approach that has not been labeled "evidence-based" cannot possibly be effective.

In the earlier section approaches to treatment, we described some of the strategies that NIDA and NIAAA have labeled "evidence-based." These include the three Project MATCH approaches (Twelve-Step Facilitation, Cognitive-Behavioral Therapy, and Motivational Enhancement Therapy). Other types of treatment approaches endorsed by NIDA and described earlier in the chapter include the Matrix Model and different types of contingency contracting, including the Community Reinforcement Approach Plus Vouchers. Multidimensional Family Therapy was briefly presented in the individual, group, and family counseling section of this chapter and is also considered an evidence-based approach according to NIDA.

Treatment and Special Populations

As with any aspect of the helping professions, the individual and group differences of clients must be considered in designing treatment. We have previously focused on the need to tailor treatment to the unique characteristics of the client rather than forcing a client to fit a particular model of treatment or addiction. Similarly, group characteristics are important to consider in treatment. This is not to imply that clients should be stereotyped simply because they are members of a particular age, gender, or ethnic group. However, demographic information may be relevant in understanding the client and in designing appropriate treatment. A comprehensive discussion of the treatment issues for all special populations would be beyond our goals for this book. We do want to acquaint you with some of these issues so you will be informed when directing your clients to treatment.

Ethnically Diverse Populations

The issues with regard to ethnically diverse populations were discussed in detail in Chapter 4, in regard not only to treatment, but to other AOD issues as well.

At this point, we want to restate several points specifically with regard to treatment. First, diversity in the treatment population and the staff is clearly beneficial for client comfort and understanding. Second, the attitude of an ethnic group toward AOD problems may present a barrier for the individual seeking treatment. For example, in some African American communities alcoholism is seen as immoral or sinful behavior, a view that is clearly incompatible with the disease concept of alcoholism. In this view, the person, not alcohol, is responsible for problems, and the use of alcohol could be controlled if the person so desired. African Americans who hold this view would be less likely to encourage and support family members and friends to seek treatment. This barrier is certainly not unique to African Americans, so many disease model programs include education for the family. Third, the customs, beliefs, and language of the group must be considered in treatment. An obvious example is the barrier presented in treatment for Spanish-speaking clients, when the treatment staff are not bilingual. With regard to Native Americans, Young (1992) stated that

> Intervention strategies must begin the realization that Native Americans represent a diverse population. Treatment modalities that prove effective among one group of Native Americans may not be useful or appropriate among another group.... In some cases...the clinician must be prepared to transcend the so-called clinical mentality through the use of indigenous healers and Native American health care practices. (p. 388)

Elderly

According to Jung (1994), the elderly are underrepresented in AOD treatment programs. This may be due to social and economic barriers to entering treatment or because a problem is not identified by the client or the family. Abrams and Alexopoulos (1987) found that alcoholism was less likely to be identified in the elderly, "in part because the impairments in social and occupational functioning attributable to alcoholism in younger people are not as obvious" (p. 1285) although "more than 20 percent of patients over 65 years old admitted to a psychiatric hospital could be considered drug dependent" (p. 1286). In addition, family members may be embarrassed by the behavior of the elderly person, and this embarrassment may cause the family to avoid bringing the use patterns of the elderly person to the attention of professionals. Finally, the type of problem that the elderly person has may be difficult to identify. Whereas alcohol misuse may be clear, many elderly persons also misuse prescription medications, which may not be obvious to the family.

As Zimberg (1978b) pointed out, the problems of the elderly are often different from those of younger clients and may require specific attention in treatment. For example, the elderly client may be experiencing an emotional reaction to retirement, feelings of bereavement from the death of a spouse and/or friends, loneliness, and physical pain from illnesses or age.

Adolescents

The senior author conducted a psychological evaluation of an adolescent in an inpatient treatment program some time ago. During the evaluation, the young man reported that he (and others, so he claimed) had learned that if they publicly (defined as being in a group) said that they had a disease and were powerless, they would be released from the program. This young man was quite rebellious (one reason the evaluation had been requested), and he refused to say that he had a disease. In fact, he told everyone that he had every intention to use again when he got out.

This adolescent's statements are indicative of some of the treatment issues for adolescents. Adolescents have difficulty relating to a concept of a life-long disease. They have rarely experienced the same level of life problems resulting from their AOD use as adults have. When they attend AA or NA meetings, they may hear stories from older adults that have little relationship to their lives (Fisher & Harrison, 1993b). If you have worked with adolescents at all, you probably know that they can be skilled at saying what they need to say to get what they want. After working with adolescents with AOD problems for some time, we have little doubt that what the young man said was true. Many of the adolescents told the staff what they wanted to hear. Finally, adolescents may reject the idea that lifestyle change is necessary. Adults who have lost jobs, families, and possessions and have been arrested for DUIs may have little difficulty accepting the need to change their lives. An adolescent who has been busted at school for smoking pot may not feel the same way. Even when the problems have been more significant, it is very difficult to convince an adolescent that he or she needs to change his or her social group. G. W. Lawson (1992) has suggested considering the developmental stage of the adolescent in treatment strategies and using alternatives to Twelve-Step groups and models when necessary. Obviously, family treatment is a very important component in the treatment of adolescents.

Persons with Disabilities

Individuals with sensory (hearing or visually impaired), motor, mental, and learning handicaps can and do have AOD problems. For example, Karacostas and Fisher (1993) found evidence that adolescents diagnosed as learning disabled had a higher rate of chemical dependency than did nonlearning disabled peers. Obviously, the nature of the disability may be a factor in the development of the substance abuse problem and is certainly a factor in treatment. For example, we worked with a young man named Stan, who became a quadriplegic at age 24 after an automobile accident. Although he had been an occasional alcohol user before the accident, Stan began heavy use of prescription pain medication, alcohol, and marijuana following his accident. He had extreme difficulty handling his grief regarding his loss of mobility and his increased dependence on others. Clearly, these were important treatment issues. Another of our clients, Lisa, had been blind since birth. To cope with social isolation in high school, Lisa began using a variety of drugs and ended up in a hospital emergency room at age 17 after an overdose. Finding a treatment program that could meet her needs was extremely difficult.

Irrespective of the model of addiction, persons with disabilities have treatment needs that require attention. We have already mentioned the grief that a person may experience, particularly if the disability was acquired later in life. With sensory handicaps, there is the obvious problem of communication. In a program with a heavy educational component, the methods of imparting information must be adapted for the sensory-impaired client. For individuals with learning disabilities, instructional strategies must be modified to accommodate the type of learning disability (Karacostas & Fisher, 1993). Individuals with intellectual handicaps may not be able to grasp abstract concepts and, therefore, may be unable to understand the disease concept. More behavioral interventions may be necessary.

Designing the treatment of persons with disabilities is clearly consistent with the notion of client/treatment matching that we will discuss later in this chapter. Rather than forcing the person to fit a treatment program (which is impossible with persons with disabilities), the treatment program must meet the client's needs. However, the complexity of treatment for persons with disabilities also indicates the need for greater prevention efforts for this population. While there are many prevention programs for nondisabled young people (see Chapter 15), few efforts have been made to design programs for young people with disabilities.

Women

While it seems ironic to talk about half of the population as a special group, most information about treatment has come from studies with predominantly male subjects (Harrison & Belille, 1987). Beckman and Amaro (1984) identified the barriers that may keep women from AOD treatment. These include the stigma of identification as an alcoholic or addict, family responsibilities, lack of child care in treatment facilities, inaccurate diagnosis because of professionals' stereotypes (belief that alcoholics/addicts are men), and negative reactions of family and friends based on stereotypes about alcoholics/addicts. Once in treatment, "their feelings may run from fear of rape to embarrassment at walking down the corridor in a bathrobe" (Royce, 1989, p. 174).

Women may also have special treatment issues that differ from those of men. For example, Rohsenow, Corbett, and Devine (1988) found that as many as three-quarters of the women in treatment may have a history of sexual abuse that may result in sexual dysfunction or posttraumatic stress disorder. Delayed stress symptoms and sexual dysfunction may precipitate relapse (Wallen, 1990). Additional treatment issues may include self-esteem, perceived powerlessness, and guilt if the woman has used AOD during pregnancy. Due to these special treatment issues, Royce (1989) has suggested all-women treatment groups, at least early in treatment. A more extensive discussion of women and their treatment is included in Chapter 11.

Gays and Lesbians

As Cabaj (1992) reported, there is an exceptionally high rate of AOD problems in the gay and lesbian population. While the reasons for this high incidence are unclear, biochemical and psychosocial explanations have been proposed (Cabaj, 1992). With regard to treatment, Cabaj (1992) stated that "Homophobia is the major consideration in meeting the treatment needs of gay men and lesbians with substance abuse problems, as well as the proper care and prevention of HIV-related infections" (p. 857). Homophobia may be related to staff attitudes or to the client's own denial and dissociation. With regard to HIV, "Treatment centers and programs may still be frightened to work with HIV-positive individuals... or may resist talking about safer sex because it is uncomfortable to talk about such matters or it is viewed as detracting from recovery issues" (Cabaj, 1992, p. 858). Another treatment issue for gays and lesbians involves social isolation "when the gay person has limited contacts who relate to him as a gay person.... Staying away from bars or parties may be difficult since they are often the patient's only social outlet" (Cabaj, 1992, p. 858). As we discussed in connection with adolescents, the development of a nonusing social group is an important treatment objective for gays and lesbians.

Criminal Justice Populations

The interest in treatment issues for individuals involved with the criminal justice system is the result of the large numbers of such people with AOD problems. In Chapter 1, we noted that 80% of adult inmates were either under the influence when they committed crimes, engaged in illegal activities to buy drugs, or had a history of alcohol or other drug problems (Center on Addiction and Substance Abuse, 1998). In 1995, 18% of all arrests were for alcohol related offenses (drunk driving, drunkenness, liquor law violations) and 10% for drug law violations. Three-quarters of the drug arrests were for possession and one-quarter were for selling (Center on Addiction and Substance Abuse, 1998).

Since there are so many arrests for drug possession and selling, many states have implemented "drug courts." Although drug courts vary widely in scope and organization, all have an underlying premise that drug use is not simply a criminal justice problem but a public health problem. Criminal justice agencies collaborate with substance abuse treatment centers and other community resources to design and implement drug court programs. The success of these programs is based on the fact that the post-arrest period can provide a good opportunity for interventions designed to break the drug-crime cycle. Drug courts may utilize a variety of models including supervised or conditional release (offender is released from pretrial custody), diversion from incarceration (offender pleads guilty but goes to treatment instead of prison), dismissal of charges if the offender successfully completes treatment, and jail-based treatment for those in custody or who fail other forms of treatment.

Treatment options for offenders may take a variety of forms. The least intensive is education, such as in DUI schools. This type of intervention is normally for people arrested for DUI but who do not have a substance use disorder. However, it should be noted that many areas do not conduct comprehensive evaluations on DUI offenders. DUI school may simply be mandated for first-time offenders. At the other end of the treatment spectrum are therapeutic communities in prison, a type of treatment discussed earlier in the chapter.

While legal involvement is a good motivator and allows for client control (e.g., random urine screening, threat of incarceration), there is also a need for comprehensive services, community links, and aftercare services for these clients. As you can imagine, the variety of life problems for criminal justice populations is immense. The treatment strategies and techniques we described earlier in the chapter must be utilized in treating this difficult population.

Clients with Co-Occurring Disorders

Similar to the interest in the treatment of criminal justice populations, clients with a substance use disorder and other mental disorders have become a focus of attention due to large numbers of individuals with "co-occurring" disorders (also referred to as "coexisting disorders" or "dual diagnosis"). According to Regier et al. (1990), about one-third of clients with a psychiatric disorder have a history of alcohol or other drug abuse. In addition, more than 50% of clients with substance use disorders have sufficient symptoms to be diagnosed with another mental disorder (Regier et al., 1990; Ross, Glaser, & Germanson, 1988). Although there is a great deal of variability in the combinations of co-occurring disorders, common examples include major depression and cocaine addiction, panic disorders and alcoholism, alcoholism and polydrug addiction and schizophrenia, and borderline personality disorder and episodic polydrug abuse (Center for Substance Abuse Treatment, 1994). In addition, Kessler et al., (1997) found that male alcoholics were most likely to have a conduct or antisocial personality disorder and female alcoholics to have an anxiety, other affective, or drug use disorder. Cocaine addiction has been associated with posttraumatic stress disorder (Najavits et al. 1998) and substance use disorders with attention deficit–hyperactivity disorder in adolescents (Milberger, Biederman, Faraone, Wilens, & Chu, 1997). These citations represent only a small portion of the rapidly growing work in this area. Therefore, you should not assume that these examples represent the only possible combinations of substance use disorders and other mental disorders.

The treatment of clients with co-occurring disorders has been problematic. According to Onken, Blaine, Genser, and Horton (1997):

> Despite the common co-occurrence of drug use disorders and mental disorders, persons who have both of these problems tend to fall between the cracks of service delivery systems. Individuals with mental disorders who seek treatment in the community may receive it within the mental health delivery system, and drug-addicted individuals may receive treatment within the drug abuse treatment system. Those requiring treatment for both mental and drug use disorders may not be able to receive comprehensive treatment in one treatment program. In the worst case scenario, the clinicians responsible for the treatment of the mental disorder may not have any idea about what is going on with the addictive disorder (e.g., treatment or severity) and the clinicians responsible for the addiction treatment may not be aware of what is happening with the mental disorder. Unfortunately, those persons who have concurrent mental and addictive disorders are not easily accommodated by the current treatment delivery system. (p. 1)

Traditionally, AOD treatment programs would assume that other mental disorders, such as depression, were secondary to the substance abuse problem or that clients with clear psychiatric problems (e.g., schizophrenia) were inappropriate for AOD treatment programs. It is true that symptoms of a mental disorder may be secondary to an AOD problem. For example, clients who abuse cocaine clearly become significantly depressed in the early stages of recovery. Individuals who abuse methamphetamine may develop symptoms that are indistinguishable from paranoid schizophrenia. Therefore, the true co-occurring disorder client may be difficult to accurately diagnose until a period of detoxification or until a very accurate history is available. Also, how should these clients be treated? Should the client be treated first for the substance abuse problem or the psychiatric problem? If the client is treated in an AOD treatment program, will the staff be trained to work with the psychiatric problem (and vice versa)?

These issues have resulted in the development of programs that supposedly can treat AOD problems along with other mental disorders. In such programs, there is a clear need for staff who are trained to work with both AOD problems and mental disorders. Unfortunately, in order to attract more patients, some programs are advertised as treating co-occurring disorders and are staffed only by AOD counselors. This practice is unethical, giving cause for the mental health professional to check on the training of the staff before referring a client to such a program.

Treatment Effectiveness

Does treatment work? This issue is complex but extremely important, given the time and expense of AOD treatment and the costs to society if people continue abusing AOD following treatment. While numerous studies have examined treatment effectiveness, making sense of the results is difficult because of several underlying problems. Before discussing some of these studies, let's look at some of these problems.

Treatment programs (for the most part) are not designed to scientifically evaluate the aspects of treatment that are most effective. This makes research immediately problematic, since there is no control over the many variables that may affect results. The numerous client variables that may impact treatment effectiveness include age, gender, duration of use, type of substances used, life problems experienced, voluntary or involuntary admission to treatment, prior treatment, client health, psychological problems, criminal activity, level of education, and income. The type of treatment environment (e.g., private, for profit; public, non-profit; hospital inpatient; free standing outpatient; therapeutic community) may impact effectiveness. To adequately research the effectiveness of a treatment program or treatment approach, a control group is necessary. Ethical (and practical) issues in the random assignment of clients to treatment must be considered when the researcher hypothesizes that one form of treatment is superior to another.

Equally as important to the issues that create barriers to well-designed research are the types of outcomes in effectiveness studies. Is client success defined by program completion, abstinence, length of sobriety, and/or reduction in life problems? What if a client completes a program, relapses, goes to a different program, and then remains abstinent? Was the first program a failure or did it contribute to the client's sobriety later on?

Fortunately, three major long-term studies have been completed to help answer the question "Does treatment work?" The Center for Substance Abuse Treatment sponsored a congressionally mandated study of treatment outcomes for clients in public-sector treatment programs. The National Treatment Improvement Evaluation Study (NTIES) (Gerstein, 1997) followed 4,411 clients in 78 treatment sites across the country for five years. Clients were from vulnerable and underserved populations such as minorities, pregnant women, youth, public housing residents, welfare recipients, and those involved in the criminal justice system. Many of the people studied did not complete treatment, which would tend to depress any positive results. In spite of these factors, there were significant reductions in AOD use 1 year after treatment regardless of the amount of time spent in treatment or the amount of treatment received. In addition, positive outcomes were found in employment income, mental and physical health, criminal activity, homelessness, and high-risk behaviors for HIV infection. This study also demonstrated that the average savings per client in the year after treatment was $9,177, which is more than three times the average cost of one treatment episode (Center for Substance Abuse Treatment, 1999b). The savings occurred in reduced healthcare and crime-related costs and increased earnings by clients. Outpatient and long-term residential treatment showed the largest cost savings, but short-term residential treatment and outpatient methadone also were cost effective.

The National Institute on Drug Abuse followed more than 10,000 clients in nearly 100 treatment programs for 2 years. The Drug Abuse Treatment Outcome Study (DATOS) (Mueller & Wyman, 1997) involved four types of treatment programs: outpatient methadone, outpatient drug-free, long-term residential, and short-term inpatient. In all treatment modalities, significant reductions occurred in the use of heroin, cocaine, marijuana, and alcohol 1 year following treatment. Positive outcomes were noted in criminal activity, depression, and employment. The outcomes were most pronounced for clients in long-term treatment but were significant for short-term clients as well.

Five-year follow-up data are available on 708 subjects from 45 programs in eight cities who met DSM criteria for cocaine dependence (Simpson, Joe, & Broome, 2002). There were large decreases in cocaine use in the first year after treatment discharge that were maintained at five years. Similarly, improvements in heavy alcohol use and criminal activity continued. The level of severity of drug use and psychosocial problems at treatment entry were predictive of long-term outcomes. However, outcomes improved in direct relationship to the level of treatment exposure (i.e., those who were in treatment longer did better).

Furthermore, data on 1,167 adolescents from the DATOS sample were also analyzed (Hser et al., 2001). At one year posttreatment, there were significant reductions in marijuana use, heavy drinking, use of illicit drugs, and criminal involvement. The clients also reported better psychological adjustment and school performance.

The third study was conducted by the National Institute on Alcohol Abuse and Alcoholism and was called "Project MATCH" (Project MATCH Research Group, 1997). This study was designed to determine if different types of alcoholics respond differently to specific treatment approaches. Over 1,700 alcoholics in outpatient treatment or aftercare were studied. The clients were matched with one of three treatment approaches based on client characteristics, including severity of alcohol involvement, cognitive impairment, psychiatric severity, conceptual level, gender, meaning-seeking, motivational readiness to change, social support for drinking versus abstinence, sociopathy, and typology of alcoholism. The three treatment approaches (Twelve-Step Facilitation, Cognitive-Behavioral, Motivational Enhancement) were described earlier in this chapter. Overall, the clients in this study demonstrated significant improvement in increased percentage of abstinent days and decreased number of drinks per drinking days. There were few differences among the treatment approaches. In spite of many efforts, researchers have been unable to identify the reasons why one approach was superior to another in the rare instances where differences were noted (Longabaugh, 2001). Positive outcomes were also noted in the use of other drugs, depression, and alcohol-related problems.

Finally, there have been outcome studies on the use of pharmacological approaches to treatment. For example, naltrexone has been shown to reduce the percentage of days a client spends drinking, the amount of alcohol consumed on a drinking occasion, and the relapse to excessive and destructive drinking (Center for Substance Abuse Treatment, 1998). Methadone has been shown to be an extremely effective treatment for opioid addiction. For example, Ball, Corty, Pet-roski, & Bond (1987) found that over 92% of methadone maintenance clients were abstinent from other opioids after 4½ years on methadone. Improved social functioning, reduced mortality and morbidity, and decreased criminal activity have also been demonstrated (e.g., Ball & Ross, 1991; Hubbard & French, 1991). Methadone treatment is also extremely cost effective, with $4 in economic benefits for every $1 spent for treatment (Parrino, 2002).

Although it is not possible to comprehensively review all treatment effectiveness research, several conclusions can be reached. Treatment does appear to have a beneficial, long-term effect on a variety of client behaviors, including AOD use. Treatment length may be related to improved outcomes, but even short-term treatment is helpful. A variety of treatment approaches and treatment settings have proven effective, and even the most vulnerable clients benefit from treatment.

Client–Treatment Matching

The results of the Project MATCH study that were discussed in the previous section seem to contradict the notion that treatment should be individualized based on client issues, needs, and characteristics. After all, matching clients with one of three treatment approaches using client characteristics did not result in significant differences in treatment outcomes. However, this does not mean that consideration of the unique needs of clients can be ignored in treatment planning. To use a very simple example, an alcoholic client has worked as a bartender for many years. He has a high school education. This client's treatment plan must include vocational guidance that takes into account his education level and previous work experience. If it does not, relapse is highly probable. The Project MATCH results did indicate that, within a highly structured treatment protocol, positive outcomes could be achieved regardless of the match between treatment approach and client characteristics. However, the study did not determine the level of effectiveness for each individual client, and there were obvious limitations in the range of client characteristics that could be studied.

We hope it does not make sense to you that AOD treatment should be the same for everyone. Unfortunately, in this particular field

> If one surveys alcoholism treatment programs with the question, "Do you tailor your treatment to the individual?", nearly all will answer "Yes." Yet many programs still consist of a relatively invariant set of treatment experiences offered to almost all clients.

> Furthermore, the treatment recommended to a client after evaluation is often determined by the door through which the person walked for assessment. Each program tends to find most clients it evaluates in need of the very kind of treatment it happens to offer. (Miller, 1989, p. 261)

Economics obviously is a factor in the fact that assessment personnel usually refer to the program they work for. At least, that is the case in for-profit treatment when the client has money or insurance. However, the failure of treatment programs to individualize treatment for clients may be related to the knowledge and skills of the treatment staff. Here's an example. We were talking to an AOD counselor about one of her clients in an outpatient program. The client had recently been transferred to an inpatient psychiatric hospital after a suicide attempt. He had a history of depression and had been taking an antidepressant medication. The counselor complained of the client's denial of his AOD problem and his inability to "admit his powerlessness" and to "work the program" (these are AA slogans). The counselor would not acknowledge the possibility that the client's AOD use might be secondary to a major depression.

Most states require only a high school diploma or GED for certification (although there are other requirements as well). While we admit to a bias (since we are counselor educators), it does make sense that an AOD counselor who knows the addiction field only through minimal training and his or her own experiences would have some difficulty managing other types of mental disorders that may exist concurrently with AOD problems. If a counselor's training and experience are limited, he or she would likely force the client to adapt to the counselor's own conceptual framework. Otherwise, the counselor would feel helpless. Perhaps this is the reason that clients are indoctrinated with the notion that they must work on their disease before any other problems can be dealt with. Inadequately prepared AOD counselors may unconsciously project this idea onto their clients because of their own insecurity with working on issues outside their comfort level. Usually, these counselors are only familiar with the disease model of addiction.

Clearly, we would like to see a comprehensive assessment of client needs and an individualized treatment plan that addresses all relevant client issues. This would necessitate that treatment programs have staff who are trained to handle the types of client problems that require attention. A uniform certification process for AOD counselors as well as more university training programs would be helpful in this effort. Fortunately, uniform certification requirements are being worked on by professional organizations such as the National Association of Alcoholism and Drug Abuse Counselors, and training centers based in colleges and universities have been funded by the Center for Substance Abuse Treatment.

Special Problems in Treatment

Recovering Individuals as Counselors

The issues raised in client-treatment matching relate to the use of recovering individuals as AOD counselors. As Royce (1989) said, "Since the first Yale Plan Clinic in 1944, recovered alcoholics have been a part of most treatment teams, whether or not they belonged to a profession or had a college degree.... The understanding and empathy those workers gained from their own experience as alcoholics has long been recognized as a valuable contribution to the recovery process" (p. 341). However, Miller (1995) stated that, "The effectiveness of counselors has been found to be unrelated to whether or not they are themselves 'in recovery'" (p. 94).

The question is not whether recovering individuals should be AOD counselors. We believe, as we indicated in the section on client-treatment matching, that the issue is training. The counselor we described in the situation with the depressed and suicidal client was not in recovery. She was poorly trained. An assumption has been made in the field that, if one is in recovery, that attribute is sufficient for effectiveness as an AOD counselor. However, we would be hard-pressed to find support for the notion that if one has attempted suicide, he or she would be an effective crisis intervention counselor. We have trained many master's level counselors who are in recovery, and we believe that the combination of personal experience and professional training can be dynamic. An individual who is well trained and has good interpersonal skills can be an effective AOD counselor, regardless of whether the counselor is in recovery. A person with little or no training and poor interpersonal skills will be ineffective, whether he or she is in recovery or not. What about the individual in recovery with little training and good interpersonal skills? This person might be a natural counselor and can undoubtedly be helpful. Lack of training is simply a factor limiting the type of client issue this counselor should work with. The outstanding natural counselors we have worked with who are in recovery and have returned for formal training have been able to recognize this limitation and have sought assistance to increase their effectiveness.

Confrontation as a Treatment Strategy

The association of confrontation with substance abuse treatment came about from the use of high levels of confrontation in therapeutic communities such as Synanon. Confrontation is seen as the therapeutic technique to break through the alcoholic/addict's denial. However, a hostile, confrontational counseling style has been found to be associated with poor long-term results (Lieberman, Yalom, & Miles, 1973).

The controversy regarding confrontation probably results from the association of this technique with hostility and aggression. In fact, some AOD counselors may use confrontation in this manner because that is what they have seen and heard. However, confrontation is simply a matter of pointing out to a client that there is a discrepancy between what he or she says and he or she means, or between what is said and what is done (Ivey, Bradford-Ivey, & Simek-Morgan, 1993). In this context, confrontation is a valuable technique in AOD treatment just as it is in other counseling situations. The inappropriate use of confrontation by counselors is a result of poor training and/or poor judgment. Hopefully, if client-treatment matching occurs, a counselor will determine the proper type of confrontation for a particular client and will not assume that all alcoholics/addicts must be confronted in a hostile and aggressive manner.

The Use of Medication

In the section of this chapter on treatment approaches, we discussed the use of different medications in the management of detoxification, and the treatment of AOD addiction. Minor tranquilizers are used to prevent the medically dangerous withdrawal symptoms suffered in the detoxification from CNS depressants. Drugs such as naltrexone and methadone are used to treat alcoholism and opioid addiction, and various nondependence-producing psychoactive drugs are used to treat disorders such as depression and bipolar disorder.

The controversy in this area is probably related to a misinterpretation of AA's position on the use of drugs by alcoholics. Royce (1989) explains this misinterpretation:

> AA rightly takes a strong stand against substituting one addictive drug for another. Overenthusiasm has trapped some AA members into incautious statements about pills that are not substitute addictions and may be medically necessary for a recovering alcoholic. Thus one sometimes hears horror stories about advice to a heart patient not to take digitalis, a diabetic not to take oral insulin, an epileptic not to take Dilantin, or a psychotic not to take lithium.... AA has never approved that kind of advice and in fact strongly disapproves. (p. 352)

It is certainly important for a physician to be made aware of the recovering status of a patient before prescribing pain medication with addictive potential, and alternatives to the use of pain medications are recommended (Royce, 1989). However, recovering persons should not be discouraged from taking medically necessary drugs.

Controlled Use

The question of whether alcoholics can learn to use alcohol in a moderate or nonproblematic manner has been a controversial issue in treatment for some time. In the early 1970s, the Sobells (Sobell & Sobell, 1973) were able to demonstrate that chronic alcoholics could successfully be taught controlled drinking in an experimental setting. Also, reports of the Rand study (Armor, Polich, & Stambul, 1978; Polich, Armor, & Braiker, 1981) indicated that many previously treated alcoholics had been drinking in a nonproblematic manner over a 4-year period. The Sobell and Sobell (1973) study has been criticized since few of the alcoholic subjects maintained controlled drinking over an extended period of time (Hester, 1995) and, as Royce (1989) noted, "The Rand report and other studies have been criticized...for using too short a time period, taking inadequate care in followup, subjective reporting, small number, sampling fallacies, lack of control group, and employing absurdly artificial settings" (p. 134). However, Sobell, Cunningham, and Sobell (1996) reported that large numbers of people with previous mild to moderate alcohol problems were able to drink in moderation without ongoing problems related to alcohol.

While the debate about controlled use makes for some fascinating reading in the field, largely because it evokes emotional as well as scholarly arguments and because it pits disease concept proponents against others, the practical issues seem more clear cut. It makes very little sense to teach a person to use alcohol in a controlled manner when the person has had numerous, serious life problems and has consistently demonstrated an inability to control alcohol use. If an individual can be diagnosed as having a substance dependence disorder based on the *DSM-IV-TR* (see Chapter 6), controlled use is not a reasonable goal. Even proponents of controlled use recognize that this is not a productive goal for everyone (e.g., Miller & Munoz, 1982). Therefore, treatment programs, particularly if they use a disease model, would oppose controlled use because their clients would usually be classified as alcoholics/addicts.

Who would be a candidate for learning to use in a controlled manner? These types of clients would more often be seen by generalist mental health professionals or AOD counselors in private practice or working in mental health clinics. Generally, the best candidates would be young, healthy drinkers, with few life problems related to alcohol, whose problems with alcohol are of recent duration and who resist abstaining. These drinkers would usually be considered at-risk drinkers (see Chapter 7).

If a client can be diagnosed with an alcohol abuse disorder (see Chapter 6), the decision as to whether or not controlled drinking is a wise option is very difficult. Therefore, we would advise any AOD counselor or mental health professional to be very cautious in working with a client on controlled use. An abstinent client has no risk of problems from use; a client who uses at any level is at risk. However, some clients will resist treatment or drop out of treatment if abstinence is demanded. If such a client fits the criteria described above, controlled use might be a treatment goal. Also, there are times when working with a resistant client on controlled use demonstrates to the client that he or she is unable to use in a nonproblematic manner. We worked with a young woman in individual counseling who had experienced a few minor problems as a result of her alcohol, marijuana, and cocaine use and would not agree to abstain. We asked her to set goals regarding her intake for 2 weeks and then to keep track of her actual use. It became very clear to her that her use was out of control since she almost always exceeded her goal. This resulted in her referral to an outpatient program and successful abstinence for at least 1 year (the last time we saw her).

Again, we suggest that controlled use be a treatment goal only when other alternatives have been explored and when it is probable that the client will experience more serious problems from an insistence on abstinence. There are various behavioral approaches to teaching controlled use including Behavioral Self-Control Training (Hester, 1995).

Natural Recovery

The fact that some people discontinue their problematic use of AOD without treatment has been documented by researchers (e.g., Sobell, Sobell, & Toneatto, 1991; Tuchfield, 1981) and is certainly something we have seen in our own experience. The question that is raised is whether the person who becomes abstinent without treatment is recovering or is a *dry drunk.* A dry drunk is defined as a person who "may exhibit any or all the feelings and behavior associated with intoxication although no alcohol is consumed" (Royce, 1989, p. 299). This is not to imply that euphoria is experienced, as can be seen in Royce's (1989) description of the symptoms of the dry drunk: "Shakes, insomnia, stiffness, headaches, and other flu-like symptoms may accompany the irritability, fatigue, depression, hunger, egocentrism, over-reaction, unexplained sadness, aimless puttering or wandering, and a host of negative emotions" (p. 299).

There has been a sense from the treatment community and Twelve-Step adherents that people who try to quit drinking or using on their own end up in the dry drunk syndrome. This sense probably arises from the same dynamics that cause treatment providers to view all alcoholics/addicts as having a disease. In other words, if you are a treatment provider or an AA member, when would you see someone who is trying to abstain on his or her own?

You would see this person when he or she was having problems (such as the dry drunk symptoms) and was referred, by self or by others, to a treatment program or to an AA meeting. It would be logical to conclude that discontinuing use without treatment or Twelve-Step support is difficult, if not impossible. However, those who discontinue problematic use without experiencing the dry drunk syndrome do not show up in treatment or at meetings. Sobell et al. (1991) suggested that natural recovery is much more frequent than has been suspected. In fact, Cunningham, Sobell, Sobell, and Kapur (1995) and Sobell et al. (1996) have identified significant numbers of people with previous alcohol problems who reported recovering without formal treatment or support groups. These researchers believe that an in-depth investigation of these "natural recovering" individuals may help identify important interventions for treatment providers.

Some research of this type has been conducted. Researchers (Granfield & Cloud, 2001) interviewed 46 formerly substance dependent men and women who recovered without treatment. They discovered that the subjects in this research had what they termed *recovery capital.* This was defined as *social capital,* or the presence of a social network or social support of family, friends, or colleagues who were available to provide help and motivation. *Physical capital* included tangible resources that provided flexibility and options for courses of recovery that did not involve formal treatment. Finally, recovery capital included *human capital,* such as knowledge, skills, and personal attributes. The researchers noted that most of their subjects had college degrees or vocational skills and that recovery capital may not be equitably available to everyone.

Summary

- Approaches to treatment include the Minnesota Model, behavioral models (aversive conditioning, covert sensitization, Behavioral Self-Control Training, Community Reinforcement Approach), Twelve-Step Facilitation, Cognitive-Behavioral Therapy, Motivational Enhancement Therapy, and pharmacological procedures.
- Treatment strategies and techniques include individual, group, and family counseling; support groups; lifestyle changes; education; and aftercare.
- Treatment occurs in therapeutic communities, inpatient and residential settings, partial hospitalization and day treatment settings, and intensive outpatient and outpatient settings.
- The National Institute on Drug Abuse has established 13 principles of effective treatment.
- Treatment must be designed individually and consider diversity issues including gender, ethnicity, age, sexual orientation, criminal justice involvement, and co-occurring mental disorders.
- A variety of studies on treatment effectiveness have found all forms of treatment to be effective in reducing alcohol and other drug use, criminal justice involvement, and healthcare utilization and in improving employment.
- Evidence-based treatment processes have been identified by federal research agencies such as the National Institute on Drug Abuse and the National Institute on Alcohol Abuse and Alcoholism.

Internet Resources

Treatment facility locator
www.findtreatment.samhsa.gov

Treatment trends
www.drugabuse.gov/infofacts/treatmenttrends.html

Evidence-based treatment
www.nfattc.org/publicationsNewsResources/ebpOnline.aspx
www.drugabuse.gov/TB/Clinical/ClinicalToolbox.html

Principles of Effective Treatment
www.drugabuse.gov/PODAT/PODATIndex.html

Further Discussion

1. How could treatment for AOD problems be improved? Design your ideal treatment program.
2. Why do you think the Principles of Effective Treatment are not utilized in every treatment program and setting across the country?

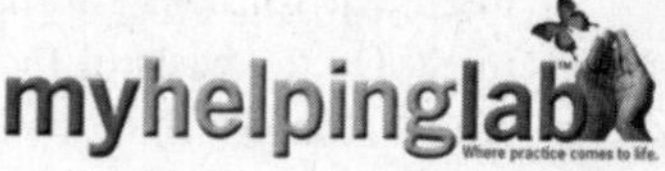

Treatment of AOD Problems

Video Lab

The following modules contain videos related to the topics in this chapter:

- Module 2, Couples Therapy
- Module 3, Cognitive Therapy
- Module 4, Reality Therapy
- Module 5, Harm Reduction Psychotherapy
- Module 6, Solution Focused Therapy

Case Study Activity

Read Substance Abuse, Case 2: A Cry for Help: A Counselor and an Alcoholic Friend.

- Review the principles of effective treatment. When you consider this man's situation, which of these principles do you suppose were *not* met? Describe a treatment plan for this man that would be consistent with the principles of effective treatment. What type of treatment setting would be the most appropriate? Why?

To access the videos and case study, log on to MyHelpingLab at www.myhelpinglab.com. Select the **Counseling & Psychotherapy** tab to locate the **Counseling Video Lab ➤ MyHelpingLab Videos by Course ➤ Addictions/Substance Abuse Counseling** modules or the **Counseling Case Archive.**

9

Relapse Prevention and Recovery

Some time ago, we met a 16-year-old girl named Anna. Anna was in an intensive outpatient treatment program for polydrug use problems, with her drugs of choice including tobacco, alcohol, marijuana, LSD, and methamphetamine. She was court-ordered to treatment following a variety of status offenses and crimes and a psychological assessment. On the basis of the assessment, Anna was diagnosed with Alcohol Abuse, Amphetamine Abuse (see Chapter 6), and posttraumatic stress disorder (PTSD). The diagnosis of PTSD was related to a history of sexual molestation by Anna's stepfather that began when she was 8 and ended when she was 13 when her biological mother discovered the molestation and divorced the perpetrator. The crime was reported, but Anna had never been in therapy. Shortly after the molestation began, Anna began to demonstrate a series of problems in school including deteriorating academic performance, fighting, and noncompliance with teachers. These problems continued until she entered treatment. Anna's biological father left the family when Anna was two and was an active alcoholic who had been in two treatment programs. He maintained sporadic contact with his daughter. Anna was slightly obese and had an acne problem. On an IQ test, she scored 88 (low average), and her academic skills were at the sixth to seventh grade level (she was a sophomore). Anna's mother was 33 years old, did not complete high school, and worked in a service position at a hotel/casino. She used alcohol and marijuana on an infrequent basis. She and Anna had a volatile relationship with a great deal of conflict. The mother noted a strong similarity between Anna and her biological father. She also expressed guilt over not discovering the sexual molestation sooner.

Anna completed her treatment program in three months. She was initially resistant and defiant. However, she bonded with a female counselor in the program and, for the first time, found support and consistency from both adults and peers. She maintained abstinence for the last two months of her program. Her mother participated in the program and began to learn about the disease of chemical dependency (which was the orientation of the program) and about her own enabling. Anna and her mother had four family counseling sessions and made a little progress. There was still a lot to do, so they were referred to a marriage and family therapist. The school counselor was invited to the discharge conference and encouraged to assist Anna in readjusting to school. She had earned just two credits in high school (that means she had passed only two classes). Anna began attending AA meetings and was encouraged to go to four to five meetings a week. She was scheduled to attend a weekly 2-hour aftercare meeting at the treatment program.

Need for Generalist Training in Relapse Prevention

Imagine that you are the marriage and family therapist whom Anna and her mother contact. Or, let's say that you are the school counselor at Anna's high school. We hope that you can identify some of the issues that might lead Anna to return to AOD use and would require attention in family therapy or at school. First, there is the history of sexual molestation, which we have discussed as a frequent issue for women in substance-abuse treatment programs. Some of the other issues include academic problems at school, conflict with mom, physical appearance (we are not making a judgment here. Just remember what it was like when you were in high school for a kid who was overweight and had acne), and contact with an actively drinking father. There are also problems that, although not explicitly stated, might be logically assumed to exist. For example, we would expect that Anna's social group involved kids who use AOD. If she returns to the same school, how will she handle her peer group? She may have some deep-seated emotional issues involving abandonment by her father and anger at her mother for not protecting her from her stepfather. Finally, given her intellectual ability and academic achievement, school may be challenging.

In Chapter 1, we gave examples of how social workers, school counselors, and marriage and family therapists work with clients with AOD problems whether or not these helping professionals work in treatment programs. The area of relapse prevention is a clear illustration of this. In Anna's case, the marriage and family therapist and school counselor would probably have more intensive and a longer duration of contact with Anna than the staff at the treatment program. Therefore, the therapist and counselor are critically important to Anna's success in recovery. She could also have a probation officer and contact with social service professionals (i.e., through vocational training programs). Their work could also impact Anna's abstinence.

Although it would be nice if there were a formal discharge staffing that included all relevant parties and a formal relapse prevention plan, our experience is that these are not the norm. The mental health professional usually has sketchy information from the client and/or treatment program and is left to develop his or her own relapse prevention plan. That is why we will spend considerable time in this chapter acquainting you with the specifics of relapse prevention.

Definition of Slip *and* Relapse

As we shall see, a need exists to differentiate a *slip* from a *relapse.* A slip is an episode of AOD use following a period of abstinence, while relapse is the return to uncontrolled AOD use following a period of abstinence. Usually, a slip or slips precede relapse, and there is some evidence (e.g., Polich, Armor, and Braiker, 1981) that slipping is the rule rather than the exception for those clients who receive AOD treatment.

The disease model of addiction and AA slogans (an alcoholic is always "one drink from a drunk") can promote the idea that a slip inevitably leads to relapse. The depiction of addiction as a progressive, chronic disease that can be managed only through abstinence may create a sense that a slip means complete deterioration to pretreatment levels of functioning. The result of clients' adopting this point of view is that, when a slip occurs (as it is likely to), the client may experience guilt, anxiety, or hopelessness. These negative emotions may lead to further, heavier use. The cognitive process of the client may go something like this: "Well, I used again. Since that means I'm back to square one, I might as well do it up right."

Regardless of the model of addiction or orientation to treatment, AOD treatment providers will tell you that a return to some level of use is a frequent occurrence (shortly, we will examine data on how frequent). Although we believe that abstinence is the safest and healthiest "level" of use, we also believe that it is foolish to ignore the reality of slips, and it is poor practice to leave clients unprepared to prevent a slip from escalating to a relapse. As we discussed in Chapter 3, there is no evidence that addiction proceeds in an inevitable progression. Therefore, there is no reason to treat a slip as a catastrophe and every reason to view a slip as a signal to the client, treatment providers, and other mental health professionals to reexamine the aftercare plan (see Chapter 8) in order to prevent slips from occurring in the future and to prevent the current slip from escalating.

Frequency of Slips and Relapse

Regardless of the researcher, drug or drugs of choice, and population studied, a consistent finding from studies is that lots of people who receive treatment for AOD problems use again after leaving treatment. For example, Miller and Hester (1980) examined 500 alcohol treatment outcome studies. They concluded that

> With regard to "average" outcome rates from treatment programs, it appears that 1/3 abstinent and 1/3 improved (but not abstinent) represent reasonable estimates of at least short-term response to treatment. A review restricted to studies with one-year follow-up data, however, suggests that 26% is a representative figure for successful outcome (abstinent plus improved) 12 months after treatment. (p. 15)

Hunt, Barnett, and Branch (1971) reported that 65% to 70% of alcoholics, heroin addicts, and smokers relapsed (defined as any level of use following treatment) within the first year and most of these occurred in the first 90 days. Hoffman and Harrison (1986) followed more than 1,900 adults from five private inpatient alcohol and other treatment programs. Two years after treatment, 54% achieved total abstinence, 18% had slips and returned to abstinence, and 28% had multiple relapses. Clients who came from high socioeconomic groups and had good social stability had the lowest relapse rates. As would be expected, stereotypic "skid row" alcoholics had the poorest prognosis.

We are not presenting these data to generate an argument (which is important from a research point of view) regarding the many factors that influence these research results. Certainly, the length of time following treatment, the type of treatment setting and methods, the method of defining *relapse,* the drug or drugs of choice, the client and the environmental characteristics, and other variables influence the data. Our point is that many, if not most, clients return to use at some point following treatment. Therefore, the issue of return to use must be a focus of treatment and aftercare.

Is Relapse in Addiction Similar to Other Chronic Conditions?

McLellan, Lewis, O'Brien, and Kleber (2000) have written a historic paper, "Drug Dependence, a Chronic Medical Illness." In their extensive review of the literature, they found that about 40% of patients treated for alcohol, opioid, or cocaine dependence were continually abstinent for one year. An additional 15% returned to a nondependent level of use. In comparison, at least 30% of adult-onset, insulin-dependent diabetic patients and 40% of adult, medication-dependent hypertensive and asthmatic patients annually require restabilization of medication and/or hospitalization because of reoccurrence of symptoms. Furthermore, these researchers found the rates of compliance with prescribed medications (40% to 60%) and with behavioral change regimens (30% to 50%) to be similar between addiction disorders and other chronic illnesses such as diabetes, hypertension, and asthma. Therefore, while the relapse rate of substance disorders is certainly a focus of attention and intervention, it really is no different than the relapse and noncompliance rates for other chronic conditions.

Models of Relapse Prevention

The Cenaps Model

The Cenaps Model was developed by Terence Gorski (president of the Cenaps Corporation) and articulated in a variety of articles and books (e.g., Gorski, 1988, 1989, 1990, 1992, 1993; Gorski & Miller, 1986). The disease concept is the underlying philosophy of the model, although the methods used are eclectic. In Gorski's words, the Cenaps model "integrates the fundamental principles of AA and the Minnesota Model Treatment [see Chapter 8] to meet the needs of relapse-prone patients" (Gorski, 1990, p. 126). The model is proposed as a formal program within AOD treatment programs.

With the disease concept as a guiding philosophy, chemical dependency is viewed as a biopsychosocial disease. This means that the disease affects biological or physical, psychological, and social functioning. Although there is a complex interaction among these areas, Gorski (1990) stated that "The physical consequence of chemical dependence is brain dysfunction…[that] disorganizes the preaddictive personality and causes social and occupational problems" (p. 126). Since the disease is chronic and affects the brain (causing psychological and social problems), total abstinence is necessary. However, this is not the exclusive goal of the model. Personality, lifestyle, and family functioning are also areas that require change for biopsychosocial health. For example,

> Being raised in a dysfunctional family can result in self-defeating personality traits or disorders. These traits and disorders do not cause chemical dependence; however, they can

> cause a more rapid progression of the chemical dependence, making it difficult to recognize and to seek treatment.... Self-defeating personality traits and disorders also increase the risk of relapse. As a result, family-of-origin problems need to be appropriately addressed in treatment. (Gorski, 1990, pp. 126–127)

Gorski (1990) differentiates clients who have completed the "primary goals" of treatment from those who have not completed these goals. These primary goals are

> (1) the recognition that chemical dependency is a biopsychosocial disease, (2) the recognition of the need for lifelong abstinence from all mind-altering drugs, (3) the development and use of an ongoing recovery program to maintain abstinence, and (4) the diagnosis and treatment of other problems or conditions that can interfere with recovery. (p. 127)

If a client has not completed the primary goals, then, in Gorski's view, a relapse prevention program is inappropriate. The relapse prevention program outlined in the Cenaps Model is for clients "who believe that they have the disease, require abstinence, and need to use recovery tools, but are unable to maintain abstinence" (Gorski, 1990, p. 127). As can be seen from the primary goals of treatment, this would limit the number of clients who would be seen as appropriate for a relapse prevention program.

According to Gorski (1990), recovery and relapse are related processes. Recovery follows a sequence of six steps:

> (1) abstaining from alcohol and other drugs; (2) separating from people, places, and things that promote chemical use and establishing a social network that supports recovery; (3) stopping compulsive self-defeating behaviors that suppress awareness of painful feelings and irrational thoughts; (4) learning how to manage feelings and emotions responsibly without resorting to compulsive behaviors or the use of chemicals; (5) learning to change addictive-thinking patterns that create painful feelings and self-defeating behaviors; and (6) identifying and changing the mistaken core beliefs about self, others, and the world that promote the use of irrational thinking. (p. 128)

The relapse process begins at step 6 and proceeds upward. For example, let's take a look at Anna's situation and see how a relapse might occur based on Gorski's model. Remember that she was sexually molested by her stepfather. Anna starts thinking about the molestation and how unfair it is that this happened to her. She believes that she must have encouraged this behavior to get attention and affection from her stepfather and blames herself for the molestation (mistaken core belief about herself, step 6). She ponders this and feels guilty, embarrassed, and victimized (painful feelings, step 5). Anna becomes sexually involved with a 22-year-old who is initially kind and attentive. When she is with this man, she feels worthwhile and does not experience the feelings of guilt, embarrassment, and victimization (managing feelings in an irresponsible manner, step 4). However, the man becomes verbally abusive and openly sees other women. Anna's painful feelings return, but she tries desperately to hang on to the relationship (self-defeating behavior, step 3). The man uses AOD, as do his friends (people, places, and things that promote chemical use, step 2). In an effort to impress the man and cope with her feelings, she returns to use (step 1).

The Cenaps Model uses a variety of procedures in relapse prevention, including client self-assessment of problems that might result in relapse, education about relapse, identification of the signs of the relapse progression, strategies to manage or modify the signs, and the involvement of others, such as family members. Techniques from cognitive, affective, and behavioral therapies are used (Gorski, 1993). Therefore, while the Cenaps Model is based on the disease concept of addiction, eclectic treatment strategies are utilized. Furthermore, techniques have been developed for involving the family and the employee-assistance counselor, and procedures have been adapted for adolescents (Bell, 1990).

A Cognitive–Social Learning Model

In contrast to the Cenaps Model, cognitive–social learning approaches to relapse prevention do not have a prerequisite requirement that the client achieve "primary goals" of treatment. Therefore, the strategies of relapse prevention in this model could be used with any client who wants to maintain a behavior change. This change may involve abstinence from AODs or a moderation in use.

The cognitive–social learning model of relapse prevention has been presented by Alan Marlatt (e.g., Marlatt & Gordon, 1985) and Helen Annis (e.g., Annis, 1986, 1990; Annis & Davis, 1988). Marlatt (1985) views addictive behaviors as "overlearned *habits* that can be analyzed and modified in the same manner as other habits" (p. 9, italics in original). This model of addiction was discussed in Chapter 3. With regard to relapse prevention, Marlatt (1985) states that those who believe in this model

> are particularly interested in studying the *determinants* of addictive habits, including situational and environmental antecedents, beliefs and expectations, and the individual's family history and prior learning experiences with the substance or activity. In addition, there is an equal interest in discovering the *consequences* of these behaviors, so as to better understand both the reinforcing effects that may contribute to increased use and the negative consequences that may serve to inhibit the behavior.... [A]ttention is paid to the social and interpersonal reactions experienced by the individual before, during, and after engaging in an addictive behavior. Social factors are involved both in the initial learning of an addictive habit and in the subsequent performance of the activity once the habit has become firmly established. (pp. 9–10, italics in original)

Although the language is different from that used by Gorski, there is a similarity between the steps of recovery and relapse delineated by Gorski and Marlatt's determinants and consequences of addictive behaviors. Both emphasize the need to attend to behavior, thoughts, and feelings (Marlatt uses the terms "social and interpersonal reactions" for feelings and "beliefs and expectations" for thoughts). As we will see later in the chapter, the similarities are probably the reason for the overlap in relapse prevention techniques between the two models.

Annis (1990) criticizes traditional solutions to relapse that emphasize

> "Booster" sessions of the same treatment...added over time to reinforce the initial effects of treatment...intensify and broaden the number of treatment components offered...[or] adoption of a model of lifelong treatment, such as that embodied in Alcoholics Anonymous (AA) and other self-help groups. (p. 117)

Rather than focus on a model of addiction, Annis argues that the principles that guide the maintenance of a behavior change may be different from the principles that determine the initiation of a change. In other words, a person may enter treatment under coercion, be exposed to and accept the disease concept of addiction, and discontinue his or her use of AOD as a result. However, this same individual may be unable to maintain abstinence. This is the population who Gorski believed was appropriate for the Cenaps Model. However, Annis (and Marlatt) conceptualize this inability to maintain the "habit" change through self-efficacy theory:

> when a client enters a high risk situation for drinking, a process of cognitive appraisal of past experiences is set in motion which culminates in a judgment, or efficacy expectation, on the part of the client of his or her ability to cope with the situation. The judgment of personal efficacy determines whether or not drinking takes place.... (Annis and Davis, 1989, p. 170)

For example, let's say Anna returns to school after treatment. One day after school, she sees a group of students with whom she previously used. They invite her to "party." She says no and the kids make fun of her. In this model, Anna makes a judgment about her ability to cope with the peer pressure. If she decides that she can handle the situation and does so (i.e., asserts herself appropriately and has a social support system), her self-efficacy is enhanced. If she does not believe she can handle the situation or does not have the skills, her self-efficacy is threatened. Annis (1990) reported a high correlation between a client's situation-specific self-efficacy ratings and relapse episodes. Using self-efficacy theory, Marlatt developed a model of relapse that involves the coping strategies that an individual utilizes in high-risk situations. A high-risk situation is defined as "any situation that poses a threat to the individual's sense of control and increases the risk of potential relapse" (Marlatt, 1985, p. 37). These high-risk situations may be either unexpected or covertly planned.

Unexpected high-risk situations are similar to the situation in which Anna runs into her former using friends. She did not plan to encounter this situation; it just happened. In Marlatt's conceptualization, if Anna does not possess an appropriate coping response to the high-risk situation, she will experience decreased self-efficacy that may result in a slip. The slip may have associated thoughts and feelings such as conflict, guilt, and blame, which Marlatt termed the "abstinence violation effect (AVE)." The probability of a slip progressing to a relapse is related to the intensity of the AVE, which, in turn, is related to factors such as the length of sobriety, the commitment to abstinence, and the knowledge of the slip by significant others.

Anna does not have an effective coping mechanism to apply. To stop the teasing, she goes with the group and smokes a little pot. Unfortunately, at aftercare the next night, she has a random urinalysis. Anna's counselor calls her to discuss her "positive" drug test. Anna has an intense AVE. She is disappointed in herself for not resisting her friends and embarrassed that her counselor found out. Due to these painful feelings, Anna begins a relapse.

If Anna did have an effective coping response to the high-risk situation, Marlatt's model predicts that she will experience increased self-efficacy and a resulting decreased probability of slipping. Let's say that Anna asserts herself appropriately with her friends and goes to aftercare that night and reports the incident to her group. She is praised and supported by her peers and her counselor. Anna feels proud of herself and her renewed confidence in her ability to remain abstinent.

High-risk situations can also be encountered due to the covert planning of the individual. This occurs when the person has a "lifestyle imbalance." Marlatt defines this as having "shoulds" that are greater than "wants." Let's use Anna again to illustrate. She is trying to make up lost credits at school, attending four to five AA meetings a week, going to aftercare, trying to get along with her mother, going to counseling, and meeting with her probation officer. She is a busy young woman. Anna is 16 years old and has the same goals as most 16-year-olds—have friends and have fun. But her "shoulds" eat up all her time. Anna starts to feel resentful and victimized. When she has felt this way before, she has used alcohol and other drugs because using helps her forget (at least temporarily) her painful feelings. Also, she starts thinking that she deserves a little fun and relaxation. Although she thinks about using, Anna also has pangs of guilt when she imagines herself doing so. So, instead of simply getting alcohol or another drug and using it, she covertly makes decisions that will place her in a high-risk situation. For example, Anna decides to go to Dorothy's house on Friday to get back some CDs that she loaned Dorothy before going to treatment. Dorothy is a former using friend, and Anna knows that there are usually kids there on Friday after school getting high. Anna gets there, sees everyone loaded, and joins in. Marlatt calls Anna's decision to go to Dorothy's house an "apparently irrelevant decision (AID)." An AID is covertly planned to result in a high-risk situation. In isolation, it seems unrelated to alcohol or other drug use.

Annis and Marlatt describe a variety of interventions to prevent slips and also to prevent slips from escalating into relapse. Some of the interventions are designed to teach coping strategies in high-risk situations, and others are directed toward global lifestyle changes. Consistent with the model, the strategies are cognitive and behavioral. Many of these will be described in the following section. For those who are interested in school counseling, Fisher and Harrison (1993b) have applied Marlatt's model and strategies to adolescents in the school setting.

Essential Components of Relapse Prevention

As we have seen from the discussion of models of relapse prevention, differences exist between the two models with regard to the definition of client readiness for relapse prevention programming. In the Cenaps Model, a client must have completed the primary goals of treatment (which involve acceptance of the disease model of addiction) to be appropriate for relapse prevention. Annis and Marlatt do not discuss prerequisite conditions for relapse prevention. However, regardless of whether the Cenaps or a cognitive–social learning model of relapse prevention is the choice, the strategies employed to prevent relapse are quite similar. Therefore, we want to describe the strategies of relapse prevention that seem to be necessary in either model. Certainly, some strategies are associated to a larger extent with a particular model, which will be highlighted. However, our goal is to emphasize the techniques that a mental health professional may have to utilize in helping clients with AOD problems to remain abstinent or avoid relapse. Keep in mind that these strategies often must be developed by generalists in schools, agencies, and private practice settings, since mental health professionals in these settings usually have the most contact with clients after formal AOD treatment has ended.

Assessment of High-Risk Situations

The first step in a relapse prevention program must be to determine the specific situations for each client that may lead to a slip. Calling these situations *high risk* denotes a high probability of use based on past experience. The type of situations that are risky varies from client to client, although Cummings, Gordon, and Marlatt (1980) found that 75% of the relapses by alcoholics, smokers, and heroin users were due to negative emotions, interpersonal conflict, and social pressure.

In Gorski's (1990) model, the first step in determining high-risk situations is a client self-assessment that "involves a detailed reconstruction of the presenting problems, the alcohol and other drug use history as well as the recovery and relapse history to identify the past causes of relapse" (p. 129). Next, an examination of the client's life history helps identify any lifestyle issues that are associated with relapse. Finally, the client's recovery and relapse history is analyzed, with the goal being to "examine each period of abstinence to identify the recovery tasks that were completed or ignored, and to find the sequence of warning signs that led back to chemical use" (p. 130).

In the cognitive-social learning model, there is a "highly individualized analysis of a client's drinking behavior over the previous year to determine the high-risk situations for heavy drinking experienced by that particular client" (Annis, 1990, p. 118). For this purpose, Annis (1982) developed a 100-item self-report questionnaire called the Inventory of Drinking Situations. Obviously, the same type of assessment would occur for clients who use drugs other than alcohol.

Anna, our 16-year-old with polydrug problems, has a number of high-risk situations. Negative emotions, such as guilt, shame, and embarrassment related to her history of sexual molestation, have resulted in AOD use in the past. She also feels unattractive and unintelligent. Interpersonal conflicts with her mother and with teachers have also been identified as high-risk situations. Finally, in the past, Anna used when she experienced social pressure from her peers. Anna's current lifestyle involves a lot of time alone, because she has not established a nonusing social group. She watches a lot of TV and movies, and she has been using food as a substitute for AOD.

Coping with High-Risk Situations

Once the high-risk situations have been identified, it is necessary for the client to have strategies to deal with these situations effectively. Education and information sharing may be useful to clients. "Relapsers need accurate information about what causes relapse and what can be done to prevent it. This is typically provided in structured relapse education sessions and reading assignments that provide specific information about the recovery and relapse process as well as relapse prevention planning methods" (Gorski, 1990, p. 130).

Daley and Marlatt (1992) recommend that clients be taught that relapse is a process and an event by reviewing the common relapse warning signs identified by recovering clients: "it [is] helpful to have relapsers review their experiences in great detail so that they can learn the connections among thoughts, feelings, events, or situations, and relapse to substance use" (p. 537).

As we saw in the Chapter 8 discussion on methods of treatment, education is rarely sufficient for long-lasting change. Individualized strategies for high-risk situations are usually needed. Gorski (1990) recommends managing high-risk situations on situational–behavioral, cognitive–affective, and core issue levels. On the situational–behavioral level, the client often must avoid the people, places, and things that are high risk and learn to modify his or her behavioral response if a high-risk situation were to occur. For example, Anna identified peer pressure as a high-risk situation. She should avoid her friends with whom she previously used. She might attend a different school following treatment, but, because this is not always possible, she may not be able to avoid these peers. Anna may need assertiveness skills training to learn how to respond to the peer pressure she encounters.

Since Annis (1990) focuses on self-efficacy as the critical component of relapse prevention, a situational–behavioral intervention from this orientation "focuses on having the client engage in homework assignments involving the performance of alternative coping responses in high-risk situations" (p. 119). A hierarchy of progressively riskier situations is developed, and coping behaviors in these situations are planned, imagined, and used when needed. The underlying rationale is that the most powerful way to change thinking about self-efficacy is behavioral performance. For Anna, this hierarchy might begin with a chance meeting with one of her using friends in the hall at school, then progress to having a group of these friends sit down with her at lunch, and finally to encountering the group on Friday afternoon on their way to "party."

On the cognitive–affective level, the irrational thoughts and intense feelings that emerge in high-risk situations may need to be challenged. For those clients in Twelve-Step recovery programs, the acronym HALT is used to advise recovering people to avoid getting too hungry, angry, lonely, or tired. The term "stinking thinking" is used to challenge irrational thoughts, and members are told to get off the "pity pot" when they are immobilized by their feelings. Daley and Marlatt (1992) recommend a worksheet that lists the relapse-related thought, a statement or statements that dispute the thought, and a new, rational thought. As an example, Anna forgets to do her homework in math one day. Her teacher points this out in front of the class and tells her that she will fail unless she "gets with the program." Anna becomes angry and tells the teacher to "shut up." She is told to leave class. On the way to the office, Anna is consumed with her anger and has an inner dialog with statements such as "Mr. C. (the teacher) hates me. He's always picking on me." "I should just get loaded. No one cares anyway." Fortunately, Anna goes to see her school counselor, who listens to her, lets her emotions reduce in intensity, and then confronts her about her responsibility in completing her homework and also the fact that she is allowing Mr. C. to control her recovery program. While not condoning the public reproof by a teacher, the counselor points out the irrationality of Anna's thinking: "I should have done my homework. It embarrassed me to have it pointed out in front of the class. I conclude that the teacher hates me, nobody cares about me, and therefore, I have an excuse to use." A more rational sequence of thoughts would be: "I need to remember to do my homework and ask for help if I'm stuck. I don't like to be embarrassed and would prefer Mr. C. handle the situation differently. None of this has anything to do with people caring about me or using."

The school counselor might also conceptualize that Anna's decision not to complete her homework was part of a covert relapse plan and constitutes the "apparently irrelevant decision" we discussed in the cognitive–social learning model. In other words, Anna covertly planned a relapse by deciding not to complete her homework in a class in which the teacher often reacts with a public reprimand. Since interpersonal conflict with teachers is a high-risk situation that Anna has identified, she has an excuse to create a conflict, thus giving her an excuse to use. In this case, it would be useful to determine how much of Anna's thoughts and feelings involve her "shoulds" being greater than her "wants" and, if this is the case, to help her to modify this disparity. In addition, the AID needs to be confronted.

On the core issue level, the psychological issues that lead to high-risk situations need to be identified. Anna has identified guilt, shame, and embarrassment as negative emotions that are high risk for her. As these feelings originate from her history of sexual molestation, there is an obvious need for therapeutic attention to this issue. Low self-esteem, depressive and anxiety disorders, and codependency are examples of other psychological issues that can result in high-risk situations.

An additional issue in coping with high-risk situations involves urges and cravings. Marlatt (1985) defines a craving as the degree of desire for the positive effects a person expects as a result of use and an urge as the intention to engage in use to satisfy the craving. As Anna leaves her math class and is experiencing intense anger, she has an urge to smoke pot to satisfy a craving for the calming effect and the dissipation of her anger. In a high-risk situation, clients often report that the cravings and urges are so powerful that they lose focus on other aspects of relapse prevention. Therefore, strategies specific to coping with urges and cravings are necessary.

Daley and Marlatt (1992) suggest a variety of strategies to cope with urges and cravings. For example, intentional cognitive strategies such as changing thoughts or self-talking through the cravings can be used. Let's say you are mulling over a conflict you had at work and are having trouble falling asleep. You say to yourself, "I'm going to stop thinking about that and think about something more pleasant." Self-talking through the craving might involve an internal dialogue such as, "OK, I know what is happening. I'm upset and I'm thinking that a drink will make me feel better. It's happened before and it will probably happen again. I can get through it." It is often helpful for the client to combine this self-talk with an inner dialogue about the negative consequences of use and the positive benefits of not using (e.g., "If I drink, I'll blow nine months of sobriety and feel terrible about myself. If I don't, I'll feel really strong and proud of myself."). For some clients, calling their AA or NA sponsor or attending a meeting is helpful, while others find that getting involved in a strenuous or pleasant activity takes their thinking away from the urges and cravings.

Support Systems

As Gorski (1990) has stated, "Relapse-prone patients cannot recover alone. It is the therapist's responsibility to involve significant others in the structured process of relapse prevention planning. Family members, Twelve-Step sponsors, and employee-assistance program counselors are significant resources who need to be involved" (p. 132). We would expand on Gorski's statement in several ways. First, the "therapist" may be you—school counselor, marriage and family therapist, social worker, mental health counselor, or rehabilitation counselor. Many treatment programs do not have a formal, structured relapse-prevention program that coordinates the necessary services and people for successful relapse prevention (one reason we want you to be familiar with relapse-prevention strategies). Second, Gorski says "therapist" as if the assumption is that all clients will have such a person. If you have been attending to the discussion in this chapter, you can see that it is essential that recovering individuals be involved with a mental health professional. The behavioral, cognitive, and affective strategies we have mentioned require the expertise of trained "helpers." Although Twelve-Step meetings are a wonderful form of support in recovery, they are not designed to individually address the needs of recovering individuals. The "core psychological issues" that may lead to relapse require the involvement of mental health professionals. Finally, for adolescents, support involves more than just family members and Twelve-Step meetings and sponsors. Imagine that Anna returns to school after treatment. As a 16-year-old, her primary goals in life are to have friends and have fun. She also sincerely wants to remain abstinent. If she does not have a school-based support group of nonusing peers and no organized activities are available that are AOD-free, it is highly probable that she will relapse, in spite of her good intentions. We believe school personnel have an obligation and a challenge to help recovering adolescents such as Anna develop school-based support.

The involvement of the family in relapse prevention is certainly critical. "Numerous studies have substantiated a positive correlation between abstinence...and the presence of family and social supports" (Daley & Marlatt, 1992, p. 537). Furthermore, "Families of the chemically dependent are more likely to support rather than sabotage an addict's recovery if they are involved in the recovery process and have an opportunity to heal from the emotional pain they experienced" (Daley & Marlatt, 1992, pp. 537–538). This is not as simple a process as it may seem. As we will see in Chapter 11, although family therapy may be necessary in many cases, constellations and dynamics of families are very complex. For example, Anna and her mother are in family therapy. But, what about her actively alcoholic biological father? He's not involved and may have some investment in Anna's returning to use in order to justify his own use pattern. In a family in which the child with an alcohol or other drug problem plays the "scapegoat" role, the family "hero" may subtly sabotage recovery to maintain the family roles (see Chapter 11).

Lifestyle Changes

At the risk of beleaguering poor Anna, let's look at other aspects of her life that require some attention. We have already mentioned the history of sexual molestation that needs therapeutic attention. In addition to the negative emotions that have been generated, implications arise with regard to her sexual behavior, choice of partners in relationships, and more. She is obese and has problems with acne, indicating a need for nutritional and hygiene advice. Her IQ is low average and her academic skills are below grade level, so she needs remediation and vocational guidance. She also needs to work on her social skills, her conflict with her mother, her relationship with her father, developing support systems at school, and more.

Does this seem like a lot of "stuff" to work on? It certainly is, and each area can lead to relapse. Now imagine a 47-year-old man who has been abusing alcohol for 25 years. Due to his use, he has physical, legal, financial, family, and vocational problems, all of which cause stress and conflict—high-risk situations for relapse.

As you can see, successful relapse prevention does not simply involve a client's ability to cope with high-risk situations. Many high-risk situations result from the lifestyle of the client and the client's inability to modify this lifestyle. Many such modifications are difficult and require significant investments of time and resources. Let's examine some of these lifestyle areas and the modifications necessary for relapse prevention.

Leisure Time. What do you do in your spare time? (We know. You are a student and you don't have spare time. Just pretend.) Do you read, exercise, have a hobby? Many people with AOD problems have had only one leisure time activity—using. When you remove AOD, these people don't know what to do with themselves. They become bored, but are avoiding their only known method to relieve boredom. We have had clients become intense workaholics after treatment to alleviate the fear of having any free time. We also find clients attending one AA meeting after another because they don't know what else to do. We recently worked with a middle-aged man who had completed an alcohol treatment program at the Salvation Army. Each day, he would work at the Salvation Army, attend an AA meeting, and then wander around the casinos in town. Not surprisingly, it wasn't long before he started to use again.

Support Systems. We have already mentioned the importance of support systems. This is certainly related to leisure time. If a recovering person has a circle of friends, he or she has something to do with his or her free time and will become involved with the interests and activities of friends. However, many recovering people have not had contact for years, if at all, with people who are nonusers. Furthermore, recovering clients are often advised during treatment to discontinue contact with friends who use but, as we will discuss, may not have developed the social and communication skills needed to develop new friendships. If the recovering person does not develop an alternative social support system, the options may be isolation or the resumption of the old relationships that involved AOD use. Certainly, Twelve-Step meetings provide a structure to meet nonusing people. However, it is essential to assist in the development of healthy support systems and to not rely solely on Twelve-Step meetings, particularly with adolescents.

Social and Communication Skills. If a client does not have appropriate social and communication skills, he or she can attend all the Twelve-Step meetings available and still not be able to develop a social network. Many people with AOD problems have not had to rely on social or communication skills to have "friends." Simply having money and alcohol or other drugs probably created a social network. They may have never been in a social situation without being under the influence. Clients might need training in listening skills, asking people questions about themselves, or practice in "small talk." We have found the lack of social skills to be a particular problem with adolescents, who normally feel awkward in new social situations. But many adult clients feel like adolescents too, because their social skill development has been truncated by their AOD use. In addition, assertiveness training and stress and anger management may be needed. Clients may have simply used AOD in situations in which stress was encountered. In the absence of using AOD, these clients may demonstrate passive or aggressive responses to conflict.

Self-Care. Anna needs advice on nutrition and hygiene in a caring and supportive way. If her self-esteem improves, she might pay more attention to this area, but she simply may not know how to eat, dress, or even wash to make herself look better. She may need an adult's help in making the best of what nature has given her. Self-care is a relapse issue because people tend to tease or reject those who are inattentive to their appearance and hygiene. Teasing and rejection can certainly elicit negative emotional states, which we discussed earlier as a significant cause of relapse. While self-care is a sensitive area and may be embarrassing to discuss, the following case illustrates the importance of this area in relapse prevention. We worked with a man who was recovering and trying to find employment. He was quite obese, sloppily dressed, and had halitosis and body odor. Needless to say, he was not having much luck in interviews. We would not have been doing a good job if we had not been honest with him about his self-care issues, especially since his discouragement over his lack of a job was a high-risk situation.

Advice on nutrition, dress, and hygiene are not the only self-care issues with which clients may need assistance. Exercise might have been neglected during the time the clients were using, and they may need guidance with the development of an exercise program. Clients may also need assistance with the discontinuation of other unhealthy addictions such as tobacco use. In addition to the health hazards of tobacco use, smoking has an effect on energy level, and the growing intolerance of smoking can have social ramifications.

Educational and Vocational Guidance. It is common for school and jobs to be affected by AOD problems. Also, these areas can be high-risk situations for many different reasons. As we saw with Anna, her scholastic aptitude and poor academic achievement contributed to making school an unpleasant experience. An unsatisfying or unpleasant job can also elicit negative emotions. Frequently, a client may be reluctant to return to the same school or to the job he or she had before treatment because the people and/or the situation there may be associated with use. With adult clients, community colleges and vocational rehabilitation can be resources for educational and vocational guidance. For school-aged clients, high schools generally have vocational counselors and school psychologists who may be of assistance with low-achieving or low-scholastic-aptitude youngsters.

Financial Planning. Clients may need financial guidance for two reasons. The first is that they may have financial problems because of their AOD use. Second, the client may have little experience with budgeting, since the priority for money was to secure the drug(s) of choice. Financial issues may require attention because they can be a source of stress, negative emotions, and interpersonal conflict. For example, a client goes through treatment and is working on remaining abstinent. For the first time in a long time, the client is taking his responsibilities seriously. Whereas creditors were ignored when the client was using, now he is making an attempt to clear up his debts, but he has no idea how to negotiate with creditors and budget his current income. Creditors are making harassing phone calls, he can't get his car fixed, and he has no money for recreation. Does this sound like a setup for relapse?

Relationships. A few years ago, we worked with a 37-year-old client named Gene who had been sober for 18 months. Gene had been using AOD since he was 14. The longest relationship he had ever been in had lasted 6 months. Due to the length of time he had been using, emotional attachment, commitment, and interdependence were all unfamiliar to Gene. He sought therapy when he slipped after the end of a short relationship with a woman he met in AA. After a couple of dates and sex, he had proposed to the woman and she had dumped him. Clearly, Gene needed some help with many aspects of relationship development and management.

Although Gene may seem to be an extreme case, relationship problems are a cause of many relapses. Recovering adults may have virtually no experience in relationships while drug free. They may not be able to make logical decisions in the face of the intense emotions that romantic relationships can generate. They may not have a basis for making decisions about potential partners. In many ways, working with adult recovering clients can be like counseling an infatuated adolescent who is "in lust" for the first time. The emotional roller coaster of relationships can be high risk for many clients.

Balance. In reading this section, you may have experienced some sense of being overwhelmed with all the areas that may need attention. Clients can have this experience as well. As a mental health professional, you might contribute to a client's frustrations if you list all the lifestyle changes a client must make to prevent relapse. Presenting a recovering client with all of these lifestyle changes at once would probably result in an immediate relapse. Certainly, these areas must be prioritized and then be worked on in increments. As we discussed in the section on covert relapse planning, if a client perceives a great imbalance between "shoulds" and "wants," this perception alone can lead to relapse. It is usually easy for clients and mental health professionals to develop long lists of "shoulds." But it is also important to help clients achieve a balance in their lives so they can have some fun and pleasure. It takes most people a number of years to mess up their lives with AOD. So in spite of a client's desire to repair everything quickly, it will probably take a number of years to clear up their lives as well.

Preventing Slips from Escalating

Earlier in the chapter, we discussed the frequency of slips and relapses. Given the fact that it is more common than not for a client to return to use following treatment, it makes sense to develop strategies to reduce the likelihood of a slip's progressing to a relapse. However, this is a sticky issue in the treatment field. Since most treatment programs are abstinence based, you might feel a hesitancy to introduce such strategies, since doing so may provide an excuse to a client to use again. The alternative to withholding these techniques is not attractive either because, if a client does slip, he or she has no "weapons" to use to prevent the slip from escalating. In fact, without the knowledge that slips are common, the client's feeling of failure might contribute to further use. As we stated earlier, the conflict, guilt, and shame a client may experience after a slip has been termed the *abstinence violation effect* (AVE) by Marlatt (1985), and "The AVE involves perceived loss of control that undermines self-efficacy and increases expectations of continued failure" (Annis, 1990, p. 121). In our own experience, we have found it useful to discuss slips, AVE, and strategies to limit slips in the context of an expectation that the client will remain abstinent. We believe that it is important to attempt to limit a client's guilt and blame if a slip occurs, so that the client will be more likely to discuss the slip with a mental health professional.

Marlatt (1985) describes strategies to limit slips. One such strategy is a relapse contract. "The purpose of this procedure is to establish a working agreement or therapeutic contract to limit the extent of use should a lapse occur" (p. 59). The contract includes an agreement to "time out" if a slip occurs. In other words, the client agrees to leave the situation when this happens. Clients can also carry reminder cards that contain specific steps, including people to call if a slip occurs. The cards also have cognitive and behavioral reminders such as "Remember, you are in control," "This slip is not a catastrophe. You can stop now if you choose," and "Imagine yourself in control." Clients may also carry a decision matrix they have developed with a counselor. The decision matrix contains the immediate and delayed consequences of use and, hopefully, would be reviewed after a slip, reminding the client of the consequences of continuing to use. Clearly, these strategies rely on preplanning that would convince a client to use the techniques immediately following a slip. If the slip continues, the cognitive impairment resulting from use would impact the effectiveness of these strategies.

Recovery

Recovery from addiction can be conceptualized as a continuous, lifelong process. It begins with an intentional action on the part of a person to discontinue the harmful use of AOD. For many people, this intentional act involves entering a treatment program (voluntarily or involuntarily) and continues with a formal aftercare and relapse-prevention program. For many others, the intentional act involves going to a Twelve-Step meeting. For others, it may involve starting a methadone maintenance program. Some people discontinue their harmful AOD use through support from a religious institution. Some people stop on their own with or without various support systems.

In other words, people start the recovery process in many different ways. There is no one right way. For those of us in the helping professions, most of the recovering people we encounter have been through formal treatment programs and/or are involved in Twelve-Step groups. These clients are the most likely to define themselves as being "in recovery." However, that does not mean that other methods of beginning the recovery process are less useful. (Although we have never encountered this situation, we might have some disagreement with the person who has moderated their use of AOD and defines himself or herself as being "in recovery.")

The concept of a continuous, lifelong process may be difficult for you. It may help if we personalize this a bit. As was said in Chapter 1, the first author of this textbook (Gary) is a recovering alcoholic and drug addict. Speaking for myself, I (Gary) see the recovery process as similar to many other therapeutic, religious, or spiritual philosophies. Personal development involves qualities and actions such as introspection, honesty, forgiveness, gratitude, humility, responsibility, and service to others. So, whether I attend Twelve-Step groups, participate in a religious program, practice yoga, read self-help books, or attend a therapy group, I will probably be encouraged to do much the same things. In other words, whether you are in recovery or not, you hear a fairly consistent message from a variety of sources about what qualities and actions are likely to produce contentment and serenity. For me, when I am actively engaged in my personal recovery program, I have that sense of contentment and serenity (most of the time). When I get distracted or lazy, I start to feel dissatisfied, restless, angry, and resentful, and I get urges and cravings. Since I don't want to go back to AOD use, I have to keep moving forward for the rest of my life. It doesn't feel like a burden. It is just my reality. I just accept it and am grateful that some wise people showed me how to have a great life without AOD.

It's a little weird to write about my personal recovery in a textbook (and I didn't include it in the first two editions). The reasons for this personal disclosure are very well expressed by William White, a leader of the recovery advocacy movement:

> The stigma of addiction—the price that even those in long-term recovery can pay in disclosing this aspect of their personal history—leads many recovering people to "pass" as a "normal," scrupulously hiding their recovery journey from members of the larger community. Some recovering people live a socially cloistered existence, interacting almost exclusively with others in recovery. Does such isolation constitute a failure at re-entry, a missed opportunity for reconciliation, and an abdication of the responsibility to teach and serve the community?
>
> The answers to these questions are not easy to answer because recovering people and their styles of recovery and the styles of living are extremely diverse....
>
> If recovering people have not fully returned to their communities, it is as much a cultural failure as a personal one. It is the cultural stigma—the very real price that can be exacted for disclosure of recovery status—that is a primary culprit here. It is time for a new recovery advocacy movement that, by removing the cultural stigma that continues to be attached to addiction/recovery, can open the doors for recovering people to return to their communities. It is time recovering people shared the boon of their recovery, not just with others seeking recovery, but with the whole community. (White, undated, pp. 1–2)

People in recovery are joining together in groups and organizations to advocate for treatment, to combat stigma, and to share the miracle of recovery with those who are still suffering from addiction, their family members, policy makers, and the entire community. Faces and Voices of Recovery is a national recovery movement, and you can find information about recovery organizations in your area. In addition, you can find out about National Alcohol and Drug Addiction Recovery Month (held each September) and the Recovery Community Services Program at the Center for Substance Abuse Treatment Web site. The internet sites are listed in the Internet Resources section.

Summary

- Relapse prevention often involves mental health professionals in addition to AOD treatment providers.
- Relapse prevention strategies common across models or approaches include assessment of high-risk situations, strategies for coping with high-risk situations, lifestyle changes, and strategies for preventing slips from escalating to relapse.
- Mental health professionals must be cautious to avoid overwhelming clients with relapse prevention activities.
- Recovery is a lifelong process that can start in many different ways, including support groups, religious or spiritual experiences, and independent efforts.
- Recovering people who choose to do so can help combat stigma, advocate for treatment services, and encourage those still suffering from AOD addiction to seek treatment by sharing their recovery experiences.

Internet Resources

General Guidelines on Relapse Prevention
www.treatment.org/Taps/Tap11/tap11chap9.html

Cenaps Model
www.tgorski.com/gorski_articles/developing_a_relapse_prevention_plan.htm

Cognitive-Social Learning Model
http://pubs.niaaa.nih.gov/publications/arh23-2/151–160.pdf

Faces and Voices of Recovery
www.facesandvoicesofrecovery.org/main/index.php

Recovery Community Services Program
http://rcsp.samhsa.gov

National Recovery Month
www.recoverymonth.gov

Further Discussion

1. You may have been asked to participate in an abstinence experience for the class you are taking. If not, you have probably tried to cut down or stop doing something before (smoking, drinking, caffeine, sugar, shopping, video games). When you have tried to cut down or stop a behavior you felt was nonproductive, what high-risk situations did you encounter? How did you handle these situations?
2. When you read about all the areas that recovering individuals have to attend to in order to avoid relapse, what occurs to you about the nature and duration of posttreatment services and support that recovering people need?

Relapse Prevention and Recovery

Case Study Activity

Read Addictions Counseling, Case 1: A Life of Substance Abuse: The Story of Josh.

- Devise a relapse prevention plan for Josh.

To access the case for this activity, log on to MyHelpingLab at www.myhelpinglab.com. Select the **Counseling & Psychotherapy** tab to locate the **Counseling Case Archive.**

10

Twelve-Step and Other Types of Support Groups

If we were to specify one characteristic of the AOD field that differentiates it from other areas in mental health, it would be the role of support groups in treatment. One would be hard-pressed to find another area in which the most common method of intervention is through groups that are organized and led by nonprofessionals. The unique contribution of support groups in the recovery of individuals with AOD problems warrants a chapter in this text for several reasons. The first and most obvious reason is that, if you work in the helping professions, you will have clients who have attended, are attending, or have been encouraged to attend some type of support group. Therefore, you need to know about such groups. Second, some inevitable conflict seems to exist between mental health professionals and those who are advocates of support groups, and this conflict requires discussion. Finally, the proliferation of support groups based on the Twelve Steps has led to considerable confusion with regard to the methods and purposes of these groups. It is estimated that there are over 15 million people participating in 500,000 Twelve-Step groups (Hemfelt & Fowler, 1990).

In Chapter 8, we discussed support groups as a component of AOD treatment programs. As we noted, Twelve-Step groups such as Alcoholics Anonymous (AA) and Narcotics Anonymous (NA) are an essential part of many, if not most, treatment programs. In particular, treatment programs that are disease-model-based will almost always require (or strongly recommend) attendance at AA or NA as part of the treatment program and aftercare plan. Family members may be encouraged to attend Al-Anon and teenagers to attend Alateen. There are CODA meetings for codependents and ACOA meetings for adult children of alcoholics. A variety of other Twelve-Step groups have developed for group support for other issues: Emotions Anonymous, Overeaters Anonymous, Sexaholics Anonymous, Spenders Anonymous, and Gamblers Anonymous.

Since Twelve-Step support groups predominate in the support group area and have generated the most confusion and controversy, we want to thoroughly discuss the origin and elements of this type of group. Because Twelve-Step support groups originated with AA, and AA meetings are the most common type of Twelve-Step group, we will spend the most time discussing the history, elements, and effectiveness of AA. We will also discuss the advantages and disadvantages of Twelve-Step groups. Finally, we want you to be aware of other types of support groups that have developed as alternatives to Twelve-Step groups.

The topic of Twelve-Step groups can generate emotions in those people who have been—or are actively—involved in these groups. A person who actively attends a group such as AA and maintains sobriety may be a fervent advocate for Twelve-Step groups. An individual who had an unfavorable reaction to this type of group may be a vocal critic. Many of you may have had some personal experience with Twelve-Step groups and have strong feelings one way or another. Therefore, before discussing AA, we would like you to keep two points in mind. First, Twelve-Step groups were not designed as treatment. As you will see from the discussion below, AA groups were developed to support alcoholics who were trying to remain sober. Many people do maintain abstinence with support from AA meetings and never go to a treatment program. As we discussed in Chapter 8, many people remain abstinent without AA and without formal treatment. There is no conflict between formal treatment and AA. Some people do both, some one or the other, and some neither. The fact that many people remain abstinent with support from AA meetings has resulted in some AA members' preaching a philosophy of "AA is the only way." This point of view is not that of AA and is, in fact, contrary to the AA philosophy.

Second, as most of you know, Twelve-Step meetings contain many references to "God" and "Higher Power." We will discuss spirituality in Twelve-Step groups later in this chapter. However, people tend to have an emotional, as opposed to a logical, reaction to anything that appears to be religious. If you have preconceptions about Twelve-Step groups because of the spiritual nature of these groups, try to put them aside as you read this chapter. We want you, as a mental health professional, to completely understand a very common type of support group and to know when such groups (or others) may be useful for clients. If you have not attended a Twelve-Step meeting before, we strongly encourage you to do so (make sure you go to an open meeting). If Twelve-Step meetings have benefited you personally, remember that each client is an individual, and what has worked for you may not work for someone else. The spiritual nature of Twelve-Step groups presents some interesting and challenging issues for mental health professionals. However, your primary concern should be to objectively assess the needs of your clients and recommend the interventions that best address those needs. To do so, you must put aside any personal preferences for or against Twelve-Step groups and objectively determine whether such groups would benefit your clients.

Alcoholics Anonymous

History of AA

An excellent history of AA is presented by Kurtz (1979). June 10, 1935, is thought of as the birthdate of AA, since that is the date that Bill Wilson, a stockbroker, and Bob Smith, a surgeon, met, and "Dr. Bob" had his last drink.

The sequence of events that brought Bill W. and Dr. Bob, the co-founders of AA, together began with the famous psychiatrist, Carl Jung, and his treatment of Roland H., an alcoholic and an American businessman. Jung had told Roland H. that he had done all that medicine and psychiatry could do. Jung suggested that he needed a spiritual awakening if he were to recover from his alcoholism. Roland H. joined the Oxford Group, a popular nondenominational religious group that sought to recapture the essence of first-century Christianity. Roland H. was able to abstain from alcohol after associating with the Oxford Group, and he convinced a friend, Edwin T., to do the same. Edwin T. was a friend of Bill W. When Bill offered Edwin a drink, Edwin replied, "I don't need it anymore. I've got religion" (Kurtz, 1979, p. 7). Bill W., an agnostic, did not immediately see the implication of Edwin's statement. However, after being admitted to a hospital for detoxification, Bill W. had a spiritual experience. Following his release, he read a book by William James, *The Varieties of Religious Experiences,* which became the foundation of the Twelve Steps. Bill W. was able to stop drinking and his life improved dramatically. During a business trip to Akron, Ohio, Bill W. had a strong desire to drink after a business deal fell through. He wanted to talk to another alcoholic, so he called an Oxford Group minister and was referred to Dr. Bob, an active alcoholic. Dr. Bob reluctantly agreed to talk to Bill W. They ended up talking for hours. Bill W. had made this contact because he needed to talk to another alcoholic to avoid drinking himself. Through this contact, Bill W. avoided relapsing and Dr. Bob stopped drinking. This was the start of the AA method of alcoholics talking to other alcoholics in order to remain sober. Bill W. had no plan or desire to change Dr. Bob. He only wanted to maintain his own sobriety.

What AA Is About

The AA preamble, which is usually read at meetings, is a good description of the purpose of AA:

> Alcoholics Anonymous is a fellowship of men and women who share their experience, strength, and hope with each other that they may solve their common problem and help others to recover from alcoholism.
>
> The only requirement for membership is a desire to stop drinking. There are no dues or fees for AA membership; we are self-supporting through our own contributions. AA is not allied with any sect, denomination, politics, organization, or institution; does not wish to engage in any controversy, neither endorses nor proposes any causes. Our primary purpose is to stay sober and help other alcoholics to achieve sobriety. (*AA Grapevine,* 1985, p. 1)

AA meetings may be closed (for AA members only) or open. Closed meetings are usually "step" meetings in which members can choose which of the twelve steps to focus on. Open meetings may be "speaker" meetings in which people voluntarily tell their stories (their histories of drinking and recovery) or discussion meetings where a topic is suggested by the meeting chair or a participant. The topics relate to some aspect of recovery or a barrier to recovery, such as "forgiveness," "anger," "humility," or "serenity."

As the AA preamble indicates, the only requirement for membership is a *desire* to stop drinking. Those who relapse are not banned but are offered support in their struggle for sobriety. The bible for AA is the book *Alcoholics Anonymous* (2001), commonly referred to as "The Big Book." Anonymity, a central concept in AA, protects the identities of members and ensures that no one person or persons become spokespeople for AA. To further the ideal of equality among members, meetings chairs rotate and there are no elected directors. Special committees and service boards are created as needed from AA members.

At AA meetings, you will hear many slogans that are amusing, catchy, or clever and are easily remembered. For example, the famous "One day at a time" is meant to reinforce the concept that sobriety is a day-to-day (sometimes minute-to-minute) process to keep the alcoholic focused on the present as opposed to the future. Other examples include "Keep it simple" (sobriety is a simple process: don't drink), "Let go and let God," and "Get off the pity pot."

When a person speaks at an AA meeting, he or she usually starts by saying, "Hi. My name is (first name of speaker) and I'm an alcoholic." The rest of the participants respond by saying, "Hi, ________." The statement of the speaker acknowledges his or her alcoholism, and the response of the participants indicates acceptance and support. At some meetings, a person may be called upon to speak. One can always say, "Hi, my name is ________, and I pass."

In the introduction to this book, we told you that we require our students to attend an AA or an NA meeting, and the students generally are impressed with the friendliness and encouragement they encounter at the meetings. However, some of the students are concerned with another aspect of AA meetings, which is the "no cross talk" rule. When someone speaks at an AA meeting, subsequent speakers do not address previous speakers. For example, one of our students was very concerned about a woman at a meeting who was emotionally distraught and disoriented in her speech. The next speaker did not react to the woman at all. As we explained, AA meetings are for support in maintaining sobriety. They are not designed to provide therapy. If cross talk were allowed, there would be a tendency for nonprofessionals to provide therapy. Also, as Bill W. discovered, he was able to avoid drinking simply by talking about himself to another alcoholic. Input and feedback from Dr. Bob was not necessary and, therefore, is not necessary at meetings.

As a helping professional, you might wonder about the advisability of eliminating feedback from members, since this can be a valuable method of growth. Although feedback does not occur in meetings, members are encouraged to seek a "sponsor." McCrady and Irvine (1989) describe sponsors as follows:

> A very important part of the AA experience is sponsorship. While anyone who wants to stop drinking can join AA, choosing a sponsor as soon as possible is encouraged as a means of maintaining sobriety. The process of sponsorship involves two alcoholics, one of whom has made more progress in recovery and who shares that experience in an ongoing manner with another who is trying to achieve or maintain sobriety. Some groups offer a temporary sponsor program, which matches a newcomer with someone until they are able to meet enough members to make their own choice. The important factor is that a newcomer not be left to flounder without introduction to the program and to each new aspect of recovery as it is experienced for the first time. (p. 157)

The Twelve Steps and the Twelve Traditions

> A.A.'s Twelve Steps are a group of principles, spiritual in their nature, which, if practiced as a way of life, can expel the obsession to drink and enable the sufferer to become happily and usefully whole.

> A.A.'s Twelve Traditions apply to the life of the Fellowship itself. They outline the means by which A.A. maintains its unity and relates itself to the world about it, the way it lives and grows. (*Alcoholics Anonymous,* 1981, p. 15)

The core of the AA program and the basis of similar groups developed on the AA model are the Twelve Steps. As a statement in the Big Book indicates, "Rarely have we seen a person fail who has thoroughly followed our path" (p. 58). It is truly astounding that these twelve statements, written more than a half-century ago, have generated so great a number of adherents, groups, and critics. We will present the Twelve Steps and comment briefly on them. If desired, you can find a thorough discussion in *Twelve Steps and Twelve Traditions* by Alcoholics Anonymous World Services. Professional analysis of the twelve steps can be found in articles such as Peteet (1993).

The Twelve Steps[1]

1. We admitted we were powerless over alcohol—that our lives had become unmanageable.
2. Came to believe that a Power greater than ourselves could restore us to sanity.
3. Made a decision to turn our will and our lives over to the care of God *as we understood Him.*
4. Made a searching and fearless moral inventory of ourselves.
5. Admitted to God, to ourselves, and to another human being the exact nature of our wrongs.
6. Were entirely ready to have God remove all these defects of character.
7. Humbly asked Him to remove our shortcomings.
8. Made a list of all persons we had harmed, and became willing to make amends to them all.
9. Made direct amends to such people wherever possible, except when to do so would injure them or others.
10. Continued to take personal inventory and when we were wrong promptly admitted it.
11. Sought through prayer and meditation to improve our conscious contact with God *as we understood Him,* praying only for knowledge of His will for us and the power to carry that out.
12. Having had a spiritual awakening as the result of these steps, we tried to carry this message to alcoholics, and to practice these principles in all our affairs.

Let us point out a couple of things about the Twelve Steps. First, alcohol is mentioned only in step 1. Steps 2 through 11 are the ways to improve a person's life. You can see how these might be applied to many issues other than alcohol. The focus is on surrender, forgiveness,

[1]The Twelve Steps and Twelve Traditions are reprinted with permission of Alcoholics Anonymous World Services, Inc. ("AAWS"). Permission to reprint the Twelve Steps and Twelve Traditions does not mean that AAWS has reviewed or approved the contents of this publication, nor that AA necessarily agrees with the views expressed herein. AA is a program of recovery from alcoholism *only*—use of the Twelve Steps and Twelve Traditions in connection with programs and activities that are patterned after AA, but which address other problems, or in any other non-AA context, does not imply otherwise.

humility, limitations, and service to others. The influence of the Oxford Group on Bill W. also is clear from these aspects of the Twelve Steps. As Miller and Kurtz (1994) stated in a fascinating article contrasting AA and models of addiction, "Practice of the 12 Steps brings a recovery characterized by growth in character traits such as honesty, humility and patience" (p. 161). In this light, the Twelve Steps can be conceptualized as a way of living.

The Twelve Traditions[2]

The Twelve Traditions govern the operation of AA. They are as follows:

1. Our common welfare should come first; personal recovery depends upon AA unity.
2. For our group purpose there is but one ultimate authority—a loving God as He may express himself in our group conscience. Our leaders are but trusted servants; they do not govern.
3. The only requirement for AA membership is a desire to stop drinking.
4. Each group should be autonomous except in matters affecting other groups or AA as a whole.
5. Each group has but one primary purpose—to carry its message to the alcoholic who still suffers.
6. An AA group ought never endorse, finance, or lend the AA name to any related facility or outside enterprise, lest problems of money, property, and prestige divert us from our primary purpose.
7. Every AA group ought to be fully self-supporting, declining outside contributions.
8. Alcoholics Anonymous should remain forever nonprofessional, but our service centers may employ special workers.
9. AA, as such, ought never be organized; but we may create service boards or committees directly responsible to those they serve.
10. Alcoholics Anonymous has no opinion on outside issues; hence the AA name ought never be drawn into public controversy.
11. Our public relations policy is based on attraction rather than promotion; we need always maintain personal anonymity at the level of press, radio, and films.
12. Anonymity is the spiritual foundation of all our Traditions, ever reminding us to place principles before personalities.

The emphasis of the Twelve Traditions is on maintaining anonymity and avoiding controversy, thereby reducing the likelihood that AA will be diverted from its mission. You will not find AA endorsing or criticizing any model of addiction or approach to treatment. There is no AA lobbyist to help pass legislation. AA has no "spokesperson" and does not solicit or accept contributions. No matter what your opinion is of AA, you have to be impressed with the singular focus of AA and its ability to maintain this focus for over 70 years.

[2]Ibid.

Elements of AA Meetings

Although there may be some variability in what you will hear and see at AA meetings, most open meetings have common elements. By describing these, we are not trying to provide a substitute for actual attendance at meetings. However, when you first go to an AA meeting, it is similar to attending a religious service of an unfamiliar denomination. You are not quite sure when to do what, and you don't want to call attention to yourself. Therefore, by describing these events, we hope you will feel prepared to attend a meeting.

Generally, people socialize for a short time before the meeting starts. Coffee and other beverages are usually available. If the meeting is not advertised as nonsmoking, be prepared for cigarette smoke. People who regularly attend the meeting may introduce themselves to those who are obviously new and offer to sit with a newcomer. Remember, last names are not used.

The meeting chair or secretary will introduce the meeting by saying something like, "Welcome to the Gemini meeting of Alcoholics Anonymous. May we have a moment of silence for those alcoholics who are still suffering." The Serenity Prayer will then be recited, "God grant me the serenity to accept the things I cannot change, the courage to change the things I can, and the wisdom to know the difference." The AA preamble is read and newcomers (those with fewer than 30 days of sobriety) and out-of-towners are given an opportunity to introduce themselves. Members participate in reading part of Chapter 3 of the Big Book, titled "More about Alcoholism" or Chapter 5, "How It Works," the Twelve Steps, and the Twelve Traditions. The chair then speaks, usually telling his or her story. If the meeting is a discussion meeting, the chair either suggests a topic of discussion, asks for suggestions, or has a member read something from AA literature. The reading selection then becomes the basis for the meeting discussion. If it is a speakers' meeting, the chair asks for volunteers or calls on people to speak. Remember, if you are called upon to speak and do not wish to, you can always say "Pass." It is nice if you say, "Hi, my name is ___ and I pass," but you don't have to. Also, don't be confused by the title "discussion meeting." It really isn't an exchange—rather, a series of speakers talking about the meaning of the topic of discussion in their sobriety. As we stated previously, cross talk is not permitted. After the discussion or speakers, AA-related announcements are made and a basket for contributions is passed around. The chair may sign attendance records for those who are court ordered to attend. "Chips" may be given to those in attendance who have achieved sobriety milestones (i.e., 30, 60, and 90 days; 6 months; 9 months) and those who have "birthdays" (anniversary of sobriety). "A Vision for You" from the Big Book is read, and participants stand in a circle, join hands, and recite the Lord's Prayer. They then say "Keep coming back. It works if you work it, so work it 'cause you're worth it," and the meeting is over. Participants usually socialize for a brief period following the meeting.

Research on AA

Two areas of research regarding AA exist that have relevance for the mental health professional. The first has to do with the characteristics of clients who are most likely to affiliate with AA. Emrick (1987) summarized the results of ten studies published since 1976 that examined this issue. According to Emrick,

> More often than not, psychosocial, alcoholism, and treatment variables were found to be either consistently unrelated to membership or to be unrelated in some samples but positively or negatively associated in others. A few variables were consistently related in one direction or another (e.g., dual addiction, use of external supports to stop drinking, and warmth of childhood environment) but firm conclusions about these variables must await more data.... Until specific affiliation characteristics are identified, prudence suggests viewing all alcoholic patients in conventional alcoholism treatment as *possible* members of AA, while at the same time recognizing that many alcohol-dependent patients recover from their alcohol problems without ever joining the organization. (p. 418, italics in original)

The second area of research has to do with the effectiveness of AA. A professional work group was formed by the Substance Abuse and Mental Health Services Administration and the Department of Veterans Affairs (2003) to examine self-help organizations. This work group reviewed the literature on the effectiveness of AA and other Twelve-Step groups and concluded the following:

> (1) Longitudinal studies associate 12-step self-help group involvement with reduced substance use and improved psychosocial functioning, (2) Twelve step self-help groups significantly reduce health care utilization and costs, (3) Self-help groups are best viewed as a form of continuing care rather than as a substitute for acute treatment services, (4) Randomized trials with coerced populations suggest that Alcoholic [sic] Anonymous (AA) combined with professional treatment is superior to AA alone.

AA and Spirituality

The effectiveness of AA has been related to elements in the group process, ego function development, empathic understanding, disintegration of pathologic narcissism, and so forth (Nace, 1992). However, as Miller and Kurtz (1994) point out, "It would be helpful for treatment and research professionals to…understand the essential nature of AA as a spiritual program of living" (p. 165). As Nace (1992) states, "Spirituality is rarely part of the lexicon of the mental health professional…" (p. 493). Therefore, the well-intentioned efforts to conceptualize the effects of AA in terms of psychological theories or processes and to research AA through traditional scientific methods may be misguided. As we mentioned at the beginning of the chapter, the broad utilization of a spiritual support program is unique in the helping professions. The mental health professional may need to be flexible in order to gain some understanding of the impact of AA on many recovering alcoholics.

Nace (1992) discusses the spiritual themes of AA: release, gratitude, humility, and tolerance. Release is clearly experienced when the alcoholic no longer feels the compulsion to drink. Gratitude results from the release from compulsion. The alcoholic's powerlessness over alcohol elicits humility, since it is a humbling experience to acknowledge one's inability to handle this drug. The theme of tolerance of differences among people and of one's own shortcomings helps the recovering individual to achieve serenity. If you now reread the Twelve Steps and Twelve Traditions, you can see the themes of release, gratitude, humility, and tolerance in these basic precepts of AA.

Misconceptions Regarding AA

In the minds of many professionals, AA is associated with a particular model of addiction and specific methods of dealing with alcoholics. For example, AA is often associated with the disease concept of addiction (see Chapter 3) and with the need to confront the denial system of alcoholics (see Chapter 8). Miller and Kurtz (1994) compare different models of addiction with AA through AA literature and the writings of Bill W. They conclude that:

> AA writings do not assert that: (1) there is only one form of alcoholism or alcohol problems; (2) moderate drinking is impossible for everyone with alcohol problems; (3) alcoholics should be labeled, confronted aggressively or coerced into treatment; (4) alcoholics are riddled with denial and defense mechanisms; (5) alcoholism is purely a physical disorder; (6) alcoholism is hereditary; (7) there is only one way to recover; or (8) alcoholics are not responsible for their condition or actions. These assertions involve outside economic, political, social, moral, legal, and disciplinary issues on which AA takes no stand. (p. 165)

However, we should note that many AA members may not be familiar with the original writings of Bill W. and therefore may perpetuate some or all of these misconceptions.

Other Twelve-Step Groups

As we mentioned earlier, many other groups have adapted the Twelve Steps to areas other than alcohol. Narcotics Anonymous (NA) was founded in 1953. AA and NA are not officially affiliated. However, NA uses the same Twelve Steps as AA, replacing "alcohol" and "alcoholism" with "drugs" and "addiction." From 1983 to 1988, there has been a 600% increase in the number of NA groups (Coleman, 1989). This increase is understandable considering the tremendous rise in illicit drug use in this country since the formation of NA. Since so many people present polydrug problems, the choice of whether to attend AA or NA has become less clear. It is probably best to let clients with polydrug problems (if one of the drugs is alcohol) attend both AA and NA meetings and decide which is most comfortable. There are also Cocaine Anonymous groups and "Double Trouble," which is a Twelve-Step program for those with co-occurring mental disorders.

When AA was founded, its members were men. The wives of the members would get together and talk about their problems. Lois W., the wife of Bill W., founded Al-Anon Family Groups in 1954. Royce (1989) describes Al-Anon:

> Al-Anon is a recovery program for people who suffer because someone close to them drinks too much. At Al-Anon meetings members learn...that their own recovery is possible whether or not the drinker seeks help or even recognizes that a drinking problem exists. (p. 280)

The Twelve Steps have been adapted for Al-Anon with step 1 being an admission that the person is powerless to control the drinking of significant others. Essentially, Al-Anon is support for family members of alcoholics. Al-Anon does not advocate that family members abandon the alcoholic or coerce the alcoholic into treatment. Rather, it is a spiritual program that encourages detachment and self-improvement. At Al-Anon meetings, you will find family members living with recovering alcoholics, those living with active alcoholics, and those who have separated from alcoholic family members. Alateen is a component of Al-Anon that was started by a teenager in 1957 and is designed for young people who are living with an alcoholic family member. There is a Big Book for Alateen (Al-Anon Family Group, 1973). In our area, Alateen meetings are held at schools, providing these young people with a convenient way to attend and experience the support of others with similar issues. At both Al-Anon and Alateen meetings you will find participants who are living with or involved with people who have addictions to drugs other than alcohol. We encourage you to attend some Al-Anon meetings so you will have first-hand experience with this type of support group.

As we mentioned previously, there are numerous other Twelve-Step groups that focus on a variety of issues and where the twelve steps are adapted for the particular focus of the group. Twelve-Step groups exist for codependency, adult children of alcoholics, eating disorders, sexual behavior, gambling, spending, and other issues.

Advantages and Disadvantages of Twelve-Step Groups

There are some obvious advantages to Twelve-Step groups. First of all, they are free. In the mental health field, this is certainly unique. Second, meetings such as AA are available at a variety of times and places (of course, this depends on the size of the area and the type of meeting). An AA member who is on either a business or pleasure trip can usually find a meeting. Third, at meetings, Twelve-Step participants find a group of people who share similar concerns and problems and who can provide group support. This type of support is helpful to many people and would be difficult for them to achieve on their own. Additionally, a social network is often developed through Twelve-Step meetings. For the recovering person, this is a useful way to make nonusing friends. Fourth, the structure and ritual of Twelve-Step meetings may be comforting and helpful to people whose lives have been chaotic and unpredictable. Finally, the spiritual nature of Twelve-Step groups, with its themes of release, gratitude, humility, and tolerance, can be a productive focus for self-improvement and general contentment with life. For one who has experienced excessive guilt, blame, and embarrassment, the spiritual themes can refocus the person on more positive emotions.

The disadvantages of Twelve-Step meetings are usually focused on the differentiation (or lack thereof) between spirituality and religion and the concept of "powerlessness." While Twelve-Step meetings are supposed to be nondenominational, the recital of the Lord's Prayer implies a Christian orientation. Those who are members of other religious groups may be alienated by this prayer. Atheists can certainly have difficulty with the notion of "Higher Power." Even though steps 3 and 11 refer to "God as we understood Him," the notion of Higher Power in Twelve-Step meetings is clearly that of the Judeo-Christian God. However, remember that AA was formed in 1935 when diversity was hardly a predominant concept. In the context of the times, it is a tribute to Bill W.'s openness that "God as we understood Him" was included. Regardless, the rituals of Twelve-Step meetings and the references to God and a Higher Power can be problematic for clients who have negative attitudes and/or experiences with organized religion or those who are not Christian.

As Miller and Kurtz (1994) pointed out, AA does not promulgate the notion that alcoholics are not responsible for their condition or actions. Although the first of the Twelve Steps contains the word "powerlessness" and the third step involves turning "our will and our lives over to the care of God," steps 4 through 8 involve taking responsibility for past wrongs and shortcomings. However, critics of Twelve-Step groups and some participants have interpreted steps 1 and 3 to mean that the Twelve-Step philosophy supports the notion that addicted individuals are not responsible for their actions. Clearly, such a view would be counterproductive for clients.

Additional disadvantages of Twelve-Step groups arise from the individuals involved in such groups rather than from the ideas themselves. As Nace (1992) states, "AA is predominantly a white, middle-class organization consisting of middle-aged married males" (p. 493). This might alienate women, ethnically diverse individuals, and young people. Groups for different demographic groups have developed in response.

Some participants in Twelve-Step groups feel so strongly about the benefits of the program that they denigrate other interventions, such as therapy or psychotropic medications. Again, there is nothing in the AA philosophy that is opposed to other forms of intervention or that preaches that AA is the only way to recovery. However, just as some adherents of religious views misinterpret the doctrines based on their personal characteristics and experiences, some Twelve-Step participants appear dogmatic.

Finally, critics of Twelve-Step groups claim that many people simply switch addictions from alcohol and other drugs to going to meetings. Certainly, attendance at Twelve-Step meetings can interfere with social, family, and occupational functioning, and, if a person continued with constant participation in spite of these consequences, this would constitute problematic behavior. Personally, we would rather see someone constantly attending meetings than committing armed robbery to get money for drugs. However, we have no doubt that compulsive Twelve-Step meeting attendance could be a barrier to mature functioning.

To close this discussion of Twelve-Step groups, we want to reemphasize our personal view that Twelve-Step meetings should not be confused with treatment. Twelve-Step groups, with the support they offer and the emphasis on spiritual development, can be an important part of a comprehensive treatment program. Some people maintain sobriety (or whatever behavior change they are focused on) without any other form of intervention or support. Others maintain these changes without ever going to a Twelve-Step meeting. As we said in Chapter 6, do a thorough assessment on every client, and (if you are involved in treatment) design treatment strategies designed to meet the client's needs. You will find that many clients can benefit from this type of free, available support group consisting of people with similar problems. Whether the group is a Twelve-Step group or one of the other groups we will now discuss depends on the needs, background, and experiences of the client. The recommendation for a support group should not depend on your own preconceptions or stereotypes.

Other Types of Support Groups

Rational Recovery

In 1988, Jack Trimpey began Rational Recovery (RR) as an alternative to AA. RR is based on the Rational Emotive Therapy of Albert Ellis. The basis of the RR program is contained in Trimpey's book, *The Small Book: A Revolutionary Alternative for Overcoming Alcohol and Drug Dependence* (Trimpey, 1992). In Trimpey's words:

> In Rational Recovery we have a comprehensive system of self-help wherein the "alcoholic" can quickly come to terms with the central issues of addiction and recovery. As in rational-emotive therapy, RR identifies several specific irrational ideas and beliefs that perpetuate the addictive behavior of alcohol-dependent people, and then RR provides the means to change one's own emotions and behavior. (p. 101)

Trimpey takes 15 "central beliefs about alcoholism" (p. 102) that he calls *irrational* and reframes them according to a rational idea. For example, the irrational belief of the alcoholic's powerlessness over alcoholic cravings and the consequent lack of responsibility for what is ingested is reframed as "I have considerable voluntary control over my extremities and facial muscles" (p. 102). Other examples involve the irrational belief that one drink will lead to "my downfall" (p. 104). The rational response is:

> as time goes by drinking appears increasingly stupid because of the obvious selfish advantages of sobriety, but, if I ever stupidly relapsed by drinking, it wouldn't be awful because I would very likely recover again—selfishly, guiltlessly, and probably very quickly. (p. 104)

Finally, the idea of turning one's life over to a Higher Power is reframed as

> dependency is my original problem, and it is better to start now to take the risks of thinking and acting independently. I cannot really "be" an "alcoholic," but just a person who has believed some of the central ideas of alcoholism. (p. 104)

RR meetings are free and are led by a coordinator who maintains contact with a mental health professional familiar with the RR program. The meetings last about 1½ hours. Cognitive strategies are used to achieve and maintain abstinence, which is the goal of RR. The compulsive and irrational thoughts that lead to drinking are conceptualized as the "Beast," and participants develop and use a "Sobriety Spreadsheet" to combat the Beast. The Sobriety Spreadsheet contains the irrational beliefs and the associated rational thoughts. Members are encouraged to use the Sobriety Spreadsheet in and out of meetings and to read *The Small Book.* In contrast to AA, participants openly exchange their views on the issues discussed. In addition, there are no sponsors, and members are discouraged from attending RR meetings for more than one year, in order to prevent dependence on meetings. Obviously, spirituality is not a focus of RR.

Galanter, Egelko, and Edwards (1993) surveyed 433 RR members to assess the program's effectiveness. In the largely well-educated and employed sample, 73% of those participants who had attended meetings for 3 months or more were abstinent for at least 30 days. Fifty-eight percent of those attending for 6 or more months had at least 6 months of abstinence.

Many Roads, One Journey

In her 1992 book, *Many Roads, One Journey: Moving beyond the 12 Steps,* Charlotte Davis Kasl argues that issues such as child abuse, sexism, racism, poverty, and homophobia are in opposition to Twelve-Step concepts such as conformity, humility, personal failings, and powerlessness. For example, an adult woman who was sexually molested as a child or has been in an abusive relationship and has a substance abuse problem may find the first of the Twelve Steps unacceptable. To admit powerlessness over anything may rekindle the feelings of powerlessness in the abusive situations.

To begin meetings, Kasl suggests an introductory reading of *Many Roads, One Journey.* We have excerpted some of the content to illustrate the philosophy of this approach:

> Our purpose in coming together is to support and encourage each other in our healing from addiction, dependency, or internalized oppression. The only requirement for membership is a desire to maintain sobriety as we each define it.... We do not impose our beliefs on others or expect others to tell us the way.... Healing is a balance between gentle self-acceptance and a firm commitment to sobriety. We overcome addiction and internalized oppression because we want to honor and enjoy the life we have been given. Healing from addiction and dependency is not about moral worth. We are all sacred children of Creation this moment.... We believe that through bonding with others, speaking genuinely from our hearts, forgiving ourselves and others, finding purpose, helping create social change, and accepting the imperfections of life, we will find a sense of fulfillment that we have sought to fill through our addictive and dependent behavior. (pp. 356–357)

Kasl has developed 16 steps for "discovery and empowerment" (p. 337). Some examples of these steps are

1. We affirm we have the power to take charge of our lives and stop being dependent on substances or other people for our self-esteem and security.
2. We come to believe that God/the Goddess/Universe/Great Spirit/Higher power awakens the healing wisdom within us when we open ourselves to that power.
3. We make a decision to become our authentic Selves and trust in the healing power of truth.
4. We examine our beliefs, addictions, and dependent behavior in the context of living in a hierarchal, patriarchal culture (p. 338).

The spiritual nature of the steps is clear, although acceptance of alternatives to God is more clearly specified than in the Twelve Steps. An emphasis is also placed on power*ful*ness, choice, and the relationship of behavior to culture.

Kasl also provides guidelines for *Many Roads, One Journey* groups. Rather than suggesting a rigid structure and rituals, the groups are more flexible. Kasl does suggest that the purpose of the group be defined, a moderator chosen, and time constraints adhered to. She also suggests a six-week commitment for new members and two-week notice when a member is leaving. Readings of poems, sayings, or other literature are recommended. However, that is the extent of structure suggested, since, as the name *Many Roads, One Journey* implies and as Kasl writes,

> Let's weave together, creating a form and a process that builds a foundation for positive change. Instead of one linear model, we can have many circles with many ways, all working toward growth, empowerment, and an ability to appreciate life. (p. 371)

Women for Sobriety

Jean Kirkpatrick found AA meetings to be rigid, dogmatic, and chauvinistic and felt that the meetings increased her desire to drink. She found hypocrisy in AA members' resistance to taking blood pressure medication or using vitamins to control the effects of alcohol withdrawal, and in the heavy use of caffeine and tobacco at meetings. After 28 years of alcoholism during which Kirkpatrick experienced hospitalization, violence, and depression, she founded Women for Sobriety in 1976. According to Kirkpatrick (1990):

> The Women For Sobriety Program... is a product of women's new awareness of self developed through the feminist movement.... Through this self-help Program, women take charge of their alcoholism.... For women to take full charge of self is a revolutionary concept. For too long, women's health has been governed by persons other than themselves.
>
> The Program challenges women to learn their strengths and values, to become aware that they are competent women, that sobriety depends upon the discovery and maintenance of strong feelings of self-value and self-worth which, ultimately, will lead to strong self-esteem. (Preface)

She believes that women begin to drink because of frustration, loneliness, emotional deprivation, and harassment, while men drink for power. In her opinion, treatment programs have not been responsive to the needs of women, and separate self-help groups are necessary to affirm women's autonomy from men.

Kirkpatrick's program emphasizes a holistic approach to recovery. She emphasizes good nutrition, meditation, and cessation of smoking. Consistent with this philosophy, coffee, sugar, and smoking are not permitted at Women for Sobriety meetings.

Kirkpatrick's 13 "statements" reflect her view that self-esteem is the "magic building block" (Kirkpatrick, 1986, p. 131) of recovery. Some examples of these statements are

1. I have a drinking problem that once had me.
2. Negative emotions destroy only myself.
3. Happiness is a habit I will develop.

12. I am a competent woman and have much to give to others. (p. 251)

In commenting on Kirkpatrick's program, Kasl (1992) writes:

> Kirkpatrick understands the need for women to have groups of their own that stress choices, the positive power of the mind, imaging, broadening one's perspective, the ability to love, and physical healing. Her approach to self-empowerment through monitoring one's thoughts is well documented in psychological research on cognitive therapy with depression. (p. 169)

Secular Organization for Sobriety/Save Our Selves (SOS)

James Christopher had his last drink on April 24, 1978. He attended AA meetings although "[I] gritted my teeth and said the Lord's prayer; after all, these AA people were *sober*" (Christopher, 1988, p. 96, italics in original). In 1985, Christopher published an article expressing his frustration with "AA's religiosity and my belief that the needs of free thinkers are not being met there" (Christopher, 1988, p. 95). In 1986, the first SOS meeting was held, and the program now has more than 20,000 members (Kasl, 1992).

While Christopher is a firm adherent to the disease concept of addiction, he rejects the notion that spirituality is a necessary component for recovery:

> My personal thoughts, feelings, and experiences within Alcoholics Anonymous were suppressed on a number of occasions, and AA was not particularly fulfilling or supportive to me as an alcoholic free thinker. I had to "go it alone" for many years. But through it all, I kept my sobriety through prioritizing it on a day-to-day basis. There is no higher power keeping me sober. I make this choice and reacknowledge it daily. No one can do it for me. (p. 95)

As indicated in Christopher's statement, the central component of the SOS program is the "sobriety priority":

> As a sober alcoholic I must daily recommit, reaffirm, reaccept, resurrender, and reacknowledge my disease and its antidote: the sobriety priority. My priority frees me up for another day of life with all its pain, sorrow, joy, fear, sickness, achievements, failures, and goals, rather than trapping me in my previous subhuman, coma-like addiction to alcohol. Sobriety is assured *only* by prioritizing it daily on a day-at-a-time basis. This keeps my addiction to alcohol under "house arrest" day to day, hopefully lifelong.
>
> I have the right to fail in any other area of my life. My sobriety priority is the one exception. (p. 51, italics in original)

Christopher suggests five secular guidelines for sobriety. These include an acknowledgement of alcoholism; choosing to remain sober one day at a time, reaching out to those who have been directly or indirectly affected by the person's alcoholism; working toward self-acceptance, change, and growth; and taking responsibility for providing meaning in life. SOS meetings are 1½ hours long with a different person acting as moderator each week. Often soft, classical music is played and a short selection from secular literature related to alcoholism is read. The group may choose a topic to discuss or have an open discussion. Meetings are closed with a short, humanistic reading. Christopher does suggest an opening for an SOS meeting, which stresses sobriety, personal growth, secularism, and humanism. He also emphasizes that his structure and suggestions may be modified as the group wishes.

Moderation Management

This behavioral change program and support group network was developed in 1994 to assist problem drinkers with modifying their use of alcohol. It was not designed for those who have been diagnosed with an Alcohol Dependence Disorder (see Chapter 6) but rather for those people who are concerned about their drinking and want to cut back or quit drinking before serious problems develop. The Moderation Management program is based on the premise that alcohol abuse is a learned behavior rather than a disease. Therefore, people can learn to use alcohol in a moderate manner.

Moderate Management advocates a nine-step program that includes attendance at (free) meetings and abstinence from alcohol for 30 days. The rest of the steps are behavioral in nature and involve tracking drinking behavior, setting drinking goals, and making positive lifestyle changes. The program neither encourages nor discourages abstinence as a goal but does acknowledge that moderation may not be a workable goal for all problem drinkers.

Summary

- Support groups organized around the Twelve Steps of Alcoholics Anonymous have grown to include groups for other drug addicts, family members, and various non-drug problems.
- Twelve-Step support groups involve a spiritual approach to recovery and a commitment to the anonymity of members.
- Alternatives to Twelve-Step groups are available for those who are uncomfortable with the Twelve Steps or a spiritual approach to recovery.
- Mental health professionals should attempt to match clients with the type of support group that matches their needs and values.

Internet Resources

Alcoholics Anonymous
www.alcoholics-anonymous.org

Narcotics Anonymous
www.na.org

Al-Anon and Alateen
www.al-anon.alateen.org

Double Trouble
www.doubletroubleinrecovery.org

Support groups other than Twelve-Step
www.womenforsobriety.org
www.secularsobriety.org
www.rational.org
www.moderation.org

Further Discussion

1. Should coerced clients (i.e., people mandated to attend treatment by courts, employers, or schools) be required to attend Twelve-Step meetings? Why or why not?
2. Do you think that recovering people can become too dependent on support group meetings? Why or why not?

Twelve-Step and Other Types of Support Groups

Video Lab

The following module contains videos related to the topics in this chapter:

- Module 1, Integrating Therapy with Twelve Steps

Case Study Activity

Read Substance Abuse, Case 2: An Emergency Room Patient Who Is a Chronic Alcoholic.

- The man in this case relapsed after 12 years of attending AA. Given the description of this man in the case, do you think that the philosophy and structure of AA contributed to his relapse? Why or why not? Do you think this man could have benefited from an alternative type of support group? If so, which one and why?
- From this case, what conclusions can you reach about the role of support groups in sustaining ongoing recovery?

To access the videos and case study, log on to MyHelpingLab at www.myhelpinglab.com. Select the **Counseling & Psychotherapy** tab to locate the **Counseling Video Lab > MyHelpingLab Videos by Course > Addictions/Substance Abuse Counseling** modules or the **Counseling Case Archive.**

11

Children and Families

In Chapter 1, we discussed a conceptualization of addiction in which the alcoholic or drug addict is in an intimate and monogamous relationship with the drug of choice. Clearly, if the primary relationship is with alcohol or other drugs, other relationships will be adversely impacted, and the effect on the family is particularly dramatic. Investigators in the field have identified a myriad of problems that occur in children in substance-abusing families as well as in the family system itself. Since the early 1980s, studies have consistently shown that children from these families suffer in a variety of ways (McIntosh, McKeganey, & MacDonald, 2003; Usher, Jackson, & O'Brien, 2005). Other studies describe the impact of AOD use in families in terms of communication and parenting style (Aquilino & Supple, 2001; Barrett & Turner, 2006; Copello, Velleman, & Templeton, 2005; Stephenson, Quick, Atkinson, & Tschida, 2005; Rangarajan and Kelly, 2006; Wills, Resko, Ainette, & Mendoza, 2004).

This is not meant to be a comprehensive review of the vast literature related to children and families in which there is an alcohol or other drug problem. Rather, these examples illustrate the obvious fact that, if a family member has an alcohol or other drug problem, the family will be affected. Individuals living in such families did not need researchers to discover this, as evidenced by the development of Al-Anon in 1954 and Alateen in 1975 (see Chapter 10). Furthermore, comprehensive treatment programs include family education and family therapy as a component of treatment (see Chapter 8). They acknowledged that alcoholism and drug addiction affect each member of the family and that successful recovery necessitates the involvement of the entire family.

As we discussed in Chapter 3, different models of addiction and, predictably, differing conceptualizations occur in families in relation to AOD problems. Some may argue that the individual with an alcohol or other drug problem is reflecting dysfunction in the family. Others see the alcohol or other drug problem as the primary cause of family dysfunction. As with other controversies in this field, both conceptualizations are probably true. In some families, dysfunction may be acted out through the abuse of AOD. For example, an adolescent female may use drugs to cope with the emotional trauma of sexual abuse. A fairly functional family may become tumultuous as a result of the father's progressive alcoholism. Regardless of the "chicken or the egg" question, we find that the understanding of families and AOD abuse is aided through a family-systems conceptualization.

You should be aware that even the definition of *family* varies across cultures. "Family" is a traditional white Anglo-Saxon Protestant definition based on an intact nuclear family, where lineage is of importance when tracing one's ancestry. According to the same author, the family, in the traditional African American population, is focused on a wide informal network of kin and community that goes beyond blood ties to include close, longtime friends. The traditional Asian American family includes the entire family group and all ancestors and all their descendants. Differences in the life cycle of the family also reflect cultural and ethnic differences. For example, McGoldrick, Giordano, and Garcia-Preto (2005) state that the traditional Euro-American family begins with a psychological being, and growth and development is measured by the human capacity for differentiation. In the traditional Asian American family, there is a social being (as opposed to a psychological being), and growth and development are measured by the capacity for empathy and connection.

A great deal of the research into alcoholic families has focused upon the Euro-American population. However, as we pointed out in Chapter 4, culturally and ethnically diverse families are at risk for AOD abuse. While there is a growing body of literature focusing on diverse family systems, there continues to be a dearth of information focusing on the effects of AOD on these family systems and structures. Notwithstanding, interesting and provocative ideas addressing this issue are appearing in the emerging professional literature. For example, Krestan (2000) writes about the issue of addiction as it relates to power and powerlessness in a multicultural society. In her conceptualizations, she maintains the importance of the sociocultural impact of power and powerlessness as they are experienced by various racioethnic groups. From this perspective, family theorists and therapists can readily see how racioethnic family structures might be affected. For instance, African American males often learn to "play the game" to get ahead in a Euro-American dominated society. When at home, they may and often do behave very differently. While the strategy of playing the game is successful for many, some individuals may experience distress at having such a marked split between home and work. This split tends to create an additional family structure for some racioethnic families. This additional structure and the concomitant stressors can increase risk factors for AOD abuse among this population.

Children's Exposure to Alcohol and Other Drugs

There are essentially two types of AOD exposure for children: prenatal and interpersonal. Both types of exposure can have dramatic effects on children. Since the 1970s, there has been an increasing concern regarding the passage of drugs through the human placenta and through the mother's breast milk. The resulting research has indicated that there are effects on the fetus when women use tobacco, alcohol, and other drugs during pregnancy. Some of these problems may remain even if the mother discontinues her use or if the child is raised in a nonusing environment (Jones, 2006). Jones asserts that the issue of drug use during pregnancy is now considered a critical health concern.

Interpersonal exposure from parental AOD use can affect a child's social and psychological development through adulthood. However, the effects on children will vary. This is due to individual and environmental differences including age of exposure, progression of use, characteristics of the child and of the AOD abuser, family dynamics, and external events. Copello, Velleman, and Templeton (2005) assert that there is also growing evidence that not all children will suffer adversely either in childhood or adulthood. Some children will develop resilience and do not develop significant problems. Therefore, it would be unwise to assume that all children who experience AOD abuse in their families of origin will exhibit similar behaviors.

Prenatal Exposure to Alcohol and Other Drugs

Similar to many issues in this field, prenatal exposure to drugs generates a great deal of publicity, and the topic of maternal use of AOD has become emotionally charged and widely publicized. With such attention focused on the topic, you can imagine that prevalence rates are difficult to determine. Who wants to admit that their drug use has impacted a helpless child? Thus, estimated rates vary. For example, Jones (2006) and data from the Substance Abuse and Mental Health Services Administration (2005) both reflect that among pregnant women, almost 10% report using alcohol, 4% report using at least one illicit drug, and 18% report smoking tobacco. Other data from the National Institute on Drug Abuse (NIDA, 2006) estimate that nearly 20% of infants are exposed to alcohol, 17% to marijuana, 5% to cocaine or heroin, and 40% to tobacco. Further, the NIDA data shows that about one-half of the pregnancies are unplanned and this population of pregnant women report more binge drinking. Half of pregnant women reported drinking in the three months prior to recognizing the pregnancy. This means that these children could have been exposed to alcohol for at least six weeks.

Lester, Andreozzi, and Appiah (2004) maintain that the effects of tobacco smoking on prenatal children can include low birthweight, intrauterine growth restriction, and sudden infant death syndrome (SIDS). Alcohol use can compromise physical growth and development as well as inducing morphological and psychological problems. It is alarming that research indicates that effects of alcohol and/or tobacco use may be greater than the effects of illicit drugs because the former are reportedly used at greater frequency than illicit drugs. In an earlier study, Sameroff and Chandler (1975) found that the accumulative effects of numerous risk factors appear to have a greater impact on child development than any risk factor taken alone. This finding is concurrent with a more recent study by Bauer, Shankaran, Bada, Lester, Wright, Krause-Steinrauf et al. (2002). These researchers maintain that prenatal exposure to AOD use and abuse is "best characterized as one of many risk factors that place the mother and child at risk for adverse outcome" (p. 127). Other risk factors include lack of prenatal care, high rates of exposure to violence, the co-occurrence of psychiatric problems, poor nutrition, and poverty. Nonetheless, the most widely researched drug relative to pregnancy is alcohol.

Fetal Alcohol Syndrome, Alcohol-Related Birth Defects, and Alcohol-Related Neurodevelopmental Disorder. The term "Fetal Alcohol Syndrome" (FAS) was first used in 1973 to depict the effects of pregnant women's alcohol abuse on the fetus. May and Gossage (2001, p. 166) estimate a prevalence rate for fetal alcohol syndrome (FAS) between 0.05% and 2.0% per 1,000 births. When combining FAS and alcohol-related birth defects (ARBD), the estimate is likely to be at least 10 per 1,000. This ratio translates into 1% of all births. However, this rate is spuriously high for any one population to accept.

According to Streissguth et al. (1991):

> Fetal alcohol syndrome (FAS) now is recognized as the leading known cause of mental retardation in the United States, surpassing Down's syndrome and spina bifida. Over 2,000 scientific reports have now appeared, confirming that alcohol is a teratogenic drug capable of producing lifelong disabilities after intrauterine exposure. Fetal alcohol syndrome does not include all individuals affected by alcohol in utero, but rather it represents the severe end of the continuum of disabilities caused by maternal alcohol use during pregnancy. (p. 1961)

Impact of Fetal Exposure to Alcohol and Other Drugs. We do not want to minimize the problems that can result from prenatal exposure to AOD. However, we also do not want you to conclude that all children prenatally exposed will have serious or permanent learning, behavioral, social, and emotional problems. Those children diagnosed as FAS have been the focus of attention for some problems, and an association has then been made with maternal alcohol use. However, many children who have been prenatally exposed to alcohol have had no identified problems. About 30% to 40% of children prenatally exposed to illegal drugs demonstrate some type of developmental delay (Jackson, 1993), which means 60% to 70% do not. We provide this caveat so that you will not jump to conclusions about a child when you learn that the mother used alcohol or other drugs during pregnancy.

Mental retardation is common, although it is not inevitable. Other associated problems that impact the academic progress and behavior of these children in school include learning disabilities, attention deficit disorder with or without hyperactivity, and motor coordination difficulty.

Implications for Intervention. Doctor (1994) has developed a training curriculum for educators who work with FAS. She emphasizes that educators should acknowledge the learning and behavioral differences of some of these children and should accommodate for these differences. For example, she suggests that a daily routine be established that minimizes transitions. However, when transitions are to occur, students should be prepared in advance. Teaching strategies should include all sensory modalities whenever possible. When an abstract concept is difficult for a student, it should be made more concrete. Sequencing, repetition, reinforcement, and structure are all emphasized. Again, the instructional and management strategies are not different from those used in working with children with a variety of learning and behavioral problems.

Although the problems demonstrated by children prenatally exposed may be serious, these problems do not seem different from those of other children not exposed. Common sense should prevail here. Prenatally exposed children did not develop suddenly after media attention was focused on them. They have always existed. Either numbers may be increasing, or our awareness may be increasing. As with many developmental, cognitive, and behavioral disorders, prevention is the most effective cure. Abstinence during pregnancy will ensure that no prenatal exposure occurs. If there is prenatal exposure, early intervention including medical care and a supportive and nurturing environment will reduce the frequency of problems. Even if a child's problems are not identified until reaching school age, appropriate educational intervention may be helpful.

Interpersonal Exposure to Alcohol and Other Drug Abuse

Fraser, McAbee, and the Committee on Medical Liability (2004) maintain that there are between 11 and 17.5 million children in the United States younger than 18 currently living with a parent with alcoholism. The number of children living in homes where other drugs are abused is relatively unknown. There is little disagreement that many children do experience negative effects as a result of being exposed to the interpersonal and environmental influences of AOD abuse in their homes (Coppello et al., 2005). Studies demonstrate that children who grow up in homes where AOD are abused can view themselves as worthless, can feel unimportant as a result of being consistently rejected, and may feel responsible for their parents' substance abuse (Towers, 1989). Around the holidays, especially, elementary school-aged children of alcoholics may become moody and "withdrawn, irritable, and certainly not ready or able to participate with the rest of the class and the teacher in holiday-related lessons and activities" (Towers, 1989, p. 20). Another result may be seen in the young child's expressed defiance toward activities of these kinds. It is thought that reasons for this behavior center on the child's anxiety regarding a family get-together or celebration in which drugs will likely be abused.

In a review of the literature, Kroll (2004) used content analysis to investigate the impact of AOD misuse on children. Findings revealed that children's lives were affected in six overarching areas: denial, distortion and secrecy; attachment—separation and loss; family functioning—conflict and breakdown, violence, abuse, and living with fear; role reversal, role confusion and child as caretaker; and what children would say that they needed.

Apart from the idiosyncratic behaviors demonstrated during or around holidays, general feelings of alienation can lead children into social isolation and reinforce the child's beliefs that they are socially incompetent. Bennett (1988), in her study of school-aged children of alcoholics, suggests that a lowering of a child's self-concept results from exposure to AOD abuse. A child who comes to school having slept little the night before because of anxiety or because of parental fighting or abuse cannot really be expected to perform well. As a result, the child's self-concept can be diminished by repeated failures at learning. A vicious cycle can be born. The result can be that the child feels hopeless, fearful, and lonely. In some cases, the effects can be fateful. For example, Whitfield (1980) estimates that 80% of all adolescent suicides are children of alcoholics. Although this estimate may be spuriously high, his estimate does underscore that parental drug abuse may be a significant covariant in adolescent suicide attempts.

More often than not and depending on the child's age when first encountering parental alcohol or other drug abuse, the impact of interpersonal and environmental exposure will be reflected in the school classroom and can affect students' hygiene, concentration, achievement, attitudes toward learning, attitudes toward teachers and others in authority, attitudes toward classmates, attendance, completion of homework assignments, and participation in extracurricular activities and sports (Lawson & Lawson, 1998; Towers, 1989).

Implications for Intervention. Counselors and social workers who work in the schools will be faced not only with student–clients who are children of alcoholics but will, as well, be consulting with teachers who attempt to teach these children. Helping teachers become familiar with the symptoms is important. Teachers need to know basic facts about AOD abuse. With some empathic guidance from school counselors and social workers, teachers can emphasize the need to make their classrooms safe havens where students can learn to overcome their difficulties and experience success. As in dealing with children affected by in utero exposure to AOD, school counselors can help teachers emphasize the need for structure in their classrooms where children can learn or reinforce appropriate social skills. Helping teachers see the need for students' healthy expression of feelings, including anger and frustration, and helping teachers see the need for activities that aim at bonding, autonomy, and problem solving can aid in helping students develop protective factors against drug abuse and can help with students' self-esteem and successes at learning in school.

In a study focusing on peer-led support groups for children of alcoholics (COA), DiCicco, Davis, Hogan, MacLean, and Orenstein (1984) reported that school children may not want to be identified as a "child of an alcoholic" per se. So identifying children as such for after-school support groups may diminish the number of participants. In both DiCicco et al. (1984) studies, the authors imply that when such groups avoid the label COA, the number of participants may increase. Thus, in schools, peer-led support groups that do not identify themselves as COA support groups may be more efficacious than if the label is used. Instead, a group might be called Concerned Others Group.

Family Exposure to Alcohol and Other Drugs

So far, we have only discussed the effects of AOD misuse on children. Substance misuse can also negatively impact other family members and disrupt a range of family dynamics and processes including family rules and rituals, routines, communication structures, social life, finances, homeostasis, and family roles (Copello et al., 2005).

Homeostasis

Regardless of ethnicity, families are dynamic systems and are influenced by changes that occur both within and outside of the family context. The larger social, political, and economic forces exert their influence in the family from the outside, while internal changes such as illness, aging, entering and leaving the family, changes occurring in the workplace, changing geographical locations, and changes in stress levels affect families from within.

Jackson (1957) used the term *family homeostasis* to describe the natural tendency of families to behave in such a manner as to maintain a sense of balance, structure, and stability in the face of change. Significant to the concept of homeostasis is the notion that, as one family member experiences change in his or her life, the entire family will be affected and will adjust in some fashion. Family members can adjust overtly and covertly in an effort to maintain this balance and will exert much effort during times when the balance is threatened. This natural resistance can be both a blessing and a bane: by facing some changes with resistance, families can avoid losing their structures and becoming chaotic systems. However, there will inevitably be times when change requires the family to adjust.

It is during these times that the family, to varying degrees, will need to reorganize its roles, rules, boundaries, and values to create a new balance that fits. If families are too resistant to change, they can become rigid and unable to adjust adequately, and family dysfunction can follow. For example, Ewing and Fox (1968) describe the alcoholic marriage as a homeostatic mechanism that is "established to resist change over long periods of time. The behavior of each spouse is rigidly controlled by the other. As a result, an effort by one person to alter typical role behavior threatens the family equilibrium and provokes new efforts by the spouse to maintain status quo" (p. 87). Alcohol is seen as playing a key role in attempting to maintain the status quo in alcoholic families.

Wegscheider (1981) believes that, in an alcoholic family, members attempt to maintain balance by compulsively repressing their feelings while developing survival behaviors, as well as emotional walls, to ward off the pain associated with the family member's drinking. If drinking is removed from the family system, the family can be thrown into chaos. For example, an alcoholic father who becomes sober may attempt to reexert his influence as head of the household, thus throwing the marriage out of the balance to which it had become accustomed. The mother is no longer needed as a buffer between the children and their father, so she fades into the background as the children begin to address their father directly. The oldest son is no longer the surrogate father and begins acting out his frustration. The relationship between the mother, who has relied upon this son for support, and her son becomes strained as the father cannot hide his jealousy over this relationship. Unless the family can adjust adequately, drinking may be initiated again to reestablish balance.

Roles

Family Roles. We pointed out in Chapter 4 the variety of roles assumed by culturally and ethnically diverse families. Roles are an important part of Euro-American families as well. Role is often defined by the individual's behaviors in performing the rights and obligations associated with a certain position, and usually involves a set of complementary expectations concerning one's own actions as well as the actions of others with whom one is involved (Shertzer & Stone, 1980). Irrespective of the presence of alcohol, one of the basic principles of family homeostasis is predictable family roles. Through these roles, family members can act out the overt and covert family rules in an effort to maintain homeostasis within the family system. According to Satir (1964), because the marital relationship is the "axis around which all other family relationships are formed" (p. 1), it is the interaction of roles in the marital relationship that influences the character of the family homeostasis.

Roles can also be further divided into affective and instrumental areas. Instrumental roles are those aimed at addressing the day-to-day human needs. The latter, affective roles, have particular significance in alcoholic or other drug-abusing families. Often in these families, there are individuals who will experience and express certain emotions for the family. For example, the alcoholic who becomes angry and sullen when drunk may be carrying the anger for other family members who have difficulty in expressing this emotion. So, when the alcoholic gets angry, things may finally be said (inappropriately or not) to other family members that might not be discussed otherwise because the sober family members do not overtly express their own hostility. In this example, the anger role is carried by the alcoholic, and the emotions of sadness and helplessness may be carried and expressed by other nonalcoholic family members.

Childhood Roles. Children in families carry two essential roles. One role is that of child. The other is the role of family member. There are roles within roles and the child assumes a variety of other roles. For example, many believe that birth order in the Euro-American family affects the child's role in the family and see the oldest child as taking on a dominant role with the second child taking on a more rebellious role. Youngest children are often used to having things done for them and take on a more passive role. While birth order alone does not determine an individual's perception of relationships, it does have an influence.

These two role structures remain fairly constant across families of varying ethnic and racial origins. However, the manner in which these roles are played out in the family as well as in the larger social contexts is different. For instance, many Latino families who immigrate to the United States may leave some of their children behind temporarily for practical and financial reasons. In these situations, the mother may tend naturally to overcompensate by showering abundant affection upon those with whom she does have contact. As a result, Latino children may appear infantilized or overprotected to Euro-American teachers and counselors when, in fact, the family's transitions and subsequent reorganization may greatly intensify these behaviors (Carter & McGoldrick, 1999). In more traditional families, children may also have bonded with their mothers, and the centrality of their position allows them to wield great power when it is used against a disengaged, authoritarian father (McGoldrick, Giordano, & Garcia-Preto, 2005). For African American youth, there may be significant family difficulties brought on by the compounding effects of poverty, racism, and the general vulnerabilities of adolescence. For those families in poverty, they will vary in structure, coping styles, and levels of resilience (McGoldrick et al., 2005). Some families may support themselves by exchanging resources within their family support systems. Ho (1992) and other researchers maintain that in many Asian American families, the roles of family members are highly interdependent. The family structure is arranged so that conflicts in the family are minimized in order not to disrupt family peace and harmony. Even when adult children marry, allegiance to their parents—especially among the adult sons—is to remain paramount. Male offspring have especially revered roles in traditional Asian American families. Native American perceptions of family are universal in that the entire universe is thought of as a family in which every member serves a useful and necessary function. The Native American child may live in several different households at various times (Iron Eye Dudley, 1992). In these traditional Native families, grandparents, aunts, uncles, and community members are all responsible for the raising of the children. One can readily see how the roles of the child in Native American families are both stable and quite varied (Atkinson, Morten, & Sue, 1998).

For alcoholic or other drug-abusing families, there is a dearth of data on childhood roles among culturally and ethnically diverse populations. Much of the research on childhood roles is the result of clinical impressions of the Euro-American population and, for the most part, the research has been reported in the popular literature. For example, Black (1981) described the roles adopted by children of alcoholic homes as based upon their perceptions of what they need to do to survive and bring stability to their lives. It was Wegscheider (1981) who described the dysfunctional family roles of "hero," "scapegoat," "lost child," "mascot," and "enabler." The hero or heroine child is often a compulsive high achiever who, through accomplishments, defocuses attention from the alcoholism in the family system. Music, sports, and academics are frequent arenas in which the heroes or heroines act out their roles, often at the expense of their own needs. Because they can often excel in one or more undertakings, they create the impression that their family must be quite well adjusted. In our own practice, we have seen many adolescents who are valedictorians, captains of sports teams, cheerleaders, and/or student government officers who come from homes where alcohol is abused. The scapegoat child is seen as acting out the family problem by demonstrating defiance and irresponsibility. The unconscious or conscious agenda for these children is to create a need for overt parental attention as they attempt to defocus from the problem of alcohol. Lost children are believed to be shy, withdrawn, and require very little attention so that the family does not have to worry about them (Wegscheider, 1981). These children often cope through avoidance that, unfortunately, leaves them isolated from the joys and richness of life, feeling unloved and unworthy of love (Kitchens, 1991; Wegscheider, 1981). The family mascot is the funny and often mischievous child who defuses the tension inherent in alcoholic families. In the classroom, this child may act out as the class clown. The enabler is the person who attempts to protect the alcoholic or drug addict from experiencing the natural and logical consequences of his or her behavior. These roles are seen as survival roles in alcoholic families and are deemed as dysfunctional or maladaptive in that they do not allow children to experience the normal, full range of emotions and behaviors. Wegscheider (1981) believes that the roles assumed by children in homes where alcohol and other drugs are present tend to be fixed or rigid. The result is family dysfunction.

Jenkins, Fisher, and Harrison (1993) studied the rigidity of roles adopted by Euro-American children from alcoholic and nonalcoholic families. The results indicated that the roles were not rigid. That is, over 75% of those coming from alcoholic homes and 60% of those having other problems (death, divorce, or abuse) indicated that they took on more than one role. In that only 30% of the other group (i.e., those reporting no family dysfunction) adopted one or more roles, Jenkins et al. concluded that "some type of dysfunctional or disrupted family history was the best indicator of whether a subject would indicate adopting a dysfunctional role or roles as children" (p. 316). Therefore, these same authors suggest that children from alcoholic families and those from families with other dysfunctions appear to be more similar than different. Interestingly, the most commonly reported role combination was that of hero and the lost child. The authors suggest that the child assuming the hero role may attempt to defocus the problem through high achievement, which would be consistent with Wegscheider's (1981) observations. The adaptation to the lost child role was seen as the child's attempting to avoid having to disclose the pain and family dysfunction when in social relationships or when there was parental conflict (Jenkins et al., 1993). Thus, there is some evidence about the validity of the adoption of childhood roles, but the notion of role rigidity is questionable.

Family Rules

All culturally and ethnically diverse families as well as Euro-American families have overt and covert contracts between their members that operate as rules governing family interactions. Barnard (1981) believes that these rules govern (1) what, when, and how family members can communicate their experiences about what they see, hear, feel, and think; (2) who has permission to speak to whom about what; (3) the extent and manner in which a family member can be different; (4) the manner in which sexuality can be expressed; (5) what it means to be a male or female; and (6) how family members acquire self-worth and how much self-worth a member can experience. In all likelihood, culturally and ethnically diverse families are governed by these same rules. The only differences between these families would revolve around what happens if the rules are broken. For example, a Euro-American family may punish the child who has talked back to his or her parents. An Asian American family might use shame to correct aberrant behavior.

Case Example

Black (1981) stated three imperatives or rules that govern alcoholic families: Don't talk; Don't trust; Don't feel. In families where alcohol and other drugs are abused, these rules form the basis for family interactions and for the alliances between individual family members and society at large. An example (in which names have been changed) can help you understand.

Tony, a very successful businessman, was married to Mary, and they had three children: Loretta, Mark, and Donnie, whose ages were 16, 15, and 9. Tony was an alcoholic, but nobody in the family believed his drinking to be problematic. That was rule 1: Do not believe that your father has a drinking problem. Every night when he arrived home after twelve hours on the job, the children would come downstairs and greet their father, then allow him to change clothes while their mother would mix their father's usual drink: his favorite scotch with crushed ice. She would have a glass of red wine. The children would leave their mother and father alone to discuss the day. That was rule 2: Do not disturb your father's ritual. Even when the children had something exciting to talk about that had occurred during the day, they were not to disrupt the ritual until it was time for dinner. Gathered around the table, with Tony nursing his second or third drink or even a beer, the children would then "report" the day to their father. The children were not allowed to leave the table until everyone, including their Dad, was finished. Sometimes, if Tony was drinking a lot, the dinner could last an entire evening. Frustrations about wasting time at dinner were not to be discussed, but, when out of exasperation, they were aired, Tony would most often respond by becoming argumentative, oppressive, threatening, and upon occasion physically abusive. This was rule 3: Your father is the head of the household and you must do exactly as he wants. When Tony lost his temper at the table, Mary would jump in to mediate between Tony and the children. Usually, the fighting occurred between Tony and Mark, the oldest son, so Mary usually wound up arbitrating between these two. While they did not like the situation, Loretta and Donnie did appreciate Mark's intervening on their behalf because it allowed dinner to be over. The shouting and threatening behavior created so much chaos that Loretta and Donnie could slip away while Mary, Tony, and Mark were fighting it out. This was rule 4: Mark is the scapegoat. Two or three times during the week, dinners would proceed in a fashion similar to that just described. Hence, rule 5: Even when things are unpleasant and could be changed, do not change the family. The weekends were just an extension of the weekdays, except on the weekends Tony would play tennis in the mornings rather than spend time with the family and would begin drinking at lunchtime. Often, he would come home drunk or noticeably high from alcohol. If he had had a good game of tennis, his mood would be pleasant; if he played poorly, he was easily agitated. The children knew enough to be gone all day Saturday to avoid whatever might occur, while Mary would do household chores until Tony came home. Because Tony and Mary would usually go out on Saturday night, the children would most often find something to do until they were sure that their dad and mom were out of the house before coming home to eat the meal their mother had prepared for them. On Saturday nights, whoever was home would sit watching television with the lights out, prepared to run to their rooms and feigning sleep at the first sign of their parents' arrival home.

It was Loretta who first asked her mother about her dad's drinking. This occurred after the school counselor had done a guidance unit on alcohol and other drugs during Loretta's fifth-period social studies class. Her mother readily confessed to having similar concerns but told Loretta that her dad worked very hard and everyone should be understanding because he was under a great deal of stress. She told Loretta not to worry and to keep this information between the two of them. Rule 6: Do not talk about your feelings about your dad's drinking problem to anyone.

As Tony's drinking progressed over the next two years, Mark became the focus of his dad's displaced hostility. Mark felt as if he could do nothing right in his father's eyes, and, during his later teen years, began to express his own hostility toward his dad. However, when Mark confronted his dad about how unreasonable he was when he drank, his father would respond by yelling, pointing his finger in his son's face, and would eventually become more angry than his son. Mark learned to back down, swallowing his pride, his feelings, and his lowered sense of self-respect. Gradually, his grades began to drop. In spite of his being a very talented golfer, Mark lost his eligibility to participate in athletics due to his grades. Having lost his friends who were busy participating in after-school sports, Mark fell into a crowd who used alcohol and other drugs, and he began drinking alcohol on the weekends and eventually began using marijuana and cocaine. Loretta continued her attempts to soothe her father's nerves by doing whatever he asked but emotionally removed herself from the family and focused her attentions on her boyfriend and her grades. She confided in Mark that she couldn't wait to get out of the house. Donnie was his mother's favorite, and Mary did everything she could to protect Donnie from her husband. Donnie was able to escape the direct wrath of his father by keeping quiet, getting straight *A*s, and devoting himself to helping his mother.

What was most confusing to Loretta, Mark, and to some extent to Donnie was how their father could be seen as so successful at work, yet be so different at home. When their father was away on business trips and the discussion about his drinking would come up during dinner, Mary would consistently respond by saying that the children's father loved them very much so they need not worry. When pressed by Loretta and Mark, their mother would usually start crying, saying that she did not know what to do, yet she would balk at suggestions to see a counselor and/or confront their dad. Loretta and Mark would comfort their mother by telling her that she was a good mother and that she did not need to cry because her children loved her. Rule 7: Believe that your mother is helpless and that you need to take care of her.

This example shows how rules are developed and maintained by family members. Nobody was supposed to confront the alcohol problem because "there was no alcohol problem." That their father loved the children was supposed to be enough. There was to be no anger. If that rule were broken, Tony would become more angry than anyone, thereby overpowering the family's anger and sending it back into a repressed state. Eventually the children, especially Loretta and Mark, learned to control their emotions—especially anger, hurt, and fear. The rigidity of the rule, "don't talk, don't trust, don't feel," led to Loretta's desire to leave the family and to never confront her father, so that her father never knew how she really felt. Mark responded to his feelings of helplessness and frustration by internalizing his shame and coming to believe that he was to blame for his father's drinking since he was usually the one who fought with his dad. As a result of his internalized shame, he began using drugs and acted out his helplessness by becoming irresponsible, thus neglecting his own desires and hopes in life. Donnie eventually became the family "hero" by getting exceptional grades and becoming involved in student government. He posed "no threat and no problem" to the family. Mary worked herself to the bone as a mediator between her children and their father, all the while attempting to become the apple of her husband's eye. Her whole life was her family, and the centrality of her position provided her with a sense of meaning in an otherwise unhappy marital situation. Because these family rules were rigid, the family system functioned to maintain itself as best it could, but there were grave consequences. In spite of the severity of the consequences, the family was unable to adjust until Tony's alcohol problem was addressed and the rules changed.

Underlying Family Themes

Reilly (1992) identifies two underlying themes that serve to fuel the interactive patterns of families experiencing drug abuse: impaired mourning and homeostasis collusion. Impaired mourning refers to the family's preoccupation with "issues of attachment and separation, loss and restoration, and death and rebirth" (p. 109). Other research suggests that oftentimes in these families there has been parental death, divorce, or abandonment (Kaufman & Kaufman, 1992) that can leave the family with an inability to transform itself to meet new challenges (Minuchin, 1974, 1992). Because of the strong sense of loss, either through abandonment, death, divorce, rejection, or neglect, concomitant with an inability to transform the experience, children never fully grieve the loss, and the family can become stuck. In the example, Tony's drinking problem precluded his ability to develop a strong attachment to his family. The ensuing abandonment left his children and his wife grieving for a relationship with him. The rules were such that any attempt to work through the grieving process would have been met with severe opposition from Tony. So the children and their mother were left to deal with the problem either indirectly or surreptitiously. As a result, the family was not able to fully grieve the loss of a functional and healthy relationship with their father.

Remember how, in Chapter 4, we discussed the issue of Native American mourning and its impact on the risk factors for AOD abuse among this population? Knowing that impaired mourning seems to be characteristic of alcoholic families in general, you can readily see how the issue of impaired mourning may have an additive effect with regard to the Native American family. That is, mourning for their lost culture has been cited as increasing the risk among Native Americans for substance abuse (Young, 1991), and impaired mourning is seen as fueling the dysfunctional interactive patterns among families once AOD are abused in the family. It would seem that mourning, in some form, can be seen as both partly causing alcoholism and helping to maintain the resulting dysfunctional family patterns in the Native American population.

When the whole family becomes stuck or unable to transform itself due to its following of the "don't talk, don't trust, don't feel" rule, as it did in this case example, family collusion can occur (Haley, 1973; Noone & Reddig, 1976). Paul (1967) points out that families who have not grieved the losses in the early cycles of their system develop a family style that reflects a lack of empathy, a lack of respect for individuality, and a tenacious and unconscious attempt to hold back the passage of time, with the concomitant need to keep individual family members in a dependent position.

Paul's (1967) study demonstrates how family collusion results from a break in the grieving process and how it reinforces the interactive patterns characteristic of families with AOD abuse. In the example, Mark turned to using AOD as a means to identify with his father. Eventually, Mark's problem became the focus of attention for the family, thereby diminishing the centrality of Tony's drinking. Mark gained much power in the family because he became a rallying point around which the family could address issues of his drug abuse. Without that rallying point, Mary might have chosen to leave the marriage. She stayed in order to help the family deal with Mark's problems. Also, the family colluded and remained stuck because they covertly reinforced Mark's drug problems. Loretta would occasionally buy marijuana for her brother and often bought him beer until he became of legal age. When she periodically found drug paraphernalia in her son's room, Mary chose to not confront Mark. And Donnie remained distant from his older brother, although he loved him deeply. While these were all conscious decisions, the family members unconsciously knew that, if Mark's problems were addressed and corrected, Tony's alcohol problems would once again become the focal point of concern as well as reminding each of their shame, grief, and helplessness. To avoid the pain, the family unconsciously colluded to keep Mark the scapegoat and the family member with the problem.

Clearly, the character and extent of family collusion in culturally and ethnically diverse families will be influenced by family values, by values regarding AOD, and by the degree of acculturation among family members. For example, we pointed out in Chapter 4 how Gilbert (1978) had noted the problems occurring in Latino/Hispanic families and Shon and Ja (1982) noted corresponding difficulties occurring in Asian American families where one well-adjusted partner marries a spouse who is less acculturated. The resulting stresses and feelings of guilt, self-doubt, and betrayal were seen as disrupting family harmony. Alcoholism or other drug abuse in that family would only add to the enormous problems inherent in acculturation. The collusion transpiring in Latino/Hispanic, African American, and Asian American families could include extended family members who likely live nearby and who probably share in childrearing, discipline, and problem solving.

Family collusion might become even more complex when you consider family or cultural values. Recall that Stevens (1973) found that drinking alcohol is an accepted way of dealing with the stresses of acculturation for Latino/Hispanic males, and that the value of *machismo* tends to strengthen that notion. In this example, should the alcoholic family member be a less acculturated male, then family collusion might include the male members of the immediate and extended family who share a common value of machismo. The resulting collusion might serve to sharpen the differences between male and female family members as well as exacerbating the generic difficulties found in the process of acculturation.

In general, the reciprocal nature of any family system suggests that, as the children impact the parents, new dynamics take place between the parents that in turn affect how the parents relate to their children (Erekson & Perkins, 1989; Liu & Kaplan, 2001). It is common in the literature on AOD abuse to find reports of how the alcoholic has impacted the spouse and/or his or her children. Erekson and Perkins (1989) and Wilson (1982) write about the effects of alcoholism upon the family and suggest that family dysfunction may be both a cause and a result of alcoholism.

Family Subsystems and Boundaries

All families, regardless of cultural or ethnicity diversity, are made up of subsystems and boundaries. For the Euro-American family, there are three essential family subsystems: the marital, the parental, and the sibling subsystems. In Native American, Asian American, African American, and Latino/Hispanic families, the family subsystems would include, to varying degrees, extended family members or other significant individuals. For example, the participation of godparents in the childrearing practices of many Latino/Hispanic families and its parallel value, known as "child-keeping," seen in many African American families, might reflect an extended parental subsystem.

The primary subsystem is the marital or couple subsystem made up of the wife and husband. This subsystem is closed in that there are certain duties and primary functions performed only by the married partners (e.g., earning money, managing the home). With the birth of a child, the marital subsystem extends to that of a parental subsystem. Interactions continue between the marital partners, which are aimed at the marriage itself (e.g., having a romantic dinner after the child is asleep) or are carried out between the spouses with an aim toward their parenting (e.g., juggling schedules around to cover child care). A third main subsystem is the sibling subsystem. The number of children, along with their ages, sexes, and interests, will suggest the number of potential sibling subsystems. In addition, African American and Latino/Hispanic families may have sibling subsystems that include cousins.

Rules or boundaries help define these various subsystems. Boundaries are like fences surrounding one's home: They define one's property and regulate the nature and type of interactions between neighbors. In essence, boundaries result from cultural and family values and define who can talk to whom, when one can talk, and what one can talk about. Regardless of cultural or ethnic background, both subsystems and boundaries need to be flexible enough to allow for adjustments to changes brought on either within the family or as a result of outside influences. However, in families where AOD are abused, boundaries are often violated (Kelley, French, Bountress, Keefe, Schroeder, Steer, Fals-Stewart, & Gumienny, 2007).

Our example of Tony and Mary reflected a disengaged family in which Tony was rather removed from his spouse and his children. The children were not allowed to talk with their father about his drinking problem and so began to disengage and live their lives emotionally distant from other family members. With the onset of Mark's drug use, the disengaged nature of the family made it very difficult to regroup in order to address the underlying issue that was Tony's alcohol abuse. Nor was the family able to find ways to deal effectively with Mark's drug use. To avoid interacting with her father, Loretta spent all of her available time with her boyfriend. Donnie, despite his strong feelings for his older brother, remained rather aloof from him because he didn't understand or like what his brother was doing. Mary, the mother, was emotionally removed from her husband after years of emotional neglect by him. She tolerated her husband's drinking patterns so that she could avoid conflict and more hurt and pain in their relationship.

The issue of disengagement is clearly culturally biased. In traditional Asian American families, the father is expected to be disengaged. Therefore, the construct of disengagement would not always be an appropriate measure of family unity. An African American male who works two jobs and is not home much in order to help get his family out of poverty may be labeled as disengaged when, in fact, his disengagement is a healthy adaptation to poverty. Likewise, "el amor de madre" (motherly love), a value highly regarded in Latino/Hispanic families, could be described as enmeshment, but this enmeshment is central to Latino/Hispanic culture and is not seen as dysfunctional behavior.

Where there is AOD abuse, all families, regardless of cultural or ethnic background, act as "the fulcrum, the pivot point, the mediator, and the interpreter between its members and their culture" (Reilly, 1992, p. 105). The family thus is seen as having a significant influence upon the socialization of its members. As a social lens, the family screens, filters out, or magnifies social influences from the outside. These influences may be antisocial.

For instance, in studying African Americans, Boyd and Homes (2002) found that the use of cocaine by fathers, brothers, partners, and uncles was highly correlated with the crack cocaine use by females in the family. Of the women family members who used crack cocaine, the data indicate that the aunt's use is associated with the other females' crack use.

Reilly maintains that the disturbed Euro-American family system needs a symptom bearer, and this would be the member who is susceptible to drug abuse. In our example, the symptom bearer was Mark, the eldest son. Reilly (1992) also believes that the family will consciously or unconsciously push this individual into antisocial, drug-abusing values as was reflected in our case example.

The Marital or Couple Subsystem. Jacob, Ritchey, Cvitkovic, and Blane (1981) found that the marital relationship where alcoholism exists reflects communication that is hostile, critical, and disapproving. As alcoholism progresses, the communication between spouses tends to increase in hostility, thereby suggesting that there is a growing cycle of hostility and resentment.

Moreover, according to Shields (1989), the partners in a Euro-American marriage where there is alcohol or other drug abuse interact with each other in extremes, and the nature of this interactive pattern is symbiotic. Symbiotic relationships are characterized by an excessive amount of projection, poor psychological boundaries, and the frequent use of blame, resentment, ambivalence, and intense love and hate (Beavers, 1985). Shields also maintains that these couples tend to be either totally in control or totally out of control and that they will either really love their partners or they will really hate them. These couples are usually elated or depressed, emotionally disengaged, and distant or emotionally enmeshed. Because each spouse's self-esteem is deleteriously affected by the other's drug abuse, a great deal of inner conflict is usually projected onto the other spouse.

Orford and Guthrie (1976) claimed that the nondrinking spouse may protect the alcoholic, may withdraw from the marriage, may safeguard the family's interests such as keeping the children out of the way, and/or may act out. Erekson and Perkins (1989) caution against rigid adherence to the findings of Orford and Guthrie, although they do maintain that clinical impressions provide some support for these conclusions. We want to draw your attention to the potential limits of this concept when applying it to culturally and ethnically diverse families. No research has been found that reflects a similar dynamic occurring in these families as that identified by Orford and Guthrie. That is not to say that the nonalcoholic spouse won't withdraw from his or her partner in an Asian American or another culturally diverse family. It is to say that we have no supporting evidence for this conclusion.

The Parent–Child Subsystem. Kaufman and Kaufman (1992) identified structural patterns in families when there is AOD abuse based upon the works of Minuchin (1974). Most of their sample was observed for over 6 months, and the research design included postgroup discussions of patterns. In addition, verbatim transcripts of all sessions were made and were analyzed to confirm initial clinical impressions. Videotapes were produced and were given to a group of experienced clinicians who rated the structural patterns they observed. The sample consisted of 75 families representing eight different ethnic groups (Latino/Hispanic, 23%; Italian, 19%; Euro-American, 18%; Jewish, 13%; African American, 10%; Irish, 9%; Greek, 1%; and Mixtures, 6%).

Kaufman and Kaufman found that of the 75 families, 88% had enmeshed (undifferentiated boundaries) mother–child relationships and 40% had enmeshed father–child relationships. Forty-two percent of the fathers were considered disengaged while only two mothers were seen as such. The mothers of addicts were seen as enmeshed across all ethnic groups. Seven of thirteen Italian fathers were described as enmeshed as were six of thirteen Jewish fathers. Puerto Rican, African American, and Euro-American fathers tended to be disengaged. The authors found that, while the sample of African Americans was too small to generalize, "most of the Black families had strong, involved mothers" (p. 39). Categorically, no relationship between the addicted family member and other family members was seen as having clear boundaries.

In a more recent study on family dysfunction and alcoholism, Dube, Anda, Felitti, Edwards, and Croft (2002) found interesting results. These researchers agree with the professional literature indicating the relationship between adult alcohol abuse and childhood abuse and family dysfunction. However, Dube et al. were interested in the impact of multiple adverse childhood experiences (ACEs) with parental alcohol abuse and later alcohol abuse. From their data, they categorized eight adverse childhood experiences associated with parental alcohol abuse. The results indicated a strong association between each of the eight adverse childhood experiences and risk for later alcohol abuse. When multiple ACEs were involved, it did not seem to matter whether parental alcohol abuse was involved or not. Compared to persons with no ACEs, those experiencing multiple ACEs were two to four times more likely to self-report adult alcoholism, marry an alcoholic, and be at risk for heavy drinking.

However, there is hope for families. Results of recent studies continue to indicate that families provide strong protective factors against AOD abuse (Kingon & O'Sullivan, 2001; Krestan, 2000). Nevertheless, there is strong indication that dysfunctional family structure imposes a significant influence on the risk for AOD use patterns among family members (e.g., Barrett & Turner, 2006; Dunn et al., 2002; Ledoux, Miller, Choquet, & Plant, 2002; Meness, 2000).

The Sibling Subsystem. Siblings do appear to have an influence on adolescent drug use in terms of providing the drug and/or modeling drug behaviors (Kaufman & Kaufman, 1992). Research on the impact of siblings upon sibling drug use has focused on Euro-Americans and has been relegated to male siblings, but one can infer that these dynamics will be operating to varying degrees between sister subsystems and sister–brother subsystems. In addition, sibling subsystems for culturally and ethnically diverse families might include cousins and/or other extended kin. Kaufman and Kaufman note three pathways of sibling influence that tend to lead to sibling drug use. An older brother is linked to his younger brother through the *personality-influence mechanism.* According to this hypothesis, the older brother's personality impacts the younger brother's personality through identification and modeling and likely leads to common values, attitudes, and behavioral orientation. So, deviance in the older brother is reflected in deviance in the younger brother. *Genetic temperamental connection* is the second pathway reported by Kaufman and Kaufman. This genetic predisposition may account for some of the similarity of values between older and younger brothers. Thus, a genetic link between male siblings may reinforce the personality-influence mechanism. The third pathway in this subsystem is called *environmental reactive mechanism* and refers to the ways in which the brothers are linked through their environment. That is, when the relationship between brothers is characterized by tension, there appears to be an increase in the intrapsychic distress in the younger brother. As a result of that distress, the younger brother may disengage from the relationship and withdraw from responsibility (Kaufman & Kaufman, 1992). In our example, Donnie's distancing from his brother exemplified the environmental reactive mechanism.

Intergenerational Transmission of Alcoholism

When examining the intergenerational processes involved in the transmission of alcoholism, the terms *adult child of alcoholic* and *codependency* immediately rise to the surface. These terms are easily recognized in the AOD field. Yet there is a family systems dimension aspect to the transmission process that is often overlooked. Thus, while these terms and concepts are discussed elsewhere in the text, this section focuses on the family system and structures related to the transmission process of alcoholism.

Family therapists will recognize Bowen's (1978) notions of the intergenerational emotional transmission process. This is the mechanism by which family rituals and rules are passed down from one generation to another. In the AOD field, the issue of intergenerational transmission of alcoholism is of keen interest as well. Lawson, Lawson, and Rivers (2001) assert that researchers consistently find a multigenerational aspect to alcoholism. These same researchers agree with the work of Steinglass, Bennett, Wolin, and Reiss (1987), who maintain that the transmission of alcoholism across generations tends to involve the whole family system over time. In other words, the transmission process is both subtle and overt, and it includes the entire system of family interactions, rituals, attitudes, and beliefs that define the family. There is no particular starting pointing, or specific ending point, or any specific nodal event that determines the origin of the process because it is an ongoing process. In general, genetics clearly play a major role in the father–son transmission of alcoholism, while family environment may be a significant factor in the transmission of alcoholism among females (Lawson et al., 2001).

In a seminal study, Wolin, Bennett, and Noonan (1979) defined family rituals as any behavior that is repetitive and stable with respect to roles and that continues over time. They theorized that rituals stabilize the ongoing family life by clarifying roles and defining boundaries. Using these definitions, the researchers were able to distinguish three types of families: distinctive, intermediate subsumptive, and subsumptive families. *Distinctive families* were those families in which rituals did not change during drinking episodes. *Intermediate subsumptive families* were characterized by a rejection of the intoxicated behavior when it was present. *Subsumptive families* were those in which drinking changed the fabric of the family and was seen as highly disrupting family life. Wolin et al. found that the type of family most likely to transmit alcoholism to the younger generation was the family whose rituals changed during the period of heaviest alcohol consumption. The intermediate subsumptive families, the ones rejecting intoxicated behavior, were found the least likely to transmit alcoholism to the younger generation. This rejection could be open or private or talking about the intoxicated behavior in a disapproving manner (Wolin et al., p. 591).

Lawson et al. (2001) describe several other studies aimed at understanding the intergenerational transmission process. For instance, they cite the Bennett, Wolin, and Reiss (1988a) study that identified several behaviors tending to decrease the likelihood that alcoholism would be transmitted downward to other generations. The researchers found that spouse selection and the establishment of new family rituals in which families participate in the community are helpful to reduce risk. Moreover, these researchers found that families who utilized a selective disengagement strategy to distance themselves from the dysfunctional aspects in their families of origin reduced the transmission of alcoholism across generations. Other researchers have also identified the importance of having a nurturing, supportive, and guiding family atmosphere in which children can feel a sense of cohesion and support as helping disrupt the intergenerational transmission process (O'Sullivan, 1991; Simmons, 1991).

Women and Alcoholism

Back, Contini, and Brady (2007) report that there has been a growing awareness of the importance of gender differences in medical treatment and research. Although Drummond (2002) conducted a meta-analysis on alcohol treatment research and found that women accounted for only 27% of the research sample subjects, there has been a significant increase in the attention paid to gender differences since 1990 (Greenfield, Brooks, Green, Kropp, McHugh et al., 2007). Attention to gender differences is very important in light of Cyr and

McGarry's (2002) review of the National Household Survey on Drug Abuse (Substance Abuse and Mental Health Services Administration, 2001) which found that women account for one-third of those abusing alcohol or having alcohol dependence.

Nevertheless, Hood (2003) noted differences in etiology and recovery, and van der Walde, Urgensen, Weltz, and Hanna (2002) maintain that there are social and psychological differences as well. In fact, in their review of the literature from 1977, van der Walde et al. show data indicating that women with substance abuse disorders have a higher number of alcohol-related conditions than males consuming an equal amount of alcohol. Specifically, women alcoholics have been found to be at higher risk for cirrhosis of the liver (Deal & Galaver, 1994) and cognitive functioning impairment (Nixon, 1994). In addition, women are at higher risk for breast cancer (Aronson, 2003), cardiovascular disease, osteoporosis, and hip fractures (Cyr & McGarry, 2002) as well as for psychiatric co-morbidity (Ziberman, Tavares, Blume, & el-Guebaly, 2003). Women drink heaviest during their midlife, and these women are more likely to be involved with a partner suffering from addiction. They are also more likely than men to present themselves in a more severe state of psychological or physical impairment, such as cardiovascular disease or cancer (Chang, 2002).

Assessment of Problems in Women

The complicated presentation of symptoms is only one factor that influences the lower rate of diagnosing alcoholism in women. Women need to seek help before a diagnosis can be rendered, and research suggest that women with alcohol problems have a difficult time coming in for help. This difficulty may be due to the stigma of alcoholism and/or the associate feelings of shame. For example, Corrigan, Miller, and Watson (2006) found that the stigma of "drug dependence" was viewed as more negative than the stigma for "other mental disorders." Beckman (1994) found shame associated with drinking and not fulfilling traditional roles to be a factor in women not seeking help.

Even when women present for help at a physician's office, research indicates many more women than men deny that they have a drinking problem or that they identify problems other than drinking (Chang, 2002). The fact that their situations may be more medically complicated when they do seek help increases the likelihood that other conditions will be identified by the patient as problematic. In many cases, a diagnosis of depression will precede substance abuse (Ambrogne, 2007). This makes a diagnosis of alcoholism more difficult. A confounding result can be a diagnosis for one disorder and a misdiagnosis for another. Hence, physicians cans be prescribing medications for one disorder that obscures the symptoms of the other (van der Walde et al., 2002).

However, a more insidious factor may be the stereotyping of the disease of alcoholism itself. Cyr and McGarry (2002) maintain that a major reason for not diagnosing women with alcohol problems is that alcoholism is seen as a male disease based on male characteristics. In essence, the cultural discourse has not overtly posited a connection between alcoholism and being female, and the myths that have resulted are hard to dispel. Three major streams of research in the professional literature have been identified by Cho and Crittenden (2006). Some research suggests that women drink more alcohol because of the multiple roles and conflicting expectations they experience when the enter the workforce. In opposition to this perspective is a second line of research holding that performing multiple roles is gratifying to women. Thus, there would not be an increased need for drinking. A third line of inquiry is that working women simply drink more because there is more opportunity. Cho and Crittendon (2006) attempted to research women and drinking and found that drinking for women is a multidimensional construct in which adult roles "differentially influence a woman's likelihood of being a drinker, if she drinks, how much alcohol she consumes, and how likely she is to become a 'problem' drinker" (p. 27). While Cho and Crittenden's research is revealing as well as promising to spawn further research, their present results further complicate the issue. More studies and more time will be needed to renarrate the cultural discourse to reflect the relationship between women and alcoholism.

The discussion above clearly points to the need for early screening of alcohol problems in women (Bradley, Boyd-Wickizer, Powell, & Burman, 1998; Cyr & McGarry, 2002). Van der Walde et al. (2002) and other researchers (e.g., Braiker, 1989; Brown, 1992) suggest that it is imperative that counselors understand the status and role that women have experienced in order to assess their issues and concerns adequately.

As discussed in Chapter 6, the CAGE is an effective screening instrument that is easy to administer and score. What is important to note is that when used to screen women the scoring on the CAGE is adjusted. The CAGE has a cutoff score of 2. This indicates a positive for alcohol disorders in both men and women. In applying this for women, Bradley et al. (1998) believe that a cutoff score of 1 point may be indicative of a problem. In addition, Bradley et al. maintain that the CAGE may not be as appropriate for racioethnic women. In their study of brief alcohol screening instruments, they found that the CAGE was relatively insensitive for racioethnic minorities. These same researchers found that as long as the cutoff scores are adjusted downward appropriately, the TWEAK and the Alcohol Use Disorders Identification Test (AUDIT) perform adequately for all female populations.

Like the CAGE, the TWEAK is an acronym (Tolerance, Worry, Eye-Opener, Amnesia, and Kut Down). Originally, the instrument was used to screen alcohol use in pregnant women. However, Cyr and McGarry (2002) believe that the TWEAK can also be valid for nonpregnant women. The questions for the TWEAK are these:

1. Tolerance: How many drinks does it take before you begin to feel the effects of alcohol? (Greater than two indicates tolerance.)
2. Worry: Have close friends or relatives worried about or complained about your drinking in the past year?
3. Eye-opener: Have you ever taken a drink to steady your nerves or to get rid of a hangover?
4. Amnesia: Has a close friend or relative ever told you about things you said or did while you were drinking that you could not remember?
5. Kut down: Have you ever felt the need to cut down on your use of alcohol?

The scoring is easy. A score of 3 likely indicates an alcohol use disorder in both men and women. A score of 2 may be indicative of a problem for females.

The AUDIT is also reported as appropriate for women in general (Bradley et al., 1998; Cyr & McGarry, 2002). It consists of 10 questions, and the scoring is straightforward. Like the other two brief screening instruments, the AUDIT is relatively user friendly. However, the scoring is more complicated that either the CAGE or the TWEAK. Leonardson, Kemper,

Ness, Koplin, Daniels, and Leonardson (2005) report that the CAGE and AUDIT have sufficient concurrent and divergent validity as well as excellent reliability coefficients for use among Native Americans, and Bedregal, Sobell, Sobell, and Simcok (2006) maintain that the AUDIT can be used effectively with Hispanic populations as can Skinner's (1982) Drug Abuse Screening Test-10 (DAST-10).

Treatment Concerns for Women

There is substantial literature establishing the fact that women are uniquely burdened by a host of issues and vulnerabilities that can impede their process of recovery (Cadiz, Savage, Bonavota, Hollywood, Butters, Neary, & Quiros, 2004). Yet, there is still a dearth of gender-based models for women's recovery (Najavits, Rosier, Nola, & Freeman, 2007), and women are still underrepresented in most substance abuse treatment programs (Greenfield, Trucco, McHugh, Lincoln, & Gallop, 2007). According to other researchers, there is strong evidence that women are less likely to enter treatment when compared to males (Greenfield, Brooks, Gordon, et al., 2007).

Clearly, the best treatment for AOD problems is primary prevention. Cadiz et al. (2004) and Schuck and Spatz (2003) suggest that efforts to increase women's sense of self-efficacy is also an important protective factor in reducing the risk for alcohol use problems. They assert that this is especially true for women who have been abused or neglected. These same researchers found that high self-efficacy was significantly associated with lower levels of alcohol symptoms among women who were abused or neglected. They suggest that interventions can be aimed at showing the importance of improving educational achievement and increased feelings of self-efficacy. Schuck and Spatz believe that this can potentially be very powerful in reducing alcohol symptoms later for these women.

When secondary or tertiary prevention is indicated, there are barriers to treatment for women (Back, Contini, & Brady, 2007). However, these same researchers maintain that once in treatment, males and females receive similar benefits. Nonetheless, many women who abuse alcohol have a history of sexual and physical abuse and are hesitant to come in to work through issues for fear that the environment will not be safe and gender sensitive. In addition, Blume (1997) found that women are often very concerned about their children and will not present themselves for treatment because of a lack of child care. Once there, these women may drop out of treatment when there is a problem with their children. In addition, Blume found that some state laws view alcohol abuse by women as child neglect or endangerment. So some women have a real fear that they will be considered unfit as a parent and risk losing their children. If a woman is pregnant, many treatment programs will not admit out of fear of being liable if something goes awry. In addition, economic concerns are seen as potentially significant barriers to treatment (van der Walde et al., 2002). Men will often divorce their alcoholic wives. This can leave a woman with few financial resources. Moreover, in a divorce, women are often left with inadequate insurance coverage, and if the alcoholic and divorced woman is unemployed, she is more likely to be uninsured (Blume, 1997).

Even though the effectiveness of culture-specific treatment for racioethnic minorities is apparent, research is mixed in terms of gender-specific treatment for women. Nonetheless, there is growing research support for gender-specific treatment for women abusing alcohol in a variety of settings (Back, Contini, & Brady, 2007; Sideman & Kirschbaum, 2002). In general, helpers who understand, utilize empathy, invoke good communication skills, and are gender-sensitive and initially less problem-focused are seen as more helpful. Regarding gender-specific treatment, van der Walde et al. (2002) believe that to understand and appreciate the issues counselors need to remember several other things in treating women of any racioethnic background. First, it is important to know that women are especially sensitive to their peers, significant others, and family members. Second, care for alcoholic women must be ongoing and focused on the individual needs of each woman. Successful treatment requires sensitivity to the plight of minority women. Finally, it is worth repeating that the stigma for women who abuse alcohol is a significant and deleterious factor. Clearly, regardless of whether treatment is gender specific, these issues need to be addressed with all women during treatment.

Family therapy has been found to be helpful in reducing problem drinking among women, as well as for other family members. Leisure therapy for women has also been reported to be effective (Hood, 2003). However, brief therapy is another issue. Moyer, Finney, Swearingen, and Vergun (2002) conducted a meta-analysis comparing brief interventions with either control or extended treatment conditions. The results of their study, as well as the results of Wutzke, Conigrave, Saunders, and Hall's (2002) study, showed little difference between brief and extended interventions. Chang (2002) found that brief interventions with women do not appear to be consistently helpful among women drinkers.

Stepfamilies: System and Structure

Since the 1980s, at least 50% of marriages, many with children, end in divorce (Jay, Freisthler, & Svare, 2004). Thus, Anderson's (1992) assertion that stepfamilies may prove to be the traditional American family of the twenty-first century is likely more true than not. The traditional notion of stepfamilies needs to reflect more contemporary occurrences in U.S. culture. According to the 2000 census (U.S. Census Bureau, 2000), the number of families reflecting two parents and those reflecting single parenting and alternative parenting arrangements, such as is the case with a gay couple, are closing the gap on one another. This means that, statistically speaking, it is almost as normal to come from a traditional two-parent family as it is to come from any number of alternative family structures. Unfortunately, research on the stepfamily system and structure does not usually include alternative forms of family structure. As of yet, there is little research on the dynamics of other forms of parenting related to AOD. So, when discussing the research on traditionally defined stepfamilies, it is important to consider those observations in a more general way when applying the findings to racioethnic groups and gay and lesbian couples.

It can be seen that stepfamilies are different in terms of the family developmental tasks. These tasks, if not accomplished, can lead to a higher risk for AOD abuse. Although a stepfamily in and of itself is not any more at risk than any other family, the unique characteristics of these families can pose problems if the tasks are disrupted or not addressed.

Stepfamilies have some key inherent differences from other families. Although many of the same problems in stepfamilies also exist in other families, stepfamilies are seen as having psychic and physical boundaries that are more permeable than those in a nuclear family (Anderson, 1992). Emotional bonds or psychic boundaries have to be loose enough to allow for affections to be expressed to both the biological parent as well as to the stepparent. The physical boundaries need to be permeable enough to allow for the revolving door of noncustodial visitation and need to be able to allow for visits of a longer duration, such as coming or leaving for an entire school year. Anderson also identifies the complexities involved in decision making in stepfamilies. Often, there needs to be a coordinated effort of two households in making plans. The stepfamily does not have the history that the nuclear family does, and sometimes children (and their parents) can experience a type of culture shock. Anderson says that this culture shock is "an acute feeling of an unfamiliar, sometimes alien, environment that is very disorienting to their basic sense of what 'my family' is" (p. 174). Because stepfamilies are born out of previous losses due to divorce or death, children (and parents) need to be able to grieve the loss adequately. However, grieving the loss is often painful, and many may be reluctant to do so when it appears that the grieving process may impinge upon the happier times of the current relationship.

In stepfamilies in which the adolescent is a drug abuser, a destructive pattern involving discipline may evolve (Anderson, 1992). The stepparent may be drawn into the disciplinarian role if the biological parent has been ineffective, and this move can result in marital strife if the biological parent steps in to protect the adolescent. Such a situation certainly reinforces the biological parent–child coalition, while continuing to exacerbate the child's feelings of guilt and stress (Jay, Freisthler, & Svare, 2004).

Helping Families

Helping families includes both equipping clinicians with appropriate and effective assessment techniques and providing families with the necessary level and structure of care. Assessing for AOD problems has been covered in detail in Chapter 6. Here, among other things, we want to draw your attention to a particular assessment strategy that can help in working with various racioethnic families. With this information, treatment concerns for many racioethnic families can be better aimed.

Barón's Integrative Cross-Cultural Model (ICM)

In discussing addiction treatment for Mexican Americans, Barón (2000) builds on the multidimensional perspectives of several researchers and presents a model aimed at helping therapists integrate the complex individual, family, and culturally related variables that underlie and color the various beliefs, cognitions, and adaptive as well as maladaptive behaviors (p. 227). When used in assessment, this model is thought to constitute a comprehensive assessment of the internal and external influences affecting racioethnic minorities.

The Cross-Cultural Model (ICM) model draws from the earlier works of Jones (1985), who conducted research on African Americans. Jones's earlier model identifies four sets of interactive factors needing to be considered with minority clients and their families. (1) personal experiences and endowments, (2) influence of native culture, (3) reactions to racial oppression, and (4) influence of the majority culture (Barón, 2000; Jones, 1985). The more recent ICM model expands the earlier approach by expanding these and reorienting them as general *domains of inquiry.* These domains of inquiry include (1) individual and systemic variables and dynamics, (2) cultural and ethnically related variables, (3) dominant group influences, and (4) minority group experiences.

Individual and systemic variables and dynamics incorporate neurobiological conditions, developmental issues, family-of-origin dynamics, childhood experiences, education, and the like. Specific to AOD issues, clients and/or their families might be queried about use, frequency, presence, tolerance and withdrawal symptoms, alcoholic family dynamics, and the centrality of AOD in the client's life. Regarding *culturally and ethnically related variables,* clinicians would likely assess the culturally based beliefs regarding AOD use and the beliefs surrounding being clean and sober. It is also important to assess differences in help-seeking behavior, family organization, family life cycle, hierarchies, gender roles, parenting styles, subsystems, and other related variables. The *dominant group influences* describe the extent to which the individual or family incorporates beliefs, values, attitudes, and patterns of behavior reflecting the dominant discourse. According to Barón, an assessment aimed at AOD abuse would focus on differences and similarities between the client's views of use, misuse, and abuse and those of the dominant culture. Included in this domain of assessment would be the identification and discussion of the client's perspectives on abstinence, sobriety, help-seeking behavior, and the Twelve-Step programs. Some understanding of the degree of congruence or incongruence with the dominant culture's view is needed. Finally, the client's experience with being a member of a minority group (*minority group experience*) should be examined. This is a type of within-minority group variance in which the assessment would become more specific to the minority person's experience as a unique minority member. According to Barón, differential treatment by members of society's dominant group as well as treatment by other minority groups related to personality development, beliefs, attitudes, and origin and maintenance of the current problem profoundly influence a minority person's experiences. Because of the differential effects on individuals, it is important to examine the prevalence and impact of these particular beliefs on a case by case basis.

The four domains are considered effective in the understanding of the significant contextual influences affecting the general experience of racioethnic minorities. When working with a racioethnic family suspected of having alcohol and other drug problems, a clinician using this ICM approach would first want to construct a profile based on three mediator variables: level of acculturation, stage of ethnic-identity development, and world view related to locus of control and responsibility. From here, the clinician can advance some hypotheses about the relative contribution of each of the four domains of inquiry (individual and systemic variables, cultural and ethnic variables, dominant group influences, and minority group experiences) that were just described. According to Barón, the ICM can be especially helpful in the early stages of assessment.

Case Example. Imagine a situation in which the ICM was used with a Mexican American couple. The Mexican American couple was referred to a mental health counselor for help with Mr. Aguilar's (husband's) drinking. The *individual and systemic variables* would reveal valuable information that could help explain why they stated they were experiencing distress over acculturating. It could reflect the fact that the Aguilars are first-generation immigrants without documents. By using the model, the clinician would easily note the Aguilars' preference to speak Spanish to one another while at home and at most places in public. The individual and systemic domain would reflect the fact that Mrs.

Aguilar's mother spoke almost exclusively Spanish. As is also common, her mother also lived with her daughter and son-in-law.

The assessment would reveal that the Aguilar's children were bilingual and more acculturated than their parents. The model would allow the interview to guide a discussion of Mr. Aguilar's beliefs about the dominant culture being misguided and that he preferred to mingle with other Mexican Americans. His beliefs were seen as both helpful and hurtful by his children.

Questions guided by interest in the individual and systemic variables could also reveal that Mr. Aguilar had been exposed to drinking at an early age. This exposure came in a culture where heavy drinking was more tolerated. As a result, Mr. Aguilar was seen as being caught between his culture of origin and the practices of his current cultural environment with regard to AOD use. He maintained that his situation was inevitable and blamed his condition on the system. To his way of thinking, drinking was an appropriate way to cope.

An assessment of the second domain, *cultural and ethnic variables*, could reveal the family's proclivity to respond to stress through culturally congruent behaviors, which reflected more tolerance. Moreover, this assessment domain would show that the family would not ordinarily go about solving problems through the help of a therapist. In assessing the impact of the Aguilars' *dominant group and minority group experiences*, it was clear that he was resentful and bitter over his adaptation woes. Perhaps, the family's most telling difficulty in seeing the problem from a different perspective was the fact that they had identified their 15 year-old-son, Enrico, who was having academic problems, as the issue.

In the treatment phase of the ICM, initial efforts were aimed at establishing credibility and an effective psychological and therapeutic contract. Motivational interviewing techniques were employed to help to create dissonance for Mr. Aguilar between his perception of what his role as a father and provider needed to be and the impact that his behavior was having on his family—and on Enrico in particular. Barón (2000) suggests the use of psychoeducational approaches as well. In this case, the psychoeducational component was actually a professional's confirmation about the existence of a problem.

It was also pointed out that Enrico was not trying to be disrespectful of his father. Through family therapy, Mr. Aguilar came to see how Enrico's behaviors were a way to signal to his father that something was wrong. The fact that Mrs. Aguilar often wanted to speak to the clinician in private reflected her own cultural conflicts. She was caught between being seen as disrespectful to her husband and her need to help him to manage his problematic drinking.

In this hypothetical case, the ICM would be able to help the clinician formulate the appropriate cultural context for the Aguilars' problems. By understanding the interplay of acculturation, ethnic identity development, and world views related to responsibility and locus of control, the clinician was able to be more effective in the planning of treatment.

Treating families with substance abuse problems is a complicated process, and treatment takes place on many different levels (Kaufman & Kaufman, 1992). Primarily, the counselor needs to decide which treatment mode will be the most efficacious. Because the plethora of research suggests that AOD abuse is a family problem, family therapy is often indicated, although not all families will want to be treated.

Edwards and Steinglass (1995), in their review of family therapy for alcoholism, conclude that family therapy is efficacious for motivating alcoholics to enter treatment.

However, once the drinker enters treatment, the authors found no difference between family therapy and individual treatment. These authors state that three factors seem to mediate the effectiveness of family therapy: gender, investment in the relationship, and perceived support from the spouse for abstinence. In addition, Edwards and Steinglass (1995) found modest benefits in having the spouse involved in aftercare.

Stanton and Stadish (1997) reviewed 1,571 cases involving an estimated 3,500 patients and family members. According to the authors (p. 182), the superordinate question was whether family-couples therapy in general (as summarized across studies) achieves a better outcome when compared with the average effect of all alternative interventions. Stanton and Stadish report that the meta-analysis results suggest that family therapy is favored over individual counseling or therapy, peer group therapy, and family psychoeducation. Family therapy tends to have higher retention rates than other treatment modalities. The authors suggest that family therapy is as effective for adults as it is for adolescents.

As previously mentioned in working with racioethnic families in Chapter 4, several authors underscore the importance of narrative approaches to individual and family treatment. Krestan (2000), Harrison (2004), and others suggest the relevancy of postmodern narrative principles in working with diverse populations. In writing about the relationship between addiction and power and powerlessness among diverse populations, Krestan discusses the influence of the dominant social discourse regarding the conceptions of power and powerlessness for racioethnic minorities. Krestan notes the particular challenges facing counselors in discussing the culturally powerless client's need to accept the concept of powerlessness in recovery (p. 35).

In general, the narrative approaches underscore the importance of the relationship in the helping process. A fundamental principle of the narrative and dialogic approaches is the ability of individuals to create a sense of power through the helping relationship. According to the theory, this power is then re-created over and over in the relationship so that it becomes a dominant reality for helpees (Abney & Harrison, 2003). In relating narrative principles to racioethnic families in need of AOD treatment, it is not so much the narrative approach to treatment that is effective as it is the adherence to the importance of the helping relationship developed in the process. Through emphasis on the relationship, it is easily seen how critical it becomes for the helper from the dominant discourse perspective to know the essential differences between themselves and those they are attempting to help. It is believed that knowing the differences in this manner is the door that opens counselors to a deepened understanding of diversity.

Krestan, Abney and Harrison, and other researchers are attempting to describe how the dominant discourse related to power, powerlessness, and difference serves to promote the narrative discourse of risk factors for addiction among racioethnic families. Researchers such as Coyhis (2000), who writes about Native Americans, and Chang (2000), writing about Asian/Pacific American addicts, are not asserting that the dominant discourse is causal. They are describing the manner in which this discourse interacts with racioethnic populations and the importance of understanding cultural differences in intervening so as to not promote the deleterious components of the dominant discourse.

In other research, Roberts and McCrady (2003) write about working with alcohol problems in intimate relationships. These researchers identify several modalities of change, such as family-involved treatment, change through referral, and change through self-help groups. These same authors claim that cognitive–behavioral therapy (CBT), motivational enhancement therapy (MET), and Twelve-Step facilitation (TSF) approaches have been empirically proven to be effective.

To their credit, Roberts and McCrady also identify and discuss alternative treatment models and programs, even though these are not empirically tested. Approaches that are designed specifically for certain populations, such as gay and lesbian clients, women, racioethnic populations, and those programs designed to use alternative spiritual, medical, or nutritional approaches, do not lend themselves to empiricism. Moreover, these treatment modalities will likely not be accepted by insurance and managed-care organizations. It should be kept in mind that these approaches are not endorsed because of managed-care decisions. It would be a mistake to assume that the models themselves are ineffective. In some cases, individuals and families can benefit from these more idiosyncratic approaches. The important thing to remember is that there is no one approach that holds the magic key to recovery for all people. Appreciating diversity means appreciating the potential benefits of diverse approaches (Chan, 2003).

Kaufman and Kaufman's Family Types

Four types of Euro-American families will likely present themselves for treatment (Kaufman & Kaufman, 1992). In one family type, members might talk openly about drinking or drugging but are more concerned with other important issues. In these families, drinking or drugging may be present but not to the degree that it is a problem, and helping professionals should focus on the presenting problems but should also attempt to emphasize the possible connection between AOD use and other problems in their lives. In the second family type, clues to alcohol and other drug-use problems may be present, but the clues are oblique and difficult to discern. In these families, the symptom bearer will probably be the child who could be involved in drug abuse. Other clues may be found in reports of drinking in the parents' families of origin, in parental role reversals, in children's attempts to protect their parents, in children's fears of talking about the family, or when the parents present themselves as overly concerned about teenage alcohol and drug abuse. The mental health professional should focus on the presenting problem and should attempt to infuse drinking or drugging into the presenting issue. The third family type is the one whose members present themselves for therapy after the alcohol or other drug abuser has completed some type of treatment program and is clean and sober. The issues here will likely be rebalancing the family system to avoid a full-blown relapse. Slips (see Chapter 9) are to be expected, so the work of the mental health professional is to help the family anticipate situations in which a slip might occur and help the family to determine effective ways to keep the slip from becoming a relapse. The fourth family type is the one presenting alcohol or other drug abuse as the major problem. In these families, alcohol or other drug abuse is the focus of the family, and the conflict will be quite open and apparent. Mental health professionals may need to take more control of these sessions if emotional reactivity is running too high.

Regardless of which family type presents itself for counseling, mental health professionals need to attend to the spousal subsystem, the parent–child subsystem, and the sibling subsystem. The reason for this is simple: Families will balance themselves. So, mental health professionals need to take into account how interventions impact these critical subsystems, the individual family members, and the family itself so that the rebalancing that inevitably will take place will be beneficial.

Kaufman and Kaufman point to situations in which individual counseling may be the preferred mode of treatment for alcoholic families. They see individual work being done in those situations in which family therapy may be misused to deny personal responsibility, psychopathology of one family member can be prevented by individual work, the parents are psychopathological to the point that helping a child cope with the psychopathology is preferred, a family member is deceitful, individual pathology remains after family intervention, and detoxification or getting the client clean and sober is needed prior to family therapy.

There are many avenues open for helping the alcohol or other drug-abusing client or family. The actively drinking or using family member should be directed to a facility where he or she can become clean and sober. Abstinence may be just an ideal for some families. Therefore, if the individual does not want to go into treatment, the family members have a decision to make: They can learn to cope better with the abusing family member, which creates a "wet" system, or they can decide to go further into an intervention (see Chapter 7) and attempt to move their family into a "dry" system. In either case, support groups for family members such as Al-Anon, Alateen, and Codependents Anonymous (see Chapter 10) can be very effective in many, but not all cases.

Summary

- Children can be exposed to AOD use and abuse while in the uterus as well as interpersonally exposed after birth.
- Prenatal exposure to AOD is a critical health concern, because Fetal Alcohol Syndrome is the leading known cause of mental retardation.
- In general, children interpersonally exposed to AOD abuse can take on survival roles that include hero, mascot, lost child, scapegoat, and/or enabler.
- Research shows that these children experience a host of problems related to loss, denial, distortion, and secrecy as well as attachment and separation, and families suffer also in terms of family functioning, violence, abuse, and living with fear.
- The dysfunctional family system will often create an environment where there is role reversal and confusion and where children are often made into caretakers, or children can become *parentified,* which is seen as an unhealthy alliance with one parent over the other.
- Children from AOD abuse families have difficulty in stating what they need or want in the family.
- Families often invoke rules such as "Don't talk, don't trust, and don't feel."
- One reason that families with AOD problems maintain dysfunction is due to underlying family themes related to impaired mourning which revolves around separation and loss as well as family collusion.
- It is clear that stepfamilies are at higher risk for AOD misuse and abuse due to a myriad of obvious reasons.

- Women present much later in the course of alcoholism and, by then, there are other medical issues that can obscure a diagnosis; however, once in treatment they benefit about the same as males.
- Although women account for one-third of those abusing AOD, alcoholism is still considered a "male" disease, and women alcoholics often go undiagnosed.
- The CAGE and AUDIT are assessment instruments and can be used effectively with the general as well as diverse populations; clinicians can also assess for AOD problems by being aware of Kaufman and Kaufman's four family types.
- While there is evidence that family-based interventions can work, family participation rates in interventions is low (between 5 and 20%).
- Culture plays an important role in determining the type of treatment for alcoholism.
- Barón's Integrative Cross-Cultural Model (ICM) for treating racioethnic minority families attends to four domains of inquiry that include individual and systemic variables and dynamics, cultural and ethnically related variables, dominant group influences, and minority group experiences.

Internet Resources

Fetal Alcohol Syndrome
www.cdc.gov/ncbddd/fas

Children of alcoholics
www.coaf.org

Stepfamilies
www.stepfamilies.info

Women and alcohol
http://pubs.niaaa.nih.gov/publications/brochurewomen/women.htm

Family AOD Treatment
www.treatment-centers.net/women's-recovery.html

Further Discussion

1. Do you know if your mother engaged in AOD use or misuse while you were in the womb?
2. Since FAS is the leading cause of mental retardation, how is it that this is still a public health crisis?
3. Why would you think that stepfamilies are at greater risk for AOD problems?
4. There are many issues related to women and AOD. What role does gender play in the identification and treatment concerns for women?
5. What are the reasons that diverse populations mistrust the treatment system, and what would you recommend be done to counter the problem?

12

Adult Children and Codependency

In the last chapter, we discussed the impact that AOD abuse has on children and families. In this chapter, we want to focus the discussion on the impact that AOD use has on the lives of adults who grew up in homes where substances were abused.

According to Juliana and Goodman (1997), scholarly writing about the effects of alcohol upon children first appeared in the late nineteenth century with a study on the possible long-term effects of fetal opioid exposure. The popular movement appears to have been initiated by interest in Cork's (1969) book *The Forgotten Children,* which examined 115 school-aged children of alcoholics and found them to be suffering from varied problems such as difficulty in expressing anger and resentment, low self-confidence, and difficulty in initiating and maintaining friendships. El-Guebaly and Offord (1977, 1979) reviewed the early empirical literature on children of alcoholics and attempted to identify problems that members of this group had across their life spans.

Intense popular interest then ensued with the publication of such books as Wegscheider's (1981) *Another Chance: Hope and Health for the Alcoholic Family,* Black's (1981) *It Will Never Happen to Me,* and Woititz's (1983) *Adult Children of Alcoholics.* As a result of these popular writings, a children of alcoholics (COA) movement began (Sher, 1991). The surging interest in COAs and adult children of alcoholics (ACOAs) has been prolific enough to have spawned a cottage industry. Essentially, the message promulgated in these popular writings is that one should confront one's chaotic childhood and work through the repressed pain (Blau, 1990).

From time to time, you may have heard people label themselves as being an "Adult Child of an Alcoholic" (ACOA) or, more simply in support groups and amongst like-minded individuals, as an "Adult Child." You may also be somewhat familiar with the term *codependency* because some adult children may describe themselves as being "codependent." There is some debate in both popular and professional circles about the benefits of such labeling. On the one hand, such a label can act as a shortcut in conversations where others are familiar and/or may be subscribing to the same sobriquet. A "shortcut" means that others "know what you mean" when you use that label. However, in professional circles, there is concern that labeling can have its own life. For example, George, La Marr, Barrett, and McKinnon (1999) studied the relationship among alcoholic parentage, self-labeling, and endorsing oneself as an ACOA. They found that parents' drinking did affect whether the subjects labeled themselves as an ACOA–codependent. However, the researchers state that it was unclear if a certain number of subjects were simply responding to the fact that "Since my parents drank, I must be an ACOA–codependent." George et al. (1999) also found that when subjects labeled themselves as codependent, they endorsed more pathological statements. In an earlier study, Sher (1991) found "strong negative stereotypes associated with the COA label, both from peer group and from mental health professionals" (p. 169).

Aside from the potentially negative consequences of labeling oneself as a COA during school-aged years, there may be some positive aspects to the labeling process for Adult Children of Alcoholics (ACOAs). Burk and Sher (1988) reviewed the literature in an attempt to determine the relevance of labeling theory for research on ACOAs. One of the possible benefits of labeling might be raising one's consciousness about the need for help. In addition, labeling oneself as an ACOA allows access to a variety of self-help support groups such as Codependents Anonymous and Al-Anon (see Chapter 10). Burk and Sher (1988) also suggest that labeling oneself as an ACOA allows for an external attribution to be made that can provide a structure for individuals' insight and understanding into their problems. Kaminer (1990) believes that identifying oneself as an adult child begins a recovery process that can lead to a lifestyle of recovery. In the final analysis, the authors of this text believe that, as long as the labeling process allows for continued growth in the individual, it might be beneficial for an individual to subscribe to such labeling. However, to label oneself as an ACOA in order to avoid personal responsibility is not helpful and can serve to maintain one's self-deprecation and self-defeating behaviors.

Adult Children of Alcoholics (ACOAs)

The labeling controversy aside, millions of adults do identify with the term and relate this to present dissatisfaction in life. Regardless of the extent to which one subscribes to the concepts of adult children, this area is a focal point of current research.

Research on ACOAs has focused on three areas. One branch of research, referred to as risk factors for later substance abuse, includes both qualitative and quantitative studies that examine the variables believed to influence ACOA's own drug or nondrug use in adulthood. The quantitative research is aimed at identifying the characteristics that predispose ACOAs to alcoholism, other drug dependence, or other substance-related problems. The qualitative writings in this area are found mainly in popular literature and focus upon identifying the personality characteristics and problematic behaviors that increase an ACOA's risk for choosing a partner with an identifiable substance abuse problem. A second branch of research focuses on identifying the clinical characteristics of ACOAs, an area that has been addressed largely in popular writings and has gained a broad popular following. The third branch of research centers on attempts to empirically validate the clinical characteristics. As you will see, the current state of these three research venues generally reveals mixed results.

Clinical Characteristics and Empirical Research

Popular writers (see Ackerman, 1983, 1987; Beattie, 1987; Black, 1981; Woititz, 1983) and professional writers (see Brown, 1988; Cermak, 1986; Goodman, 1987) have identified some of the characteristics distinctive to an adult child of an alcoholic. These characteristics are based upon the assumption that children see parental behavior as a reflection of the child's own sense of self-worth (Ackerman, 1983). In general, characteristics of ACOAs are seen as emanating from dysfunctional family systems and include excessive use of denial, all-or-nothing thinking, exaggerated need for control, avoidance of anger and other feelings, avoidance of self-disclosure, lack of trust, and difficulty with intimate relationships (Brown, 1988; Sher, 1991). Cermak (1984) and McKearn (1988) identified depression, isolation, rage, avoidance of feelings, survival guilt, anxiety reactions, sleep disturbances and nightmares, and intrusive thoughts as being symptomatic of ACOAs. These characteristics are essentially moderating variables thought to influence one's vulnerability to developing both intrapsychic and interpersonal problems. The characteristics identified through clinical impressions relate more to one's problems in adulthood that may, but do not necessarily, include substance abuse.

There was a spate of empirical research conducted in the 1980s that addressed various aspects of ACOAs. Fisher, Jenkins, Harrison, and Jesch (1992; 1993) and D'Andrea, Fisher, and Harrison (1994) found many investigations to be helpful. However, they found several limitations to the studies. Some studies did not have sophisticated statistical analyses, and others had small sample sizes. Moreover, the majority of the studies conducted during this period used comparison groups of ACOAs and non-ACOAs. These studies may have begged the question because it was assumed that ACOAs were, in fact, different from non-ACOAs. Fisher et al. (1992) found that ACOAs are "not as codependent as they are described by clinicians and that codependency does not occur more frequently in ACOAs than in other adults" (p. 32). In addition, Fisher et al. (1993) found that ACOAs may not be that different from other adults who reported significant problems in their family of origin, and D'Andrea et al. (1994) maintain that ACOAs may not be as pathological as described by Black (1981) and others. Rather than categorically countering the popular notions about ACOAs being doomed to repeat the patterns found in their substance-abusing homes, there is more recent evidence that ACOAs may present different risk factors for substance abuse and other issues.

Risk Factors

There remains some question as to the strength of the association between substance abuse in one's childhood home and the development of problems later in life. However, studies do demonstrate that an association does exist. Some studies address psychiatric symptoms and contend that ACOAs have lowered self-esteem and a heightened risk for substance abuse (Watt, 2002). Other research reflects ACOAs as having higher risk for developing substance abuse problems and depressive symptoms, antisocial behavior, anxiety disorders, and relational difficulties (Beesley & Stoltenberg, 2002; Harter, 2000). Kelley et al.

(2007) studied female ACOAs and non-ACOAs and found that the former group experience boundary violations (parentification) and also reported having more responsibility for caretaking in their families of origin. Although popular notions that ACOAs would have more relational troubles, studies examining relationship patterns among ACOAs present mixed results, and many studies do not draw from random samples.

Nonetheless, Watt found that ACOAs are less likely to marry, more likely to be in unhappy marriages, and more likely to divorce. Olmsted, Crowell, and Waters (2003) report that sons of alcoholics have increased risk for alcoholism. Yet, neither alcoholism nor marriage to an alcoholic is an inevitable outcome for ACOAs. More specifically, these researchers report that both males and females whose parents were alcoholic are more likely to marry moderate-to-severe alcoholics. Perhaps the most controversial assertion made about ACOAs is that their relational difficulties can be described as "codependent." Because of the overwhelming popularity of this observation, we will discuss the notion of codependency in detail later in this chapter. It needs to be noted here that codependency is variously described as boundary problems that often result in enmeshed relationships (see Chapter 11) and codependents engage in dysfunctional relationships in a variety of forms. While it may be somewhat true that ACOAs have boundary issues in their adult relationships, it cannot be seen as being caused by their families of origin. Family therapists see many couples' boundary problems that may be associated with other variables mitigated by a more generalized anxiety in contemporary couples that translates into power and control issues.

Assessment and Treatment Considerations

Assessment of ACOAs

Berkowitz and Perkins (1988) reviewed the means by which ACOAs have been identified in the professional literature and found that there are both broad and strict definitions of ACOAs. Clinical diagnosis of parental alcoholism reflects the more strict definition whereas the children's perceptions of parental drinking problems mirrors a broader definition. An example of a broad definition is that used in the Russell, Henderson, and Blume (1985) study in which an ACOA is "any person, adult, or child who has a parent identified in any way as having a significant problem related to alcohol use" (p. 1). According to Berkowitz and Perkins, the more strict definition is likely to exclude many individuals whose parents are alcoholic but who have not been formally diagnosed. The more broad definition, based upon the child's perceptions, may also reflect an inaccurate number of ACOAs because the child may see his or her parents only infrequently or may see his or her parent drink only occasionally.

A detailed instrument is the CAST (Jones, A. C., 1985), which stands for Children of Alcoholics Screening Test. This is a diagnostic instrument containing 39 items that ask questions related to parental problems with alcohol, and is designed to measure the chaotic and inconsistent behaviors and experiences of the alcoholic home such as emotional instability, inconsistent child care, family conflict, and lack of close, intimate, and trusting relationships between parents and children (Williams & Collins, 1986). Dinning and Berk (1989) attempted to extend the validity of the CAST and reported significant negative correlations between CAST scores, family cohesion, and family support, and positive correlations between CAST scores and family conflict. They also reported differing means for male and females. In a more recent study, Lease and Yanico (1995) did not find the gender differences, but did find support for a shortened version of the CAST, which correlates highly with family disruption. In an attempt to demonstrate construct validity for a single-item question asking whether "a parent may have had or may have an alcohol abuse problem" (p. 207), Berkowitz and Perkins compared subjects' responses on the CAST to the subjects' responses to that single question and found that the single question reliably classifies ACOAs.

Others have used simple, single-item questions as well. For example, DiCicco, Davis, and Orenstein (1984) asked whether one had ever wished that either or both of his or her parents would drink less and found that this single item identified ACOAs reliably over time. In another study, Biek (1981) asked subjects whether their parents' drinking caused problems for them and found this single question accurately selected ACOAs. The results of using a single question to classify ACOAs is summarized in the study by Berkowitz and Perkins in which they assert that

> studies suggest that it is possible to identify most adolescents from alcohol-abusing families by using a single, objective question focusing on the child's perception of the parent's drinking and that this method produces prevalence rates similar to those obtained from a more detailed diagnostic instrument such as the CAST [Jones, 1985] and large-scale national surveys. (p. 207)

Implications for Intervention

Empirical studies on prevention and treatment of ACOAs are significantly lacking (Williams, 1990). Nevertheless, Williams describes two essential goals in intervening with ACOAs. The first goal is to identify and address early symptoms of problem drinking, and the second goal is to identify dysfunctional behaviors and coping skills that may be predisposing risk factors for drinking or other adult problems.

Aside from the mixed results reflected in the empirical research, group settings seem to be preferred for families identified as having alcohol issues (Hawley & Brown, 1981; Morehouse, 1986). ACOAs may benefit from the same support groups that are identified and discussed in Chapter 10, which include Codependents Anonymous (CODA) and Al-Anon. Other self-help groups, such as Sex Addicts Anonymous and Emotions Anonymous, could be used as well, depending upon the identified problem.

The mixed results of empirical studies do not suggest that specific interventions should be identified for ACOAs, because it is unclear whether such a group exists whose individual members are significantly different from other adults with dysfunctional family backgrounds. Nevertheless, being associated with alcohol or other drug abuse either directly, as in the case of the alcoholic, or indirectly, as in the case of many ACOAs, has been shown to be problematic. In terms of helping clients, mental health professionals may want to provide information regarding AOD use as well as help clients clarify their values about use so that they may make decisions regarding abstention or moderation. Many clients who were raised in homes with alcohol abuse may not identify themselves as ACOAs, so counselors need to be careful about using jargon that may create client resistance. Mental health professionals who use the label ACOA may leave their clients with the impression that this is a widely accepted clinical syndrome, but such a posture would be misrepresenting the empirical findings about ACOAs.

Adults who were raised in families with substance abuse, physical or sexual abuse, and/or parental death or divorce do seem different from adults with no such history. Moreover, recall from Chapter 11 that a characteristic of families with alcohol or other drug abuse is unresolved grief. This grief, coupled with poor communication skills and a lack of role-modeling on how to express feelings, may leave these clients predisposed to difficulty in trusting the counselor. Because ACOAs may control their emotions and attempt to control others as well, it is advisable that mental health professionals focus on developing a strong and deep rapport with the ACOA client.

The George et al. (1999) study focused on analyzing the traits of ACOAs. They found seven factors:

1. Difficulty with intimacy
2. Discomfort with feelings
3. Self-esteem
4. Indecisiveness
5. Friendship troubles
6. Romance management
7. Giving into the needs of others

As mentioned, while these factors do not reliably differentiate ACOAs from others who grew up in homes with chronic stress, these seven factors seem to be a very good jumping off point when clinicians are initiating discussions with clients. These constructs are broad enough to apply to diverse populations.

ACOAs and Diversity

George et al. (1999) demonstrated the blurred boundary between ACOA and codependency. This is reflected in the popular movement of ACOA–codependency. However, when the singular ACOA–codependency concept is applied to racioethnic and other populations, its validity does not hold. A distinction needs to be made between the two terms. Codependency is a Western concept and is not easily translated into non-European and collectivist cultures. Linking the concept with ACOA is not a helpful perspective when working with many diverse populations either.

With respect to African Americans, Rodney (1995) found that the African American ACOAs in her study reported significantly more drinking problems and less healthy family environments and social support than non-ACOAs. However, no differences were reported in the mastery of developmental tasks such as autonomy, mature interpersonal relationships, and purpose. In a later study that examined the ACOA construct for African Americans, Rodney (1996) found several inconsistencies for African Americans in the professional literature. She concludes that clinicians should stop believing that certain characteristics of ACOAs are common to all adult children of alcoholics. Mintz, Tracey, and Kashubeck (1995) reported similar concerns for the characteristics of women ACOAs. Specifically, they studied the relationship of parental alcoholism to eating disorder symptomology and substance abuse in a nonclinical sample of undergraduate women and found that not all ACOAs are alike nor do they all suffer from psychological problems. In another study, Stout and Mintz (1996) examined women and eating disorders and found that there were no group differences on eating disorder symptomology, but reported differences in terms of distress arising from interpersonal problems and the prevalence of abuse. Kelly and Myers (1996) corroborate the finding of the earlier Mintz et al. (1995) study by reporting that there were no differences between female undergraduate children of alcoholics and nonalcoholics on depression nor on coping differences.

Codependency

The term *codependency* arrived in our popular nomenclature in the early 1980s. Originally referring to the coalcoholic (Whitfield, 1984), this notion was broadened through the popular writings of Black (1981), Friel (1984), and others who described a variety of compulsive behaviors. With the possible exception of transactional analysis and the famous phrase, "I'm okay-you're okay" (Harris, 1969), few movements in the mental health field have generated so much popular interest and so much professional controversy as has the codependency movement.

The fields of chemical dependency and mental health were beginning to enjoy a healthy, although somewhat acrid at times, relationship once the notion of the dually diagnosed patient became vogue in professional circles and more routine. However, it was the phenomenon of the patient with a coexisting disorder that sent shudders down the spine of the community mental health system—administrators and clinicians alike, because this dually diagnosed patient suggested the chicken-or-the-egg idea: What caused what? Which was the primary diagnosis? Did the alcohol or other drug problem create the mental disorder or was it the other way around? If patients were active in their addictive behaviors during the time of their entry into the mental health system, what was the proper treatment plan? The very real complications resulting from having a co-existing disorder caused the fear that the financial backbone of community mental health centers would be broken. That a professional could be treating the wrong problem was a good possibility.

One direct result of the numbers of such dual diagnoses was a bringing together of chemical treatment providers and mental health providers under one roof. Although it was not an easy operation in terms of administrative logistics, great strides were made by mental health centers to do exactly that. Staff meetings, which were once held to discuss mental health cases, now included addictions counselors whose training was quite different from that of their mental health colleagues. The friction that resulted was to be expected, because often mental health professionals had to move their offices or generate other concessions in order to make room for their new colleagues. As each group became more familiar with and received direct benefits from the work of the others, issues of turf and prestige gradually gave way to more amiable working relationships. Patients began to receive improved care, and with this came shared respect for each professional group. It appeared that all was well.

Then the chemical dependency field introduced the concept of codependency, and whatever strides had been made in the salubrious relationship between the mental health field and the addiction field turned sour once again. The definition and characteristics of codependency were seen by many mental health professionals as a new name for an old mental health disorder, which once again brought problems of professional boundaries into sharp focus. However, the problem was not only that the chemical dependency field was seen as trespassing onto the field of mental health nor was it only that those in the addictions field were being trained to treat codependency: The problem was more the issue of whether codependency actually existed. And if it did exist, questions about what constituted codependency would become the next cause of battle.

Some of the fiery debate was fueled by differences over the disease concept inherent in the popular views of codependency. Recall that, in Chapter 3, one's view of alcoholism as being a disease or nondisease was seen to have profound implications for identification and treatment. Moreover, remember how the discriminating variable casting one into a disease or nondisease orientation essentially revolved around one's view of "loss of control" (with the disease model claiming the centrality of a loss of control). Well, the voracity with which mental health professionals have debated the disease concept has been duplicated in the debate over codependency: Are people responsible for the root of their codependency? In other words, are individuals seen as more responsible for how they manage their impulses rather than being responsible for the impulse itself?

Another source of debate centered on the traits of a codependent person. Does codependency really exist, or is it another name for a diagnosis already identified in the *DSM-IV* under Borderline Personality Disorder, Dependent Personality Disorder, Post-traumatic Stress Disorder? Is codependency essentially a thematic variation on one of these disorders? Does it simply extend the boundaries of an already established diagnosis so that codependent characteristics lie more along one pole of a continuum in a given disorder?

Furthermore, some feminists argue that the perennial influence of the *codependency* hypothesis suggests that it is a social construct and is heavily influenced by traditional assumptions of gender. For instance, Douglas and Minton (1993) report that many feminists maintain the view of a society that demands that women be nurturing, caring, and sensitive to others' needs. Yet, these are the very characteristics deemed dysfunctional when viewed through a *codependency* paradigm. Perhaps this contentious issue surrounds the notion of whether codependency is a progressive disease.

Definitions of Codependency

Definitions of the term *codependency* are influenced by the degree to which one subscribes to the concept. That is, staunch proponents of the concept may see everyone and almost all of our institutions as codependent. For example, Giermyski and Williams (1986) state that enthusiastic proponents of the concept see codependency

> as a primary disease present in every member of an alcoholic family, which is often worse than alcoholism itself, has its own physical manifestations and is a treatable diagnostic category. Its presence is recognized in individuals, among institutions, in hospitals as well as judicial and legal systems, in schools and even in the Federal Communications Commission (FCC). The last two are viewed as afflicted with codependency because schools expel students for drug-related offenses, and the FCC has not yet banned wine and beer commercials. (p. 7)

Cermak (1986) noted that efforts to define codependency have included metaphoric and interpersonal approaches as well as those approaches based upon ego psychology, behaviorism, and combinations of behaviorism and intrapsychic dynamics. For example, Anderson (1987) uses a metaphor to state that "being codependent is like being a life guard on a crowded beach, knowing that you cannot swim, and not telling anyone for fear of starting a panic" (p. 16). More formalized definitions of codependency are found in the interpersonal approaches of Black (1981) and Weigscheider (1985). Black talks about rules operating in the family structure that prohibit the honest expression of feelings regarding alcoholism and the alcohol-dependent family member. Weigscheider discusses codependency in terms of it being a preoccupation and dependence upon another person or object. Examples of codependency include individuals who are in a significant relationship with an alcoholic, those having one or more alcoholic parents or grandparents, and those who grew up in a family where there was systematic repression of feelings. Schaef (1987) presents a definition that depicts the belief in the progressive nature of codependency. She sees codependency as a disease emanating from an "addictive process" similar to that of alcoholism. This addictive process, unless confronted in much the same manner as alcoholism, can lead to a type of spiritual death—a life aimed at existing rather than thriving—or physical death (Schaef, 1987).

Friel (1984) extended the interpersonal approaches to include codependency and emphasized the impact of such behaviors upon the ego functioning of individuals. These authors maintain that codependency is an emotional and behavioral pattern of interactive coping resulting from one's protracted exposure to a restrictive environment that does not allow the open or direct expression of feelings about oneself or other family members. For example, children who are consistently told that the mother's or father's drinking binges are not problematic, even in the face of drunken rages and subsequent physical abuse, will grow up confused about their reality. Any attempt to talk about the problem when the parents were sober would likely be met with cognitive resistance: "There is no problem." Any attempt to talk about the problem when the parent(s) were drinking is likewise met with physical abuse. Hence, these children often learn to keep their feelings and thoughts about the parents' drinking to themselves. This fear of talking would be introjected and thus carried into one's adult life and relationships.

Whitfield (1984) believes that codependency is a disease of lost selfhood, and that it is the most common type of addiction that people develop. Whitfield (1984) states that codependence develops whenever there is "suffering and/or dysfunction that is associated with or results from focusing on the needs and behavior of others" (p. 19). An intrapsychic approach is reflected in Cermak's (1986) definition in which he sees a codependent person as having a personality disorder based upon an excessive need to control self and others. Other symptoms include neglecting one's own needs, boundary distortions centered on approach and avoidance in intimate relationships, attraction to other individuals demonstrating codependent characteristics, denial, a constricted or restricted emotional expression, low-level and persistent depression, and stress-related physical ailments.

As Irvine (1999, p. 29) and others point out (e.g., Krestan & Bepko, 1990), codependency's "definitional ambiguity should not be taken to be "so vague as to be meaningless." Nonetheless, Irvine maintains that one cannot simply ascribe any and all meanings to it. She goes on to say that the constitution of one person's codependency is really defined by what the person sees as troublesome in his or her own history. According to the same researcher, codependency can stand for different issues in an individual's life. For instance, it might mean a series of loveless and oppressive relationships. In another case, codependency might mean distant, aloof, and isolating interpersonal response patterns to others. In yet another instance, codependency might reflect a sense of chronic low self-esteem and boundary problems in relationships (Watt, 2002).

Characteristics of Codependent Individuals

Several authors have advanced codependent characteristics, and, like the definitions, these characteristics range from less formal to more pedantic (see Kitchens, 1991; Schaef, 1987; Whitfield, 1984). Potter-Efron and Potter-Efron (1989) identified eight characteristics of codependence: (1) Fear is indicated by a preoccupation with the problems of others, an avoidance of interpersonal risk, a general mistrust of others, persistent anxiety, and manipulative attempts to change another's behavior, especially drinking behavior; (2) Shame and guilt are characterized by a persistence of shame and guilt about another's behavior, self-loathing, isolation, and an appearance of superiority that masks low self-worth; (3) Prolonged despair relates to a generalized pessimism toward the world and feelings of hopelessness about changing one's current situation. One may also demonstrate a low sense of self-worth that stands in direct opposition to one's actual accomplishments; (4) Anger is often present but may be expressed in a passive-aggressive manner. One may also fear that becoming angry will mean a loss of control. Another characteristic of anger is that it is persistent; (5) Denial is usually rather consistent, especially when it involves family pain such as drinking behavior. Denial is also demonstrated by a consistent minimization of problems and the use of justifications or rationalizations aimed at protecting the person from perceived or real consequences; (6) Rigidity is identified by cognitive, behavioral, moral and spiritual, and emotional inflexibility; (7) Identity development is also impaired. This is usually seen as an inability to take care of one's own emotional needs and as having an excessive need for others to validate one's self-worth. Along with this need is an obsessive concern about how one is perceived by others; (8) Confusion about what is normal and what is real is another behavioral pattern. Confusion is also indicated by one's gullibility and indecisiveness.

More recently, Irvine (1999) summarized the characteristics of codependent individuals in a similar, yet different, way. She sees codependency as involving these factors:

- Difficulty in identifying feelings
- Minimizing, altering, or denying feelings
- Difficulty in making decisions

- Feelings of embarrassment for receiving recognition, praise, or gifts
- Punctuated sensitivity to the feelings of others, along with assuming the same feelings
- Extreme loyalty, remaining in harmful situations too long
- Putting aside of personal interests and hobbies to do what others want
- Thought and emotional patterns of feeling responsible for other people and other peoples' experiences (e.g., their feelings, thoughts, and actions)
- Anticipation of other people's needs
- Thoughts that they are not quite good enough

In examining the definitions and characteristics, Doweiko (2002) states that the core aspect of codependency includes four elements: *overinvolvement, obsessive attempts to control, the extreme tendency to use external sources for self-worth, and the tendency to make personal sacrifices.* In codependency, overinvolvement with the abusing family member is coupled with an obsessive attempt to control the abusing member's behaviors. Using external sources for self-worth is similar to Whitaker's notion of "looking elsewhere" mentioned in an earlier section. The issue of personal sacrifices comprises those behaviors aimed at "curing" the abusing family member, in which the helper is seen as "saintly."

According to Kitchens (1991), eight indicators can help to determine the severity of codependence: (1) the extent to which the client equates performance with self-value; (2) the extent to which the client equates self-worth with taking care of others' needs; (3) the extent to which the client believes he or she is helpless to control what happens in life; (4) the extent to which the client attempts to feel more powerful or more in control of life than is actually the case; (5) the extent to which the client ruminates about dysfunctional family of origin behavior; (6) the extent to which the client continues to protect or defend against any criticism of his or her parents in the face of contradictory information; (7) the extent to which the client experiences unexplained or overwhelming anger; and (8) the extent to which the client feels stuck in his or her relationships.

Assessing for Codependency

In its heyday in the 1980s and early 1990s, codependency was not formally recognized in the *DSM-IV.* The fact that codependency does not appear in the *DSM-IV-TR* (APA, 2000) continues to reflect the lack of formal professional acknowledgment. Nevertheless, mental health professionals should not categorically dismiss the concept. While the lack of formal acknowledgment in the early years hindered the development of sophisticated assessments of codependency, the same cannot be said today. The lack of appearance in the *DSM-IV-TR* has not deterred more recent efforts to legitimize the concept and assessment of codependency.

During the period from the mid-1980s to the mid-1990s, assessing codependency in clients was relatively informal, and professionals and nonprofessionals alike used a few notable nonstandardized instruments. However, the subjectivity and informality in the early years of the codependency movement were not categorical and should not be mistaken for a complete lack of validity. In the early years, the differences in the assessment of codependency were probably attributed to variations in the general assessment skills of practitioners, rather than being attributed to differences over the meaning and definition of codependency. While it is true that clinicians often assessed codependency simply through their subjective clinical impressions of the client, these impressions were partly guided by the professional works of Kitchens (1991), who also cautioned mental health professionals to combine subjective and objective assessment procedures. Interestingly, Harkness and Cotrell (1997) show that the pioneers may have been accurate in their assessments of codependency. These researchers studied over 2,000 practitioners worldwide and found a remarkable agreement and consistency in the meaning and definition of codependency across practitioner subjects.

Similar to the popularity enjoyed by subjective clinical assessments, the early psychometric instruments demonstrated an abundance of informal face validity, as well as significant concurrent validity. In the first place, the "formal" instruments were easy to administer and score and used language and situations to which clients and nonclients could easily relate. For instance, the Friel Codependent Assessment Inventory (Friel, 1985) contains 60 true–false items. The items essentially list various aspects of codependency, such as those outlined by Irvine (1999) and presented earlier in this chapter. The total score is measured by tabulating the number of True responses. Scores can range from "Few Codependent Concerns" (less than 20 True responses) to "Severely Codependent" (more than 60 True responses). Kitchens (1991) developed A Codependence Test that has 25 Likert-type questions, and scores can range from "Healthy" (a score of less than 25) to "Severe Codependence" (a score greater than 75). Gossett (1988) and a staff of graduate students, at the Institute for the Study of the Family and Addictive Disorders at the University of North Texas, developed the Orientation to Life Inventory. The authors state that the 50-item instrument, although unpublished, measures a client's internal consistency or denial of codependence through the use of a type of validity scale, as well as measuring three different aspects of codependence: cognitive rigidity, emotional disintegrity, and extreme normative expectations. As with other instruments, scores on this scale range from "Healthy" to "Severe Codependence." Unfortunately, none of the instruments mentioned above report reliability or validity coefficients. Thus, should you, as a mental health professional, choose to administer an instrument, you are advised to use these instruments with extreme caution. Probably the best use of these assessment devices is for the mutual identification of problematic areas occurring in the client's life. Asking the client to share his or her impressions of the assessment results can help focus on areas that might need attention.

Current research has focused on validating some of the earlier psychometric instruments. For instance, Lindley, Giordano, and Hammer (1999) attempted to validate the Spann–Fischer Codependency Scale (1991). The results indicated a strong convergent validity for the Spann–Fischer instrument. Fuller and Warner (2000) used the Spann–Fischer and the Potter-Efron Codependency Assessment (Potter-Efron & Potter-Efron, 1989) and studied the relationship of these instruments with self-reported chronic family stress. Results of their study showed that women had higher codependency scores on the Spann–Fischer than did the sample of male subjects. This study raises questions about potential gender bias in the instrument, and this issue will be addressed later in the chapter.

In another study, Zetterlind and Berglund (1999) aimed to establish concurrent and construct validity for codependency. These researchers wanted to establish concurrent validity for codependency for Cermak's (1986) *DSM*-type criteria. The researchers cross-referenced several instruments that measured such variables as social interaction, coping behavior style, hardship, and trait personality features. The results indicate that Cermak's ideas are, indeed, associated with scores on coping styles, such as fear withdrawal and hardship.

Aside from these efforts to update assessments published in the early years of the codependency movement, a review of the current professional literature reveals continued interest in the introduction of new empirically tested psychometric assessments for codependency. For instance, Harkness, Swenson, Madsen-Hampton, and Hale (2001) studied the reliability and validity of a clinical rating scale for codependency. The researchers developed an example-anchored rating scale, based on how clinicians generally construe the term *codependency* in practice. The researchers administered the instrument to a group of practicing counselors. The design controlled for gender and called for counselors to be randomly assigned to one of four groups. The findings suggest that the rating scale yields reliable and valid clinical evaluations of codependency without appreciable gender bias.

The Holyoake Codependency Index (HIC) (Dear & Roberts, 2000) is a 13-item scale that measures the extent to which a person endorses or rejects codependent sentiments. It is comprised of three scales: external focus, self-sacrifice, and reactivity. *External focus* is defined as the tendency to rely on other people in order to obtain approval and a sense of self. *Self-sacrifice* is the tendency to regard others' needs as more important than one's own needs. *Reactivity* is the degree to which one feels overwhelmed by a partner's problematic behavior. According to the authors of the index, these subscales were derived from factor analysis of key themes using a clinical sample of mostly females. Dear & Roberts (2002) then replicated the earlier study using a mixed-gender sample of undergraduate university students (aged 18 to 56). Results indicate that the scales hold for both males and females.

As you can see, arguments can be made about the consistency in the validity and reliability of assessment instruments throughout the history of the codependency movement. One current trend in research in assessment is to conduct concurrent validity and reliability studies as ancillary, yet important components, of other research questions. Lindley et al.'s (1999) study is an example. In this study, the researchers validate the Spann–Fischer scale while primarily looking at the relationship between codependency and age, gender, self-confidence, autonomy, and succorance. These studies, and others like them, provide opportunities for enhancing the clinical assessment of codependency.

Implications for Mental Health Professionals

As far as the controversy is concerned, the mental health profession has the last word for now: The *DSM-IV* does not include codependency in its nomenclature on personality disorders. This may or may not dissuade others from adhering to the concept of codependency, but this omission does make a clear statement that may intensify the chasm that exists over the use of the term between mental health practitioners and those practitioners in the chemical dependency field.

A close examination of the concept of codependency and the criticism surrounding the term and its corollaries will likely indicate that much of the argument involves degrees of acceptance. Even though little empirically based research has been conducted on the subject per se, Giermyski and Williams (1986) maintain that

> It would be a mistake to deny that living or even working side by side with a drug dependent person causes stresses and problems or that wives and children as well as other members of families of drug dependent individuals undergo deprivations and stresses, that they suffer indignities, that such problems deserve help, and that help should be offered. However, the authors wonder if the term "codependency" has not been given connotations far exceeding justification, whether or not the implications (systematic, theoretical, and practical) at the level of the delivery of needed services have been sufficiently examined and the consequences considered. (p. 7)

In this sense, the very least that can be said about the concept of codependency is that it has helped to describe a variety of interpersonal and intrapersonal dynamics in a language that many can understand. In that alcohol and other drugs are rampant in our society across every economic and social line, the concept of codependency may currently be best operating as a paradigm attempting to make sense out of the confusing, paradoxical, and often deleterious effects of one's extended drug involvement and its impact on others. Whether intuitively understood or empirically proved, it is safe to say that the characteristics identified as codependent operate in almost all of us at one time or another. Differences between individuals exist in incidence, degree, and persistence. Our society is based upon competition and achievement. You, as a reader of this book, might be termed an overachiever, but, it is often overachievers who are in positions to help others. The need for belonging to powerful groups, identified as indicative of an antisocial and narcissistic personality disorder (Kitchens, 1991), can be functional, and decisions that affect us all are made by groups of powerful people. We all need humor in our lives, so the histrionic personality identified as maladaptive is necessary for us to have perspective on our lives. Compulsivity is almost a given in undergraduate and graduate school, isn't it? Does that mean you are maladaptive for choosing to go to college or graduate school? The point we are making here is that codependent characteristics, per se, are not inherently good or bad. Sometimes behaving codependently is appropriate, very adaptive, and can lead to satisfaction with oneself and others. Sometimes these same characteristics can lead to problems. An inflexible adherence to codependency as well as an inflexible avoidance of it may become problematic. The advice given here is for you to remain open to the client and to employ an understanding of codependency as it relates to the well-being of that client. Categorically disregarding the presence of codependent behaviors may limit the amount and kind of information being presented by clients and can lead to less than efficacious results in counseling. Moreover, since thousands upon thousands attend CODA meetings and adhere to the principles of codependency as outlined in *The Coda Book,* a limited or myopic understanding of the larger social, political, and economic implications of codependency for women and racioethnic minorities is questionable practice.

Mental Health Professionals' Own Codependency

In a recent study, Martsolf (2002) sampled 149 males and females whose ages ranged from 23 to 73. The sample included nurses, family physicians, psychologists, and social workers. The results of the study indicate a relatively low incidence of codependency in this sample. This stands in contrast to a preliminary study conducted by Fisher and Harrison (1993a), which assessed codependent characteristics of graduate students in a master's degree counseling program. We found that these prospective mental health professionals reported more codependent characteristics than did students in other graduate programs. Moreover, the graduate students in the mental health profession were more likely to have come from an alcoholic home. This preliminary study suggests that mental health professionals' codependency may be a potential problem in a counseling relationship.

Even though these are only two studies (and both are limited in their own ways), some interesting implications are apparent. Given that the pathological discourse of codependency in this culture has been around long enough to be seen and experienced as oppressive by many in the helping professions, one wonders whether there is now a tendency to be hesitant in identifying oneself as codependent. Given this possibility, Fisher and Harrison's earlier study of graduate students occurred when there was widespread interest in the concept, and helping professionals were thought to be potential codependents because of the nature of the work they performed. During the time in which Fisher and Harrison (1993a) conducted their preliminary study, the stigma of codependency was not as harsh as feminists accused it of being in the 1990s. Thus, in the past, a questionnaire measuring codependency in a population that reflected low incidence may well have been due to a lack of subjects' identification with codependent characteristics. Currently, the stigma of being codependent has many pathological connotations. This has created a situation in which both male and female subjects (mental health practitioners included) who are being assessed for codependency may not want to see or be seen as codependent. The fear is that being seen or identifying oneself as codependent will indicate a degree of pathological relating.

Professional Enabling. The dynamics that transpire between client and mental health professional in sessions may also reflect the professional's codependent behaviors and may result in a type of professional enabling of your client's maladaptive behaviors. Weigscheider (1981) sees attempts to keep an alcoholic from experiencing logical or natural consequences as enabling (see Chapter 11). Miller (1989) believes that enabling reinforces another's dysfunctional behavior. Thus, your attempts to keep clients from experiencing the natural consequences of their actions can be framed as professional enabling and can reinforce maladaptive client behaviors. You might perceive a client's desire to return to a dysfunctional relationship as reflecting your failure to effect client change. By personalizing the client's progress, you might strongly advise the client to avoid returning to the dysfunctional relationship and become angry with the client if the advice is not heeded. You might also over-identify with the experience of the client, resulting in an enmeshed relationship with the client. The loss of these interpersonal boundaries can diminish the effectiveness of the helping process, or at least confound the process. For example, you might identify with the client's feelings of helplessness in changing an alcoholic partner's behaviors. Rather than recognizing and working with the enabling aspects of the client's behaviors, you might prematurely attempt to steer the client into solutions rather than helping him or her gain insight into how his or her behaviors actually enable or reinforce the partner's alcoholism. In this manner, the client is kept from experiencing the consequences of his or her own behaviors.

We could continue with protracted examples of mental health professionals' potential codependent behaviors. Suffice it to say that codependency in the profession can be problematic. Training programs go a long way in helping mental health professionals understand the parameters of interactions with clients. Yet, if you come from a home where there was alcoholism or other family dysfunction, you may be more prone at times to behaving codependently with clients. Personal work can increase awareness of your codependent behaviors and can help you arrive at some strategies and solutions. It may well be that our profession attracts those who have experienced much of the same pain that clients will have experienced. Your experiences with your own pain and codependency can significantly increase the potential for accurate empathy with your clients and, therefore, can be of potential benefit. The extent of the benefit to clients will likely be related directly to the amount of your own work on codependency issues.

Relationship of ACOA, AA, Al-Anon, and Codependency

In her book, *Codependent Forevermore*, Irvine (1999) discusses ACOAs and codependency. She states that "codependency and the support group Codependents Anonymous exist today because of the trail blazed by Adult Children of Alcoholics" (p. 19). Thus, for Irvine, the two movements are related. For her, the debate is essentially focused on the extent that the relationship is complementary and/or supplementary.

However, the relationship between ACOA–codependency and AA and Al-Anon is more acrimonious. It goes beyond the fact that AA and Al-Anon were in existence first. According to Irvine, the Adult Child does *not* belong to AA. This is because AA exists for the alcoholic who wishes to become clean and sober and remain so. Second, the ACOA–codependency movement poses a cultural narrative that is in direct opposition to the discourse and tenets of AA and Al-Anon. The ACOA–codependency movement takes the focus off the alcoholic and places the focus on outside factors, specifically on genetic and/or interpersonal factors leading to addictions. In other words, adults who abuse alcohol are seen in the ACOA–codependency movement as doing so because of their childhoods and/or because of some genetic predisposition or proclivity. By locating some, if not all, of the control outside the abuser, a dramatic and deep chasm between ACOA and AA and Al-Anon is drawn.

There is another structural difference that is even more pronounced at the macrolevel, and Irvine (1999) again provides insight. She says that the AA discourse is a conservative narrative. This means that it conforms more closely to the larger social narrative. If blame is to be had at all (remember that in AA blame is seen as a process to be worked), one could feasibly "blame" it on the bottle—not society. From this perspective, the narrative of ACOA–codependency is anti-AA. This is so because, if blame is to be had in codependency, the "blame" is placed on the family. This difference in world views, concomitant with the obvious ensuing implications for treatment and recovery, is hard to understate.

On yet another front, the relationship between ACOA and codependency is an interesting one. According to research results (e.g., Dube, Anda, Felitti, Edwards, &

Croft, 2002), it is imperative that mental health therapists not confuse codependency with alcohol or being in a relationship with a person with AOD problems. Individuals can be codependent without being in a relationship where there is AOD use. For instance, Cullen and Carr (1999) studied the differences between young adults on a measure of codependency. Results indicated that those high on codependency scores reported significantly more family-of-origin problems. Yet the problems were not necessarily alcohol related. The family-of-origin problems included such things as relationships with chemically dependent partners, parental mental health problems, problematic intimate relationships, and personal psychological problems (for example, compulsivity). Moreover, there was no significant difference among those scoring high on codependency levels and the reporting of physical or sexual abuse.

The results of these studies suggest that codependency is one component of a wider multigenerational family systems issue. Thus, it is quite possible that ACOAs may be codependent. Yet not all codependents are ACOAs.

Critics of the ACOA–Codependency Movement

Popular Criticism. The ACOA–codependency movement's narrative was seen (and still is seen by many) as pitting children of any age against parents. The movement is seen as attacking the core structure of family. More significantly, the ACOA–codependency movement is seen as blaming *all families and all parents of all children.* Ironically, and to their credit, proponents of the movement adroitly point to the rigidity of the critics' "all or nothing" perspective as demonstrating the very dysfunction of dualistic thinking firsthand. Thus, the separation between AA and Al-Anon is reiterated with the larger social narrative.

Clearly and from a social perspective, any new discourse that runs counter to the larger, prevailing discourse is enough to spawn criticism. It is to be expected, because societies remain stable through the dialectical processes of homeostasis and change. However, at the outset, the ACOA–codependency movement was seen as significantly altering the traditional Euro-Caucasian discourse on families regarding one's position in the family structure. The antifamily nature of the new narrative also had significant structural implications for families themselves.

The movement had its emphasis on confrontation. Rightly or wrongly, it was seen as a movement of "parent bashing." At that time in history, blaming one's (somewhat elderly) parents ran diametrically opposite to the discourse calling for being grateful to one's parents (usually fathers) for fighting World War II and bringing peace and prosperity to the world. The movement was seen by some women and mothers as a movement that discredited their choices, their sacrifices for their family, and, in some cases, their livelihoods. (As you will see, the feminist researchers had critics of their own.) As such, a core basic orientation of the ACOA–codependency movement was seen as crossing the decades old narrative of "healthy and loving families" (of the 1940s through the 1980s).

Professional Criticism. As the ACOA–codependency movement grew, professional researchers became interested in studying the concept. After all, from a strict research perspective, the ability to identify, isolate, and profile a (albeit reputed) significantly large segment of society (ACOAs) for study was quite appealing. Yet the enthusiasm in being able to identify and isolate this population waned significantly as researchers designed studies and published results. Enormous methodological challenges in studying ACOA–codependency needed to be overcome. Many of the same problems remain today (Jacobs, Windle, Seilhamer, & Bost, 1999).

In the early 1980s, there was little problem in defining the terms *COA* and *ACOA*. The definitions were very precise and clear: COA meant a child of a parent who abuses alcohol, and ACOA meant an adult child of a parent who drank alcohol excessively. However, such a precise definition would eventually narrow the subject pool and create a diminished ability to generalize results. The problems were numerous. For instance, there would be difficulties attributing length of exposure to alcohol and the subsequent effects that it had. Second, since many alcoholics also used other drugs, this condition limited the population of alcohol-only users. Third was the issue of the validity of self-reports. Were the subjects reporting their patterns accurately? Fourth, even if one could argue in favor of self-reports, self-reports were (and are always) about events in the past. The validity of recollection was significant at the time, and debate continues in the courts. Today, the validity of self-reports is challenged under the rubric *recovered memories.* Fifth, assuming that one could validly recall an event and reliably self-report it, Goodman (1987) and then Windle and Searles (1990) argue that such things as parental inconsistencies, double-bind messages, the covert expression of feelings, shame, mistrust, and the existence of childhood roles occur in everyone's life. Therefore, since these experiences are ubiquitous, one should not attribute these characteristics solely to COAs and ACOAs.

From the outset of the movement, researchers were not interested in undertaking studies demonstrating the clinical characteristics of COAs, ACOAs, and codependency (Giermyski & Williams, 1986). Thus, if one were to examine the professional journals in the early 1980s, one would find a dearth of systematic and empirically based studies. Today, this has changed somewhat. There is moderate professional research interest in the topic of ACOA–codependency per se.

At the same time, it is important to understand the sequence of the growth and development of the ACOA–codependency movement. Alcoholics Anonymous came first, followed in order by Al-Anon, ACOA, CODA, and Gamblers Anonymous (GA) and other Twelve-Step recovery programs. This chronology is interesting because it reflects the importance of the ACOA and CODA recovery programs. CODA is the bridge connecting the earlier and more conservative programs of AA and Al-Anon with the other addictions that will be discussed in Chapter 14. As such, the ACOA–codependency narrative has had a significant background effect on the upstream research studies of alcohol, alcoholism, children of alcoholics, fetal alcohol syndrome, and other substance abuse. The downstream effects on research affect studies of gambling and other addictions.

Codependency and Diversity

Feminist Critiques of Codependency

As you would expect, codependency has been thoroughly critiqued from researchers in the fields of sociology and women's studies. There is a range of criticism, and most of it relates to white women. The feminist criticisms of codependency can fall into three broad categories: gender bias, the codependency discourse, and victimization and victimhood.

Most of the vociferous objections have come from those who see codependency as perpetuating a state of victimhood. From the manner in which many of these researchers write, it is easy to generalize many of their findings to racioethnic women. However, it is critical to note that, while feminists would readily agree about the presence of the oppression of women on an international scale, they would also agree that the West has tended to dominate both the theoretical and practical aspects of the feminist movement. Hence, the grand narrative of feminism is the story of Western endeavor and relegates the experience of non-Western women to the margins of feminist discourse (Kurian, 1999, p. 66).

In the United States culture, traditional feminism is not necessarily an appropriate voice for some or many racioethnic women. This does not mean that the criticisms advanced by feminists about codependency are irrelevant for the minority populations. It means that some of the criticisms discussed by feminists will be relevant and can be loosely generalized to minority populations. Some criticisms will not be able to be appropriately generalized. Perhaps equally important to note is that the codependent discourse affects both males and females. It just affects them differently. To our way of thinking, the impact of the codependent discourse in general is potentially more harmful to the population of women in general than it is to men. This is due to the social, political, and economic barriers that women face in today's culture.

Gender Bias. Researchers are in agreement that, given the multiple meanings of codependency, it is largely a social construct, as much perceiver as perceived (Harkness & Cotrell, 1997). Harkness and Cotrell (p. 473) and Rice (1992) believe that the concepts of codependency and enabling reflect a Twelve-Step culture perspective of the world. With this perspective as a backdrop, feminist critiques of gender bias in codependency argue against its many forms. The crux of their argument is that the concept of codependency is prejudicial toward women on social, political, and economic fronts. It is also claimed that the issue of gender bias and codependency is critical because the consequences for all women are serious (Hurcom, Copello, & Orford, 2000).

A review of the literature on gender bias and codependency reveals that the very notion of gender is a questionable construct and narrative. For instance, Butler (1990) believes that gender is not represented as "real," but as a boundary that is politically regulated. In agreeing with the principles of Butler's work, Phoca (1999) goes on to say that, since there is no essential masculine or feminine subject, both genders can take up masculine and feminine subject positioning. In essence, this perspective blurs the boundaries surrounding gender in the traditional sense.

Although you may not agree with these researchers, the implications of this blurring of boundaries for the AOD field are important to understand. The blurring of gender boundaries directly affects the definitions of codependency, as well as favorably affecting the ability of codependency research results to be generalized to larger populations. For instance, the AOD field has adopted a gender-neutral definition of codependency, such as the use of "adult," "person," "individual," and "family member." In other words, the definitions of codependency do not include or use the gender-driven terms "women" or "men" or any of their derivatives. Thus, the gender lines do not exist and, theoretically, anyone could be codependent.

Yet, in spite of these gender-neutral definitions, earlier studies conducted by Krestan and Bepko (1990) and Parker (1980) showed that the traditional views of addiction and codependency were rather traditional in that they usually reflected male substance abusers connected with helpful females. These helpful females, who were seen as also depending on addicted men, were labeled as codependent. In more current research, Babcock (1995), Babcock and McKay (1995), and Dear and Roberts (2002) reviewed the definitions and various meanings of codependency and enabling and assert that these concepts continue to be framed by traditional views of male and female. These researchers, along with others (e.g., Hurcom et al., 2000; Krestan & Bepko, 1990), argue that the existing structures of codependency nurture the development of caretaking and self-sacrifice in women while, at the same time, keeping men from developing those same qualities.

One of the main consequences of this misidentification and gender bias is the fact that the use of such words as "(codependent) person" and/or "(codependent) adult" has failed to successfully assign codependency or codependent traits evenly across males and females. For instance, it is a fact that males receive treatment for alcoholism far more often than do women. It is a tragic irony that this treatment differential occurs in spite of the fact that women, who are significantly underrepresented in studies of AOD abuse, may have higher rates of alcoholism or other substance abuse problems than are reported in the professional literature and databases. Hence, from this gender-bias perspective, not only does the concept of codependency propel women into stereotypic roles, but it also is seen as helping to mask their AOD abuse. At the same time, gender bias is hindering the development of nurturing qualities in the male population.

The Codependency Discourse. Several researchers (e.g., Babcock, 1995; Babcock & McKay, 1995; Krestan, 2000; Krestan & Bepko, 1990; Taleff & Babcock, 1998) write about the nature of discourse in our culture as it relates to codependency. Taleff and Babcock (1998) review the literature in the AOD field and identify five dominant discourses that guide the AOD culture. Two of these dominant narratives relate directly to the concept of codependency. According to Taleff and Babcock (pp. 34–39), the dominant discourses "in AOD work" are these:

- Blame the client for treatment failure
- Blame the victim
- Closeness equals pathology
- Too much knowledge is bad (don't think, it will get you in trouble)
- Never trust the client (all addicts are cons and manipulators)

Blaming the victim and closeness equals pathology relate directly to the codependency issue. In examining family systems theory and treatment approaches, Babcock and McKay (1995) believe that the notion of codependency has been the most blatant example of blaming the victim. Hurcom et al. (2000) believe that role-specific behaviors that result from a partner being addicted do more than blame. They pathologize the behavior. This followed the research of Taleff and Babcock (1998), who concluded that the AOD field tends to blame family members for the ongoing addiction (p. 37).

This research stream strongly characterizes an essential concern regarding the codependency discourse and feminism. Through this pathological narrative, helping is not perceived as a well-meaning, misguided, and yet unsuccessful attempt to thwart off the addict's self-destruction. Rather, codependency is an insidious strategy used by the addict's significant other(s) aimed at perpetuating the addiction. The discourse of blame and pathology results in the fact that cultural closeness, love, anxiety, and feminine nurturing are ignored. On a core assumptive level, the argument is that the paradigm reflects that people who are engaging in codependent behaviors are insidious and not to be trusted. Women engaging in these behaviors are posited as untrustworthy as well as antifeminine, because their natural tendency to nurture is now seen as unhealthy and is to blame for the addiction.

These researchers, as well as Krestan and Bepko (1990), see the need to understand the phenomenon of *closeness* as a way of overcoming the problems with this perspective. Clinicians need to be able to distinguish between normal, healthy closeness and pathological closeness or dependency. Moreover, clinicians need to assess families with AOD problems in terms of the amount of healthy *interdependence* that exists. If clinicians have a simplistic understanding of the gender-bias issue and codependency, they will miss what is clearly a complex phenomenon.

Victimization and Victimhood. A related issue is the social discourse of victimization and victimhood. This broad, social narrative is different from the AOD discourses identified by Taleff and Babcock (1998). Nevertheless, the social discourse of victimization clearly has significant implications for the meanings of codependency.

For example, Irvine (1999) presents a subtle and powerful argument regarding the dominant social discourse and victimization as a response. She maintains that it is the individuals "left or abandoned" who are the ones most often claiming the status of victimhood. Moreover, these "victims" are more likely to be unemployed, have fewer commitments to family, and less commitment to service in CODA (p. 148). Through this perspective, victimization and victimhood are structurally tied to the person's position with regard to who "left the relationship first" (p. 148). This same researcher maintains that victims usually have fewer social–structural resources available to them. As a result, the narrative of victimization initially responds to and then, ironically, augments these very social–structural losses. Irvine (1999) sees this as a failure of our larger social structure to protect individuals from these social losses and resulting isolation. Given these insightful assertions, it is appropriate for counselors to assess the extent to which victimization is state and the extent to which it might be more of a trait in individuals with AOD abuse issues (Irvine, 1999, pp. 156–157).

At the core assumptive level, victimization and victimhood place individuals, mostly women and racioethnic minorities, underneath the dominant discourse. This is because this discourse, in which these groups are portrayed as always seeking, presupposes an absence of something. Among other things, this seeking behavior is a "less than" position. The result is a vicious cycle that continues to isolate individuals from the mainstream and into a constant search to balance the scale.

Although not considered a feminist researcher, McWhorter (2000) cautions against the benefits of victimization and victimhood. McWhorter's work in the field of race and race relations and his views on victimization and victimhood are germane to this discussion. He believes that one of the very real dangers facing African Americans today is the *cult of victimhood.* According to McWhorter (2000), also cited in Harrison, 2004, a cult of victimology has become a keystone of cultural blackness and treats victimhood not as a problem to be solved, but as an identity to be nurtured.

Victimology is the result of calling attention to victimhood in black America, where the view is "less toward solutions and more toward fostering and nurturing an unfocused brand of resentment and sense of alienation from the mainstream" (McWhorter, p. 2). McWhorter sees the cult of victimology as an unconscious process, although not necessarily one that is the result of white political chicanery. Victimology infects the subconscious to the point that it makes it all but impossible for one to be open to all sides of an issue. Victimology has become a cultural keystone, likened to religion or bigotry, and one of the more deleterious effects is that it is passed on from one generation to another. According to McWhorter (2000), victimology is an expression of insecurity at its core. Subsequently, the insecurity manifests itself by calling attention to the faults of others through blaming. At the same time, Harkness and Cotrell (1997) remind mental health counselors that the victim narrative has a salubrious effect as well. People suffering from the effects of AOD abuse in the family need some shelter from the storm. Victimization and victimhood provide that shelter and comfort—albeit temporarily. Hence, clinicians should not categorically dismiss the full understanding of the dynamics of victimhood.

Harkness and Cotrell (1997) also advance a thoughtful critique of codependency from feminist perspectives. These researchers agree with the views of Irvine (1999) and Krestan and Bepko (1990) regarding the issues of pathologizing and blame. Citing the works of Asher (1992), Collins (1993), and others, Harkness and Cotrell discuss the notion that codependency is reoppressing women through the recapitulation of patriarchal politics of power in recovery. These same researchers also maintain that, from a certain feminist perspective, the cure for codependency is equally as toxic as the disease itself. They agree with Collins in asserting that the recovery is toxic because it is based on the core basic assumption of subordination.

The argument is similar to the argument about powerlessness and recovery for racioethnic minorities discussed in Chapter 11. The argument is based on the idea that recovery is toxic because codependent persons must assume a stance of powerlessness in order to become free from addiction. This powerlessness is layered by the experience of powerlessness in the sociopolitical realm. Thus, feminist concerns about codependency and recovery reflect the subtle and powerful social realm impacting the identification and treatment of women in need.

Codependency and Collectivist Cultures

According to many researchers, studies are also needed that examine codependency in women of other cultures. In terms of assessing codependency in women of diverse cultures, Gayol and Lira (2002) conducted a study aimed at validating an instrument for assessing codependency in Mexican women. Gayol and Lira used a sample of 230 Mexican women (aged 18 to 65 years). The Codependency Instrument (ICOD) was designed to assess codependency in this female population. The authors used a sample of 41 women to determine the ability of the instrument to discriminate between codependency and noncodependency. The results demonstrate that the instrument is a valid and reliable method for screening probable cases of codependency in couple relationships in Mexican women. The research results also indicate a higher proportion of codependency women whose relationships included either an alcoholic partner or one who was abusive.

The Self and Boundaries. Central to codependency is the concept of self and the subsequent issue of boundaries (Kelley et al., 2007; Watt, 2002). When codependency first appeared in Western culture and was embraced as a popular movement, it was criticized as being antimarriage, antireligion, and antisocial. These same criticisms exist today, although not necessarily in the same vociferous form. Essentially, these arguments center on codependency's overemphasis on the self. Codependency is seen as a relational problem in which a person's self is not complete, not satisfied, and not fulfilled until entering into relation with something or someone. As Whitaker says, this leads these individuals to constantly be "looking somewhere else" for fulfillment.

Once in relationships, codependent individuals were encouraged to set boundaries and, if the need arose, were encouraged to disassociate from marital partners and organized religion and, instead, focus on one's own needs. The concept of selfishness was reframed into the idea that it is better to be selfish than to be selfless. Codependents were selfless and needed to become more independent. However, Kim (1996) maintains that Americans [sic] have created the fantasy that they can live independent lives. For this researcher, Americans believe that being independent is equivalent to being free. In this manner, dependency becomes a negative characteristic and is viewed as a "failure to be autonomous."

Because of the collective nature of many non-Western peoples, it is imperative that mental health professionals understand that the notions of boundaries, such as independence and dependence, are culturally defined. To punctuate the point, Kwon (2001, p. 49) states that codependency theorists have failed to describe the cultural matrix of relationality, since their Western views of selfhood conflict with those of Korean and other Asian philosophies at a core assumptive level. For instance, the self in Asian culture is configured entirely differently from Western notions. In general, Asian peoples have strikingly different construals of such constructs as the self, others, and of the interdependence of the two. In turn, these construals can influence and sometimes determine the nature of individual experience, including motivation and emotion (Kwon, p. 43). The significant impact of these different construals is reflected in the quote by Kim (1996), also cited in Kwon (2001, p. 46). Kim says that if one used the Western notions of codependency to examine Korean or Asian family enmeshment, the resulting blurred ego boundaries and diminished ego strength should be reflected in higher rates of psychopathology in Asia and Korea than in the United States. Kim (1996) states that there are no data to support this view. In another illustration, Kwon (2001) says that many Americans say to their children who refuse to eat their supper, "Think of all the starving children in Africa and how blessed you are to be *different* from them." In Asia, Kwon says that the same story would go, "Think about the *farmer* who worked so hard to grow this rice for you. Think about how bad the *farmer* will feel if you do not eat your supper. The farmer's efforts will have been in vain!" Kwon says that both statements seem to involve others (starving kids and farmers). However, the starving kids are only *compared* to American children; they are not *related*.

The notion of relatedness is central in Asian societies. According to Kim, Americans have been cultured into setting boundaries in relation to others. Moreover, this awareness of boundaries has been deeply and inextricably woven into a cultural imperative of *autonomy and self-control.* Relationality becomes odious in that it would force some Americans to surrender this cultural ideal. A final example illustrates Kwon's (2001) views.

> When I first came to the United States and was becoming acquainted with American culture, I was bewildered when told by an American friend of mine, "Hey, leave me alone!" At the time, I asked myself a question, "Have I ever told *anyone*, 'please leave me alone'?" In my memory, I had never insisted on setting my boundary by saying, "Leave me alone." (p. 42)

In many collective cultures, the fundamental relatedness of the person is emphasized. In other words, the selfhood of the individual is sought more from a relational than from the internal attributes of rugged individualism. This difference clearly requires a reworking of the notion of blurred boundaries when working with some Korean or Asian individuals and families. Ego boundaries are established to separate or differentiate ourselves from others, and relational boundaries are created when we form our own sense of self in relation to others (Kwon, 2001). Kwon (2001) says that Koreans are not used to expressing *themselves.* They are accustomed to engaging in appropriate action that has their self-evaluations focused on normative information such as, "Is it appropriate or does it please others?" Many Asians are taught to feel more comfortable fitting in, rather than being separate or unique.

Therefore, it is not surprising to hear Carr (1997) state that it is more problematic for Koreans to work with self-identity and relatedness than it would be for them to work with identity and autonomy from others. In other words, the problems encountered in that culture move in a different direction than those occurring in America. With respect to mental health, codependent Americans have problems with others and need to be separating from them. Koreans and other Asians have problems because they are alone with the self. (In actuality, it would be more accurate to say that "they are alone and have no self" and need to be joining with others.) For Americans, the difficulty is in the separation. For Koreans, the difficulty is in the joining.

Relationship between Social Oppression and Codependency. Borovoy (2000) and Kwon (2001) are both interested in the impact of the larger social narratives on the meanings of codependency for women in Asian cultures. Borovoy states that since alcoholism in Japan has become more of a social concern the notion of codependency is becoming a more significant issue. Borovoy agrees with many feminist researchers in believing that the codependency narrative pathologized women in the 1980s. Moreover, Borovoy agrees with Kwon in maintaining that the Western meanings of codependency do not transfer well to the Japanese (Asian) culture.

In Japan, the American version of codependency is seen as normal and not viewed as a compromise of the self. Borovoy goes on to state that the codependency discourse in Japan is reminiscent of its postwar national ideologies. These ideologies reflect the value of a familylike (codependent?) intimacy holding together Japanese society. This dominant discourse also implores its social members to develop a highly cultivated sensitivity to social demands.

Kim (2002) is also interested in the impact of a codependent discourse on women of Korea and other Asian cultures. Kim took an accepted feminist perspective in noting the significant influence that social oppression has on codependency. Kim develops a concept of codependency that is derived from the Korean notion of *jong-sok-euee-jon,* known as "subjugated dependency" (p. 2569). In this context, codependency in Korean women is seen as resulting from the oppressive Confucian patriarchy in marriage and family systems. The hypothesis of this qualitative study was that there would be a strong relationship between the persistence of Confucian patriarchal values and practices in the Korean family structure and females' disposition to codependency in their marriages. Results confirmed the hypothesis for this sample: There is a positive relationship between codependency and the practices of Confucian patriarchal values.

The studies underscore the significance of being sensitive to cultural differences when applying the essential concepts of Western codependency to collective cultures, specifically for women in Korea and Japan. Borovoy (2000) believes that Japanese women who define themselves as codependent need to distinguish between socially valued interdependence and unhealthy or systematically exploitive forms of asymmetrical ties. Borovoy believes that, in this way, these codependent women can reject the exploitive demands of society while continuing to function in familial and neighboring communities (p. 94).

Summary

- The 1980s witnessed a spate of interest in the concept of Adult Children of Alcoholics (ACOAs) and codependency, concepts that, although different, many associate together.
- Early studies comparing difference between ACOAs and non-ACOAs were replete with methodological flaws such as small and nonrandomized samples and the use of elementary statistics to interpret results; other researchers assert that many studies beg the question since research also shows there may be no difference in these populations.
- The clinical characteristics exhibited by ACOAs include low self-esteem, depressive symptoms, antisocial behavior, anxiety disorders, parentification, and relational difficulties characterized by blurred and enmeshed boundaries.
- Other traits include difficulty with intimacy, discomfort with emotions, indecisiveness, and excessively giving into the needs of others.
- There is some evidence that ACOAs are at higher risk for substance abuse.
- Studies of relational patterns of ACOAs reflect that both males and females tend to marry less, have more issues if married, and have higher divorce rates.

- The CAST is the Children of Alcoholics Screening Test and is reliable in classifying ACOAs.
- Intervening with ACOAs includes the identification and addressing of early symptoms of problematic drinking and dysfunctional behavior and should also include the development of appropriate coping skills to replace those that may predispose clients to relational issues.
- There are many definitions of codependency, and these definitions are influenced by the degree to which one subscribes to the concept ; many who do not subscribe believe the characteristics have already been identified in various *DSM-IV-TR* diagnostic classifications.
- Many see codependency as an addiction that is chronic, progressive, and fatal, characterized in codependent individuals by fear, shame and guilt, protracted despair, anger that is expressed directly or in a passive-aggressive manner, denial and/or minimalization of feelings, rigidity, confusion over what is normal, extreme or excessive loyalty, overly anticipating the needs of others, and feeling overly responsible.
- Feminists criticize the concept of codependency asserting that the discourse blames the client for failure, blames the victim, equates closeness with pathology, and advocates for therapists to not totally trust their clients.
- Codependency does not translate well into collective culture narratives because of the emphasis upon "We"; in Asian cultures many see a positive and unhealthy relationship between codependency and Confucian patriarchal values.
- The Holyoake Codependency Index (HCI) has acceptable levels of validity and reliability for assessing codependency; other instruments are The Friel Codependent Assessment Inventory and The Codependency Test but these lack the necessary validity and reliability to be used clinically by professionals.
- Regarding treatment concerns, the client's use of the label ACOA and/or the term "codependent" can be helpful in that they are easy to understand by individuals and many are familiar with the concepts.
- Mental health professionals should remain aware of their own proclivities towards behaving codependently with their clientele.
- While helpful in treating, there is tension between AA and the other groups over codependency because AA places responsibility for problems externally on alcohol and Co-Dependents Anonymous (CODA) and Adult Children of Alcoholics (ACA) place responsibility on the person.

Internet Resources

Adult Children of Alcoholics
www.acoas.com.co

Codependency
www.nmha.org/go/codependency

Holyoake Codependency Index
www.taylorandfrancis.metapress.com/index

Further Discussion

1. What are your views of Adult Children of Alcoholics? Is there such a concept?
2. Why is there so much opposition in the professional community about ACOAs?
3. To what extent does the label of ACOA and/or Codependent provide a self-fulfilling prophecy?
4. What is beneficial about labeling oneself as an ACOA and/or Codependent?
5. Codependency has been criticized for gender bias. To what extent do you agree or disagree with those claims?
6. In what ways do mental health professionals' codependency help or not help this population?

13

HIV/AIDS

HIV/AIDS was first referred to as "slim disease." It first appeared on the shores of Lake Victoria in Uganda. Some thirty-three years later, those infected with HIV/AIDS are still in desperate need for a solution. Although medicine is routinely available, it is estimated that less than 5% of the 40 million people living with the virus throughout the world have access to these medications.

According to Primm (1992), five cases of *Pneumocystis carinii* pneumonia were reported to the Centers for Disease Control (CDC) in Atlanta in May 1981. In December of that same year, more than 100 cases of Kaposi's sarcoma (a form of cancerous skin lesion) were reported in homosexual men. The unusual occurrence of these two maladies caused suspicion and spawned further investigation, so that in September 1982, the Centers for Disease Control identified and labeled the acquired immunodeficiency syndrome (AIDS) as resulting from HIV infection. Although the White House Conference for a Drug Free America barely mentioned HIV in 1988, the Presidential Commission on the Human Immunodeficiency Virus Epidemic issued a separate report calling for increased research into treatment modes, increased treatment capacity, strengthening of primary and secondary prevention and early intervention programs, and an aggressive outreach program in HIV-related prevention and education.

Incidence and Prevalence

According to UNAIDS (2006), there are approximately 39.5 million people living with HIV worldwide. Of these, about 37 million are adults and 2.3 million are children under 15 years of age. Cases are split about evenly for males and females. Of world HIV cases, 63% reside in sub-Saharan Africa. Worldwide, young people 15–24 account for approximately 40% of the new cases each year. Since 2004, individuals living with HIV increased in every region of the world. The greatest increases are found in eastern Asia, central Asia, and eastern Europe, whose rates increased one-fifth since 2004. There are between 1,039,000 and 1,185,000 people in the United States living with HIV infection (Centers for Disease Control and Prevention, 2007a), and approximately 40,000 are infected each year. It is even more alarming that about one-quarter of the total HIV-infected population do not know they are infected. The result is that these individuals are unknowingly continuing to spread this disease. As sad as these statistics are, HIV/AIDS cases are often complicated by the presence of AOD and infectious diseases, including pneumonia, tuberculosis, and sexually transmitted diseases.

Based on data from 33 states (those with sufficient reporting systems), it was found that in 2005, the estimated rate of HIV/AIDS was 19.8 per 100,000 people. This reflects an increase of 7%. From 2001 to 2005, rates for HIV/AIDS cases in children less than 13 years of age had decreased. The rate remained stable for persons 65 years or older. However, the largest number of cases occurred for persons aged 35 to 39 years. From 2001 to 2005, African American and Hispanic rates decreased. Still, African Americans accounted for 49% of all HIV/AIDS cases diagnosed in 2005. Rates increased among Euro-Americans, Asian/Pacific Islanders, and Native Americans/Alaskan Natives. Currently, rates of HIV/AIDS cases among their respective populations are as follows: Hispanics, 27.8 per 100,000; Native Americans/Alaskan Natives, 10.4; Euro-Americans, 8.8; and, Asian/Pacific Islanders, 7.4 per 100,000.

Males having sex with males continued to increase as a category from 2001 to 2005. Yet, a decrease was noted among intravenous drug users (IDUs). Nonetheless, males having sex with males and persons exposed through high-risk heterosexual contact accounted for 81% of all HIV/AIDS cases diagnosed in 2005. The rates of increase for males and females was the same (7%). In spite of these rates, HIV/AIDS is a chauvinistic disease in that women are more easily infected than men. Moreover, women die of AIDS quicker than men (CDC, 2006c, 2001, 1994). As has been the case in the past, if you practice risky behavior in South Dakota or some other more rural state, your odds of becoming infected are not as great as they are if you practice the same behavior in New York, Los Angeles, or Washington, DC (CDC, 2001).

Myths and Facts about HIV and AIDS

Because of the severity of the AIDS epidemic, rumors and misinformation about the disease abound. In general, three areas of interest and of potential misinformation can be identified. One area is information about HIV itself—what it is, what it does, and how an individual infected with HIV will appear to others. Another area of concern relates to how HIV is transmitted, and the third area focuses on the workplace—what employers can and cannot do regarding a worker with HIV or AIDS.

The HIV Virus

Human immunodeficiency virus is known as HIV. The virus attacks a person's immune system, thereby damaging the individual's ability to fight off other opportunistic diseases such as pneumonia or cancers. Once an individual is infected with HIV, it may take years for acquired immunodeficiency syndrome (AIDS) to develop. Individuals infected with HIV develop a characteristic serum antibody response that can usually be detected between two weeks and six months following exposure (Selwyn, 1992). However, it is possible for as much as six months to two years to pass before one's body begins producing detectable HIV antibodies (Pimentel & Lamendella, 1988). Roughly 5% of all HIV-infected people remain free from AIDS-related diseases (Hooker, 1996).

Testing for HIV. The HIV antibody test reflects only exposure to the AIDS virus, but this exposure does not mean that the person will develop the AIDS disease. It is possible for a person to test positive for HIV antibodies and suffer no detectable immune system damage, feel healthy, and not develop full AIDS disease. The incubation period between HIV infection and AIDS is 7 to 10 years (Hooker, 1996; Selwyn, 1992). However, once individuals have been infected with HIV, there is a great likelihood they will develop AIDS; the only unknown factor is when this will occur, since the progression of illness is unpredictable. Of the HIV infections diagnosed in 2004, 39% were diagnosed with AIDS within 12 months. The most vulnerable populations for this diagnosis were those older than 35 and IDUs. Although early detection of HIV and medical treatment can slow the progression of AIDS significantly, medical treatment cannot stop AIDS from developing.

Diagnosis of AIDS and AIDS Related Complex. AIDS and AIDS Related Complex (ARC) are medical diagnoses indicating a specific set of characteristic symptoms. A diagnosis of AIDS is made when any of 12 opportunistic infections (e.g., *Pneumocystis carinii* pneumonia) and/or any of three malignancies (e.g., Kaposi's sarcoma) are reliably diagnosed in the absence of any other known cause for immunodeficiency (CDC, 1994). AIDS Related Complex refers to the condition of those individuals who have damaged immune systems and some specific symptoms, which include night sweats, weight loss, and lymphoma, but who do not have any of the opportunistic infections associated with AIDS. An individual may be diagnosed as having AIDS Related Complex and be sick some of the time with less serious opportunistic infections than those found in AIDS cases. Individuals with AIDS or AIDS Related Complex may show signs of a disease, but they will not always be sick. Thus, an individual may test antibody positive but show no signs of opportunistic diseases. On the other hand, an individual may have full-blown AIDS where any number of opportunistic infections may be present.

To date, there is no known vaccine currently available that can prevent HIV infection. There is also no known cure for AIDS. Although new information is being discovered every day, as of 2007, no cure for AIDS has been found.

Transmission of HIV

There is consensus and certainty about how AIDS is transmitted, and no new information regarding this issue is expected. Anyone infected with HIV can infect others. According to World Health Communications (1988), "HIV is transmitted primarily during sexual contact through parenteral exposure to blood and blood products, and from mother to child during the perinatal period" (p. 10). Hence, "The virus must be transmitted from the blood stream of a person with AIDS to the blood stream of another person" (Pimentel & Lamendella, 1988, p. 42).

Because of the screening of blood now used in hospital settings, it is rare for someone to become infected through a transfusion or blood clotting factors. Babies born to HIV-infected women may become infected before or during birth or through breast-feeding after birth. Although unusual, healthcare workers have been infected with HIV after being stuck with needles containing HIV-infected blood or after infected blood gets into a worker's open cut or a mucous membrane, such as the eyes or inside of the nose. There has been only one instance of a patient being infected by a healthcare worker in the United States, and this involved HIV transmission from one infected dentist to six patients (CDC, 2007b). According to the CDC, research involving more than 22,000 patients of 63 HIV-infected physicians, surgeons, and dentists found no other case of this type of transmission in the United States.

Living with a Person with HIV/AIDS. With some precautions, living with a person infected with HIV or AIDS is almost completely safe. There have been only rare occurrences of infection, and those cases were found to have resulted from contact between skin or mucous membranes and infected blood. The CDC (2007b) does provide guidelines for prevention of transmission:

- Wear gloves during contact with blood or other body fluids that could possibly contain visible blood, such as urine, feces, or vomit.
- Be sure to cover cuts, sores, or breaks on both the caregiver's and patient's exposed skin with bandages.
- Immediately wash hands and other parts of the body after contact with blood or other body fluids.
- Surfaces soiled with blood should be disinfected immediately and appropriately.
- Avoid sharing razors, toothbrushes, or other objects or engaging in practices that increase the likelihood of blood contact.
- Needles and other sharp instruments should be used only when medically necessary and handled according to recommendations for healthcare settings. Do not put caps back on needles by hand or remove needles from syringes. Dispose of needles in puncture-proof containers out of the reach of children and visitors.

Kissing. There is no known risk of transmission through either closed-mouth or "social kissing." However, "French" or open-mouth kissing is different. The CDC recommends against engaging in this activity with a person known to be infected because of the possibility of an open wound in the mouth. Nevertheless, the risk of acquiring HIV during open-mouth kissing is believed to be very low. CDC has investigated only one case of HIV infection that may be attributed to contact with blood during open-mouth kissing.

Biting. There was one incident of transmission through biting that the CDC investigated in 1997, and since then there have been other reports. However, in all of the reports, there was evidence of severe trauma with extensive tissue tearing and damage and the presence of blood. Biting is not a common way of transmitting HIV. In fact, the CDC reports numerous cases of bites that did *not* result in HIV infection.

Saliva, Tears, and Sweat. Although HIV has been found in saliva and tears in very low quantities from some AIDS patients, this does not mean that it can be transmitted. In fact, contact with saliva, tears, or sweat has never been shown to result in transmission of HIV.

Environmental Contact. There is also no known evidence of HIV being transmitted through such things as eating utensils, drinking glasses, telephones, swimming pools, toilet seats, or computer keyboards. Touching, hugging, shaking hands, or being in the same proximity with an HIV-infected person poses no risk.

Insects. Studies conducted by researchers at CDC and elsewhere have shown no evidence of HIV transmission through insects. This is the case even in areas where there are many cases of AIDS and large populations of insects such as mosquitoes. Lack of such outbreaks, despite intense efforts to detect them, supports the conclusion that HIV is not transmitted by insects. Since HIV lives for only a short time inside an insect it does not reproduce nor survive in insects. HIV is not found in the feces of insects either.

Sexual Contact. When condoms are used reliably, they have been shown to prevent pregnancy up to 98 percent of the time among couples using them as their only method of contraception. Similarly, numerous studies among sexually active people have demonstrated that a properly used latex condom provides a high degree of protection against a variety of sexually transmitted diseases, including HIV infection. Condoms are classified as medical devices and are, thus, regulated by the Food and Drug Administration (FDA). Condom manufacturers in the United States test each latex condom for defects, including holes, before it is packaged. However, only latex or polyurethane condoms provide a highly effective mechanical barrier to HIV. Natural skin condoms may contain natural pores and are not recommended for prevention of HIV. Women should consider using the female condom when a male condom cannot be used.

Working or Interacting with HIV-Infected Individuals. There is no known risk of HIV transmission to coworkers, clients, or consumers from contact in industries such as food-service establishments. In fact, an HIV-infected food service worker (e.g., cook, waitress, bartender) need not be restricted from work unless they have other infections or illnesses (such as diarrhea or hepatitis A) for which any food-service worker, regardless of HIV infection status, should be restricted.

Likewise, there is no evidence of transmission from a personal-service worker to a client or vice versa. This includes hairdressers, barbers, cosmetologists, and massage therapists. There has been no known instance of HIV transmission through tattooing or body piercing. There is theoretically a risk of HIV infection from this process, though, if unhealed piercings come into contact with an infected person's blood. Healing from various piercings can take weeks or months. Workers using needles for tattooing, piercing ears or other body parts, or for acupuncture, should use them only once. Although the risk of HIV infection is low in these situations, the Hepatitis B virus has been transmitted through some of these practices (CDC, 2007b).

Living with an HIV-infected person may also pose a threat in the case of co-occurrence of tuberculosis (Selwyn, 1992). Although prolonged exposure to TB is normally necessary for infection to occur, it is very important that infected individuals cover their mouths and noses when coughing and to take all of the prescribed TB medication (Washington State Department of Health, 1996). Because of the risk of TB infection to household members, it is recommended that all who live with an HIV-infected individual be screened for TB and followed up.

Survival and Mortality. Walker (2002) believes that the gender differential in AIDS deaths is associated with a decrease in the mortality of males with AIDS. In particular, this researcher maintains that the advent of antiretroviral medications is the main cause of the decrease in death among males. Moreover, another factor explaining the gender differential is the idea that antiretroviral medications are not fully utilized by women. Duerr (1997) sees reasons for this lack of utilization as stemming from limited access, as well as from patient and provider knowledge or attitudes about the treatment. In rural areas, there may be other reasons. For example, transportation might be a serious issue. In addition, Walker maintains that in rural areas there is a sense of independence that can preclude seeking help—for instance, the women in her study who believed that caregiving to other women with AIDS might prevent that woman from caring for herself (Walker, 2002, p. 311).

As demonstrated by the statistics reviewed earlier in the chapter, the CDC (2007a) reports that from 2001 to 2005, the estimated number of HIV/AIDS cases decreased among children age 14 and under. However, rates of HIV/AIDS increased among the 15 to 19 year olds. The survival rates were intermediate among male and female adolescents who had heterosexual contact with someone known to be at high risk or actually HIV-infected. Mortality was greatest among those HIV-infected male and female adolescents who were injecting drugs.

Risk Factors and High-Risk Populations

General Risk Factors

From the statistics cited at the beginning of this chapter, it seems as though race and gender are risk factors for HIV-infection. Using race only, the African American and Hispanic populations of the United States are at greatest risk for HIV infection. In general, women are more susceptible than men for HIV infection. However, this does not sufficiently tell the story of who gets HIV/AIDS. When these racial and gender risk factors are coupled with such things as sexual orientation, protected sex practices, alcohol and other drug use, and the intravenous injection of drugs, the risk increases dramatically.

The CDC (2006b) has identified general risk factors for HIV and sees individuals at risk from the following:

- Sharing needles, syringes, cotton, or water with others while injecting drugs or steroids
- Engaging in unprotected sex, including vaginal, anal, or oral, with men who have sex with other men, with multiple partners, and/or with anonymous partners
- Exchanging sex for drugs or money
- Receiving a blood transfusion or clotting factor between 1978–1985
- Receiving diagnosis or being treated for hepatitis, tuberculosis (TB), or a sexually transmitted disease (STD)
- Having unprotected sex with anyone who has any of the risk factors listed above

Co-Infection: HIV Infection and Other Diseases

Since HIV was first diagnosed, an association between HIV infection, drug use, tuberculosis (TB), and sexually transmitted diseases (STDs) has been found. Anyone can get TB: people of all races and colors, rich and poor, of any age. Despite a decline in TB nationwide, rates have increased in certain states, and elevated TB rates continue to be reported in certain populations (e.g., foreign-born persons and racial/ethnic minorities). People with HIV also seem to be at higher risk for TB as well as at higher risk for STDs. TB is a very lethal disease for those with HIV. It is estimated that at least one-third of the 39.5 million people who have HIV are also infected with TB. Tuberculosis is treatable, and it can usually be cured even in those living with HIV. However, according to the CDC (2005a), there are some strains of TB that are particularly resistant to the common antibodies used to treat them. As such, the 37th Union World Conference on Lung Health held in Paris in 2006 featured the interaction between HIV and TB with the caveat that we need prompt and accurate diagnosis in order to combat the new strains of TB.

Sexually transmitted diseases (STDs) or sexually transmitted infections (STIs) remain a major public health challenge in the United States, and Weinstock (2004) and the CDC (2006) estimate that 19 million new infections occur each year, almost half of them among young people ages 15 to 24. In general, individuals who are infected with STDs are at least two to five times more likely to acquire HIV if they are exposed through sexual contact. However, the risk may be increased up to tenfold, especially where an STI such as syphilis, cancroids, or herpes causes inflammation or open sores on the genital or perineal area of either partner.

Health problems for women with STDs tend to be more severe than those for men. This is due mainly to the fact that many STDs are asymptomatic in the early stages and, therefore, often go undetected and untreated. Hooker (1996) explains that most STDs are more easily transmitted to women than to men, and the rate of infection reveals that women are twice as likely to contract gonorrhea, chlamydia, chancroid, or hepatitis B during a single act of unprotected intercourse with an infected partner. When putting these statistics together with those depicting HIV among women and adolescents, one can readily see that these two populations are at great risk.

The close parallel between HIV infection and AIDS, TB, and sexually transmitted diseases is clearly disturbing. Reasons for such high rates of exposure and infection have been studied by various human interest groups such as the National Institutes of Health, the Centers for Disease Control and Prevention, the World Health Organization, and others. In general, risk for these diseases is correlated with sociopolitical issues. Factors such as immigration (from areas where TB and STDs are prominent), increased poverty, homelessness, IV drug use, limited access to healthcare, and living in communities with a high prevalence of STDs all have been identified as high-risk factors (CDC, 1996; Hooker, 1996).

Risk Factors for Women

In the United States, the proportion of women among new HIV or AIDS diagnoses has increased sharply from 15% before 1995 to 27% in 2004. According to Mphande-Finn and Sommers-Flanagan (2007) and the CDC (2007a), AIDS among women is on the rise and is partly related to the fact that women are approximately twice as likely as men to contract HIV during vaginal intercourse. Whereas males most often contract HIV through homosexual contact, nearly 80% of new HIV cases in women are caused by heterosexual intercourse. Malow, Dévieux, Rosenberg, Dyer, and St. Lawrence (2006) assert that rates of HIV infection are increasing rapidly among reproductive age, non-substance-injecting women, and Theall, Mitchell, Ludwick, Brown, and Kissinger (2004) concur by stating that 85% of HIV-infected women are between 15 and 44 years of age. A U.S. Department of Health and Human Services (HHS) Public Health Report (2004, p. 2) found that most women with HIV are racial and ethnic minority women living in urban inner cities who are disproportionately affected by poverty, crime, and social disorganization and represent the most disenfranchised sector of our society. According to the same report, rates of psychiatric disorders among HIV-infected women (53% for any disorder) are higher than for their noninfected counterparts. Of these disorders, a diagnosis of substance abuse disorder occurred in 25% to 66% of these women, 15% had a major depressive disorder, and approximately 35% had posttraumatic stress disorder (PTSD).

The World Health Organization (2007) believes that gender norms impact a women's vulnerability to HIV. The cultural discourse allows males to have more sexual partners than women and encourages older males to have sex with younger females, and the statistics showing higher infection rates for younger women than for younger men seems to bear this out. Women may want their partners to use condoms, yet women often lack the power to make them do so. In that one-third of women with HIV report PTSD, it is clear that physical, emotional, and sexual violence also contribute to the vulnerability for women. The impact of such a narrative is seen in several venues. For example, forced sex can contribute to tears and lacerations and, thus, put women at greater risk for HIV infection. Moreover, violence and/or the threat of it can prevent the negotiation of safer sex practices and can prevent women from sharing the results of HIV-positive tests.

According to the CDC (2007b) and UNAIDS (2006), approximately 75% of women newly diagnosed with HIV were infected during unprotected sex. More often than not, these women were infected by male partners who had engaged in risky sexual behaviors. Twenty percent of women diagnosed with HIV in 2004 acquired it during unsafe injection drug use.

Although it appears to be a heterosexual issue for women, lesbian women have a small risk for becoming infected with HIV, too. An advisory panel for the Centers for Disease Control maintains that there are some risk factors for lesbian women that include substance abuse, sex with gay or bisexual men, artificial insemination, and sexually transmitted diseases (CDC, 1994).

Culturally and Ethnically Diverse Populations

Only seven countries are estimated to have more people living with HIV than the United States (UNAIDS, 2006). According to the CDC (2007a) data from HIV and AIDS prevalence and incidence surveys continue to reflect the disproportionate and differential impact of the HIV epidemic on racial and ethnic minority populations.

The overwhelmingly high incidence of HIV in minority populations may be partly explained by the concentration of IV drug abuse in those populations. However, because of the paucity of research into minority drug abuse (see Chapter 4), one can really only surmise reasons for this remarkably high incidence. Another factor identified as being associated with a higher incidence of HIV infection among minorities is the general distrust of the healthcare system by these groups, especially minority women, that may heighten resistance for preventive help (O'Leary & Jemmott, 1995; Ullery & Carney, 2000).

The CDC (2007a), UNAIDS (2006), and Myers, Javanbakht, Martinez, and Obediah (2003) found African Americans as having the highest overall HIV prevalence, HIV incidence, and HIV mortality. Moreover, this population "has the greatest number of years of potential life lost to the disease" (Myers et al., 2003, p. 66). These same researchers see several continuing factors implicated as contributors to sexual risk taking among African Americans. Among these factors are such issues as low socioeconomic status, sexual orientation, HIV serostatus, substance use or abuse, and psychosocial factors such as self-esteem and perceived loss of control (see Chapter 4). Although African Americans comprise 12% of the United States population, they made up 50% of the new HIV cases reported in 2001 (Hasnain, Levy, Mensah, & Sinacore, 2007; National Institute on Drug Abuse, 2002). The majority of cases among youth and young adults is made up of African Americans as well.

Adolescents

Teens at increased risk for HIV infection include runaways and homeless youth, gay and bisexual youth, youth in juvenile facilities and adult jails, those in foster care, injecting drug users, crack cocaine users, those who have been sexually assaulted, out-of-school youth, and minority youth (Hooker, 1996). While these risk factors are self-explanatory, there is at least one hidden implication of great significance. Capuzzi and Gross (1996) report that children and adolescents who were sexually abused were found more likely to engage in activities that increased their risk for HIV infection. Specifically, females who were sexually abused were three times more likely to have injected drugs and five times more likely to have had intercourse before the age of 13. The males who reported sexual abuse were nine times more likely to report injecting drugs and nearly four times as likely to have initiated sexual intercourse before the age of 13.

Other High Risk Groups

The Homeless. The homeless present another population at high risk for HIV because of their high incidence of drug abuse. As you can imagine, statistics for this population and drug abuse and/or HIV are hard to determine. Since behavior associated with drug abuse is the largest single factor in the spread of HIV infection, this population remains at very high risk. Because TB rates are somewhat correlated with HIV rates, it is interesting to note that in 2003, 6.3% of reported TB cases in the United States were among homeless persons (CDC, 2005a). When compared with the general population, the homeless have a greater risk for latent TB infection (LTBI) and progression to active disease. These factors, concomitant with the issues of poor hygiene, inadequate nutrition, lack of medical care, crowded shelters, and the unsanitary conditions that prevail among this population all contribute significantly to their high risk.

Alcohol Users, Other Drug Users, and Clients in Treatment Centers. Substance abuse is related to a wide spectrum of medical disorders, and this is especially true with regard to HIV infection, other infectious diseases such as hepatitis C virus (HCV), and sexually transmitted infections. A variety of studies published in professional journals maintain that 30 to 40% of injection drug users are HIV-infected, 60 to 90% are HCV-infected, and approximately 90% have at least one type of STI (e.g., Brown, Kritz, Goldsmith, Bini, Rotrosen, Baker, Robinson, & McAuliffe, 2006; Francis, 2003). It is important to note that the risky practices of this population place them and others at substantial risk for these and other infections.

As you might surmise, the incidence of HIV among those in drug treatment centers is high. However, Sorenson and Batki (1992) note that only a small minority of drug abusers are in drug treatment. Brown et al. found that testing for these infections is prevalent among drug abuse treatment programs. However, there is very little education and almost no counseling for patients. By the time that HIV-infected individuals enter treatment, their HIV-related problems may be already beyond the reach of most human service systems. As we demonstrated earlier in this chapter, an equally alarming issue is that a great number of those with HIV infection do not know they are infected!

Those in the Penal System. The issues and implications surrounding HIV/AIDS in drug treatment centers are mirrored for prisoners and penal institutions. According to Kantor (2006), nearly 7 million people in the United States lived under the jurisdiction of the criminal justice system, and more than 2.2 million were in jail or prison in 2004. Fifty-seven percent of federal prisoners were incarcerated for drug-related offenses in 2001. Because of the association between drug use and HIV, it should be clear that prisoners are at exceptional risk for infection. As you would expect, female prisoners who have practiced prostitution, which frequently is associated with injection drug use and contact with HIV-infected sex partners, are at additional risk for HIV infection. The AIDS prevalence in 2003 was more than 3 times higher in state and federal prisons (0.51%) than in the general U.S. population (0.15%). Astonishingly, between 20% and 26% of people living with HIV/AIDS in the United States have spent time in the correctional system.

Primm (1992) and Kantor (2006) caution that no precise count of HIV cases in prisoners is available. Incarceration numbers usually reflect those currently in prison; criminals who are on probation and parole may go undetected or, at least, are underrepresented in any reports. Prisoners often enter a high-risk system with little or no knowledge about HIV because many HIV information campaigns "may miss many drug abusers (and their sexual partners) because criminal justice records and arrest or conviction charges are poor indicators of drug abuse" (Primm, 1992, p. 617). Even if individuals do not actually enter jail (many criminals charged and arrested with minor infractions are routinely released back into the community), the problem is that many of these individuals may have drug-abuse problems and may already be infected with HIV.

Kantor maintains that the rate of HIV infection among racial minorities is even more punctuated in prison than in the at-large population. In the general population, 40% of AIDS cases were among blacks and 40% were among whites, whereas in prison, 58% of AIDS cases were among blacks and only 18% were among whites. There is a paucity of evidence describing the transmission of HIV in prison. However, tattooing, sex, and injection drug use do occur, and if the guidelines (discussed earlier) are not followed, infection can occur.

Assessment of Clients for HIV and AIDS: Signs and Symptoms

As you saw earlier in this chapter, early detection and medical treatment can forestall the onset of AIDS and ARC, although to date nothing can eliminate the probability of AIDS once a person has been infected with HIV. Although the diagnosis of HIV can be made only by positive tests for the HIV antibody, several indicators might suggest the presence of the infection in clients who have not undergone medical testing for the virus. Therefore, it is important that you, as mental health professionals, be aware of issues that suggest the presence of HIV in order to urge high-risk clients to be tested and, hopefully, to receive appropriate medical intervention if they show early stages of infection. When risk factors are coupled with other signs and symptoms, it is crucial that every attempt be made to refer the client for assessment of HIV infection. These other signs and symptoms include physical anomalies and neuropsychiatric disturbances.

Physical Signs and Symptoms

It is customary for mental health professionals to initially elicit a psychosocial, drug, and brief medical history from their clients. In the course of that interview, clients may mention many symptoms that, to them, may seem unrelated to the risk of HIV infection. These signs and symptoms may include complaints of fever, unexplained weight loss or loss of appetite, night sweats, general malaise, coughing and/or shortness of breath, swollen lymph nodes, recurrent or persistent sinusitis, abdominal pain, diarrhea, and visual changes such as visual field defects (Barthwell & Gibert, 1993). Other symptoms that should alert you to the possibility of HIV may be dermatological conditions such as genital warts, rashes, herpes zoster (shingles), and psoriasis (U.S. Department of Health and Human Services, 1990). Although these symptoms are not diagnostic nor unique to HIV, these coupled with a history of substance abuse may help guide your efforts in evaluating the possibility of HIV infection.

Helping HIV-Infected Clients

Clients with HIV can manage only the disease process and the disease itself. So, once a client is diagnosed with HIV or AIDS, your concern as a mental health professional will be to focus on helping the client attempt to manage and cope with the disease. Remember, the only way to know whether a client is infected is to be tested for HIV. Mental health professionals should not rely on symptoms alone because many people who are infected with HIV do not have symptoms for many years. Someone can look and feel healthy but still be infected.

In all cases, it is critical that clients adhere to the medications prescribed for HIV infection. This is because of the fact that the virus can replicate and mutate readily, and if doses are missed, the virus can quickly begin to replicate. In general, individuals can adhere to treatment of chronic diseases about 80% of the time and still be successful. However, with HIV, this level does not work. Patients need to be adhering almost 100% of the time in order to keep the virus from replicating. The absence of treatment means that almost all those infected with HIV will eventually get AIDS.

In general, helping the HIV-infected client focuses on assisting the client in understanding and accepting the changes that are occurring and will occur in his or her life. Educating the client about the disease and treatment is also important, as is the emphasis on the fact that AIDS is not necessarily fatal. This last statement is critical because general misconceptions about the disease are held by the public and by many HIV-infected individuals. For example, an HIV-infected client of one of the authors stated during the second group therapy session, "Having HIV is like living with a time bomb. The only thing you know is that the bomb will go off. You never know when or where you'll be in life when it goes off. All you know is just that it will explode someday and you'll die."

Because practice settings offering HIV care vary according to local resources and needs, it is important that mental health professionals have some knowledge of the resources that are available for each patient in order to avoid fragmentation of care. Clearly, a single source, capable of providing comprehensive care for all stages of HIV infection, is preferred. However, this is often not the case. In every case involving HIV-infected clients, mental health professionals should make concerted efforts to avoid long delays between diagnosis of HIV infection and access to additional medical and psychosocial services.

The Centers for Disease Control and Prevention (2006b) and the World Health Organization (2007) outline an approach to helping HIV-infected clients. This approach is called *palliative care therapy,* and it is indicated for clients who are living with an incurable illness. The aim of this approach is to help provide the best quality of life to clients and to offer support and comfort to loved ones. Palliative care is based on work conducted with hospice cancer patients and addresses emotional, psychological, and spiritual needs. Because HIV patients will probably suffer from severe pain at some point, pain control is a central focus of palliative care. Palliative caregivers affirm life and help clients see that dying is a natural process that can neither be hastened nor postponed.

The CDC Treatment Guidelines for HIV (2006b) recommend the following for counseling persons with HIV:

- Counseling should include the behavioral, psychosocial, and medical implications of HIV infection.
- Providers should be acutely aware of medical and psychosocial conditions that may be emergent.
- Providers should address other issues such as psychiatric disorders, emotional distress, or substance abuse.
- Providers should follow up on recommendations given to clients.
- Patients should be educated about what to expect from the medical community.

Regarding the medical community, clients need to know that they will be asked for a detailed medical history that will include sexual and AOD history. They will be given a complete physical examination and blood tests will be conducted. Included will be an assessment for other infectious diseases such as STIs, TB, and HCV. It is also likely that the medical facility will conduct a urinalysis as well as a chest radiograph.

Psychosocial Concerns of HIV-Infected Clients. Clients with HIV will be distressed when they are first informed of a positive HIV test result. The changes in their lives will likely be all-encompassing and overwhelming. According to the CDC (2006c), changes will include 1) accepting the possibility of a shortened life span, 2) coping with the stigmatization, 3) the need to develop and adopt new strategies for maintaining physical and emotional health, and 4) initiating changes in behavior to prevent HIV transmission to others. In addition, many persons will require assistance with making reproductive choices, gaining access to health services, confronting possible employment or housing discrimination, and coping with changes in personal relationships.

The larger narratives or social discourses shaping the values for males and females in the U.S. culture both create and help to solve issues related to helping clients with HIV/AIDS. This is clearly the situation for women from a feminist perspective. For example, DeMarco, Miller, Patsdaughter, Chisolm, and Grindel (1998) point out that women have learned to use silence as a generalized way to cope when they feel disempowered. Adherence to this discourse can have drastic effects for women with HIV/AIDS. In these cases, keeping silent can result in death. In other cases, the potential for early death is present if an HIV/AIDS-infected client uses silence. Moreover, the social narrative that guides the caregiving values for women in the mainstream culture can be deleterious as well. If a mother who has been socialized to ignore her needs while caring for others ignores her HIV/AIDS issues, she can bring more harm to herself.

In some cases, the social narratives are in conflict with more personal ones and serve to present barriers and challenges to the treatment of infected individuals. This is clearly the case in Walker's (2002) research. The rural women in Walker's study leaned more toward a rugged independence, which runs counter to the larger social discourse for many women. This was seen as presenting problems in the identification and treatment of that population.

The issue of stigma and stigmatization is another serious concern. The CDC (2007a), UNAIDS (2006), and Hoffman (1996) state that one of the defining characteristics of the HIV epidemic has been the perpetual association with stigma. One stigma related to the epidemic is homophobia (Trezza, 1994). Hoffman also reports that the disease has always been associated with death and with certain stigmatized groups such as gay men and injecting drug users. However, as the epidemic shifts, HIV is being increasingly associated with groups that are more marginalized—economically impoverished people of color, for instance. Hoffman also reports that, aside from the social stigma, there is also a legal aspect of the stigma relating to the protection of the public at large, the interpersonal stigma, and the internalized stigma that diminishes self-esteem.

According to Brown, Macintyre, and Trujillo (2003) and Macintyre, Brown, and Sosler (2001), the AIDS stigma undermines preventive efforts on both public and private levels. These researchers assert that the stigma negatively affects condom use, HIV test-seeking behaviors, care-seeking behavior on diagnosis, quality of care provided to HIV-positive patients, and perception and treatment of persons living with HIV/AIDS by communities, families, and various partners. Nothing is more important to the recovery effort than social support, and nothing so distinctly divides survivors who seem to do well from those who seem to do poorly than the level of social support that exists (Odets, 1995; Springer & Lease, 2000).

Vital in the approach to helping drug-abusing clients with HIV is a coordinated effort among the psychological, medical, social services, legal, pastoral and religious, peer support groups, significant family members, and other community-based service networks (Selwyn, 1992). The plethora of services required by these clients is due to the myriad tasks needing attention once the individual has AIDS. Selwyn (1992) purports that, for the young heterosexual HIV population, there will be issues surrounding childbearing, child support and custody, and orphanhood that will need to be addressed. These family issues will likely require the assistance of social and legal services. Legal services may also be needed in helping to determine a person who will be designated as having power of attorney (POA) for the client; also, this necessity should be addressed before the onset of delirium or AIDS dementia complex, which can leave the client adjudicated as incompetent. The HIV-infected client may be reluctant to ask for help in seemingly unimportant areas of his or her life. This neglect can impact surviving loved ones, so the term *coordinated effort* takes on special significance. Such coordinated effort can also help to identify the services needed to avoid a duplication of services, an issue that might increase client reluctance in asking for assistance.

Another area of concern is the client's sexuality and the risk of HIV transmission. Understanding the sexual aspects of the disease is of paramount importance, and frank communication between you as the mental health professional and your client is essential. Human touch is essential to everyone, and the client should be encouraged to hug his or her loved ones as well as to engage in safe sex. However, if an individual has already been exposed to HIV infection and has unprotected sexual relations with another infected individual, an acceleration of the disease process may be experienced. So it is critical to emphasize the importance of safer sex practices among already infected HIV clients.

Clients tend to do better and remain longer in the home setting when they have a caretaker (World Health Communications, 1988). Therefore, home health care and other supportive systems should be explored. Often these supportive networks are nontraditional; therefore, some exploration of community resources may be indicated. Identifying individuals and services that the client can access during a time of crisis can help allay fears regarding how he or she will be cared for. One of the goals of this identification is to help the HIV client avoid isolation, and many community, volunteer-based support systems are available for assistance. Ideally, these systems allow the client to live freely within his or her physical limitations.

Emotional Concerns. Certainly, client reactions to having a catastrophic illness will be of paramount importance to mental health professionals working with this group of clients. This work may include helping clients prepare for death. It is also important to help clients examine their quality-of-life issues, with a focus on establishing a philosophical understanding about what is acceptable in terms of work and disability status. Regardless of the extent to which one can work or one wants to work, delaying hospitalization as long as possible is recommended (World Health Communications, 1988).

Clients who have HIV may present a number of emotional reactions that can include anxiety, stress-distress syndrome, panic reactions, suicidal ideation, rumination, depression, and a plethora of defense mechanisms such as denial, anger, guilt, and isolation (Joseph & Bhatti, 2004; Springer & Lease, 2000; World Health Communications, 1988). These reactions have been gleaned from clinical impressions in working with HIV-infected clients as well as from studies on opiate addicts with AIDS or ARC. For example, Batki, Sorensen, Faltz, and Madover (1988) and Rounsaville, Weissman, Kleber, and Wilbur (1982) have identified that addicts with AIDS or ARC use denial as a defense mechanism and are also angry, isolated, and depressed.

Nord (1997) writes about the initial shock and denial experienced by people with multiple AIDS-related loss. After shock and denial comes overload and confusion, having to face reality, and reinvestment and recovery. This same author goes on to point out various multiple AIDS-related losses, including loss of family and friends, personal history, future, security, emotional range and well-being, hope, interest in life, self-esteem, roles, spirituality and assumptions, community, and celebration and sexual freedom.

Denial would certainly be a component of any client's grieving process when confronted with HIV. In HIV-infected, drug-abusing clients, however, denial about drug abuse as well as about having HIV may become more pronounced (Sorensen & Batki, 1992), and, as a result, clients and counselors can face a double-whammy of denial. However, it can be helpful for mental health professionals to understand that denial may only be a component of a larger construct of ambivalence: ambivalence about drug abuse and/or ambivalence about having HIV. In Chapter 7, we discussed the motivational interviewing techniques of Miller and Rollnick. One premise used in these techniques is that clients may be more accurately described as being ambivalent rather than being in denial about drug abuse. The client may actually sense that drugs may be a problem but may not be sure of the extent of the problem—or even if a problem truly exists. While this concept was originally intended for application to drug abusers, Miller and Rollnick's (1991) notion of ambivalence can apply as well to both HIV-infected drug-abusing clients and to those infected clients not abusing drugs. So, rather than being in denial about HIV infection per se, clients may be seen as experiencing ambivalence, and the techniques to reduce ambivalence described in Chapter 7 can be helpful and easily adapted to working with HIV-infected individuals. It should be noted, however, that denial and/or ambivalence can also be present in clients who are at high risk for HIV, and, if issues of denial and ambivalence are mishandled, it could be that they would refuse to be tested or refuse medical treatment or counseling interventions.

Anger displayed by people with HIV is to be expected, and in many cases is a sign of healthy adaptation to having been infected. However, it is possible that infected individuals could inappropriately displace their anger onto healthcare workers, family members, significant others, and at their healthcare management. Covert expression of this anger may be seen in individuals' missing appointments, in their refusal to comply with medical or counseling interventions, in their continued drug abuse, and/or in the selling of their medications. Some of this anger may be due to fear and mistrust of the system and of the care providers. This is exemplified by one of the author's own experiences: When running therapy groups for HIV-infected clients, a few group members attended only sporadically. Attendance became more stable only after the author had been "checked out" (clients' words) by other group members who passed the information along.

Nord (1997) points out that AIDS-related multiple losses create severe trauma and bring up such existential issues as being versus nonbeing, isolation versus a desire for connection, and meaning versus meaninglessness. Concomitantly, mood disturbance such as depression, a phenomenon already common among drug abusers, is exacerbated in HIV-infected individuals (Sorensen & Batki, 1992). Moreover, isolation is characteristic of drug-abusing, HIV-infected individuals. According to Sorensen and Batki (1992), isolation occurs in two ways: First, if the person's drug abuse already places him or her outside of mainstream society, HIV only pushes him or her further away; and, second, if the individual already has difficulty in initiating and maintaining healthy social contacts (as is rather common in drug abusers), then this difficulty may be a significant barrier to treatment. Because of the isolation factor, outreach programs designed to identify high-risk individuals for testing and counseling need to be aggressive and skillfully handled.

While recent advances in medication are slowly changing the status of HIV/AIDS from a terminal illness to a chronic illness, the spiritual issues that HIV-infected persons cope with continue to prevail (Holt, Houg, & Romano, 1999). These researchers identify three broad spiritual themes that may come up in counseling: (1) terminal illness, postdeath existence, and the meaning of life, (2) religious disenfranchisement from God or a higher power ("Why did I get AIDS?"), and (3) cross-cultural spiritual and religious issues in society and families of origin.

In general, these three spiritual themes will be relevant for all individuals. At the same time, the individual's psychosocial development and cultural mores will influence the manner in which these themes are presented and processed. Given the overrepresentation of racioethnic populations with HIV/AIDS, the diverse cultural spiritual beliefs and practices are obviously critical for counselors to consider. For example, mid to late adolescents are already working with issues related to the meaning of life. An aging individual is asking the same questions from the other direction. While both individuals are experiencing questions about the meaning of life, an adolescent's perspective is different from that of an aging person, and the conversations that occur in counseling with the adolescent will be different from the conversations with an older adult.

One difference between the two conversations would relate to the discussion with the older client regarding the client's comorbid health conditions. The multiple losses in physical health experienced by the aging population in general can become overwhelming when HIV/AIDS is present. Because of this situation, Orsulic-Jeras, Shepherd, and Britton (2003) believe that a strengths-based approach can be effectively used with aging HIV-infected individuals. Conversations with adolescents would not normally relate to their physical deterioration.

Medical Concerns. We have already discussed the medical concerns related to helping HIV-infected clients and suggested that the medical questions that clients have should be referred to medical personnel. Here, it is important to note that mental health professionals will most likely be confronted with complaints of side effects by their HIV-infected clients who are prescribed any of the anti-HIV agents just discussed. These side effects may increase client resistance to treatment and should be explored with clients who can be reminded that early intervention with these chemotherapies have been shown to slow the disease process (Selwyn, 1992).

Pain management, a focus of palliative therapy, might also be a potential problem because HIV-infected clients will still frequently require analgesia for the pain syndrome that often accompanies the opportunistic infections (Selwyn, 1992). Because drug-abusing HIV-infected clients probably have access to illegal drugs that can be used to numb the pain, this is one issue counselors need to keep in mind when and if their clients talk about pain. With the drug-abusing HIV-infected client, self-medication with AZT and antibiotics may also be a problem, since both can be purchased on the street. Again, clients should be warned of the dangers of self-medicating.

Yoga is gaining interest as a treatment for HIV/AIDS (Foster, 1999; Stukin, 2003). Counselors might encourage clients of any age with HIV/AIDS to inquire about the benefits of yoga. According to Foster (1999) and Stukin (2003), yoga can help with the side effects of the disease as well as of medications. Stukin does not believe it is necessary for someone with HIV to take specially designed classes in yoga, but it might be beneficial. Counselors can suggest that clients utilize the Internet and/or inquire at local community colleges and universities to gather information and resources about yoga.

Issues in the Workplace. In that the number of persons living with HIV/AIDS (PLWHA) increased 519% between 1990 and 2003 (Hergenrather, Rhodes, & Clark, 2006), and given that the general increases have been in the 24 to 64 age range, it is clear that the number of HIV-infected individuals in the workplace has increased and will continue to grow. This has created a need for more complex systems of delivery that includes vocational services and vocational rehabilitation. Conyers (2004) studied employment and HIV/AIDS and noted various motivations to work among the study participants. Reasons that HIV/AIDS patients gave for wanting to work included 1) the hope of increased mental health, 2) regaining a vocational identity, 3) meeting financial needs, 4) concern about the impact of unemployment on families and loved ones, and 5) decreasing fear related to the loss of needed services. Hergenrather et al. concur with Conyers and add that social skills are increased through employment.

Participants in the Hergenrather et al. study identified four impediments to employment for PLWHA. There was the fear that they would not have the ability to adhere to prescribed medical treatment because they might get so involved in work as to forget to medicate. Second was a lack of workplace accommodations. Loss of Medicaid was also identified as was the lack of HIV/AIDS education in the workplace.

According to the U.S. Department of Justice, Civil Rights Division (2007), PLWHA are protected under the Americans with Disabilities Act of 1990 (ADA). According to the ADA, private employers with 15 or more employees *may not discriminate in any employment practice* against qualified individuals with disabilities. This means that, for example, a restaurant may not fire a waitress upon notification that she is HIV positive, nor can a university fire a physical education instructor because her or his boyfriend has AIDS. Although prospective employees with HIV/AIDS have concerns about accommodations, the ADA requires employers to make "reasonable accommodations" to those having a disability. This means that employers are required to modify any aspect of the job so that the PLWHA can perform the essential functions of the job. This would include restructuring the job, modifying work schedules, acquiring or modifying equipment, and the reassignment to a vacant position for which the PLWHA is qualified. For example, an HIV-positive individual might be granted longer lunches in order to keep medical appointments and required to make up the time in flexible ways.

Obviously, the employer would have to know that the employee is disabled in order to make accommodations. This brings up very complex issues. Conyers and Boomer

(2005) maintain that research indicates that the vast majority of PLWHA choose *not* to disclose their status because of fears of discrimination. Other reasons for not disclosing include a desire for privacy, concerns about the overall work environment, and fear of other repercussions (p. 190). At the same time, PLWHA may *choose to* disclose in order to access social support, assert personal identity, and accommodate a desire to be open.

HIV-Related Issues Specific to the Helping Professional

Confidentiality

From our discussion here (see also Chapter 5), you can readily see that a person with HIV/AIDS has a right to keep his or her HIV status confidential. At the same time, certain issues of HIV testing warrant special consideration. Although some states have resolved the issue of mandatory HIV testing for certain personnel, such testing remains the subject of heated debate in other states (Barthwell & Gibert, 1993). Essentially, the debate centers on mandatory versus voluntary and anonymous versus confidential testing for HIV. Anonymous testing assigns a unique identifiable code to each person tested, so that the results are not traceable to an individual. Confidential testing links an individual by name to the test result, so that the laws protecting confidentiality protect the test results. According to the Revised Recommendations for HIV testing of Adults, Adolescents, and Pregnant Women in Health-Care Settings (Branson, Handsfield, Lampe, Janssen, Taylor, Lyss, & Clark, 2006) as well as the Centers for Disease Control and Prevention (Barthwell and Gibert, 1993) and many other professional healthcare associations that represent the public interest, voluntary and confidential or anonymous testing for individuals at high risk for HIV infection are strongly urged.

The confidentiality of testing is not an issue when it comes to sexually transmitted and other communicable diseases such as TB. However, because of the strong co-occurrence of these diseases among the HIV-infected population (Selwyn, 1992), you should assess for the presence of these diseases during the assessment phase of your work with clients who are at high risk for HIV infection and urge your clients to be tested.

Currently, federal law requires all who enter the military to be tested for HIV as well as requiring testing for HIV of all organ and tissue donors, all blood donors, persons seeking immigration to the United States, and federal prisoners (U.S. Preventive Services Task Force, 1989). Laws that relate to issues such as mandatory testing, confidentiality, reporting of results, and notification vary by state. Because of the statute idiosyncracies concomitant with the catastrophic effects of the disease itself, mental health professionals should take great care in becoming informed of these issues with their clients and learn to handle such clients delicately.

Harm Reduction and Needle Exchange

Another issue that can confront you as a mental health professional relates to the controversial issue of needle exchange in which drug-injecting addicts can receive clean needles so as to diminish the risk of sharing needles that might be carrying HIV. Alan Marlatt believes that "we will never get ahead of AIDS and our drug problems. People think that the solution, a softer drug policy or legalization, is worse than the problem. Our ways of handling these problems are not working and they may be making them worse" (Manisses Communication Group, Inc., 1994, p. 1).

The more moderate approach advocated by Marlatt is based on a European approach called *harm reduction.* Taking a middle-of-the-road approach between prohibition and legalization, the harm reduction approach would include methadone programs for heroin addicts and nicotine replacement therapy for tobacco users, and would attempt to control such addictive or excessive behaviors as binge drinking and overeating. Harm reduction also includes legalized needle-exchange programs as well as including "a more humane approach to drug problems and [would] begin to soften criminal penalties for drug use" (Manisses Communication Group, Inc., 1994, p. 5). The CDC (2005b), Kleinig (2006), Maddow (2002), and Marlatt & VandenBos (1997) believe that a harm reduction approach offers the at-risk populations simple behavioral solutions that can dramatically reduce the danger associated with high-risk activities, and these simple behavioral skills can help prevent the spread of AIDS (through needle-exchange programs and safe-sex and condom-use programs). Safe tattooing information and materials, along with bleach and disinfection materials, would also be included in the harm reduction approach.

Summary

- There is still no cure for HIV/AIDS, and a great number of those with HIV infection do not know they are infected.
- Only seven countries are estimated to have more people living with HIV than the United States.
- In the United States from 2001 to 2005, the estimated number of HIV/AIDS cases decreased among children age 14 and under; rates of HIV/AIDS increased among 15 to 19 year olds.
- AIDS among women is on the rise and is partly related to the fact that women are approximately twice as likely as men to contract HIV during vaginal intercourse.
- Approximately 75% of women newly diagnosed with HIV were infected during unprotected sex and, more often than not, were infected by male partners who had engaged in risky sexual behaviors; 20% of women diagnosed with HIV in 2004 acquired it during unsafe injection drug use.
- Most women with HIV are racial and ethnic minority women living in urban inner cities who are disproportionately affected by poverty, crime, and social disorganization and represent the most disenfranchised sector of our society.
- Rates of psychiatric disorders among HIV-infected women (53% for any disorder) are higher than for their noninfected counterparts; a diagnosis of substance abuse disorder occurs in 25 to 66% of HIV-infected women.
- Mortality is greatest among those HIV-infected male and female adolescents who were injecting drugs.
- The risk of co-infection is on the rise.

- Of injection drug users, 30 to 40% are HIV-infected, 60 to 90% are HCV-infected, and approximately 90% have at least one type of STI.
- By the time that HIV-infected individuals enter treatment, their HIV-related problems may be already beyond the reach of most human service systems.
- With proper precautions, there is minimal to no risk of becoming infected with HIV when living with a person who is infected.
- The number of HIV-infected individuals in the workplace has increased and will continue to grow; persons living with HIV/AIDS are protected under the Americans with Disabilities Act, 1990 (ADA), and employers are required to make "reasonable accommodations."
- Reasons that HIV/AIDS patients give for wanting to work include: 1) the hope of increased mental health, 2) regaining a vocational identity, 3) meeting financial needs, 4) concern about the impact of unemployment on families and loved ones, and 5) decreasing fear related to the loss of needed services.
- Employers need to know of the disability in order to make workplace accommodations but the vast majority of PLWHA choose *not* to disclose their status because of fears of discrimination and because of a desire for privacy, concerns about the overall work environment, and the fear of other repercussions.
- In treating the HIV/AIDS client, the CDC Treatment Guidelines for HIV recommend that counseling persons with HIV should include the behavioral, psychosocial, and medical implications of HIV infection.
- It is important that mental health professionals have some knowledge of the resources that are available for each patient in order to avoid fragmentation of care; providers should also follow-up on recommendations given to clients, and patients should be educated about what to expect from the medical community.
- Providers should also be acutely aware of medical and psychosocial conditions that may be emergent and should address other issues such as psychiatric disorders, emotional distress, and substance abuse.
- The World Health Organization also outlines an approach to helping HIV-infected clients called *palliative care therapy* for clients who are living with an incurable illness in order to help provide the best quality of life to clients and to offer support and comfort to loved ones.
- There is continued interest in secondary and tertiary prevention efforts that include needle exchange programs and other forms of harm reduction.

Internet Resources

HIV/AIDS and disabilities in the workplace
www.ada.gov/pubs/hivqanda.txt

Women and HIV/AIDS
www.who.int/gender/hiv_aids/en

HIV/AIDS and co-infections
www.unaids.org/en/MediaCentre/PressMaterials/FeatureStory/20061124_TB+and+HIV_en.asp

HIV/AIDS
www.cdc.gov/hiv/resources/factsheets/index.htm

Palliative therapy
www.cdc.gov/std/treatment/2006/hiv.htm

Further Discussion

1. What is your experience with HIV/AIDS? Do you know anyone who is infected?
2. How comfortable would you be interacting with a person living with HIV/AIDS (PLWHA) in a social situation?
3. Would this be different if you were working with a PLWHA?
4. Even though HIV/AIDS is protected under the Americans with Disabilities Act, how far should employers and employees go to accommodate a PLWHA?
5. Women have a higher mortality rate with HIV/AIDS, and they are often undiagnosed when they have alcohol problems. What impact has gender had on the development of treatment for HIV/AIDS when most researchers are male?

14

Gambling and Other Addictions

Lynn is a 44-year-old professional woman who has lived in Las Vegas for over 20 years. Lynn started gambling in her mid-twenties. For many years, Lynn's gambling could be described as recreational. She would go to casinos with friends, play video poker, and socialize. She never lost more than she could afford. At 32, Lynn married for the second time. She and her husband started using cocaine and gambling more and more frequently. They ran up debt on their credit cards. Lynn's husband developed an addiction to cocaine and Lynn left him. He shot himself to death shortly after they separated. After this traumatic event, Lynn stopped using cocaine and curtailed her gambling. However, in her late thirties, she remarried and started gambling with her third husband. Lynn's gambling started to spiral out of control. She applied for numerous credit cards and took out cash advances on them. To hide her activity, Lynn got a post office box so that her husband wouldn't see the mail. She borrowed money from her parents and friends, making up believable stories to justify the loans. Lynn had a job in which she had a lot of independence, and she spent considerable work time in local bars that had video poker machines. When she finally could not hide her debts any longer, she told her husband. Lynn's husband took care of their debts and made Lynn promise to only gamble with him on weekends. Lynn tearfully agreed and was able to moderate her gambling for a short time. However, within a year, Lynn was gambling out of control and had accumulated over $200,000 in debt. She couldn't sleep and was contemplating suicide.

This true story does have a happy ending. Lynn has not gambled in many years and regularly attends Gamblers Anonymous. She has cleaned up all her debts, has a demanding professional career, and enjoys an upper-middle-class lifestyle. It's a far cry from the chaos of compulsive gambling, which involved continuous lying, cheating, and stealing. You may be thinking that this kind of problem only happens in places like Las Vegas and Atlantic City. You would be wrong.

Prevalence of Gambling and Gambling Problems

In 1997, Congress established the National Gambling Impact and Policy Commission. On June 18, 1999, the National Gambling Impact Study Commission's Final Report was released. The Commission studied the following types of gambling: convenience gambling and stand-alone electronic gambling devices, lotteries, casinos, riverboat casinos, Native American tribal gambling, pari-mutuel wagering (horse racing, greyhound racing, jai alai), sports wagering, and Internet gambling. The commission examined gambling regulations, problem and pathological gambling,[1] and the impact of gambling on people and places. Recommendations were made in each area studied. Except where there are other references, the following information is from the National Gambling Impact Study Commission's Final Report (1999).

Prior to the establishment of the National Gambling Impact and Policy Commission, the last federal study of gambling had been conducted in 1976. The growth of gambling in the United States since that time has been astounding. Some form of legal gambling is now available in 48 states and the District of Columbia. There are lotteries in 42 states and Washington, DC, pari-mutuel racetracks and betting in 43 states, and authorized casino gambling in 28 states (including casinos on Native American reservations). In addition, Internet gambling sites provide an opportunity to gamble without ever leaving the house. In 1982, Americans lost $10.4 billion to gambling. In 1997, that figure had increased to more than $50 billion. Since 1973, state lottery sales have increased from $2.0 billion to $34 billion in 1997. Per capita lottery sales have gone from $35 per person in 1973 to $150 per person in 1997. Prior to 1990, there were only two destination casinos in the United States: Atlantic City and Nevada. Now there are more than 100 riverboat and dockside casinos and more than 260 casinos on Native American reservations.

As we did for alcohol and other drug problems, we will eventually specify criteria for gambling addiction. However, the number of individuals identified by the commission as having gambling problems is instructive at this point to indicate the scope of the problem. According to the commission's report, an estimated 2.5 to 3.2 million adults met the criteria for pathological gambling (analogous to alcohol and other drug dependence) in their lifetime, and 1.1 million adolescents (12 to 18 years) were estimated to be pathological gamblers. Petry, Stinson, and Grant (2005), who surveyed more than 43,000 adults as part of the National Epidemiological Survey of Alcohol and Related Conditions (NESARC), found that the prevalence rate of pathological gambling was estimated at 0.4% of the general U.S. population. This estimate differs from that of Welte, Barnes, Wieczorek, Tidwell, and Parker (2001), who found the lifetime prevalence rate to be 2.0%. Jacobs (2004; 2000) suggests that approximately 66% of underage youth have gambled in regulated and licensed gambling venues, and studies show that adolescents have pathological gambling rates two to four times those of adults. In a meta-analysis of the literature on disordered gambling in college students, Blinn-Pike, Worthy, and Jonkman (2007) found that 7.89% of college students had gambling problems. Gambling problems among those with psychiatric disorders have also been studied. In a large national community survey conducted by Statistics

[1]As will be described in this section, the terms *pathological* and *compulsive* gambling will be used interchangeably.

Canada (el-Guebaly, Patten, Currie, Williams, Beck, Maxwell, and Wang, 2006), it was found that of those who had engaged in gambling in the previous 12 months, 5.8% had low-severity and 2.9% had moderately high-severity gambling problems. In the same study, if gambling problems had comorbidity with mood and anxiety disorders, the rate of problematic gambling was 1.7 times higher. If substance abuse disorders were taken into account, the rate was 2.9 times higher. The Statistics Canada researchers and others (e.g., Zimmerman, Chelminski, and Young, 2006) conclude that the comorbidities of substance abuse and/or mood/anxiety disorder reflect higher risk for gambling problems.

Social and Economic Costs

The National Gambling Impact Study Commission's final report includes a chapter on gambling's impact on people and places. The report acknowledges the difficulties in determining cause and effect relationships between gambling and economic and social impacts. However, an attempt was made to describe both positive and negative effects of gambling on people and communities. For example, casino gambling has resulted in increased employment and income; increased tax revenues; enhanced tourism and recreational opportunities; and rising property values in some economically depressed communities. Some Native American tribes have used casinos to rebuild infrastructure, diversify holdings, and reduce unemployment. However, most of the major economic benefits of gambling seem to be limited to casino gambling and pari-mutuel wagering, because these forms of gambling employ the most people and often attract tourists. Other forms of gambling (e.g., lotteries) simply redistribute income among state or local residents. In many cases, lotteries have been shown to be a form of regressive taxation. In other words, those people least able to afford to play lotteries spend proportionately more than those who can afford it. The commission also examined the impact of gambling on the following social problems.

Crime. The relationship between crime and gambling has been difficult to establish because of methodological problems in studies designed to examine this relationship. In testimony before the commission, anecdotal incidents related pathological gambling and crime. "The Commission heard repeated testimony of desperate gamblers committing illegal acts to finance their problem and pathological gambling, including a Detroit man who faked his own son's kidnapping to pay back a $50,000 gambling debt, a 14-year hospital employee who embezzled $151,000 from her employer for gambling, and the wife of a Louisiana police officer who faced 24 counts of felony theft for stealing to fund her pathological gambling" (pp. 7–13).

Financial and Other Economic Impact. According to the commission, nearly one-fifth of pathological gamblers have filed for bankruptcy compared to 4.2% of nongamblers. In Iowa, 19% of Chapter 13 bankruptcies involved gambling debt. Three-quarters of the Iowa counties with the highest bankruptcy rates had gambling facilities in or near them. In a study involving Southern Nevada (Las Vegas), the Commission estimated the amount of bankruptcy debt losses and civil court costs at $10,000 per pathological gambler. In addition, these researchers estimated the cost of missed work, productivity losses, forced terminations, and unemployment compensation at $6,000 per pathological gambler.

With 20,000 to 40,000 pathological gamblers in Southern Nevada, the financial and other economic impact was estimated to be between $320 million and $640 million.

Suicide. According to the National Council on Problem Gambling (1997), nearly 20% of pathological gamblers have attempted suicide, and Zangeneh and Hason (2006) give similar figures of 18 to 20% of gamblers reporting suicide attempts. This is higher than the suicide rate for any other addictive disorder. The commission heard testimony that a survey of Gambler's Anonymous members showed that two-thirds had contemplated suicide, 47% had a firm plan, and 77% stated that they have wanted to die. It should also be noted that Nevada regularly has the highest suicide rate in the nation. While gambling problems cannot be clearly established as a primary cause, they would certainly be suspected.

Homelessness. The Commission heard testimony associating gambling problems and homelessness. In interviews with 7,000 homeless persons in Las Vegas, 20% reported gambling problems. In a survey of Chicago homeless providers, 33% reported that gambling was a contributing factor to homelessness of people in their program. Finally, the Atlantic City Rescue Mission told the commission that 22% of its residents were homeless due to gambling.

Abuse and Neglect. The news stories on the more dramatic cases of abuse and neglect related to gambling are depressing. Recently, in Las Vegas, a three-year-old was stabbed to death in her home while her mother and stepfather were gambling. Several years ago, a young girl was sexually assaulted and killed in a Southern Nevada casino bathroom in the early morning hours. Her father had left her in the video game section of the casino while he gambled. The commission reviewed two studies that showed that between 25% and 50% of pathological gamblers had abused their spouses. Increases in domestic violence were noted in communities after the advent of casinos. Finally, the commission report stated:

> Children of compulsive gamblers are often prone to suffer abuse, as well as neglect, as a result of parental problems or pathological gambling. The Commission heard testimony of numerous cases in which parents or a caretaker locked children in cars for an extended period of time while they gambled. In at least two cases, the children died. (pp. 7–28)

Internet Gambling. In addressing the U.S. House of Representatives in 2006, the executive director of the National Council on Problem Gambling, Keith White, stated that between January and March of 2006 the National Problem Gambling Helpline received over 30,000 calls of which 8% were for problematic Internet gambling. The predominant age range was 18 to 25. He also cited statistics from the Annenberg Foundation reflecting 600,000 youths (age 14 to 22) gambling online on a weekly basis. In that same report, White estimated the social cost of problem gambling from bankruptcy, divorce, job loss and criminal justice costs at $6.7 billion in 2005. We will discuss Internet addiction later in this chapter. However, suffice it to say here that the Internet makes gambling more available than ever before. Wood, Williams, and Lawton (2007) cite four main reasons why gamblers prefer online to land-based gambling: 1) convenience; 2) an aversion to land-based atmospheres; 3) preference for the pace of online gambling; and 4) the potential for higher wins. Although available, Internet gambling is regulated to some extent through the Unlawful Internet Gambling Enforcement Act passed into law in October 2006. This law prohibits financial transactions from banks and credit card companies to the Internet casinos, poker rooms, and sports betting sites.

Definitions of Gamblers and Problem Gambling

Perhaps the most well known model for conceptualizing gamblers was developed by Robert Custer (Custer & Milt, 1985). Custer described six types of gamblers:

1. *Professional gambler.* This relatively rare type of gambler is not usually considered one who has a gambling problem. However, many people with gambling problems may have a fantasy about becoming or the illusion of being a professional gambler. The true professional gambler controls the amount of time spent gambling and the amount of money wagered.
2. *Antisocial gambler.* The antisocial gambler is also relatively rare. This is the individual who is involved with cheating to win at gambling. This may involve the popular shell game that you have most likely seen on television or at the movies, marking cards, or rigging slot machines. This type of gambler may develop a gambling problem but, obviously, has antisocial personality issues as well.
3. *Casual social gambler.* As the label implies, this type of gambler is one who does not experience problems from gambling. Gambling may be a regular activity (e.g., buying a weekly lottery ticket) or part of the person's recreation (e.g., periodic trips to Las Vegas). The casual social gambler would not lose more than intended or find it difficult to stop gambling.
4. *Heavy social gambler.* For this type of gambler, recreation involves gambling. While the heavy social gambler may rarely lose more money than intended, he or she spends a great deal of time in gambling or gambling-related activities. For example, someone involved with sports betting may spend hours going over point spreads, injury reports, scouting reports, and trades in order to make "educated" bets. The gambling and associated behavior of this type of gambler can affect vocational functioning and family relationships because of the amount of time spent on preparing for gambling and following bets (i.e., watching games).
5. *Relief-and-escape gambler.* Custer described this type of gambler as the one who gambles to escape life problems or life situations. Problem gamblers may be lonely, anxious, or depressed and use gambling as a method to numb themselves against negative feelings. This is similar to the way some people use alcohol and other drugs to temporarily dull unpleasant emotions.
6. *Compulsive gambler.* The compulsive gambler is preoccupied with gambling and with getting money to gamble. He or she cannot control the amount of time spent gambling or the amount of money lost gambling. According to Custer, gambling becomes the most important aspect of the person's life. The compulsive gambler may engage in illegal activity to get the money to gamble.

There are several different models for defining gambling problems. Shaffer et al. (1997) described three levels of gambling. Level 1 gamblers experience few or no adverse consequences as a result of gambling. Level 2 gamblers experience negative consequences related to gambling, but do not meet *DSM-IV-TR* criteria for pathological gambling (see the next section). Level 2 gamblers may either progress to level 3, remain at level 2 indefinitely, or become level 1 gamblers or abstainers. Level 3 gamblers do meet *DSM-IV-TR* criteria for pathological gambling. The following section gives a more thorough description of these criteria.

Assessment and Diagnosis

Much of what you read in Chapter 6 about the screening and assessment of alcohol and other drug problems is applicable to gambling. Most importantly, if a person has experienced problems in school or job, family, and other relationships, with finances or the law or in other areas as a result of gambling, then that person has a gambling problem. Helping professionals should consider gambling as a possible causal factor for the presenting problems of clients and should ask about gambling in the psychosocial history.

As with alcohol and other drug problems, screening and assessment instruments have been developed for gambling problems. For a thorough discussion of these instruments, we suggest you read the chapter on this topic in *Best Possible Odds: Contemporary Strategies for Gambling Disorders* by William McCown and Linda Chamberlain (McCown & Chamberlain, 2000).

The best known screening instrument is the South Oaks Gambling Screen (SOGS) (Lesieur & Blume, 1987). According to McCown and Chamberlain (2000), the SOGS is highly correlated to the *DSM-IV* diagnosis of pathological gambling, is easily scored, can be used by helping professionals in generalist settings, and can be used with older adolescents and college students. A score of 3 or more indicates that the client is a "potential pathological gambler," and a score of 5 or more is indicative of a "probable pathological gambler." However, Weibe and Cox (2005) caution against using the SOGS with the older adult population until it can be further refined for this at-risk population.

In our own clinical work, we have found that the Twenty Questions used by Gamblers Anonymous are very useful for screening and client self-awareness. As with the SOGS and other self-report inventories, clients can easily lie to either minimize or exaggerate their symptoms in response to these questions. However, for clients and family members with genuine questions or concerns about gambling, we believe that the Twenty Questions are helpful. According to Gambler's Anonymous, most compulsive gamblers answer yes to at least seven questions.

1. Did you ever lose time from work or school due to gambling?
2. Has gambling ever made your home life unhappy?
3. Did gambling affect your reputation?
4. Have you ever felt remorse after gambling?
5. Did you ever gamble to get money with which to pay debts or otherwise solve financial difficulties?

6. Did gambling cause a decrease in your ambition or efficiency?
7. After losing, did you feel you must return as soon as possible and win back your losses?
8. After a win, did you have a strong urge to return and win more?
9. Did you often gamble until your last dollar was gone?
10. Did you ever borrow to finance your gambling?
11. Have you ever sold anything to finance gambling?
12. Were you reluctant to use gambling money for normal expenditures?
13. Did gambling make you careless of the welfare of yourself and your family?
14. Did you ever gamble longer than you had planned?
15. Have you ever gambled to escape worry or trouble?
16. Have you ever committed or considered committing an illegal act to finance gambling?
17. Did gambling cause you to have difficulty sleeping?
18. Do arguments, disappointments, or frustrations create within you an urge to gamble?
19. Did you ever have an urge to celebrate any good fortune by a few hours of gambling?
20. Have you ever considered self-destruction as a result of your gambling?

The term *pathological gambling* is used in the *DSM-IV-TR* to describe a severe gambling problem. As we have seen, Shaffer et al. use *level 3* to define the most serious type of gambling problem; Custer and Gamblers Anonymous use *compulsive gambling.* While there might be some academic debate about the most appropriate terminology or subtle differences between terms, we think it is fair to say that these three terms are essentially equivalent. The *DSM-IV-TR* does not have the equivalent diagnosis of *abuse,* as is the case with alcohol and other drugs. Terms like *level 2 gambler* or *problem gambler* are the closest descriptors.

The *DSM-IV-TR* describes pathological gambling as follows:

Diagnostic criteria for 312.31 Pathological Gambling

A. Persistent and recurrent maladaptive gambling behavior as indicated by five (or more) of the following:

(1) is preoccupied with gambling (e.g., preoccupied with reliving past gambling experiences, handicapping or planning the next venture, or thinking of ways to get money with which to gamble)
(2) needs to gamble with increasing amounts of money in order to achieve the desired excitement
(3) has repeated unsuccessful efforts to control, cut back, or stop gambling
(4) is restless or irritable when attempting to cut down or stop gambling
(5) gambles as a way of escaping from problems or of relieving a dysphoric mood (e.g., feelings of helplessness, guilt, anxiety, depression)
(6) after losing money gambling, often returns another day to get even ("chasing" one's losses)

(7) lies to family members, therapist, or others to conceal the extent of involvement with gambling
(8) has committed illegal acts such as forgery, fraud, theft, or embezzlement to finance gambling
(9) has jeopardized or lost a significant relationship, job, or educational or career opportunity because of gambling
(10) relies on others to provide money to relieve a desperate financial situation caused by gambling

B. The gambling behavior is not better accounted for by a Manic Episode.

You can clearly see the relationship between these criteria and the criteria for substance use disorders. The first criterion involves preoccupation, the next two are equivalent to increasing tolerance and lack of control, and the final three involve trouble as a result of gambling. The similarities between pathological gambling and substance use disorders raise this question: Is pathological gambling really an addiction?

Pathological Gambling: Addiction or Behavioral Disorder?

Many people have difficulty seeing pathological or compulsive gambling as an addiction, similar to alcoholism or drug addiction. It is easy to see why. With alcohol or other drugs, *substances* are introduced into the body and changes in neurotransmitters result. In other words, there are observable biological and chemical changes in the body. Drug dependence can be observed in the laboratory in nonhuman animals. Tolerance and withdrawal can be observed in humans.

With gambling, no substance enters the body. However, researchers have been able to demonstrate that changes in the brain occur during gambling, and these changes are similar to what occurs when drugs are ingested (e.g., Breiter, Aharon, Kahneman, & Shizgal, 2001). As we noted in Chapter 6, tolerance and withdrawal are not necessary conditions to define addiction. However, compulsion to engage in the activity, inability to predict when control will be lost, and continued involvement in the activity regardless of negative consequences are the necessary and sufficient conditions to define addiction to alcohol or other drugs. Compulsive or pathological gambling certainly is defined by these conditions. Clinically, we have seen individuals whose lives have been just as devastated as for the most serious alcoholic or drug addict. We have known cases of people committing suicide due to the problems resulting from compulsive gambling. We know people who lost every material possession they ever had and became homeless as a result of their gambling. We interviewed a famous compulsive gambler who lost more than $40 million in the Atlantic City casinos and lived on the charity of family and friends. In spite of the enormity of these losses and the condition of his life, this man continued to spend his Social Security money on lottery tickets.

The point is that the question of whether compulsive gambling is a "real" addiction is academic. For clinicians, it doesn't make any difference. If someone meets the criteria for pathological gambling, that person needs help. From our point of view, the etiology on the condition and neurochemical correlates are irrelevant. However, theoretically, there could be treatment implications if pathological gambling is viewed as a behavioral disorder. One could conceivably use techniques of behavior modification and contingency management to moderate gambling behavior. Our argument would be: Why do this? Gambling is not necessary. There are many other forms of recreation. It is not too challenging to avoid gambling establishments and opportunities. You don't show up at a party and have someone offer you a video poker machine. As with alcohol and other drugs, you can be absolutely sure that a person will not have problems if abstinence is followed. With any process that involves moderate or controlled use, there is a probability of problems. Why risk it? And, if abstinence is the most logical course, it doesn't matter if compulsive or pathological gambling is a true addiction or a behavioral disorder.

Treatment, Resources, and Support

Treatment

While there are similarities between treatment for substance use disorders and treatment for pathological or compulsive gambling, there are also significant differences. One practical difference is that health insurance rarely covers treatment for gambling problems. Furthermore, there is no federal support for compulsive gambling treatment as there is for alcohol and other drug treatment. Since problem gamblers almost always seek help only when the problem has become severe, they generally have accumulated large debts and cannot afford to pay for treatment. Therefore, unless a family member or friend has the financial resources to pay for treatment (which is usually expensive), the cost of treatment is prohibitive.

In some states, a portion of the taxes levied on casinos, race tracks, lotteries, or gambling devices is used to provide treatment for compulsive gamblers. For example, Oregon allocates a portion of their lottery proceeds to publicly supported compulsive gambling treatment. However, Nevada, unquestionably the state with the highest proportion of problem gamblers, currently has no public support for compulsive gambling treatment.

As with treatment for substance use disorders, compulsive gambling treatment can take place in inpatient or outpatient settings and usually includes a component for family members and/or significant others. According to McCown and Chamberlin (2000), inpatient treatment, often in a hospital setting,

> may be medically necessary for a client who has experienced a major life disruption—a vocational, financial, or marital disaster associated with either excessive gambling or suicidal attempts. Inpatient treatment probably is also indicated if the patient is experiencing insomnia, anxiety attacks, depression, mania, tangential thinking, extreme grandiosity, suicidal thinking, or frequent dissociative experiences. (p. 115)

Additionally, McCown and Chamberlin (2000) point out that inpatient treatment may also be necessary for many compulsive gamblers because they tend to be more impulsive and give in to cravings more frequently than alcoholics and drug addicts. Furthermore, a period of isolation may provide relief from the pressure of creditors, loan sharks, and gambling associates.

Outpatient treatment for compulsive gamblers is also available and has the obvious advantages of less expense than inpatient treatment and more convenience for those who continue to work and have families. However, as McCown and Chamberlain (2000) point out, there are no biological tests for gambling equivalent to drug testing for substance abusers. Therefore, the compulsive gambler could, theoretically, continue to gamble undetected while in treatment. However, we would point out that drug testing is not routine or random in many outpatient alcohol or other drug treatment programs. Perceptive clinicians can usually see the warning signs of slips and relapses, and the chronically relapsing client rarely remains in treatment.

Toneatto and Ladouceur (2003) summarize the literature on gambling treatment and maintain that studies show good response by gamblers to treatment and that most can benefit from it. However, Westphal (2006) studied attrition rates and found attrition rates of 23.5% for short-term pharmacological treatment; 42% for psychosocial interventions, 50.4% for long-term pharmacological treatment, 67.5% for Gamblers Anonymous, and 75% for community multimodal approaches. Westphal concludes that if the estimation of treatment effects have been based on patients who complete treatment, then treatment effects may be overestimated. Finally, Westphal asserts that attrition in gambling treatment is flourishing and is a substantial issue that varies across treatment sites, approaches, and modalities over more than two decades of investigation.

Resources

The National Council on Problem Gambling (www.ncpgambling.org) is a nonprofit organization whose mission is "to increase public awareness of pathological gambling, ensure the widespread availability of treatment for problem gamblers and their families, and to encourage research and programs for prevention and education" (from the website). The council administers programs and services, including a 24-hour confidential hotline (800-522-4700), a gambling-specific certification program for treatment professionals, an academic journal (*Journal of Gambling Studies*), literature distribution, and sponsorship of research and conferences. The National Council on Problem Gambling has 34 state affiliates. On their website, you can link to a state affiliate. It should be noted that the council maintains a neutral stance on gambling and receives financial support from the gambling industry.

Support

Gambler's Anonymous (GA) is the best known and most widely utilized source of support for compulsive gamblers. GA was established in 1957 and is based on the Twelve Steps and Twelve Traditions of Alcoholics Anonymous. We have discussed Twelve-Step groups thoroughly in Chapter 10. One difference between GA and AA is that more members of AA have been involved in a formal treatment program than those in GA. The reason is simple. There simply aren't as many treatment options for compulsive gamblers. Therefore, for many people with gambling problems, GA may be the *only* form of assistance they receive.

While there are some differences in format and language, open GA and open AA meetings have many similarities. The Twelve Steps and Twelve Traditions are read, people introduce themselves by saying, " Hi, my name is _______ and I am a compulsive gambler," and members share their experience, strength, and hope with each other. Cross-talking is not allowed and there is a sponsorship program. McCown and Chamberlain (2000) argue that GA is less spiritual and more pragmatic than AA and that GA meetings (particularly closed meetings) are more confrontational than AA. We have not found this to be true, but our experience with GA is less extensive than with AA.

A unique part of the GA program is the *pressure relief* group. After about 30 days of continuous abstinence, a member can request a pressure relief group meeting. The meeting usually includes the GA member, the spouse or significant other, the sponsor, and other GA members with long-term recovery. The group helps the new member develop a budget and a plan for repayment of debts. Members of the group may contact creditors and assist in debt negotiation. The spouse or significant other (assuming that he or she doesn't have a gambling problem) is encouraged to take control of the household finances. The new member is given an allowance and removed from credit card and bank accounts.

There are also Gam-Anon meetings, the equivalent of AlAnon, for the family and significant others.

Other Addictions

While the purpose of various support groups and Twelve-Step programs is to help gamblers abstain, there are other compulsive problems for which abstention is not an option or would be very difficult. These problems include compulsive behaviors around eating, sex and love, the Internet, and work. To some researchers, the fact that the latter behaviors cannot be dealt with through abstention is reason enough to eliminate them from the field of addictions and addictive behaviors. Moreover, many researchers have argued that the term *addiction* should be applied only to issues related to the ingestion of AOD (Young, 2004). In any case, the extension of a model of addiction from substances to behaviors remains controversial (Morahan-Martin, 2005; Yellowlees & Marks, 2005).

It is important for mental health professionals to formulate an opinion about whether behaviors other than AOD use can be classified as addictions. Because of the content in many popular magazines, books, and television talk shows, it is quite likely that you will encounter clients who believe they are addicted to gambling, food, work, the Internet, or relationships. While there is little disagreement among professionals that excessive engagement in these and other behaviors can result in a variety of problems, there is controversy about whether these behaviors can be classified as addictions. We believe that it is important for you to be informed about the different arguments in this controversy so that you can develop your own view. After outlining the arguments pro and con regarding the existence of other addictions, we will describe pathological eating, sex and love, Internet use, and work behaviors. Finally, we will present information on assessment and treatment issues.

Two Points of View about Other Addictions

In preparing to write this book, we submitted a prospectus that included a proposed table of contents. One reviewer was particularly impressed with the fact that we had included a chapter on other addictions. This reviewer commented that this area was usually neglected in books in the AOD field. Another reviewer was quite critical of our inclusion of this topic and chastised us for creating the impression that behaviors such as overeating, excessive gambling, and other behaviors were addictions. This was a clear demonstration to us that there are different points of view on the topic of other addictions and that these perspectives are expressed with considerable fervor.

Critics of Other Addictions

There are three main groups who discount the notion that behaviors related to eating, excessive work or Internet use, and sexual compulsions can be addictions. One group claims that classifying compulsive behaviors as *addictions* is inappropriate because these behaviors are already well defined in the mental health field. The debate is similar to the one regarding codependency that was discussed in Chapter 12. It can be argued that compulsions involving sex are already identified in the *DSM-IV.* For example, the sexual disorders called *paraphilias* include many of the sexual behaviors often referred to as *addictive* (e.g., exhibitionism, fetishism, voyeurism). Furthermore, the criteria for Histrionic Personality Disorder include "interaction with others [that] is often characterized by inappropriate sexually seductive or provocative behavior" (APA, 2000, p. 657), suggesting that those who are "addicted" to sex may have a personality disorder. Therefore, no new diagnostic category of sex addiction is necessary. For other interpersonal relationship problems, such as the compulsive need for love and attention, critics of other addictions point out that these symptoms may also be characteristic of a personality disorder, such as Dependent Personality Disorder, Narcissistic Personality Disorder, or Histrionic Personality Disorder, or may be classified as an Other Condition That May Be a Focus of Clinical Attention (e.g., Partner Relational Problem). Similarly, Pathological Gambling is already classified as an Impulse-Control Disorder Not Elsewhere Classified, and there is an Eating Disorders category in the *DSM-IV-TR.*

A second group of critics of "other addictions" are the same people who view alcohol and other drug problems as bad habits, willful misconduct, or irresponsible and irratinal behavior (Drewnowski & Bellisle, 2007). These conceptualizations have been described in Chapter 3 and may be held by professionals promoting a certain theoretical model of addiction or by lay people who see addictive behaviors from a moral model. For example, Alan Marlatt has written extensively regarding a social learning model of addictive behaviors (see Chapters 3 and 9). In his words, "addictive behaviors represent a category of 'bad habits' including such behaviors as problem drinking, smoking, substance abuse, overeating, compulsive gambling, and so forth" (Marlatt, 1985, p. 9).

Finally, there are also "purists" who see addiction from a medical model and restrict this label to those who are dependent on alcohol or other drugs. From this point of view, the demonstration of tolerance and withdrawal (see Chapter 2) in an individual who uses alcohol and/or other drugs is indicative of addiction. Since physiological tolerance and withdrawal cannot be shown in regard to behaviors such as overeating, gambling, and sex, these behaviors cannot be thought of as "addictions." Purists see the use of the term *addiction* when applied to behaviors different from alcohol and other drug use as diminishing the disease model of addiction.

Somewhere in between these groups of critics are Stanton Peele and Archie Brodsky who, in their book on love addiction (Peele & Brodsky, 1991), claim that love addiction—and any other addiction—is not a disease. These authors maintain that while putting love addiction in a disease model gave it a broad, popular appeal that was helpful in the 1980s, there is now a need to redefine what is meant by the addictive process.

Peele and Brodsky (1991) maintain that an addiction is an experience that takes on significant meaning and power with respect to an individual's needs, desires, beliefs, expectations, and fears. Further, these authors maintain that compulsive, dependent attachments arise from the punctuated contrast between the void and anxiety that people experience in the totality of their lives and the immediate fulfillment they expect will occur when engaged with the addictive object or sensation.

Proponents of Other Addictions

The proponents of other addictions point out the similarities between alcoholics and drug addicts and those who engage in excessive behaviors other than AOD use. For example, Yellowlees and Marks (2005) and Young (2004) associate problematic Internet use and Internet addiction. Carnes (2001), and Tripodi (2006) present research linking compulsive sexual practices with sexual addiction.

If you go back to Chapter 6 and review the criteria for Substance Dependence from *DSM-IV-TR,* you will see that only three of the criteria are necessary for the diagnosis. Even if we ignore the first two criteria, since they involve the controversial topics of tolerance and withdrawal, it is still easy to see that a client who overeats, gambles too much, is constantly changing sex partners, or uses the Internet excessively would meet the criteria for dependence if that behavior were substituted for the word *substance.* For example, Steve, a compulsive gambler with whom we worked, often gambled more money than he intended and tried to cut down on his gambling on many occasions. His marriage and job were adversely affected by his gambling. With these symptoms, it could be argued that Steve was dependent on gambling.

A less scientific argument to support the similarity of behavioral addictions to alcohol and other drug addictions is the development of Twelve-Step support groups for overeaters, gamblers, and "sex addicts" (see Chapter 10). Because Twelve-Step groups are based on the principles of Alcoholics Anonymous, and because these groups have helped many people with problem behaviors in many areas other than alcohol and other drugs, it is argued that these "other" behaviors should be seen as addictions. It is clear that someone can feel powerlessness over eating, gambling, or sex, which is consistent with the first of the Twelve Steps.

Finally, proponents of other addictions contend that adoption of this concept has resulted in organized efforts to help people with these problems. Popular books and talk shows, the heightening awareness of mental health professionals, and the development of support groups have all helped people label their problems. While some people believe that the labeling process is used as an excuse for problematic behavior, the opposite may be true. For example, if you have some troubling physical symptoms that you cannot explain, it is often comforting to receive a diagnosis of the condition, even if there is no cure. Perhaps you find out that you are hypoglycemic. You will always have the condition, but you can modify dietary habits to reduce the unpleasant symptoms. Similarly, if Steve identifies himself as a gambling addict, he may believe that he will always be a gambling addict but that he also has some resources for help (e.g., Gamblers Anonymous). Therefore, the open discussion about problems involving eating, gambling, and sex has resulted in many people acknowledging that they have one of these problems, that many people share their problem, and that there is help for those with these problems.

Food Addiction: The Eating Disorders

We eat to survive. We eat for a variety of other reasons as well, such as in celebration, for enjoyment, for social acceptance, or to relieve boredom. We also eat to win affection, as reflected in the often-heard phrase, "The way to a man's heart is through his stomach." Our eating is often ritualized: hot dogs at a sporting event, popcorn at the movies, snacking in front of the television, or setting aside meals as the time when the family can meet to discuss family issues or the day's events. Ritualistic eating can likewise be reflected in a tradition of overeating at Thanksgiving or other holidays. Eating patterns also vary: Some may eat when they feel stress or to avoid painful feelings, while others may restrict their intake under the same circumstances. It can safely be said that most of us, at one time or another, eat for reasons other than to survive.

You are probably most familiar with the eating disorder anorexia nervosa, described by Bruch (1986) as the relentless pursuit of thinness, and bulimia nervosa, described as chronic episodes of binge eating followed by purging. These two disorders are cited in the *DSM-IV-TR* under the section Eating Disorders (p. 539). Our cultural preoccupation with food, thinness, and its relationship with success has been cited as a cause of the increase in the incidence of eating disorders—especially among women (Schwartz, Thompson, & Johnson, 1983). However, there are other disordered eating patterns such as chronic obesity, binge eating, and chronic overeating that are not yet cited in the *DSM-IV.* These eating behaviors can eventually become problematic as well.

Over recent decades, eating disorders have become the most widespread mental health concern in young women (Newton & Ciliska, 2006). Recent estimates suggest that clinically diagnosable eating disorders such as anorexia nervosa and bulimia nervosa, affect from 0.5 to 2.8% of the United States population (Hudsen, Hiripi, Pope, & Kessler, 2007). These same researchers maintain that eating disorders are among the most lethal psychiatric illnesses and kill up to 20% of those afflicted.

In U.S. culture, being overweight is a symbol of illness and ugliness, and being slim represents health, beauty, and success. The pressures to be thin have resulted in a substantial proportion of adolescents from a variety of ethnic backgrounds, regardless of gender (although females make up a disproportionate number of those with an eating disorder), to engage in excessive weight control behaviors (Lynch, Heil, Wagner, & Havens, 2007). Dissatisfaction with one's body in terms of size, shape, and form can lead to personal distress and/or psychosocial impairment about one's body image. In some cases, this leads to body image disturbances (BID). It is this disturbance that is seen as a significant causative factor in the development of disordered eating and eating disorders.

Body Image

According to Cash (1997, p. 2) and Vocks, Legenbaurer, Rüddel & Troje (2007), body image does not refer to what you actually look like. Body image is a phrase that refers to an individual's *personal relationship* with his or her body. This relationship is formed around beliefs, perceptions, thoughts, feelings, and actions that are associated with physical appearance.

Body image is affected by strong sociocultural factors. Levine and Smolak (2001) state that body image is a complex synthesis of psychophysical elements that are perceptual, emotional, cognitive, and kinesthetic in nature. Body image is seen as integral to gender identity, and disturbances in it can cause interpersonal anxiety and self-consciousness.

According to Cash (1997), one's attitude toward one's body and the emotional and cognitive elements are more amenable to change than is one's perception. In fact, the perception of one's body size and shape is considered difficult, if not impossible, to change. This same researcher sees a disturbed body image as lowering one's self-esteem. In addition, Cash asserts that roughly one-third to one-fourth of one's self-esteem is related to appearance.

Cash sees that body image disturbances can also influence body dysmorphic disorder and clinical depression. While you are probably somewhat familiar with major depressive states, body dysmorphic disorder may be unfamiliar. Essentially, it is the disorder of *imagined ugliness* at the same time when others look at these individuals and see them as okay or even beautiful or handsome. Researchers have demonstrated the association between disturbances in body image and eating disorders, including anorexia nervosa, bulimia nervosa, and binge-eating disorder (e.g., Cummins & Lehman, 2007; Dounchis, Hayden, & Wilfley 2001; Levine & Smolak, 2001; Lynch, Heil, Wagner, & Havens, 2007).

While men's body image has not received the attention in the professional literature as has women's body image, Levesque and Vichesky (2005) report that males experience body image dissatisfaction as well. In particular, gay males, as opposed to heterosexual males, may have pronounced concerns with body image and can be at high risk for eating disorders. In a different stream of research, Lynch et al. (2007) maintain that in spite of the lack of agreement on the source of racioethnic and cultural differences related to eating problems, there is clearly a link between body mass index, body concerns, and risk of eating disorders among these various groups. However, the strength of that association varies from one ethnic group to another. It stands to reason that as we are able to prevent body image disturbance we will also witness a diminishing number of eating disorders.

Chronic Obesity

Chronic obesity is a worldwide epidemic (Coutinho, Moreira, Spagnol, & Appolinario, 2007). *Obesity* occurs when one is 20% over the desirable weight for one's height (Burrows, 1992), and *chronic obesity* occurs when individuals are at least 20% overweight for protracted periods of time. In general, there are mild, moderate, and severe degrees of obesity. However, it is important to be sensitive to diversity issues regarding obesity in that different cultures value different body types. For example, Becker (2007) cites the fat phobia among Hong Kong Chinese who appear to meet the qualifications for anorexia, and Lynch et al. (2007) cite studies demonstrating variations in attitudes toward eating, the meaning of food and meals, culturally related eating behaviors, as well as cultural influences on individuation, maintenance of control, and emotional expression.

According to the Centers for Disease Control and Prevention (CDC, 2007c), the prevalence of overweightness and obesity has increased sharply for both adults and children in the United States. These increasing rates are concerning in that being overweight or obese increases the risk for many diseases and health conditions, such as hypertension, Type 2 diabetes, coronary heart disease, stroke, gallbladder disease, osteoarthritis, sleep apnea, respiratory problems, and some cancers (endometrial, breast, and colon) (CDC, 2007; Dounchis, Hayden, & Wilfley, 2001; Levine & Smolak, 2001). Because of this, Jarosz, Dobal, Wilson, and Schram (2007) state that the reduction of obesity is one of the most important public health objectives for the twenty-first century.

Some research suggests that obesity has a genetic component and that obesity in childhood has a strong positive correlation with weight status in adulthood (Brownell & Stunkard, 1978; Robinson & Killen, 2001). However, Burrows qualifies this assertion by stating that a high fat cell count in infancy and childhood is predictive of adult obesity only when other factors such as overeating and inactivity persist. In addition to the genetic component and ensuing environmental factors leading to obesity in adulthood, two other avenues lead to this condition: a pattern of chronic binge eating or chronic overeating. Chronic overeating occurs when individuals routinely eat more than they need to eat in order to be healthy. Whenever you sit at a dinner table and say to yourself or to others, "I am so full, but I don't want that last piece of chicken to go to waste," you are engaging in overeating. Imagine if you were to repeat this at every meal—that is the experience of the chronic overeater. In contrast to chronic overeating, binge eating involves consumption of large and unnecessary quantities of food in one sitting and in a relatively short amount of time. Movies that depict first-century Romans lying on their couches and engaged in an eating orgy show a good example of binge eating. Although binge eating and obesity commonly co-occur, the relationship of one to the other is not always causal. For example, Gormally, Black, Dastrom, and Rardin (1982) estimated that only 50% of those seeking treatment for obesity indicated a pattern of binge eating at least once per week.

Chronic Binge Eating. Binge-eating disorder (BED) is a newly recognized entity that is characterized by uncontrollable consumption of food without any inappropriate compensatory behaviors (Coutinho et al., 2007). Bennett and Dodge (2007) assert that there is mounting evidence to include chronic binge eating as a third type of eating disorder. Estimates of the prevalence of binge eating suggest that it affects between 2 and 5% of Americans in any 6 month period. BED mostly affects women ages 46 to 55 and affects African Americans at the same rate as Euro-Americans. There are no reliable statistics related to other ethnic groups (National Institutes of Health, 2007).

Symptoms include eating an excessive amount of food within a discrete period of time with a sense of lack of control over eating during the episode. Generally, the binge-eating episodes include eating much more rapidly than normal; eating until feeling uncomfortably full; eating large amounts of food when not feeling physically hungry; eating alone because of being embarrassed by how much one is eating; and feeling disgusted with oneself, depressed, and/or feeling guilty after overeating. Individuals with BED are distressed about the binge-eating behavior. Binge-eating disorder is not associated with regular use of inappropriate compensatory behaviors such as purging or fasting. Although similar to bulimia (discussed later in this chapter), the main difference between them is that individuals with binge-eating disorder do not purge their bodies of excess calories. Hence, it would be expected that individuals with this disorder would be overweight for their age and height.

Bennett and Dodge (2007) claim that even though BED is most common in people who are overweight, it can affect people with appropriate weight as well. Adult females comprise about two-thirds of those with BED. BED is on the rise among teenagers, too. Symptoms can include a child eating a lot of food very quickly, feelings of shame and disgust about the amount of food ingested, a pattern of eating in response to emotional stress, eating late at night in secret, and hiding food containers in one's room.

Depression often accompanies BED (National Institutes of Health, 2007). A vicious cycle can occur where one becomes depressed and binges, which then creates more depression and more binging. According to Robinson and Killen (2001) and Striegel-Moore, Dohm, Kraemer, Schreiber, Taylor, and Daniels (2007), binge eating episodes can be triggered by feelings of anger, sadness, boredom, or anxiety. In addition, Bennett and Dodge have demonstrated that feeling embarrassed and feeling out of control are two distinguishing features delineating binge eating and BED from chronic overeating.

Chronic Overeating. Excessive intake of one's favorite food, intake of a food substance with a particularly high calorie count, or excessive intake of fats are forms of overeating (hyperphagia). However, we most often consider it to be overeating when individuals engage in a pattern of eating large quantities of food. In general, overeating is defined as the degree of food intake that brings in more energy than is needed for an individual to function (Striegel-Moore & Rodin, 1986).

Much of the research on overeating involves obese individuals. This research focuses on the effects of diffuse anxiety, uncontrollable arousal, uncontrollable life stress, emotional sensitivity, and physiological bases of food preferences and their relation to obesity (e.g., Brownell & Foreyt, 1985; Slochower, 1983). However, Wansink and Kim (2005) suggest that packaging and container size also affect overeating. In general, studies indicate that high, uncontrollable anxiety coupled with available food produces overeating (Slochower, 1983), and when a person eats in response to the anxiety, his or her anxiety level is lowered (Bruch, 1986). Overeating as a means of "stuffing" feelings or to relieve painful feelings has also received some support in the professional literature. For example, Slochower (1983) found that obese individuals may have more difficulty in spontaneously describing or labeling emotional experiences. She goes on to say,

> If the obese person is relatively unable to deal with emotions via the cognitive labeling process, then his or her sense of helplessness and distress would persist until an alternative stress-reducer was found. In this sense, overeating may represent an unconscious attempt to

> reassert control in the face of emotional helplessness, thereby suppressing that highly painful state. (p. 98)

The issue of control is apparent in this quote on obesity. Control is also an issue when discussing more pathological forms of eating, such as anorexia nervosa and bulimia nervosa.

Bulimia Nervosa and Anorexia Nervosa

According to Goodman, Blinder, Chaitin, and Hagman (1988), there have been no extensive reports of childhood anorexia or bulimia associated with purging. However, the adolescent and adult population present a different picture. Reports show the incidence of anorexia and bulimia to be less than 5% of high school and college women, although other estimates state that 80% to 90% of adolescent and young adult women have concerns about weight or are dieting (Freeman, 1992; Kitsantas, Gilligan, & Komata, 2003). There is evidence that eating disorders occur throughout the lifespan for women. Cause for alarm is signaled by studies that have demonstrated that only a minority of college women have normal eating habits (Hesse-Biber, 1989; Mintz & Betz, 1988). Kashubeck, Walsh, and Crowl (1994) believe that many college campuses may promote disordered eating behaviors by emphasizing perfection, competition, and physical attractiveness. The presence of such sociocultural pressures is at least partially responsible in the development of eating disorders during adolescence. Researchers in the field generally agree. However, early childhood trauma, unmerciful teasing about body size and shape, and other factors also influence the pressures leading to the final development of the illness (Kitsantas et al., 2003; Robinson & Killen, 2001).

Humphreys, Clopton, and Reich (2007) maintain that there is a link between eating disorders and obsessive-compulsive disorder (OCD). They estimate that between 15 and 41% of those with eating disorders also suffer from OCD. Newton and Ciliska (2006) cite increased risk of serious comorbidity with other disorders as well such as depressive and anxiety disorders, substance abuse, suicide attempts, general psychological distress, impaired social (interpersonal) functioning, and a reduced quality of life. It is clear that there are serious health consequences from prolonged bulimia nervosa and anorexia nervosa.

Bulimia Nervosa. Bulimia nervosa (BN) emerged as a new disorder in the 1970s, and incidence rates rose from the 1980s to early 1990s, with concerns being expressed that this disorder might be affecting increasingly larger numbers of adolescents. These same researchers state that current prevalence rates reflect that between 1.1 to 4.2% of females have bulimia nervosa in their lifetime. Males represent approximately 5 to 15% of people with anorexia or bulimia and an estimated 35% of those with binge-eating disorder (U.S. Department of Health and Human Services, 2007).

In general, bulimia nervosa is characterized by recurrent episodes of binge eating where the person experiences a lack of a sense of control and eats an excessive amount of food within a discrete period of time. There is also recurrent inappropriate compensatory behavior in order to prevent weight gain. This includes self-induced vomiting or misuse of laxatives, diuretics, enemas, fasting, or excessive exercise. The fact that people with bulimia nervosa usually weigh within the normal range for their age and height is interesting.

This is due to the compensatory behaviors that keep weight down. Individuals with this disorder can fear gaining weight and can feel intensely dissatisfied with their bodies to the point of having BID. Often, compensatory behaviors occur in secrecy. During the episode, individuals report feeling disgusted and ashamed when they binge, yet relieved once they purge. According to the *DSM-IV-TR,* specific diagnostic criteria for bulimia nervosa include recurrent episodes of binge eating, recurrent inappropriate compensatory behavior aimed at preventing weight gain, binge eating and inappropriate compensatory behaviors occurring on the average two times per week for three months, the overinfluence of body shape and weight upon one's self-evaluations, and that the disturbance does not occur exclusively during periods of anorexia nervosa.

Rogers and Petrie (2001) found that women with bulimia generally have a diminished ability to regulate tension, have lowered impulse control, have a need for immediate gratification, and have a lowered sense of worth. Forbush, Heatherton, and Keel (2007), Brouwers and Wiggum (1993), and others report an association with perfectionism and an array of eating disorders in women. Forbush et al. found that the associations were strongest for fasting and purging and, for males, perfectionism was associated more with fasting than for other disordered eating.

Brouwers and Wiggum (1993) see internal conflict as abounding within the bulimic population. An individual with bulimia often gets caught up in a psychic no-win situation, in which one side of her insists that she must eat only the right foods and the other side begs for spontaneity with food and a natural acceptance of herself. The classic case of this conflict is the binge–purge cycle, in which the person eats a large quantity of food spontaneously (the "all") followed by purging ("the nothing"), or is seen as a client when she tells herself that she can eat anything and everything since she can always purge (Neuman & Halvorson, 1983).

In most cases, bulimia will result after a period of anorexia. Again, it is an "all or nothing" thought process. In other words, these individuals say to themselves, "I won't eat anything today (nothing)." Eventually, the body must receive nourishment, and the bulimic person, after a period of starvation, will gorge with food (all).

Anorexia Nervosa. Garfinkel and Kaplan (1986) state,

> Anorexia is an increasingly common complex order . . . that overrides the patient's physical and psychological well-being. . . . Pursuing a thin body becomes an isolated area of control in a world in which the individual feels ineffective; the dieting provides an artificially dangerous sense of mastery and control. As the weight loss progresses, a starvation state ensues, which eventually develops a life of its own, leading to features of anorexia nervosa. (p. 266)

According to the U.S. Department of Health and Human Services (2007), approximately 0.5 to 3.7% of females suffer from anorexia nervosa in their lifetime. In general, anorexia nervosa is characterized by resistance to maintaining body weight at or above a minimally normal weight for age and height, an intense fear of gaining weight or becoming fat, even though underweight, and disturbances in the way in which one's body weight or shape is experienced. There may also be negative self-evaluations related to one's body weight as well as a denial of the acute crisis resulting from severe underweight.

There are two types of anorexia nervosa: restrictive anorexia and bulimic anorexia. As you would expect, bulimic anorexia is characterized by the use of compensatory measures such as purging. However, the main difference between bulimic anorexia and bulimia nervosa is that the former does not binge before purging. Individuals with the restrictive type of anorexia nervosa can restrict the amount of food intake and/or can engage in excessive exercise.

It is interesting to note that individuals with restrictive anorexia do not suffer from a loss of appetite. Rather, they are "frantically preoccupied with food and eating . . . [they] deliberately, seemingly willfully, restrict their food intake and overexercise. These girls are panicky with the fear that they might lose control over their eating" (Bruch, 1986, p. 331). As a result, the actual process of eating can become obsessive, and unusual eating habits will develop. These habits can include such things as assessing or weighing the portion of food, restricting the foods that one eats to only a few, and/or avoiding food and even missing meals.

Traditionally, eating disorders have been seen as a disorder of adolescents and young women. However, recent research suggests that eating disorders can often occur across the life span (Brandsma, 2007). Exact figures are difficult to determine in that many older women will not seek treatment. In some cases, these individuals are treated for depression and/or anxiety, while the eating disorder goes undiagnosed. The opposite can be true in other cases where the rise in incidence is due to better recognition among diagnosticians. Morley and Castele (1985) believe that a diminished sense of smell and taste concomitant with appetite disorders contribute to the incidence among female elderly. Goodman, Blinder, Chaitin, and Hagman (1988) assert that anorexia in the elderly can be present in the absence of depression. Bereavement can influence appetite or eating altogether in this population.

Even though it would be unusual for anorexia nervosa to be found in a woman over the age of 25, the same can be said for the incidence of anorexia nervosa in African Americans and Latino/Hispanic populations. For example, Goodman et al. (1988) found that only 5% of the reported cases of anorexia nervosa were reflected in these ethnically diverse populations. Regarding anorexia in women over the age of 25, Dally (1984) maintains that these anorexics tend to come from upper-middle-class families. Other researchers found anorexic women over the age of 25 to have had stress secondary to childbirth or marriage (Kellett, Trimble, & Thorley, 1976) or death of a spouse (Price, Giannini, & Colella, 1985).

The course and outcome of anorexia nervosa vary across individuals. This means that some will recover after a single episode. Others can have a fluctuating pattern of gaining weight and relapsing. Still others can experience this chronically with a concomitant deterioration of their body. Males can experience anorexia. However, the proportion of females to males with anorexia is approximately 10 to 1 (Lindblad, Lindberg, and Hjern, 2006). Males with anorexia often display perfectionism, obsessions, passive dependencies, and antisocial characteristics (Anderson & Michalide, 1983).

According to the DHHS (2007), the mortality rate for individuals with anorexia has been estimated at 0.56% per year, or approximately 5.6% per decade. This means that death due to anorexia is about 12 times higher than the annual death rate due to all causes of death among females ages 15 to 24 in the general population. Suicide, cardiac arrest, or electrolyte imbalance are the most common causes of death.

Addiction to Sex and Love

Gulsun, Gulcat, and Aydin (2007) maintain that researchers continue to debate whether sex addiction is the same as compulsive sexual behavior. Regardless of which side is right, these same researchers assert that the symptoms of sexual addiction, compulsive sexual behavior, and substance addiction are similar and respond similarly to treatment.

Sex and love addiction is seen by many as comprising three addictions: addiction to love, addiction to sex, and addiction to love and sex. No doubt you have heard about (or even seen) the sex videos of celebrities such as Paris Hilton, Pamela Anderson, and others that are posted on various websites. When Brittany Spears and her cohorts are photographed exiting from automobiles in revealing clothing and compromised positions, there are questions about who is addicted to sex: the stars or the paparazzi? Even those who stalk the stars could be considered, among other things, as addicted to love. The media is replete with stories of a spouse attempting to kill the other in order to be able to carry on with a lover. Even members of the U.S. Congress have been exposed (or outed) by former prostitutes or madams as recently as 2007.

Griffin-Shelley (1991) writes that our physical and psychological identity is made up in part by sex and love, and "Letting go of sex and love, even for a short amount of time, seems [to addicts] like giving up [their] whole identity" (p. 19). According to Forward (1986) and Norwood (1985), sex addictions are gender free and cut across all socioeconomic lines, racioethnic groupings, and sexual orientations. The compulsive behavioral problems of sex addiction can include excessive masturbation, preoccupation with pornography, excessive sexual relations, and engaging in prostitution.

Sex and love addiction combines sex and love and can reflect individuals who involve themselves in numerous affairs in spite of promises to the contrary. More often than not, these individuals may use sex in attempting to get the love they feel they need. In many of these cases, sex is only the enticer, or the avenue through which other emotional, intellectual, or spiritual needs are met. But the act of sex does not characterize all individuals addicted to sex and love. Being in a primary relationship and compulsively fantasizing about others is also characteristic of those addicted to sex and love. Constantly fantasizing about someone other than the one to whom a person is making love also reflects a sex and love addiction.

Even without sexualizing the relationship, many sex and love addicts maintain that they compulsively engage in emotional affairs. For example, one of our clients told us of a time when she was paralyzed at a traffic light on a busy street trying to decide whether she should drive by her fantasy lover's office "just to see him, not to talk to him." She remained immobilized for an entire light cycle, with cars honking on both sides of her while she engaged in an internal debate about whether to drive straight ahead or whether to turn and drive by his office. (She drove straight ahead.)

Regarding sex and love addiction, Griffin-Shelley (1991) writes,

> The habit of thinking or fantasizing and then having to compulsively act out is like the binge/purge cycle of the bulimic. As thoughts fill the addict with excitement, anticipation, and energy, he or she feels closer and closer to losing control. When the rush into action takes place, it consumes the person with the passion of the moment, and all reason and rationality are lost in the explosion. What a "rush." What a release. What an orgasm. The guilt, shame, remorse

> come later. For the time being, the addict feels fulfilled. The pattern of riding the wave of sexual and romantic excitement to the crash on the beach is worth the ride and is difficult to give up. Ordinary life pales in comparison to the highs and lows of the obsession/compulsion routine. (p. 80)

For sex and love addicts, the consequences can be profound. Losses can include serious financial problems, being fired from a job for sexual harassment, and relationship breakups. Kasl (2002) includes other consequences such as issues related to health (STDs), as well as educational, parental, safety, and spiritual issues. Emotional consequences can revolve around guilt, resentment, suicidal ideation, depression, fear, self-loathing, and a diminished sense of self-worth.

Even in the face of such catastrophic consequences, individuals with sexual addiction persist. For instance, a national network broadcasts a television show *To Catch a Predator* that (while controversial) demonstrates the power of sexual addiction (among other disorders). In this series, a house in an everyday neighborhood in a variety of cities is set up for the purpose of catching predators who have made contact with "minors" online. (The "minors" are actually actors and actresses). The show airs weekly, and in spite of it being on primetime national television, there are numerous males who visit the various houses and are confronted by a news anchor while a crew films the interactions. Then the perpetrators are usually arrested. What is amazing and what supports the gravity of the sexual addiction is that some men are arrested more than once. So, even after getting caught on national television, some continue and get caught again in the same trap on the same show!

Clearly, the rise of the Internet in the early 1980s has completely altered the landscape for sexual and love addiction. MySpace is not only used socially for relationships and for sharing information, it is used by sexual predators to lure minors into meetings. YouTube gets sexual postings daily. There are disgruntled ex-lovers who post nude pictures of themselves or their former lovers as a way of getting even. A related issue is the use of the Internet for pornography or cybersex and online affairs (cyberaffairs) increasing at an alarming rate (Beard, 2005; Young, 2004).

Internet Addiction

It is clear that cybersex and cyberaffairs, while reflecting a high incidence rate, represent only one dimension of compulsive Internet use. These two issues are really symptoms of what might be considered a comorbidity of sexual addiction and Internet addiction. That means that addiction to the Internet is primary, and the particular use of the Internet, such as use for cybersex and/or cyberaffairs are only manifestations of a deeper issue. Problematic use of the Internet is found in every age, social, educational, and economic bracket. The hackneyed view that Internet addiction was relegated to young, introverted, computer-oriented males is no longer valid (Beard, 2005).

As with the "other" addictions, there is professional debate as to whether compulsive use of the Internet is an addiction. Morahan-Martin (2005) says that the relationship between Internet use, Internet addiction, and compulsive Internet use is nuanced, and the difference between the terms is more than semantic. It reflects the appropriate caution used by researchers, given the state of research. Morahan-Martin also believes that the fear of new technologies contributes to the confusion about whether it is better to think of Internet abuse as symptomatic of problems such as depression or loneliness. This same researcher maintains that the field might be better off by referring to the various problems with Internet use as *Internet-enabled pathologies.* You could expect that even with the debate about the term concomitant with its implications for diagnosis and assessment, researchers do report similar symptoms across all definitions.

According to Suhail and Bargees (2006) and Young (2004), Internet use in the United States has grown from less than 50% of Americans in 2000 to about 68% by 2004. Morahan-Martin (2005) maintains that there are 700 million users worldwide, with 103 million people from China alone going online (Cao & Su, 2006). There are estimates that between 5.9 and 13% of these users exhibit disturbed behavior on the Internet (Morahan-Martin, 2005). Young (2004) sees new areas of research on excessive use of online instant messaging, chat rooms, interactive games, eBay, and online shopping.

Chou, Condrom, and Belland (2005) conducted a review of the literature on Internet addiction and identified the nature of these Internet users. These researchers found that the Internet was used for 1) sex, 2) an altered state of consciousness, 3) achievement and mastery, 4) belonging, 5) relationships, and 6) self-actualization and transcendence of self. Philaretou, Mahfouz, and Allen (2005) maintain that there are several dynamics that individuals have when engaged in the Internet. There are online behaviors, which are characterized by use being either utilitarian or experiential. Purchasing travel and paying bills exemplify utilitarian behavior. Using the Internet for pleasurable feelings are experiential examples. There is also the dynamic of virtual experience, user control, vividness, customization, telepresence, flow experiences, and temporal/spatial dimensions. All of these combine to make the interaction between human and computer complex and inviting.

In that behaviors accomplish goals for individuals, it may be that Internet addiction provides anonymity and escape from emotional difficulties such as depression and anxiety, occupational stresses such as burnout and sudden layoffs, or personal hardships related to relationships. Generally, excessive use of the Internet often only exacerbates these problems.

Gamblers addicted to the Internet may have more serious gambling problems than other gamblers (British Broadcasting Company, 2002). According to the BBC report, the reason is that, since Internet addiction can occur in private, these gamblers may go deeper into their addiction and be able to hide their addiction longer. Although there is a paltry number of studies on Internet gambling addiction, this research does suggest that those with Internet gambling problems may be more likely to be unmarried and have lower socioeconomic and education levels (Ladd & Petry, 2002).

Rather than taking a pathological approach toward Internet addiction, Hall and Parsons (2001) lean more toward a mental health model approach. These researchers see these issues of Internet addiction as problems affecting the lives of otherwise healthy people and state that "excessive Internet use is a benign problem in living" (p. 314). Hall and Parsons see their definition as reflecting a more "holistic framework that complements our understanding of the client's world" (p. 314).

Hall and Parson have a good point. Yet it may be that the client's addiction to the Internet also includes being addicted to gambling on the Internet: the double-whammy. In this case, where does the gambling addiction end and the addiction to the Internet begin, and vice versa? This co-occurring addiction may only get worse as increasing numbers of individuals log onto the Internet.

There is an increase in research efforts focused on specific symptoms of *cybersex compulsion* (Waskul, 2004). Research reveals 6.5% of male Internet users spend at least six hours per week engaging in cybersex. Orzach (2004) identifies specific psychological and psychical symptoms that include the following: a) euphoria and sense of well-being while online; b) feeling unable or unwilling to stop; c) an increasing desire to stay online or to go online; d) experiencing feelings of emptiness, distress, or irritability when prevented from going online; e) lying to others about extent of use; f) carpal tunnel syndrome; g) dry eyes; h) neglect of personal hygiene; i) migraines; j) sleep disturbances; k) experiencing more general problems related to work and/or school; and l) neglecting interpersonal relationships.

Impact of Internet Abuse on Relationships, Students, and Workers

Cyberaffairs are defined as a romantic and/or sexual relationship that are initiated and maintained online (Young, 1999). According to this researcher, online affairs differ dramatically from in vivo affairs in several ways. In cyberaffairs, individuals can be more honest, open, forthright, less inhibited, and can be more culturally diverse (which augments the perceived glamour). The impact of cyberaffairs on existing real-life relationships can be dramatic and can include: a change in sleep patterns, a new demand for privacy, ignoring other responsibilities, lying, personality changes, loss of interest in sex, and a declined investment in the real-life relationship. The declined interest in one's real-life relationship is often reflected by no longer valuing rituals, no longer taking vacations together, an avoidance of making long-range plans together, and a general distancing between partners with the concomitant loss of intimacy. A profound effect is found in the works of Carnes (2001) and Cooper, Delmonico and Burg (2000) who maintain that cybersex may actually speed up the process of addiction in individuals who otherwise would not have addictive disorders.

Ceyhan, Ceyhan, and Gürcan (2007) assert that university students were one of the first groups identified as having problems with Internet addiction. Research conducted internationally also reveals that teachers, librarians, computer coordinators, and college administrators are now recognizing that all of the money put into technological endeavors for education can be abused by students (Cao & Su, 2006; Young, 2004). College counselors have argued that college students have become the most vulnerable population due to these increases in technological resources. This observation may be borne out in that several studies show the extent of the problem. For example, Chou and Hsiao (2000) found 5.9% of Taiwan college students were addicted to the Internet, and Wu and Zhu (2004) cite 10.65% of Chinese college students are addicted. Studying Korean senior high school students, Yang, Choe, Baity, Lee, & Cho (2005) found 4.9% used the Internet excessively. In the United States, Morahan-Martin and Schumacher (2000) maintain that 8.1% of U.S. college students are abusing the Internet.

Young (2004) sees several factors that influence the rise in Internet addiction among college students. These include having free and unlimited use; huge blocks of unstructured time with no or very little monitoring; institutional values that encourage the use of technology for readings, assignments, viewing syllabi online, and taking online courses; higher drinking ages that restrict locations to meet others; and the social intimidation that some students can feel when they arrive on large campuses. Studies have shown that 58% of students who use the Internet excessively suffer from poor study habits or late-night logins (Young, 2004, 1998). Aside from institutional structures that seem to invite Internet abuse, novelty seeking among adolescents in Taiwan was found to be a significant predictor associating Internet addiction and substance abuse (Ko, Ye, Chen, Chen, Wu, & Yen, 2006).

Employee abuse of the Internet is also of concern to researchers and employers alike, and there is some evidence that the phenomenon is of epidemic proportions. One of the problems in identifying the prevalence of Internet addiction in the workplace is the difficulty in gathering subjects for scientific study. As a result, there are many informal estimates that lack statistical power. Also, information is often gathered in a non-scientific manner. Moreover, many studies are conducted by companies that hope to gain from the statistics. Given these caveats, the Queen's University in Belfast conducted a survey of 350 companies from the United States, Australia, and the United Kingdom and found that 28% percent of those surveyed admitted downloading sexually explicit content while on the job (Sullivan, 2004).

The impact of Internet abuse on the workplace is multifaceted. For example, the loss of productivity is staggering. Stewart (2001) sees the loss to revenues in the billions. There is also negative publicity associated with class action suits or individual lawsuits that claim sexual harassment in the workplace as a result of pornography or other content being passed around. There are also legal liabilities involved. This means that as Internet abuse is increasingly being touted as an addiction, it makes those abusing the Internet at work disabled. With protection under the American Disabilities Act, an employee may in turn sue their former employer for wrongful termination.

Due to the increasing demand and availability of computers and the Internet in the workplace, the problems associated with abuse will continue to rise (Nie & Erbing, 2000). To combat this, a new industry that focuses on spy software and the development of Internet policies in the workplace has been spawned and is flourishing. It seems as though the Internet not only has changed the landscape of sex and love addiction, it has changed and complicated the construct of workaholism as well. Workaholics, especially those who bring work home, may actually be bringing Internet-based addictive behaviors home instead of the work. Nonetheless, there still remains a discrete issue related to the traditional notions of workaholism.

Addiction to Work: Workaholism

Because the Internet provides opportunities for individuals to work more at home, it also provides opportunities for excessive work. Robinson (2000, p. 29) sees work as possibly being the "great unexamined therapy issue of our time." This researcher says that, for some, work is the venue in which real life takes place. It can become the secret repository where an individual's life drama and primary emotional experiences take place.

As a student, you probably have engaged in compulsive work behaviors. These behaviors will most often occur around exam time or when assignments are due. If you are also a homemaker, you probably understand clearly the meaning of the cliché "A woman's work is never done." Remember the phrase "The early bird catches the worm?" Many of us have subscribed to the tenets of these phrases. However, some believe these phrases to be rules to follow and believe these dictums to be essential to one's very own sense of well-being or survival.

According to Oates (1971), a workaholic is

> a person whose need for work has become so excessive that it creates noticeable disturbance or interference with his [sic] bodily health, personal happiness, and interpersonal relations, and with his [sic] smooth social functioning. (p. 4)

Since Oates's definition was first published, the term *workaholism* has infused itself into the mainstream U.S. cultural narrative. One would think that because of this infusion, our scientific understanding of the concept would have increased. According to McMillan, O'Driscoll, and Burke (2003) and Taris, Schaufeli, and Verhoeven (2005), the professional field is only slowly coming into its own. Although workaholics are seen as people who work excessively hard, the motivation for such hard work varies across individuals. A strong inner drive, considered by many as the root cause of this affliction (Burke, 2000), may also be mediated by other factors. These include external factors, contextual issues that impact one's finances, poor relationships, the organizational culture itself, and the pursuit of promotion.

Taris et al. (2005) reviewed the literature and organized their findings along four dimensions: workaholism and the nonwork domain, workaholism at work, workaholism and health, and workaholism as a type-A behavior and commitment. Their findings reveal that while the effects of workaholism appear to have a negative impact on the person's nonwork domain, there is no evidence that this leads to higher rates of divorce (p. 40). Early research demonstrated that workaholics spend more time on their work than others (e.g., McMillan, Brady, O'Driscoll, & Marsh, 2002). Nonetheless, Taris et al. claim that current research is rather inconclusive. Workaholics might actually work harder than their counterparts. Yet, they work harder without the concomitant rewards for their efforts. The same researchers maintain that this reflects the strong inner drive that characterizes workaholics. Health is the one dimension where research is consistent: Workaholics do report higher levels of stress and health complaints. It is interesting to note that the professional literature on the relationship between type-A behavior and workaholism shows only modest correlations. This suggests that type-A and workaholism are not that closely associated. Still, it can be hard to work with a person who is a workaholic.

According to Machlowitz (1980), a workaholic can be detrimental to the work environment by being difficult to work with, being excessively competitive, and demanding a great deal from others while, at the same time, being critical of them, and can avoid delegating tasks and responsibilities to others. Franzmeier (1988) believes that workaholics who attempt to lighten their workload might find that they suffer from anhedonia—the inability to feel pleasure after pleasure has been postponed too long. Franzmeier maintains that the workaholic can experience a type of pleasure atrophy similar to the atrophy of an unused muscle. Kiechel (1989) agrees by saying that the workaholic is not able to enjoy leisure time.

Scott, Moore, and Miceli (1997) reviewed the early literature on workaholics and identified 30 different characteristics. Noting the variability of definitions as a mitigating factor, they nevertheless found both positive and negative characteristics attributed to the workaholic. For instance, whereas some workaholics are preoccupied with work, desperate for control, driven to power, perfectionistic, rigid, intensely competitive, and afraid of failure, other workaholics are seen as optimistic, resourceful, adaptable, extremely committed, good at making lists, passionate and enthusiastic about work, and good at ascending hierarchies. Thus, while the authors of this text will present this information in terms of workaholism being an "other addiction," there are clearly conflicting ideas about where workaholics actually fit into the scheme of things.

Styles of Workaholism

Robinson (2000) identifies four predominant styles of workaholism. These four styles help therapists to organize their thoughts about a given client's symptoms. At the same time, the clients themselves will likely present with a combination of styles or with alternating styles. The *bulimic workaholic style* reflects a perfectionistic orientation toward work. Individuals who use this style often cycle through procrastination, work binges, and exhaustion. It is hard for these individuals to get started. However, once a deadline approaches, they can work excessively to the point of staying up nights to finish before falling into bed from exhaustion.

A second style is the *relentless workaholic style.* This style mirrors the dictum "It has to be finished yesterday" (Robinson, 2000, p. 37). While the bulimic style reflects procrastination, the relentless style reflects just the opposite. These individuals start early. One reason for this might be the fact that the relentless style of workaholism is also characterized by taking on too much work. Saying no is as difficult as prioritizing. Moreover, these individuals can complete projects long before deadlines without much input from coworkers.

Those who invoke an *attention-deficit workaholic style* are seen as using the adrenaline of overwhelming work pressure as a focusing device (Robinson, 2000, p. 37). Living on the brink of chaos and destruction, persons use this style to get high from the rush of new ideas. Whereas projects are completed early by those using the relentless style, the attention-deficit style reflects a plethora of unfinished projects.

Finally, in the *savoring workaholic style* individuals move slowly, methodically, and in an overly scrupulous manner. Projects are savored in and of themselves. When projects are close to completion, additional work is generated because these individuals have difficulty distinguishing when a job is good enough.

If you are a student, the bulimic style probably sounds familiar. This is especially true for those times when you are watching television, playing video games, or otherwise occupied while feeling excessive guilt over not doing what should be done. Remember, this experience does not mean that you are a workaholic. Workaholism and maladaptive styles of workaholics lie on a continuum. Moreover, according to Scott, Moore, and Miceli (1997), "It is critical that researchers avoid making value judgments about workaholism based on the negative connotations that often accompany this term" (p. 308). One should be aware of the multiple meanings of the term. These same authors go on to say that, depending on the type of workaholism identified in the literature (compulsive dependency or perfectionism or achievement orientation), a workaholic may be seen as either good or maladaptive. Mental health professionals need to be aware of the differential effects of workaholic behaviors on such things as job satisfaction, self-esteem, absenteeism, turnover, organizational citizen behavior, commitment, and job performance. Functionality is a key to working with individuals with compulsive work behavior patterns. For some, workaholism may work. For instance, Scott, Moore, and Miceli (1997) studied cases in which workaholism seems to work well for people. In analyzing more than 50 research articles on workaholism, these authors found that at least some workaholics are perfectly happy with their status. In addition, many can (and often do) do quite well in jobs that reward hands-on management, a high standard of work quality and that allow for independent work.

Assessment and Treatment Issues

Assessment

As we stated in Chapter 6, assessment is crucial in planning for treatment. Individuals with other addictions will probably reflect problems in a variety of areas such as physical health, psychological and social functioning, reproduction and sexuality, cross-addictions, and family relationships. However these same problems may also exist in individuals whose behaviors are not addictive. For example, the client who comes in to work on grieving the intense feelings of a lost relationship may or may not be a sex and love addict. Such a determination will result from exploring thematic patterns in the client's various relationships. Clearly, questions addressing an individual's eating, gambling, sex and love issues, and work habits should be included in your routine psychosocial history. The nature and extent of information gathering in these areas will, of course, depend on the presenting problem. However, as you gather such data, facts disclosed about a client's family of origin or a client's current behavioral patterns may suggest areas for further exploration. For example, in listening to a bright, thin, college-aged woman with a family history of perfectionism and conflict, you might want to ask her about her eating patterns or about her attitudes regarding eating.

Eating Disorders. Cummins, Simmons, and Zane (2005) reviewed the literature in their study of eating disorders in Asians and maintain that the multitude of ways to define eating disorders raises questions about the relevancy of diagnostic criteria for all groups. These researchers maintain that it is vital that assessments used to measure eating disorders are culturally sensitive. Western-based criteria might not be germane or even relevant to Asian and other diverse populations. These same researchers assert that it is important to study *symptom patterns* rather than diagnostic criteria. This is because that even when differences among groups are found, researchers are left to surmise as to the actual patterns of differences in the presentation of an eating disorder.

Fairburn, Cooper, and Shafran (2003) go further and state that the classifications of anorexia nervosa, bulimia nervosa, and eating disorder not otherwise classified share similar psychopathological mechanisms to a degree that a transdiagnostic approach to assessment and treatment is more appropriate. Even though the professional literature addressing the impact of sociocultural factors on eating disorders is cloudy, little doubt exists as to the importance of a culture-centered understanding of eating disorders for accurate assessment. The Eating Disorder Inventory (EDI-3) (Garner, 2005) is a popular 91-item standardized test that is easy to administer in order to assess and treat eating disorders in white women ages 13 to 53. There are three eating disorder specific scales and nine general psychological scales that are highly relevant to eating disorders. The test yields six composites. One is eating disorder specific, while the remaining five reflect ineffectiveness, interpersonal problems, affective problems, overcontrol, and general psychological maladjustment.

In general, Hill and Pomeroy (2001) believe that those with anorexia nervosa tend to minimize their symptoms and the medical complications. Quite often, seeking professional help comes only after the individual has experienced pressure from family members and cohorts at work or school. Behavioral and attitude changes often accompany anorexia nervosa and bulimia nervosa and include an increased interest in cooking, nutrition, and concomitant increase in exercise. Mental health professionals will want to examine the client's family for evidence of enmeshment, overprotectiveness, rigidity, lack of conflict resolution, and the involvement of the client in unresolved marital and family conflicts. In addition, information about weight loss is critical in assessing the severity of anorexia nervosa and bulimia nervosa.

Cash (1997), Dounchis, Hayden, and Wilfley (2001), Levesque and Vichesky (2005), and others have demonstrated the impact of body image on eating disorders. Hence, clinicians need to be aware of the need to assess body image as it relates to the client's eating patterns. In doing so, clinicians need to keep in mind that ethnicity and sexual orientation play a significant part in body image. This is especially true when considering that Dounchis et al. (2001) and Lynch, et al. (2007) report that body dissatisfaction is more pervasive in nonwhite females within the United States than originally thought. For instance, Allison (2002) found that binge eating, age, and black racial status are *positively correlated* with heightened scores in body mass index (BMI). For Asian subjects, racial status is *negatively correlated* with BMI. At the same time, other research suggests that binge eating may not be the significant and sole variable accounting for being overweight in the African American community (Dounchis et al., 2001). Patterson et al. (1997) point to the differences in physical maturation and sexual development as a significant factor influencing research results. In general, it is important for clinicians to contextualize treatment approaches so that they reflect the larger issues influencing diverse clients with body image disturbance and eating disorders.

Addiction to Sex and Love, the Internet, and Work. We stated in Chapter 6 that a simple rule for determining whether a behavior is problematic is to ask yourself the question, "Does a normal drinker drink like this client?" For sex and love addiction, the mental health counselor can assess the normality of the client's relationship with a spouse or companion, the client's past and present extended family environment, other intimate relationships both present and past, and the client's relationships with strangers (Logan, 1992).

Clinicians will also want to examine the client's history of sexual abuse and its relationship to current acting out behaviors. Southern (2002) found that there is a relationship between chemically dependent women who have no prior memory of sexual abuse and are having a pattern of sexual acting out. Southern found that the women in his study reported their mothers as being unsafe, that there was tension and stress in the family of origin, and that clients experienced isolation. Valenti (2002) concurs with Southern's findings and reports that sexually addicted women are significantly more likely to come from families of origin where they experienced abandonment, abuse, physical punishment, crisis, chaos, and depression. These issues clearly could be significant areas for mental health clinicians to explore with clients.

Regarding Internet addiction, Hall and Parsons (2001) outline four key areas in need of assessment: Internet usage, usage content, environmental distress, and comorbidity. Regarding Internet usage, these researchers say that it is difficult to determine because of the tendency to underreport the hours spent on the Internet. It is suggested that the assessment might include other significant social contacts, such as friends and family members, in order to get a more accurate picture of usage. Individuals who are Internet dependent spend an inordinate amount of time online engaged in social activities such as participating in chat rooms, newsgroups, and various bulletin boards. Nondependent individuals spend more time on email and web browsing.

Beard (2005) presents a model to conceptualize problematic Internet use. It is based upon the biopsychosocial model of addiction that we discussed in Chapter 3. Beard's model integrates genetic, psychological, biochemical, familial, cultural, and environmental dynamics. This same researcher presents 72 questions that can be used for assessment. These questions address the following: presenting problem (21 questions), biological areas (17), psychological areas (12), social areas (16), and relapse prevention (6). Thatcher and Goolam (2005) developed the Problematic Internet Use Questionnaire (PIUQ). These researchers conducted an exploratory factor analysis study and identified three subscales: online preoccupation, adverse effects, and social interactions. Currently, the instrument should not be used for clinical screening because the predictive validity of the instrument has yet to be established. The reason we mention it is because this seems to be a promising measure for future use and because of its alignment with Young's (2004) eight criteria for Internet addiction, discussed next.

Young (2004) believes that since there is no formal disorder of Internet Addiction, clinicians and researchers should use the criteria for pathological gambling as a frame. Young cites the following criteria in the form of eight questions (p. 404):

1. Do you feel preoccupied with the Internet in terms of thinking about previous online activity or anticipating the next online session?
2. Do you feel the need to use the Internet for increasing amounts of time to achieve satisfaction?
3. Have you repeatedly made unsuccessful attempt to control, cut back, or stop Internet use?
4. Do you feel restless, moody, depressed, or irritable when attempting to cut down or stop Internet use?
5. Do you stay online longer than originally intended?
6. Have you jeopardized or risked the loss of a significant relationship, job, or educational or career opportunity because of the Internet?
7. Have you lied to family members, therapists, or others to conceal the extent of involvement with the Internet?

8. Do you use the Internet as a way of escaping from problems or relieving a dysphoric mood (e.g. feelings of helplessness, guilt, anxiety, depression)?

There are a few measures used to assess workaholism. The early works of Spence and Robbins (1992) diverges from the later work of Robinson (1999). Referred to as the Workaholism Battery, Spence and Robbins postulate that there is a workaholic triad consisting of work involvement, drive, and work enjoyment. Toward that end, they identify *true workaholics* (high on involvement and drive, low on enjoyment), *work enthusiasts* (high on enjoyment and involvement, low on drive), and *enthusiastic workaholics* (high on enjoyment, involvement, and drive). Workaholism can also be assessed using the Work-Addiction Risk Test (WART) (Robinson, 1999). It is a 25-item, self-administered test that assesses work habits. The higher the score, the more likely one is a workaholic. Flowers and Robinson (2002) conducted a discriminate analysis on the WART and found that it has five dimensions: (a) compulsive tendencies, (b) control, (c) impaired communication/self-absorption, (d) inability to delegate, and (e) self-worth.

Treatment

Eating Disorders. In that there are various types of eating disorders, with only anorexia nervosa and bulimia nervosa appearing in the *DSM-IV-TR,* you can understand the difficulty in treating this disorder from a structural sense. Insurance companies do not readily pay for in-patient treatment of eating disorders. Perhaps, the reason for this is the lack of agreement on what constitutes recovery from an eating disorder. Noordenbos and Seubring (2006) maintain that due to the various definitions of "recovery" related to eating disorders, therapists and other mental health professionals should understand that prioritizing the criteria for recovery may vary among clients. Weight is clearly an issue. However, how much weight needs to be regained in order to be "recovered" is questionable. A pound of weight versus a half-pound of weight is significant for an eating disorder client. In any case, Noordenbos and Seubring state that weight needs to be taken into account with other factors such as age, gender, racioethnicity, height, bone structure, as well as one's physical constitution.

Nevertheless, eating disorders can be treated and a healthy weight restored. From your reading, it is clear that eating disorders require a comprehensive treatment plan that addresses medical and psychological issues. This often includes medical monitoring (including medical management), psychosocial and psychological interventions, and some nutritional counseling. With anorexia nervosa, there are three main phases of treatment: a) cessation of weight loss and the restoration of weight; b) addressing the psychological issues related to body image, depression, anxiety, and compulsive behaviors; and c) achievement of long-term remission and rehabilitation. Medications should be administered after the client has experienced some weight gain.

For bulimia nervosa and binge-eating disorder, the treatment strategies are similar. The primary goal is to reduce or eliminate the cycle of binging and purging (for bulimia) and the binging (for binge-eating disorder). While in-patient treatment is often recommended for anorexia, bulimia nervosa and binge-eating disorder can be treated through individual psychotherapy (especially cognitive-behavioral or interpersonal psychotherapy), group psychotherapy that uses a cognitive-behavioral approach, and family or marital therapy. The goals include attempts to establish a pattern of regular, nonbinge meals. Therapy also aims to improve the client's attitudes about their eating disorder as well as addressing the often co-occurring mood disorder.

Faith, Saelens, Wilfley, and Allison (2001) found that research focusing on family-based treatment approaches are the most popular, when compared to medical, educational, and school-based program studies. These researchers, as well as Jelalian and Saelens (1999), maintain the efficacy of these approaches in both short- and long-term treatment of weight issues.

As we pointed out in Chapter 8, it is critically important for mental health professionals to determine the client's learning style or learning capacity before initiating psychoeducational approaches. In addition to individual, family, and group psychotherapy, Twelve-Step support groups, such as Overeaters Anonymous (OA), may be of some help to clients whose problems include binge eating and overeating. These support groups can be especially helpful with relapse prevention, since clients with full-blown anorexia nervosa and bulimia nervosa will probably have problems in other areas of functioning. Specifically, support groups may help with important issues related to the initiation of pathological eating behaviors. For example, clients with eating disorders may demonstrate codependent behaviors or complain of other family dysfunction, factors that trigger compulsive eating behavior. Learning how to identify these triggers concomitant with hearing about how others deal with them may help to prevent a relapse.

Addiction to Sex and Love, the Internet, and Work. In treating individuals with compulsive behaviors related to such things as sex and love, the Internet, and work, we recommend a multifaceted approach. These approaches should include the client's self-examination of his or her attitudes and beliefs about compulsive behaviors. In terms of client engagement and brief interventions, it is important for mental health counselors to pay attention to their own world views about body and body image. Moreover, Freeman (1992) advocates the need for establishing baselines, timelines, and plans for evaluating the overall effectiveness of the treatment approach. Clients can be asked to maintain a log. This log can be used to identify events that involve food, relationships, the Internet, and work, along with identifying the concomitant feelings and experiences. In general, individuals with these various compulsions can benefit by having their families involved in the treatment plan (e.g., Freeman, 1992; McCown & Chamberlin, 2000; McGoldrick & Gerson, 1985; Nie & Erbing, 2000). Clearly, the timing of this involvement is critical.

Special considerations influence the treatment of compulsive behaviors around sex and love. For instance, imagine a lesbian woman being treated for sexual addiction, compulsivity, and codependency. While knowledge and interpersonal skills are needed to counsel lesbian women, numerous dynamics need further understanding. According to Manley and Feree (2002), these include understanding patterns of sexual addiction in lesbian relationships and basic knowledge of the issues, such as personal homophobia and feelings of oppression, experienced daily by lesbian women. In addition, there needs to be an awareness of the level of internalized oppression in the lesbian client. From our perspective, the social discourse regarding individuals with gay and lesbian orientations presents a difficult challenge for many. It is important to have dialogue with clients about these issues in order to more fully understand their experience of the coming-out process, along with the subculture dynamics. Manley and Feree also suggest that the need for a broad understanding of the dynamics of oppression can be helpful in facilitating the client's integration (p. 191).

McCarthy (2002) sees the opportunity to include women in the disclosure, assessment, treatment, recovery, and relapse prevention process for men addicted to sex. Women are viewed as vital in rebuilding couple trust, intimacy, and sexuality. Milrad (1999) believes that couples can benefit in couples therapy for the treatment of codependence and sex addiction. She urges mental health clinicians to understand the beginning recovery stages of codependency, because the stages relate to the dynamics that couples often experience in dealing with a sex-addicted spouse. Feree (2002) believes that more and more women within Christian circles will seek treatment for sexual compulsions. Clinicians need to understand ways to help this special population.

As mentioned, sex and love addiction has been greatly influenced by the Internet, and Bergner and Bridges (2002) examined the significance of heavy pornography use in romantic relationships. As you would expect, discovering that a partner is heavily involved in Internet pornography creates conditions for substantial reappraisal of the relationship. Feelings of worthlessness, being weak and stupid, sexually undesirable, and of living a lie are common reactions of their partners. While the nonaddicted partner's focus would likely be on changing the addictive behaviors of the partner, it is more effective if therapists help reframe the situation and provide a clearer understanding of the issue, help the partner become more objective, and help the person be less devastated about it. For the addictive partner, Freeman (1992) and Hall and Parsons (2001) see the need for cognitive interventions.

Cognitive approaches can also be effective with those with compulsive work behaviors. For instance, Robinson (2000, p. 37) sees the bulimic workaholic style benefiting from the disputation of irrational beliefs about needing to be perfect. Those with a more relentless work style may benefit by focusing on impulse control, forethought, and attention to detail. Deliberately slowing down, such as slowing one's walking or driving speed, is also an effective treatment approach. Sometimes a medical evaluation might be needed for individuals who work compulsively. This is especially important if the person has trouble focusing on finishing or becomes easily bored with projects at work. It is important to remember that some workaholics make it difficult for other workers in the workplace. So, with the savoring workaholic person, it will probably be important to help him or her to learn the advantages of teamwork, cohesion, and trusting fellow workers.

Summary

- Pathological gambling lifetime prevalence rates are between 0.4% and 2.0% of the general population.
- Sixty-six percent of underage youth have gambled and rates of gambling problems are 2 to 4 times greater than for adults.
- Eight percent of college students have gambling problems.
- The cost of problem gambling is approximately $6.7 billion per year.

- The rise of Internet use has created a new gambling industry, and Internet gamblers prefer this venue because of convenience, aversion to land-based gambling, the pace of online gambling, and the potential for higher wins.
- There is a significant increase for gambling problems among those with a co-occurring psychiatric disorder, and higher rates of suicide are reported for pathological gamblers.
- Types of gamblers include professional, antisocial, casual social, heavy social, relief-and-escape, and compulsive gamblers.
- The South Oaks Gambling Screen is the best known assessment of pathological gambling.
- While treatment of gambling problems approximates the approaches for other addictions, most insurance does not cover gambling treatment.
- In treatment, gamblers have very high attrition rates.
- Pathological gamblers can benefit from 12-Step groups for gamblers, such as Gamblers Anonymous and Gam-Anon (similar to Al-Anon).
- "Other Addictions" include eating disorders, compulsive work, Internet abuse, and sex and love addiction, although not all professionals agree that these are addictions because the symptoms are already covered under various Axis II diagnoses in the *DSM-IV-TR*.
- Proponents of other addictions see the benefits as calling attention to a variety of problems associated with work, the Internet, and sex and love.
- Eating disorders include chronic binge eating, anorexia nervosa, bulimia nervosa, chronic overeating, and binge eating.
- Only anorexia nervosa and bulimia nervosa are formal diagnoses in the DSM-IV-TR, but some researchers are calling for a Binge-Eating Disorder (BED) diagnosis.
- Eating disorders are prevalent in women across their lifespans, most often diagnosed in younger females; males have lesser rates.
- Body Image Disturbance (BID) is strongly associated with all of the eating disorders, including chronic overeating and binge eating.
- Eating disorders are often medical emergencies, and mental health professionals need to refer clients for medical workups when they suspect these problems.
- Internet addiction creates problems at the workplace and at home.
- Cybersex and cyberaffairs are results of Internet addiction and are considered double addictions in that there can be an addiction to the Internet without addiction to cybersex or cyberaffairs.
- There are four types of workaholics: bulimic workaholic (characterized by perfectionistic and work binging), relentless workaholic (starting early and finishing up late), attention-deficit workaholic (living on the brink of chaos with a lot of adrenaline), and savoring workaholic (loves the work).
- Workaholics may not always be type-A personalities.
- Workaholics tend to have strong internal drives that are more related to their behaviors than the pursuit of accomplishment and praise.
- Cognitive-behavioral treatments and the utilization of in-patient treatment facilities are effective in working with those afflicted with other addictions.

Internet Resources

Gambling addiction
www.ncpgambling.org

Assessment for Internet addiction
www.netaddiction.com

Eating disorders
www.edap.org

Workaholism
www.workaholics-anonymous.org

Further Discussion

1. How often have you gambled? Can you see how a person could become addicted to it?
2. What is your experience with disordered eating?
3. To what extent does the cultural narrative play in the initiation and maintenance of disordered eating and eating disorders?
4. Do you know anyone who leaves the table immediately after eating? If so, what do you think is going on?
5. When you are on the Internet, what are the alluring features of the interaction between you and the computer?
6. To what extent do you think that Internet use should be monitored in the workplace?
7. In what ways has cyberporn and cyberaffairs affected people or couples that you know?
8. Now that you know there can be a difference between type-A personalities and workaholism, can you distinguish between the two in your own experience?

15

Prevention

If you have read this text in sequence, you can see that most of the book involves topics related to the abuse of AOD. This reflects our view regarding the need for mental health professionals to acquire this information, given the frequency of AOD abuse in our society. However, this frequency is related to the effectiveness of efforts to prevent AOD abuse. Therefore, do not conclude that prevention is less important than the other topics in this book because there is only a single chapter devoted to this topic. On the contrary, we believe that prevention is critically important from both policy and program standpoints. In particular, those of you who are planning to work in public schools as counselors or social workers should go beyond the information in this chapter. Also, there is a growing number of prevention specialists who work for public and private organizations involved with substance abuse prevention. These professionals also need a more thorough understanding of this field than is found in this chapter. The section on Prevention Resources is a good place to start.

Why Are Prevention Efforts Needed?

This is not a difficult question to answer. You could provide the same answer that we can. As you have read this text, you have received information on the problems caused by the abuse of AOD. So, if you take some action or actions that decrease the frequency of abuse, logically, the associated problems should also be reduced. For example, if there is a reduction in the number of people who chronically abuse alcohol, there should be a concomitant reduction in the number of people with medical problems resulting from chronic alcohol abuse. Therefore, prevention efforts designed to reduce the number of people who will end up abusing alcohol for many years are important and beneficial.

Most prevention efforts are directed toward young people. Again, this is logical because people generally make decisions about their use of tobacco, alcohol, and other drugs before they reach adulthood. As you know, it is illegal for people under 18 to use tobacco, for those under 21 to use alcohol, and for any age to use "street" drugs. Therefore, an examination of survey data on the use of tobacco, alcohol, and other drugs by young people can provide information on the need for substance abuse prevention.

Although there are several prominent surveys conducted annually on the use of tobacco, alcohol, and other drugs by young people, the information in the following table is from the "Monitoring the Future" (MTF) study (Johnston, O'Malley, & Bachman, 2006). MTF is a survey conducted by the University of Michigan and is funded by the National Institute on Drug Abuse. In 2006, 47,000 8th, 10th, and 12th graders were surveyed. MTF has been conducted for the past 31 years, which makes trends easy to identify.

Although there are numerous ways to look at the data generated by these surveys, we find it helpful to compare 30-day prevalence rates, which mean that a respondent has said that the substance in question has been used in the past 30 days. The following table is a report of 30-day prevalence data on 8th, 10th, and 12th graders from 2006, as well as changes since last year and since 1991.

30-Day Prevalence and Change-in-Use Patterns

	Year	*8th graders*	*10th graders*	*12th graders*
Cigarettes	2006	8.7	14.5	21.6
	2005–2006	–0.6	–0.4	–1.6
	1991–2006	–5.6	–6.3	–6.7
Alcohol	2006	17.2	33.8	45.3
	2005–2006	0.1	0.6	–1.7
	1991–2006	–7.9	–9.0	–8.7
Marijuana	2006	6.5	14.2	18.3
	2005–2006	–0.2	–0.9	–1.4
	1991–2006	3.3	5.5	4.5
Other illicit drugs	2006	3.8	6.3	9.8
	2005–2006	–0.2	0.0	–0.5
	1991–2006	0.0	0.8	2.7

The MTF survey generates much more data than are reported here. However, even this small sample contains interesting information on substance use by young people and has implications for the prevention field. Clearly, tobacco and alcohol use are far more frequent than illicit drug use. While that is not surprising, it certainly indicates that prevention efforts must involve the legal drugs in our society. The trend has been decreases in tobacco and alcohol use and increases in marijuana and other illicit drugs. Finally, young people frequently believe that "everybody" is using. However, most young people report that they do *not* use tobacco, alcohol, or illicit drugs.

Policy Issues in Prevention

Drug Free?

On a surface level, it might seem that prevention scarcely needs a policy discussion. After all, most people would agree that preventing AOD misuse, especially by young people, is positive and that's the only policy that is necessary. Clearly, the issues are more complicated. For example, federal agencies often set "drug-free" goals. The Center for Substance Abuse Prevention developed a teleconferencing initiative called "Let's Help Youth Stay Drug-Free." However, *drug-free* does not include tobacco or alcohol. As was seen in the MTF survey, tobacco and alcohol are by far the most widely used drugs by young people. In addition, these legal substances (for adults) cause more harm to society than all illegal drugs combined. Unfortunately, the illogical dichotomy of legal/illegal drugs persists. So, while *drug-free* may be politically popular, this concept may divert attention and resources from efforts to prevent the use of tobacco and alcohol by young people.

An alternative conceptualization to drug-free is the harm-reduction model. This model is based on the premises that drug use (including tobacco and alcohol) cannot be eliminated from our society, that the misuse or abuse of any drug can cause harm, and that there are strategies that can be implemented to reduce the harm caused by misuse or abuse. A widely publicized example of a harm-reduction strategy is needle exchange. In this example, there is acknowledgment that some people are intravenous drug users who will not discontinue their use. By sharing needles with others, these hardcore drug users spread diseases such as hepatitis and HIV. The distribution of clean needles should reduce needle-sharing as a cause of infection. In fact, these programs have been successful in reducing the spread of AIDS (Hurley, Jolley, & Kaldor, 1997; Singer, 1997; Vlahov et al., 1997). However, in spite of the evidence supporting needle exchange programs, the federal government will not fund these programs.

Harm-reduction efforts are also directed at the legal drugs in our society. Sobriety checkpoints and designated driver publicity campaigns are intended to reduce the harm caused by alcohol-impaired drivers. Sting operations to identify and penalize retailers who sell tobacco to minors are designed to reduce the access of tobacco to young people. If a minor has trouble purchasing cigarettes, he or she will smoke less or not at all.

Some harm-reduction processes involving alcohol use by minors are quite controversial. For example, some parents of teenagers may allow alcohol use at parties to discourage drinking and driving. Parents who allow this are engaging in a dangerous activity since it is a crime to contribute to the delinquency of a minor. In addition, in many cases they are enabling alcohol abuse. On prom and graduation nights, organizations such as Mothers Against Drunk Driving (MADD) may organize volunteers to drive for impaired students. This is certainly a difficult issue since no one wants a situation in which an impaired minor is involved in an accident, and responsible adults do not want minors to drink. Reconciling these issues is a dilemma for parents.

Gateway Drugs

Related to these issues is the fact that federal prevention efforts have not focused on gateway drugs as much as they should. Gateway drugs are those that precede the use of other drugs and are usually considered to be alcohol, tobacco, and marijuana[1] (Kandel, 1989). In

[1]Recent research (e.g., RAND Drug Policy Research Center, 2002) has raised questions about whether marijuana is a gateway to other illicit drug use.

fairness, more recent publications from the Center for Substance Abuse Prevention now refer to "alcohol, tobacco, and other drug problems," but this has not always been the case. As we will discuss, the reasons for the lack of focus on tobacco and alcohol probably are related to political pressure as opposed to best practice. It makes sense to focus on gateway drugs in prevention programs because it is rare that a drug user begins with drugs such as cocaine or heroin (New York State Division of Alcoholism and Alcohol Abuse, 1989). A young person usually begins drug use with tobacco or alcohol, since these drugs are readily available and their use is perceived as dangerous, exciting, and adultlike. Once a young person "takes the plunge" (begins use), it is much easier to go on to the next class of drugs. Furthermore, Hawkins, Catalano, and Miller (1992) have shown that the age of first use of any drug is related to later drug abuse by adolescents. Finally, alcohol and tobacco cause more health and related problems than other drugs. For example there are over 500,000 deaths annually associated with tobacco and alcohol as opposed to 23,500 deaths annually from all of the currently illegal drugs combined (Fisher, 2006).

For all these reasons, it makes sense to focus on preventing the initiation of use of gateway drugs. However, the alcohol and tobacco industries have powerful lobbies that present constant barriers to prevention efforts. To give you one simple example, the tobacco industry is allowed to market a product that has no medically useful purpose, is highly addicting, and kills 400,000 people a year. A product with these characteristics would never be allowed to be introduced today, and the failure to ban the promotion of tobacco is unconscionable. Since the tobacco master settlement agreement in 1998, cigarette advertisements in youth magazines increased by $54 million (Turner-Bowker & Hamilton, 2000). Obviously, alcohol is also marketed widely. In 2002, the alcohol industry spent over $1.7 billion on advertising, including over $1 billion on television advertising. The beer industry alone spent $972 million on television ads (Alcohol Policies Project, 2003). In comparison, the federal government's National Media Campaign spent $185 million in 2002 to convince young people to avoid illicit drugs, about one-tenth of what the alcohol industry spent to convince young people to drink. Of course, the alcohol industry claims that it does not target underage drinkers. However, according to a review of literature conducted by the Center on Alcohol Marketing and Youth at Georgetown University, the amount of beer and hard liquor advertising in magazines increases with a magazine's youth readership. Furthermore, 12-year-olds who were more aware of beer advertising held more favorable views on drinking and expressed an intention to drink as adults more often than children who were less aware of these ads. Finally, young people who were exposed to and enjoyed alcohol advertisements were more likely to drink than other youth (Center on Alcohol Marketing and Youth, 2005). The alcohol industry does place "responsibility" advertising on television. However, between 2001 and 2003, there were 761,347 product ads for alcohol on television and 24,161 responsibility ads. Alcohol companies spent 27 times more on product ads than on responsibility ads and 12- to 20-year-olds, on average, saw 779 commercials encouraging alcohol use compared to 9 discouraging drinking (Center on Alcohol Marketing and Youth, 2005). Therefore, any efforts designed to prevent young people from initiating alcohol or tobacco use are directly countered by the marketing of these products. Legislators are heavily lobbied and receive campaign contributions from the alcohol and tobacco industries and have little motivation to pass laws that restrict or prohibit advertising. The attempt by the 1998 Congress to pass a comprehensive tobacco bill is an excellent example. The tobacco companies launched a successful effort to defeat this bill. So research indicates that we need prevention efforts that focus on the gateway drugs, but federal and state government officials do not want to upset the tobacco and alcohol industries. Furthermore, prevention efforts are sabotaged by the sophisticated marketing of tobacco and alcohol. Can you see how policy affects prevention?

Supply versus Demand

The White House Office of National Drug Control Policy (ONDCP) is responsible for the development, management, and implementation of all federal programs involving illicit drugs. These programs are broadly classified as being "supply reduction," including domestic law enforcement, interdiction, and international efforts, or "demand reduction," including treatment and prevention. Our federal public policies regarding illicit drugs are demonstrated by how monetary resources are distributed between supply reduction and demand reduction. Domestic law enforcement includes agencies such as the Drug Enforcement Administration. Interdiction involves efforts by the Coast Guard and Customs and Border Protection to stop illegal drugs from entering the United States. International efforts include the initiatives in Colombia to destroy coca plants and in Afghanistan to stop the growing of poppies. Most treatment and prevention dollars are distributed to states by block grants administered by the Center for Substance Abuse Treatment and the Center for Substance Abuse Prevention, both in the Substance Abuse and Mental Health Services Administration in Health and Human Services.

In the fiscal year 2008 budget proposal, ONDCP allocated 64.4% of the budget to supply reduction and 35.6% to demand reduction (Office of National Drug Control Policy, 2007). In contrast, the 2002 budget was 56% supply reduction and 44% demand reduction (Fisher, 2006). If you think that this increasing amount of money devoted to supply reduction is a function of the philosophy of the Bush administration, you would be incorrect. The Clinton administration regularly allocated about two-thirds of the drug control budget to supply reduction (Fisher, 2006).

With this large proportion of financial resources allocated to law enforcement and military initiatives, it would be expected that the supply of illicit drugs in this country would be significantly disrupted. However, that is not the case. Since 2001, the Department of Justice has issued an annual report called the "National Drug Threat Assessment" on the availability of illicit drugs in this country. According to these reports, the availability of heroin, cocaine, methamphetamine, and marijuana has not been reduced in the United States at all (Fisher, 2006). A statement from the 2007 report illustrates the problem:

> Despite the fact that the highest recorded level of cocaine interdiction and seizure was recorded in 2005—the fifth consecutive record-setting increase—there have been no sustained cocaine shortages or indications of stretched supplies in domestic drug markets. These seemingly inconsistent trends suggest greater source country supply than was previously estimated, an assertion supported by a recent upwardly revised cocaine production estimate for 2005. (U.S. Department of Justice, 2006, p. 3)

Another federal report has examined the price and purity of illegal drugs over time. If supply reduction efforts were successful, economic laws would predict that the price of these drugs would increase and/or the purity would decrease. Neither has happened. In fact, the price of cocaine has dropped more than 50% since the creation of the ONDCP (Fisher, 2006).

With all the competing interests for federal funds, it would certainly make sense to reprioritize the proportion of money allocated to supply reduction and demand reduction. We now have ample evidence to conclude that the amount of money devoted to supply reduction is not justified. This money would be better spent on prevention and treatment.

Legalization. Legalization is an extremely controversial policy issue and one that generates highly emotional arguments from each side. Proponents of legalization argue that crime, violence, and diseases would be reduced. If all drugs were legal, the profitability of black-market distribution would be reduced and those who inject drugs could always use clean needles. The quality of currently illegal substances could be controlled to prevent contamination. The number of people incarcerated for possession or for crimes related to the need to buy drugs would be reduced. More money would be available for prevention and treatment due to reduced prison populations and the decreased need to interrupt drug supplies.

Opponents of legalization counter by saying that the use of currently illegal drugs would increase, especially among youth. There would be more social problems resulting from drug use because of the increased access. They doubt that black-market distribution would decrease because it would still be easier to buy drugs on the street than from the government. Therefore, violence and crime would still characterize drug distribution. Both sides use the experience of history (e.g., prohibition) and policies from European countries to support their arguments.

As with many controversial issues, legalization is not as simple as either side would have you believe. First, drugs are legal. Alcohol and nicotine are drugs. Many other drugs with addictive potential are distributed with a physician's prescription. The legalization issue usually involves marijuana, cocaine, methamphetamine, and heroin. Second, many proponents of legalization are actually supporting *decriminalization.* Decriminalization involves allowing individuals to possess small amounts of currently illegal drugs for personal consumption. Distribution would remain illegal. This would prevent the arrest, prosecution, and incarceration of individuals who use drugs but do not commit other crimes. Third, the concept of legalization can have numerous operational definitions from unlimited and uncontrolled access and distribution to highly controlled access and distribution. Clearly, the consequences of legalization would be dependent on these processes. Finally, it makes little sense to discuss the legalization of marijuana, cocaine, methamphetamine, and heroin together. As we discussed in Chapter 2, the acute and chronic effects of these drugs are quite diverse, and the concept of dangerousness is vastly different.

We believe that it makes more sense to advocate for a logical and comprehensive discussion of our policies regarding alcohol, tobacco, and illicit drugs than to discuss the legalization of illegal drugs in isolation from other substances. For example, if marijuana were legal and marketed and distributed as alcohol and tobacco are, we have little doubt that use would dramatically increase. We believe that the legalization issue, although fun to discuss, is a diversion from a focus on all the drugs (legal and illegal) we abuse.

Prevention Classification Systems

The Institute of Medicine Classification System

This classification system is based on the target population of prevention activities. Universal prevention strategies are directed toward the entire population of a country, state, community, school, or neighborhood. The goal is to deter the onset of substance abuse by providing all individuals in the population with the information and skills perceived as necessary to prevent substance abuse. There is no screening to assess the risk of substance abuse by subsets of the population because everyone is assumed to be at risk for substance abuse and capable of benefiting from the prevention activities. For example, a national media campaign is part of the federal government's prevention efforts. The television advertisements created as a part of this campaign are directed at all people who view them. School-based prevention programs that are implemented in the classroom are considered universal prevention.

Selective prevention strategies are targeted at subsets of a population who are considered at risk for substance abuse. For example, children of alcoholics or addicts, students who are failing academically, and abused children are considered "high risk" because research has shown that these children have a higher probability of later substance abuse than other children (Hawkins, Catalano, & Miller, 1992). The risk factors may be biological, psychological, social, or environmental, and the targeted subgroups may be determined by age, gender, family history, or place of residence (i.e., high-drug-use neighborhoods). The only criterion for inclusion is membership in the selected subgroup. Therefore, some individuals may be at low personal risk for substance abuse while others may already be involved with alcohol or other drug use or abuse. A mentoring program for children from a low-income, high-drug-use neighborhood is an example of a selective prevention strategy. Another example of a selective prevention strategy would be a support group for children of alcoholics and addicts.

Indicated prevention strategies are directed toward individuals who have demonstrated the potential for substance abuse based on their behavior. For example, a minor in possession of tobacco, alcohol, or other drugs would fit this criterion. It is important to determine if the individual is a substance abuser or substance dependent because the latter would indicate the need for treatment (see Chapter 6). Other indicated behaviors include involvement with the juvenile justice system for nonalcohol or other drug-related offenses, dropping out of school or excessive truancy, and conduct disorders. Examples of indicated prevention strategies include social skills classes for juvenile offenders, drug education for minors in possession, and family counseling.

Classification by Prevention Strategy

The Center for Substance Abuse Prevention (CSAP), the federal agency that coordinates prevention efforts throughout the country, has utilized a prevention classification system based on six strategies. This system is not in conflict with the Institute of Medicine system since a strategy may be targeted to universal, selective, or indicated populations. The six strategies are as follows:

Information Dissemination. This involves communication of the nature, extent, and effect of substance use, abuse, and addiction on individuals, families, and communities. In addition, these strategies may involve information on prevention programs and services. One-way communication between a source and an audience, with limited or no contact between the two, characterizes information dissemination. Public service announcements, didactic instruction, audiovisual materials, displays of drugs, and publications are examples of information dissemination.

Education. These activities are designed to build or change life and social skills—such as decision making, refusal skills, assertiveness, and making friends—that are usually thought to be associated with substance abuse prevention. Education is differentiated from information dissemination in that there is interaction between the facilitator or instructor and the participants. In addition, there is an expectation that participants will develop skills from the education strategies. Most school-based prevention programs are considered to be education, although they may include an information dissemination component. Programs designed to improve parenting skills are also examples of education strategies.

Alternatives. These strategies involve the development of activities that are incompatible with substance use. This is based on the assumption that young people may use AOD because of boredom or lack of access to other activities. Therefore, if there are healthy, productive, and fun activities, young people will participate in these activities rather than in AOD use. In addition, this participation may expose high-risk youth to positive role models and provide an expanded view of the possibilities for the future. Midnight basketball is often used as an example of an alternative strategy. Another common alternative strategy is the development of after-school programs, designed to provide a supervised, productive program for young people at a time when much of the youth crime is committed (3 to 7 P.M.).

Problem Identification and Referral. This strategy is generally targeted to indicated populations who have been identified as using tobacco, alcohol, or other drugs or who have engaged in other inappropriate behaviors. Depending on the nature and severity of the problem, referrals may be made to educational programs, family therapy, or other forms of treatment. For young people who are caught in possession of tobacco, alcohol, or other drugs, consequence may be combined with mandatory education.

Community-Based Processes. These strategies involve the mobilization of communities to more effectively provide prevention services. Interagency collaborations, coalition building, and networking are considered community-based strategies. For example, representatives from county government, social services, juvenile justice, education, the faith community, and the business community may join together to develop seamless (i.e., no barriers to access services from different agencies) services for youth.

Environmental Approaches. Within this strategy are the written and unwritten standards, codes, laws, and attitudes that impact substance use and abuse in a community. The clearest examples are laws regarding tobacco and alcohol. States and counties have very different laws relating to the taxation and distribution of tobacco and alcohol.

A social service organization that relies on alcohol-related events (e.g., wine tasting) to raise funds is communicating a value that is counterproductive for prevention. An environmental strategy would be to lobby this organization to change its fund-raising activities. Another example would be efforts to prohibit university campus newspapers from accepting advertisements that promote excessive alcohol use.

Classification by Risk and Protective Factors

David Hawkins and his colleagues at the University of Washington have done a considerable amount of work on the identification of factors that are associated with an increased probability of AOD abuse (risk factors) or with a decreased probability of AOD abuse (protective factors) (e.g., Hawkins et al., 1992). This conceptualization has become so popular that many states build their prevention systems by assessing the extent of each risk factor in their communities and then by designing prevention strategies to reduce these risk factors (Wong, Catalano, Hawkins, & Chappell, 1996).

Risk factors have been organized by community, family, school, and individual or peer categories. Community risk factors include the availability of tobacco, alcohol, and other drugs; community laws and norms favorable toward substances; community mobility (i.e., frequent movement of people in and out of the community); low neighborhood attachment and community disorganization; and extreme economic deprivation. Family risk factors include a family history of problem behaviors, family management problems, family conflict, and parental attitudes toward and involvement with substance use. In the school area, the risk factors are early and persistent antisocial behavior, academic failure beginning in elementary school, and lack of commitment to school. Finally, individual or peer risk factors include alienation and rebelliousness, association with peers who engage in problem behaviors, favorable attitudes toward problem behaviors, early initiation of problem behaviors; and constitutional factors (i.e., genetic predisposition to addiction or sensation seeking).

In spite of being exposed to multiple risk factors, some young people do not develop problems with alcohol or other drugs. There seem to be certain protective factors that buffer youngsters by reducing the impact of the risk factors or by changing the way in which the individual responds to the risks. These protective factors have been categorized as individual characteristics, bonding, and healthy beliefs and clear standards. The individual characteristics include gender (females are more protected than males), a resilient temperament, a positive social orientation, and intelligence. Obviously, these individual characteristics are difficult or impossible to change. Bonding involves the attachment to positive families, friends, school, and community. The beneficial aspects of bonding cannot be overemphasized. A child who develops a bond to positive role models or healthy systems can overcome the disadvantages of exposure to risk factors. To facilitate the development of bonding, children need the opportunity to bond, the skills to take advantage of the opportunity, and recognition for making efforts to bond. For those of you who wonder if you can make a difference in a young person's life, this information on bonding should be a strong affirmation that you can have a major impact. Healthy beliefs and clear standards go hand-in-hand with bonding. The people and systems to which young people bond must communicate positive values and hold young people accountable for their behavior. Protection is enhanced when clear standards of behavior are expressed and consequences are applied for violations of these standards.

Although the risk and protective factor model is logical, a caution is necessary. Much of this research is correlational rather than causal. To illustrate, let's look at one family risk factor: family conflict. Family conflict has been identified as a risk factor because there is evidence that children from families in which there is excessive family conflict have a higher probability of developing substance abuse problems (and other problems as well) than children who come from families in which there is minimal family conflict. However, this does not mean that family conflict causes substance abuse problems or that reducing family conflict will prevent a child from developing a substance abuse problem. Perhaps the family conflict is due to the substance abuse of one or more of the caretakers in the family. As a result of some type of intervention, perhaps the family learns to resolve its problems in a more reasonable manner. However, the caretaker continues to abuse substances. In this instance, family conflict is just one symptom of dysfunction in the family system as a result of substance abuse. Therefore, treating one symptom is not likely to affect the development of substance abuse (or other problems) in the children.

It should be noted that a causal relationship between risk and protective factors and substance abuse is not proposed in the model developed by Hawkins and his colleagues. However, many intervention programs designed to reduce risk factors and increase protective factors have been based on an assumption that such a causal relationship exists. In our view, there is a complex interaction between all these factors. As we will discuss in the next section, the development of prevention strategies and programs should be based on research on what works.

What Works in Prevention

Evaluation of Prevention Programs

Attempts to measure the success of prevention programs have resulted in some controversy. The prevailing attitude regarding prevention programs is summarized in a statement made by Botvin and Botvin (1992): "Until recently, virtually all efforts to develop effective substance abuse prevention approaches have failed" (p. 910). However, this perceived failure may be due to the evaluation problems in this area as opposed to (or in addition to) the prevention approaches themselves.

Several issues need to be considered in evaluating prevention programs. Clearly, local, state, and federal government entities are interested in evaluating the success of prevention programs because of the money spent on the programs. As you might imagine, the typical method for evaluating success is the implementation of a prevention program in classrooms or schools and to later see whether the kids who were involved in the program use AOD to a lesser extent than kids who were not involved in the program. One problem is that the initiation of use by young people depends on a complex interaction of personal, familial, cultural, and societal variables. To expect a school-based prevention program to singularly impact a behavior influenced by so many variables is unrealistic. Second, we know that attitudes and behavior can be influenced by a consistent, long-term, and comprehensive effort. For example, when many of us were young, cars did not have seat belts. Seat belts were then made optional, but we still never used them. Today, they are standard features in all cars, and many states have legislation requiring their use. So, our children don't even think about it. When they get in the car, they put on their seat belts. We do, too. However, this change in attitude and behavior in adults who grew up with seat-belt-free cars was accomplished through a long-term process involving public policy (legislation) and public awareness. Similarly, school- and community-based prevention programs should be viewed as a part of long-term, consistent, comprehensive prevention efforts and not as isolated "cures" for the problem of tobacco, alcohol, and other drug use by young people.

However, we believe that the effectiveness of prevention efforts would be enhanced if the contradictory messages were less pervasive. Marketing of tobacco and alcohol products, positive depictions of tobacco, alcohol, and drug use in the media, and modeling by adults and peers are powerful influences on young people. It is not currently possible, given financial and practical constraints, for the prevention community to counteract creative and funny beer commercials, cigarette smoking in youth-oriented movies, and mom and dad smoking a joint with their friends in the living room. At this point in time, the prevention message is not consistent or comprehensive. Finally, school-based prevention programs are often viewed in a similar manner to other programs in a school. If you want to evaluate a new reading program, you compare the reading performance of the children in the new program with the performance of children in another program. However, we would argue that prevention programs are different. For example, imagine that you begin a prevention program that costs $10,000 in materials and training. In the entire school, only one student who would have become dependent on tobacco, alcohol, or other drugs is impacted and avoids use. You will have more than made up for the money invested in the program by preventing the financial and societal impact on healthcare, work productivity, the legal system, and family members that this person would have caused. We are not arguing that prevention programs should be purchased and implemented without careful evaluation. We are arguing that prevention programs should not be blamed for failing to solve a complex and multifaceted problem.

Because of the importance of the problem and the money spent on prevention, the federal government has become very interested in determining which prevention strategies and programs are the most effective. For example, the National Institute on Drug Abuse has a publication on principles of effective prevention (National Institute on Drug Abuse, 2004). In addition, Paglia and Room (1998) presented an excellent review of the prevention literature, and Tobler (1992) and Tobler and Stratton (1997) conducted meta-analyses of school-based prevention programs. From these sources, conclusions regarding effective (and ineffective) prevention strategies can be reached. We will present these conclusions for each of the six CSAP strategies.

Information Dissemination. School-based information dissemination methods have been unsuccessful in impacting tobacco, alcohol, and other drug use. As Botvin and Botvin (1992) stated:

> studies have rather consistently indicated that informational approaches do *not* reduce or prevent tobacco, alcohol, or drug use; they indicate quite clearly that increased knowledge has virtually no impact on substance use or on intentions to engage in tobacco, alcohol, or drug use in the near future. (p. 914, italics in original)

Similarly, Tobler (1992) found that prevention programs that only presented information did increase knowledge of participants but had no effect on attitudes and drug use. This is not surprising when you consider the analogy of the prevention of heart disease. Most Americans know that quitting smoking, regular aerobic exercise, reducing fat in the diet, and so forth will reduce the risk of heart disease. However, this information alone is usually insufficient to result in a significant behavior change for most people. Similarly, simply learning about the negative consequences of using tobacco, alcohol, and other drugs does not affect the reasons for use by most young people.

Although information dissemination alone is not sufficient, providing accurate information is an important component for school-based prevention programs. Paglia and Room (1998) recommend an emphasis on the short-term adverse effects of use, rather than on the long-term effects. The reasoning is that, from a developmental standpoint, young people are impacted more by short-term effects, particularly those that involve social attractiveness. Additionally, information on health risks and consequences of use should be based on research and should be delivered in a nonjudgmental manner (Bachman, Johnston, & O'Malley, 1991). Scare tactics and moral lecturing have not been shown to be effective and may actually have a detrimental effect if the information is in conflict with the personal experience of students.

As might be expected, information dissemination via the mass media should be aired at times when young people are likely to be listening or watching. The use of authority figures and exhortations has not been shown to be effective. As with school-based information dissemination, short-term risks involved in substance use should be emphasized (Brounstein, Zweng, & Gardner, 1998).

Education. In contrast to previously discussed school-based prevention programs that are "information only," Tobler (1992) has categorized some school-based programs as affective. This model is based on the assumption that young people use AOD because of low self-esteem, inadequate social skills, and ambiguous values. Through discussion and activities involving feelings, values, and self-awareness, an attempt is made to improve self-concept and social skills and to clarify the students' values.

The results from Tobler's (1992) meta-analysis show that prevention programs that used only affective education were ineffective in impacting knowledge, attitudes and values, self-reported drug use, or decision-making, assertive, and refusal skills. Furthermore, drug incident reports, school grades and attendance, and achievement test scores also were unaffected. Approaches that combine cognitive (information dissemination) and affective approaches did have a positive effect on knowledge of participants but a negligible effect on the other outcomes. Part of the problem with this approach to prevention may be the consistent finding that very little relationship has been established between self-esteem and drug use (Clayton, Leukefeld, Grant, Harrington, & Cattarello, 1996; Coggans & McKellar, 1994; Schroeder, Laflin, & Weis, 1993).

Another educational approach to prevention is based on the environmental influences on young people that result in the initiation of tobacco, alcohol, and other drug use. Family use patterns (including parents and siblings), peer pressure, and media all may influence young people to use (or not to use). Social resistance skills approaches (also called *social influence* or *refusal skills* approaches) have been developed to counteract environmental influences. According to Botvin and Botvin (1992),

> these interventions were designed to increase students' awareness of the various social influences to engage in substance use. A distinctive feature of these prevention models is that they place more emphasis on teaching students specific skills for effectively resisting both peer and media pressures to smoke, drink, or use drugs. (p. 916)

According to Botvin and Botvin (1992), social resistance skills approaches generally contain the following components: recognizing situations in which there is a high probability that a young person will experience peer pressure to use, formulating strategies to avoid these high-risk situations, teaching students what to say and how to say it when confronted with peer pressure, and developing awareness of techniques used by the media to encourage use by young people. Peers are frequently used in implementing these programs, since peers, particularly older adolescents with perceived status, may be more influential than teachers or other adults. Information dissemination, with a focus on prevalence of use by young people, is used to counter the argument that "everyone is doing it."

In evaluating social resistance skills approaches, Botvin and Botvin (1992) report that these programs have been associated with reductions in tobacco, alcohol, and marijuana use for up to three years. However, long-term follow-up studies have shown that these reductions are not maintained over time. Tobler (1992) found that programs using peers as implementors had a positive impact on knowledge, attitudes, self-reported drug use, and skills. However, no beneficial effect was noted on drug incident reports or on indirect measures of use such as school grades and attendance. The age group of the students, number of training sessions, use of booster sessions, instructional materials, and characteristics of the students may all impact evaluation of these programs, and Botvin and Botvin suggest that additional research is necessary to clarify the variables that are important for success.

Competency enhancement approaches are more comprehensive than the other approaches and focus on the interaction between the individual and environment in the prevention of substance use by young people. Competency enhancement approaches emphasize the development and use of personal and social skills that are directly related to substance use but that are also applicable to many other adolescent problems. According to Botvin and Botvin (1992), competency enhancement approaches

> typically teach two or more of the following:
>
> 1. General problem-solving and decision making skills
> 2. General cognitive skills for resisting interpersonal or media influences
> 3. Skills for increasing self-control and self-esteem
> 4. Adaptive coping strategies for relieving stress and anxiety through the use of cognitive coping skills or behavioral relaxation techniques

5. General social skills
6. General assertive skills

> These skills are taught using a combination of instruction, demonstration, feedback, reinforcement, behavioral rehearsal (practice during class), and extended practice through behavioral homework assignments. (p. 320)

Evaluation studies of competency enhancement approaches seem generally positive. In a summary of these studies, Botvin and Botvin (1992) report reductions in initiating use of tobacco, alcohol, and marijuana. Effectiveness has been demonstrated using many types of trainers (e.g., peers, teachers, project staff) as well as with ethnically diverse groups. With booster sessions, the effects have been maintained for up to six years (Botvin, Baker, Dusenbury, Botvin, & Diaz, 1995). However, this long-term follow-up study has been criticized for failing to report negative results and for issues regarding sample selection (Brown & Kreft, 1998; Gorman, 1998).

In reviewing the literature on school-based prevention, Paglia and Room (1998) and Brounstein et al. (1998) have presented some general guidelines in the structure, content, and delivery of prevention education. The recommendations include prevention programming throughout the grades, with the greatest emphasis on the median ages of first use (late elementary school and middle school). While long-term programs are superior to short-term programs, periodic booster sessions following the completion of programs are necessary to maintain benefits. Information presented should be factual. If the instructor does not know an answer, this should be admitted to students. Students should have the opportunity to discuss the reasons why people use AOD, alternatives to meeting these needs, and the dangers and benefits to using and not using. While both short-term and long-term effects should be presented, the short-term effects should be emphasized. Perceptions regarding "everybody does it" should be challenged with data. An interactive style of presentation is most beneficial, including cooperative learning, role-plays, and group exercises. Peer facilitators can be effective if they are trained and are perceived as credible. The instructional atmosphere should be tolerant and free from moralizing and scare tactics. Finally, as Paglia and Room (1998) state, "*most importantly, anything taught in the school must be reinforced in the community by parents, media, and health policies*" (p. 16, italics in original).

While there are many commercially prepared school-based prevention programs, the Drug Abuse Resistance Education (DARE) program should be specifically mentioned. The DARE program is unique among school-based prevention programs with its use of police officers as instructors. The program was developed by Daryl Gates, former Los Angeles Chief of Police. DARE officers are trained in child development, classroom management, teaching techniques, and communication skills prior to classroom instruction. The program consists of 17 lessons delivered to fifth- and sixth-grade students offering information about AOD, refusal skills, decision making, alternatives to drug use, resistance to peer pressure, and self-esteem enhancement (DARE America, 1991). There are ten follow-up lessons in junior high and an additional nine lessons in high school.

According to DARE America (1991), the nonprofit organization that coordinates DARE, over 5 million children a year participate in the program. Ennett et al. (1994) report that DARE is the most widely used prevention program in the United States. However, in a long-term evaluation study in 36 schools in Illinois, they found limited support for DARE's impact on drug use immediately following the program and no support for continuing impact on drug use one to two years following the program. There was a positive effect on self-esteem but no effect on peer resistance skills. Similarly, Clayton, Cattarello, and Johnstone (1996) conducted a five-year follow-up of DARE in Lexington, Kentucky, and found no significant differences in tobacco, alcohol, or marijuana use among 10th graders who had received the DARE program and students who had received other types of school-based prevention programs.

A meta-analysis of eight evaluation studies of DARE found the program less effective than more interactive prevention programs on measures of drug knowledge, drug attitudes, social skills, and drug use (Ennett, Tobler, Ringwalt, & Flewelling, 1994). Due to these results, the DARE curriculum has been revised.

A variety of education programs focused on the family have also been hypothesized to prevent substance use among youth. These programs can involve parent education, parenting skills training, parent support groups, and family therapy. It is particularly useful to combine school-based prevention programs with family-based programs. Most studies of family-based prevention have focused on "high-risk" families. An example of such a program is the Strengthening Families Program (Kumpfer, Williams, & Baxley, 1997). Parent, child, and family skills training was targeted to substance abusing families with children in the 6 to 10 year range. Improvements were found in the problem behaviors of the children, in intentions to use AOD, in parenting skills, in family communication, and in family conflict.

A major research problem with high-risk family-focused programs is the recruitment and retention of families. In spite of this problem, programs "that include parenting skills and children's skills training and structured family sessions, may be effective in reducing risk factors and strengthening protective factors which etiological models link to drug use. However, whether these types of effects actually become translated into the prevention of substance use or abuse among youth has yet to be confirmed by long-term empirical evaluations" (Paglia and Room, 1998, p. 22).

Alternatives. The research evidence regarding the effectiveness of alternative activities is mixed.

Botvin and Botvin (1992) indicate that entertainment, vocational, and social alternatives programs have been associated with more rather than less substance use, although academic, religious, and sports activities are associated with less use. They report that evaluations of alternatives programs have failed to demonstrate an impact on adolescent use. In contrast, Tobler's (1992) meta-analysis of alternatives programs for high-risk youth showed positive effects on skills and behavior, including school grades, school attendance, and independent reports of observed drug use.

According to the review of literature conducted by Brounstein et al. (1998), alternatives should be part of a comprehensive prevention plan that includes other activities with proven effectiveness. However, when alternative activities are being developed, they must be attractive to the target group or participation will not occur. Therefore, young people must be involved in the planning process. Not surprisingly, the more intensive the activity (in terms of both hours required and length), the more effective it is.

Carmona and Stewart (1996) and Tobler (1986) point out that alternative activities serve a more general purpose than just providing something else to do besides using substances. For some high-risk youth, alternative activities are an opportunity for personal development and positive bonding to adults and the community. The development of these protective factors may be beneficial in a variety of ways. One type of alternative activity that is popular is mentoring. Mentoring programs provide young people, particularly high-risk youth, with structured time with positive adult role models. Mentoring programs have been associated with reductions in substance use; increases in positive attitudes toward others, the future, and school; and increased school attendance. As would be expected, the more highly involved the mentor, the greater the impact. It is particularly important to screen and train potential mentors. Clearly, mentors must be positive role models and must complete their commitment to the young people in the program. Many of the high-risk youth in these programs have been disappointed by adults in the past and should be protected from having similar experiences with mentors.

Problem Identification and Referral. There are certain important factors to consider in the development of any problem identification and referral system. First, experimental users should be differentiated from problematic users. Although any use of tobacco, alcohol, or other drugs by a minor is a problem, experimentation is not uncommon and does not require intensive intervention. A significant consequence combined with education is usually the appropriate level of intervention for experimental use. In addition, if experimental users are placed in more intensive programs, they will be grouped with problematic users. This could have the unintended consequence of enabling further use. Because of these issues, problem identification and referral programs must have valid procedures and trained personnel to determine where the individual is on the use continuum (see Chapter 6).

Substance use among young people is often associated with other problems, including family dysfunction, school failure, sexual activity, and violence. Therefore, a problem identification and referral program must be prepared to screen for other problems in addition to substance use and must have adequate referral resources to assist the targeted individuals. This may include very concrete issues such as transportation. For example, a 15-year-old female was referred to a guidance team at her high school after she was found in possession of marijuana. She admitted to frequent, unprotected sex with a variety of partners. The young woman was receptive to a referral to the local health department for contraception and testing for sexually transmitted diseases, but she had no way to get there. Fortunately, school personnel were able to arrange public transportation.

Community-Based Processes. Community-based coalitions are formed to improve the nature and delivery of services to the community (comprehensive service coordination), generate community activism to address substance-related problems (community mobilization), or to perform both functions (community linkage). Comprehensive service coordination requires the involvement of the leaders of the organizations in the coalition, whereas community mobilization is dependent on grassroots activists and community citizens. In order to elicit change at a systems or individual-behavior level, community partnerships must have a clear and shared vision of their objectives, commitments to participate from all partnership members, participation from diverse community groups, and comprehensive prevention activities directed at a large number of individuals.

Appropriate organization, leadership, and evaluation have been shown to be important components in successful community partnerships. While committees are usually necessary, those with specific purposes sustain higher levels of involvement than those with elaborate structures. A dynamic leader may be effective but this type of individual cannot normally be replaced. Therefore, opportunities for leadership roles from a variety of participants are helpful. Community coalitions are also advised to implement evidenced-based prevention strategies and to incorporate procedures for measuring the effectiveness of their strategies.

Environmental Approaches. The approaches in this category generate a great deal of discussion in the prevention community and in state and federal governments. Environmental approaches have demonstrated a direct impact on the use of tobacco and alcohol and on the problems associated with the use of these substances. However, environmental strategies have not been as effective in regard to illicit drugs, as we saw in the earlier discussion in this chapter on supply reduction efforts.

Increasing the taxes on tobacco and alcohol is one type of environmental strategy. Tax increases have resulted in reductions in the use of both tobacco and alcohol as well as reductions in associated problems, such as alcohol-related traffic accidents. The tobacco legislation considered by the 1998 Congress included a significant tax increase on tobacco and was bitterly fought (and defeated) by the tobacco industry. Moreover, efforts to increase the price of illicit drugs through law enforcement efforts have not been successful.

Laws regarding the purchase of tobacco and alcohol by minors have also been effective. When the minimum purchase age for alcohol was raised to 21 in all states, alcohol consumption among minors decreased, as did alcohol-related problems. Sting operations, using underage individuals who attempt to purchase tobacco or alcohol, are effective in increasing retailer compliance with restricting sales to minors. In addition, "use and lose" laws that result in driver's license suspension for minors convicted of an alcohol or drug violation have also been shown to increase compliance with minimum-purchase-age laws.

Deterrence laws and policies have also been shown to be effective in reducing alcohol-related accidents and underage drinking and driving. These include lowering the blood-alcohol level from .10 to .08 or lower, enforcement of drinking and driving laws, sobriety checkpoints, and zero tolerance for alcohol use by underage drivers. While sobriety checkpoints do not result in high levels of detection, publicizing that they will occur seems to have a deterrent effect.

Local communities can also implement proven environmental strategies by placing restrictions on the location and number of retail outlets authorized to sell tobacco and/or alcohol. Neighborhoods have been able to disrupt illicit drug sales through citizen surveillance and through pressure on landlords who own property where drug sales occur.

Training for individuals who serve alcohol (i.e., bartenders) and clerks who sell tobacco and alcohol is an effective strategy when it is combined with law enforcement efforts. Training is intended to educate servers and clerks about the laws, as well as teach them to identify intoxication and false identification and to provide skills in refusing to serve or sell.

Although environmental strategies are clearly effective in reducing the use of tobacco and alcohol, the involvement of community coalitions is usually essential to implement these strategies. Since many require action by policy makers and since many policy makers receive campaign contributions from the tobacco and alcohol industries, pressure from community groups is often necessary.

Further information on environmental approaches is available from Stewart (1997). This document is an extremely thorough review of the literature in this area.

Evidence-Based Prevention

In Chapter 8, we discussed evidence-based treatment and commented that some states will only fund evidence-based strategies and approaches. This same situation, perhaps even to a greater extent, exists in the prevention field, which in contrast to the treatment field, has had for some time now a formal process in place to determine if a prevention program is worthy of being called "evidence-based." The Substance Abuse and Mental Health Services Administration documents this in "The National Registry of Evidence-Based Programs and Practices" (NREPP). While this registry is not currently limited to substance abuse prevention programs, it was initially started as a process to determine which prevention programs could be called "model programs" and continues to list many more substance abuse prevention programs than treatment programs or other types of prevention programs.

To be included on NREPP, a program goes through a formal review process. The minimum requirements are as follows:

1. The intervention demonstrates one or more positive outcomes ($p < .05$) in mental health and/or substance use behavior among individuals, communities, or populations.
2. Intervention results have been published in a peer-reviewed publication or documented in a comprehensive evaluation report.
3. Documentation (e.g., manuals, process guides, tools, training materials) of the intervention and its proper implementation is available to the public to facilitate dissemination. (SAMHSA, 2007).

To review the evidence-based programs on NREPP, go to http://nrepp.samhsa.gov.

Prevention Resources

The Center for Substance Abuse Prevention has an online prevention resource called PREVline (ncadi.samhsa.gov). This site contains resources, referrals, conferences, data, and much more. Included on PREVline is the National Clearinghouse for Alcohol and Drug Information (NCADI). NCADI has federal prevention publications available, generally at no cost. If you are not online, the NCADI toll-free phone number is 1-877-SAMHSA7. In addition, there are five Centers for the Application of Prevention Technologies (CAPT) in the United States. These centers are funded by the Center for Substance Abuse Prevention and are designed to help states and community-based organizations apply evidence-based prevention strategies. Each CAPT covers a different region of the country. You can find information about your regional CAPT at www.captus.org. In addition, each state has a single state agency for treatment and prevention coordination. There will be some staff in this agency involved with prevention efforts.

Finally, for those of you who are interested in exploring the prevention field in more depth, we recommend a textbook by Hogan, Reed-Gabrielsen, Luna, and Grothaus (2003), *Substance Abuse Prevention: The Intersection of Science and Practice.*

Summary

- Public policies regarding tobacco, alcohol, and other drugs have an impact on prevention efforts.
- Prevention activities are classified by the target audience (universal, selective, indicated) or the type of prevention strategy (information dissemination, education, alternative activities, problem identification and referral, community-based processes, environmental).
- The Risk and Protective Factor theory is widely used to identify variables associated with the increased or decreased probability of AOD abuse.
- Evidence-based prevention programs have been identified through a federal review process.

Internet Resources

National Registry of Evidence-Based Programs and Practices
http://nrepp.samhsa.gov

Centers for the Application of Prevention Technologies
http://captus.samhsa.gov/home.cfm

Prevention principles
www.drugabuse.gov/Prevention/principles.html

National Clearinghouse for Alcohol and Drug Information (NCADI)
http://ncadi.samhsa.gov

Further Discussion

1. What would be the advantages and disadvantages of parents teaching their children to drink responsibly?
2. After reading the risk factors for adolescent substance abuse, do you think it is possible to significantly reduce these risk factors? How would you design a prevention program to accomplish this?
3. Is the goal of "drug-free" schools realistic? If so, how would you go about accomplishing this? If not, how would you minimize the harm from adolescent drug use? Do you include tobacco and alcohol in your definition of "drug-free"? Why or why not?

References

AA Grapevine. (1985). New York: Alcoholics Anonymous Grapevine.

Abadinsky, H. (2007). *Drug abuse: An introduction* (6th ed.). Chicago: Nelson-Hall.

Abney, P. C., & Harrison, T. C. (June 19, 2003). RESOURCERY counseling: A model for the 21st century. Paper presented at the annual convention of the International Association of Phenomenology, Constructivism, and Psychotherapy. Bari, Italy.

Abrams, R. C., & Alexopoulos, G. (1987). Substance abuse in the elderly: Alcohol and prescription drugs: Over-the-counter and illegal drugs. *Hospital and Community Psychiatry, 39,* 822–823.

Ackerman, R. J. (1983). *Children of alcoholics. A guidebook for educators, therapists, and parents.* New York: Simon & Schuster.

Ackerman, R. J. (1987). *Same house, different homes: Why adult children of alcoholics are not all the same.* Deerfield Beach, FL: Health Communications.

Adelman, S. A., & Weiss, R. D. (1989). What is therapeutic about inpatient alcoholism treatment. *Hospital and Community Psychiatry, 40,* 515–519.

Agras, W. S. (1987). *Eating disorders: Management of obesity, bulimia, and anorexia nervosa.* New York: Pergamon Press.

Al-Anon Family Group (1973). *Alateen: Hope for children of alcoholics.* New York: Al-Anon Family Group Headquarters.

Alcohol (in Korean). Fifty-nine authors, fifty-nine essays. (1978). Gi So Rhim Publishing.

Alcohol Policies Project, Center for Science in the Public Interest (2003). *Alcoholic-beverage advertising expenditures. Fact sheet.* Retrieved March 27, 2007 from www.cspinet.org/booze/FactSheets/AlcAdExp.pdf

Alcoholics Anonymous (3rd ed.). (2001). New York: Alcoholics Anonymous World Services.

Alcoholics Anonymous: Twelve steps and twelve traditions (1981). New York: Alcoholics Anonymous World Services.

Allen, J. P., Litten, R. Z., Fertig, J. B., & Babor, T. (1997). A review of research on the Alcohol Use Disorders Identification Test (AUDIT). *Alcoholism: Clinical and Experimental Research, 21,* 613–619.

Allen, R. (1996). Alcoholism in the elderly. *Journal of the American Medical Association, 275*(10), 797–801.

Allison, S. K. (2002). A path model using codependency and binge eating as mediating variables with selected biographic correlates to explain body mass index in a nursing sample. *Dissertation Abstracts International, 63*(2-B), Section B, 757. (Order Number AAI3042860).

Ambrogne, J. A. (2007). Managing depressive symptoms in the context of abstinence: Findings from a qualitative study of women. *Perspectives in Psychiatric Care, 43*(2), 84–92.

American Heart Association, (1999). *Cigarette and tobacco smoke: Biostatistical fact sheets* [Online]. Retrieved October 11, 2007 from www.amhrt.org/statistics.

American Psychiatric Association. (2000). *Diagnostic and statistical manual of mental disorders-IV-Text Revised.* Washington, DC: American Psychiatric Association.

American Temperance Union. (n.d.). *Temperance tract for the freedman.* New York: Author.

Andersen, A. E., & Michalide, A. D. (1983). Anorexia nervosa in the male: An underdiagnosed disorder. *Psychosomatics, 24,* 1066–1069, 1072–1075.

Anderson, G. L. (1987). *When chemicals come to school.* Greenfield, WI: Community Recovery Press.

Anderson, J. Z. (1992). Stepfamilies and substance abuse: Unique treatment considerations. In E. Kaufman & P. Kaufman (Eds.), *Family therapy of drug and alcohol abuse* (2nd ed., pp. 172–189). Boston: Allyn and Bacon.

Andre, J. M. (1979). *The epidemiology of alcoholism among American Indians and Alaska Natives.* Albuquerque, NM: U.S. Indian Health Services.

Annis, H. M. (1982). *Inventory of drinking situations.* Toronto: Addiction Research Foundation of Ontario.

Annis, H. M. (1986). A relapse prevention model for treatment of alcoholics. In W. R. Miller & W. Heather (Eds.), *Treating addictive behaviors: Process of change* (pp. 407–433). New York: Plenum.

Annis, H. M. (1990). Relapse to substance abuse: Empirical findings within a cognitive-social learning approach. *Journal of Psychoactive Drugs, 22,* 117–124.

Annis, H. M., & Davis, C. S. (1989). Relapse prevention. In R. K. Hester & W. R. Miller (Eds.), *Handbook of alcoholism treatment approaches: Effective alternatives* (pp. 171–182). New York: Pergamon.

Aquilino, W. S., & Supple, A. J. (2001). Long-term effects of parenting practices during adolescence on well-being outcome in young adulthood. *Journal of Family Issues, 22,* 289–308.

Archambault, D. L. (1992). Adolescence: A physiological, cultural, and psychological no man's land. In G. W. Lawson & A. W. Lawson (Eds.). *Adolescent substance abuse: Etiology, treatment, and prevention* (pp. 11–28). Gaithersburg, MD: Aspen Publications.

Armor, D. J., Polich, J. M., & Stambul, H. B. (1978). *Alcoholism and treatment.* New York: John Wiley & Sons.

Aronson, K. (2003). Alcohol: A recently identified risk factor for breast cancer. *Canadian Medical Association Journal, 168,* 1147–1148.

Asher, R. (1992). *Women with alcoholic husbands: Ambivalence and the trap of codependency.* Chapel Hill, NC: University of North Carolina Press.

Atkinson, D. R., Morten, G., & Sue, D. W. (1998). *Counseling American minorities* (5th ed.). Boston: McGraw-Hill.

Attneave, C. (1982). American Indians and Alaska Natives families: Emigrants in their own homeland. In M. McGoldrick, J. K. Pierce, & J. Giordano (Eds.), *Ethnicity and family therapy* (pp. 55–83). New York: Guilford Press.

Austin, A. A. (2004). Alcohol, tobacco, other drug use, and violent behavior among Native Hawaiians: Ethnic pride and resilience. *Substance Use and Misuse, 39*(5), 721–746.

Babcock, M. (1995). Critiques of codependency: History and background issues. In M. Babcock & C. McKay (Eds.), *Challenging codependency: Feminist critiques* (pp. 3–27). Toronto: University of Toronto Press.

Babcock, M., & McKay, C. (1995). *Challenging codependency: Feminist critiques.* Toronto: University of Toronto Press.

Babor, T. F., de la Fuente, J. R., Saunders, J., & Grant, M. (1992). *AUDIT: The alcohol use disorders identification test: Guidelines for use in primary health care.* Geneva, Switzerland: World Health Organization.

Bachman, J. G., Johnston, L. D., & O'Malley, P. O. (1991). How changes in drug use are linked to perceived risks and disapproval: Evidence from national studies that youth and young adults respond to information about the consequences of drug use. In L. Donohew, H. E. Sypher, & W. J. Bukoski (Eds.), *Persuasive communication and drug abuse prevention* (pp. 133–155). Hillsdale, NJ: Erlbaum.

Bachman, J., Wallace, J., O'Malley, P., Johnston, L., Kurth, C., & Neighbors, H. (1991). Racial/ethnic differences in smoking, drinking and illicit drug use among American high school seniors. *American Journal of Public Health, 81,* 372–377.

Back, S. E., Contini, R., Brady, K. T. (2007). Substance abuse in women: Does gender matter? *Psychiatric Times, 24*(1), 48–58.

Backer, T. (1991). Drug abuse services and EAPs: Preliminary report on a national study. *National Institute on Drug Abuse, Drug abuse services research series, No. 1: Background papers on drug abuse financing and services research*

-244). Rockville, MD: U.S. Depart- ı Health and Human Services.

ı, F., & Lundwall, L. (1975). Dropping out ıreatment: A critical review. *Psychological ulletin, 82,* 738–783.

, J. C., Corty, E., Petroski, S. P., & Bond, H. (1987). Treatment effectiveness: Medical staff and services provided to 2,394 patients at methadone programs in three states. *National Institute on Drug Abuse: Research Monograph Series #76,* 175–181.

Ball, J. C., & Ross, A. R. (1991). *The effectiveness of methadone maintenance treatment: Patients, programs, services and outcomes.* New York: Springer-Verlag.

Barnard, C. P. (1981). *Families, alcoholism, and therapy.* Springfield, IL: Charles C Thomas.

Barnes, G. M., Farell, M. P., & Cairns, A. (1986). Parental socialization factors and adolescent drinking behaviors. *Journal of Marriage and the Family, 48,* 27–36.

Barón, M. (2000). Addiction treatment for Mexican-American families. In J. Krestan (Ed.), *Bridges to recovery. Addiction, family therapy, and multicultural treatment* (pp. 219–252). New York: The Free Press.

Barrett, A. E., Turner, R. J. (2006). Family structure and substance use problems in adolescence and early adulthood: Examining explanations for the relationship. *Addiction, 101,* 109–120.

Barthwell, A. G., & Gibert, C. L. (1993). *Screening for infectious diseases among substance abusers. Treatment improvement protocol (TIP) series, No. 6.* Rockville, MD: U.S. Department of Health and Human Services.

Batki, S. L. (1990). Drug abuse, psychiatric disorders, and AIDS: Dual and triple diagnosis. *Western Journal of Medicine, 152,* 547–552.

Batki, S. L., Sorensen, J. L., Faltz, B., & Madover, S. (1988). Psychiatric aspects of treatment of intravenous drug abusers with AIDS. *Hospital and Community Psychiatry, 39,* 439–441.

Bauer, C. R., Shankaran, S., Bada, H. S., Lester, B., Wright, L. L., Krause-Steinraug, H. Smeriglio, V. L., Finnegan, L. P. Maza, P. L., & Verter, J. (2002). The maternal lifestyle study: Drug exposure during pregnancy and short-term maternal outcomes. *American Journal of Obstetrics and Gynecology, 186,* 487–495.

Beard, K. W. (2005). Internet addiction: A review of current assessment techniques and potential assessment questions. *CyberPsychology & Behavior, 8*(1), 7–14.

Beattie, M. (1987). *Codependent no more: How to stop controlling others and start caring for yourself.* Center City, MN: Hazelden.

Beavers, W. R. (1985). *Successful marriage: A family systems approach to couples therapy.* New York: W. W. Norton.

Becker, A. E. (2007). Culture and eating disorders classification. *International Journal of Eating Disorders.* Retrieved July 24, 2007 from http://0-www3.interscience.wiley.com.innopac.library.unr.edu/cgi-bin/fulltext/114295153/PDFSTART

Beckman, L. J. (1994). Treatment needs of women with alcohol problems. *Alcohol Health & Research World, 18,* 206–211.

Beckman, L. J., & Amaro, H. (1984). Patterns of women's use of alcoholism treatment agencies. In S. C. Wilsnack & L. J. Beckman (Eds.), *Alcohol problems in women: Antecedents, consequences, and intervention* (pp. 319–348). New York: Academic Press.

Bedegral, L. E., Sobell, L. C., Sobell, M. B., & Simcok, E. (2006). Psychometric characteristics of a Spanish version of the DAST-10 and the RAGS. *Addictive Behaviors, 31,* 309–319.

Beesley, D., & Stoltenberg, C. D. (2002). Control, attachment style, and relationship satisfaction among adult children of alcoholics. *Journal of Mental Health Counseling, 24,* 281–298.

Beidler, R. J. (1989). Adult children of alcoholics: Is it really a separate field for study? *Drugs and Society, 3,* 133–141.

Bell, T. L. (1990). *Preventing adolescent relapse: A guide for parents, teachers, and counselors.* Independence, MO: Independence Press.

Bennett, L. A. (1988). Problems among school-age children of alcoholic parents. *DATA, Brown University Digest of Addiction Theory and Application, July,* 9–11.

Bennett, L. A., Wolin, S. J., & Reiss, D. (1988a). Deliberate family process: A strategy for protecting children of alcoholics. *British Journal of Addiction, 83,* 821–829.

Bennett, L. A., Wolin, S. J., & Reiss, D. (1988b). Cognitive, behavioral, and emotional problems among school-age children of alcoholic parents. *American Journal of Psychiatry, 145,* 185–190.

Bennett, S., & Dodge, T. (2007). Ethnic-racial in feelings of embarrassment associated with binge eating and fear of losing control. *International Journal of Eating Disorders, 40*(1), 454–459.

Bergner, R. M., & Bridges, A. J. (2002). The significance of heavy pornography involvement for romantic partners: Research and implications. *Journal of Sex and Marital Therapy, 28,* 193–206.

Berkowitz, A., & Perkins, H. W. (1988). Personality characteristics of children of alcoholics. *Journal of Consulting and Clinical Psychology, 56,* 206–209.

Bettes, B. L., Dusenbury, L., Kerner, J., James-Ortiz, S., & Botvin, G. L. (1990). Ethnicity and psychosocial factors in alcohol and tobacco use in adolescence. *Child Development, 61,* 557–565.

Biek, J. D. (1981). Screening test for identifying adolescents adversely affected by a parental drinking problem. *Journal of Adolescent Health Care, 2,* 107–113.

Black, C. (1981). *It will never happen to me.* Denver: MAC.

Blau, M. (1990). Adult children: Tied to the past. *American Health, 9,* 56–65.

Blinn-Pike, L., Worthy, S. L., & Jonkman, J. N. (2007). Disordered gambling among college students: A meta-analytic synthesis. *Journal of Gambling Studies, 23*(2), 175–183.

Blume, S. (1988). Compulsive gambling and the medical model. Special issue. Compulsive gambling: An examination of relevant models. *Journal of Gambling Behavior, 3,* 237–247.

Blume, S. A. (1997). Women and alcohol: Issues in social policy. In S. Wilsnack & R. Wilsnack (Eds.), *Gender and alcohol* (pp. 462–477). New Brunswick, NJ: Rutgers Center for Alcohol Studies.

Bombardier, C. H., Blake, K. D., Ehde, D. M., Gibbons, L. E., Moore, D., & Draft, G. H. (2004). *Multiple Sclerosis, 10,* 35–40.

Borovoy, A. (2000). Recovering from codependence in Japan. *American Ethnologist, 28*(1), 94–118.

Botvin, G. J., Baker, E., Dusenbury, L., Botvin, E. M., & Diaz, T. (1995). Long-term follow-up results of a randomized drug abuse prevention trial in a White middle-class population. *Journal of the American Medical Association, 27* 1106–1112.

Botvin, G. J., & Botvin, E. M. (1992). School-based and community-based prevention approaches. In J. H. Lowinson, P. Ruiz, R. B. Millman, & J. G. Langrod (Eds.), *Substance abuse: A comprehensive textbook* (2nd ed., pp. 910–927). Baltimore: Williams & Wilkins.

Bourne, P. G. (1973). Alcoholism in the urban Negro population. In P. G. Bourne & R. Fox (Eds.), *Alcoholism: Progress in research and treatment* (pp. 211–226). New York: Academic Press.

Bowen, M. (1971). The use of family theory in clinical practice. In M. J. Haley (Ed.), *Changing families: A family therapy reader* (pp. 159–192). New York: Grune & Stratton.

Bowen, M. (1978). *Family therapy in clinical practice.* New York: Jason Aronson.

Boyd, C. J., & Holmes, C. (2002). Women who smoke crack and their family substance abuse problems. *Health Care for Women International, 23,* 576–586.

Boyd, M. B., Mackey, M. C., Phillips, K. D., & Travakoli, A. (2006). Alcohol and other drug disorders, comorbidity and violence in rural African American women. *Issues in Mental Health Nursing, 27,* 1017–1036.

Boyle, C. A. (1998). Alcohol consumption by pregnant women in the United States during 1988–1995. *Obstetrics and Gynecology, 92,* 187–192.

Bradley, K. A., Boyd-Wickizer, J., Powell, S. H., & Burman, B. L. (1998). Alcohol screening questionnaires for women: A critical review. *Journal of the American Medical Association, 280,* 166–171.

Bradshaw, J. (1988). Compulsivity: The black plague of our day. *Lears Magazine, 42,* 89–90.

Braiker, H. (1989). Therapeutic issues in the treatment of alcoholic women. In S. Wilsnack & L. J. Beckman (Eds.), *Alcohol problems in women* (pp. 349–365). New York: Guilford Press.

Brandsma, L. (2007). Eating disorders across the lifespan. *Journal of Women and Aging, 19*(1–2), 155–172.

Branson, B. M., Handsfield, H. H., Lampe, M. A., Jassen, R. S., Taylor, A. W., Lyss, S. B., & Clark, J. E. (2006). *Revised recommendations for HIV testing of adults, adolescents, and pregnant women in health-care settings.* Retrieved July 24,

… www.cdc.gov/mmwr/preview …ml/rr5514a1.htm

…E. (1985). Special clinical psychothera-…c concerns for alcoholic and drug addicted …ividuals. In T. E. Bratter & G. G. Forrest …Eds.), *Alcoholism and substance abuse: Strategies for clinical intervention* (pp. 523–574). New York: The Free Press.

…ray, G. A. (1989). Obesity: Basic considerations and clinical approaches. *Dissertation Monographs, 35,* 449–537.

Breiter, H. C., Aharon, I., Kahneman, A. D., & Shizgal, P. (2001). Functional imagery of neural responses to expectancy and experience of monetary gains and losses. *Neuron, 30,* 619–639.

British Broadcasting Company. (March 17, 2002). *Internet gambling TA breeds addiction.* Retrieved August 2, 2003 from http://news.bbc.co.uk/1/hi/health/1872731.stm

Britton, P. J., Cimini, K. T., & Rak, C. F. (1999). Techniques for teaching HIV counseling: An intensive experiential model. *Journal of Counseling and Development, 77,* 171–176.

Brookoff, D., O'Brin, K. K., Cook, C. S., Thompson, T. D., & Williams, C. C. (1997). Characteristics of participants in domestic violence. *Journal of the American Medical Association, 277,* 1369–1373.

Brooks, M. K. (1992). Ethical and legal issues of confidentiality. In J. H. Lowinson, P. Ruiz, R. B. Millman, & J. G. Langrod (Eds.), *Substance abuse: A comprehensive textbook* (pp. 1049–1066). Baltimore: Williams & Wilkins.

Brounstein, P. J., Zweug, J. M., & Gardner, S. E. (1998). *Science-based practices in substance abuse prevention: A guide.* Rockville, MD: Center for Substance Abuse Prevention.

Brouwers, M., & Wiggum, C. D. (1993). Bulimia and perfectionism: Developing the courage to be imperfect. *Journal of Mental Health Counseling, 15,* 141–149.

Brower, K. J., Blow, F. C., Young, J. P., & Hill, E. M. (1991). Symptoms and correlates of anabolic-androgenic steroid dependence. *British Journal of Addiction, 86,* 759–768.

Brown, E. R. (1992). Program and staff characteristics of successful treatment. In M. N. Kilbey & K. Ashgar (Eds.), *Methodological issues in epidemiological, prevention, and treatment research on drug exposed women and their children* (pp. 305–313). Rockville, MD: National Institute on Drug Abuse.

Brown, J. H., & Kreft, I. G. (1998). Zero effects of drug prevention programs: Issues and solutions. *Evaluation Review, 22,* 3–14.

Brown, L., Macintyre, K., & Trujillo, L. (2003). Interventions to reduce HIV/AIDS stigma: What have we learned? *AIDS Education and Prevention, 15,* 49–69.

Brown, L. S., & Alterman, A. I. (1992). African Americans. In J. H. Lowinson, P. Ruiz, R. B. Millman, & J. G. Langrod (Eds.), *Substance abuse: A comprehensive textbook* (2nd ed., pp. 861–867). Baltimore: Williams & Wilkins.

Brown, L. S., Kritz, S. A., Goldsmith, R. J., Bini, E. J., Rotrosen, J., Baker, S., Robinson, J., & McAuliffe, P. (2006). Characteristics of substance abuse treatment programs providing services for HIV/AIDS, hepatitis C virus infection, and sexually transmitted infections: The National Drug Abuse Treatment Clinical Trials Network. *Journal of Substance Abuse Treatment, 30,* 315–321.

Brown, S. (1988). *Treating children of alcoholics: A developmental perspective.* New York: John Wiley & Sons.

Brownell, K. D., & Foreyt, J. P. (1985, November). Unpublished Obesity Workshop conducted at Association for the Advancement of Behavior Therapy Convention, Chicago.

Brownell, K. D., & Stunkard, A. J. (1978). Behavioral treatment of obesity in children. *American Journal of Diseases in Children, 132,* 403–412.

Bruch, H. (1973). *Eating disorders: Obesity, anorexia nervosa, and the person within.* New York: Basic Books.

Bruch, H. (1986). Anorexia nervosa: The therapeutic task. In K. D. Brownell & J. P. Foreyt (Eds.), *Handbook of eating disorders* (pp. 328–332). New York: Basic Books.

Brunswick, A. F. (1979). Black youths and drug use behavior. In G. M. Beschner & A. S. Friedman (Eds.), *Youths drug use: Problems, issues, and treatment* (pp. 443–490). Lexington, MA: Lexington Books.

Burk, J. P., & Sher, K. J. (1988). The "forgotten children" revisited: Neglected areas of COA research. *Clinical Psychology Review, 8,* 285–302.

Burke, R. J. (2000). Workaholism and divorce. *Psychological Reports, 86,* 219–220.

Burns, C. M., & D'Avanzo, C. E. (1993). *Alcohol and other drug abuse in culturally diverse populations: Hispanics and Southeast Asians. Faculty resource.* Washington, DC: Cosmos Corporation.

Burrows, B. A. (1992). Research on the etiology and maintenance of eating disorders. In E. M. Freeman (Ed.), *The addiction process: Effective social work approaches* (pp. 149–160). White Plains, NY: Longman.

Butler, J. (1990). *Gender trouble: Feminism and the subversion of identity.* London: Routledge.

Cabaj, R. P. (1992). Substance abuse in the gay and lesbian community. In J. H. Lowinson, P. Ruiz, R. B. Millman, & J. G. Langrod (Eds.), *Substance abuse: A comprehensive textbook* (2nd ed., pp. 852–860). Baltimore: Williams & Wilkins.

Cable, L. C. (2000). Kaleidoscopes and epic tales: Diverse narratives of adult children of alcoholics. In J. Krestan (Ed.), *Bridges to recovery. Addiction, family therapy, and multicultural treatment* (pp. 45–76). New York: The Free Press.

Cadiz, S., Savage, A., Bonavota, D., Hollywood, J., Butters, E., Neary, M., & Quiros, L. (2004). *The portal project: A layered approach to integrating trauma into alcohol and other drug treatment for women.* Retrieved August 3, 2007 from www .haworthpress.com/web/ATQ

Caetano, R. (1990). Hispanic drinking in the U.S.: Thinking in new directions. *British Journal of Addictions, 85,* 1231–1236.

Caetano, R., Clark, C., & Tam, T. (1998). Alcohol consumption among racial/ethnic minorities. *Alcohol Health & Research World, 22,* 233–238.

Cao, F., & Su, L. (2006). Internet addiction among Chinese adolescents: Prevalence and psychological features. *Child: Care, Health and Development, 33*(3), 275–281.

Capuzzi, D., & Gross, D. R. (Eds.). (1996). *Youth at risk.* Alexandria, VA: American Counseling Association.

Carmona, M., & Stewart, K. (1996). *A review of alternative activities and alternatives programs in youth-oriented prevention. (CSAP Technical Report No. 13).* Rockville, MD: Center for Substance Abuse Prevention.

Carnes, P. J. (2001). Cybersex, courtship, and esca lating arousal: Factors in addictive sexual desire. *Sexual Addiction and Compulsivity, 8,* 45–78.

Carr, A. (1997). *Family therapy and systemic consultation.* Lanham, MD: University Press of America.

Carter, B., & McGoldrick, M. (1999). *The expanded family life cycle.* Boston: Allyn and Bacon.

Cartwright, B. Y., & D'Andrea, M. (2005). A personal journey toward culture-centered Counseling. *Journal of Counseling and Development, 83,* 214–221.

Cash, T. F. (1997). *The body image workbook. An 8-step program for learning to like your looks.* Oakland, CA: New Harbinger.

Center for Substance Abuse Treatment. (1993). *Screening and assessment of alcohol and other drug-abusing adolescents (Treatment Improvement Protocol Series #3).* Rockville, MD: Center for Substance Abuse Treatment.

Center for Substance Abuse Treatment. (1994). *Assessment and treatment of patients with coexisting mental illness and alcohol and other drug abuse (Treatment Improvement Protocol Series #9).* Rockville, MD: Center for Substance Abuse Treatment.

Center for Substance Abuse Treatment. (1995a). *Planning for alcohol and other drug abuse treatment for adults in the Criminal Justice System (Treatment Improvement Protocol #17).* Rockville, MD: Center for Substance Abuse Treatment.

Center for Substance Abuse Treatment. (1995b). *Purchasing managed care services for alcohol and other drug treatment: Essential elements and policy issues (Treatment Improvement Protocol #16.)* Rockville, MD: Center for Substance Abuse Treatment.

Center for Substance Abuse Treatment. (1998). *Naltrexone and alcoholism treatment (Treatment Improvement Protocol #28).* Rockville, MD: Center for Substance Abuse Treatment.

Center for Substance Abuse Treatment. (1999a). *Brief interventions and brief therapies for substance abuse (Treatment Improvement Protocol #34).* Rockville, MD: Center for Substance Abuse Treatment.

stance Abuse Treatment. (1999b). *Na- aluation data services (NEDS). The costs :nefits of substance abuse treatment. Find- from the National Treatment Improvement aluation Study (NTIES).* Retrieved June 8, 2003 rom http://neds.calib.con/products/pdfs/cost-ben.pdf

enter on Addiction and Substance Abuse. (2001). *CASA releases shoveling up: The impact of substance abuse on state budgets.* Retrieved February 2, 2001 from www.casacolumbia.org/newsletter1457/newsletter_show.htm?doc_id=47445

Center on Addiction and Substance Abuse. (1998). *Behind bars: Substance abuse and America's prison population.* Retrieved October 11, 1997 from www.casacolumbia.org

Center on Alcohol Marketing and Youth. (2005). *Alcohol marketing and youth. Fact sheets.* Retrieved March 27, 2007 from http://camy.org/factsheets/index.php?FactsheetID=1

Centers for Disease Control. (1994, May). *HIV/AIDS prevention: Facts about the human immunodeficiency virus and its transmission.* Atlanta, GA: U.S. Department of Health and Human Services/Public Health Service.

Centers for Disease Control. (1996, February). *HIV and AIDS trends in the epidemic.* Atlanta, GA: U.S. Department of Health and Human Services/Public Health Service.

Centers for Disease Control. (1997). *HIV/AIDS surveillance report 1997 [On-line].* Retrieved September 17, 1995 from www. us.unaids.org/highband/document/epidemio/report97.html

Centers for Disease Control and Prevention. (1993). *HIV/AIDS surveillance report,* July 5, 10–11.

Centers for Disease Control and Prevention. (2000). Deaths: Final data for 1998. Retrieved April 18, 2003 from www.cdc.gov/nchs/data/nvs48_11.pdf

Centers for Disease Control and Prevention. (2001). *What's up with HIV/AIDS?* Atlanta, GA: Centers for Disease Control and Prevention Reports.

Centers for Disease Control and Prevention (2005a). *Tuberculosis transmission in a homeless shelter population, 2000–2003.* Retrieved August 8, 2007 from www.cdc.gov/mmwr/preview/mmwrhtml/mm5406a4.htm

Centers for Disease Control and Prevention (2005b). *Access to Sterile Syringes.* Retrieved August 8, 2007 from www.cdc.gov/idu/facts/aed_idu_acc.htm

Centers for Disease Control and Prevention (2006a). *Fetal alcohol spectrum disorders.* Retrieved August 4, 2007 from www.cdc.gov/nvbddd/fas/fasask.htm

Centers for Disease Control and Prevention (2006b). *Sexually Transmitted Diseases Treatment Guidelines 2006.* Retrieved August 8, 2007 from www.cdc.gov/std/treatment/2006/hiv.htm#hiv1#hiv1

Centers for Disease Control and Prevention (2006c). *Trends in Reportable Sexually Transmitted Diseases in the United States, 2005: National Surveillance Data for Chlamydia, Gonorrhea, and Syphilis.* Retrieved August 7, 2007 from www.cdc.gov/std/hiv/STDFact-STD&HIV.htm#WhatIs

Centers for Disease Control and Prevention (2007a). *Revision of the 2005 HIV/AIDS surveillance report.* Retrieved August 5, 2007 from www.cdc.gov/hiv/topics/surveillance/resources/reports/2005report/default.htm

Centers for Disease Control and Prevention (2007b). *HIV and Its Transmission.* Retrieved August 7, 2007 from www.cdc.gov/hiv/resources/factsheets/transmission.htm

Centers for Disease Control and Prevention, (2007c). *Preventing obesity and chronic diseases.* Retrieved August 1, 2007 from www.cdc.gov/search.do?queryText=chronic+obesity&action=search&searchButton.x=22&searchButton.y=8

Cermak, T. L. (1984). Children of alcoholics and the case for a new diagnostic category of codependency. *Alcohol, Health and Research World, 8,* 38–42.

Cermak, T. L. (1986). *Diagnosing and treating codependence: A guide for professionals with chemical dependents.* Minneapolis: Johnson Institute.

Ceyhan, E., Ceyhan, A. A., & Gürcan, A. (2007). The validity and reliability of the Problematic Internet Usage Scale. *Educational Sciences: Theory and Practice, 7*(1), 411–416.

Chafetz, M. E. (1964). Consumption of alcohol in the Far and Middle East. *New England Journal of Medicine, 271,* 297–301.

Chan, J. G. (2003). An examination of family-involved approaches to alcoholism treatment. *Family Journal, 11,* 129–138.

Chang, G. (2002). Brief interventions for problem drinking and women. *Journal of Substance Abuse Treatment, 23,* 1–7.

Chang, P. (2000). Treating Asian/Pacific American addicts and their families. In J. Krestan (Ed.), *Bridges to recovery. Addiction, family therapy, and multicultural treatment* (pp. 192–219). New York: The Free Press.

Charuvastra, V. C., Dalali, I. D., Cassuci, M., & Ling, W. (1992). Outcome study: Comparison of short-term vs. long-term treatment in a residential community. *International Journal of the Addictions, 27,* 15–23.

Chasnoff, I. J., Anson, A. R., Moss Iaukea, K. A. (1998). *Understanding the drug-exposed child: Approaches to behavior and learning.* Chicago: Imprint Publications.

Chasnoff, I. J., Griffith, D. R., Freier, C., & Murray, J. (1992). Cocaine/polydrug use in pregnancy: Two year follow-up. *Pediatrics, 89,* 284–289.

Chi, I., Lubben, J. E., & Kitano, H. H. (1989). Differences in drinking behavior among three Asian-American groups. *Journal of Studies on Alcohol, 50,* 15–23.

Chittenden, H. (1935). *American fur trade of the far west: A history of pioneer trading posts and early fur companies of the Missouri Valley and Rocky Mountains and of the overland commerce with Santa Fe.* (Vol. 1). New York: Barnes & Noble.

Cho, Y. I., & Crittenden, K. S. (2006). The impact of adult roles on drinking among women in the United States. *Substance Use and Misuse, 41,* 17–34.

Chou, C., Condron, L, Belland, J. C. (2005). A review of the research on Internet addiction. *Educational Psychology Review, 17*(4), 363–388.

Chou, C., & Hsaio, M. C. (2000). Internet addiction, usage, gratification, and pleasure experience: The Taiwan college students' case. *Computers in Education, 35*(1), 65–80.

Christopher, J. (1988). *How to stay sober: Recovery without religion.* Buffalo, NY: Prometheus Books.

Clayton, R. R., Cattarello, A. M., & Johnstone, B. M. (1996). Effectiveness of Drug Abuse Resistance Education (DARE): 5-year follow-results. *Preventive Medicine, 25,* 307–318.

Clayton, R. R., Leukefeld, C. G., Grant-Harrington N., & Cattarello, A. (1996). DARE (Drug Abuse Resistance Education): Very popular but not very effective. In C. B. McCoy, L. R. Metsch, & J. A. Inciardi (Eds.), *Intervening with drug-involved youth* (pp. 101–109). Thousand Oaks, CA: Sage.

Cloud, W., & Granfield, R. (2001). Natural recovery from substance dependency: Lessons for treatment providers. *Journal of Social Work Practice in the Addictions, 1,* 83–104.

Codependents Anonymous. (1995). *The CODA book.* Phoenix, AZ: Coda Service Office.

Coggans, N., & McKellar, S. (1994). Drug use amongst peers: Peer pressure or peer preference. *Drugs: Education, Prevention, and Policy, 1,* 15–24.

Coleman, E. (1982). Family intimacy and chemical abuse: The connection. *Journal of Psychoactive Drugs, 14,* 153–158.

Coleman, P. (1989). Letter to the editor. *Journal of the American Medical Association, 261,* 1879–1880.

Collins, B. (1993). Reconstructing codependency using self-in-relation theory: A feminist perspective. *Social Work, 38,* 470–476.

Conyers, L. M. (2004). Expanding understanding of HIV/AIDS and employment: Perspectives of a focus group. *Rehabilitation Counseling Bulletin, 48*(1), 5–18.

Conyers, L., & Boomer, K. B. (2005). Factors associated with disclosure of HIV/AIDS to employers among individuals who use job accommodations and those who do not. *Journal of Vocational Rehabilitation, 22,* 189–198.

Cook, C. C. (1988). The Minnesota model in the management of drug and alcohol dependency: Miracle, method, or myth? (Part I: The philosophy of the programme). *British Journal of Addiction, 83,* 625–634.

Cooney, N. L., Zweben, A., & Fleming, M. F. (1995). Screening for alcohol problems and at-risk drinking in health-care settings. In R. K. Hester & W. R. Miller (Eds.), *Handbook of alcoholism treatment approaches: Effective approaches* (2nd ed., pp. 45–60). Boston: Allyn and Bacon.

...monica, D., & Burg, R. (2000). Cy... ...sers, abusers, and compulsives: New ...s and implications. *Sexual Addiction and ...ulsivity: The Journal of Treatment and ...vention, 7*(1–2), 5–30.

...r, S. E., & Robinson, D. A. G. (1987). Use of the Substance Abuse Subtle Screening Inventory with a college population. *Journal of American College Health, 36,* 180–184.

Copello, A. G., Velleman, R. D. B., & Templeton, L. J. (2005). Family interventions in the treatment of alcohol and drug problems. *Drug and Alcohol Review, 24,* 369–385.

Corbett, K., Mora, J., & Ames, G. (1991). Drinking patterns and drinking-related problems of Mexican-American husbands and wives. *Journal of Studies on Alcohol, 52,* 215–222.

Corey, G. (1990). *Theory and practice of group counseling* (3rd ed.). Belmont, CA: Brooks/Cole.

Cork, M. (1969). *The forgotten children: A study of children with alcoholic parents.* Toronto: Addiction Research Foundation.

Corrigan, P. W., & Miller, F. E. (2006). Blame, shame, and contamination: The impact of mental illness and drug dependence stigma on family members. *Journal of Family Psychology, 20*(2), 239–246.

Coutinho, W. F., Moreira, R. O., Spagnol, C., & Appolinario, J. C. (2007). Does binge eating disorder alter cortisol secretion in obese women? *Eating Behaviors, 8*(1), 59–64.

Coyhis, D. (2000). Culturally specific addiction recovery for Native Americans. In J. Krestan (Ed.), Bridges to recovery. *Addiction, family therapy, and multicultural treatment,* (pp. 77–114). New York: The Free Press.

Coyhis, D., & White, W. L. (2002). Alcohol problems in Native America: Changing paradigms and clinical practices. *Alcoholism Treatment Quarterly, 20,* 157–165.

Crago, M., & Shisslack, C. M. (2003). Ethnic differences in dieting. *Eating Disorders, 11,* 289–304.

Creager, C. (1989). SASSI Test breaks through denial. *Professional Counselor, July/August,* p. 65.

Cullen, J., & Carr, A. (1999). Codependency: An empirical study from a systemic perspective. *Contemporary Family Therapy, 21,* 505–526.

Cummings, C., Gordon, J. R., & Marlatt, G. A. (1980). Relapse: Strategies of prevention and prediction. In W. R. Miller (Ed.), *The addictive behaviors: Treatment of alcoholism, drug abuse, smoking and obesity* (pp. 291–321). New York: Pergamon Press.

Cummins, L. H., Lehman, J. (2007). Eating disorders and body image concerns in Asian American women: Assessment and treatment from a multicultural and feminist perspective. *Eating Disorders, 15,* 217–230.

Cummins, L. H., Simmons, A. M., & Zane, N. (2005). Eating Disorders in Asian Populations: A Critique of Current Approaches to the Study of Culture, Ethnicity, and Eating Disorders. *American Journal of Orthopsychiatry, 75*(4), 443–453.

Cunningham, J. A., Sobell, L. C., Sobell, M. B., & Kapur, G. (1995). Resolution from alcohol problems with and without treatment: Reasons for change. *Journal of Substance Abuse, 7,* 365–372.

Custer, R., & Milt, H. (1985). *When luck runs out: help for compulsive gamblers and their families.* New York: Facts on File.

Cyr, M. G., & McGarry, K. A. (2002). Alcohol use disorder among women. *Postgraduate Medicine, 112,* 31–40.

Daley, D. C., & Marlatt, G. A. (1992). Relapse prevention: Cognitive and behavioral interventions. In J. H. Lowinson, P. Ruiz, R. M. Millman, & J. G. Langrod (Eds.), *Substance abuse: A comprehensive textbook* (2nd ed., pp. 533–542). Baltimore: Williams & Wilkins.

Dally, P. (1984). Anorexia tardive—late onset marital anorexia nervosa. *Journal of Psychosomatic Research, 28,* 423–428.

D'Andrea, L. M., Fisher, G. L., & Harrison, T. C. (1994). Cluster analysis of adult children of alcoholics. *The International Journal of the Addictions, 29,* 565–582.

DARE America. (1991). *D.A.R.E. will teach over 5 million children drug resistance skills in 1991.* Los Angeles: Author.

Davis, R. A. (2001). A cognitive-behavioral model of pathological Internet use. *Computers and Human Behavior, 17,* 187–195.

de la Rosa, M. R., Holleran, L. K., Rugh, D., & MacMaster, S. A. (2005). Substance Abuse among

U.S. Latinos: A review of the literature. *Journal of Social Work Practice in the Addictions, 5*(1/2), 1–20.

de la Rosa, M., Rugh, D., & Rice, C. (2006). An analysis of risk domains associated with drug transitions of active Latino gang members. *Journal of Addictive Diseases, 25*(4), 81–90.

Deal, S. A., & Galaver, J. (1994). Are women more susceptible than men to alcohol-induced cirrhosis? *Alcohol, Health, and Research World, 18,* 189–191.

Dear, G. E., & Roberts, C. M. (2000). The Holyoake Codependency Index: Investigation of the factor structure and psychodynamic properties. *Psychological Reports, 87,* 991–1002.

Dear, G. E., & Roberts, C. M. (2002). The relationship between codependency and femininity and masculinity. *Sex Roles, 46,* 159–165.

Delgado, M. (2002). Latinos and alcohol: Treatment considerations. *Alcoholism Treatment Quarterly, 20,* 187–192.

Delva, J., Wallace, J. M., O'Malley, P., Bachman, J. G., Johnston, L. D., & Schulenberg, J. E. (2005). The epidemiology of alcohol, marijuana, and cocaine use among Mexican American, Puerto Rican, Cuban American, and other Latin American eighth grade students in the United States: 1991–2002. *American Journal of Public Health, 95*(4), 696–702.

DeMarco, R. F., Miller, K. H., Patsdaughter, C. A., Chisolm, M., & Grindel, C. G. (1998). From silencing the self to action: Experiences of women living with HIV/AIDS. *Health Care for Women International, 19,* 539–552.

Desire for drugs fuels crime. (1991, August 26). Associated Press.

Deutsch, H. (1945). *The psychology of women: A psychoanalytic interpretation.* Vol II. New York: Grune and Stratton.

DeWit, D. J., Adlaf, E. M., Offord, D. R., & Ogborne, A. C. (2000). Age at first alcohol use: A risk factor for the development of alcohol disorders. *American Journal of Psychiatry, 157*(5), 745–750.

Diamond, G. S., & Liddle, H. A. (1996). Resolving a therapeutic impasse between parents and adolescents in Multidimensional Family Therapy. *Journal of Consulting and Clinical Psychology, 64,* 481–488.

DiCicco, L., Davis, R., & Orenstein, A. (1984). Identifying the children of alcoholics from survey responses. *Journal of Alcohol and Drug Education, 30,* 1–17.

DiCicco, L., Davis, R. B., Hogan, J., MacLean, A., & Orenstein, A. (1984). Group experiences for children of alcoholics. *Alcohol Health and Research World, 8,* 20–24.

Dinning, W. D., & Berk, L. A. (1989). The children of alcoholics screening test: Relationship to sex, family environment, and social adjustment in adolescents. *Journal of Clinical Psychology, 45*(2), 335–339.

Doctor, S. (1994). *Fetal alcohol syndrome, fetal alcohol effect, fetal drug effect: Educational implications. A training-curriculum for educators and other service providers.* Reno, NV: Washoe County School District.

Dodds, S., Nuehring, E. M., Blaney, N. T., Blakely, T., Lizzotte, J., Lopez, M., Potter, J. E., & O'Sullivan, M. J. (2004). *Integrating mental health services into primary HIV care for women: The whole life project.* Public Health Report, January 2004/February 2004. Washington, DC: U.S. Department of Health and Human Services.

Doering, P. L., Davidson, C. L., & LaFauce, L. (1989). Effects of cocaine on the human fetus: A review of clinical studies. *Annals of Pharmacotherapy, 23,* 639–645.

Douglas, J. J., & Minton, H. L. (1993, August 20–24). *Codependency: Innovation or status quo?* Paper presented the Annual Convention of the American Psychological Association. Ontario, Canada.

Douglass, F. (1855). *My bondage, my freedom.* New York: Ortin and Mulligan.

Dounchis, J. Z., Hayden, H. A., & Wilfley, D. E. (2001). Obesity, body image, and eating disorders in ethnically diverse children and adolescents. In J. K. Thompson & L. Smolak (Eds.), *Body image, eating disorders, and obesity in youth* (pp. 67–98). Washington, DC: American Psychological Association.

Doweiko, H. E. (2002). *Concepts of chemical dependency* (5th ed.). Pacific Grove, CA: Brooks/Cole.

..., & Bellisle, F. (2007). Is sweetness ...? *Nutrition Bulletin, 32*(Suppl. 1), ...

...d, D. C. (2002). Meta-analysis in alcohol ...ment research: Does it help us to know ...hat works? *Addiction, 97,* 297.

...ois, W. E. B. (1928). Drunkenness. *The Crisis, 35,* 348.

...ube, S. R., Anda, R. F., Felitti, V. J., Edwards, V. J., & Croft, J. B. (2002). Adverse childhood experiences and personal alcohol abuse as an adult. *Addictive Behaviors, 27,* 713–725.

Duerr, A. (1997). *Report from the national conference on women and HIV.* Atlanta, GA: Centers for Disease Control and Prevention.

Dunn, M. G., Tartar, R. E., Mezzich, A. C., Vanyukov, M., Kirisci, M., & Kirillova, G. (2002). Origins and consequences of child neglect on substance abusing families. *Clinical Psychology Review, 22,* 1063–1090.

Dunst, C. J., Trivette, C. M., & Deal, A. G. (1988). *Enabling and empowering families: Principles and guidelines for practice*. Cambridge, MA: Brook-line Books.

Ebberhart, N. C., Luczak, S. E., Avanecy, N., & Wall, T. L. (2003). Family history of alcohol dependence in Asian Americans. *Journal of Psychoactive Drugs, 35*(3), 375–377.

Ebrahim, S. H., Diekman, S. T., Floyd, L., & Decoufle, P. (1999). Comparison of binge drinking among pregnant and non-pregnant women. *American Journal of Obstetrics and Gynecology, 180,* 1–7.

Ebrahim, S. H., Luman, E. T., Floyd, R. L., Murphy, C. C., Bennett, M. M., & Boyle, (1998). Defects. *Alcohol Research and Health, 25,* 159–167.

Edwards, M. E., & Steinglass, P. (1995). Family therapy treatment outcomes for alcoholism. *Journal of Marital and Family Therapy, 21*(4), 475–509.

Ehlers, C. L., & Wilhelmsen, K. C. (2007). Genomic screen for substance dependence and body mass index in southwest California Indians. *Genes, Brain & Behavior, 6*(2), 184–191.

el-Guebaly, N., & Offord, D. R. (1977). The offspring of alcoholics: A critical review. *American Journal of Psychiatry, 134,* 357–365.

el-Guebaly, N., & Offord, D. R. (1979). On being the offspring of an alcoholic: An update. *Alcoholism: Clinical and Experimental Research, 3,* 148–157.

el-Guebaly, N., Patten, S., Currie, S., Williams, J., Beck, C. Maxwell, C., & Wang, J. (2006). Epidemiological associations between gambling behavior, substance use and mood and anxiety disorders. *Journal of Gambling Studies, 22*(3), 275–287.

Emerson, E. & Turnball, L. (2005). Self-reported smoking and alcohol use among adolescents with a mild intellectual disability. *Journal of Intellectual Disabilities, 9*(1), 58–69.

Emrick, C. (1987). Alcoholics Anonymous: Affiliation processes and effectiveness as treatment. *Alcoholism: Clinical and Experimental Research, 11,* 416–423.

Ennett, S. T., Rosenbaum, D. P., Flewelling, R. L., Bieler, G. S., Ringwalt, C. L. & Bailey, S. L. (1994). Long-term evaluation of drug abuse resistance education. *Addictive Behaviors, 19,* 113–125.

Ennett, S. T., Tobler, N. S., Ringwalt, C. L., & Flewelling, R. L. (1994). How effective is drug abuse resistance education? A meta-analysis of project DARE outcome evaluations. *American Journal of Public Health, 84*, 1394–1401.

Erekson, M. T., & Perkins, S. E. (1989). System dynamics in alcoholic families. Special issue. Codependency: Issues in treatment and recovery. *Alcoholism Treatment Quarterly, 6,* 59–74.

Ewing, J. A., & Fox, R. E. (1968). Family therapy of alcoholism. In F. Messerman (Ed.), *Current psychiatric therapies* (pp. 86–91). New York: Grune & Stratton.

Ewing, J. A., & Rouse, B. A. (1970, February). *Identifying the hidden alcoholic.* Paper presented at the 29th International Congress on Alcoholism and Drug Dependence, Sydney, Australia.

Eysenck, H. J. (1957). *The dynamics of anxiety and hysteria.* New York: Praeger.

Fairburn, C. G., Cooper, Z., & Shafran, R. (2003). Cognitive behaviour therapy for eating disorders: A "transdiagnostic" theory and treatment. *Behaviour Research and Therapy, 41,* 509–528.

Faith, M. S., Saelens, B. E., Wilfley, D. E., & Allison, D. B. (2001). Behavioral treatment of childhood and adolescent obesity: Current statue, challenges, and future directions. In J. K. Thompson & L. Smolak (Eds.), *Body image, eating disorders, and obesity in youth* (pp. 313–340). Washington, DC: American Psychological Association.

Falicov, C. J. (1982). Mexican families. In M. McGoldrick, J. K. Pierce, & J. Giordano (Eds.), *Ethnicity and Family Therapy* (pp. 134–163). New York: Guilford Press.

Feldstein, S. W., & Miller, W. R. (2007). Does subtle screening for substance abuse work? A review of the Substance Abuse Subtle Screening Inventory (SASSI). *Addiction, 102,* 41–50.

Feree, M. C. (2002). Sexual addiction and co-addiction: Experiences among women of faith. *Sexual Addiction and Recovery, 9*(4), 285–293.

Fernandez, F., & Levy, J. K. (1990). Diagnosis and management of HIV primary dementia. In D. G. Ostrow (Ed.), *Behavioral aspects of AIDS* (pp. 235–246). New York: Plenum.

Fernandez, F., & Ruiz, P. (1992). Neuropsychiatric complications of HIV infection. In J. H. Lowinson, P. Ruiz, R. B. Millman, & J. G. Langrod (Eds.), *Substance abuse: A comprehensive textbook* (2nd ed., pp. 775–786). Baltimore: Williams & Wilkins.

Fingarette, H. (1988). *Heavy drinking: The myth of alcoholism as a disease.* Berkeley, CA: University of California.

Fisher, G. L. (2006). *Rethinking our war on drugs: Candid talk about controversial issues.* Westport, CN: Praeger.

Fisher, G. L., & Harrison, T. C. (1992). Assessment of alcohol and other drug abuse with referred adolescents. *Psychology in the Schools, 29,* 172–178.

Fisher, G. L., & Harrison, T. C. (1993a). *Codependent characteristics of prospective counselors as compared to other graduate students.* Paper presented at American Counseling Association National Conference, Atlanta, GA, March.

Fisher, G. L., & Harrison, T. C. (1993b). The school counselor's role in relapse prevention. *School Counselor, 41,* 120–125.

Fisher, G. L., Jenkins, S. J., Harrison, T. C., & Jesch, K. (1992). Characteristics of adult children of alcoholics. *Journal of Substance Abuse, 4,* 27–34.

Fisher, G. L., Jenkins, S. J., Harrison, T. C., & Jesch, K. (1993). Personality characteristics of adult children of alcoholics, other adults from dysfunctional families, and adults from nondysfunctional families. *International Journal the Addictions, 28,* 477–485.

Fisher, J. C., Mason, R. L., & Fisher, J. V. (1976). A diagnostic formula for alcoholism. *Journal c Studies on Alcohol, 37,* 1247–1255.

Fleming, M. F., Mundt, M. P., French, M. T., Baier-Manwell, L., Stauffacher, E. A., & Lawton-Berry, K. F. (2002). Brief physician advice for problem drinkers: Long-term efficacy and benefit-cost analysis. *Alcoholism: Clinical and Experimental Research, 26,* 36–43.

Flowers, C. P., & Robinson, B. (2002). A structural and discriminant analysis of the Work Addiction Risk Test. *Educational and Psychological Measurement, 62*(3), 517–526.

Floyd, R. L., Zahniser, C., Gunter, E. P., & Kendrick, J. S. (1991). Smoking during pregnancy: Two year follow-up. *Pediatrics, 89,* 284–289.

Forbush, K., Heatherton, T. F., & Keel, P. K. (2007) Relationships between perfectionism and specific disordered eating behaviors. *International Journal of Eating Disorders, 40*(1), 37–41.

Foreyt, J. P., Poston, W. C. S., Winebarger, A. A., & McGavin, J. K. (1998). Anorexia nervosa and bulimia nervosa. In E. J. Mash & R. A. Barkley (Eds.), *Treatment of childhood disorders* (2nd ed., pp. 647–691). New York: Guilford Press.

Forward, S. (1986). *Men who hate women and women who love them.* New York: Basic Books.

Foster, B. (1999). The mind-body connection. *Body Positive, 12*(9), 1–5. Retrieved April 4, 2003, from www.thebody.com/bp/sept99/yoga.html

Francis, H. (2003). Substance abuse and HIV infection. *Topics in Medicine, 11,* 20–24.

Franzmeier, A. (1988). To your health. *Nation's Business, 76,* 73.

Fraser, J. J., & McAbee, G. N. (2004). Dealing with the parent whose judgment is impaired by alcohol or drugs: Legal and ethical considerations. *Pediatrics, 114*(3), 869–873.

Fredrickson, G. M. (1971). *The Black image in the White mind: The debate on Afro-American character and destiny, 1817–1914.* New York: Harper and Row.

Freehling, W. W. (1968). *Prelude to civil war: The nullification controversy in South Carolina, 1818–1836.* New York: Harper & Row.

...(Ed.). (1992). *The addiction process: ...social work approaches.* White Plains, ...gman.

...985). Codependency assessment inven... A preliminary research tool. *Focus on ...mily, May/June,* 20–21.

... J. C. (1984). *Co-dependency and the search for identity: A paradoxical crisis.* Pompano Beach, FL: Health Communications.

Fukuyama, M., & Inoue-Cox, C. (1992). Cultural perspectives in communicating with Asian/Pacific Islanders. In J. Wittmer (Ed.), *Valuing diversity and similarly: Bridging the gap through interpersonal skills* (pp. 93–112). Minneapolis, MN: Educational Media Corporation.

Fuller, J. A., Warner, R. M. (2000). Family stressors as predictors of codependency. *Genetic, Social and General Psychology Monographs, 126*(1), 5–23.

Fuller, R. K., & Gordis, E. (2001). Naltrexone treatment for alcohol dependence. *New England Journal of Medicine, 345,* 1770–1771.

Galanter, M., Egelko, S., & Edwards, H. (1993). Rational recovery: Alternative to AA for addiction? *American Journal of Drug and Alcohol Abuse, 19,* 499–510.

Galizio, M., & Maisto, S. A. (1985). *Determinants of substance abuse: Biological, psychological and environmental factors.* New York: Plenum Press.

Garfinkel, P. E., & Kaplan, A. S. (1986). Anorexia nervosa: Diagnostic conceptualizations. In K. D. Brownell & J. P. Foreyt (Eds.), *Handbook of eating disorders* (pp. 266–282). New York: Basic Books.

Garfinkel, P. E., Moldofsky, H., & Garner, D. M. (1980). The heterogeneity of anorexia nervosa: Bulimia as a distinct subgroup. *Archives of General Psychiatry, 37,* 1036–1040.

Garner, D. M. (2005). *Eating Disorder Inventory-3. Professional manual.* Odessa, FL: Psychological Assessment Resources.

Garner, D. M., & Bemis, K. M. (1982). A cognitive behavioral approach to anorexia nervosa. *Cognitive Theory and Research, 6,* 1–27.

Gaudia, R. (1992). Compulsive gambling: Reframing issues of control. In E. M. Freeman (Ed.), *The addiction process: Effective social work approaches* (pp. 237–248). White Plains, NY: Longman.

Gayol, G. N., & Lira, L. R. (2002). Construction and validity of the codependency instrument (ICOD) for Mexican women. *Salud Mental, 25*(2), 38–48.

George, W. H., La Marr, J., Barrett, K., & McKinnon, T. (1999). Alcoholic parentage, self-labeling, and endorsement of ACOA-codependent traits. *Psychology of Addictive Behaviors, 13*(1), 39–48.

Gerstein, D. R. (1997). *Final report: The National Treatment Improvement Evaluation Study.* Rockville, MD: Center for Substance Abuse Treatment.

Giermyski, T., & Williams, T. (1986). Codependency. *Journal of Psychoactive Drugs, 18,* 7–13.

Gilbert, M. J. (1978). *Five week alcoholism ethnography conducted in three Spanish speaking communities.* Sacramento, CA: State Office of Alcoholism.

Gilbert, M. J., & Cervantes, R. C. (1986). Patterns and practices of alcohol use among Mexican Americans: A comprehensive review. *Hispanic Journal of Behavioral Sciences, 8,* 1–60.

Gilley, B. J., & Co-Cké, J. H. (2005). Cultural investment: Providing opportunities to reduce risky behavior among gay American Indian males. *Journal of Psychoactive Drugs, 37*(3), 293–298.

Ginzburg, H. M., Weiss, S. H., MacDonald, M. C., & Hubbard, R. L. (1985). HTLV-III exposure among drug users. *Cancer Research, 45* (Suppl.), 4605–4608.

Goodman, R. W. (1987). Adult children of alcoholics. *Journal of Counseling and Development, 66,* 162–163.

Goodman, S., Blinder, B. J., Chaitin, B. F., & Hagman, J. (1988). Atypical eating disorders. In B. J. Blinder, B. F. Chaitin, & R. S. Goldstein (Eds.), *The eating disorders: Medical and psychological bases of diagnosis and treatment* (pp. 393–404). New York: PMA.

Gordon, J. U. (Ed.). (1994). *Managing multiculturalism in substance abuse services.* Thousand Oaks, CA: Sage.

Gormally, J., Black, S., Dastrom, S., & Rardin, D. (1982). The assessment of binge-eating severity among obese persons. *Addictive Behaviors, 7,* 47–55.

Gorman, D. M. (1998). The irrelevance of evidence in the development of school-based drug prevention policy, 1986–1996. *Evaluation Review, 22,* 118–146.

Gorski, T. T. (1988). *The staying sober workbook: A serious solution for the problem of relapse.* Independence, MO: Independence Press.

Gorski, T. T. (1989). *Passages through recovery: An action plan for preventing relapse.* Center City, MN: Hazelden.

Gorski, T. T. (1990). The Cenaps model of relapse prevention: Basic principles and procedures. *Journal of Psychoactive Drugs, 22,* 125–133.

Gorski, T. T. (1992). Creating a relapse prevention program in your treatment center. *Addiction & Recovery, July/August,* 16–17.

Gorski, T. T. (1993). Relapse prevention: A state of the art overview. *Addiction & Recovery, March/April,* 25–27.

Gorski, T. T., & Miller, M. M. (1986*). Staying sober: Guide to relapse prevention.* Independence, MO: Herald House.

Gossett, G. (1988). Unpublished seminar report, March, 1988. Denton, TX: University of Texas.

Granfield, R., & Cloud, W. (2001). Social context and "natural recovery": The role of social capital in the resolution of drug-associated problems. *Substance Use and Misuse, 36,* 1543–1570.

Greenfield, S. F., Brooks, A. J., Gordon, S. M., Green, C. A., Kropp, F., McHugh, R. K., Lincoln, M., Hein, D., Miele, G. M. (2007). Substance abuse treatment entry, retention, and outcome in women: A review of the literature. *Drug and Alcohol Dependence, 86*(1), 1–21.

Greenfield, S. F., Trucco, E. M., McHugh, R. K., Lincoln, M., & Gallop, R. J. (2007). The women's recovery group study: A stage 1 trial of women-focused group therapy for substance use disorders verses mixed-gender group drug counseling. *Drug and Alcohol Dependence, 90*(1), 39–47.

Griffin, J. E. (1993). *Using Faces II to predict a shelter-seeker's return to an abusive relationship.* Unpublished doctoral dissertation, University of Nevada, Reno, NV.

Griffin-Shelley, E. (1991). *Sex and love.* New Yor Praeger.

Griffith, D. R. (1989). *Neurobehavioral effects of intrauterine cocaine exposure Ab Initio.* Boston: University of Massachusetts, Amherst, and Boston Children's Hospital.

Griffith, D. R. (1990). *Developmental follow-up of cocaine-exposed infants to three years.* Paper presented at the International Society for Infant Studies Conference, Montreal.

Griffith, D. R. (1992). Prenatal exposure to cocaine and other drugs: Developmental and educational prognoses. *Phi Delta Kappan, 74,* 30–34.

Grinspoon, L., & Bakalar, J. B. (1994). The war on drugs—a peace proposal. *New England Journal of Medicine, 330,* 357–360.

Grofer, J., Penne, M., Pemberton, M., & Folsom, R. (2003). Substance abuse treatment need among older adults in 2020: The impact of the aging baby-boom cohort. *Drug and Alcohol Dependence, 69,* 127–136.

Grube, J. W., & Wallack, L. (1994). Television beer advertising and drinking knowledge, beliefs, and intentions among schoolchildren. *American Journal of Public Health, 84*, 254–259.

Gulsun, M., Gulcat, Z., & Aydin, H. (2007). Treatment of compulsive sexual behavior with clomipramine and valproic acid. *Clinical Drug Investigations, 27*(3), 219–223.

Gurnack, A. M., & Johnson, W. A. (2002). Elderly drug use and racial/ethnic populations. *Journal of Ethnicity in Substance Abuse, 1*(2), 55–71.

Gwirtsman, H. E., Roy-Byrne, P., Lerner, L., & Yager, J. (1984). Bulimia in men: Report of three cases with neuroendocrine findings. *Journal of Clinical Psychiatry, 45,* 78–81.

Haley, J. (1973). *Uncommon therapy: The psychiatric techniques of Milton H. Erickson, M.D.* New York: Ballantine Books.

Hall, A. S., & Parsons, J. (2001). Internet addiction: College student case study using best practices in cognitive behavior therapy. *Journal of Mental Health Counseling, 23,* 312–327.

Hall, W. & Pacula, R. L. (2003). *Cannabis use and dependence: Public health and public policy.* Cambridge, UK: Cambridge University Press.

Halpern, H. M. (1982). *How to break your addiction to a person.* New York: Bantam Books.

... (1989). A critical review of object ...theory. *American Journal Psychiatry,* ...2–1560.

...A., Laughren, T., & Racoosin, J. (2006). ...idality in pediatric patients treated with an...epressant drugs. *Archives of General Psychiatry, 63,* 332–339.

...son, G., Venturelli, P. J., & Fleckenstein, A. E. (2006). *Drugs and society* (9th ed.). Boston: Jones and Bartlett.

Hardoon, K. K., Gupta, R., & Derevensky, J. L. (2004). Psychosocial Variables Associated With Adolescent Gambling. *Psychology of Addictive Behaviors, 18*(2), 122–142.

Harkness, D., & Cotrell, G. (1997). The social construction of codependency in the treatment of substance abuse. *Journal of Substance Abuse Treatment, 14,* 473–479.

Harkness, D., Swenson, M., Madsen-Hampton, K., & Hale, R. (2001). The development, reliability, and validity of a clinical rating scale for codependency. *Journal of Psychoactive Drugs, 33,* 159–171.

Harman, M. J., Armswoth, M. W., Hwang, C., Vincent, K. R., & Preston, M. A. (1995). Personality adjustment in college students with a parent perceived as alcoholic or non-alcoholic. *Journal of Counseling and Development, 73*(4), 459–462.

Harper, F. D. (Ed.). (1976). *Alcohol abuse and Black America*. Alexandria, VA: Douglass Publishers.

Harper, F. D. (1978). Alcohol use among North American Blacks. In Y. Israel, F. B. Glaser, H. Kalant, R. E. Popham, W. Schmidt, & R. G. Smart (Eds.), *Research advances in alcohol and drug problems* (Vol. 4, pp. 349–364). New York: Plenum Press.

Harper, M. (2006). Ethical multiculturalism: An evolutionary concept analysis. *Advances in Nursing Science, 29*(2), 110–124.

Harris, T. A. (1969). *I'm okay–you're okay.* New York: Avon Books.

Harrison, P. A., & Belille, C. A. (1987). Women in treatment: Beyond the stereotype. *Journal of Studies on Alcohol, 48,* 574–578.

Harrison, T. C. (2004). *Consultation for contemporary helping professionals.* Boston: Allyn and Bacon.

Harter, S. L. (2000). Psychosocial adjustment of adult children of alcoholics: A review of the recent empirical literature. *Clinical Psychology Review, 20,* 311–337.

Harter, S. L., & Vanecek, R. J. (2000). Cognitive assumptions and long-term distress in survivors of childhood abuse, parental alcoholism, and dysfunctional family environment. *Cognitive Therapy and Research, 24*(4), 445–472. Retrieved August 18, 2007 from harvard.edu/doa/html/meta.htm

Harwood, H. (2000). *Updating estimates of the economic costs of alcohol abuse in the United States: Estimates, update methods, and data.* Report prepared by the Lewin Group for the National Institute on Alcohol Abuse and Alcoholism. Rockville, MD: National Institutes of Health. Based on Harwood, H., Fountain, D., & Livermore, G. (1998). *The economic costs of alcohol and drug abuse in the United States 1992.* Report prepared for the National Institute on Drug Abuse and the National Institute on Alcohol Abuse and Alcoholism, National Institutes of Health, Department of Health and Human Services. NIH Publication No. 98–4327. Rockville, MD: National Institutes of Health.

Hasnain, M., Levy, J. A., Mensah, E. K., & Sinacore, J. M. (2007). Association of educational attainment with HIV risk in African American injection drug users. *AIDS Care, 19*(1), 87–91.

Hawkins, D. M. (1986). Understanding reactions to group instability in psychotherapy groups. *International Journal of Group Psychotherapy, 36,* 241–260.

Hawkins, J. D., Catalano, R. E., & Miller, J. Y. (1992). Risk and protective factors for alcohol and other drug problems in adolescence and early adulthood: Implications for substance abuse prevention. *Psychological Bulletin, 112,* 64–105.

Hawkins, J. D., Lishner, D. M., & Catalano, R. E. (1985, April). *Childhood predictors and the prevention of adolescent substance abuse.* Presented at the National Institute on Drug Abuse research analysis and utilization system meeting, etiology of drug abuse: Implications for prevention.

Hawkins, J. D., Lishner, D. M., Catalano, R. E., & Howard, M. O. (1985). Childhood predictors of adolescent substance abuse: Toward an empirically grounded theory. Special issue. Childhood and chemical abuse: Prevention and intervention. *Journal of Children in Contemporary Society, 18,* 11–48.

Hawley, N. P., & Brown, E. L. (1981). The use of group treatment with children of alcoholics. *Journal of Contemporary Social Work, 62,* 40–46.

Hayes, C. L. (1998). Spots for adults appeal to children. *New York Times* (national edition), March 26, C5.

Hayford, S. M., Epps, R. P., & Dahl-Regis, M. (1988). Behavior and development patterns in children born to heroin-addicted and methadone-addicted mothers. *Journal of the National Medical Association, 80,* 1197–1200.

Heather, N. (1995). Interpreting the evidence on brief interventions for excessive drinkers: The need for caution. *Alcohol and Alcoholism, 30,* 287–296.

Hegedus, A. M., Alterman, A. I., & Tarter, R. E. (1984). Learning achievement in sons of alcoholics. *Alcoholism: Clinical and Experimental Research, 8,* 330–333.

Hemfelt, R., & Fowler, R. (1990). *Serenity: A companion for twelve step recovery, complete with New Testament, Psalms, Proverbs.* Nashville, TN: Nelson Publishing.

Herd, D. (1991). The paradox of temperance: Blacks and the alcohol question in nineteenth-century America. In S. Barrows & R. Room (Eds.), *Drinking: Behavior and belief in modern history* (pp. 354–375). Berkeley: University of California Press.

Hergenrather, K. C., Rhodes, S. D., & Clark, G. (2005). The employment perspectives study: Identifying factors influencing the job-seeking behavior of persons living with HIV/AIDS. *AIDS Education and Prevention, 17*(2), 131–142.

Hergenrather, K. C., Rhodes, S. D., & Clark, G. (2006). Windows to work: Exploring employment seeking behaviors of persons with HIV/AIDS through PhotoVoice. *AIDS Education and Prevention, 18*(3), 243–258.

Hesse-Biber, S. (1989). Eating patterns and disorders in a college population: Are college women's eating problems a new phenomenon. *Sex Roles, 20,* 71–89.

Hester, R. K. (1995). Behavioral self-control training. In R. K. Hester & W. R. Miller (Eds.), *Handbook of alcoholism treatment approache[s]: Effective alternatives* (2nd ed., pp. 148–175). Boston: Allyn and Bacon.

Hibbard, S. (1987). The diagnosis and treatment of adult children of alcoholics as a specialized therapeutic population. *Psychotherapy, 24,* 779–785.

Higgins, S. T., Budney, A. J., Bickel, H. K., Badger, G., Foerg, F., & Ogden, D. (1995). Outpatient behavioral treatment for cocaine dependence: One-year outcome. *Experimental & Clinical Psychopharmacology, 3,* 205–212.

Hill, A. (1989). Treatment and prevention of alcoholism in the Native American family. In G. Lawson & A. Lawson (Eds.), *Alcoholism & substance abuse in special populations* (pp. 247–272). Rockville, MD: Aspen.

Hill, K., & C. Pomeroy, C. (2001). Assessment of physical status of children and adolescents with eating disorders and obesity. In J. K. Thompson & L. Smolak (Eds.), *Body image, eating disorders, and obesity in youth* (pp. 171–192). Washington, DC: American Psychological Association.

Hines, P. M., & Boyd-Franklin, N. (1982). Black families. In M. McGoldrick, J. Pierce, & J. Giordano (Eds.), *Ethnicity and family therapy* (pp. 84–107). New York: Guilford Press.

Hispanic Health Council. (1987). *Conference proceedings: Alcohol use and abuse among Hispanic adolescents.* Hartford, CT: Hispanic Health Council.

Ho, M. K. (1992). *Minority children and adolescents in therapy.* London: Sage.

Hoffman, M. A. 1996. *Counseling clients with HIV disease.* New York: Guilford Press.

Hoffman, N. G., & Harrison, P. A. (1986). *CATOR 1986 report: findings two years after treatment.* Minneapolis, MN: CATOR.

Hogan, J. A., Reed-Gabrielsen, K., Luna, N., & Grothaus, D. (2003). *Substance abuse prevention: The intersection of science and practice.* Boston: Allyn and Bacon.

Hollar, D., & Moore, D. (2004). Relationship of substance use by students with disabilities to long-term educational, employment, and social outcomes. *Substance Use and Misuse, 39*(6), 931–962.

...g, B. L., & Romano, J. L. (1999). ...s can clearly punctuate the spiritual ... of individuals. *Journal of Counseling ...evelopment, 77,* 160–170.

...H. (2003). Women in recovery from alco...ism: The place of leisure. *Leisure Sciences, ...5,* 51–80.

...ker, T. (1996). *HIV/AIDS, facts to consider: 1996.* Denver, CO: National Conference of State Legislatures.

Horney, K. (1937). *The neurotic personality of our time.* New York: Norton.

Horney, K. (1945). *Our inner conflicts: A constructive theory of neurosis.* New York: Norton.

Hser, Y., Grella, C. E., Hubbard, R. L., Hsieh, S. C., Fletcher, B. W., Brown, B. S., et al. (2001). An evaluation of drug treatment for adolescents in four U.S. cities. *Archives of General Psychiatry, 58,* 689–695.

Hubbard, R. L., & French, M. T. (1991). New perspectives on the benefit-cost and cost-effectiveness of drug abuse treatment. In W. S. Cartwright & J. M. Kaple (Eds.), *Economic costs, cost-effectiveness, financing and community-based drug treatment* (NIDA Research Monograph #113, pp. 94–113). Rockville, MD: National Institute on Drug Abuse.

Hudsen, J., Hiripi, E., Pope, H., & Kessler, R. (2007). The prevalence and correlates of eating disorders in the national comorbidity survey replication. *Biological Psychiatry, 61,* 348–358.

Humphrey, L. L. (1989). Observed family interactions among subtypes of eating disorders using structural analysis of social behavior. *Journal of Consulting and Clinical Psychology, 57,* 206–214.

Humphreys, J. D., Clopton, J. R., & Reich, D. A. (2007). Disordered eating behavior and obsessive- compulsive symptoms in college students: Cognitive and affective similarities. *Eating Disorders, 15,* 247–259.

Hunt, W. A., Barnett, L. W., & Branch, L. G. (1971). Relapse rates in addiction programs. *Journal of Clinical Psychology, 27,* 455–456.

Hurcom, C., Copello, A., & Orford, J. (2000). The family and alcohol: Effects of excessive drinking and conceptualizations of spouses over recent decades. *Substance Use & Misuse, 35,* 473–502.

Hurley, S. F., Jolley, D. J., & Kaldor, J. M. (1997). Effectiveness of needle-exchange programmes for prevention of HIV infection. *Lancet, 349,* 1797–1800.

Inaba, D. S., & Cohen, W. E. (2000). *Uppers, downers, all arounders: Physical and mental effects of drugs of abuse* (4th ed.). Ashland, OR: Cinemed.

Institute of Medicine. Stratton, K. R., Howe, C. J., & Battaglia, F. C. (Eds). (1996). *Fetal alcohol syndrome: Diagnosis, epidemiology, prevention and treatment.* Washington, DC: National Academy Press.

Iron Eye Dudley, J. (1992). *Choteau Creek: A Sioux reminiscence.* Lincoln, NE: University of Nebraska Press.

Irvine, L. (1999). *Codependent forevermore.* Chicago: University of Chicago Press.

Ivey, A. E., Bradford-Ivey, M., & Simek-Morgan, L. (1993). *Counseling and psychotherapy: A multicultural perspective* (3rd ed.). Boston, MA: Allyn and Bacon.

Ivey, A. E., D'Andrea, L., Bradford-Ivey, M., & Simek-Morgan, L. (2007). *Counseling and psychotherapy: A multicultural perspective* (6th ed.). Boston, MA: Allyn and Bacon.

Jackson, D. D. (1957). The question of family homeostasis. *Psychiatric Quarterly Supplement, 31,* 79–90.

Jackson, S. A. (1993). *Educating young children prenatally exposed to drugs and at risk.* Washington, DC: Office of Educational Research and Improvement.

Jacob, T., Ritchey, P., Cvitkovic, J. F., & Blane, H. T. (1981). Communication styles of alcoholic and non-alcoholic families when drinking and not drinking. *Journal of Studies on Alcohol, 42,* 466–482.

Jacobs, D. F. (2000). Juvenile gambling in North America: An analysis of long term trends and future prospects. *Journal of Gambling Studies, 16,* 119–152.

Jacobs, D. F. (2004). Youth gambling in North America: Long term trends and future prospects. In J. Derevensky & R. Gupta (Eds.), *Gambling problems in youth: Theoretical and* applied perspectives (pp. 1–24). New York: Kluwer Academic/Plenum.

Jacobs, M. R., & Fehr, K. O'B. (1987). *Addiction Research Foundation's drugs and drug abuse: A reference text* (2nd ed.). Toronto, Canada: Addiction Research Foundation.

Jacobs, T., Windle, M., Seilhamer, R. A., & Bost, J. (1999). Adult children of alcoholics: Drinking, psychiatric, and psychosocial status. *Psychology of Addictive Behaviors, 13*(1), 3–21.

Jacobson, G. R. (1989). A comprehensive approach to pre-treatment evaluation: I. Detection, assessment and diagnosis of alcoholism. In R. K. Hester & W. R. Miller (Eds.). *Handbook of alcoholism treatment approaches: Effective alternatives* (pp. 17–43). New York: Pergamon Press.

James, T., & Goldman, M. (1971). Behavior trends of wives of alcoholics. *Quarterly Journal of Studies on Alcohol, 32,* 373–381.

Jarosz, P. A., Dobal, M. J., Wilson, F. L., & Schram, C. A. (2007). Food cravings and disordered eating among urban obese African American women. *Eating Behaviors, 8*(3), 374–381.

Jay, S., Freisthler, B., Svare, G. M. (2004). Drinking in young adulthood: Is the stepparent a risk factor? *Journal of Divorce and Remarriage, 41*(2/3), 99–114.

Jelalian, E., & Saelens, B. E. (1999). Intervention for pediatric obesity: Treatments that work. *Journal of Pediatric Psychology, 24,* 223–248.

Jellinek, E. M. (1952). Phases of alcohol addiction. *Quarterly Journal of Studies on Alcohol, 13,* 673–684.

Jellinek, E. M. (1960). *The disease concept of alcoholism.* New Haven, CT: Hillhouse Press.

Jenkins, S. J., Fisher, G. L., & Harrison, T. C. (1993). Adult children of dysfunctional families: Childhood roles. *Journal of Mental Health Counseling, 15,* 310–319.

Johnson, G. M., Shontz, F. C., & Locke, T. P. (1984). Relationships between adolescent drug use and parental drug behavior. *Adolescence, 19,* 295–298.

Johnson, J. L., & Rolf, S. (1988). Cognitive functioning in children from alcoholic and nonalcoholic families. *British Journal of Addiction, 83,* 849–857.

Johnson, V. E. (1973). *I'll quit tomorrow.* Toronto, Canada: Harper and Row.

Johnson, V. E. (1986). *Intervention: How to he[lp] someone who doesn't want help. A step-by-ste[p] guide for families and friends of chemically dependent persons.* Minneapolis, MN: Johnson Institute Books.

Johnston, L. D., O'Malley, P. M., & Bachman, J. G. (2003). *Monitoring the Future national survey results on adolescent drug use: Overview of key findings, 2002* (NIH Publication No. 03-5374). Bethesda, MD: National Institute on Drug Abuse.

Johnston, L. D., O'Malley, P. M., & Bachman, J. G. (2006). *Monitoring the Future national survey results on drug use, 1975–2005. Volume I: Secondary school students* (NIH Publication No. 06-5883). Bethesda, MD: National Institute on Drug Abuse.

Johnston, L. D., O'Malley, P. M., Bachman, J. G., & Schulenberg, J. E. (2006). *Trends in 30-day prevalence of use of various drugs for eighth, tenth, and twelfth graders.* Retrieved March 27, 2007 from www.monitoringthefuture.org/data/06data/pr06t3.pdf

Jones, A. C. (1985). Psychological functioning in black Americans: A conceptual guide for use in psychotherapy. *Psychotherapy, 22,* 363–369.

Jones, A. S. (2007). Maternal alcohol abuse/dependence, children's behavior problems, and home environment: Estimates from the national longitudinal survey of youth using propensity score matching. *Journal of Studies on Alcohol and Drugs, 68*(2), 266–275.

Jones, H. E. (2006). Drug addiction during pregnancy: Advances in maternal treatment and understanding child outcomes. *Current Directions in Psychological Science, 15*(3), 126–130.

Jones, J. W. (1985). *Children of alcoholics screening test.* Chicago: Camelot Unlimited.

Jones-Saumty, D., Hochhaus, L., Dru, R., & Zeiner, A. R. (1983). Psychological factors of familial alcoholism in American Indians and Caucasians. *Journal of Clinical Psychology 39,* 783–790.

Joseph, E. B., Bhatti, R. S. (2004). Psychosocial problems and coping patterns of HIV seropositive wives of men with HIV/AIDS. Retrieved July 24, 2007 from www.haworthpress.com/web/SWHC

...odman, C. (1997). Children of substance-...using parents. In J. H. Lowinson, P. ... B. Millman, & J. G. Langrod (Eds.), *...nce abuse: A comprehensive textbook* (... ed., pp. 808–815). Baltimore: Williams & ...kins.

..., R. M. (2005). *A primer of drug action: A concise, nontechnical guide to the actions, use and side effects of psychoactive drugs* (10th ed.). New York: W. H. Freeman and Company.

Jung, J. (1994). *Under the influence: Alcohol and human behavior.* Pacific Grove, CA: Brooks/Cole.

Kaminer, W. (1990). Chances are you're codependent too (p. 16). *New York Times Book Review, February 1.*

Kandel, D. B. (1989). Issues of sequencing of adolescent drug use and other problem behaviors. *Journal of Drug Issues, 3,* 55–76.

Kanoy, K., & Miller, B. C. (1980). Children's impact on the parental decision to divorce. *Family Relations, 29,* 309–315.

Kantor, E. (2006). *HIV transmission and prevention in prisons.* Retrieved August 5, 2007 from http://hivinsite.ucsf.edu/InSite?page=kb-07-04-3#S2X

Karacostas, D. D., & Fisher, G. L. (1993). Chemical dependency in students with and without learning disabilities. *Journal of Learning Disabilities, 26,* 491–495.

Kashubeck, S., Walsh, B., & Crowl, A. (1994). College atmosphere and eating disorders. *Journal of Counseling and Development, 72,* 640–645.

Kasl, C. D. (1989). *Women, sex, and addiction: A search for love and power.* New York: Ticknor & Fields.

Kasl, C. D. (1992). *Many roads, one journey: Moving beyond the 12 steps.* New York: Harper Collins.

Kasl, C. S. (2002). Special issues in counseling lesbian women for sexual addiction, compulsivity, and sexual codependency. *Sexual Addiction and Compulsivity, Special Issue: Women and Sexual Addiction, 9*(4), 191–208.

Kaslow, R. A., Blackwelder, W. C., & Ostrow, D. G. (1989). No evidence for a role of alcohol or other psychoactive drugs in accelerating immunodeficiency in HIV-1-positive individuals. *Journal of the American Medical Association, 261,* 3424–3429.

Kaufman, A. (1975). Gasoline sniffing among children in a Pueblo Indian village. *Pediatrics, 51,* 1060–1065.

Kaufman, E., & Kaufman, P. (1992). From psychodynamic to structural to integrated family treatment of chemical dependency. In E. Kaufman & P. Kaufman (Eds.), *Family therapy of drug and alcohol abuse* (pp. 34–45). Boston: Allyn and Bacon.

Kelinig, J. (2006). Thinking ethically about needle syringe programs. *Substance Use and Misuse, 41*(6–7), 815–825.

Kelleher, K., Chaffin, M., Hollenberg, J., & Fischer, E. (1994). Alcohol and drug disorders among physically abusive and neglectful parents in a community-based sample. *American Journal of Public Health, 84,* 1586–1590.

Keller, M. (1972). On the loss-of-control phenomenon in alcoholism. *British Journal of Addiction, 67,* 153–166.

Kellett, J., Trimble, M., & Thorley, A. (1976). Anorexia nervosa after the menopause. *British Journal of Psychiatry, 128,* 555–558.

Kelley, M. L., French, A., Bountress, K., Keefe, H. A., Schroeder, V., Steer, K., Fals-Stewart, W., & Gumienny, L. (2007). Parentification and family responsibility in the family of origin of adult children of alcoholics. *Addictive Behaviors, 32,* 675–685.

Kelly, V. A., & Myers, J. E. (1996). Parental alcoholism and coping: A comparison of female children of alcoholics with female children of non-alcoholics. *Journal of Counseling and Development, 74*(5), 501–504.

Kerr, B. (1994). Review of the Substance Abuse Subtle Screening Inventory. In J. C. Conoley & J. C. Impara (Eds.), *The supplement to the eleventh mental measurements yearbook* (pp. 249–251). Lincoln, NE: University of Nebraska Press.

Kessler, R. L., Crum, R. M., Warner, L. A., Nelson, C. B., Schulenberg, J., & Anthony, J. C. (1997). Lifetime co-occurrence of DSM-III-R alcohol abuse and dependence with other psychiatric disorders in the National Comorbidity Survey. *Archives of General Psychiatry, 54,* 313–321.

Kiechel III, W. (1989, April 10). The workaholic generation. *Fortune,* pp. 50–52.

Kim, H. J. (2002). Codependency: The impact of Confucian marriage and family structure on women in Korea. *Dissertation Abstracts International: Section B: The Sciences and Engineering, 63*(5-b), 2569.

Kim, L. I. (1996). Korean ethos. *Journal of Korean American Medical Association, 2,* 13–23.

Kim, S. (1991). *Cultural competence for evaluators working with Asian American communities: Some practical considerations.* Unpublished manuscript, Database Evaluation Research, Charlotte, NC.

King, L. M. (1982). Alcoholism: Studies regarding Black Americans: 1977–1980. In *Alcohol and health monograph No. 4: Special Populations Issue* (pp. 385–410). Rockville, MD: National Institute on Alcohol Abuse and Alcoholism.

Kingon, Y. S., & O'Sullivan, A. L. (2001). The family as protective asset in adolescent development. *Journal of Holistic Nursing, 19,* 102–121.

Kingree, J. B., & Sullivan, B. F. (2002). Participation in Alcoholics Anonymous among African Americans. *Alcoholism Treatment Quarterly, 20*(3–4), 175–186.

Kirby, D. G. (1989). Immigration, stress, and prescription drug use among Cuban women in South Florida. *Medical Anthropology, 10,* 287–295.

Kirkley, B. G. (1986). Bulimia: Clinical characteristics, development, and etiology. *Journal of the American Dietetics Association, 4,* 468–472, 475.

Kirkpatrick, J. (1986). *Goodbye hangover, hello life: Self-help for women.* Canada: Collier Macmillan Canada.

Kirkpatrick, J. (1990). *Turnabout: New help for the woman alcoholic.* New York: Bantam Books.

Kitano, H. H. L. (1982). Alcohol drinking patterns: The Asian Americans. In *U.S. Department of Health and Human Services, Alcohol and Health, Monograph 4, Special Populations Issue* (pp. 411–430). Rockville, MD: National Institute on Alcohol Abuse and Alcoholism.

Kitchens, J. A. (1991). *Understanding and treating codependence.* Upper Saddle River, NJ: Prentice Hall.

Kitsantas, A., Gilligan, T. D., & Komata, A. (2003). College women with eating disorders: Self-regulation, life satisfaction, and positive/negative fect. *Journal of Psychology, 137*(4), 381–395.

Klar, H. (1987). The setting for psychiatric treatmen In A. J. Frances & R. E. Hales (Eds.), *American Psychiatric Association Annual Review* (Vol. 6, pp. 336–352). Washington, DC: American Psychiatric Association Press.

Knop, J., Teasdale, T. W., Schulsinger, F., & Goodwin, D. W. (1985). A prospective study of young men at high risk for alcoholism: School behavior and achievement. *Journal of Studies on Alcohol, 46,* 273–278.

Ko, C., Yen, J., Chen, C., Chen, S., Wu, K., & Yen, C. (2006). Tridimensional personality of adolescents with Internet addiction and substance use experience. *Canadian Journal of Psychiatry, 51*(14), 887–894.

Krestan, J. (2000). Addiction, power, and powerlessness. In J. Krestan (Ed.), *Bridges to recovery. Addiction, family therapy, and multicultural treatment* (pp. 15–44). New York: The Free Press.

Krestan, J., & Bepko, C. (1990). Codependency: The social reconstruction of the female experience. *Smith College Studies in Social Work, 60,* 216–232. Also reprinted in Babcock and McKay, 1995.

Kroll, B. (2004). Living with the elephant: Growing up with parental substance misuse. *Child and Family Social Work, 9,* 129–140.

Kubler-Ross, E. (1969). *On death and dying.* New York: Macmillan.

Kumpfer, K. L., & Baxley, G. B. (1997). *Drug abuse prevention: What works.* Rockville, MD: National Institute on Drug Abuse.

Kumpfer, K. L., Trunnell, E. P., & Whiteside, H. O. (1990). Biopsychosocial model: Application to the addictions field. In R. Engs (Ed.), *Controversies in the addiction's field: Volume One* (pp. 55–67). Dubuque, IA: Kendall/Hunt.

Kumpfer, K. L., Williams, M. K., & Baxley, G. B. (1997). *Drug abuse prevention for at-risk groups.* Rockville, MD: National Institute on Drug Abuse.

Kurian, A. (1999). Feminism and the developing world. In S. Gamble (Ed.), *Feminism and postfeminism* (pp. 66–79). New York: Routledge.

Kurtz, E. (1979). *Not-God: A history of Alcoholics Anonymous.* Center City, MN: Hazelden.

f... 0). Twelve step programs. In T. J. ... Ed.), *Working with self-help* ... 18). Silver Spring, MD: NASW Press.

... (2001). Codependence and interdepen... : Cross-cultural reappraisal of boundaries ... relationality. *Pastoral Counseling, 50*(1), ...–52.

..., G. T., & Petry, N. M. (2002). Disordered gambling among university-based medical and dental patients: A focus on Internet gambling. *Psychology of Addictive Behaviors, 16*(1), 76–79.

Larkin, J. R. (1965). *Alcohol and the Negro: Explosive issues.* Zebulon, NC: Record Publishing.

Lawson, A., & Lawson, G. (1998). *Alcoholism and the family.* Gaithersburg, MD: Aspen.

Lawson, A. W. (1992). Intergenerational alcoholism: The family connection. In G. W. Lawson & A. W. Lawson (eds.), *Adolescent substance abuse: Etiology, treatment and prevention* (pp. 41–70). Gaithersburg, MD: Aspen.

Lawson, G. W. (1992). Twelve-step programs and the treatment of adolescent substance abuse. In G. W. Lawson & A. W. Lawson (Eds.), *Adolescent substance abuse: Etiology, treatment and prevention* (pp. 219–229). Gaithersburg, MD: Aspen.

Lawson, G. W., Lawson, A. W., & Rivers, P. C. (2001). *Essentials of chemical dependency counseling* (3rd ed.). Gaithersburg, MD: Aspen.

Lawson, G. W., Peterson, J. S., & Lawson, A. W. (1983). *Alcoholism and the family: A guide to treatment and prevention.* Gaithersburg, MD: Aspen.

Lease, S. H., & Yanico, B. J. (1995). Evidence of validity for the children of alcoholics screening test. *Measurement and Evaluation in Counseling and Development, 27*(4), 200–210.

Ledoux, S., Miller, P., Choquet, M., & Plant, M. (2002). Family structure, parent-child relationships, and alcohol and other drug use among teenagers in France and the United Kingdom. *Alcohol and Alcoholism, 37,* 52–60.

Lemert, E. M. (1964). Forms and pathology of drinking in three Polynesian societies. *American Anthropology, 66,* 361–374.

Leonardson, G. B., Kemper, E., Ness, F., Koplin, B. A., Daniels, M. C., & Leonardson, G. A. (2005). Validity and reliability of the AUDIT and CAGE-AID in Northern Plains American Indians. *Psychological Reports, 97*(1), 161–166.

Leshner, A. I. (2000). Treating the brain in drug abuse. *NIDA Notes, 15,* 1.

Lesieur, H. R., & Blume, S. B. (1987). The South Oaks Gambling Screen (SOGS): A new instrument for the identification of pathological gamblers. *American Journal of Psychiatry, 144,* 1184–1188.

Lester, B. M., Andreozzi, L., & Appiah, L. (2004). Substance use during pregnancy: Time for policy to catch up with research. *Harm Reduction Journal, 1,* 5–49.

Levesque, M. J., Vichesky, D. R. (2006). Raising the bar on the body beautiful: An analysis of the body image concerns of homosexual men. *Body Image 3*(2), 45–55.

Levine, M. P., & Smolak, L. (2001). Primary prevention of body image disturbances and disordered eating in childhood and early adolescence. In J. K. Thompson & L. Smolak (Eds.), *Body image, eating disorders, and obesity in youth* (pp. 237–260). Washington, DC: American Psychological Association.

Levinson, D. J. (1978). *The seasons of a man's life.* New York: Knopf.

Lex, B. W. (1987). Review of alcohol problems in ethnic minority groups. *Journal of Consulting and Clinical Psychology, 55,* 293–300.

Lieberman, M. A., Yalom, I. D., & Miles, M. B. (1973). *Encounter groups: First facts.* New York: Basic Books.

Lin, R. K. (Ed.). (1997). Local and national outcomes from Community Partnerships to Prevent Substance Abuse. *Evaluation and Program Planning, 20*(3), 293–377.

Lindblad, F., Lindberg, L., & Hjern, A. (2006). Anorexia nervosa in young men. *International Journal of Eating Disorders, 39*(8), 662–666.

Lindley, N. R., Giordano, P. J., & Hammer, E. D. (1999). Codependency: Predictors and psychometric issues. *Journal of Clinical Psychology, 55*(1), 59–64.

Lipscomb, W. R., & Trochi, K. (1981). *Black drinking practices study: Report to the Department of Alcohol and Drug Programs.* Berkeley, CA: Source.

Liu, X., & Kaplan, H. B. (2001). Role strain and illicit drug use: The moderating influence of commitment to conventional values. *Journal of Drug Issues, 31*(4), 833–856.

Logan, S. M. L. (1992). Overcoming sex and love addiction: An expanded perspective. In E. M. Freeman (Ed.), *The addictive process: Effective social work approaches* (pp. 207–222). White Plains, NY: Longman.

Longabaugh, R. (2001). How does treatment work? *Brown University Digest of Addiction Theory and Application, 20,* 8.

Lopez, F. (1994). *Confidentiality of patient records for alcohol and other drug treatment* (Technical Assistance Publication, #13). Rockville, MD: Center for Substance Abuse Treatment.

Loro, A. D. (1984). Binge-eating: A cognitive-behavioral treatment approach. In R. C. Hawkins, W. J. Fremouw, & P. F. Clement (Eds.), *The binge–purge syndrome: Diagnosis, treatment, and research* (pp. 183–210). New York: Springer.

Lurie, N. O. (1971). The world's oldest on-going protest demonstration: North American Indian drinking patterns. *Pacific Historical Review, 40,* 311–332.

Lynch, W. C., Heil, D. P., Wagner, E., & Havens, M. D. (2007). Ethnic differences in BMI, weight concerns, and eating behaviors: Comparison of Native American, White, and Hispanic adolescents. *Body Image, 4*(2), 179–190.

Machlowitz, M. (1980). *Workaholics: Living with them, working with them.* Reading, MA: Addison-Wesley.

Macintyre, K., Brown, L., & Sosler, S. (2001). "It's not what you know, but who you knew": Examining the relationship between behavior change and AIDS mortality in Africa. *AIDS Education and Prevention, 13*(2), 160–174.

Madden, P. A., & Grube, J. W. (1994). The frequency and nature of alcohol and tobacco advertising in televised sports, 1990 through 1992. *American Journal of Public Health, 84,* 297–299.

Maddow, R. (2002). *Pushing for progress. HIV/AIDS in prisons.* Washington, DC: National Minority AIDS Council.

Mahler, M. S. (1975). *The psychological birth of the human infant: Symbiosis and individuation.* New York: Basic Books.

Malcolm, B. P., Hesselbrock, M. N., & Segal, B. (2006). Multiple substance dependence and course of alcoholism among Alaska Native men and women. *Substance Use and Misuse, 41,* 729–741.

Maletta, G. (1982). Alcoholism and the aged. In Pattison & E. Kaufman (Eds.), *Encyclope handbook of alcoholism* (pp. 192–223). Ne York: Gardner Press.

Malow, R. M., Dévieux, J. G., Rosenberg, R., Dyer, J. G., & St. Lawrence, J. (2006). Integrated HIV care: HIV risk outcomes of pregnant substance abusers. *Substance Use and Misuse, 41,* 1745–1767.

Manisses Communication Group, Inc. (1994). *Alcoholism and Drug Abuse Weekly.* Retrieved September, 22, 2003, from manissess.com/2newsletters/newsletters/adaw/adaw.htm

Manley, G., & Feree, M. C. (2002). Special issues in counseling lesbian women for sexual addiction, compulsivity, and sexual codependency. *Sexual Addiction & Compulsivity, 9*(4), 191–209.

Manning, D. T., Balson, P. M., & Xenakis, S. (1986). The prevalence of Type A personality in the children of alcoholics. *Alcoholism: Clinical and Experimental Research, 10,* 184–189.

Marcus, A. M. (1986). Academic achievement in elementary school children of alcoholic mothers. *Journal of Clinical Psychology, 42,* 372–376.

Marino, T. M. (1995). Writing your way out of trouble. *Counseling Today,* February 8, 10.

Markides, K. S., Ray, L. A., Stroup-Benham, C. A., & Trevino, F. (1990). Acculturation and alcohol consumption in the Mexican-American population of southwestern U.S. *American Journal of Psychiatric Health, 80,* (Suppl), 42–46.

Marlatt, G. A. (1985). Relapse prevention: Theoretical rationale and overview of the model. In G. A. Marlatt & J. R. Gordon (Eds.), *Relapse prevention: Maintenance strategies in the treatment of addictive behaviors* (pp. 3–70). New York: Guilford Press.

Marlatt, G. A., Demming, B., & Reid, J. B. (1973). Loss of control drinking in alcoholics: An experimental analogue. *Journal of Abnormal Psychology, 81,* 223–241.

Marlatt, G. A., & Gordon, J. R. (Eds). (1985). *Relapse prevention: Maintenance strategies in the treatment of addictive behaviors.* New York: Guilford Press.

Marlatt, G. A., & VandenBos, G. R. (Eds.). (1997). *Addictive behaviors.* Washington, DC: American Psychological Association.

okorni, J. L., Long, T., & Teti,). Maternal depression and cognires of 9-year-old children prenatally to cocaine. *The American Journal of and Alcohol Abuse, 33,* 45–61.

D. S. (2002). Codependency, boundaries, professionalism. *Orthopaedic Nursing, 1*(6), 61–68.

tsolf, D. S., Sedlak, C. A., & Doheny, M. O. (2005). Codependency and related health variables. *Archives of Psychiatric Nursing, 14*(3), 150–158.

May, P. A., & Gossage, J. P. (2001). Estimating the prevalence of fetal alcohol syndrome: A summary. *Alcohol Research & Health, 25,* 159–167.

McCarthy, B. W. (2002). The wife's role in facilitating recovery from male compulsive sexual behavior. *Sexual Addiction and Recovery, 9*(4), 275–285.

McCarthy, J. C. (1988). The concept of addictive disease. In D. E. Smith & D. R. Wesson (Eds.), *Treating cocaine dependency* (pp. 21–30). Minneapolis, MN: Hazelden.

McCown, W. G., & Chamberlain, L. L. (2000). *Best possible odds: Contemporary treatment strategies for gambling disorders.* New York: John Wiley & Sons.

McCrady, B. S., & Irvine, S. (1989). Self-help groups. In R. K. Hester & W. R. Miller (Eds.), *Handbook of alcoholism treatment approaches: Effective alternatives* (pp. 153–169). Elmsford, NY: Pergamon Press.

McCrystal, P., Percy, A., & Higgins, K. (2007). Substance use behavior of young people with a moderate learning disability: A longitudinal analysis. *The American Journal of Drug and Alcohol Abuse, 33,* 155–161.

McDermott, D. (1984). The relationship of parental drug use and parent's attitude concerning adolescent drug use to adolescent drug use. *Adolescence, 19,* 89–96.

McDougall, J. (1989). *Theaters of the body: A psychoanalytic approach to psychosomatic illness.* New York: Norton.

McGillicuddy, N. B. (2006). A review of substance use research among those with mental retardation. *Mental Retardation and Developmental Disabilities Research Reviews, 12,* 41–47.

McGoldrick, M. (1998). *Re-visioning family therapy: Race, culture, and gender in clinical practice.* New York: Guilford Press.

McGoldrick M., & Gerson, R. (1985). *Genograms in family assessment.* New York: Norton.

McGoldrick, M., Giordano, J. & Garcia-Preto, N. (2005). *Ethnicity and family therapy* (3rd ed.). New York: Guilford Press.

McIntosh, J. G., McKeganey, N., & MacDonald, F. (2003). Exposure to drugs among pre-teenage school children. *Addiction, 98,* 1615–1625.

McKearn, J. (1988). Post-traumatic stress disorder: Implications for the treatment of family members of alcoholics. *Alcoholism Treatment Quarterly, 5,* 141–144.

McLellan, A. T., Lewis, D. C., O'Brien, C. P. , & Kleber, H. D. (2000). Drug dependence, a chronic medical illness: Implications for treatment, insurance, and outcome evaluation. *Journal of the American Medical Association, 284,* 1689–1695.

McLellan, A. T., Luborsky, L., O'Brien, C. P., & Woody, G. E. (1980). An improved diagnostic instrument for substance abuse patients: The Addiction Severity Index. *Journal of Nervous and Mental Disorders, 168,* 26–33.

McMenamin, J. P., & Tiglio, A. D. (2006). Not the next tobacco: Defenses to obesity claims. *Food and Drug Law Journal, 61,* 445–518.

McMillan, L. H. W., Brady, E. C., O'Driscoll, M. P., & Marsh, N. (2002). A multifaceted validation study of Spence and Robbins' (1992) Workaholism Battery. *Journal of Occupational and Organizational Psychology, 75,* 357–368.

McMillan, L. H. W., O'Driscoll, M. P., & Burke, R. J. (2003). Workaholism: A review of theory, research, and future directions. In C. L. Cooper & I. T. Robertson (Eds.), *International Review of Industrial and Organizational Psychology, 18,* 167–189.

McMillen, J. S., McMillen, B. J., Simeonsson, R. J. (2002). Risk behaviors among students with and without disabilities: The North Carolina high school YRBS. In *Proceedings of the First CDC Conference on Birth Defects, Developmental Disabilities, and Disability and Health.* Atlanta, GA, September, 17–19, 2002. Atlanta, GA: Centers for Disease Control and Prevention.

McWhorter, J. H. (2000). *Losing the race: Self sabotage in black America.* New York: The Free Press.

Meness, M. M. (2000). The specificity of disrupted processes in families of adult children of alcoholics. *Alcohol and Alcoholism, 35,* 361–367.

Milberger, S., Biederman, J. Faraone, S. V., Wilens, T., & Chu, M. P. (1997). Associations between ADHD and psychoactive substance use disorders: Findings from a longitudinal study of high-risk siblings of ADHD children. *American Journal on Addictions, 6,* 318–329.

Milbrodt, T. (2002). Breaking the cycle of alcohol problems among Native Americans: Culturally-sensitive treatment in the Lakota community. *Alcoholism Treatment Quarterly, 20*(1), 19–43.

Miller, D., & Jang, M. (1977). Children of alcoholics: A 20-year longitudinal study. *Social Work Research and Abstracts, 13,* 23–29.

Miller, G. A. (1983). *Substance Abuse Subtle Screening Inventory.* Bloomington, IN: SASSI Institute.

Miller, G. A. (1997). *The Substance Abuse Subtle Screening Inventory-3 manual.* Spencer, IN: Spencer Evening World.

Miller, W. R. (1989). Matching individuals with interventions. In R. K. Hester and W. R. Miller (Eds.), *Handbook of alcoholism treatment approaches: Effective alternatives* (pp. 261–272). New York: Pergamon Press.

Miller, W. R. (1995). Increasing motivation for change. In R. K. Hester and W. R. Miller (Eds.), *Handbook of alcoholism treatment approaches: Effective alternatives* (2nd ed., pp. 89–104). Boston: Allyn and Bacon.

Miller, W. R., & Hester, R. K. (1980). Treating problem drinkers: Modern approaches. In W. R. Miller (Ed.), *The addictive behaviors: Treatment of alcoholism, drug abuse, smoking, and obesity* (pp. 11–141). New York: Pergamon Press.

Miller, W. R., & Hester, R. K. (1995). Treatment for alcohol problems: Toward an informed eclecticism. In R. K. Hester & W. R. Miller (Eds.), *Handbook of alcoholism treatment approaches: Effective alternatives* (2nd ed., pp. 1–11). Boston: Allyn and Bacon.

Miller, W. R., & Kurtz, E. (1994). Models of alcoholism used in treatment: Contrasting AA and other perspectives with which it is often confu *Journal of Studies on Alcohol, 55,* 159–166.

Miller, W. R., & Munoz, R. F. (1982). *How to co trol your drinking* (rev. ed.). Albuquerque, NM University of New Mexico Press.

Miller, W. R., & Rollnick, S. (1991). *Motivational interviewing: Preparing people to change addictive behavior.* New York: Guilford Press.

Miller, W. R., Westerberg, V. S., & Waldron, H. B. (1995). Evaluating alcohol problems in adults and adolescents. In R. K. Hester & W. R. Miller (Eds.), *Handbook of alcoholism treatment approaches: Effective approaches* (2nd ed., pp. 61–88). Boston: Allyn and Bacon.

Milrad, R. (1999). Coaddictive recovery: Early recovery issues for spouse of sex addicts. *Sexual Addiction and Recovery, 6,* 125–136.

Mintz, L. B., & Betz, N. E. (1988). Prevalence and correlates of eating disordered behaviors among undergraduate women. *Journal of Counseling Psychology, 35,* 463–471.

Mintz, L. B., Tracy, L. S., & Kashubeck, S. (1995). Relations among parental alcoholism, eating disorders, and substance abuse in nonclinical college women: Additional evidence against the uniformity myth. *Journal of Counseling Psychology, 42*(1), 65–70.

Minuchin, S. (1974). *Families and family therapy.* Cambridge, MA: Harvard University Press.

Minuchin, S. (1992). Constructing a therapeutic reality. In E. Kaufman & P. Kaufman (Eds.), *Family therapy of drug and alcohol abuse* (pp. 1–14). Boston: Allyn and Bacon.

Morahan-Martin, J. (2001). Impact of Internet abuse for college students. In C. Wolfe (Ed.), *Learning and teaching on the World Wide Web* (pp. 191–219). San Diego, CA: Academic Press.

Morahan-Martin, J. (2005). Internet abuse: Addiction? Disorder? Symptom? Alternative explanations? *Social Science Computer Review, 23*(1), 29–48.

Morahan-Martin, J., & Schumacher, P. (2000). Incidence and correlates of pathological Internet use among college students. *Computers in Human Behavior, 16,* 13–29.

Morehouse, E. R. (1986). Counseling adolescent children of alcoholics in groups. In R. Ackerman (Ed.), *Growing in the shadow* (pp. 125–142). Pompano Beach, FL: Health Communications.

. McCrady, B. S. (1992). Curative ...cohol and drug treatment: Behav- ... disease model perspectives. *British ...of Addiction, 87,* 901–912.

..., & Castele, S. C. (1985). Death by star- ...n: The Sepulveda Grecc Method No. 6. *...iatric Medicine Today, 4,* 76–78, 83.

..., A., Finney, J. W., Swearingen, C. E., & Vergun, P. (2002). Brief interventions for alcohol problems: A meta-analytic review of controlled investigations in treatment-seeking and non-treatment-seeking populations. *Addiction, 97,* 279–293.

Mphande-Finn, J. T., & Sommers-Flanagan, J. S. (2007). The experience of HIV/AIDS among rural women in the northwestern United States: A qualitative analysis. *Journal of Community Psychology, 35*(1), 3–11.

Mueller, M. D., & Wyman, J. R. (1997). Study sheds new light on the state of drug abuse treatment nationwide. *NIDA Notes, 12,* 1, 4–8.

Muula, A. D., Mfutso-Bengo, J. M. (2005). When is public disclosure of HIV sertopositivity acceptable? *Nursing Ethics, 12*(3), 288–294.

Myers, H. F., Javanbakht, M., Martinez, M., & Obediah, S. (2003). Psychosocial predictors of risky sexual behaviors in African American men: Implications for prevention. *AIDS Education and Prevention, 15*(Supplement A), 66–79.

Nace, E. P. (1987). *The treatment of alcoholism.* New York: Brunner/Mazel.

Nace, E. P. (1992). Alcoholics Anonymous. In J. H. Lowinson, P. Ruiz, R. B. Millman, & J. G. Langrod (Eds.), *Substance abuse: A comprehensive textbook* (2nd ed., pp. 486–495). Baltimore: Williams & Wilkins.

Najavits, L. M., Gastfriend, D. R., Barber, J. P., Reif, S., Muenz, L. R., & Blaine, J., et al. (1998). Cocaine dependence with and without PTSD among subjects in the National Institute on Drug Abuse Collaborative Cocaine Treatment Study. *American Journal of Psychiatry, 155,* 214–219.

Najavits, L. M., Rosier, M., Nolan, A. L., & Freeman, M. C. (2007). A new gender-based model for women's recovery from substance abuse: Results of a pilot outcome study. *The American Journal of Drug and Alcohol Abuse, 33*(1), 5–11.

Napoli, M., Marsiglia, F. F., & Kullis, S. (2003). Sense of belonging in school as a protective factors against drug abuse among Native American urban adolescents. *Journal of Social Work Practice in the Addictions, 3*(2), 25–41.

National Center on Addiction and Substance Abuse. (2001). *Shoveling up: The impact of substance abuse on state budgets.* Retrieved April 18, 2003, from www.casacolumbia.org/publications1456/publications_show.htm?doc_id=47299

National Council on Problem Gambling (1997). *Problem and pathological gambling in America: The national picture.* Washington, DC: The Council.

National Gambling Impact and Policy Study Commission. (1999). *National Gambling Impact Study Commission's final report, June 18, 1999.* Retrieved March 11, 2003, from http://govinfo.library.unt.edu/ngisc/reports/fullrpt.html

National Institute of Justice. (2001). Arrestee drug abuse monitoring program, 2000 annualized site reports. Retrieved April 18, 2003 from www.ojp.usdoj.gov/nij/adam

National Institute on Alcohol Abuse and Alcoholism. (2000). *Executive summary on improving the delivery of alcohol treatment and prevention services: A national plan for alcohol services research.* Retrieved June 8, 2003 from www.niaaa.nih.gov/publications/exsum/html

National Institute on Alcohol Abuse. (2001). *Number of deaths and age-adjusted death rates per 100,000 population for categories of alcohol-related (A-R) mortality, United States and States, 1979–1996.* Retrieved April 18, 2003 from www.niaaa.nih.gov/databases/armort01.txt

National Institute on Drug Abuse. (1998). *NIDA Capsule: Marijuana Update* [On-line]. Retrieved August 12, 2004 from www.health/org/pubs/caps/Marijuana.htm

National Institute on Drug Abuse. (1999). *Principles of drug addiction treatment: A research-based guide.* Washington, DC: National Institute of Health.

National Institute on Drug Abuse. (2001). *NIDA Capsule: HIV-AIDS update.* Retrieved August 2, 2003 from www.health.org/pubs/qdocs/hiv/prevent

National Institute on Drug Abuse. (2002). *NIDA capsule: HIV/AIDS update on African Americans.* Retrieved March 6, 2003, from www.drugabuse.gov/Infofax/DrugAbuse.html

National Institute on Drug Abuse. (2004). *Lessons from prevention research. NIDA InfoFacts.* Retrieved March 28, 2007 from www.nida.nih .gov/pdf/infofacts/Prevention04.pdf

National Institute on Drug Abuse. (2006). *National Institute on Drug Abuse Conference: Children of Parents in the Criminal Justice System: Children at risk. Bethesda, Nov. 6, 2006.* Retrieved August 9, 2007 from www.drugabuse.gov/whatsnew/meetings/children_at_risk/powerpoint/Mullen.ppt+

National Institutes of Health. (1997). *Report to the Director: Workshop on the medical utility of marijuana, February 19–20, 1997* [On-line]. Retrieved August 12, 2004 from www.health.org/pubs/qdocs/marij/medicalmarijuana.l

National Institutes of Health. (2004). Use of AOD in American Indians, Alaska Natives, and Native Hawaiians. *Mental Health Research NIH Guide, 22*(6).

National Institutes of Health. (2007). *Binge eating disorder.* Retrieved July 5, 2007 from http://win .niddk.nih.gov/publications/PDFs/bingedis10.04.pdf

National Leadership Coalition on AIDS. (March, 1993). Employee attitudes about AIDS, a national survey. In T. Hooker (Ed.), *HIV/AIDS, Facts to consider: 1996* (pp. 87–113). Washington, DC: National Conference of State Legislatures.

Neuman, P. A., & Halvorson, P. A. (1983). *Anorexia nervosa and bulimia: A handbook for counselors and therapists.* New York: Van Nostrand Reinhold.

New York State Division of Alcoholism and Alcohol Abuse. (1989). *The gateway to other drug use.* Buffalo, NY: Research Institute on Alcoholism.

Newton, M. S., & Ciliska, D. (2006). Internet-based innovations for the prevention of eating disorders: A systematic review. *Eating Disorders, 14*(5), 365–385.

Nie, N. H., & Erbing, L. (2000). *Internet and society: A preliminary report.* Palo Alto, CA: Stanford Institute for Quantitative Study of Society.

Nixon, S. J. (1994). Cognitive deficits in alcoholic women. *Alcohol, Health and Research World, 18,* 228–231.

Noone, R., & Reddig, R. (1976). Case studies in the family treatment of drug abuse. *Family Process, 15,* 325–332.

Noordenos, G., & Seubring, A. (2006). Criteria fo[r] covery from eating disorders according to [p]tients and therapists. *Eating Disorders, 1*[…] 41–54.

Nord, D. (1997). *Multiple AIDS-related loss.* Washington, DC: Taylor & Francis.

Norwood, R. (1985). *Women who love too much: When you keep wishing and hoping he'll change.* New York: Pocket Books.

Oashi, K., & Nishimura, H. (1978). *Alcoholic problems in Japan.* Paper presented at the 9th World Congress of Sociology, Uppsala University, Sweden.

Oates, W. (1971). *Confessions of a workaholic.* New York: World.

O'Connor, P. G., & Kosten, T. R. (1998). Rapid and ultrarapid opioid detoxification techniques. *Journal of the American Medical Association, 279,* 229–234.

Odets, W. (1995). *In the shadow of the epidemic: Being HIV-negative in the age of AIDS.* Durham, NC: Duke University Press.

O'Farrell, T. J. (1995). Marital and family therapy. In R. K. Hester & W. R. Miller (Eds.), *Handbook of alcoholism treatment approaches: Effective alternatives* (2nd ed., pp. 195–220). Boston: Allyn & Bacon.

Office of Applied Studies. (2002). *National and state estimates of the drug abuse treatment gap: 2000 National Household Survey on Drug Abuse* (NHSDA Series H-14, DHHS Publication No. SMA 02–3640). Rockville, MD: Substance Abuse and Mental Health Services Administration.

Office of National Drug Control Policy. (2002). *Pulse check.* Retrieved August 31, 2003 from www.whitehousedrugpolicy.gov/publications/drugfact/pulsechk/nov02/powder_cocaine

Office of National Drug Control Policy. (2007). *Table 1: Federal drug control spending by function,* FY2006-FY2008. Retrieved March 27, 2007 from www.whitehousedrugpolicy.gov/publications/policy/08budget/tbl_1.pdf

Ohlms, D. L. (1983). *The disease concept of alcoholism.* Belleville, IL: Gary Whiteaker Corporation.

O'Leary, A., & Jemmott, L. S. (1995). General issues in the prevention of AIDS in women. In A. O'Leary & L. S.D. Jemmott (Eds.), *Women at risk: Issues in the primary prevention of AIDS* (pp. 1–12). New York: Plenum Press.

...owell, J. A., & Waters, E. (2003). ...ting among adult children of alcohol-...holics. *Family Relations, 32,* 64–71.

..., Blaine, J. D., Genser, S., & Horton, ...(1997). Introduction to treament of drug-...dent individuals with comorbid mental dis-...ers. *National Institute on Drug Abuse Re-...arch Monograph Series #172,* 1–3. Rockville, MD: National Institute on Drug Abuse.

...man, A. M., & Kirschenbaum, D. A. (1984). Bulimia: Assessment of eating, psychological and family characteristics. Unpublished manuscript. In E. M. Freeman (Ed.), *The addiction process: Effective social work approaches* (pp. 1–113). White Plains, NY: Longman.

Orford, J., & Guthrie, S. (1976). Coping behavior used by wives of alcoholics: A preliminary study. In G. Edward, R. D. Hawks, & M. MacCafferty (Eds.), *Alcohol dependence and smoking behavior* (pp. 136–143). Lexington, MA: The Haworth Press.

Orsulic-Jeras, S., Shepherd, J. B., & Britton, P. J. (2003). Counseling older adults with HIV/AIDS: A strength-based model of treatment. *Journal of Counseling and Development, 25,* 233–244.

Orzack, M. H. (2004). *Computer compulsion services.* Retrieved July 24, 2007 from www.computercompulsion.com

O'Sullivan, C. (1991). Making a difference: The relationship between childhood mentors and resiliency in adult children of alcoholics. *Family Dynamics of Addiction Quarterly, 1,* 46–59.

Owen, B. (2004). Women and imprisonment in the United States: The gendered consequences of the U.S. imprisonment binge. In B. Price & N. Sokoloff (Eds.), *The criminal justice system and women* (2nd ed., pp. 195–206). New York: McGraw-Hill.

Paglia, A., & Room, R. (1998). *Preventing substance use problems among youth: A literature review and recommendations.* Paper presented at the Alcohol Policy XI Conference, May 10–13, 1998, Chicago.

Palfai, T., & Jankiewicz, H. (1997). *Drugs and human behavior* (2nd ed.). Dubuque, IA: W. C. Brown.

Paltrow, L. M. (2004). The war on drugs and the war on abortion. In B. Price & N. Sokoloff (Eds.), *The criminal justice system and women* (2nd ed., pp. 165–194). New York: McGraw-Hill.

Parker, F. (1980). Sex-role adjustment in women alcoholics. In C. Eddy & J. Ford (Eds.), *Alcoholism in women* (pp. 6–15). Dubuque, IA: Kendall/Hunt.

Parrino, M. W. (2002). Methadone maintenance and other pharmacotherapeutic interventions in the treatment of opioid dependence. *Drug Court Practitioner Fact Sheet, III,* 3.

Patterson, M., Stern, S., Crawford, P., McMahon, R., Similo, S., Schreiber, G., et al. (1997). Sociodemographic factors and obesity in preadolescent black and white girls: NJLBI's growth and health study. *Journal of the National Medical Association, 89,* 594–600.

Pattison, E. M., & Kaufman, E. (1982). The alcoholism syndrome: Definitions and models. In E. M. Pattison & E. Kaufman (Eds.), *Encyclopedic handbook of alcoholism* (pp. 3–30). New York: Gardner Press.

Paul, N. (1967). The use of empathy in the resolution of grief. *Perspectives in Biology and Medicine, 2,* 153–169.

Pedersen, P. B. (2002). Ethics, competence, and other professional issues in culture-centered counseling. In P. B. Pedersen, J. Draguns, W. Lonner, & J. Trinble (Eds.), *Counseling across cultures* (5th ed., pp. 3–28). Thousand Oaks, CA: Sage.

Peele, S. (1984). The cultural context of psychological approaches to alcoholism: Can we control the effects of alcohol? *American Psychologist, 39,* 1337–1351.

Peele, S. (1988). On the diseasing of America. *Utne Reader, 30,* 67.

Peele, S. (1989). *Diseasing of America: Addiction treatment out of control.* Lexington, MA: Lexington Books.

Peele, S., & Brodsky, A. (1991). *Love and addiction* (2nd ed.). New York: Signet.

Perry, S. W., & Tross, S. (1984). Psychiatric problems of the AIDS patients in New York Hospital: Preliminary report. *Public Health Report, 99,* 200–205.

Peteet, J. R. (1993). A closer look at the role of a spiritual approach in addictions treatment. *Journal of Substance Abuse Treatment, 10,* 263–267.

Petry, N. M. (2007). Gambling and substance use disorders: Current status and future directions. *American Journal on Addictions, 16*(1), 1–9.

Petry, N. M., Stinson, F. S., & Grant, B. F. (2005). Comorbidity of DSM-IV pathological gambling and psychiatric disorders: Results from the National Epidemiologic Survey on Alcohol and Related Conditions. *Journal of Clinical Psychiatry, 66,* 564–574.

Philaretou, A. G., Mahfouz, A. Y., & Allen, K. R. (2005). Use of Internet pornography and men's well-being. *International Journal of Men's Health, 4*(2), 149–169.

Phillips, L. (2006). Literature review of research in family systems treatment of sexual addiction. *Sexual Addiction and Compulsivity, 13*(2/3), 241–246.

Phoca, S. (1999). Feminism and gender. In S. Gamble (Ed.), *Feminism and postfeminism, 1999* (pp. 55–65). New York: Routledge.

Pimentel, R., & Lamendella, J. (1988). *Perspectives: AIDS in the workplace.* Northridge, CA: Milt Wright & Associates.

Polich, J. M., Armor, D. M., & Braiker, H. B. (1981). *The course of alcoholism: Four years after treatment.* New York: Wiley.

Polich, J. M., Ellickson, P. L., Reuter, P., & Kahan, J. P. (1984). *Strategies for controlling adolescent drug use.* Santa Monica, CA: Rand Corp.

Pomerleau, O., Pertschuk, M., Adkins, D., & Brady, J. P. (1975). A comparison of behavioral and traditional treatment for middle-income problem drinkers. *Journal of Behavioral Medicine, 1,* 187–200.

Potter-Efron, R. T., & Potter-Efron, P. S. (1989). Assessment of codependency with individuals from alcoholic and chemically dependent families. *Alcohol Treatment Quarterly, 6,* 37–57.

Price, W. A., Giannini, A. J., & Colella, J. (1985). Anorexia nervosa in the elderly. *Journal of the American Geriatric Society, 33,* 213–215.

Primm, B. J. (1992). Future outlook: Treatment improvement. In J. H. Lowinson, P. Ruiz, R. B. Millman, & J. C. Langrod (Eds.), *Substance abuse: A comprehensive textbook* (2nd ed., pp. 612–627). Baltimore: Williams & Wilkins.

Prochaska, J. O., & DiClemente, C. C. (1982). Transtheoretical therapy: Toward a more integrative model of change. *Psychotherapy: Theory, Research, and Practice, 19,* 276–288.

Project MATCH Research Group (1997). Matching alcoholism treatments to client heterogeneity: Project MATCH posttreatment drinking outcomes. *Journal of Studies on Alcohol, 58,* 7–29.

RAND Drug Policy Research Center. (2002). *Using marijuana may not raise the risk of using harder drugs.* Retrieved August 31, 2003 from www.rand.org/publications/RB/RB6010

Rangarajan, S., Kelly, L. (2006). Family communication patterns, family environment, and the impact of parental alcoholism on offspring self-esteem. *Journal of Social and Personal Relationships, 23,* 655–671.

Rawson, R., Shoptaw, S., Obert, J. L., McCann, M., Hasson, A., Marinelli-Casey, P., et al. (1995). An intensive outpatient approach for cocaine abuse: The Matrix Model. *Journal of Substance Abuse Treatment, 12,* 117–127.

Regier, D. A., Farmer, M. E., Rae, D. S., Locke, B. Z., Keith, S. J., & Judd, L. L., et al. (1990). Comorbidity of mental disorders with alcohol and other drug abuse: Results from the Epidemiologic Catchment Area (ECA) study. *Journal of the American Medical Association, 264,* 2511–2518.

Reilly, D. M. (1992). Drug-abusing families: Intrafamilial dynamics and brief triphasic treatment. In E. Kaufman & P. Kaufman (Eds.), *Family theory of drug and alcohol abuse* (pp. 105–119). Boston: Allyn and Bacon.

Reilly, N. P., Bocketti, S. P., Maser, S. A., & Wennet, C. L. (2006). Benchmarks affect perceptions of prior disability in a structured interview. *Journal of Business and Psychology, 20*(4), 489–500.

Rice, J. (1992). Discursive formation, life stories, and the emergence of codependency: Power/knowledge and the search for identity. *Sociological Quarterly, 33,* 337–364.

Rimmele, C. T., Howard, M. O., & Hilfrink, M. L. (1995). Aversion therapies. In R. K. Hester & W. R. Miller (Eds.), *Handbook of alcoholism treatment approaches: Effective alternatives* (2nd ed., pp. 134–147). Boston: Allyn and Bacon.

Roberts, L. J., & McCrady, B. S. (2003). *Alcohol problems in intimate relationships: Identifica-*

tion and intervention. A guide for marriage and family therapists. Washington, DC: National Institute of Health (Publication No. 03-5284).

Robins, L. N., & Guze, S. B. (1971). Drinking practices and problems in urban ghetto populations. In N. K. Mello & J. H. Mendelson (Eds.), *Recent advances in studies of alcoholism* (pp. 825–842). Rockville, MD: National Institute on Alcohol Abuse and Alcoholism.

Robins, L. N., & Przybeck, T. R. (1985). Age of onset of drug use as a factor in drug and other disorders. In C. L. Jones & R. J. Battjes (Eds.), *Etiology of drug abuse: Implications for prevention* (DHHS Publication No. 85-1335, pp. 178–192). Washington, DC: U.S. Government Printing Office.

Robinson, B. (2000). Chained to the desk. *Family Therapy Networker, 24*(4), 26–33.

Robinson, B. E. (1999). The Work Addiction Risk Test: Development of a tentative measure of workaholism. *Perceptual and Motor Skills, 88,* 199–210.

Robinson, T. N., Killen, J. D. (2001). Obesity prevention for children. In J. K. Thompson & L. Smolak (Eds.), *Body image, eating disorders, and obesity in youth* (pp. 237–260). Washington, DC: American Psychological Association.

Rodney, E. H. (1995). A profile of collegiate Black adult children of alcoholics. *Journal of College Student Development, 36*(3), 228–235.

Rodney, E. H. (1996). Inconsistencies in the literature on collegiate adult children of alcoholics: Factors to be considered for African Americans. *Journal of American College Health, 45*(1), 19–25.

Rodning, C., Beckwith, L., & Howard, J. (1990). Attachment in play in prenatally drug-exposed children. *Developmental Psychopathology, 1,* 277–289.

Rogers, R. L., & Petrie, T. A. (2001). Psychological correlates of anorexic and bulimic symptomatology. *Journal of Counseling and Development, 79,* 178–187.

Roget N., & Johnson, M. (1995). *Pre and post treatment planning in the substance abuse treatment case management process.* Carson City, NV: Bureau of Alcohol and Drug Abuse.

Rohsenow, D. J., Corbett, R., & Devine, D. (1988). Molested as children: A hidden contribution to substance abuse? *Journal of Substance Abuse Treatment, 5,* 13–18.

Room, R. (2005). Multicultural contexts and alcohol and drug use as symbolic behavior. *Addiction Research and Theory, 13*(4), 321–331.

Ross, H. E., Glaser, F. B., & Germanson, T. (1988). The prevalence of psychiatric disorders in patients with alcohol and other drug problems. *Archives of General Psychiatry, 48,* 43–51.

Ross, L. (2004). Native women, mean-spirited drugs, and punishing policies. *Social Justice, 31*(4), 54–63.

Rounsaville, B. J., Weissman, M. M., Kleber, H. D., & Wilbur, C. (1982). Heterogeneity of psychiatric diagnosis in treated opiate addicts. *Archives of General Psychiatry, 39,* 161–166.

Royce, J. E. (1989). *Alcohol problems and alcoholism: A comprehensive survey* (Rev. ed.). New York: The Free Press.

Russell, M., Henderson, C., & Blume, S. (1985). *Children of alcoholics: A review of the literature.* New York: Children of Alcoholics Foundation.

Sager, C., Brown, H., Crohn, H., & Walker, L. (1983). *Treating the remarried family.* New York: Brunner-Mazel.

Sameroff, A. J., & Chandler, M. J. (1975). Reproductive risk and the continuum of caretaking causality. In F. D. Horowitz (Ed.), *Review of child development research: Vol. 3* (pp. 187–244). Chicago, IL: The University of Chicago Press.

Sanders, M. (2002). The response of African American communities to alcohol and other drug problems: An opportunity for treatment providers. *Alcoholism Treatment Quarterly, 20*(3-4), 167–173.

Satir, V. M. (1964). *Conjoint family therapy: A guide to theory and technique.* Palo Alto, CA: Science and Behavioral Books.

Scaturo, D. J., Hayes, T., Sagula, D., & Walter, T. (2000). The concept of codependency and its context within family systems theory. *Family Therapy, 27,* 63–70.

Schable, B., Diaz, T., & Chu, S. (1995). Who are the primary caretakers of children born to HIV-infected mothers? Results from a multi-state surveillance project. *Pediatrics, 95,* 511–515.

Schaef, A. W. (1987). *When society becomes addict.* San Francisco: Harper & Row.

Schroeder, D. S., Laflin, M. T., & Weis, D. L. (1993). Is there a relationship between self-esteem and drug use? Methodological and statistical limitations of the research. *Journal of Drug Issues, 23,* 645–665.

Schuck, A. M., & Spatz, W. C. (2003). Childhood victimization and alcohol symptoms in women: An examination of protective factors. *Journal of Studies on Alcohol, 64,* 247–257.

Schultz, E. (1994). If you use firm's counselors, remember your secrets could be used against you. *Wall Street Journal, May 26,* C2.

Schwartz, D. M., Thompson, M. G., & Johnson, C. (1983). Anorexia and bulimia: The sociocultural context. *International Journal of Eating Disorders, 1,* 20–36.

Schwartz, R. H. (1987). Marijuana: An overview. *Pediatric Clinics of North America, 34,* 305–317.

Scientific American. (1996). *Deaths due to alcohol* [On-line]. Retrieved June 4, 1999 from www.health.org/pressrel

Scott, K. S., Moore, K. S., & Miceli, M. P. (1997). An exploration of the meaning and consequences of workaholism. *Human Relations, 50*(3), 287–314.

Selwyn, P. A. (1992). Medical aspects of human immunodeficiency virus infection and its treatment in injecting drug users. In J. H. Lowinson, P. Ruiz, R. B. Millman, & J. G. Langrod (Eds.), *Substance abuse: A comprehensive textbook* (2nd ed., pp. 744–774). Baltimore: Williams & Wilkins.

Selwyn, P. A., & Batki, S. L. (1995). *Treatment for HIV-infected alcohol and other drug abusers.* Rockville, MD: U.S. Department of Health and Human Services.

Selwyn, P. A., Feingold, A. R., & Iezza, A. (1989). Primary care for patients with human immunodeficiency virus (HIV) infection in a methadone treatment program. *Annals of Internal Medicine, 111,* 761–763.

Selzer, M. L. (1971). The Michigan Alcohol Screening Test: The quest for a new diagnostic instrument. *American Journal of Psychiatry, 127,* 1653–1658.

Seybold, K. C., & Salomone, P. R. (1994). Understanding workaholism: A review of causes and counseling approaches. *Journal of Counseling and Development, 73,* 4–9.

Shaffer, H. J, Hall, M. N., & Bilt, J. V. (1997). Estimating the prevalence of disordered gambling behavior in the United States and Canada: A meta-analysis. Retrieved March 11, 2003 from www.hms.harvard.edu/doa/html/meta.htm

Sher, K. (1991). *Children of alcoholics: A critical appraisal of theory and research.* Chicago: University of Chicago Press.

Shertzer, B., & Stone, S. C. (1980). *Fundamentals of counseling* (3rd ed.). Boston: Houghton Mifflin.

Shields, P. (1989). The recovering couples group: A viable treatment alternative. *Alcoholism Treatment Quarterly, 6,* 135–149.

Shon, S. P., & Ja, D. Y. (1982). Asian families. In M. McGoldrick, J. Pierce, & J. Giordano (Eds.), *Ethnicity and family therapy* (pp. 208–228). New York: Guilford Press.

Sideman, L. M., & Kirschbaum, E. (2002). The road to recovery: A gender-responsive program for convicted DUI females. *Corrections Today, 64,* 84–89.

Simeonsson, R. J., McMillen, B. J., McMillen, J. S., & Lollar, D. (2002). *Risk behaviors among middle school students with and without disabilities. The North Carolina middle school YRBS.* In Proceedings of the 130th Annual Meeting of the American Public Health Association. Philadelphia, PA, November 9–13. Washington, DC: American Public Health Association.

Simmons, G. M. (1991). Interpersonal trust and perceived locus of control in the adjustment of adult children of alcoholics. (Doctoral dissertation, California School of Professional Psychology, Fresno). *Dissertation Abstracts International, 37*(11), 5812 (University Microfilms No. AAC7710809).

Simpson, D. D., Joe, G. W., & Broome, K. M. (2002). A national 5-year follow-up of treatment outcomes for cocaine dependence. *Archives of General Psychiatry, 59,* 538–544.

Singer, M. (1997). Needle exchange and AIDS prevention: Controversies, policies and research. *Medical Anthropology, 18,* 1–12.

Skinner, H. A. (1982). The drug abuse screening test. *Addictive Behaviors, 7,* 363–371.

Sloboda, Z., & David, S. L. (1997). *Preventing drug use among children and adolescents: A research-based guide.* Rockville, MD: National Institute on Drug Abuse.

Slochower, J. A. (1983). *Excessive eating.* New York: Human Sciences Press.

Sobell, L. C., Cunningham, J. A., & Sobell, M. B. (1996). Recovery from alcohol problems with and without treatment: Prevalence in two population surveys. *American Journal of Public Health, 86,* 966–972.

Sobell, L. C., & Sobell, M. B. (1973). A self-feedback technique to monitor drinking behavior in alcoholics. *Behavior Research and Therapy, 11,* 237–238.

Sobell, L. C., Sobell, M. B., & Toneatto, T. (1991). Recovery from alcohol problems without treatment. In N. Heather, W. R., Miller, & J. Greeley (Eds), *Self-control and addictive behaviors* (pp. 198–242). New York: Pergamon Press.

Sorensen, J. L., & Batki, S. L. (1992). Management of the psychosocial sequelae of HIV infection among drug abusers. In J. H. Lowinson, P. Ruiz, R. B. Millman, & J. G. Langrod (Eds.), *Substance abuse: A comprehensive textbook* (2nd ed., pp. 788–793). Baltimore: Williams & Wilkins.

Sorenson, J. L., Costantini, M. F., & London, J. A. (1989). Coping with AIDS: Strategies for patients and staff in drug abuse treatment programs. *Journal of Psychoactive Drugs, 21,* 435–440.

Southern, S. (2002). A qualitative case study of two chemically dependent women with compulsive sexual behaviors. *Sexual Addiction and Recovery, 9,* 231–249.

Spence, J. T., & Robbins, A. (1992). Workaholism: Defintion, measurement, and preliminary results. *Journal of Personality Assessment, 58*(1), 160–179.

Springer, C. A., & Lease, S. H. (2000). The impact of multiple-AIDS related bereavement in the gay male population. *Journal of Counseling and Development, 78,* 297–304.

Stampp, K. (1956). *The peculiar institution: Slavery in the ante-bellum south.* New York: Alfred A. Knopf.

Stanton, M. D., & Stadish, W. R. (1997). Outcome, attrition, and family-couples treatment for drug abuse: A meta-analysis and review of the controlled, comparative studies. *Psychological Bulletin, 122,* 170–190.

Stanton, M. D., & Todd, T. C. (1992). Structural-strategic family therapy with drug addicts. In E. Kaufman & P. Kaufman (Eds.), *Family therapy of drug and alcohol abuse* (pp. 46–62). Boston: Allyn and Bacon.

Steer, R. A., Shaw, B. F., Beck, A. T., & Fine, E. W. (1977). Structure and depression in Black alcoholics. *Psychological Reports, 41,* 1235–1241.

Steinglass, P., Bennett, L. A., Wolin, S. J., & Reiss, D. (1987). *The alcoholic family.* New York: Basic Books.

Stephenson, M. T., Quick, B. L., Atkinson, J., & Tschida, D. A. (2005). Authoritative parenting and drug-prevention practices: Implications for antidrug ads for parents. *Health Communication, 17*(3), 301–321.

Sterne, M., & Pittman, D. J. (1972). *Drinking practices in the ghetto.* St. Louis: Washington University, Social Science Institute.

Sterne, M. W. (1967). Drinking patterns and alcoholism among American Negroes. In D. J. Pittman (Ed.), *Alcoholism* (pp. 66–98). New York: Harper & Row.

Stevens, E. P. (1973). Marianismo: The other face of machismo in Latin America. In A. Pescatello (Ed.), *Female and male in Latin America: Essays* (pp. 89–102). Pittsburgh: University of Pittsburgh Press.

Stewart, K. G. (1997). Environmentally oriented alcohol prevention policies for young adults. In *Substance Abuse and Mental Health Services Administration, Center for Substance Abuse Prevention, Secretary's Youth Substance Abuse Prevention Initiative: Resource papers. Prepublication documents* (pp. 107–158). Rockville, MD: Author.

Stewart, S. (2001). Internet acceptable use policies: Navigating the management, legal, and technical issues. *Information Systems Security, 9*(3), 46–53.

Stivers, R. (2000). *Hair of the dog: Irish drinking and its American stereotype* (Rev. ed.). New York: Continuum.

Stout, M. L., & Mintz, L. B. (1996). Differences among nonclinical college women with alcoholic mothers, alcoholic fathers, and nonalcoholic parents. *Journal of Counseling Psychology, 43*(4), 466–472.

Streigel-Moore, R. H., Dohm, F., Kraemer, H. C., Schreiber, G. B., Taylor, C. B., & Daniels, S. R. (2007). Risk factors for binge eating disorder. *International Journal of Eating Disorders, 40*(1), 481–487.

Striegel-Moore, R. H., & Rodin, J. (1986). The influence of psychological variables in obesity. In K. D. Brownell & J. P. Foreyt (Eds.), *Handbook of eating disorders* (pp. 99–121). New York: Basic Books.

Striegel-Moore, R. H., Silberstein, L. R., & Rodin, J. (1986). Toward an understanding of risk factors for bulimia. *American Psychologist, 41,* 246–263.

Streissguth, A. P., Aase, J. M., Clarren, S. K., Randels, S. P., LaDue, R. A., & Smith, D. F. (1991). Fetal alcohol syndrome in adolescents and adults. *Journal of the American Medical Association, 265,* 1961–1967.

Streissguth, A. P., Sampson, P. D., & Barr, H. M. (1989). Neurobehavioral dose-response effects of prenatal alcohol exposure in humans from infancy to adulthood. *Annals of the New York Academy of Sciences, 562,* 145–158.

Strober, M., Salkion, B., & Burroughs, J. (1982). Validity of bulimia-restricter distinction in anorexia nervosa parental personality characteristics and family psychiatric morbidity. *Journal of Nervous and Mental Disease, 170,* 345–351.

Stukin, S. (2003). Health, hope and HIV. Yoga Journal. Retrieved April 4, 2003, from www.yogajournal.com/health/581.cfm

Substance Abuse and Mental Health Services Administration. (1998). New study examines expansion of mental health/substance abuse insurance benefits. Press release from the Substance Abuse and Mental Health Services Administration, March 24, 1998. www.samhsa.gov/press

Substance Abuse and Mental Health Services Administration. (2001). National household survey on drug abuse. Retrieved July 6, 2003 from www.samhsa.gov.oas/nhsda2k1nhsda/vol1/chapter7.htm

Substance Abuse and Mental Health Services Administration. (2005). *Substance use during pregnancy: 2002–2003 update.* Rockville, MD: SAMSHA.

Substance Abuse and Mental Health Services Administration. (2006a). National survey on drug use and health. Retrieved March 23, 2007 from www.samhsa.gov/oas/nsduh.htm

Substance Abuse and Mental Health Services Administration. (2007). *Drug Abuse Warning Network, 2005: National estimates of drug-related emergency room department visits.* Retrieved March 26, 2007 from https://dawninfo.samhsa.gov/files/DAWN-ED-2005-Web.pdf

Substance Abuse and Mental Health Services Administration, Office of Applied Studies. (2006b). Treatment Episode Data Set (TEDS). Highlights—2005. National Admissions to Substance Abuse Treatment Services, DASIS, Series: S-36, DHHS Publication No. (SMA) 07-4229, Rockville, MD: Department of Health and Human Services.

Substance Abuse and Mental Health Services Administration, Office of Applied Studies. (2006c). *National survey of substance abuse treatment services.* Retrieved April 11, 2007 from http://oas.samhsa.gov/DASIS/2k5nssats.cfm.

Substance Abuse and Mental Health Services Administration and Department of Veterans Affairs. (2003). *Self-help organizations for alcohol and drug problems: Towards evidence-based practice and policy. Workgroup on substance abuse self-help organizations.* Retrieved August 16, 2003 from www.chce.research.med.va.gov/chce/pdfs/Vasma_feb1103.pdf

Sue, D. (1987). Use and abuse of alcohol by Asian Americans. *Journal of Psychoactive Drugs, 19,* 57–66.

Suhail, K., & Bargees, Z. (2006). Effects of excessive Internet use on undergraduate students in Pakistan. *CyberPsychology and Behavior, 9*(3), 297–307.

Sullivan, B. (2004). *Porn at work problem persists.* Retrieved August 3, 2007 from www.msnbc.msn.com/id/5899345

Super, D. E. (1990). A life-span, life-space approach to career development. In D. Brown, L. Brooks, & Assoc. (Eds.), *Career choice and development: Applying contemporary theories to practice* (2nd ed., pp. 197–261). San Francisco: Jossey-Bass.

Szyrynski, V. (1973). Anorexia nervosa and psychotherapy. *American Journal of Psychotherapy, 27,* 492–505.

Taggart, L., McLaughlin, D., Quinn, B., & McFarlane, C. (2007). Listening to people with intellectual disabilities who misuse alcohol and drugs. *Health and Social Care in the Community, 15*(4), 360–368.

Taleff, M. J., & Babcock, M. (1998). Hidden themes: Dominant discourse in the alcohol and other field. *International Journal of Drug Policy, 9,* 33–41.

Tani, N., Haga, H., & Kato, N. (1975). A survey of concern for drinking and alcoholics. First report: Students of junior high school. *Japan Journal of Alcohol Studies, 10,* 35–40.

Taris, T. W., Schaufeli, W. B., Verhoeven, L. C. (2005). Workaholism in the Netherlands: Measurement and implications for job strain and work-nonwork conflict. *Applied Psychology: An International Review, 54*(1), 37–60.

Tarter, R. E., Jacob, T., & Bremer, D. A. (1989). Cognitive status of sons of alcoholic men. *Alcoholism: Clinical and Experimental Research, 13,* 232–235.

Tarter, R. E., & Schneider, D. U. (1976). Models and theories of alcoholism. In R. E. Tarter & A. A. Sugerman (Eds.), *Alcoholism: Interdisciplinary approaches to an enduring problem* (pp. 202–210). Reading, MA: Addison-Wesley.

Thatcher, A., & Goolam, S. (2005). Development and psychometric properties of the Problematic Internet Use Questionnaire. *South African Journal of Psychology, 35*(4), 793–809.

Theall, K. P., Mitchell, C., Ludwick, M., Brown, B., & Kissinger, P. (2004). Factors associated with maternal-child separation among HIV-infected mothers. *AIDS Patient Care and STDs, 18*(9), 509–519.

Tobler, N. S. (1986). Meta-analysis of 143 adolescent drug prevention programs: Quantitative outcome results of program participants compared to a control or comparison group. *Journal of Drug Issues, 16,* 537–567.

Tobler, N. S. (1992). Drug prevention programs can work: Research findings. *Journal of Addictive Diseases, 11,* 1–28.

Tobler, N. S., & Stratton, H. H. (1997). Effectiveness of school-based drug prevention programs: A meta-analysis of the research. *Journal of Primary Prevention, 18,* 71–128.

Toneatto, T., & Ladouceur, R. (2003). Treatment of pathological gambling: A critical review of the literature. *Psychology of Addictive Behaviors, 42,* 92–99.

Toneatto, T., & Millar, G. (2004). Assessing and treating problem gambling: Empirical status and promising trends. *Canadian Journal of Psychiatry, 49*(8), 517–525.

Torres, S. (1993). Cultural sensitivity: A must for today's primary care provider. *Advance for Nurse Practitioners, 1,* 16–18.

Towers, R. L. (1989). *Children of alcoholics/addicts.* Washington, DC: National Education Association.

Trezza, G. R. (1994). HIV knowledge and stigmatization of persons with AIDS: Implications for the development of HIV education for young adults. *Professional Psychology, 25,* 141–148.

Trimpey, J. (1992). *The small book: A revolutionary alternative for overcoming alcohol and drug dependence.* New York: Delacorte Press.

Tripodi, C. (2006). Long term treatment of partners of sex addicts: A multi-phase approach. *Sexual Addiction and Compulsivity, 13,* (2/3), 269–288.

Tuchfield, B. S. (1981). Spontaneous remission in alcoholics: Empirical observations and theoretical implications. *Journal of Studies on Alcohol, 42,* 626–640.

Tucker, R. (2006). Review of ethnicity and family therapy. *Psychology and Psychotherapy: Theory, Research, and Practice, 79*(2), 306–307.

Turner-Bowker, D., & Hamilton, W. L. (2000). *Cigarette advertising expenditures before and after the master settlement agreement: Preliminary findings.* Massachusetts Department of Public Health and Abt Associates, Inc. Available from Cesar Fax, Volume 9, Issue 26.

Twerski, A. J. (1983). Early intervention in alcoholism: Confrontational techniques. *Hospital and Community Psychiatry, 34,* 1027–1030.

Ullery, E. K., & Carney, J. S. (2000). Mental health counselors' training to work with persons with HIV disease. *Journal of Mental Health Counseling, 22,* 334–342.

UNAIDS. (2006). *Global summary of the AIDS epidemic.* Retrieved August 7, 2007 from http://data.unaids.org/pub/EpiReport/2006/2006_EpiUpdate_en.pdf

UNAIDS. (2007). *Joining forces to tackle TB and HIV.* Retrieved August 7, 2007 from www.unaids.org/en/MediaCentre/PressMaterials/FeatureStory/20061124_TB+and+HIV_en.asp

UNAIDS and World Health Organization. (1997). *Report on the global HIV/AIDS epidemic* [Online]. Retrieved February 26, 2004 from www.us.unAIDS.org/highband/document/epidemic/report97.html

U.S. Bureau of the Census. (2000). Washington, DC: U.S. Government Publications.

United States Department of Education. (1998). *Safe and drug-free schools and communities: National Programs* [On-line]. Retrieved June 4, 1999 from www.ed.gov/programs.html

U.S. Department of Health and Human Services. (1990). *Pregnancy and infant health.* Health United States and Prevention profile. Rockville, MD: Author.

U.S. Department of Health and Human Services. (2003). *2001 National Household Survey on Drug Abuse* (NHSDA). Washington, DC: Author.

U.S. Department of Health and Human Services. (2004). Integrating mental health services into primary HIV care for women: The whole life project. *Public Health Report, 119,* 48–59.

U.S. Department of Health and Human Services (2007). *Eating away at health.* Retrieved on July 5, 2007 from www.nimh.nih.gov/publicat/eatingdisorders.cfm?textSize=L

U.S. Department of Justice. (2007). *Questions and answers: The American with Disabilities Act and persons with HIV/AIDS.* Retrieved August 8, 2007 from www.ada.gov/pubs/hivqanda.txt

U.S. Department of Justice, Civil Rights Division, Disability Rights Section. (2007). *Questions and answers: The Americans with Disabilities Act and persons with HIV/AIDS.* Retrieved August 8, 2007 from www.ada.gov/pubs/hivqanda.txt

U.S. Department of Justice, National Drug Intelligence Center. (2006). *National drug threat assessment 2007.* Retrieved March 27, 2007 from www.usdoj.gov/dea/concern/18862/2007.pdf

U.S. Preventive Services Task Force. (1989). *Screening for infection with human immunodeficiency virus. Guide to clinical preventive services.* Baltimore: Williams & Wilkins, Eds.

Usher, K., Jackson, D., & O'Brien, L. (2005). Adolescent drug abuse: Helping families survive. *International Journal of Mental Health Nursing, 14*(3), 209–214.

Vaillant, G. E. (1983). *The natural history of alcoholism.* Cambridge, MA: Harvard University Press.

Valenti, S. A. M. (2002). Family-of-origin characteristics among women married to sexually addicted men. *Sexual Addiction and Recovery, 9,* 263–274.

van der Walde, H., Urgensen, F. T., Weltz, S. H., & Hanna, F. J. (2002). Women and alcoholism: A biosocial perspective and treatment approaches. *Journal of Counseling and Development, 80,* 145–153.

Van Gorp, W. G., Miller, E., Satz, P., & Visscher, B. (1989). Neuropsychological performance in HIV-1 immunocompromised patients. *Journal of Clinical and Experimental Neuropsychology, 11,* 35.

Vannicelli, M. (1986). Alcohol, hormones, and health in post-menopausal women. *Alcohol, Health, and Research World, 18,* 185–188.

Vincent, K. R. (1985). *Diagnostic inventory of personality and symptoms (DIPS).* Richland, WA: Pacific Psychologicals.

Vlahov, D., Junge, B., Brookmeyer, R., Cohn, S., Riley, E., Armenian, H., & Beilenson, P. (1997). Reductions in high-risk drug use behaviors among participants in the Baltimore needle exchange program. *Journal of Acquired Immune Deficiency Syndrome, 16,* 400–406.

Vocks, S., Legenbaurer, T., Rüddel, H., & Troje, N. (2007). Eating to live. *International Journal of Eating Disorders, 40*(1), 59–66.

Wadden, T. A., & Stunkard, A. J. (1987). Psychopathology and obesity. *Annals of the New York Academy of Science, 499,* 55–65.

Walker, J. (2002). Rural women with HIV and AIDS: Perceptions of service accessibility, psychosocial, and mental health counseling needs. *Journal of Mental Health Counseling, 24,* 299–316.

Wallace, J. (1994). Modern disease models of alcoholism and other chemical dependencies: The new biopsychosocial models. *Drugs and Society: A Journal of Contemporary Issues, 8,* 69–87.

Wallen, J. (1990). *Issues in alcoholism treatment.* In R. C. Engs (Ed.), *Women: Alcohol and other drugs* (pp. 103–109). Dubuque, IA: Kendall/Hunt.

Walters, K., & Simoni, J. (2002). Reconceptualizing Native women's health: An indigcnist' stress-coping model. *American Journal of Public Health, 92*(4), 520–524.

Wansink, B., & Kim, J. (2005). Bad popcorn in big buckets: Portion size can influence intake as much as taste. *Journal of Nutrition Education and Behavior 37*(5), 242–246.

Ward, D. A. (1990). Conceptions of the nature and treatment of alcoholism. In D. A. Ward (Ed.), *Alcoholism: Introduction to them and treatment* (pp. 4–16). Dubuque, IA: Kendall/Hunt Publishing.

Warner, E. A., Kosten, T. R., & O'Connor, P. G. (1997). Pharmacotherapy for opioid and cocaine abuse. *Medical Clinicians of North America, 81,* 909–925.

Washington State Department of Health. (1996). *Tuberculosis fact sheet* [On-line]. Retrieved August 8, 2004 from www.doh.wa.gov/Topics/TB.html

Waskul, D. D. (2004). *Net.seXXX: Readings on sex, pornography, and the Internet.* New York: Peter Lang.

Watt, T. T. (2002). Marital cohabiting relationships of adult children of alcoholics. *Journal of Family Issues, 23*(2), 246–265.

Wegscheider, S. (1981). *Another chance: Hope and health for the alcoholic family.* Palo Alto, CA: Science and Behavior Books.

Weibe, J. M. D., & Cox, B. J. (2005). Problem and probable pathological gambling in older adults assessed by the SOGS-R. *Journal of Gambling Studies, 21*(1), 205–221.

Weinstock, H. (2004). Sexually transmitted diseases among American youth: Incidence and prevalence estimates, 2000. *Perspectives on Sexual and Reproductive Health, 36*(1), 6–10.

Weinstock, J., Ledgerwood, D. M., & Petry, N. M. (2007). Association between post treatment gambling behavior and harm in pathological gamblers. *Psychology of Addictive Behaviors, 21*(2), 344–356.

Weisner, T. S., Weibel-Orlando, J. C., & Long, J. (1984). "Serious drinking," "White man's drinking," and "teetotaling": Drinking levels and styles in an urban American Indian population. *Journal of Studies on Alcohol, 45,* 237–250.

Welte, J., Barnes, G., Weiczorek, W., Tidwell, M. C., & Parker, J. (2001). Alcohol and gambling pathology among U.S. adults. Prevalence, demographic patterns and comorbidity. *Journal of Studies on Alcohol, 62,* 706–712.

Westermeyer, J., & Baker, J. M. (1986). Alcoholism and the American Indian. In N. J. Estes and M. E. Heinemann (Eds.), *Alcoholism: Development, consequences, and interventions* (pp. 273–282). St. Louis, MO: C. V. Mosby Company.

Westermeyer, J., Yargic, I., & Thuras, P. (2004). Michigan Assessment-Screening Test for Alcohol and Drugs (MAST/AD): Evaluation in a clinical sample. *American Journal on Addictions, 13,* 151–162.

Westermeyer, J. O. (1991). Cultural perspectives: Native Americans, Asians and new immigrants. In J. H. Lowinson, P. Ruiz, R. B. Millman, & J. G. Langrod (Eds.), *Substance abuse: A comprehensive textbook* (2nd ed., pp. 890–896.) Baltimore: Williams & Wilkins.

Western Regional Center for Drug-Free Schools and Communities. (1995). *Confidentiality of records in student assistance programs.* Portland, OR: Author.

Westphal, J. R. (2006). The evidence base supporting the subtyping of gamblers in treatment. *International Journal of Mental Health and Addiction, 5*(2), 127–140.

White, W. L. (2001). *The rhetoric of recovery advocacy: An essay of the power of language.* Retrieved April 26, 2003 from www.efavor.ogr/ADVOCACY.htm

White, W. L. (n/d). *Recovery as a heroic journey.* Retrieved June 21, 2003 from www.efavor.org/ADVOCACY.HTM

Whiteside, M. (1989). Remarried systems. In L. Combinck-Graham (Ed.), *Children in family contexts: Perspectives on treatment* (pp. 135–160). New York: Guilford Press.

Whitfield, C. L. (1980). Children of alcoholics: Treatment issues. *State Medical Journal, 29,* 86–91.

Whitfield, C. L. (1984). *Alcoholism, other drug problems and spirituality: A transpersonal approach.* Baltimore: The Resource Group.

Whyte, K. S. (2006). *Statement of the National Council on Problem Gambling regarding current Internet gambling legislation.* Presented to the United State House of Representatives, Committee on the Judiciary, Subcommittee on Crime, Terrorism, and Homeland Security, April, 12, 2006.

Wilens, T. E., Faraone, S. V., Biederman, J., & Gunawardene, S. (2003). Does stimulant therapy of attention-deficit/hyperactivity disorder beget later substance abuse? A meta-analytic review of the literature. *Pediatrics, 111,* 179–185.

Wilk, A. I., Jensen, N. M., and Havighurst, T. C. (1997). Meta-analysis of randomized control trials addressing brief interventions in heavy alcohol drinkers. *Journal of General Internal Medicine, 12,* 274–283.

Williams, C. N. (1990). Prevention and treatment approaches for children of alcoholics. In M. Windle & J. S. Searles (Eds.), *Children of alcoholics. Critical perspectives* (pp. 187–216). New York: Guilford Press.

Williams, C. N., & Collins, E. W. (1986). The connection between alcoholism, child maltreatment, and family disruption. In S. H. Lease & B. J. Yanico (1995), Evidence of validity for the children of alcoholics screening test. *Measurement and Evaluation in Counseling and Development, 27*(4), 200–210.

Williams, M. (1986). Alcohol and ethnic minorities: Native Americans: An update. *Alcohol Health and Research World, 11,* 5–6.

Wills, T. A., Resko, J. A., Ainette, M. G., & Mendoza, D. (2004). Role of parent support and peer support in adolescent substance use: A test of mediated effects. *Psychology of Addictive Behavior, 18,* 122–134.

Wilson, C. (1982). The impact on children. In J. Orford & J. Harwin (Eds.), *Alcohol and the family* (pp. 151–166). New York: St. Martin's Press.

Windle, M., & Searles, J. S. (1990). *Children of alcoholics. Critical perspectives.* New York: Guilford Press.

Winnicott, D. W. (1965). *The maturational process and the facilitating environment.* New York: International Press.

Woititz, J. G. (1983). *Adult children of alcoholics.* Pompano Beach, FL: Health Communications.

Wolin, S. J., Bennett, L. A., & Noonan, D. L. (1979). Family rituals and recurrence of alcoholism over generations. *American Journal of Psychiatry, 136,* 589–593.

Wolpe, J. (1958). *Psychotherapy by reciprocal inhibition.* Palo Alto, CA: Stanford University Press.

Wolpe, J. (1969). *The practice of behavior therapy.* New York: Pergamon Press.

Wong, S. C., Catalano, R. F., Hawkins, J. D., & Chappell, P. J. (1996). *Communities that care prevention strategies: A research guide to what works.* Seattle, WA: Developmental Research and Programs.

Wood, R. T., Williams, R. J. and Lawton, P. K. (2007). Why do Internet gamblers prefer online versus land-based venues? *Journal of Gambling Issues.* Retrieved August 5, 2007 from www.camh.net/egambling/issue20/07wood.htm

World Health Communications. (1988). *Management of HIV disease. Treatment team workshop handbook.* New York: World Health Communications.

World Health Organization. (2007). *Women and HIV/AIDS.* Retrieved August 7, 2007 from www.who.int/gender/hiv_aids/en

Wright, P. H., & Wright, K. D. (1990). Measuring codependents' close relationships: A preliminary study. *Journal of Substance Abuse, 2,* 335–344.

Wu, H. R., & Zhu, K. J. (2004). Path analysis on related factors causing Internet addiction disorder in college students. *Chinese Journal of Public Health, 20,* 1363–1364.

Wutzke, S. E., Conigrave, C. M., Saunders, J. B., & Hall, W. D. (2002). The long-term effectiveness of brief interventions for unsafe alcohol consumption: A 10-year follow-up. *Addiction, 97,* 665–675.

Yamaguchi, R., Johnston, L. D., & O'Malley, P. M. (2003). The relationship between student illicit drug use and school drug-testing policies. *Journal of School Health, 73,* 159–164.

Yang, C. K., Choe, B. M., Baity, M., Lee, J. H., & Cho, J. S. (2005). SLC-90-R and 16PF profiles of senior high school students with excessive internet use. *Canadian Journal of Psychiatry, 50,* 407–414.

Yellowlees, P. M., & Marks, S. (2005). Problematic Internet use or Internet addiction? *Computers in Human Behavior, 23,* 1447–1453.

Yoon, Y. H., Yi, H., Grant, B. F., Stinson, F. S., & Dufour, M. C. (2002). *Surveillance report #60: Liver cirrhosis mortality in the United States, 1970–99.* Rockville, MD: National Institute on Alcohol Abuse and Alcoholism, Division of Biometry and Epidemiology.

Young, K. (1999, January). Internet addiction: Symptoms, evaluation and treatment. In L. Vande Creek & T. Jackson (Eds.), *Innovations in clinical practice: A source book* (Vol. 17, pp. 19–31). Sarasota, FL: Professional Resource.

Young, K. S. (1996). *Internet addiction: The emergence of a new clinical disorder.* Paper presented at the 104th Meeting of the American Psychological Association, Toronto, Canada, August, 1996.

Young, K. S. (1998). *Caught in the act: How to recognize the signs of Internet addiction and a winning strategy for recovery.* New York: John Wiley.

Young, K. S. (1999). The evaluation and treatment of Internet addiction. In L. VandeCreek & T. Jackson (Eds.), *Innovations in clinical practice: A source book* (pp. 17, 19–31.). Sarasota, FL: Professional Resource Press.

Young, K. S. (2004). Internet addiction. *American Behavioral Scientist, 48*(4), 402–415.

Young, T. J. (1991). Native American drinking: A neglected subject of study and research. *Journal of Drug Education, 21,* 65–72.

Young, T. J. (1992). Substance abuse among Native American youth. In G. W. Lawson & A. W. Lawson (Eds.), *Adolescent substance abuse: Etiology, treatment and prevention* (pp. 381–390). Gaithersburg, MD: Aspen.

Zangeneh, M., & Hason, T. (2006). Suicide and gambling. *International Journal of Mental Health and Addiction, 4*(3), 191–193.

Zetterlind, U., & Berglund, M. (1999). The rate of codependence in spouses and relatives of alcoholics on the basis of the Cermak codependence scale. *Nordic Journal of Psychiatry, 53,* 147–151.

Ziberman, M. L., Tavares, H., Blume, S. B., & el-Guebaly, N. (2003). Substance use disorders: Sex differences and psychiatric comorbidity. *Canadian Journal of Psychiatry, 48,* 5–14.

Zimberg, S. (1978a). Principles of alcoholism psychotherapy. In S. Zimber, J. Wallace, & S. B. Blume (Eds.), *Practical approaches to alcoholism psychotherapy* (pp. 3–21). New York: Plenum Press.

Zimberg, S. (1978b). Psychosocial treatment of elderly alcoholics. In S. Zimberg, J. Wallace, & S. B. Blume (Eds.), *Practical approaches to alcoholism psychotherapy* (pp. 237–254). New York: Plenum Press.

Zimmer, L., & Morgan, J. P. (1997). *Marijuana myths, marijuana facts.* New York: Lindesmith Center.

Zimmerman, M., Chelminski, I., & Young, D. (2006). Prevalence and diagnostic correlates of DSM_IV pathological gambling in psychiatric outpatients. *Journal of Gambling Studies, 22*(2), 255–262.

Index